The Acquisition of Private Companies and
Business Assets

The Acquisition of Private Companies and Business Assets

Seventh Edition

William J L Knight

Senior Partner, Simmons & Simmons

LAW & TAX

© WJL Knight 1997

ISBN 0752 002929

Published by
FT Law & Tax
21–27 Lamb's Conduit Street
London WC1N 3NJ

A Division of Pearson Professional Limited

Associated offices
Australia, Belgium, Canada, Hong Kong, India, Japan, Luxembourg,
Singapore, Spain, USA

First published 1975
Seventh edition 1997

A CIP catalogue record for this book is available from the British Library.

Printed in Great Britain by Biddles Ltd, Guildford.

Contents

Preface to the Seventh Edition

Although, for the first time, this edition deals with the acquisition of business assets, the aim of this book remains the same—to provide a guide for the practising solicitor who is engaged in the acquisition or disposal of a private company. We hope that the book will continue to be of interest to accountants, bankers and others involved in acquisitions.

The book was last revised in October 1992. The period since then has been one of change in legislation, regulation and case law as the law has caught up with the changes in the market place resulting from the intense takeover activity of the late 1980s. This period has produced the four longest Finance Bills ever enacted introducing, among other things, a new regime for corporate debt and foreign exchange gains and losses as well as yet more anti-avoidance legislation. The Stock Exchange Rules have been revised; the USM has been abolished in favour of AIM; rules relating to public offers of unlisted securities have changed; there are, as usual, proposals for change in the accounting treatment of acquisitions; the Pensions Act 1995 has been introduced and important decisions such as *Barclays Bank v British & Commonwealth* and *Thomas Witter v TBP Industries*, together with an increasing body of case law in the field of negligent mis-statement, have clarified the law relating to a number of aspects of acquisitions.

This edition seeks to take account of all these changes. A new chapter 10 deals with the mechanics of assets transactions, but apart from that the approach we have taken to the introduction of the commentary on assets acquisitions is to deal with these matters at the end of each chapter. In some cases, for example competition law and investigations and warranties, there is little or no distinction to be made between the two forms of transaction and they are dealt with together.

The law of acquisitions is a moving target. As this edition goes to press a new government is preparing its first budget and the Queen's speech predicts changes in competition law. The life of this edition promises to be as full of change as that of its predecessor.

This book is the work of a team. It could not have been written without tremendous contribution and support from our colleagues at Simmons & Simmons. Particular thanks go to Nick Cronkshaw (who has updated all sections on tax, as well as contributing the new section on the taxation of asset transactions), Michael Wyman (coping with the ever changing pensions legislation) and Sarah Bowles (precedent agreements, including notes), as well as Jenny Block (competition), Adrian Crawford (employment), Nic Heald (property), Roy Montague Jones (Europe) and Michael Clarkson (environment), with support from other members of the firm's environment department. Thanks are also due to Jonathan Downey, for his review and updating of the insolvency chapter, Stephen Parkinson of Ernst & Young for his review of the accounting chapter and Lucian Pollington, on secondment from Simmons & Simmons to the Stock Exchange, who has reviewed the chapter on listed companies. Also to Paul Barton (intellectual property), Martin Scott and Monica Ma (pensions), Heather Savage and Simon Yates (tax deed) and Peter Williams, Ian Hammond, Howard Mather, Claire Burnett-Scott, Richard Binns and Sarah Bowles (again) for responding to various requests to read different sections; to trainees Sarkis Zeronian, Cathya Djanogly, Zoe Fountain and Pierre Agyeman; and for secretarial support from within the firm—most especially Karen Saunders.

Author's royalties from this edition will be divided between Children's Express—the children's news agency and Argyle Primary School at King's Cross in London.

Subject to our errors and omissions, the law stated is that in force in England on 1 May 1997.

Bill Knight
Jane Newman

May 1997

Table of Cases

Table of Statutes

Table of Statutory Instruments

European Legislation

Chapter 1

Introduction

There are approximately 1.1 million active companies registered in Great Britain and of these only about 13,300 are public companies. Although these figures give no guide to the proportion of the nation's business which is carried on through private companies, they give some indication of the popularity of the private company as a vehicle for trade and investment.

This book deals, mainly from the point of view of a purchaser, with the legal aspects of the acquisition of the share capital of a company where the selling shareholders are few enough to enable negotiations to be carried on with them individually and with the equivalent legal considerations if, instead of acquiring the share capital of the company from its shareholders, the purchaser acquires some or all of the company's assets or business from the company itself. The company whose shares or assets are to be acquired (called the 'target' throughout this book) in such a transaction may be a public company but is more likely to be private. Public companies are recognisable by the inclusion in their name of the words 'public limited company' or 'plc' and the privilege they enjoy is the right to issue shares to the public. All other companies are private companies.

When those who trade or invest through a private company come to dispose of their business they are faced with a choice of methods. The target can sell its assets, or the shareholders can sell their shares in the target. The latter approach is popular, not only because it is a simpler transaction involving a transfer of ownership only of the shares in the target, but also for tax reasons. Factors which commonly weigh on the parties' minds when considering the choice of structure, shares or assets, include:

(a) *Tax* A sale of shares will normally involve individual shareholders in a charge to capital gains tax on any gain realised, but if a company sells its capital assets the company will pay corporation tax on any net gains realised and it will then be difficult to pass the consideration to individual shareholders without further taxation (eg capital gains tax on a deemed disposal of their shares in a winding up). Vendors will, therefore, often

1

wish to sell shares rather than procure a sale of assets by the target, and a purchaser who wishes to preserve the benefit of tax losses available to the target will certainly buy shares rather than assets. These issues, and other tax considerations, are considered further on p 253. Continued availability of the target's losses is considered at p 313.

(b) *Liabilities* A company is a person with the capacity to incur contractual, tortious and even criminal liability which will need to be evaluated by the purchaser of shares. The purchaser of assets is able to select only those it wishes to acquire and will not generally inherit the vendor's liabilities (although there are exceptions to this rule eg employees may transfer with the business (*see* Chapter 6), and property or environmental liabilities may become the responsibility of the purchaser). In addition, an assets transaction is sometimes used where the target's exposure to liabilities is uncertain or where there is doubt as to its ability to meet warranty claims (*see* Chapter 16).

(c) *Partial sale* If only part of the vendor company's business is to be sold eg it is one of several divisions through which the vendor carries on business, an assets sale may be the only practical course.

(d) *Non-transferable contracts, rights and licences* The sale of the target's shares will sometimes be obviously preferable where the target has contracts, rights or licences which require consent, or are subject to pre-emption rights, on transfer.

While these factors will affect the choice of structure, one or more factors will often be compelling. The vendor or purchaser may require advice as to the preferred approach, but debate between the parties is remarkably rare

Although investigation may go some way to establish whether or not the target owns the assets which it is said to own, the most intensive and searching enquiries cannot conclusively establish the extent of the liabilities which the target owes. It is therefore the practice for the purchaser to require warranties and indemnities from the vendors in respect of the target's affairs. These are considered in Chapter 9 and, insofar as they relate to taxation, in Chapter 14.

Acquisitions of business assets also typically include warranties as to ownership of the assets to be acquired and charges or other factors affecting them. Such matters are also addressed in Chapter 9. Other matters specifically affecting business acquisitions are found in Chapters 9, 10 and 12.

1.1 Regulation of acquisitions

The regulations which affect a take-over bid for a listed company are not normally applicable to the acquisition of a private company and will not apply to an acquisition of assets. The City Code on Take-overs and Mergers applies to listed and unlisted public companies considered by the Panel to be resident in the United Kingdom, the Channel Islands or the Isle of Man but applies to private companies only if:

(a) their equity share capital has been listed on the London Stock Exchange at any time during the ten years prior to the relevant date; or

(b) dealings in their equity share capital have been advertised in a newspaper on a regular basis for a continuous period of at least six months in the ten years prior to the relevant date; or

(c) their equity share capital has been subject to a marketing arrangement as described in the Companies Act 1985, s 163(2)(*b*) at any time during the ten years prior to the relevant date (eg their shares have been dealt in on the Unlisted Securities Market or the Alternative Investment Market); or

(d) they have filed a prospectus for the issue of equity share capital at the Companies' Registry at any time during the ten years prior to the relevant date.

In each case, the relevant date is the date on which an announcement is made of a proposed or possible offer for the target or the date on which some other event occurs in relation to the target which has significance under the Code.

The City Panel appreciates that the provisions of the Code may not be appropriate to all statutory and chartered companies or to all private companies falling within the categories listed above and will, therefore, apply the Code with a degree of flexibility in suitable cases.

The Code also applies if the transaction amounts to a reverse take-over of a listed company. A reverse take-over involves the acquisition for shares by a listed company of an unlisted one in circumstances in which the number of shares issued as consideration by the listed company is so great that a change in the control of the listed company results. In those cases the Panel claims authority and expects full compliance with the Code.

Although the rules and regulations of the London Stock Exchange may affect the transaction, if the target is unlisted they will apply only if either the vendor or purchaser is a listed company (*see* Chapter 11).

Taxation apart, there is little legislation which has specific application to the transfer of ownership of private companies. The Stock Transfer Act 1963 prescribes a form of transfer which may be used and some sections of the Companies Act 1985 (notably s 151: *see* Chapter 5) place restraints upon some aspects of the transaction; but there is, for instance, no legislation which implies any term into an agreement for the sale of shares. Schemes of arrangement under the Companies Act 1985, s 425 are rarely used as a method of acquiring a private company in the circumstances with which this book deals and equally rare is the application of s 428 *et seq* of that Act for the purpose of acquiring the shares of dissenting minority holders.

Those who are concerned in a professional capacity with the sale and purchase of shares in private companies must consider whether they are carrying on investment business within the meaning of the Financial Services Act 1986 and therefore need to be authorised under its provisions. Activities constituting investment business are described in Sched 1 to the Act, and those which might be relevant are para 12 (dealing in investments as principal or agent), para 13 (arranging deals in investments) and para 15 (advising investors or potential investors on the merits of purchasing or selling an investment). Paragraph 21 of Sched 1, however, provides that paras 12, 13 and 15 do not apply in relation to the acquisition or disposal of shares in a body corporate other than an open-ended investment company if (in summary) more than 75 per cent of the voting share capital of the body corporate is involved in the transaction and the acquisition and disposal is between parties each of whom is a body corporate, a partnership, a single individual, or a group of connected individuals. For this purpose, a 'group of connected individuals' means people who are connected to the directors and managers of the target by being close relatives of them. 'Close relative' means a spouse, child, parent, brother or sister. If less than 75 per cent of the target is involved in the transaction, or if even one of the shareholders is not connected to a present director or manager (eg if one of them is a former director's widow), then the exemption will not apply and, apparently, will not apply to those involved on either side.

Solicitors who advise on acquisitions can take some comfort from para 24 of Sched 1 which provides that para 15 (giving advice) does not apply to advice which is given in the course of a profession and the giving of which is a necessary part of other advice or services given in the course of carrying on that professional business. The paragraph goes on to provide that advice is not to be regarded as falling within the exemption if it is remunerated separately from other advice. It is to be assumed that para 15 is intended to catch advice given on the acquisition or sale of shares as an investment and not, eg, tax advice or advice about warranties and indemnities. In the case of an acquisition of a private company it is quite difficult to differentiate between the legal advice on the contract and commercial advice upon the merits of the shares as an investment. In this sense, the exception given in para 24 should be helpful. In any event, the problem does not exist for solicitors who are certified by the Law Society in its capacity as a recognised professional body as they are authorised persons. In their case, giving advice as to the merits of an investment in a private company in this context is likely to be 'incidental' within the meaning of the Solicitors Investment Business Rules 1988 and will not constitute discrete investment business.

Solicitors who contact shareholders in order to get them to join in a sale of shares will be wary of the Financial Services Act 1986, s 56 which forbids unsolicited calls 'by way of business' and renders unenforceable investment agreements entered into as a result of a prohibited 'cold call'. The Solicitors Investment Business Rules 1995, r 12 contain an exception which provides that cold calling is not prohibited if it complies with the practice rules, but the relevant rules (Solicitors' Code 1990) are very narrow in scope, and do not seem to cover such approaches. The s 56 prohibition forbids the firm from procuring or endeavouring to procure an agreement as well as from entering into one.

Section 57 of the Financial Services Act 1986 is relevant where the acquisition involves a circular to shareholders or other investment advertisement. These issues are dealt with on p 27.

Neither the City Code on Take-overs and Mergers, nor the Financial Services Act 1986, apply to the sale by the target of its business assets or their acquisition by the purchaser, although may be Financial Services Act considerations if the business assets of the target include any of the investments described in Sched 1, Part I, to the Act or if its activities fall within Sched 1, Part II.

Chapter 2

Acquisition Structures

Apart from the decision whether to acquire assets or shares, here are a number of factors which, time and again, affect the structure of an acquisition. They are, in no particular order:

Shareholder approval and ABI guidelines
Share premium account
Roll-over relief
Intra-group transfers
The Companies Act 1985, s 151
Preference shares in the target

Most of these issues are dealt with in more detail elsewhere in this book: their treatment here is only an outline, focusing on points which often arise in practice and are of particular reference to the share acquisition. This chapter concludes with examples which show the interaction of some of the elements.

2.1 Shareholder approval and ABI guidelines

These issues arise where the purchaser or the vendor is a listed company. Shareholder approval can be required either because the acquisition itself requires approval or because the creation or allotment of share capital in association with the acquisition requires approval. These issues are dealt with in more detail in Chapter 11, but essentially, approval will be required under the London Stock Exchange *Yellow Book* if the transaction is Super Class 1 (more than 25 per cent of profits or assets) or a related party transaction (a transaction with a director or substantial shareholder). The Companies Act will require a shareholders' meeting if it is necessary to increase capital, or to disapply the Companies Act 1985, s 89 which requires that issues for cash must be approved by special resolution unless first offered to existing shareholders. The Companies Act 1985, s 320 provides that shareholder approval is required if the transaction is with a director or a person connected with a director. This mirrors related party requirements but applies to all companies, listed or not (p 25).

Where shareholder approval of the transaction itself is required, there is little that can be done except to comply. Almost invariably, the acquisition agreement will be entered into before the notice of meeting and explanatory circular are sent to shareholders and completion of the acquisition will be conditional upon the passing of the necessary resolution (although there is a technical problem with s 320 (*see* p 25)). The vendors will try to secure, as far as they can, that the directors of the purchaser will recommend the transaction to their shareholders. Directors should not bind themselves to act in breach of their fiduciary duties and therefore, it used to be generally thought that, if circumstances change between contract and completion, directors must be free to change their recommendation (see *John Crowther Group v Carpets International* [1990] BCLC 460). In *Fulham Football Club v Cabra* (1994) 1 BCLC 363 the Court of Appeal made it clear, however, that directors can bind themselves as to the future exercise of their fiduciary powers, citing with approval the Australian case of *Thorby v Goldberg* (1964) 112 CLR 597 where the court said:

> If, when a contract is negotiated on behalf of a company, the directors think it in the interests of the company as a whole that the transaction should be entered into and carried into effect they may bind themselves by the contract to do whatever is necessary to effectuate it.

The *Fulham* decision should not be taken to overrule *John Crowther* which, the court said, might be justified on its own facts. Directors will seek to avoid such undertakings, where they can.

The questions of increase of capital and authority to allot raise more complicated issues. An increase of capital will normally involve an ordinary resolution, requiring 14 clear days' notice, as will authority to allot under the Companies Act 1985, s 80. A disapplication of s 89 however will require a special resolution and 21 clear days' notice and this may have adverse timetable implications. If the acquisition is a major one and, for market reasons, a rights issue is required, s 89 will fall to be considered because, of course, a rights issue is an issue for cash. However, it is probable (although not axiomatic) that the purchaser will have in place a general authority, passed at its latest annual general meeting, which will permit a rights issue of existing authorised share capital, even where the rights issue does not comply with the strict statutory requirements of s 89 *et seq*. Therefore, provided there is sufficient unissued share capital of the class required, a rights issue will not, of itself, require a shareholders' meeting. However, in practice, it is only the largest acquisitions which would be funded by a rights issue and it often happens therefore that the acquisition is Super Class 1, requiring shareholder approval of the acquisition itself.

Similarly, a vendor placing, in which the shares in the target are acquired in consideration for shares in the purchaser which are placed with placees whose cash payment is used to pay the vendors, will not in practice require shareholder approval unless the transaction itself requires approval (eg because it is Super Class 1). So long as the purchaser has sufficient unissued share capital it is likely that it will also, in practice, have authority to allot the capital under the Companies Act 1985, s 80 and as the issue is technically not an issue for cash, the s 89 authority is not in point. The guidelines issued by the investment committee of the Association of British Insurers and others may, however, require an open offer to be made to shareholders.

The ABI guidelines indicate practices which its members will support. Broadly speaking, these guidelines are designed, among other things, to ensure that major issues of shares do not take place at a discount unless offered to existing shareholders. The guidelines require disapplication of the Companies Act 1985, s 89 to be reviewed annually and to be limited to 5 per cent of the existing issued capital, with a cumulative limit of 7.5 per cent for non pre-emptive issues for cash in any rolling three year period. As a result, companies are not able to fund acquisitions by means of cash placings to selected shareholders but must structure issues for cash as rights issues or accept the need for a meeting to pass a special resolution to disapply s 89, bearing in mind that institutional shareholders may well be inclined to oppose the resolution if the shares are placed at a discount of more than 5 per cent (although prior consultation with the investment committee of the ABI is always possible). The guidelines are reinforced by the *Yellow Book*, paras 9.18 and 9.20 (continuing obligations) and para 14.8 which repeat the requirement to offer shares on a pre-emptive basis and the requirement for annual (ie every 15 months) renewal of the general disapplication of pre-emption rights. ABI guidelines also limit the amount of unissued capital over which there is s 80 authority to allot to the lesser of either one third of existing issued capital or the unissued ordinary share capital, but of itself this will not normally impede an acquisition, as any acquisition requiring capital in excess of that limit is likely to need an ordinary resolution seeking approval for some other reason.

Partly as a result of this regime, the vendor placing is a popular method of using shares to fund an acquisition. A vendor placing involves the allotment of shares in the purchaser to the vendors in consideration for shares in the target. The consideration shares are then placed (sold) for cash by the purchaser's bank or broker. Thus the purchaser funds the acquisition through a share issue while the vendors receive cash. A vendor placing is not a cash issue of shares and therefore does not require s 89 disapplication (*see further* p 244). However, ABI guidelines do not permit placings involving more than 10 per cent of the company's issued share capital or a discount greater than 5 per cent unless clawback is offered. Clawback is an offer to existing shareholders of the shares to be placed. The 5 per cent discount is calculated by comparing the mid-market price with the offering price net of the commission charged by the bank or broker undertaking responsibility for the placing. The London Stock Exchange will require an open offer to be open for 15 business days, but apart from that there are no prescribed formalities, unless listing particulars are required (*see* p 219).

2.2   Share premium account

Whether or not any particular acquisition is accounted for on consolidation according to the acquisition method of accounting or the merger method of accounting is decided according to the appropriate accounting rules (to be found in the Companies Act 1985, Sched 4A, para 7 *et seq* and FRS 6). These are summarised in Chapter 8 and aspects of the debate remain, as usual, to be finally implemented by the introduction of a new standard at the time this book goes to print. The requirement to have a share premium account gives rise to problems. In the barest possible outline, the problem can be summarised by saying that acquisition accounting gives rise to goodwill on consolidation where the price paid for the target exceeds the value of the target's assets. Writing off goodwill through the profit and loss account depresses earnings and purchasers will wish to deal with the goodwill in some other way, normally by writing it off against reserves (although it is this aspect of the accounting treatment that is to change). Share premium account is not available to be used as reserve against which goodwill can be written off so that creation of a large share premium account as a result of an acquisition is unwelcome because it has the indirect effect of depressing future earnings.

The Companies Act 1985, s 131 provides that it is not necessary to create a share premium account where the company issuing the consideration shares 'has secured at least a 90 per cent equity holding in another company in pursuance of an arrangement providing for the allotment of equity shares in the issuing company ...' (*see* p 125).

Where the equity share capital of the target is divided into different classes, s 131 does not apply unless the requirements are satisfied in relation to each of the classes taken separately. Where the arrangement involves the acquisition of non-equity shares in the target, relief extends to the issue of consideration shares in exchange for those non-equity shares.

Where it is not possible to structure the acquisition so as to avoid the need to create a share premium account, eg because it must be funded through a rights issue, it is possible to apply to the court to reduce capital by writing down the share premium account (see, for example, *Re Thorn EMI plc* (1988) 4 BCC 698). This procedure produces a reserve against which goodwill can be written off, as required under current (but probably not future) accounting rules.

2.3   Roll-over relief

Tax can affect the structure of an acquisition in so many ways that it is difficult to pick out points that have overriding significance. Issues which affect the taxation of vendors are dealt with in Chapter 12.

In cases where the vendors accept shares or debentures as consideration for their shares, and intend to retain them, then it is clearly important to obtain roll-over relief. The conditions for roll-over relief are dealt with in detail on p 264. There is no difficulty in complying with them in a normal acquisition because as a result of the exchange the purchaser will hold more than one-quarter of the ordinary share capital of the target. One problem which sometimes causes structural difficulties however is that the shares must be issued by the purchasing company, ie the company which will hold, directly, more than one-quarter of the ordinary share capital of the target. Thus, if a listed purchaser wishes to acquire a company through one of its subsidiaries, arrangements can be made to issue shares in the parent to the vendors to satisfy the consideration, but the exchange is not eligible for roll-over relief because the consideration shares are not shares in the direct purchaser. In such a case, if relief is to be obtained, the target can be acquired by the purchaser and sold down to the subsidiary subsequently, but sometimes it may be necessary for shares in the subsidiary to be issued to the vendors and then for the parent to buy back the shares in the subsidiary by means of a subsequent exchange for shares in the parent. Shares which are issued to vendors momentarily in this way and then repurchased are sometimes called 'flip flops'.

Tax requirements can give rise to movements of assets or shares in the target within a vendor group prior to the sale. This can arise for a number of reasons, for example the requirement to sell shares in, or assets of, the target to a company with capital losses, before the shares or assets are sold outside the group, thus crystallising the gain in a company which is able to offset losses against the gain arising on the sale. Where part only of the business is to be sold, tax and commercial considerations may dictate that assets are removed from the target and then the target itself sold, as opposed to the alternative option of selling to the purchaser out of the target that part of the business which is to be sold. For the corporate lawyer, these intra-group transactions raise problems of their own, and they are referred to below.

2.4   Intra-group transfers

Transferring assets inside a group before a company is sold causes more problems than are generally realised. Take a simple case in which a parent wishes to transfer the target inside the group so that it can be sold by a company which has capital losses against which the gain can be set. The price at which the target is transferred intra-group will have no effect on the taxation of the sale, and the normal reaction is to transfer the target at book value ie for a consideration equal to the value at which the shares in the target stand in the books of the vendor group, and to leave the consideration outstanding on loan account.

Suppose target T is owned by the vendor's subsidiary S, and it is proposed that the shares in T are to be transferred to be held directly by vendor V before they are sold. To start with the obvious, the directors of S have a fiduciary duty to S not to dispose of the corporate assets at less than fair market value. Provided S is solvent, this does not in practice present any difficulty. In *Rolled Steel Products (Holdings) Ltd v British Steel Corporation* [1986] 1 Ch 246 it was held that the shareholders can unanimously ratify an act by directors which, although technically within the powers of the company contained in its memorandum, is done to serve a purpose other than the interests of the company. In this case, the court would probably be willing to imply the consent of V, as the sole shareholder, although for their own protection the directors of S should insist on the written instructions of V.

What gives rise to more difficulty in practice is the question of distributable profits. *Aveling Barford Ltd v Perion Ltd* (1989) 5 BCC 677 is authority for the proposition that a sale of property by a company at an undervalue to one of its shareholders or to a company controlled by one of its shareholders is a distribution of the amount of the undervalue. If, for example, the book value of T in the books of S is £750,000 but its market value is £1,000,000, then a transfer by S to V of the shares in T for £750,000 will amount to a distribution by S to V of £250,000. *Aveling Barford* was a case involving a company which had no distributable reserves and was decided on the basis of the common law rules relating to distributions. If carried to their logical conclusion and applied in the context of the statutory restrictions on distribution the principles followed in that case give rise to a number of problems for companies which are solvent but whose reserves are not sufficient to cover the distribution.

Under s 263 of the Companies Act 1985, a distribution may be made only out of profits available for the purpose and under s 270, distribution must be justified by reference to the latest annual accounts or interim accounts if the annual accounts do not show sufficient reserves. Thus, if S has reserves of less than £250,000, a sale of the property at book value will, if considered a distribution, apparently be unlawful. Nevertheless the £250,000 represents a profit, albeit unrealised and unrecorded, of S and ordinary principles of company law ought to require that S should be free to distribute that profit by distribution of the asset itself, so long as S is solvent after the distribution so that the interests of creditors are protected. It is clear that, if S were to declare a dividend *in specie* of T, S would need reserves of only £750,000 (ie the book value of T) to cover the distribution. Thus, if V were to make a capital contribution of £750,000 to S, creating the necessary reserves, T could then be distributed back to V, creating the same economic result as a sale at £750,000. Incidentally, the capital contribution would not increase the base cost of S for capital gains tax purposes.

The Companies Act 1985, s 276 ought to help. It says that when a company makes a distribution of or including a non-cash asset and any part of the amount at which that asset is stated in the accounts relevant for the purposes of the distribution represents an unrealised profit, that profit is to be treated as a realised profit for the purpose of determining the lawfulness of the distribution. Thus, if T in fact stood in the books of S at its market value of £1,000,000, then S would have an additional unrealised profit of £250,000 which could be treated as realised for the purposes of determining the lawfulness of the distribution. As the amount of the distribution is only £250,000 it will be covered by the profit. To this it can be objected that it is not clear that s 276 applies to a deemed distribution of the *Aveling Barford* type, nor is it clear that the asset stated in the accounts is the asset which is distributed; it is the undervalue which is distributed, not the asset itself. The more robust view is that once transactions are treated as distributions they ought to be so treated for all purposes, including s 276 and, construing s 276 reasonably broadly, the asset in fact distributed is the property (or that part of the property which is not paid for) and that is the same asset which is stated in the accounts at an amount which includes an unrealised profit.

Unfortunately, s 276 is of no help where the asset has not been revalued but is shown at its original cost. To take advantage of s 276 a revaluation is necessary and it may be said that it seems artificial to revalue the asset to market value, draw up accounts, and then sell the asset at its original book value. However, the act of drawing up accounts does provide some safeguards. As a matter of common law, directors should not make distributions where they know that losses have been incurred which would have the effect, if accounts were prepared, of reducing reserves below the level of the distribution. The drawing of accounts is, however, of some additional protection because it forces these issues to be considered. Similarly, if a capital contribution were made to increase reserves, as suggested above, accounts would be required before the asset could be distributed. Thus the obvious ways through the *Aveling Barford* maze do involve some additional protection for creditors. On the other hand it must be said that the accounting recognition of an *Aveling Barford* distribution raises very difficult questions. Suppose S had the necessary reserves, would they be reduced by £250,000 after the transfer of T at book value? In practice they will not. The transfer will be accounted for as a transfer at book value and, on the assumption that the shareholders approve there will be no objection as the transfer will be otherwise lawful. After all the asset which is distributed (the under value) was never recognised in the first place.

Pending further authority it is not clear how the proposition in *Aveling Barford* interacts with the statutory restrictions on distributions. Where reserves are insufficient the safest course is to transfer the asset at market value. This will then result in a realised profit which is available to be distributed back to the parent once accounts are drawn which comply with s 270. In such a case it is better to pay cash for the asset as there can then be no doubt that the profit is 'realised'. Whether or not the profit is regarded as realised where the consideration is left outstanding on loan account will, however, depend on accounting principles (see s 262(3)) and advice from the auditors should be sought. If money is borrowed from an external source in order to finance the transaction, care needs to be taken to ensure stamp duty relief will be available (*see* p 281).

Where the transfer is by the target itself there is an over-riding consideration. As will be seen below, the Companies Act 1985, s 151, has the practical effect of requiring the transfer of assets in these cases to be made at market value, for cash payable on completion.

2.5   The Companies Act 1985, section 151

Section 151 is dealt with in detail in Chapter 5. Problems arise where a target company itself is a party to any transaction which is entered into for the purpose of the sale. Thus, where the purchaser is not to acquire some of the target's assets, and they are transferred out of the target to the vendors or within the vendor group prior to the sale of the target, then in addition to the points discussed above under the heading of 'Intra-group transfers' (section 2.4), the question will arise as to whether the transfer constitutes unlawful financial assistance.

Financial assistance is defined by s 152 (p 44) and the most satisfactory method of resolving a s 151 problem is to ensure that the transaction in question is not caught by the definition. Those parts of the definition which often cause a problem in structuring transactions are ss 152(1)(*a*)(iii) and (iv). Subsection (iii) refers to 'financial assistance given by way of loan or any other agreement under which any of the obligations of the person giving the assistance are to be fulfilled at a time when in accordance with the agreement any obligation of any other party to the agreement remains unfulfilled'. Subsection (iv) refers to 'any other financial assistance given by a company the net assets of which are thereby reduced to a material extent or which has no net assets'.

The first point to note is that if the assistance falls within s 151 will be infringed whatever the amount of the assistance whereas financial assistance falling within subs (iv) involves a breach of the section only where the net assets of the target are reduced to a material extent. So where the target transfers an asset to the vendor before the sale and the price is not paid at completion, s 151 will be infringed irrespective of the amount involved, while if the price is paid in full at completion, it is only if the price is less than the market value of the asset and the difference is material in relation to the net assets of the target that financial assistance will be given. Incidentally, although the financial assistance may be said in this case to be given to the vendor rather than the purchaser, it is in breach of the section nevertheless.

For this purpose 'net assets' are defined by s 152(2) as the aggregate of the company's assets, less the aggregate of its liabilities (including provisions as liabilities). It follows that reduction in net assets is not to be calculated by reference to the book value of the net assets but to their actual value and it is not safe to assume that net assets will not be reduced by a sale at book value. Of course, selling even at 'market value' does involve risk. If, despite all precautions to ascertain fair market value, the sale is in fact at less than market value, and the difference is such as to reduce the target's net assets materially, then the section will be infringed. It seems unlikely however that in such a case, where the parties are acting *bona fide*, a criminal prosecution would be successful. Also, the reference to 'material' reduction gives a margin for error.

If the amount of this undervalue is a distribution on *Aveling Barford* principles, then, so long as the target has sufficient distributable reserves, it may be said to be 'a distribution of a company's assets lawfully made' within s 153(3)(*a*) and thus outside the ambit of s 151 altogether. Given the penal nature of the section however, there is no doubt that a sale at market value is the safer course.

However fair the price, if it is left outstanding on loan account, the transaction will fall within subs (iii) and will constitute financial assistance. The cautious view is that the issue of eg debenture stock in satisfaction of the price does not mean that the transaction falls outside subs (iii). Looking at the transaction as a whole, there is a covenant to pay which is not satisfied at the time of completion. However, there is no authority on this point and a court might well hold, for example in a case which involved the issue of a listed security, that the issue of the security did fulfil the obligations of the purchaser of the assets.

Similar considerations arise where the target is to acquire an asset which is to be included in the sale. If the target pays more than a fair market price for the asset, then the assets will have been reduced, and title to the asset must be passed to the target at the time of the payment if subs (iii) is to be avoided. Transfers into the target at less than market value can cause tax problems (*see* p 310).

Cases sometimes arise in which the vendor wishes to have the benefit of a future successful realisation of an asset which the purchaser is disinclined to value highly, for example, the benefit of a claim which is to be pursued by the target. To avoid s 151 problems, it is necessary that this is dealt with by adjustment to the purchase price rather than by the target accounting to the vendor for the benefit it receives. This is the obverse of the case in which the target is to be compensated by the vendor for some liability if it is brought home. For tax reasons, it is normally advantageous to deal with these problems also by way of adjustment to the purchase price (*see* p 335).

2.6 Preference shares of the target

Where the target has preference shares, they often result from a past money-raising exercise and may be owned by a number of shareholders. The purchaser will consider whether or not these shares need to be acquired as part of the acquisition. Experience shows that there are advantages in acquiring preference shares at the same time as acquiring 100 per cent of the target's equity share capital because, although the preference shares may have very limited rights, they can cause problems in two respects. First, their continued existence will mean that the principle in *Rolled Steel* cannot apply so that even after the purchaser owns 100 per cent of the target, it will not be possible for the target to enter into transactions for any purpose other than for its own benefit. This may cause practical problems where the target would otherwise be expected to enter into transactions to serve the purposes of the group of which it now forms a part. Secondly, it should be borne in mind that if the target wishes to give financial assistance for the purpose of the acquisition of its shares or shares in its holding company, then holders of not less than 10 per cent in nominal value of the issued share capital of any class may apply to the court to object to the transaction. This is a risk which exists even when the shares are non-voting.

It may not be straightforward for the purchaser to acquire the preference shares by agreement with the holders. However, if the purchaser acquires 90 per cent pursuant to an offer to the whole class, then the purchaser will be able to apply the provisions of the Companies Act 1985, s 428 to acquire the minority. Even if the purchaser cannot achieve 90 per cent acceptance the target can reduce its share capital and pay off the preference shares. To do this, the purchaser will wish to ensure that following the acquisition it can procure the passing of the necessary special resolution. The procedure involves an application to the court under the Companies Act 1985, s 165, but in *House of Fraser v ACGE Investments* [1987] AC 387 it was held, confirming earlier authorities, that a reduction of capital which involves the return of capital to preference shareholders in priority to others in accordance with the rights attaching to those shares does not amount to a variation of rights. Therefore, although it may well be that the rights attaching to the shares will allow the shareholders to vote at the meeting to pass the necessary special resolution, in the absence of any special provisions in the articles deeming the reduction to be a variation of class rights, it is not necessary to have a separate meeting of the preference shareholders and if they are outvoted at the company meeting they will be paid off whether they like it or not. Of course, this involves paying off the shares at par, and where the coupon is low it may be less advantageous than a purchase at market value.

2.7   Examples

2.7.1   Example 1 (Intra-group transfers)

V plc agrees to sell its wholly owned subsidiary T Limited to P plc for £5,000,000. T owns a subsidiary TS which carries on a business which P does not want and V wishes to retain. TS stands in the books of T at £500,000 and it is agreed between V and P that, before the sale of T, TS should be transferred to another subsidiary of V, VS Limited, at book value. Opinions differ as to the market value of TS. In the absence of a purchaser for TS, it is unlikely that a definitive view can be obtained. V's auditors' advice, based on experience of the industry, is that a reasonable price for TS would be around £750,000.

In order to reduce the capital gains tax on the sale, it is intended that T should pay a dividend to V of £1,000,000 being the entire amount standing to the credit of T's reserves. (*See* p 268 for the taxation treatment of this.) This dividend is paid and lent back by V to T. The agreement between V and P is now that on completion, P will pay £4,000,000 for shares in T and will lend £1,000,000 to enable it to discharge its indebtedness to V at the same time.

In order to comply with the Companies Act 1985, s 151, TS must be transferred to V for at least £750,000, payable in cash on completion of that transfer. If this is done, then in terms of the deal with P, V will be the loser by the excess of the price paid over book value. The solution is either to persuade P to increase the price for T by the excess on the basis that T will have that amount in cash in excess of P's expectations, or if P will not do this, to pay a further dividend from T to V before the contracts are exchanged. However, the previous dividend will have exhausted T's distributable reserves and although the sale of TS will throw up a realised profit of £250,000, the latest accounts of T will not show sufficient distributable reserves to pay the additional dividend. It will therefore be necessary to draw up further interim accounts under the Companies Act 1985, s 270(4) and only the amount of distributable profit there shown can be paid by way of dividend. Drawing up accounts may of course create a number of problems, in particular verification of stock levels, and although the accounts need not be audited (as it is a private company), the auditors should be asked to give some comfort about the level of reserves.

2.7.2 Example 2 (Vendor Placing)

P plc agrees to buy T Limited from a number of individual shareholders. These shareholders want cash but P wishes to finance the issue through the allotment of shares. P therefore arranges a vendor placing under which it allots new shares in P to placees in consideration for the transfer of shares in T and arranges in the placing that the placees pay the exact amount of purchase money which the vendors require. The transaction is Super Class 1 for P and the amount of the issue exceeds the ABI guidelines.

The elements of the transaction are that P exchanges contracts with the vendors, conditional upon a resolution of approval being passed by P shareholders. At the same time P instructs its merchant bank (MB) to place the consideration shares and MB agrees with P that it will do so, subject to listing. Whether the contract between P and V will provide that P is bound to produce the cash on completion, or whether the contract is capable of rescission if the placing collapses will be a matter of negotiation. Because the issue exceeds ABI guidelines, MB will offer the shares to the existing shareholders of P *pro rata*, before allocating them to placees. This offer will be contained in the circular to shareholders which P sends out to explain the transaction and to convene the meeting. MB will place the shares with the placees subject to claw-back. When the resolutions are passed the consideration shares will be allotted, subject to listing, whereupon the transaction will be completed and the price paid by MB on behalf of placees to the vendor. These issues are dealt with in greater detail on p 237 *et seq.*

If some of the vendors wish to receive shares in P this can easily be accommodated under this structure, but if they want some other consideration eg loan notes to enable them to roll-over their capital gains to the next financial year, then a more complicated structure is required if P wishes to finance the acquisition (including the cost of redeeming the loan notes) through a market operation (*see* Example 3).

A cendor placing will not require a share premium account, because P has secured a 90 per cent equity holding in T in pursuance of an arrangement providing for the allotment of equity shares in P.

If the transaction is not conditional upon shareholder approval or on any other condition (eg OFT clearance) but it is still necessary to make the open offer to shareholders under the ABI guidelines then a number of difficult points arise. The purchaser will probably insist on being paid on completion. MB will place the shares but the final identity of the persons who will take them will not be known until the expiry of the open offer 15 business days later. The key point is that MB will have parted with the money at the beginning of the period and if something goes wrong will end up bearing the risk. These issues are analysed further at p 242.

2.7.3   Example 3 (Cash, shares and loan stock)

If the vendors want loan notes but the purchaser wishes to fund the acquisition wholly in shares then more complicated structures are necessary. One possibility is for MB to form a subsidiary. The subsidiary contracts to make the acquisition for cash and loan notes in the subsidiary, guaranteed by the purchaser. The purchaser agrees with MB to acquire the MB subsidiary for shares which MB then places in the market (with or without an open offer as appropriate under ABI guidelines). MB applies the proceeds of the placing to subscribe additional share capital in the MB subsidiary which is included in the sale to the purchaser. Thus, the purchaser issues shares and acquires a new company which has contracted to buy the target and owns the cash proceeds of the placing operation. The vendors have loan notes issued by the MB subsidiary and guaranteed by the purchaser, and the MB subsidiary has sufficient cash, as a result of the market operation, to pay for the target and to redeem the loan notes when they fall due.

Should the vendors want shares in the purchaser as well, then roll-over relief can be achieved by the use of flip flops. Some of the vendor shares in the target can be acquired by the MB subsidiary in exchange for shares in the MB subsidiary, which are then acquired by the purchaser from the vendors, in exchange for shares of the purchaser, at the same time as the purchaser acquires the remaining share capital of the MB subsidiary from MB.

Clearly this is a complicated structure, but it does achieve a share for share exchange for the purchaser (with merger relief and no s 89 problems) and a cash, loan note and share deal for the vendors with full roll-over relief. It is expensive in terms of stamp duty, because it involves the acquisition of the target by the MB subsidiary, the acquisition of the MB subsidiary by the purchaser, and (unless the SDRT saving structure is adopted (*see* p 244)) the stamp duty costs inherent in the placing exercise (in total three lots of stamp duty/SDRT). Some of the stamp duty can be avoided by incorporating the MB subsidiary as a Channel Islands company. This structure also has a certain amount of flexibility in the amount of money raised. Because all the cash (net of the bank's commissions) raised in the placing exercise goes into a company which is acquired by the purchaser, it is possible to raise rather more cash than is immediately required for the acquisition. This, however, will be subject to market reaction.

Chapter 3

Consents and Approvals

There are many cases in which it is necessary or desirable to obtain some consent or approval before acquisition and those which most commonly arise in practice are outlined below.

Many issues of consent or approval require consideration irrespective of the form of acquisition (eg shares or assets), whereas others are specific to either one form or the other. This chapter considers first those issues of general application followed by those issues of specific application to share and asset acquisitions.

3.1 All acquisitions

3.1.1 Consents required under contracts

The acquisition may have an impact on, or be affected by, a range of contracts which have been entered into by the vendor or the purchaser. Separately, the acquisition may affect contracts which are part of the acquisition itself eg contracts entered into by the target company or which form part of the business assets of the vendor to be acquired by the purchaser. Any such contract may make it necessary to obtain prior consent for the acquisition.

In the first instance, for example, loan agreements of the vendor may require the obtaining of consent of creditors or trustees for loan stockholders, as such agreements may contain clauses which restrict the disposal of a substantial part of its undertaking and assets. Alternatively, if the consideration for the acquisition is shares to be issued by the purchaser, the purchaser's advisers should consider whether the terms of any agreements entered into by the purchaser will be infringed by the issue of the shares. For instance, deeds constituting convertible loan stocks may restrict the issue of further share capital by the purchaser.

As far as the contracts which form part of the subject matter of the acquisition are concerned, the issue of consents under contracts arises both in the context of a share acquisition and an asset acquisition. The question of consent is slightly different in each of these cases: on the sale of the corporate target the question is whether any of the target's contracts contain provisions entitling the contract to be terminated, or accelerating rights under it, in the event of a change of control. For example it may be a term of loans made to a target company that they become repayable if control of that company changes. If the purchaser wishes the target to continue to enjoy the benefit of those loans, the consent of the lender should be obtained. Another example is where the target is party to joint venture arrangements, which typically restrict or trigger rights (eg under options) when control of one of the parties changes. By contrast, where the transaction involves the acquisition of business assets, it will involve transferring the benefit of contractual arrangements of the target business to the purchaser and in such case the purchaser will wish to consider whether there are any material contracts which cannot be transferred to the purchaser without consent, and accordingly whether consents to assignment or novation should be sought (*see further* Chapter 10 at p 209). While the question of whether consents are necessary or desirable is different for a share or asset transaction it should be noted that in either case it is likely to be the same category of contracts which require attention: if a contract contains a change of control clause which the purchaser considers significant, it will very often fall into that category of contracts for which assignment requires consent from a third party. In practice therefore, while consents under contracts inevitably require greater attention on an acquisition of business assets, the distinction is rarely as great as it may first appear.

In either case, approaching another party for consent may lead to that other party opening up negotiations for new contract terms as a condition of giving its consent. For confidentiality reasons and to protect its own business relations in the event that negotiations for the sale of the target break down, the vendor will often be reluctant to allow approaches to be made from anyone whose consent might be needed until a late stage, and perhaps only once contracts have been exchanged.

A further point to note, although not strictly a matter of consent, is where the target company or business participates in arrangements which are available only to members of the vendor's group, of which the target will need the benefit after completion. In such cases arrangements will need to be made to ensure that the target company or business will continue to have the benefit of these, or equivalent, arrangements after completion. These could include administration (eg payroll) services for which the purchaser may need short term assistance until its own arrangements are in place, or more permanent trading arrangements which had previously operated on an informal basis between group companies. In other cases severance from group arrangements will be necessary: the purchaser will wish to check that any guarantees given by a corporate target in respect of the vendor's banking arrangements, or other commitments, are released at completion and a vendor will wish to make arrangements for its release from guarantees of the target's obligations.

It is not possible to give an exhaustive list of the consents which may be required under or as a result of contracts because it will depend upon the particular terms of the previous contracts entered into by the vendor, purchaser and target and the extent to which they will affect, or be affected by, the sale. A warranty is often taken in order to prompt disclosure of contracts under which consents may be required or other arrangements (eg severance) may be necessary (*see* the Agreement for Sale (Shares), warranty 2.9 on p 413 and *see* also the Agreement for Sale (Assets), warranty 2.8 on p 573).

Consents may be required under articles of association, being a contract between shareholders. The articles of association of the target company (or, in the case of a sale of business assets, the vendor) may contain provisions which necessitate approval by the target (or vendor) shareholders. Where the acquisition is of all the shares in the target company, it is usual to deal with such matters in the sale agreement (to which all shareholders should be a party) which will typically include a waiver of any such rights (*see* the Agreement for Sale (Shares) cl 2.3 on p 381. If a purchaser is to acquire some only of the target's shares (including, for example, where a class of deferred or preference shares are to be left with existing shareholders) it should ensure that any consents or waivers required under the articles of association are obtained.

An acquisition of business assets will require consideration of a corporate vendor's articles of association, which may restrict the powers of the directors to sell without having first obtained certain approvals from the vendor's shareholders. Vendors financed by venture capital or which have been the subject of a management buyout will commonly have articles which give rise to a requirement for such approvals. Also, it should be noted that while directors will generally have delegated to them under the company's articles of association the management of the company, consideration should be given to whether such power extends to the sale of all of its assets with a view to the winding up of the vendor, when it may be prudent for the vendor's shareholders to approve the sale. See *Re Emmadart* [1979] Ch 540.

3.1.2 Special qualifications of the target

The conduct of certain types of activity is regulated or requires that the operator has a licence or other qualification. If the target business operates in a regulated sector or has any such licence or qualification it is likely that the purchaser will wish to preserve it or will need to obtain a licence or qualification of its own. Whether the acquisition is of the target's shares or of its business the issue of such industry and regulatory approvals will need to be considered. In the first instance, the issue will usually be whether any approval to the change of control will be required and in the second, it will generally be a question of whether (if the purchaser is already involved in the relevant industry) its existing licences and authorisations are broad enough to accommodate the business acquired or (if it is not) whether, and by when, a new licence or authorisation must be sought. In some instances, licences may be transferable with the business although more usually a transfer would be equivalent to an application for a new licence.

Examples of where regulatory licences or authorisations may be required are:

(a) the consent of the Council of Lloyd's to change of control of a Lloyd's broking company, underwriting management company and corporate members; change of control of an insurance broker will otherwise require consent under the Insurance Brokers (Registration) Act 1977;

(b) if the target is an insurance company the consent of the Secretary of State to a change in control may be required under the Insurance Companies Act 1982, Part II (as amended by the Insurance Companies (Third Insurance Directives) Regulations 1994). The transfer of insurance business is also regulated under the Insurance Companies Act 1982 and such a transfer may only be to a purchaser which is itself authorised under that Act to carry on insurance business;

(c) if the target carries on investment business it will be sensible to check that its continued authorisation under the Financial Services Act 1986 will not be affected by the change of ownership; members of SFA, IMRO and the PIA will, for example, require clearance from those organisations on any change of controller;

(d) a change in the controller of a bank will require the approval of the Bank of England under the Banking Act 1987.

The above is by no means exhaustive and the purchaser should ensure that it is fully aware of the regulatory environment in which the target operates, since a variety of other industries will require licensing considerations to be addressed. In some cases licences are held personally or the requirements may be applicable not only to the business which is carrying on the licensed activity, but also individuals involved in it (eg liquor licensing and gaming licences), when it will be important that the relevant employees are transferred to the purchaser and that other conditions of the licence are satisfied. Royal warrants (which are held by named individuals in relation to a business) are another example, although there is also a requirement to notify changes of control.

One further point to note, on a share acquisition, is whether any subsidiary of the target is regulated or has any such licence which will be affected by change of control.

Apart from those licences which are fundamental to the conduct of the business, the purchaser will, of course, wish to ensure, as part of its investigation, that all other permits and recognitions necessary or desirable for the conduct of the business are in place and (where relevant) transferable to it, eg waste disposal licences and trade association memberships.

3.1.3   Competition clearances

Acquisitions involving certain industries (eg newspaper) will automatically require clearance from the competition authorities. Other acquisitions may give rise to competition issues, depending on their size and the market shares involved. Competition issues should always be addressed at an early stage. A detailed discussion of competition issues is contained in Chapter 4.

3.1.4   Shareholder approvals

Purchaser

If the purchaser is a company, the approval of its own shareholders may be required for the acquisition. If the consideration for the acquisition is the issue of shares in the purchaser, an ordinary resolution may be required to increase the share capital and, unless the consideration shares can be issued under an existing general authority for the issue of share capital, an ordinary resolution will also be required to authorise the issue of the shares under the Companies Act 1985, s 80.

The statutory pre-emption rights conferred by the Companies Act 1985, s 89, which require new issues of shares to be offered first to existing shareholders, do not apply in cases where the shares are, or are to be, wholly or partly paid up otherwise than in cash (s 89(4)) (eg where the consideration is represented by the target shares or business assets, although in the latter case see the discussion of Companies Act 1985, s 103 below). It may, however, be the case that the purchaser's articles contain pre-emption rights or that there are some other relevant restrictions on the issue of share capital.

If the vendor is a director of the purchaser (or of the purchaser's holding company) or a person 'connected' with such a director within the meaning of the Companies Act 1985, s 346, shareholders' approval will normally be required under the Companies Act 1985, s 320, unless the value of the shares is less than the lower of £100,000 and 10 per cent of the purchaser's relevant assets. The section forbids a company from entering into 'an arrangement' for the purchase in these circumstances unless 'the arrangement is first approved' by the company in general meeting. Thus it would seem that a conditional contract (ie conditional on shareholder approval) is forbidden and the resolution should be passed before the contract is entered into. This can have significant implications where circumstances change between the time the notice convening the meeting is despatched and the passing of the resolution. If the parties are not bound to proceed, they may change their minds. Approval by the shareholders of the purchaser's holding company will be required under s 320 if the vendor is, or is connected with, a director of the purchaser's holding company. Section 321 provides some exceptions to the requirement of shareholder approval under s 320, including intra-group transfers, transactions in the course of winding up (if not a member's voluntary winding up) and arrangements with persons in their capacity as members.

The Companies Act 1985, s 104 imposes conditions (including the approval of shareholders) for the acquisition of 'non-cash assets' from subscribers to the memorandum of a newly incorporated public company within two years of its being issued with a certificate to do business, and from a member of a company registered or re-registered as a public company within two years from such registration or re-registration.

If the purchaser (or its holding company) is a listed company, the approval of shareholders for the transaction may be required by the Stock Exchange listing rules (contained in the *Yellow Book*) if the acquisition is Super Class 1 or a related party transaction. These matters are dealt with in Chapter 11. If the purchaser is a public company which is itself the subject of a take-over bid, r 21 of The City Code on Take-overs and Mergers may require shareholder approval for an acquisition.

Vendor

Approval of the vendor's shareholders may also be required under the Companies Act 1985, s 320 if the purchaser is a director of the vendor (or its holding company) or is connected with such a director, and the value of the shares or business assets exceeds the requisite value referred to above. Similarly, shareholder approval may be required under the Stock Exchange *Yellow Book* if the vendor or its holding company is listed or, being a public company, it is otherwise subject to a take-over bid. Shareholder approval may be required under the terms of a corporate vendor's articles of association (*see* 'Consents required under contracts' at section 3.1.1 *above*).

Target (corporate)

Apart from any consent which may be required as a result of provisions contained in a target company's articles of association (*see* section 3.1.1 *above*), any concurrent corporate action by the target may require shareholder approval eg a financial assistance whitewash under the Companies Act 1985, ss 155–158 or any repurchase of shares under ss 162–170.

3.1.5   The Companies Act 1985, section 103

Although not strictly a question of consent or approval, this provision is conveniently dealt with here.

Where the purchaser is a public company and the consideration includes an allotment of shares in the purchaser, s 103 provides that unless the transaction is exempt, the non-cash consideration must be valued by an independent person who must make a report to the purchaser, with a copy to the allottees. Failure to do this is visited with alarming consequences, namely, that the allottees become liable to pay for their shares in cash. However, there is an exception applicable where the acquisition is of shares in a target company: s 103(3) exempts an arrangement providing for the allotment of shares on terms that the whole or part of the consideration is to be provided by the transfer of all or some of the shares, or of all or some of the shares of a particular class, in another company. Section 103(4) provides, however, that this exemption does not operate unless it is open to all the holders of the shares in the target to take part in the arrangement (disregarding for such purpose shares held by, or by a nominee of, the purchaser). The exception in s 103(3) and (4) does not apply where shares are issued for other assets and accordingly s 103 is one reason why an acquisition of business assets is rarely financed directly by an exchange of shares with the vendor (*see further* p 251).

The exception from the requirement of valuation under s 103(3) and (4) is in practice helpful to facilitate transactions where the financing of a share acquisition is to be provided by an issue of the purchaser's shares. There are, however, some points to note. In a case where some of the shareholders are to sell their shares for cash and others are to sell for shares then, unless the transaction is structured so that each shareholder of the target can participate in the arrangement providing for the allotment of shares, an expert's report must be obtained. If, however, the shares which are to be acquired for cash are acquired in one transaction and the share for share transaction is carried through subsequently, it seems that an expert's report is not required as, in considering the second transaction (which is the one providing for the allotment of shares), the shares already acquired by the purchaser can be disregarded. The cautious practitioner will not, however, separate artificially what is, in truth, a single transaction or arrangement in order to avoid an expert's report. In view of the draconian consequences of failure to comply with the sections, it is safer to obtain the report. A further point to note is that under s 103(4), for the exception to apply, the arrangement must be open to all the relevant shareholders in the target. This means the registered shareholders and if shares are held beneficially by someone else, it is important to ensure that the nominee also becomes party to the arrangement so as to meet the requirements of the section.

3.2 Share acquisitions

3.2.1 The Financial Services Act 1986

Where the shares of the target are widely held it may be decided to effect the acquisition by an offer, rather than by acquisition agreement binding all parties. Minority shareholders who do not accept the offer may be compulsorily acquired if the requirements of ss 428–430F are met. Any circular offer to shareholders is likely to amount to an investment advertisement within the meaning of the Financial Services Act 1986, s 57 and, if that is the case, the circular may not be issued unless it is issued by an authorised person or unless its contents have been approved by an authorised person.

Article 3 of the Financial Services Act 1986 (Investment Advertisements) (Exemptions) Order 1996 (SI No 1586) provides that s 57 does not apply to an investment advertisement 'issued or caused to be issued by a body corporate … if the only persons to whom the advertisement is issued, other than persons to whom it may otherwise lawfully be issued are reasonably believed to be … members of … the body corporate … and the advertisement contains no invitation or information which would make it an investment advertisement other than an invitation or information relating to [shares, debentures or other defined investments in that body corporate or others in the same group]'. A similar exemption was contained in s 14(3)(*a*)(iii) of the Prevention of Fraud (Investments) Act 1958 but the view was always taken that where a company circulated an offer on behalf of a bidder, the bidder committed an offence under the Prevention of Fraud Act by causing the document to be circulated. The exemption contained in the Order, however, is wider than the old exemption and it may be that bidders who arrange for the bid circular to be sent out by the target will obtain the benefit of the exemption, at least in the case of a cash bid. If the offer included investments as consideration, the exception would not apply, as the circular would then relate to investments other than those in the body corporate issuing the circular.

However, the cautious practitioner will note that the Financial Services Act 1986 (Investment Advertisements) (Exemptions) (No 2) Order 1995 (SI No 1536) contains two exemptions which specifically address the problem of private company acquisitions and may conclude that the draftsman did not intend the exception under art 3 of the first Order to be used in these circumstances. Article 4 of the second Order provides that s 57 does not apply to certain investment advertisements in relation to a take-over offer if it is an offer for all the shares in, or the shares comprised in the equity or non-equity share capital of, a private company target. The conditions which must be satisfied before an offer comes within the scope of the Order are quite complicated, but the principal ones are these:

(a)   the terms of the offer must be recommended by all the directors of the target (other than any director who is also a director of the offeror);

(b)   if the offeror holds 50 per cent or less of the voting rights of the target and makes an offer for debentures or for non-equity share capital then the offer must include or be accompanied by an offer made by the offeror for the rest of the shares comprised in the equity share capital; and

(c)   an offer for equity share capital must be conditional upon acquiring 50 per cent or more of the voting rights.

The target must be a private company and the exemption will not apply if any shares comprised in the equity share capital of the target are or have at any time within the period of ten years immediately preceding the date of the offer been:

(a) listed or quoted on an investment exchange (in the United Kingdom or elsewhere); or

(b) shares in respect of which information has, with the agreement or approval of any officer of the target, been published for the purpose of facilitating deals in them, indicating prices at which persons have dealt or were willing to deal in them other than persons who were, at the time the information was published, existing members of a relevant class; or

(c) subject to a marketing arrangement which accorded to the company the facilities referred to in s 163(2)(*b*) of the Companies Act 1985; or

(d) the subject of an offer (whether in the United Kingdom or elsewhere) in relation to which a copy of the prospectus was delivered to the relevant registrar of companies (ie in accordance with s 41 of the Companies Act 1948, s 64 of the Companies Act 1985 or Part II of the Public Offers of Securities Regulations 1995).

For this purpose members of a relevant class are existing members or debenture holders of the target or employees or, in each case, their family members.

It will be noted that if the target is resident in the United Kingdom and any of these conditions is not satisfied it is likely that the Take-over Code will apply to an offer for its equity share capital (*see* p 2).

The offer must be accompanied by advice from an independent financial adviser. The Order contains detailed requirements about the contents of the offer and these are referred to in the notes to the specimen offer in Chapter 18.

Article 5 of the second Order gives a wider exemption for investment advertisements which are issued in connection with the sale or purchase of shares in a company which falls within Sched 1, para 21 to the Financial Services Act 1986 (*see* p 4), ie a transaction involving more than 75 per cent of the voting shares which is between parties each of whom is a body corporate, a partnership, a single individual or a group of connected individuals.

It should also be noted that under s 47 of the Financial Services Act 1986 it is a criminal offence punishable by a term of imprisonment not exceeding seven years, for any person knowingly or recklessly to make a statement, promise or forecast which is misleading, false or deceptive or dishonestly to conceal any material fact if that person makes the statement, promise or forecast or conceals the fact for the purpose of inducing another person…to enter or offer to enter into an investment agreement (which will include an agreement for the acquisition of shares in a private company). The section is not confined to written statements.

3.2.2 Consents under the Taxes Acts

The purchaser will normally seek advance clearance under the Taxation of Chargeable Gains Act 1992, s 138, where the consideration for the acquisition is shares and the vendors will wish to 'roll over' their capital gains into new shares (*see* p 265). Other sections under which clearances may be sought, because of possible adverse tax consequences, are the Income and Corporation Taxes Act 1988, s 707 (*see* p 277) s 765 (*see* p 279) and s 776 (*see* p 277).

3.3   Asset acquisitions

The principal areas of consent in the context of an asset acquisition are consents under contracts and regulatory licences and authorisations, both of which are considered above. The latter is considered above at p 23 under the heading 'Special qualifications of the target' and merits particular note, since it will be important, where the purchaser is not already engaged in the relevant business, to obtain licences to carry on the relevant business in order that, with immediate effect from completion, the purchaser is able to carry on business in compliance with the relevant legislation. The necessary licences should be applied for as early as possible in order that they are available at completion. In many instances the fact that the purchaser is to acquire an existing (licensed) business will, of course, be of relevance to the application and some licences may by their terms be transferable to it.

Apart from industry-specific consents, there are a range of other more general licences which the purchaser may need to consider. Licences under the Consumer Credit Act 1974 and the Data Protection Act 1984 are not infrequently required.

A particular area for the purchaser of assets is where leasehold or other consents are required for the transfer of property interests. These are considered in detail in Chapter 10 at p 198.

Chapter 4

Competition Law

Competition law plays an increasingly important role in the strategic planning of acquisitions. The carrying out of the acquisition can be affected by competition law in at least four ways: by the law controlling restrictive agreements and by the law controlling mergers, each under the United Kingdom and European Community systems respectively. These are considered in turn.

4.1   United Kingdom law affecting agreements

Acquisition agreements frequently contain clauses which are intended to restrict the conduct of the parties and, depending on the circumstances, their competitive activity. There may be continuing supply or purchase requirements or licences of intellectual property rights. However, the most common restrictions are covenants limiting competition. The purchaser is likely to demand a covenant from the vendor against competing with the target and may seek to extend this covenant to retiring directors or former individual shareholders of the vendor. For its part, the vendor, if it is continuing to operate in related businesses, may seek covenants from the purchaser against competing with any business retained by the vendor. Issues will arise as to the scope (both in terms of subject matter and geographical extent) and duration of these covenants.

4.1.1   Restraint of trade

Restrictive covenants can be invalidated by the common law doctrine of restraint of trade. If the doctrine does apply (as will usually be the case in this context) then a covenant will be upheld by the courts only to the extent that (i) it is necessary to protect a legitimate interest of the person wishing to enforce it, (ii) it is no more than is reasonable between the parties to protect that interest and (iii) it is reasonable in the public interest. The courts have recognised that the purchaser of a company or business has a legitimate interest in ensuring that the vendor does not immediately undermine the value of the transferred asset. However, the purchaser should take care to ensure that the covenants designed to achieve this are no broader—in terms of activities covered, geographical scope and duration—than necessary to provide reasonable protection. The question of what is reasonable will necessarily depend largely on the facts of each case. In practice most covenants which are acceptable under s 21(2) of the Restrictive Trade Practices Act 1976 or which are covered by the 1989 Orders (these aspects are explained in detail below) are unlikely to be invalidated by the common law, but restraint of trade remains as a trap for the unwary if covenants which are excessive in scope or duration are included. In view of this it is normal and prudent practice to draft each covenant in a form which permits it to be severed from the remainder under the usual English law rules; a court would not rewrite a covenant to make it more reasonable.

4.1.2   The Restrictive Trade Practices Act 1976

Despite the promises of reform contained in the 1989 White Paper *Opening Markets: New Policy on Restrictive Trade Practices* (Cm 727) and repeated in the DTI's Consultation Paper on the implementation of the Government's proposals (*Tackling Cartels and the Abuse of Market Power, March 1996*), the Restrictive Trade Practices Act 1976 remains the principal statute controlling the legality of restrictions in agreements. It is highly formalistic and applies only where two or more persons carry on business in the manufacture or supply of goods in the United Kingdom and two or more parties to the agreement accept certain statutorily defined restrictions. Restrictions to which the Act applies include those which relate to the price to be charged for goods, the terms or conditions on which they are to be supplied and the persons to whom or from whom they are to be supplied. A non-competition covenant of the type usually contained in an acquisition agreement clearly falls within the category of defined restrictions. There is a parallel but separate system controlling agreements relating to services.

Particulars of agreements falling within the control must be furnished within three months to the Director General of Fair Trading on Form RTP(C), (obtainable from the Office of Fair Trading, Field House, Bream's Buildings, London EC4 1PR). There is no longer a requirement to furnish before the restrictions take effect but, in the meantime, it is unlawful for a party who carries on business in the United Kingdom to give effect to, enforce or seek to enforce the agreement in respect of any such restrictions. Failure to furnish before the three month deadline expires renders all the restrictions unenforceable.

The Director General places the agreement on the public register of restrictive agreements and is obliged to refer it to the Restrictive Practices Court to declare whether or not it is in the public interest. In the meantime, although presumed to be against the public interest, an agreement registered in due time can be operated and enforced.

The Director General's duty is subject to certain exceptions and in practice acquisition agreements are either dealt with under these exceptions or exempted from the Act under the statutory instruments described below. The main exception is s 21(2) of the Act which relieves the Director General of his obligation to refer an agreement to the court if the Secretary of State for Trade and Industry gives directions to the effect that the restrictions in the agreement are too insignificant to require investigation by the court. This is an important provision and most registrable agreements are dealt with in this way. Other exceptions are s 21(1)(*b*)(i) where the agreement has been terminated altogether, and s 21(1)(*b*)(ii) where all the relevant restrictions have been removed (known as 'filleting' the agreement). In practice the Director General often applies a combination of these sections and the parties will be asked to remove objectionable or excessive restrictions while those remaining will be regarded as economically insignificant.

4.1.3 The 1989 Orders

The formalistic nature of the statute required a large number of acquisition agreements to be furnished to the Office of Fair Trading (OFT) under the Restrictive Trade Practices Act even though the restrictions they contained were innocuous and raised no public interest issues. For example, an agreement under which the vendors were a husband and wife, both covenanting not to compete with the purchaser, would frequently be registrable. This situation tied up considerable resources at the OFT. Accordingly, two statutory instruments were passed in 1989 (the Restrictive Trade Practices (Sale and Purchase and Share Subscription Agreements) (Goods) Order 1989 (SI No 1081) and the Restrictive Trade Practices (Services) (Amendment) Order 1989 (SI No 1082) which sought to exclude most vendor covenants from the scope of the 1976 Act. Two orders were necessary because of the separate systems controlling goods and services.

The orders provide that an agreement for the sale or purchase of shares in a company or the transfer of the whole of an interest in a business will be exempt from the 1976 Act if:

(a) 50 per cent or more of the issued share capital or the whole of the vendor's interest in a business is transferred;

(b) no pricing restrictions are imposed;

(c) restrictions are accepted only by vendors, their affiliates or by individual persons;

(d) any restrictions only limit competition by those accepting them with the business which is sold; and

(e)   the restrictions do not last more than five years from the date of the agreement or not more than two years after the expiry of any relevant employment or services contract, whichever date is the later.

The orders apply to acquisitions of assets, as well as shares, provided that these assets comprise a business as defined in the orders. Although the need to furnish particulars is much reduced by these orders, they are, like the 1976 Act itself, highly formalistic and considerable care is needed to make sure an acquisition agreement is exempted by them. In particular the orders do not apply if any restriction is accepted by the purchaser.

4.1.4   Deregulation

Pending the proposed abolition of the Restrictive Trade Practices Act, the government sought to reduce the burden of compliance further by introducing, in March 1996, two categories of non-notifiable agreements, one based on the combined annual turnover of the parties and their affiliates in the UK, and the second determined by the applicability of EC legislation exempting certain categories of agreement from the EC competition rules. Only the former (the Restrictive Trade Practices (Non-notifiable Agreements) (Turnover Threshold) Order 1996 (SI No 348)) is relevant here and the threshold is set at £20 million. A non-notifiable agreement does not have to be furnished to the OFT unless the Director General serves notice that he wants to review it.

The 1996 order applies only to agreements made on or after 19 March 1996 and, although designed to reduce the number of economically insignificant agreements furnished, the complexities of the turnover calculation may make parties reluctant to rely upon it.

4.1.5   Practical points

In practice, it remains a painstaking task to make sure that an acquisition does not fall foul of the 1976 Act. The exercise is also rather unrewarding as no real public interest issues arise and no sale or purchase agreement has ever found its way to the Restrictive Practices Court. The problem for those involved is that covenants which may be material to the deal in question can be rendered unenforceable by failure to furnish. Key practical points to remember are:
(1)   When considering the possible application of the 1976 Act, the arrangement as a whole must be considered, not only the specific contract containing the covenants.
(2)   Particulars cannot validly be furnished late. It has thus become customary to include a clause in the agreement providing that, if the inclusion of any restrictions makes it subject to registration under the 1976 Act, the coming into effect of those restrictions is suspended until particulars have been duly furnished to the Director General of Fair Trading. It is advisable to retain this suspensory wording despite the recent introduction of a three

month time limit for furnishing particulars referred to above, given that it is still unlawful to enforce or give effect to the restrictions before doing so.

(3) It is possible to furnish particulars of an acquisition on a 'fail-safe' basis but this practice is open to abuse. It is the job of the parties' legal advisers to form their own view on the possible application of the 1976 Act and to furnish particulars only in cases of genuine doubt, and with some explanation of the basis of that doubt. The OFT does not appreciate receiving voluminous acquisition documentation without any indication of why it may be registrable. (The OFT provides an optional annex to Form RTP(C) which can be used to identify the restrictions in question).

(4) The parties may often be concerned that their agreements may appear on a public register but it is possible to apply to the Secretary of State to have confidential business secrets deleted before the documents are placed on the register. This application must be made at the time particulars are furnished.

4.2 EC law affecting agreements

4.2.1 Restrictive covenants

The control of restrictive covenants under EC law is based on quite different principles from those of the United Kingdom Restrictive Trade Practices Act and is in some respects closer to the common law restraint of trade doctrine. This is not the place for an exhaustive account of EC competition law. For our purposes it is enough to be aware that the relevant principles are contained in Arts 85 and 86 of the Treaty of Rome and in the 1989 Merger Regulation (*see* section 4.4 below). Article 85 controls and (under para (1)) prohibits agreements and concerted practices which prevent, restrict or distort competition to a noticeable degree within the common market and which are liable to have an appreciable effect on trade between member states. An agreement can be exempted under para (3) of Art 85 if it has beneficial effects but this power is reserved exclusively to the European Commission and normally requires an individual notification on Form A/B. Article 86 prohibits the abuse of a dominant position and can sometimes apply to acquisitions. Both articles apply directly in the United Kingdom and can be invoked in the courts; there is no system of registration and the prohibition is backed by the power of the European Commission to impose heavy fines.

Restrictive covenants in acquisition agreements can fall within Art 85(1). As a general rule, however, they will fall outside the Article if they are no more restrictive than is necessary to secure the successful transfer of the business in question, ie they must be limited in scope, duration and geographical extent. The Commission first applied this view in its *Reuter/BASF* decision ((76/743/ EEC) [1976] 2 CMLR D44) in 1976 and the Court of Justice adopted a similar approach in the *Nutricia* case some ten years later (Case 42/84 *Remia BV and Others v EC Commission* [1985] ECR 2545). The Commission subsequently stated in the *Thirteenth Competition Policy Report* that for business transfers including know-how and goodwill, a five year restriction would be acceptable but where goodwill only was transferred, two years would usually be the maximum permissible.

These limits on duration are only rules of thumb but are not very different from the United Kingdom practice. The covenant must also be limited to the economic activity and geographical area of the business being sold. As with the United Kingdom system, the acceptance of a covenant by the purchaser will change matters considerably and will make it much more likely that the agreement will fall within Art 85.

4.2.2   Ancillary restrictions

The Commission confirmed its approach to restrictive covenants in the context of acquisitions in its 1990 *Notice regarding restrictions ancillary to concentrations* ([1990] OJ C203). This Notice explains the favourable attitude which the Commission will take to restrictions accepted in the context of a merger and which are directly related and necessary to its implementation. Although technically limited to acquisitions subject to the new EC Merger Regulation (dealt with in section 4.4), the Notice clearly applies to restrictions of the kind previously considered in the *Reuter* and *Nutricia* cases, as well as to other restrictions such as supply and purchase obligations and intellectual property licences, and to that extent indicates the Commission's attitude to restrictions in the context of acquisitions generally.

4.2.3   The acquisition as a whole

For a time the Commission tried to apply Art 85 to acquisitions as such. In the so-called *Philip Morris* decision (Cases 142 and 156/84 *BAT and Reynolds v Commission* [1987] ECR 4487) it applied Art 85 to an agreement for the acquisition by a tobacco undertaking of a minority interest in a competitor. Whether or not as a result of this move, the Commission was eventually given direct merger control powers, which are considered in section 4.4. The possibility remains of Art 85 being applied in certain circumstances to an agreement between competing undertakings where one purchases a minority stake in the other with the object or effect of restricting competition between them or indeed to any acquisition agreement forming part of a wider cartel arrangement.

4.2.4   How to decide whether Article 85 applies

It is often difficult to know for certain when Art 85 applies to an agreement. The agreement must restrict competition to a noticeable degree and also be liable appreciably to affect trade between member states. The Commission has issued a *Notice on agreements of minor importance* ([1986] OJ C231/2) (currently under review) laying down turnover and market share criteria below which Art 85 will not apply but many private companies have businesses big enough to fall outside this Notice. It may be doubtful that the proposed removal of the turnover criterion will make a great difference to the utility of the Notice in the context of most acquisition agreements. Given the growth of trade between the United Kingdom and other member states, the increasing removal of barriers to further trade and the geographical scope of covenants commonly included in acquisition agreements, the application of Art 85 is becoming more likely.

If the parties feel compelled to include restrictive covenants going beyond the limits laid down by the Commission or which cannot be regarded as ancillary to the acquisition itself, the only safe course is to notify the agreement to the Commission on Form A/B seeking exemption under Art 85(3). A quick outcome is unlikely but informal approaches to the Commission may help.

4.3   UK merger control

4.3.1   Jurisdiction

UK merger control is contained in the Fair Trading Act 1973 as most recently amended by the Companies Act 1989. In essence mergers which involve the taking over of assets with a gross value (worldwide) exceeding £70 million or which involve the creation or increase of a market share of 25 per cent or more in any given description of goods or services in the United Kingdom or a substantial part of it qualify for investigation by the Monopolies and Mergers Commission. If found by the Commission to be against the public interest, qualifying mergers can be prohibited by the Secretary of State or allowed subject to conditions. If the Commission clears the merger the Secretary of State must allow it to proceed. Although the Commission must consider whether the merger is in the broadest sense against the public interest, the main test is whether the merger will restrict competition to an unacceptable degree. The same concern governs decisions whether or not to refer a merger to the Commission. Private company and business acquisitions frequently fall within the scope of this control. Even if the assets test is not met, market shares depend on market definitions and some of these have on occasion been narrow if not arcane.

The acquisition of a controlling interest is clearly a merger but the regime also applies to the acquisition of a sufficient interest to control the policy of a company or even of an interest sufficient to confer the ability materially to influence the policy of a company (as a rule of thumb any holding over 10 per cent could, depending on the circumstances, give rise to material influence).

4.3.2 Procedure

There is no compulsory pre-notification of mergers under the Fair Trading Act. The regime can, however, be applied to mergers 'in contemplation' as well as to completed mergers and it is usual practice to give prior notice to the Mergers Secretariat of the OFT of any merger where reference to the Monopolies and Mergers Commission is a serious possibility. Such notice can be a formal request for 'confidential guidance' (given by letter to the requesting party without any party outside government being informed) or merely an informal clarification. Once the acquisition is in the public domain, and particularly if it is conditional on not being referred to the Commission, a formal clearance is normally requested. This leads to the OFT conducting a summary enquiry following which the acquisition is either cleared or referred to the Commission by the Secretary of State. The time for obtaining such clearance is not definite and can range from a few weeks to several months, although in 1994 the OFT adopted administrative timetables for dealing with qualifying mergers. These provide for the Director General to advise the Secretary of State within 39 working days (19 days in relation to requests for confidential guidance) in the expectation that the Secretary of State should be able to take a decision within a further six working days in either case. Adherence to these timetables is dependent upon receipt of a satisfactory and complete submission.

The 1989 Companies Act introduced a more formal, though still voluntary, pre-notification system. By filing a merger notice in the prescribed form, a timetable is set in train under which if no reference is made to the Commission after a given period, the merger is deemed to be cleared. The initial period is 20 working days but this can be extended by a further period of 15 days (35 working days in all). In round figures the parties are guaranteed an outcome within about seven weeks from filing. There are provisions for extending the period if false or insufficient information is provided and the period cannot start to run until the merger is in the public domain and the requisite fee has been paid (*see below*). The Director General can reject a merger notice in certain circumstances (for example if he believes the parties do not propose to carry out the merger) and the 'automatic clearance' procedure ceases to apply if the parties either complete the merger during the period or if either party merges with any other party (whether or not that unrelated merger restricts competition).

The Office's enquiries lead to a recommendation by the Director General of Fair Trading which the Secretary of State normally (though not invariably) follows. If the Director General recommends that a merger be referred to the Commission but considers the adverse effects could be avoided or remedied if the parties agreed to give either divestment or behavioural undertakings, the Secretary of State now has the power to accept such formal undertakings instead of making an MMC reference. The power to accept behavioural undertakings is relatively recent and there is considerable reluctance on the part of the authorities to take advantage of it. Structural remedies are still generally perceived as more appropriate in merger cases and pose fewer problems in terms of ongoing monitoring and enforcement.

The Secretary of State has only four months (recently reduced from six months) to make a reference to the MMC from the date the merger is completed or from the time all material facts relating to the merger have been brought to the attention of the authorities (whichever is the later).

Fees, ranging from £5,000 to £15,000, depending on the value of the assets taken over, are chargeable for (i) a reference decision by the Secretary of State, (ii) a decision not to refer, and (iii) the use of the merger notice procedure. In the latter case the fee must be paid on filing, ie some time earlier than the date for payment if the informal procedure is used. In each case a controlling interest must be acquired, not a lesser interest.

4.3.3   Specific Sectors

There are special regimes governing the acquisition of newspapers and water or sewerage companies and acquisitions in the coal and steel sectors which require prior authorisation under the Treaty of Paris (*see below*). Newspaper mergers are subject to compulsory pre-notification to the Department of Trade and Industry under pain of criminal liability and mergers involving water or sewerage companies are subject to a particularly rigorous regime requiring automatic reference to the Commission.

4.3.4   Practical points

An unexpected reference to the Commission can be a bruising experience for the parties and prior contact with the OFT will normally (but not always) limit the uncertainty. Where there is good ground for believing the authorities will wish to refer the acquisition to the Commission, there is no real alternative to making the agreement conditional on non-reference and presenting the strongest possible case to the OFT against a reference (*see* the Agreements for Sale at p 375 and p 501). Doing nothing and hoping for the best is not advisable.

4.4   EC merger control

4.4.1   Jurisdiction

Since the EC Merger Regulation (Council Regulation 4064/89 published in [1990] OJ L257) came into force on 21 September 1990 the European Community has controlled mergers ('concentrations' in Community parlance) which have a Community Dimension. These are defined by reference to turnover thresholds; the definition is satisfied if:

(a)   the parties' aggregate worldwide turnover exceeds 5 billion ECUs (currently about £3.9 billion); and

(b)   at least two of the parties have EC-wide turnover exceeding 250 million ECUs (currently about £200 million).

However, if each of the parties achieves two-thirds or more of its aggregate EC-wide turnover in one and the same member state, there is no Community Dimension. Commission Regulation 3384/94 ([1994] OJ L377) and a Commission Notice ([1994] OJ C385) give some guidance on how to calculate these turnover figures. There are special methods of calculation for banks, other credit institutions and insurance undertakings. The Commission has also published guidance Notices on the meaning of the term 'concentration' and the notion of 'undertakings concerned' (which identifies which companies are to be taken into account in determining jurisdiction).

The European Commission is currently seeking to extend the scope of the Merger Regulation by lowering the worldwide and EC-wide turnover thresholds.

4.4.2   Substantive assessment

Concentrations with a Community Dimension are (with a few exceptions) exclusively subject to the EC regime (ie national merger controls are disapplied). Under this regime a merger will be prohibited if it creates or strengthens a dominant position as a result of which effective competition would be significantly impeded in the common market or in a substantial part of it. As such the test is a stringent one and few mergers have been prohibited by the Commission outright (for example *Aerospatiale/Alenia/de Havilland,* IV/M053), although a number of others have only been allowed subject to conditions.

4.4.3   Procedure

If a merger falls within the Regulation it must be pre-notified on Form CO to the EC Commission under pain of fines. The EC Commission conducts an initial enquiry lasting four weeks. If it finds serious grounds for thinking the merger may be incompatible with the common market it initiates a more thorough investigation which lasts up to four months. At the end the EC Commission will either clear or prohibit the merger by decision.

4.4.4   One stop shop

In principle, the EC regime is a 'one stop shop' and national authorities (eg the OFT and the Monopolies and Mergers Commission) cannot interfere. However, there is a limited right for national authorities to investigate factors other than competition and a right for national authorities to request the Commission to pass consideration of a merger back to them. This is confined to cases where there is a distinct national market and the merger's effects are confined to that market. The Commission can, and on occasion does, refuse such requests. The practical effect of this provision is to require the parties to an acquisition whose main effects are felt in the United Kingdom but which, on a turnover basis, falls within the Merger Regulation to keep both the OFT and the European Commission fully informed of the details of the acquisition.

4.4.5 Joint ventures

The Merger Regulation applies a test of 'decisive influence' and covers both the acquisition of and a change in the nature of such influence. It applies to joint ventures which are concentrative in nature and the Commission has published a guidance Notice on the complexities of the distinction between concentrative and collaborative joint ventures. It is quite possible for the acquisition of a significant interest in a company to be considered as a merger under the UK merger control regime but as a collaborative joint venture under EC law and subject to Art 85 (see for example the *Allied/Carlsberg* case (1992)). The European Commission is seeking reforms in this area.

4.4.6 Practical points

Whether acquisitions and disposals of a company or business assets are subject to EC merger control will depend on whether the relevant turnover thresholds are fulfilled. It is essential to analyse the relevant turnover figures well in advance of the date the agreement is supposed to take effect. The EC Commission's Merger Task Force (a separate Directorate within Directorate General IV) makes a practice of giving informal guidance on whether the Merger Regulation applies and on more substantive issues and it is very advisable to take advantage of this openness.

4.4.7 The European Coal and Steel Community

Although the EC merger regime is relatively new, control under the Treaty of Paris of mergers involving undertakings in the coal and steel sectors has applied for over 45 years. Article 66 of the ECSC Treaty subjects relevant mergers to prior authorisation by the EC Commission and the control applies even if only one of the parties is an ECSC undertaking.

The nature and scope of the control differs in detail from that of the Merger Regulation. Decision 25–67, last amended in 1991, provides reasonably generous exemption by category, depending on the tonnages of coal or steel products involved. The Commission has wide powers to order the separation of unauthorised mergers and acquisitions and to impose penalties. Unlike EC competition law, the Commission's exclusive jurisdiction does not depend on there being any effect on trade between member states or a Community dimension. The Treaty of Paris will expire in 2001 and ECSC mergers will then fall under the general regime of the Treaty of Rome.

4.4.8   Other EC aspects

The enactment of the Merger Regulation and the confirmation by the European Commission that it will apply the doctrine of ancillary restraints in the context of mergers have largely overtaken the previous attempts by the Commission to apply Arts 85 and 86 to acquisitions, but there are still areas of uncertainty. Thus, for mergers which fall below the Merger Regulation thresholds, the Regulation disapplies the Commission's powers to investigate and act under Council Regulation 17 of 1962. This still leaves open the possibility of proceedings in a national court under Art 86 based on the doctrine established in the *Continental Can* case (Case 6/72 [1973] ECR 215) which prohibits the strengthening of a dominant position by the acquisition of competitors.

Joint ventures which are collaborative rather than concentrative in nature (*see above*) will have to be considered under Art 85 but detailed consideration of this and the Commission's proposals for reform is outside the scope of this chapter.

4.4.9   European Economic Area

In 1992 the European Community and its member states entered into an agreement with most of the EFTA states (barring Switzerland which voted not to ratify the agreement and, for a time, Liechtenstein) which contained competition rules almost identical to those contained in the Treaty of Rome, including a merger control regime. The EEA agreement also established procedures for co-operation between the Community institutions and their counterparts newly established in EFTA.

Following the accession of Austria, Finland and Sweden to the EC, the EEA agreement is likely to have little practical relevance in the future. However it will always be advisable to consider these parallel rules whenever an acquisition involves companies which are based in or have substantial operations in Norway, Iceland and Liechtenstein.

4.4.10   Other Merger Control

Many countries, including most Member States of the EEA, have systems of merger control in place. These vary considerably in their nature and effect and a detailed description is beyond the scope of this chapter. Following the introduction of the EC Merger Regulation, these national systems should be relevant only where the tests for a Community Dimension are not met. However, if that is the case and if there is any reason to suppose that an acquisition will have effects in or will involve businesses located in another such country, it would be prudent to seek local advice. This will enable any necessary applications to be made in good time and avoid any unanticipated adverse consequences.

Chapter 5

Financial Assistance

This chapter is exclusively concerned with share acquisitions and is of no application to a transaction which is limited to the sale and purchase of business assets.

Any transaction proposed to be entered into by the target company, whether before, at, or after its acquisition, should be examined with care in light of Companies Act 1985, s 151, which prohibits a target from giving financial assistance before or at the same time as an acquisition of its shares. Section 151(1) provides that:

> ...where a person is acquiring or is proposing to acquire shares in a company, it is not lawful for the company or any of its subsidiaries to give financial assistance directly or indirectly for the purpose of that acquisition before or at the same time as the acquisition takes place.

Section 151(2) further prohibits financial assistance given after the acquisition:

> ...where a person has acquired shares in a company and any liability has been incurred (by that or any other person), for the purpose of that acquisition, it is not lawful for the company or any of its subsidiaries to give financial assistance directly or indirectly for the purpose of reducing or discharging the liability so incurred.

The section is penal, and the criminal and civil consequences of a breach are set out below (p 60).

The law as it presently stands was introduced by the Companies Act 1981. The provisions re-enact, with significant change, the Companies Act 1948, s 54. A good proportion of the case law in this area is in respect of the old law and is of limited value in considering the application of s 151 (other than in respect of the consequences of a breach). One general point which should not be overlooked, however, is that the articles of many companies will restate s 54 of the 1948 Act (see eg reg 10 of the pre-1981 Act Table A). It may be appropriate to amend the articles of the target by deletion of any such provision. The restrictions on giving financial assistance in the 1985 Act are in certain respects less restrictive than the old law and such a prohibition in the articles may inhibit reliance on the current law.

5.1   The prohibition against giving 'financial assistance'

The purpose of the section has been said to be the protection of creditors and minority shareholders. With this in mind, there are some transactions which are plainly objectionable, and are clearly prohibited by s 151(1). If a purchaser does not have the cash to finance the acquisition, but the target does, creditors and minority shareholders in the target may be adversely affected if the purchaser were able to take a loan from the target, and use the proceeds of the loan to acquire the target from the vendor.

Section 151 prohibits a target or its subsidiaries from giving 'financial assistance'. Financial assistance is defined in s 152(1)(*a*):

(a) 'financial assistance' means
  (i)   financial assistance given by way of gift,
  (ii) financial assistance given by way of guarantee, security or indemnity, other than an indemnity in respect of the indemnifier's own neglect or default, or by way of release or waiver,
  (iii) financial assistance given by way of loan or any other agreement under which any of the obligations of the person giving the assistance are to be fulfilled at a time when in accordance with the agreement any obligation of another party to the agreement remains unfulfilled, or by way of the novation of, or the assignment of rights arising under, a loan or such other agreement, or
  (iv) any other financial assistance given by a company the net assets of which are thereby reduced to a material extent or which has no net assets.

The section provides a partial definition; a transaction proposed to be undertaken by the target company or its subsidiary which falls within one of the sub-definitions set out in s 152(1)(*a*)(i)–(iv) above will often be caught, but to be prohibited the transaction must also constitute 'financial assistance' since, for example, s 152(1)(*a*)(i) refers not simply to a 'gift', but to 'financial assistance given by way of gift'.

The expression 'financial assistance' itself has no technical meaning. The frame of reference for the expression is 'the language of ordinary commerce. One must examine the commercial realities of the transaction and decide whether it can properly be described as the giving of financial assistance by the company' (Hoffmann J in *Charterhouse v Tempest Diesels* [1986] BCLC 1 (a case on the old law), at p 10). It follows that, although a transaction which falls within one of the descriptions contained in s 152(1)(*a*) will satisfy the technical element of the definition, it is also necessary, before a transaction falls within the scope of s 151, to show that someone is being assisted, in a financial way, by the transaction. This approach to the non-technical limb of 'financial assistance' was endorsed by the Court of Appeal in *Barclays Bank plc and others v British & Commonwealth Holdings plc* [1996] 1 BCLC 1, at p 40. That case concerned a scheme for redemption of B&C's shares, failing which the shareholder could exercise an option to put the shares on a company formed and financed by a number of banks. B&C gave a covenant to the banks to maintain certain asset ratios, breach of which would give rise to a claim in damages by the banks against B&C. It was held that the covenant did not amount to an indemnity within s 152(1)(*a*)(ii), but was it 'any other' financial assistance under s 152(1)(*a*)(iv)? The Court of Appeal first considered whether financial assistance, in its ordinary commercial sense, had been given. The court adopted a similar approach to that taken in two Australian cases (set out in the judgment at pp 40–41), drawing a distinction between a covenant which was given for the purpose of giving financial assistance, and a covenant given to reassure the shareholder or to induce it to enter into the transaction. The court held that financial assistance, in the commercial sense, had not been given. Some reservation to the B&C decision has been expressed (see Palmer's Company Law, 25th edn, para 6.505 (April 1996)). However, it is undeniably good law in its underlying principle and will assist practitioners when advising on *bona fide* obligations by the company which are intended to reassure, or induce, rather than give the recipient 'financial assistance'.

While the non-technical term 'financial assistance' appearing in ss 152(1)(*a*)(i)–(iv) does not have a recognised legal significance and it should be given its ordinary commercial meaning, where other terms used in those sub-sections have a recognised legal significance those terms should be interpreted accordingly. So, for example, 'indemnity' in s 152(1)(*a*)(ii) is a contract under which one party agrees to keep the other harmless against loss *(Yeoman Credit Ltd v Latter* [1961] 2 All ER 294), and does not extend to an arrangement which gives rise to payment of an equal amount by way of damages for breach.

Financial assistance may be given not only to the purchaser of the shares in the target, but also to the vendor and, presumably, any other person (*Armour Hick Northern Ltd v Whitehouse* [1980] 1 WLR 1520). Financial assistance may cost the target nothing. So, for example, where the target purchases assets from the purchaser at their market value to put the purchaser in funds to enable it to make the acquisition, the target itself is not in a worse position, but the purchaser selling the assets to the target now has the cash funds to enable it to make the acquisition and so has been financially assisted: see *Belmont Finance Corporation Ltd v Williams Furniture Ltd (No 2)* [1980] 1 All ER 393. As Buckley LJ said, in the Court of Appeal (at p 402):

> If [the target] buys something from [the purchaser] without regard to its own commercial interests, the sole purpose of the transaction being to put [the purchaser] in funds to acquire shares in [the target], this would, in my opinion, clearly contravene the section, even if the price paid was a fair price for what is bought, and a *fortiori* that would be so if the sale to [the target] was at an inflated price.

The judge went on to say that if the transaction was in the genuine commercial interests of the target, the fact that the target entered into the transaction partly with the object of putting the purchaser in funds to acquire its own shares or with knowledge of the purchaser's intended use of the proceeds might involve no contravention of the section, but he did not wish to express a concluded opinion on that point. The law has changed since *Belmont*, and a court would now take a different approach. Provided it was decided that there was financial assistance in the non-technical sense, that case would now turn on whether there was any material reduction in the company's net assets and if there was, whether it would fall within one of the exceptions (*see below*). Interesting questions arise where a target with no, or negative, net assets enters into a transaction which assists a party to the share acquisition, but as a result of which the target is plainly better off. 'Any other' financial assistance is prohibited by a company with no net assets (s 152(1)(*a*)(iv)) which, of course, includes a company whose liabilities exceeds its assets; however, in such case it may be possible to argue, looking to Hoffmann J in *Tempest Diesel*, that no financial assistance has been given. Alternatively, there may be assets (and liabilities) not reflected in the company's books which should be taken into account in determining whether, for the purpose of the section, the company in fact has no net assets.

Transactions which are financial assistance within the meaning of s 152(1)(*a*) will be prohibited if they are 'for the purpose of' the acquisition of the shares in the target (or, in the case of s 151(2), reducing or discharging a liability incurred for that purpose). Transactions by the target or its subsidiaries in the ordinary course of their business and transactions entered into wholly for some other purpose will not be affected, but any transaction thought to be outside the scope of the section for these reasons but which is, nonetheless, to be entered into in the context of a share acquisition should be examined with care—any transaction which is entered into by a member of the target group in the course of a transaction in the target's shares or which is a step in an overall scheme or a term of the bargain between the parties is likely to be 'for the purpose' of the acquisition, whether it is to occur before or after the acquisition of the shares. It is generally thought that the section can apply even if no acquisition of shares ultimately takes place.

Financial assistance will be prohibited if given directly for the purpose of the acquisition, or indirectly. So, for example, a loan made by the target to a subsidiary of the purchaser, rather than to the purchaser itself, will be prohibited if its purpose is to finance the acquisition. Section 151 will not, however, prohibit financial assistance being given to a target by its parent or 'sister' companies. The application of the sections to overseas companies also merits mention: while it is clear from a literal reading of s 151, taken with the statutory definition of 'subsidiary' in s 736, that the prohibition would extend to an overseas subsidiary giving assistance for the purpose of an acquisition of shares in its English parent company, the courts have held that the section is limited to assistance given by subsidiary *companies*, ie English companies: *Arab Bank plc v Mercantile Holdings Ltd* [1993] BCC 816. Nor, it seems, is financial assistance by an English subsidiary of an overseas company prohibited as it is a necessary requirement of the section that there is, or is proposed, an acquisition of shares in a *company*, defined for that Part of the Act as a company formed and registered under the Act. This is probably a defect in the statute, and is inconsistent with the reasoning of Millet J in *Arab Bank* who, it seems, only reluctantly reached such a conclusion (if indeed he did) 'I can see no possible reason or justification for excluding such a case from the prohibition and, if this was indeed the result of the recasting of the statutory language in 1981, I think that it must have been inadvertent'. Where an English subsidiary is called upon to take part in such a transaction the parties should satisfy themselves that the transaction is not otherwise unlawful (for example because it involves a return of capital to shareholders without the sanction of the court, contrary to the rule in *Trevor v Whitworth* (1887) 12 App Cas 409, recently discussed in *Barclays Bank v B&C*) or *ultra vires*. Although s 151 does not apply to overseas companies, practitioners should be aware that assistance given by an overseas subsidiary may involve assistance by the English parent, for example, ratification by the parent or, more obviously, a waiver of dividend.

It is often the case that a target is 'groomed' for sale—particularly where, prior to its sale, it is part of a group of companies. In that case, it is not uncommon for inter-company balances to be settled, prior to, or as part of, the sale arrangements, or for assets (for example, premises owned but not used or required for use by the target group) to be moved between group companies. Assets removed from the target group can be removed by way of pre-sale dividend (although *see* p 268 for the tax treatment of pre-sale dividends). This would not infringe s 151 if the target had sufficient distributable reserves (s 153(3)(*a*)). Alternatively they might be sold to another group company. The sale of an asset intra-group may be prohibited if it results in material reduction in the net assets of the target (s 152(1)(*a*)(iv)) or if there are deferred payment terms (s 152(1)(*a*)(iii)).

To decide whether or not there has been a material reduction in net assets under s 152(1)(*a*)(iv), it is necessary to look at actual or 'fair' value, not book values, of the assets in question (this is apparent from s 152(2), when compared with s 154(2)) and it seems clear that if an asset is sold in consideration for some obligation or entitlement which would not normally be reflected in the company's books, that obligation or entitlement should nonetheless be regarded as part of the company's net assets when determining whether there has been a material reduction. In *Parlett v Guppys (Bridport)* (1996) *The Times,* 8 February the financial assistance under consideration was an agreement (as part of a resolution of disputes involving family companies) under which salary, bonus and pension payments were to be paid to Mr Parlett, the chairman and managing director of the companies in return for the transfer of shares owned by him in one of the companies ('Estates'), to be held jointly by himself and his two sons. When considering whether the arrangement involved a material reduction in net assets of Estates, the Court of Appeal considered that the services to be rendered by Mr Parlett should be taken into account as an asset of the company, even though they would not be shown in the accounts of Estates. The Court of Appeal also rejected the suggestion that, in determining the extent of any reduction in net assets for the purpose of s 152(1)(*a*)(iv), the value of future payments should be taken into account, instead agreeing that, on the assumption the services to be provided were worth the amount to be paid for them, the reduction in net assets should be measured only by that part of the payment that had fallen due. The difficulty was that the court found that the amount payable as salary and bonus, in the absence of the transfer of shares, would have been substantially lower. Ultimately, it did not need to decide the point but it seems likely that, to the extent of the overpayment, the present value of overpayments in the future should be used as a basis for determining any net asset reduction. If assets are transferred at less than their actual value there will be financial assistance unless the reduction in net assets of the target is not material. There is no guidance in the Act as to what is meant by 'material', although it is generally thought among practitioners to mean a reduction of between 1 and 5 per cent of total net assets. That is to say that all would agree that a reduction of less than 1 per cent is immaterial and all would agree that a reduction of more than 5 per cent is material. Some suggest that the test is not only relative but also absolute and that, for example, a reduction in net assets of more than £100,000 would always be material, irrespective of the size of the target, but that is not a view shared by the author. Such judicial comment as there is on the point does not take matters much further, although it might be thought to favour the 'relative' approach. In *Parlett v Guppys*, Nourse LJ, noting that Counsel were disposed to agree that a reduction of 5 per cent or more would have been material, said 'there can be no rule of thumb in such a matter … the question is one of degree to be answered on the facts of the particular case'. The practitioner must continue to apply common sense.

If the liabilities of the target exceed its assets, all forms of financial assistance under subheading (iv) are forbidden, whether or not the net assets of the target are reduced. Following *Belmont,* this would appear to be the case irrespective of the fairness of the transaction to the target, and the financial assistance would be permissible only if one of the exceptions were available.

Every transaction should be considered on its own facts. It is possible that a sale at gross undervalue might, to the extent of the undervaluation, be treated as a gift (even if the undervalue is not material in the context of s 152(1)(*a*)(iv)), and so constitute the giving of financial assistance within the meaning of s 152(1)(*a*)(i), where materiality is irrelevant (see, for example, *Plaut v Steiner* (1989) 5 BCC 352). The overpayment of salary and bonus in *Parlett v Guppys* was not, it seems, regarded as a gift. In a more flagrant case the payment of 'bonuses' in *Re Hailey Group Ltd* [1993] BCLC 459 were regarded as a gift. An asset sale which does not give rise to a material reduction in net assets will not be financial assistance if the terms of sale of the asset provide for all consideration to be paid at completion. If there is any deferral of consideration or if any part of the consideration is left outstanding to be calculated by reference to profits or some other post-completion adjustment, then the transaction is likely to fall within s 152(1)(*a*)(iii) and, as a result, be prohibited. Also, particular care should be taken where the transfer of assets is intra-group; if there is a transfer of assets which gives rise to any reduction in net assets (even if not material) then, as described on p 11, it may be treated as a distribution by the target company and, in the absence of adequate distributable reserves, be unlawful.

It is also prohibited, under s 151(2), to give financial assistance after the acquisition of shares in the target, if the assistance is given for the purpose of reducing a liability incurred for the purpose of that acquisition. Accordingly, it will be unlawful for a person who borrows to finance the acquisition of shares in the target, to use the assets of the target to reduce his borrowings. The scope of the prohibition in s 151(2) is widened by s 152(3), which extends the definition of the reference to a person 'incurring a liability' in s 151(2), to include the case where that person '[changes] his financial position by making an agreement or arrangement (whether enforceable or unenforceable, and whether made on his own account or with any other person) or by any other means'. The section also extends the meaning of the reference in s 151(2) to financial assistance being given for the purpose of reducing or discharging a liability incurred by a person for the purpose of the acquisition to include assistance given 'for the purpose of wholly or partly restoring his financial position to what it was before the acquisition took place'.

Section 152(2), when taken with s 152(3), thus has the effect of prohibiting a transaction under which a purchaser who has not borrowed (ie has not incurred a liability to finance the acquisition, but has financed it out of its own resources) receives assets from the target for example, by way of purchase at an undervalue. The effect would be wholly or partly to restore the purchaser's position to what it was before the acquisition took place and is prohibited. Such a transaction will be permissible if the target has adequate distributable reserves (see s 153(3)(*a*)) but to fall within the exception the transaction ought to be documented as a distribution (*see* p 14).

Issues under s 151(2) most commonly arise in the case where third party finance is used by a purchaser and the lender requires a guarantee from the target, or security over the target's assets is to be taken to support the acquisition finance. Guarantees or security given at, or immediately before, the time of acquisition are plainly within s 151(1). It is not immediately obvious, on the wording of s 151(2), that a guarantee or security given after the acquisition has the effect of 'reducing or discharging' the liability of the purchaser, or of any other person who incurred that liability for the purpose of the acquisition. It cannot be right that what is prohibited at the time of acquisition is permitted a day later, and the usual practice would be to treat the giving of any such guarantee or security following the acquisition of the target as falling within the scope of s 151(2); it will often be a lender's requirement that upstream security be given by the target and it is said (based on the extended definitions of s 152(3)), that the purchaser has incurred a liability by agreeing to procure security from the target, which is 'reduced or discharged' when the security is given. Accordingly, where available, use is made of the 'whitewash' procedure under ss 155–158 to ensure that such guarantees and security are lawfully given; indeed, any lender will, properly advised, insist on the whitewash procedure being followed (*see* p 54). It will be necessary to show that the guarantee is given *bona fide* in the interests of the target, which is not easy. The principle in *Rolled Steel* may be relevant (*see* p 12).

A further difficulty with s 151(2) is that the prohibition on giving financial assistance after the acquisition has taken place is not limited in time. Therefore, any financial assistance given after the transaction has occurred remains prohibited if it is for the purpose of reducing or discharging a liability incurred for the purpose of the acquisition. In practice, this can cause problems with the refinancing of funds borrowed for an acquisition, where new money is borrowed partly for one purpose (the refinancing), and partly for another, lawful, purpose (say, for group working capital purposes). It may not be safe to assume that any guarantee or security is being taken solely for the working capital purpose, rather than refinancing the purchase of the shares. If security was given at the time of acquisition it will, necessarily, have been the subject of a s 155 'whitewash' (*see below*). Where the original statutory declaration provides for variations to the terms of the financing it may be possible, depending on the facts, to say that the original whitewash also covers the refinancing. The possibility of future refinancing when preparing the statutory forms should not be overlooked (as to preparation of the forms, *see further below* p 56). Where, however, the target is giving guarantees or security for the first time then unless it is clear that the obligations secured in the refinancing are wholly unconnected to the acquisition, a 'whitewash' of the security should be undertaken. A difficult example is the case where the security is given to support, or refinance, a facility which was available for the acquisition but not drawn on if the purchaser has then made use of the facility for other purposes, having used up his available cash resources for the acquisition, when it is difficult to be satisfied that the refinancing is not within the extended scope of s 151(2).

One practical point to note is that the question of refinancing may not come up until several months after the acquisition has been completed and indeed, the first the lawyers may know of it may be when requested to review documentation or give opinions to the lenders. The purchaser then finds he must incur further cost by the whitewash (or worse, that the security may not be given at all). There is great merit in drawing the restrictions and the requirements of s 151 and the whitewash procedure firmly to the purchaser's attention before completion of the acquisition.

5.2 Exceptions to the prohibition

Transactions which are, on the face of it, prohibited by s 151 might fall within one of the exceptions set out in s 153 or be capable of approval under the 'whitewash' procedure in ss 155–158.

Section 153(3) provides that certain arrangements which might otherwise be prohibited are exempt. While this chapter considers in detail only those exceptions of relevance in the context of an acquisition, consideration should always be given to any proposal which might otherwise fall within the ambit of s 151, to see if it might be restructured so as to fall within one of the other exceptions. The exceptions provided by s 153(3) are:

(a) a distribution of a company's assets by way of dividend lawfully made or a distribution made in the course of the company's winding up,

(b) the allotment of bonus shares,

(c) a reduction of capital confirmed by order of the court under section 137,

(d) a redemption or purchase of shares [made in accordance with Chapter VII of Part V of the Act],

(e) anything done in pursuance of an order of the court under section 425 (compromises and arrangements with creditors and members),

(f) anything done under an arrangement made in pursuance of section 110 of the Insolvency Act 1986 (acceptance of shares by liquidator in winding up as consideration for sale of property), or

(g) anything done under an arrangement made between a company and its creditors which is binding on the creditors by virtue of Part I of the Insolvency Act 1986.

Further exceptions are contained in s 153(4), namely:

(a) where the lending of money is part of the ordinary business of the company, the lending of money by the company in the ordinary course of its business;

(b) the provision by a company, in good faith in the interests of the company, of financial assistance for the purpose of an employees' share scheme,

(bb) without prejudice to paragraph (b), the provision of financial assistance by a company or any of its subsidiaries for the purposes of or in connection with anything done by the company (or a company in the same group) for the purpose of enabling or facilitating transactions in shares in the first-mentioned company between, and involving the acquisition of beneficial ownership of those shares by, any of the following persons—

  (i)   the *bona fide* employees or former employees of that company or of another company in the same group; or

  (ii) the wives, husbands, widows, widowers, children or stepchildren under the age of eighteen of any such employees or former employees,

(c) the making by a company of loans to persons (other than directors), employed in good faith by the company with a view to enabling those persons to acquire fully paid shares in the company or its holding company to be held by them by way of beneficial ownership.

In practice, the exception which is of particular relevance in the context of a share acquisition is that set out in s 153(3)(*a*) (distributions by way of dividend). Dividend restrictions contained in the Companies Act 1985, Part VII will limit the extent to which a substantial dividend may be paid, and the tax treatment of pre-sale dividends should be considered (*see* p 268). However, where there are sufficient distributable reserves, s 153(3)(*a*) is a useful exception. The value of the target can be reduced (so reducing the purchase price to be paid by the purchaser without actually reducing cash received by the vendor) if a cash dividend is paid to the vendor prior to sale; if assets are to be transferred to the vendor's group, this could be effected by dividend *in specie* using, where appropriate, s 276 of the Act to treat unrealised profits on the relevant asset as realised (*see* p 13). Similarly, borrowings incurred by a purchaser for the purpose of the acquisition may lawfully be repaid out of the proceeds of dividends declared after completion by the target (although it should be borne in mind that payment of an abnormal dividend following an acquisition may have adverse tax consequences (*see* p 273) and may require a write down in the value of the shares acquired (*see* p 131)).

Section 153(4)(*a*) provides an exception for lending transactions where the lending of money is part of the ordinary business of the target. The exception is of limited scope and in practice available only for banking and similar institutions, and rarely for other types of company. See *Steen v Law* [1963] 3 All ER 770 for an example of where the defence (on the old law) was raised without success.

Section 153(1) provides an exception from the prohibition on giving financial assistance (for transactions at the same time as or before the acquisition of the target company's shares) where:

(a) the company's principal purpose in giving that assistance is not to give it for the purpose of any such acquisition, or the giving of the

assistance for that purpose is but an incidental part of some larger
purpose of the company, and

(b) the assis tance is given in good faith in the interests of the company.

Section 153(2) provides a similar exemption from s 151(2) for transactions
occurring post-acquisition.

The exception set out in subss 153(1) and (2) was explained by the House
of Lords in *Brady v Brady* [1988] 2 All ER 617. Subsection (*a*) provides two
alternative exceptions. The first is where the company's principal purpose in
giving the assistance is not to give it for the purpose of the acquisition of its
shares, where the exception contemplates a principal and subsidiary purpose
(of the type envisaged by Buckley LJ in the *Belmont* case, and upon which he
was unwilling to express an opinion). The second exception contained in sub-
section (*a*) is where the assistance given 'is but an incidental part of some larger
purpose' of the company. This was given a narrow construction by the House
of Lords in *Brady*. It seems clear, however, that to fall within the exception, the
transaction which otherwise amounts to financial assistance should be for an
identifiable corporate purpose of the target, which is not the share acquisition.
It is not always easy to see what a company's purpose is. Lord Oliver, delivering the judgment of the House of Lords said (at p 633):

> … if [s 151] is not, effectively, to be deprived of any useful application,
> it is important to distinguish between a purpose and the reason why a pur-
> pose is formed. The ultimate reason for forming the purpose of financing
> an acquisition may, and in most cases probably will, be more important
> to those making the decision than the immediate transaction itself. But
> 'larger' is not the same thing as 'more important' nor is 'reason' the same
> as 'purpose'. If one postulates the case of a bidder for control of a public
> company financing his bid from the company's own funds, the obvious
> mischief at which the section is aimed, the immediate purpose which it
> is sought to achieve is that of completing the purchase and vesting con-
> trol of the company in the bidder. The reasons why that course is consid-
> ered desirable may be many and varied. The company may have fallen
> on hard times so that a change of management is considered necessary to
> avert disaster. It may merely be thought, and no doubt would be thought
> by the purchaser and the directors whom he nominates once he has con-
> trol, that the business of the company would be more profitable under his
> management than it was heretofore. These may be excellent reasons but
> they cannot, in my judgment, constitute a 'larger purpose' of which the
> provision of assistance is merely an incident. The purpose and the only
> purpose of the financial assistance is and remains that of enabling the
> shares to be acquired and the financial and commercial advantages flow-
> ing from the acquisition, while they may form the reason for forming the
> purpose of providing assistance are a by-product of it rather than an in-

dependent purpose of which the assistance can properly be considered to be an incident.

As Lord Oliver said, the concept of a 'larger purpose' is not altogether easy to grasp or to apply to any particular set of facts. However, it does seem helpful if the transaction which involves the financial assistance is desirable for its own sake, from the target's point of view. Where a target purchases assets from the purchaser following completion of the acquisition and the purchaser utilises the purchase price to reduce or discharge a loan raised for the purpose of the acquisition, financial assistance will be given in breach of s 151 if the target's net assets are thereby reduced to a material extent. If, however, there are good business reasons for acquiring these assets it may be possible to show that it was not the principal purpose of the target to reduce or discharge the liability, but rather to acquire the assets in question. This could be a larger purpose, of which the giving of financial assistance could be merely an incident. In practice, it would obviously be helpful to show that there are compelling reasons to justify the target in making this purchase even though its net assets would be thereby reduced.

Except in the clearest of cases advisers will, in view of the decision in *Brady v Brady*, generally be reluctant to rely on s 153(1) or (2). It may be desirable, therefore, to sanction transactions under s 155 *et seq*, where those sections can be brought into play.

One example where s 153(1) has commonly been relied upon in the past, however, is in relation to the payment of commissions and fees and the giving of warranties in a typical vendor placing. This is considered in more detail at p 64.

5.3   Whitewash for private companies

A further relaxation from the prohibition on financial assistance is contained in ss 155–158, which sets out the requirements for the so-called 'whitewash' procedure.

The whitewash provisions are available only to private companies, in relation to the acquisition of shares in that company, or in that company's holding company, provided also that the holding company is itself a private company, and there is no intermediate 'plc' in the chain of ownership. Companies already incorporated as a plc can, where practicable, be reregistered as private companies under s 53 of the Companies Act 1985 so as to avail themselves of the procedure. This may be timed to coincide with the passing of any resolutions necessary to effect the whitewash, but the company must have been reregistered when the financial assistance is given. It should be borne in mind that the usual practice of the Registrar of Companies is to await the expiration of the 28 day period during which an application under s 54 of the Companies Act 1985 for cancellation of the resolution to reregister the company may be made. However, if the Registrar is satisfied that the company may be reregistered and no person is able to bring such an action it may be possible, by arrangement, to accelerate the reregistration.

The whitewash procedure may be adopted to enable a company to give financial assistance only if that company has net assets which are not thereby reduced, or to the extent that they are reduced, if the assistance is provided out of distributable profits (s 155(2)). Unlike s 152(1)(*a*)(iv), when considering whether the net assets of the private company have been reduced, and the availability of distributable reserves for the purpose of conducting a whitewash, it is the book value and not the market value of net assets that is relevant (s 155(2), applying s 154(2)). On the face of it, a company which shows a deficit on the book value of its net assets cannot benefit from the whitewash procedure. However, there seems no reason why there should not be a revaluation of assets which are understated in the books (and, naturally, of any assets which are overstated), in order to satisfy s 155(2). Any revaluation reserve which arises will not represent a distributable profit. Difficulty can arise, where the financial assistance in question is the giving of a guarantee or involves some other contingent liability, with the extent to which that guarantee or liability should be provided for. In requiring provision to be made for certain liabilities, s 154(2)(*b*) adopts the wording of Companies Act 1985, Sched 4, para 89, which applies to the drawing up of statutory accounts. Amounts to be provided as liabilities, for the purpose of determining net assets, include 'any amount retained as reasonably necessary for the purpose of providing for any liability or loss which is either likely to be incurred or certain to be incurred but uncertain as to amount or as to the date on which it will arise'. In the case of guarantees, except in the case where the target is guaranteeing a liability of a company which is insolvent or whose ability to meet its obligations is in doubt, no provision will usually be necessary.

The whitewash procedure requires a special resolution of the company which is giving the financial assistance and, where the financial assistance is given for the purpose of an acquisition of shares in its holding company, a special resolution of that holding company and all intermediate holding companies is required. However, no special resolution of any wholly owned subsidiary is required. It is possible, therefore, to eliminate the requirement for a special resolution under the whitewash in respect of assistance given immediately after the transfer of shares to the purchaser, if that company becomes the wholly owned subsidiary of the purchaser.

The directors of the company giving the assistance and, where the assistance is being given by a subsidiary, the directors of the holding company whose shares are being acquired and of all intermediate holding companies must swear a statutory declaration in the prescribed form and complying with the requirements of s 156. This applies whether or not there is also a requirement for a special resolution.

The statutory declaration must be given by the directors of the company giving assistance on form 155(6)a, or if the company is a holding company of the company giving the assistance, on form 155(6)b. It must be sworn by all the directors of the company (s 156) and the forms contemplate that all the directors should swear the same declaration. Perhaps not surprisingly, completion of these standard forms for the large variety of transactions which involve financial assistance on occasion gives rise to practical difficulties. Questions arise, for example, where directors cannot be physically present. Can separate forms be used? Can the forms be sworn on separate days? What if a director is in a foreign jurisdiction? The generally accepted course is, if at all possible, to ensure that all directors of a particular company are present and make their declaration on the same form. Apart from compliance with what seems to be the strict requirements of the section, there are other sound reasons for this approach so that the company and lenders (whose security will be dependent on the declaration) can be satisfied, as far as possible, that the procedures have been followed. It is good practice to minute the board meeting at which the decision to give the assistance is made in some detail and for the auditors, who are required to deliver a certificate in support of the declaration, to be present. However, if a director cannot be present, it is thought acceptable that he make his declaration on a separate, but identical, form. Clearly he should have access to the same information as other directors in doing so and ideally, he should participate in the board meeting by telephone. Swearing different forms on different days is also to be avoided. It seems unlikely that a court would invalidate assistance for this reason if it can be shown that the second declaration is properly one and the same with the first and that the same information was available to that director as for the others but there seems little point in leaving open the possibility of challenge, quite apart from the impact on other requirements of the section, such as the time periods in ss 156 and 157, and whether a single auditors' report would then suffice. It is not uncommon for the directors to change immediately before the declarations are made, since it is the directors at the time of the declaration who should make it. Proposals for a director to resign temporarily so that he need not give the declaration and then for his later reappointment should be avoided. If a director refuses to make the declaration and is removed in order that the others can do so, the efficacy of the declaration by the remaining directors should not be impaired. However, it would be wise for them to take note of the former director's reasons for objecting and to minute carefully their own decision to proceed. A director who makes a statutory declaration under s 155 without having reasonable grounds for the opinion expressed in it is liable to imprisonment, or a fine, or both (s 156(7)).

Minor, technical, deficiencies in preparing the declarations will, it seems, be tolerated, but are plainly to be avoided. In *Re NL Electrical Ltd v 3i plc* [1994] BCLC 22 the incorrect version of the statutory form was used which was then filed out of time. In *Re SH & Co (Realisations) 1990 Ltd* [1993] BCLC 1309, a case 'close to the line' (but where the declaration was held as valid), the particulars of financial assistance required to be given on form 155(6)a referred only to the giving of a debenture and omitted to refer to the guarantee or charges also given. It will be the lawyers' task to prepare the form 155(6)a or b, and complete the particulars of the assistance. It was suggested that solicitors responsible for completing the form should err on the side of caution and include fuller information.

The statutory declaration (s 156(2)) to be given by the directors requires them to state that:

> ... the directors have formed the opinion, as regards the company's initial situation immediately following the date on which the assistance is proposed to be given, that there will be no ground on which it could then be found to be unable to pay its debts; and either if:
> (a) it is intended to commence the winding up of the company within 12 months of that date, that the company will be able to pay its debts in full within 12 months of the commencement of the winding up, or
> (b) in any other case, that the company will be able to pay its debts as they fall due during the year immediately following that date.

In determining whether a company is able to pay its debts, the directors are required to take into account those same liabilities as would be relevant to that question under the Insolvency Act 1986, s 122 (s 156(3)). It is suggested that the better (but not universally held) view is that only those liabilities which are likely to crystallise within the 12 month period need be taken into account for this purpose. The section would, however, benefit from clarification in this respect. The directors should have reasonable grounds for believing their declaration. It is desirable that the directors have available properly prepared projections upon which they can base their opinion, particularly where directors of the target who are to continue as directors after the target is acquired have not yet had any detailed involvement in the target's business plan for the period after completion. If the purchaser cannot produce and support its projections for the target some other comfort should be sought such as a commitment or undertaking to fund the company throughout the period of the declaration.

The whitewash procedure is almost always undertaken at a late stage in the transaction, often with some considerable pressure to get what can be seen as a tedious formality out of the way. Nonetheless the process is important and the experienced adviser will help the directors pause and think before making the declaration. Unlike technical defects in wording of other parts of the form, the solvency declaration for s 156(2) purposes would seem to be the principal function of the form, and defects with this part of it may well be problematic.

The directors' statutory declarations are required by s 156(4) to have annexed to them a report addressed to the directors by the auditors of the company in question, stating that the auditors have 'enquired into the state of the affairs of the company, and that they are not aware of anything to indicate that the opinion expressed by the directors in the declaration as to any of the matters mentioned in s 156(2) is unreasonable in all the circumstances'. Where it is proposed that the whitewash is to be undertaken, the auditors should be contacted in good time to ensure that they will be able to give their report under s 156(4). If it is possible to arrange that the whitewash is undertaken in conjunction with the auditors' work on the statutory audit, the costs of preparation of the report are likely to be minimised.

Careful planning of the completion procedure is necessary if, as part of the completion meeting on an acquisition, financial assistance is to be given by the target or any of its subsidiaries in relation to which the 'whitewash' procedure is to be followed. It will often be the case that the purchaser will wish to change the auditors at completion, and in such case may prefer the incoming auditors to give the report under s 156(4) supporting directors' statutory declarations. Similarly, directors associated with the vendor will commonly resign at completion and the purchaser's directors appointed (*see above*). It will be necessary to ensure that the resignations and appointments of the new directors and auditors have taken effect at the time that the statutory declarations are given.

The whitewash procedure is straightforward in the case of a wholly owned subsidiary, where there is no requirement for a resolution to sanction the assistance. Where there are minority shareholders, particularly those who do not agree to the proposals, implementation of the financial assistance may be impeded. Section 157(2) permits an application to be made to the court for cancellation of the special resolution by (in the case of a company limited by shares) the holders of not less (in the aggregate) than 10 per cent in nominal value of the company's share capital or any class of it, unless the person proposing to make the application has consented to or voted in favour of the resolution. The application must be made within 28 days of the passing of the resolution (s 54(3), applicable by virtue of s 157(3)). One catch in s 157(2) is that 10 per cent in nominal value of 'any class' of the company's shares may bring an action for cancellation of the resolution. So where a resolution is unanimously passed by the holders of voting shares, holders of non-voting shares may nevertheless have the right to object. Wherever possible, therefore, it is advisable to ensure that, even in the case of non-voting shares, the holders of 90 per cent or more of each class of such shares consent to the resolution. It should be noted that the existence of a minority shareholder entitled to vote on a resolution, if he dissents or cannot be located, will result in a 28 day delay in giving the financial assistance. Where third party acquisition finance has been arranged, this may be a considerable problem and in such case every effort should be made to eliminate a minority holding.

The Act imposes a strict timetable for the giving of financial assistance which has been sanctioned by the whitewash procedure, and there are various procedural requirements which affect the time at which the transaction constituting financial assistance can be entered into. In summary, the requirements are as follows:

(1)   Convene the extraordinary general meeting to pass a special resolution. A

resolution is required for the company giving the assistance, and if given for the purpose of an acquisition of shares in a holding company, also of that and any intermediate holding company. Special resolutions are not required where the company concerned is a wholly owned subsidiary. Where written resolution or short notice procedures are adopted, the 21 day notice period will be curtailed.

(2) The directors must swear the statutory declaration, accompanied by the auditors' report, no more than seven days before the passing of the special resolution. The statutory declaration and auditors' report is to be filed within 15 days after the declaration is made unless a special resolution is passed, when they are to be filed together (s 156(5)).

(3) On the date of the declaration or no more than seven days thereafter, the special resolution (if required) must be passed. Note s 157(4), which provides the draconian consequence that the resolution will not be effective unless the directors' statutory declaration was available for inspection at the meeting at which the resolution was passed.

(4) Within 28 days of passing the special resolution, any application to court objecting to the passing of a resolution must be made (s 157(3)).

(5) Financial assistance may be given not earlier than the expiry of four weeks from the date on which the special resolution (if any) is passed (or where more than one special resolution is required, the date the last resolution is passed) and not later than the expiry of the period of eight weeks beginning with the date of the directors' statutory declaration (or where there is more than one, the earliest of the declarations). Financial assistance may be given immediately where there is no requirement for any special resolution, or where the resolution was passed unanimously by all persons entitled to vote in favour of it.

There are some peculiarities in the timing requirements of ss 157 and 158: it is necessary to have a delay of four weeks after passing of the special resolution if a single member has not voted in favour of that resolution, even where, under s 157(2), his holding is not sufficient to apply to court for the cancellation of the resolution. Conversely, if the special resolution has been passed unanimously by the holders of all voting shares then even if there are holders of non-voting shares who could apply to court for cancellation of the resolution, there is no necessity to have a four week delay before implementing the financial assistance.

Finally, it has been recommended that solicitors to a target avoid giving certificates of compliance as to the statutory provisions to a lending bank for whom they do not act otherwise than in the form of a legal opinion with the usual assumptions and limitations (see *Law Society's Gazette*, 1993, 90(25), 30–31). Lending banks commonly require the auditors to prepare a non-statutory report (in addition to the statutory report under s 156(4)) confirming their opinion as to compliance with certain requirements of the whitewash. The

ICEAW issued a Technical Release in September 1994 (FRAG 26/94) concerning the content of such non-statutory reports.

5.4   Consequences of breach

Section 151 provides substantial criminal penalties for breach. If a company acts in contravention of the section, the company is liable to a fine and every officer of the company in default is liable, upon conviction on indictment, to imprisonment for up to two years, or a fine, or both.

It is reasonable to suppose that the civil consequences of breach will be similar to the consequences of contravening s 54 of the 1948 Act. These were severe. Those who were party to a breach could be called upon to compensate the company. The action could be brought either under the head of the tort of conspiracy or as a breach of a constructive trust (*Belmont Finance Corp Ltd v Williams Furniture Ltd* [1978] 3 WLR 712). The company could sue, even though it was a party to the conspiracy, if the essence of the transaction was to deprive the company improperly of part of its assets. An individual minority shareholder could sue on behalf of the company (*Wallersteiner v Moir* [1974] 1 WLR 991). Constructive trustee risk will be a concern for anyone involved in the transaction, not just the direct parties. A recipient of the company's money is liable to be held as constructive trustee if the person 'knew' he was receiving trust money (see *Eagle Trust plc v SBC Securities Ltd (No 2)* [1996] BCLC 121 where a constructive trust relationship was unsuccessfully claimed). The approach of the English courts to the constructive trust issues in that case (but almost certainly not the result) seems likely to have altered following the decision of the Privy Council in *Royal Brunei Airlines v Tan* [1995] 3 All ER 97. For 'accessory liability' it seems that some form of dishonesty, judged objectively, on the part of the accessory will be required before he is liable to account as constructive trustee.

After some judicial dispute it was settled that security given in breach of the section was invalid (see *Victor Battery Co v Curry's* [1946] 1 Ch 242; *Selangor United Rubber Estates v Craddock (a bankrupt) (No 3)* [1968] 2 All ER 1073; and *Heald v O'Connor* [1971] 2 All ER 1105). A guarantee of indebtedness incurred by the target in breach of the section was void unless it amounted to an indemnity which, on its proper construction, was intended to apply even if the loan were unenforceable (see *Yeoman Credit v Latter* [1961] 2 All ER 295 cited in *Heald v O'Connor* at p 1110). An indemnity given by the target is now of course prohibited under s 152(1)(*a*)(ii).

The unlawful elements of the transaction will be severed leaving, if it is possible, the lawful elements in tact including the share transaction itself (*South Western Mineral Water Ltd v Ashmore* [1967] 2 All ER 953).

5.5   Examples

Set out below are some examples of s 151 considerations which might arise in the context of an acquisition of shares in a private company:

5.5.1   The sale of assets by the target to the vendor

If the consideration for the sale of the assets is cash, paid on completion of the sale, it is unlikely that the transaction will be prohibited by s 151 unless there is a material reduction in the value of the target's net assets. If, however, any part of the consideration of the sale is left outstanding—for example as an inter-company loan—then the transaction will be prohibited financial assistance within the meaning of s 152(1)(*a*)(iii). Where the consideration is discharged by the issue to the company giving the assistance of a loan note or other debt security it is unlikely that this will be sufficient to take the arrangement outside the scope of s 152(1)(*a*)(iii). If, however, the consideration issued by the purchaser is its marketable debt security (and perhaps also if it is satisfied by the assignment to the company of loan stock), it seems that a court ought more readily to regard the indebtedness as cash equivalent and so outside the scope of the section, although the point has not been decided.

Similar difficulties can arise where the transaction provides for a post-completion adjustment (for example, by reference to a stock-take or where a lease cannot be assigned pending landlord's consent). In such case if there is a deferral of the consideration receivable by the target, then the section may be infringed. It may be possible to restructure the transaction so as to take it outside the scope of s 152(1)(*a*)(iii) by ensuring that title does not pass from the target until the adjustable element has been determined, or by ensuring the only post-closing adjustments are obligations of the target, not the purchaser.

5.5.2   The acquisition of assets by the target from the purchaser

If the consideration for the acquisition is a cash payment by the target, and the purpose of the transaction is to put the purchaser in funds to enable it to purchase the target's shares, the transaction will be 'financial assistance', and will be prohibited by s 151 if it falls within one of the sub-definitions of s 152(1)(*a*). For example, if the target pays for the assets before title is transferred to it, then it will be prohibited by reason of s 152(1)(*a*)(iii), or if the target has no net assets or the transaction will result in a material reduction in its net assets, it will be prohibited by reason of s 152(1)(*a*)(iv).

5.5.3   Repayment of existing indebtedness

Where the target is part of a group of companies, it may be an obligation of the target to repay intra-group indebtedness at completion. Since the repayment of the indebtedness will not give rise to a reduction in the target company's net assets, the indebtedness already being reflected as a liability in the target company's balance sheet, it is difficult to see how this will give rise to financial assistance within the meaning of s 152(1)(*a*). This is particularly the case where the intra-group indebtedness is 'on demand' since the group companies will be entitled at any time to make a demand and claim repayment of the debt (*Gradwell (Pty) Ltd v Rostra Printers Ltd* [1959] 4 SALR 419, cited in *Belmont*). However, where the intra-group indebtedness is not repayable until a future date, then it is possible that the acceleration of repayment might give rise to the giving of financial assistance. For example, if the target company could not readily replace the intra-group borrowing, or if the intra-group borrowing is on better terms than borrowings it could obtain elsewhere, it is possible this might result in a reduction in its net assets which, if the target has no net assets or if the reduction is material, may be prohibited as falling within s 152(1)(*a*)(iv).

5.5.4 *Ex gratia* payments to employees

It is not uncommon for payment to be made to an officer or employee of the target, in connection with the sale of the target. Payments by the target will reduce its net assets and will often, directly or indirectly, affect the amount of consideration payable by the purchaser. If such a payment is made as compensation on termination of employment arising upon change of ownership, it will generally be in discharge or compromise of the target's legal liability to the employee and not constitute unlawful financial assistance under s 151. If, however, the payment is in excess of what may reasonably be regarded as the target's liability to the ex-employee, that excess payment could be prohibited if it results in a material reduction in the target's net assets (s 152(1)(*a*)(iv)) (and any such payments to a director should comply with s 312). If it is not *bona fide*, it could be prohibited as a gift even if not material. It is difficult to see how such a payment might be exempt under s 153. The difficulty could readily be avoided (assuming the vendor is indirectly financing the payment by a reduction in the purchase price) if the vendor paid any excess compensation. If the vendor is to fund the *ex gratia* payment in circumstances where he will pay tax on the disposal proceeds, then a reduction in the price to represent the cost of the payment will give him a tax deduction for that cost. If, however, the vendor will not obtain such a deduction, or the purchaser is to fund the cost the parties may wish the payment to be made by the target so that the target obtains a tax deduction against its trading profits.

Similar considerations will apply where 'loyalty' or similar bonuses are payable to staff who are to remain in the target's employment. The vendor may wish that payments are made to staff of its former subsidiary as a means of allowing them to participate in the sale proceeds or in recognition of past service. Any such payment will fall to be considered under s 151 (being a gift under s 152(1)(*a*)(i) or resulting in a material reduction in net assets under s 152(1)(*a*)(iv)). It does not seem unreasonable for some part of the employee's bonus payment to be made by a target in connection with a change of ownership, since loyalty of staff during a time of uncertainty is important. It might be arguable, in such a case, that any such payment will fall within s 153(1) or (2), although difficult issues of judgement will arise for the target directors as to what is reasonable in the circumstances. These issues will not necessarily be eliminated if the target is put in funds by the vendor so as to enable it to make the payment. The target plainly cannot borrow the funds from the vendor as this would not increase its net assets from which to make the payments, and the money must therefore be contributed by gift (capital contribution) or subscription for share capital. Section 151 problems will not be eliminated if the target is free to use the funds as it wishes, so this excludes subscription for share capital (which, when subscribed, represents funds freely available to the target). Generally, however, only a subscription for share capital will result in the payment increasing the vendor's base cost for tax purposes. It may not be possible to marry together tax considerations and the requirements of s 151 in such a situation. If the bonus is structured as an agreement to pay for future services (ie salary increase) it will not be financial assistance, provided it is *bona fide*, and not an overpayment.

5.5.5 Management fees

Where the target is leaving a group of companies, management charges may be levied by other group companies. If the management charge levied on sale is at the usual rate, and is a reasonable charge for services genuinely provided to the target, then this is unlikely to cause a problem. Where the charge is a one-off or increased charge at the time of sale, the excess payment may be prohibited by reason of s 152(1)(*a*)(i) or (iv). Management charges are often preferred over dividends as a means of realising an income from a subsidiary. Where the subsidiary has insufficient distributable profits, any excess management charge (ie that part unrepresented by a genuine supply of services) may be unlawful (applying *Aveling Barford v Perion, see* p 12). Where distributable reserves are adequate, however, consideration should be given to paying any doubtful management charge by way of dividend. Section 153(3)(*a*) exempts a dividend *lawfully* made. Aside from the requirement (s 263(3)) that the company has profits available for distribution, the dividend must be justifiable by reference to the relevant accounts. It may not be sufficient for the purpose of s 153(3)(*a*), to show with hindsight that the company had sufficient available profits. Care must also be taken to ensure that where any 'management fee' exceeds that which would be payable on a *quantum meruit* basis, it is not a distribution for tax purposes. If it is, then the payment will not be deductible for tax purposes and in the absence of a group income election, the target will be obliged to account for ACT (*see further* p 269). Another common tax trap is to forget that, save where the payer and recipient of the management charge are in the same VAT group, management charges attract VAT.

5.5.6   Surrender of group relief

Where a target leaves a group, it is usual for parties to agree arrangements in relation to past trading losses of the target, to the extent that they have not already been utilised. Losses arising in respect of any accounting period ending prior to the date of acquisition may either be carried forward and set against future trading profits of the target, or alternatively they may be surrendered to members of the vendor's group to offset the corporation tax liability of those companies. Although unutilised tax losses would not be recognised in the target's books (except to the extent that there are profits against which they may be offset), such losses nevertheless represent an asset of the target. The surrender by the target of unutilised losses to members of the vendor's group would be prohibited by s 151 if the target had no net assets, or if it resulted in a material reduction in the target's net assets. If, therefore, substantial losses were surrendered without payment having been received by the target, it would appear that there would be a breach of s 151. It is suggested therefore, that any arrangement for the surrender of losses by a target should occur only where the target receives payment for those losses. It is not necessarily the case that the target should receive an amount equal to the face value of the tax credit arising upon use of the losses; it would seem reasonable that if the losses are surrendered to the vendor and the target receives payment on a date earlier than the date upon which the target would be able to make use of those losses then a discounted payment in respect of the losses could be made. The discount could be substantial in a case where it is not certain when, if ever, losses would be available for utilisation by the target. Furthermore, if the target is deprived of the ability to use the losses (for example where they are not able to be carried forward, *see* p 313, then it is suggested that any subsequent surrender to the vendor's group could be made for a nominal payment only without infringing the section. See *Charterhouse v Tempest Diesel* for a case involving surrender of tax losses.

5.5.7   Warranties and indemnities in underwriting agreements

Where a private company is to be acquired by a public company, the public company may wish to use its shares to finance the acquisition. This could be achieved by financing the acquisition in a number of ways, for example by a vendor placing, or alternatively the acquirer could separately raise acquisition finance by way of cash placing or rights issue (*see* Chapter 11). The public company will arrange with its financial adviser for the issue of its shares to be underwritten and in the underwriting agreement the financial adviser will usually require warranties to be given by the public company and also an indemnity in favour of the financial adviser in relation to its role in the underwriting. In such a case, the public company incurs a liability in connection with the issue of its shares, and consideration should be given to the application of s 151.

The giving of warranties by a public company in connection with an underwriting agreement is unlikely to amount to financial assistance, unless, at the time of giving the warranty, the company knows itself to be in breach of the warranties as a result of which there may be a material claim against the company giving rise to a material reduction in its net assets under s 152(1)(*a*)(iv), or if the warranties are designed and intended to provide a financial payment; this would be unusual, but warranties can take effect as covenants or undertakings.

Indemnities are more difficult. On the face of it, an indemnity is financial assistance within the meaning of s 152(1)(*a*)(ii) and it is unlikely that the indemnity will fall within the exemption provided by that section, which permits an indemnity limited to the indemnifier's (ie the public company's) neglect or default, as this will generally be unacceptable to the financial adviser. Financial assistance by way of indemnity is not qualified by any test of materiality and in this sense, therefore, it is irrelevant that any liability under the indemnity may not be material.

Indemnities in vendor placing agreements entered into in connection with an acquisition are generally considered to fall within the scope of the 'larger purpose' exception in s 153(1) as being an incidental part of some larger purpose of the company, and given in good faith and in the interests of the company, where the 'larger purpose' of the company is the acquisition of the target. It seems more difficult to justify the indemnity on these grounds, however, in the case of a rights issue or cash placing but it seems, following the Court of Appeal's decision in *Barclays Bank v B&C* that in a normal case such indemnities may be regarded as an inducement to the financial adviser to enter into the placing or underwriting agreement and not financial assistance. What ought to be made clear, however, is that the indemnity does not extend to the underwriting risk or loss that is accepted by the financial adviser. Surprisingly, indemnities are not always clear on the point.

Prior to *B&C*, the analysis based on s 153 was not wholly satisfactory. One point arose from art 23 of the Second Directive on Company Law which prohibits a public company from advancing funds, making loans, or giving security 'with a view' to an acquisition of its shares, and has no exception of the type contemplated by s 153. The decision of the European Court of Justice in *Marleasing SA v La Commercial Internacional de Alimentacion SA* [1992] (C-106/89) 1 CMLR 305 rendered uncertain the extent to which a company can rely on any exception from a prohibition imposed by a Directive, in a case where the Directive does not contemplate that exception. The extent to which the *Marleasing* decision has an effect on ss 151–158 of the Companies Act 1985 is not clear.

5.6   Future reform

The consequences of breaching s 151, including the criminal sanctions, can sometimes lead to an overcautious, formalistic approach to the section and there have been calls for its discriminalisation. In late 1996, the DTI issued a consultative document inviting comment on proposals for change of the sections. The proposals include some important relaxations, including radical revision of financial assistance provisions applying to private companies so that such assistance will be permitted provided it is not 'materially prejudicial' to the company. It is hoped the result will remove difficulties experienced by practitioners under the existing sections (without, it is hoped, introducing new uncertainty). The scope for change affecting public companies is limited, since legislation affecting those companies has its origin in European law. It remains to be seen how far the proposals will find their way into the law.

Chapter 6

Employees

6.1 Share acquisitions

It is often a term of an acquisition that key employees of the target enter into service agreements with the target on completion of the acquisition. The Agreement for Sale, cl 5.2 (0)(5) (*see* p 383), takes account of this. By itself, the acquisition of the target will normally have no effect upon existing contracts of service between the target and its employees. A share acquisition will not constitute a transfer of an undertaking as defined in the Transfer of Undertakings (Protection of Employment) Regulations 1981 (SI No 1794), but these will be considered in connection with asset acquisitions. It is only in the rare case where a contract of service has a specific provision relating to a take-over of the target that the contract will be affected. However, the purchaser should have in mind that in the event of a change in employer (eg upon a transfer of employment between companies in a group, but no change in the terms of employment other than the names of the parties), there is a statutory requirement to inform employees so transferred of the nature of the change within one month (Employment Rights Act 1996).

The purchaser should also consider whether there are any collective agreements between the target and any trade union and whether any trade union is recognised. In the event of the target proposing to dismiss employees by reason of redundancy the target is under a duty to consult appropriate employee representatives who may be independent trade unions recognised by it or elected employee representatives and to inform the Secretary of State in relation to proposed redundancies (Trade Union and Labour Relations (Consolidation) Act 1992, ss 188–198).

It is commonplace for changes in the target's employees to take place after an acquisition. Such changes may involve dismissal of the target's employees either actually or constructively, eg, where terms of employment are changed without an employee's consent and the employee resigns, accepting the breach of his contract of employment. Unlawful dismissal may be unfair (as defined in the Employment Rights Act 1996, ss 94 and 95) or wrongful at common law.

67

If the target's articles provide that an executive director ceases to be an executive director upon the termination of his directorship (eg by an ordinary resolution of the target pursuant to the Companies Act 1985, s 303) it has been held that it will nevertheless be a breach of his service contract if the target removes him from office as a director (see *Shindler v Northern Raincoat Co Ltd* [1960] 1 WLR 1038).

The reasons for changes in the target's employees may include a decision to reorganise the target's management structure, prompted by economic or technical considerations, or there may be circumstances which justify dismissal by reason of redundancy as defined in the Employment Rights Act 1996, s 139. Where redundancy is involved the target may become liable to make redundancy payments under the Employment Rights Act 1996. As redundancy payments will be calculated by reference to the length of employee's continuous employment and age, a purchaser contemplating redundancies will wish to have details of the employees' length of continuous employment, age and remuneration for the purpose of calculating the amount likely to be due, together with details of any collective agreements or other agreements relating to redundancy entered into by the target. In ascertaining the employees' length of continuous employment the purchaser will have in mind the provisions which deem service to have continued notwithstanding a change in employer, eg upon the change in ownership of a business or upon a transfer of employment between associated companies in a group (see the Employment Rights Act 1996, ss 210–219 and 231).

In order to avoid a claim for unfair dismissal, the purchaser will need to bear in mind the general provisions for fairness of dismissal contained in the Employment Rights Act 1996, s 98. The extent to which the target, as employer of the employees concerned, has in the particular circumstances, including the size and administrative resources of the target's undertaking, acted reasonably or unreasonably in treating the reason or reasons for dismissal as sufficient reasons for dismissing the employees concerned will be particularly relevant. Where the reason for dismissal is redundancy, particular attention will need to be paid to the selection of employees who are to be made redundant, so that there is no unfair dismissal on the ground of redundancy as contemplated by the Employment Rights Act 1996, s 105.

Where there has been an unlawful dismissal of an employee, such as a senior employee of the target, it will be necessary to calculate the amount which the employee would recover if he sued the target for damages for wrongful dismissal or for compensation for unfair dismissal. The following summary may be of assistance.

6.1.1   Damages for wrongful dismissal

The calculation of damages for wrongful dismissal will be appropriate when the contract of employment of the employee concerned has been terminated unlawfully. For example, the notice required by the contract may not have been given or a fixed term of employment may have been ended prematurely without lawful cause. No damages for wrongful dismissal will be due if the employer was entitled to terminate employment without notice, as in the case of gross misconduct by the employee.

It is first necessary to ascertain the unexpired period of the contract of employment or, if the contract is not for a fixed term, the length of notice which, according to the contract, the employee would have been entitled to receive and serve, if his employment has not been prematurely terminated.

It is then necessary to ascertain the value of the employee's entitlement (including fringe benefits which the employer is contractually bound to provide) throughout the unexpired period of employment or notice period (see *Beach v Reed Corrugated Cases Ltd* [1956] 1 WLR 807; *Bold v Brough, Nicholson & Hall Ltd* [1964] 1 WLR 201; *Lavarack v Woods of Colchester Ltd* [1967] 1 QB 278; and *Shove v Downs Surgical plc* [1984] ICR 532). If the employee is entitled to commission, this must be taken into account if dismissal would result in a breach of a contractual obligation to provide the employee with an opportunity to earn the commission (see eg *Newman (RS) Ltd, Re Raphael's Claim* [1916] 2 Ch 309). Where the employee has lost the use of a car provided by the target for his private purposes as well as for business the employee is entitled to be compensated. One method of assessing such a loss is to calculate the cost of purchasing and running a comparable car for the unexpired period of the contract of employment or notice period as appropriate. Loss of pension rights will need to be calculated. The terms of the employee's contract of employment and any relevant pension scheme will need to be reviewed. Loss of pension rights may be calculated in numerous ways. For example, a broker may be requested to establish the capital cost of purchasing an annuity to cover the difference between the pension receivable by the employee if he had retired at the end of the fixed term contract of employment or notice period and the pension to which he is actually entitled. Generally compensation will not be due for injury to feelings and reputation (*Addis v Gramophone Co Ltd* [1909] AC 488; *O'Laoire v Jackel International Ltd (No 2)* [1991] IRLR 170 and *Malik v BCCI SA* [1995] IRLR 375).

Then the employee's prospective earnings (if any) over the remaining term of the contract of employment or notice period should be calculated. There is no need to include in this calculation anticipated future salary increases unless these were provided by contract. The employee is of course under a duty to mitigate his loss and, if he takes proceedings against the target and damages are not to be reduced, he will have to show that he has made attempts to obtain suitable alternative employment. This is the most difficult of all figures to quantify in advance. Each case must be considered on its merits; for example, highly qualified technical personnel will probably find it easier to obtain alternative employment than executives of advancing age with no special qualifications. It may be that the target itself or, where the purchaser is a company, some other company in the purchaser's group will make the employee an offer of alternative employment. It is hard to generalise, but it should be remembered that an employee is not necessarily bound to accept employment of a lower status (see *Yetton v Eastwoods Froy Ltd* [1967] 1 WLR 104). He is, however, under a duty to take reasonable steps to seek out other employment as quickly as possible and all benefits received from alternative employment actually obtained or which ought reasonably to have been obtained must be taken into account. The employee's duty to mitigate loss is not, however, an onerous one (see *Fyfe v Scientific Furnishings Ltd* [1989] ICR 648).

By deducting the amount which the employee can reasonably be expected to earn in alternative employment from the remuneration that he would have received under the contract of employment, a net total entitlement will be ascertained. It is then necessary to make a deduction from this amount to account for the accelerated payment. Further amounts may be deducted from this capital sum in respect of the possibility of serious illness which would have resulted in a premature determination of the employment and the employee's national insurance contributions. Unemployment benefits will be deductible (*Westwood v Secretary of State for Employment* [1985] AC 20). No deduction can be made for pension benefits (see *Smoker v London Fire and Civil Defence Authority* [1991] 2 AC 502).

The incidence of taxation must be taken into account. In *British Transport Commission v Gourley* [1956] AC 185 the court ruled that the object of awarding damages should be to put the plaintiff in the same position as if the particular wrong had not occurred. Accordingly a deduction should be made for tax. The taxation of payments by way of compensation for loss of office is governed by the Income and Corporation Taxes Act 1988, ss 148 and 188. The first £30,000 of a compensatory payment is not subject to tax in the hands of the employee. Any part of a compensatory payment which exceeds £30,000 is taxable in full as earned income. Where the compensatory payment exceeds the tax free limit, the case of *Shove v Downs Surgical plc* [1984] 1 ICR 532 suggests that an attempt should be made to estimate the net amount which would have been received by the employee after deduction of tax from gross income had he continued to be employed. The net amount would represent his actual loss. The liability to tax on the damages should be taken into account so that the actual amount received equals so far as possible the net or actual loss suffered.

6.1.2   Compensation for unfair dismissal

Calculation of the amount which a leaving employee would recover if he presented a claim to an industrial tribunal alleging unfair dismissal by the target and claiming compensation (as opposed to re-engagement or reinstatement) will be by reference to the provisions contained in the Employment Rights Act 1996, Part X, especially ss 118–127.

In the event of a finding of unfair dismissal an industrial tribunal has jurisdiction to make the following awards. The figures below are derived from the Employment Protection (Increase of Limits) Order 1995 (SI No 1953) which came into force on 27 September 1995. In the past these limits have been reviewed annually although in 1996 no increase was made.

Basic award

This award is calculated in a similar way to a redundancy payment on the basis of the employee's age, period of continuous employment and pay. The rules for calculating a week's pay are in the Employment Rights Act 1996, ss 220–224. The maximum week's pay which may be used for this calculation is £210 per week. The maximum entitlement under this head is £6,300.

Compensatory award

The compensatory award is such amount as the tribunal considers just and equitable having regard to the loss sustained by the employee insofar as that loss relates to the unfairness of the dismissal. *Norton Tool Co Ltd v Tewson* [1973] 1 All ER 183 is one of the authoritative pronouncements on the calculation of such compensation. Under this head fall to be considered matters similar to, but not identical with, those already considered in relation to an amount which the employee would recover if he sued the target successfully for wrongful dismissal. The assessment of loss is calculated by reference to criteria which include: the immediate and future loss of remuneration, the loss related to the manner of the dismissal, the loss of protection in respect of unfair dismissal deriving from the length of employment, expenses, pensions and loss of certain fringe benefits. The employee is under a duty to mitigate his loss and a deduction may be made accordingly. If the employee received social security benefit during a period which coincided with the period following his dismissal, then the tribunal will not deduct such benefit from the amount of its award but will warn the employer not to pay over to the employee a prescribed amount of the total award. The prescribed amount represents the tribunal's estimate of the social security benefits and other similar payments likely to have been received by the employee. The employer will subsequently receive a notice from the Secretary of State stating whether the prescribed amount is to be paid to him or to the employee (Employment Protection (Recoupment of Unemployment Benefit and Supplementary Benefit) Regulations 1977 (SI No 674) as amended by SI 1980 No 1608). The maximum sum currently payable in respect of a compensatory award is £11,300.

Additional award

A tribunal may make a further award where an employer has failed to comply with an order to reinstate or re-engage the employee or where there is a finding of unfair dismissal for certain reasons (eg trade union activities). The maximum entitlements are £5,460 and £10,920 (Employment Rights Act 1996, s 117).

Special award

A special award may be made where the dismissal related to trade union membership. The award is 104 weeks' (actual) pay or £13,775, whichever is the greater, subject to a maximum of £27,500. Where there is a failure to reinstate or re-engage and the employer cannot show that it was impracticable to comply with the order, the tribunal may award up to £20,600 or 156 weeks' (actual) pay, whichever is the greater.

Since certain of the items taken into account in calculating the compensation payable following an unfair dismissal will be the same as those taken into account in calculating the amount which the employee would recover if he sued the target for wrongful dismissal, an appropriate deduction may be made for the latter calculation. There is authority for the view that redundancy payments should be deducted from damages for wrongful dismissal but the position with regard to set off between wrongful dismissal damages and unfair dismissal compensation is not entirely clear (see *O'Laoire v Jackel International Ltd* [1990] ICR 197). The amount of a basic award will be reduced by the amount of any redundancy payment award made by an industrial tribunal in respect of the same dismissal or in respect of any payment made by the employer to the employee on grounds that the dismissal was by reason of redundancy (Employment Rights Act 1996, s 122(4)). If the amount of any payment made by the employer to the employee on the ground that the dismissal was by reason of redundancy exceeds the amount of any basic award which would be payable but for the above provision, that excess will go to reduce the amount of any compensatory award (Employment Rights Act 1996, s 123 (7)).

The calculation with regard to a claim for unfair dismissal will not have to be made at all if the leaving employee belongs to one of the classes excluded by statutory provision from having a right not to be unfairly dismissed (see the Employment Rights Act 1996, ss 196–201). If a claim or claims by a leaving employee of the target are settled, then certain statutory provisions should be borne in mind. If it is contemplated that a payment by way of compensation for loss of office is to be made to a director, then the provisions of the Companies Act 1985, ss 312–316, will be relevant. Section 312 provides that a payment must be approved by the target in general meeting. Where the payment is made in connection with an acquisition, s 314 provides that unless it is approved by the selling shareholders before completion the payment will be held in trust for them by the director. The sections do not apply to a *bona fide* payment by way of damages for a breach of contract or by way of pension (including any 'superannuation gratuity or similar payment') (s 316(3)).

In *Taupo Totara Timber Co v Rowe* [1978] AC 537 the Privy Council held that an Australian equivalent of s 312 did not apply to payments to a director in connection with an employment held by him, nor to payments which the company was contractually bound to make. In addition it may be relevant to consider the Companies Act 1985, s 320, which provides that a company shall not enter into an arrangement whereby the company acquires one or more non-cash assets of the requisite value from a director or connected person unless the arrangement is first approved by resolution of the company in general meeting. Having reference to the definitions of 'non-cash asset' and 'the transfer or acquisition of a non-cash asset' in s 739, it is arguable that the discharge of the target's liability for damages for breach of contract could amount to the acquisition of a non-cash asset by the company. It is suggested, however, that s 320 will not apply in a normal case. If the payment and the acquisition are not independent of each other, the payment may not be deductible in calculating the taxable income of the target (see *Snook (James) & Co v Blasdale* [1952] 33 TC 244; *Peters (George) & Co v Smith* (1963) 41 TC 264 and *Smith (George J) & Co v Furlong* [1969] 45 TC 384), and may involve 'financial assistance' by the target in breach of the Companies Act 1985, s 151 (*see* Chapter 5).

If it is made a provision of the settlement agreement with the leaving employee that he is precluded from presenting a complaint to or bringing any proceedings before an industrial tribunal, eg, for unfair dismissal, such a provision will be void (Employment Rights Act 1996, s 203). Accordingly, regard should be had to the procedures available under the Act whereby a conciliation officer may be requested to 'take action' in connection with any agreement to refrain from presenting a complaint of unfair dismissal as a result of which such an agreement may not be void (see s 203(2)(*e*)). Alternatively, a legally binding agreement may be entered into by a legally advised employee (see s 203(3)).

6.2 Asset acquisitions

The acquisition of assets without money does not involve any transfer of employees. However, if the transaction is a business transfer for the purposes of the Transfer of Undertakings (Protection of Employment) Regulations 1981 employees may be transferred.

The Transfer of Undertakings (Protection of Employment) Regulations 1981 apply to 'a transfer from one person to another of an undertaking situated immediately before the transfer in the United Kingdom or a part of one which is so situated' (reg 3(1)). The transfer of an undertaking may be effected by a series of two or more transactions and may take place whether or not any property is transferred.

The meaning of 'undertaking' is very wide. It includes undertakings which are not in the nature of a commercial venture and may include:
(a) a contract relating to the provision of services such as the running of a

staff canteen (see *Rask v ISS Kantineservice A/S* [1993] IRLR 133);

(b) the activities of a charitable foundation (*Dr Stichting (Sophie Redmond) v Bartol* [1992] IRLR 366);

(c) the grant of leases or licences or the grant or surrender of franchises (see *Foreningen af Arbejdsledere i Danmark v Daddy's Dance Hall A/S* [1988] IRLR 315);

(d) the contracting out of services (see *Wren v Eastbourne Borough Council* [1993] IRLR 425).

In deciding whether a transaction constitutes a business transfer for the purposes of the Transfer of Undertakings (Protection of Employment) Regulations 1981 the following issues must be considered:

(a) the type of undertaking or business;

(b) the transfer or otherwise of tangible assets such as plant, machinery and stocks;

(c) the value of any intangible assets;

(d) whether staff are to be taken over;

(e) the transfer or otherwise of customers;

(f) the similarity between activities before and after the transfer; and

(g) the length of any interruption in the business activities.

No one criterion is conclusive and each must be considered in the overall assessment of the transaction. The underlying question is whether an identifiable economic entity is transferred.

Although the Regulations were thought to apply in most cases where services were contracted out, the decision of the European Court of Justice in *Ayse Suzen v Zehnacker Gebaudereinigung GmbH Krankenhausservice, Lefarth GmbH* [1997] IRLR 255 suggests that in future this will only be the case where tangible or intangible assets or employees are transferred as well as the activity which is contracted out.

The effect of reg 5 is broadly that employees of the vendor immediately before the transaction are automatically transferred to the purchaser on completion of the transaction. The purchaser acquires liabilities for employees including liability for redundancy payments and unfair dismissal and contractual claims. Collective agreements with a recognised trade union will pass to the purchaser (reg 6). Rights under or in connection with occupational pension schemes relating to old age, invalidity or survivors' benefit are specifically excluded but other rights under such schemes (for example, benefits payable on redundancy) will be transferred. Criminal liabilities are not transferred (reg 5(4)). The continuity of employment of employees transferred is not broken by the transfer.

Liabilities relating to employees employed by the vendor immediately before the transfer are transferred (see reg 5(3)): 'immediately before' means at the time of the transfer (see *Secretary of State for Employment v Spence* [1987] QB 179). Where exchange and completion of the agreement are on different dates the transfer will take place on completion.

Liabilities relating to employees of the vendor who are dismissed before the transfer for a reason connected with the transfer will pass to the purchaser unless the reason for the dismissal is an economic, technical or organisational reason involving changes in the workforce within reg 8(2) (see *Lister v Forth Dry Dock Engineering Company Ltd* [1989] IRLR 163).

It is not possible for the parties to contract out of the Regulations. However, employees do have a right of objection to the transfer under reg 5(4A) and reg 5(4B). The effect of an employee exercising his right of objection is that his contract of employment of the employee with the vendor is terminated but the employee is not treated as having been dismissed. The vendor may continue to employ the employees following the transfer (see *Direct Radiators v Howse and Shepherd* (unreported) EAT 130/86). To achieve this it will sometimes be necessary to agree changes to the employees' contracts of employment before the transfer takes place.

The purchaser will often wish to reorganise the business following the acquisition or have the vendor reorganise the business before the transfer. Any dismissal for a reason connected with the transfer to which the Regulations apply will be automatically unfair unless it is for an economic, technical or organisational reason involving changes in the workforce. Any dismissal in connection with a reorganisation carried out prior to the transfer with a view to obtaining a better price will not be for an economic, technical or organisational reason involving changes in the workforce and will be automatically unfair (see *Wheeler v Patel and J Golding Group of Companies* [1987] IRLR 211). While reducing the number of employees to save costs will usually be an economic, technical or organisational reason involving changes in the workforce, reducing salaries or making other changes to terms of employment in order to reduce costs will not because it does not involve 'changes in the workforce' so the dismissal of an employee who refuses to accept such a change to his contract of employment may be automatically unfair (see *Berriman v Delabole Slate Ltd* [1985] IRLR 305).

In practice, the most reliable solution to the question of reorganisation is usually for all the employees to be transferred to the purchaser who will then carry out any reorganisation following the transfer. The costs of such reorganisation are taken into account at the time of negotiating the price of the transaction. However, particular care now needs to be taken when changing terms and conditions of employment because the prohibition against contracting out of the Regulations may go so far as to make any variation in the terms of a contract of employment to the detriment of the employee ineffective where the variation is carried out for a reason connected with the transfer, even if the employee consents to the change (see *Wilson v St Helens Borough Council* [1996] IRLR 320; *Meade and Baxendale v British Fuels Ltd* [1996] IRLR 541). Whether the transfer is the reason for the change in terms will be a matter of evidence in each case. Although the period of time between the transfer and the dismissal is technically irrelevant to the issue, in practice, it will probably be an important consideration. The purchaser would be well advised to formulate any detailed proposals after a transfer had taken place, wherever possible identifying a reason other than the transfer itself for the changes.

It is usual for the purchaser to carry out due diligence on the business to establish the liabilities it will be acquiring or to obtain appropriate warranty protection, or both. It is also usual for the purchaser to seek protection through indemnities from claims arising prior to the transfer for which liability is transferred to the purchaser by virtue of the Regulations. The vendor may seek a similar indemnity for claims arising after the transfer which are asserted against the vendor in error.

Under reg 10 there is a duty on both vendor and purchaser to provide specified information concerning the transfer to employee representatives who may be either a recognised trade union or representatives elected under the terms of the Regulations as modified by the Collective Redundancies and Transfer of Undertakings (Protection of Employment) (Amendment) Regulations 1995 (SI No 2587). The information which must be provided to representatives is as follows:

(a) the fact that the relevant transfer is to take place, when, approximately, it is to take place and the reasons for it;

(b) the legal, economic and social implications of the transfer for the affected employees;

(c) the measures which the party envisages he will, in connection with the transfer, take in relation to those employees or, if he envisages that no measures will be so taken, that fact; and

(d) if the employer is the vendor, the measures which the purchaser envisages he will take in relation to any of those employees who are transferred to the purchaser by reason of the transfer or, if the purchaser envisages that no measures will be taken, that fact.

The information must be provided to representatives long enough before the transfer to enable consultations to take place. The information must be provided to representatives of any employees affected by the transfer: this includes those employees transferred by reason of the transfer, but it also covers other employees of either the vendor or the purchaser who are affected by the transfer. The vendor and purchaser have a duty to provide information only to their own employees. However, under reg 10(3) the purchaser is under a duty to provide information to the vendor about any measures which the purchaser proposes to take in connection with employees of the vendor who will be transferred to the purchaser by virtue of reg 5.

If the employer of any affected employees envisages taking measures which affect his own employees then he has a further duty to enter into consultations with the employee representatives with a view to reaching agreement. If an employer fails to carry out its duty to inform and consult with employee representatives an award of up to four weeks' pay can be made to each affected employee on application to the industrial tribunal. Although a purchaser who envisages taking measures in respect of employees of the vendor following their transfer to him is under no legal obligation to enter into consultations about those measures in practice he will usually do so.

6.2.1 Key contractual provisions

The effect of the Regulations is that the contract of employment of an employee is deemed originally to be made between the purchaser and the employee in question. This may cause serious difficulties if, for example, the contract of employment contains a provision relating to bonus or profit sharing calculated by reference to the profits of the employer where the purchaser is a much bigger company than the vendor, or in relation to restrictive covenants where the effect of the transfer may be that the restrictive covenant is no longer appropriate to protect the legitimate business interest in question and so will no longer be enforceable.

Prior to the transfer the purchaser should consider what changes need to be made to the contracts of employment of any employees who will be transferred to deal with these difficulties and, if possible, agree changes with the relevant employees prior to completion. Such changes to the terms of the contracts of employment will clearly be for a reason connected with the transfer; it is not clear whether such changes will be ineffective as an attempt to contract out of the effect of the Regulations (see *Wilson v St Helens Borough Council* and *Meade and Baxendale v British Fuel Ltd* (above)).

Chapter 7

Pensions

Commercially, occupational pension scheme assets and liabilities may be viewed as assets and liabilities of the target company or business.

In a share transaction the target company may have its own scheme or it may participate in a group scheme of the vendor. Where it has its own scheme, the purchaser will be concerned with the funding of the past service liabilities and any contingent liabilities, such as for sex discrimination. If the target company participates in the vendor's scheme, it will have to withdraw from it either at completion or at the end of any transitional period which may be agreed in order, eg, to give the purchaser time in which to make alternative pension arrangements for the target company's employees. Following the target company's withdrawal, a transfer payment will usually be made from the vendor's scheme to the target employees' new scheme. The purchaser will be concerned as to adequacy of that transfer payment and any remaining liabilities of the target company in connection with the vendor's scheme. Whether the target company has its own scheme or participates in the vendor's scheme, the purchaser may also be concerned as to how the benefits under that scheme compare with those under any existing scheme it operates, particularly if the target employees are to be transferred to that scheme. Of particular importance to the purchaser will be the effect which future contribution rates will have on profits.

An asset acquisition gives rise to similar considerations. As it involves the employment of the target employees being transferred to the purchaser, it is necessary where the scheme is specific to them to arrange for it to be transferred to the purchaser. Likewise, if the target employees are members of the vendor's group scheme, it is necessary to arrange for the purchaser to become a participating employer under that scheme if the target employees' membership is to be maintained during a transitional period. More generally, an asset acquisition gives greater flexibility than a share acquisition with regard to future service benefits as a result of occupational pensions being excluded from the operation of the Transfer of Undertakings (Protection of Employment) Regulations 1981 (SI No 1794).

Whether a share or asset acquisition, a vendor will be concerned mainly with the financial implications of any agreement on pensions. It will wish to retain, or obtain value for, any pension scheme surplus. It may also be concerned to protect the target employees' pension expectations, at least for past service.

There are numerous types of scheme: tax approved/non-approved; funded/unfunded; final pay/money purchase. In addition, an employer may contribute directly to a personal pension scheme taken out by the employee. In practice, however, most pension issues concern funded approved schemes and these are considered first in this Chapter under the following headings:

(a) Background: *types of scheme, tax regime, and contracting-out;*
(b) Control of scheme;
(c) Principal employer;
(d) Member-nominated trustees;
(e) Funding of final pay benefits: *minimum funding requirement, funding on an 'ongoing concern' basis, target with own final pay scheme and group final pay schemes;*
(f) Shortfall and excess clauses;
(g) Transitional period: *Inland Revenue requirements, contracting-out, Pensions Act 1995 and general considerations;*
(h) Exposure after participation ends: *debt on employer, sex equality, vendor's scheme rules and Inland Revenue;*
(i) Effecting transfer to new scheme: *advising employees of options, trustees' duty, statutory transfer right, contracting-out, transfers without consent, Inland Revenue consent, stamp duty Inland Revenue limits and variation of benefits;*
(j) Transfer of Undertakings Regulations 1981.

This Chapter then considers other types of schemes and the general question of sex equality and concludes with a checklist. The following headings are used:

(a) Money purchase schemes;
(b) Non-approved arrangements;
(c) Personal pension schemes;
(d) Sex equality: *Article 119 of the Treaty of Rome, part-timer claims, Pensions Act 1995, limitation periods, common issues on acquisitions and asset acquisitions;*
(e) Pensions checklist.

This Chapter is written as if the provisions of the Pensions Act 1995 which are due to come into force on 6 April 1997 were already in force. It should be noted that at the time of writing not all the regulations to be made under the Act have been promulgated and generally the process of interpretation is continuing.

7.1 Background

7.1.1 Types of scheme

Funded approved schemes may provide benefits on a final pay (defined benefits) or a money purchase (defined contributions) basis. If final pay, the scheme will provide for each year of pensionable service a pension from normal pension age of a sixtieth or some other fraction of final pensionable pay, being the level of pensionable pay at or near retirement. If money purchase, the scheme will provide whatever pension can be bought for the employee on retirement with the pension contributions paid by or in respect of him and the investment return on those contributions. In addition, both types of scheme will usually provide life cover and other ancillary benefits.

7.1.2 Tax regime

It is generally an Inland Revenue requirement that a funded approved scheme is established under irrevocable trusts (Income and Corporation Taxes Act 1988, s 592). Such a scheme is known as an 'exempt approved scheme'. As a condition of approval, benefits may not exceed certain limits (IR12 (1991)). Approval carries with it many tax advantages: the employer is entitled to corporation tax relief on its contributions in respect of its employees and former employees; the employees are not charged to tax on any contributions made for them by their employer and are entitled to income tax relief on their own contributions; income from and capital gains on the scheme investments are also exempt from tax. However, the exemption does not extend to income derived from trading. Where the target has its own scheme, the purchaser should consider whether, having regard to the scheme investments, a warranty should be sought that the trustees have not traded.

7.1.3 Contracting-out

Lower national insurance contributions (employer and employee) are payable where the scheme members are contracted-out of the state earnings related pension scheme. To be contracted-out the employer must hold a contracting-out certificate for the relevant scheme or be named in a holding company certificate for that scheme.

Members may be contracted-out on a salary-related or money purchase basis. To contract-out on a salary-related basis as from 6 April 1997, the scheme must provide pensions which are certified by the scheme actuary to be broadly equivalent to, or better than, the statutory standard. The rights (other than voluntary contributory benefits) which accrue after 5 April 1997 under a contracted-out salary-related scheme are known as 'section 9(2B) rights'. If contracted-out on a money purchase basis the rebate in national insurance contributions must be applied to provide money purchase benefits, known as protected rights.

The rebate in national insurance contributions differs depending on the basis of contracting-out. In both cases it is based on earnings between the lower and upper earnings limits (for the tax year 1997/98 £3,224 and £24,180 respectively). For members contracted-out on a salary-related basis, the rebate as from 6 April 1997 is 3 per cent for employers and 1.6 per cent for employees. For members contracted-out on a money purchase basis the rebate comprises a flat rate of 1.5 per cent for employers and 1.6 per cent for employees and an age-related rebate of up to 5.9 per cent. The flat rate rebates (salary-related and money purchase) are made by reduced national insurance contributions. The age-related rebate will be paid by the Department of Social Security after the end of the tax year to which they relate. If before payment is made the protected rights are transferred to another contracted-out scheme (money purchase or salary-related) or to an appropriate personal pension scheme or to an overseas scheme the age-related rebate will, subject to certain conditions, be paid to that other scheme (The Occupational Pension Schemes (Contracting-out) Regulations 1996 (SI No 1172), reg 37(6)).

Prior to 6 April 1997 contracted-out members of final pay schemes accrued what are known as guaranteed minimum pensions (GMPs). These are broadly equivalent to the reduction in the state earnings related pension as a result of the members being contracted-out. Contracted-out members of money purchase schemes accrued protected rights, although the conditions which attach to these are slightly different (eg pension increases) from those which attach to protected rights accrued after 5 April 1997.

7.2   Control of scheme

As it is established under trust, a funded approved scheme is not under the control of the sponsoring employer. This point, although obvious, is all too often forgotten by the vendors and purchasers when considering issues concerning the transfer or use of pension funds.

The scheme will be governed by its constitutory documents and by overriding legislation. The trustees' duties are clear. They are required to administer the scheme in accordance with those documents and that legislation. They should exercise their powers and discretions with a view to furthering the purposes of the scheme. They should act *bona fide* in the interests of the members and other beneficiaries, holding the balance fairly between them. If, as is usually the case, the employer is entitled to any residual surplus on winding up the employer will also be a beneficiary but it is not thought that it should be regarded for most purposes as having a competing interest with those of the members and other beneficiaries.

The employer will have only such powers as are given to it under the scheme's governing documents. Even in relation to those powers the employer does not have complete discretion. Although often vested in the employer, the power to change trustees is generally regarded to be fiduciary in nature (*Re Skeat's Settlement* (1889) 42 ChD 522 and *Simpson Curtis Pension Trustees Limited v Readson Limited* [1994] OPLR 231). It also takes effect subject to the member-nominated trustee requirements under the Pensions Act 1995 (*see* p 85). In particular, a member-nominated trustee appointed pursuant to arrangements made under s 16 of the Pensions Act 1995 may be removed only from office with the agreement of all the other trustees (s 16(3)(*b*)). Where alternative arrangements to the member-nominated trustee requirements have been adopted pursuant to s 17, the power to change trustees should be exercised to give effect to those arrangements (*see* p 86).

Other powers vested in the employer may be fiduciary. In *Mettoy Pension Trustees Ltd v Evans* [1990] 1 WLR 1587 a power to augment benefits out of surplus assets on winding up was held to be fiduciary. The employer was, therefore, under a duty to consider, without regard to its own financial interests, whether and if so how to exercise the power. The judge's reasoning was that if the employer was not under such a duty the power would have been illusory from the viewpoint of the members who were not volunteers. The case might, it is thought, have been decided differently had it been after the duty of 'good faith' was first applied to pension schemes.

This duty of 'good faith' has evolved from the implied term in every contract of employment:

> that the employers will not, without reasonable and proper cause, conduct themselves in a manner calculated or likely to destroy or seriously damage the relationship of confidence and trust between employer and employee...

(*Woods v WM Car Services (Peterborough) Ltd* [1981] ICR 666 at 670, approved by the Court of Appeal in *Lewis v Motorworld Garages Ltd* [1986] ICR 157). The duty was held to apply 'as much to the exercise of his rights and powers under a pension scheme as they do to the other rights and powers of the employer' *per* Browne-Wilkinson VC (as he was then) in *Imperial Group Pension Trust Ltd v Imperial Tobacco Ltd* [1991] 2 All ER 597. In that case the Vice-Chancellor said it was not necessary to base a claim in contract as, construed against the background of the employment contract, the pension scheme deed and rules themselves are to be taken as being implicitly subject to the limitation that the rights and powers of the employer can be exercised only in accordance with the duty of 'good faith'. To comply with this duty an employer should exercise (or not exercise) its rights and powers under a pension scheme in such a way as will not destroy or seriously damage the relationship of trust and confidence between the employer and its employees and former employees. These rights and powers should be exercised (a) with a view to the efficient running of the scheme and (b) not for some collateral purpose. The Vice-Chancellor added that the employer 'can have regard to its own financial interests but only to the extent that, in so doing, it does not breach the obligation of good faith…'. As the duty arises under the pension scheme deed and rules (and not under the employment contract) it is thought that the duty is owed by any company with rights and powers under the scheme even if it is not the employer or former employer of the member or other beneficiary concerned.

Under some schemes the power to determine the amount of a transfer payment or the funds to be applied on a partial winding up is vested in the principal employer alone. Whether in exercising such a power the principal employer would be under a duty of 'good faith', as in the *Imperial* case or under a fiduciary duty, as in the *Mettoy* case, is uncertain. In the *National Grid Group plc v Group of the Electricity Supply Pension Scheme* (1997) *unreported*, the scheme rules provided that in the event of a surplus being declared following an actuarial valuation, the principal employer 'shall make…arrangements to deal with the surplus'. The Pensions Ombudsman held that this placed the principal employer under a duty of good faith 'approaching a fiduciary duty' which precluded the principal employer preferring its own interests. It is not thought this halfway house between the two duties is correct but further clarification is required.

7.3   Principal employer

The consequences of a transaction under the scheme rules turn on the identity of the principal employer and whether it is a share or an asset acquisition.

A scheme is, in effect, attached to the principal employer. Certain key powers, such as the amendment power, are usually vested in the principal employer. Other companies (participating employers) may participate in the scheme but only if they are in the same group as the principal employer or are associated with it through a permanent community of interests (eg common management or shareholders, interchangeable or jointly employed staff or interdependent operations (IR12, para 21.1)).

In the event that the participating employer ceases to be eligible to continue in the scheme it must withdraw, although normally the Inland Revenue will agree to it continuing in the scheme for a limited period while alternative pension arrangements are made for its employees (*see* p 96).

In a share acquisition, if the target company is the principal employer the purchaser will, in effect, take over the scheme. If the target company is just a participating employer it will have to withdraw from the scheme although, as discussed below, where the scheme relates wholly or mainly to its employees it may be possible for the target company to be substituted as the principal employer.

In the case of an asset acquisition, the employees in the relevant undertaking will normally become employed by the purchaser (Transfer of Undertakings (Protection of Employment) Regulations 1981 (SI No 1794), reg 5). They therefore cease to be employed by an employer participating in the scheme. As a result, they will normally become entitled to leaving service benefits, although some schemes provide for enhanced benefits where a member does not leave service voluntarily, while some others provide for a partial winding up. In any event, the scheme will remain with the vendor unless the principal employer is changed.

Whether a change in principal employer is permissible depends on the circumstances. In *Re Courage Group's Pension Schemes* [1987] 1 All ER 528, Millett J said, (at p 542):

> The validity of any purported exercise of such [a power of substitution of principal employer] depends on the purpose for which the substitution is made. The circumstances must be such that substitution is necessary or at least expedient in order to preserve the scheme for those for whose benefit it was established; and the substituted company must be recognisably the successor to the business and workforce of the company for which it is to be substituted. It is not enough that it is a member of the same group as, or even that it is the holding company of, the company for which it is substituted ....

Moreover, before agreeing to a change, the trustees should review the other options open to them. They should proceed in such a way as they consider best promotes the purposes of the scheme and holding the balance fairly between each beneficiary is in the best interests of the beneficiaries when viewed as a whole. Where the scheme relates wholly or mainly to the target's employees, the trustees may (and, probably, in most cases, should) agree to the change unless there are special factors which militate against this (eg if there were concerns as to the financial status of the purchaser or if a large surplus would become available for distribution if the substitution was not made and the benefits of such distribution outweigh the disadvantage of not having a continuing scheme for future service benefits).

Where the principal employer is to be changed, this is usually accomplished by a simple deed of substitution. The deed should be executed before completion so as to prevent rights crystallising at completion.

7.4 Member-nominated trustees

The Pensions Act 1995 introduces the requirement for member-nominated trustees. Broadly, at least one-third of the trustees must be member-nominated with a minimum, if the scheme has at least 100 members, of two. Member-nominated trustees are appointed for a term of between 3 and 6 years. A member-nominated trustee who is a member on appointment must cease to be a trustee if he ceases to be a member. Otherwise, he may be removed only with the unanimous consent of all the other trustees (s 16). The term 'member' includes pensioners and deferred members (s 124). Similar provisions for member-nominated directors apply where a company is sole trustee of a scheme or all the trustees are companies (s 18 and The Occupational Pension Schemes (Member-nominated Trustees and Directors) Regulations 1996 (SI No 1216 as amended by The Personal And Occupational Pension Schemes (Miscellaneous Amendments) Regulations 1997 (SI No 786)) (the 'MNT Regulations'), Sched 3, para 7).

If the same company acts as sole trustee of two or more schemes those schemes to which the member-nominated director requirements apply are treated as one. This single scheme treatment is generally mandatory. (Pensions Act 1995, s 18(8) and the MNT Regulations, reg 5(1) and Sched 3.)

Member-nominated trustees and directors must be nominated and selected in accordance with procedures laid down in appropriate rules or, in default, prescribed by regulations. The appropriate rules may provide for any form of nomination and selection process, including ballot, nomination by unions, appointment by the employer. They must, however, be approved under the statutory consultation procedure.

As an alternative to the member-nominated trustee and director requirements, the employer may propose alternative arrangements for selecting the trustees. These may take almost any form. Again, they must be approved under the statutory consultation procedure (ss 17 and 19).

Under the statutory consultation procedure, active members and pensioner members must be consulted. The trustees have discretion whether to consult some or all of the deferred members. Approval may be obtained by direct ballot. Alternatively, the approval process may involve a circular to the members being consulted, followed by a period for objections. Approval will be regarded as having been obtained unless 10 per cent (or 10,000 if less) of the members consulted object, in which case a ballot must be held.

In the normal course, the appropriate rules or, as the case may be, the alternative arrangements continue for six years. They may, however, be terminated by the trustees on the happening of a relevant event if the trustees consider it would be detrimental to the interests of the scheme members to continue them. The relevant events are:

(a) a group of members is transferred to or from the scheme without their consent (*see* p 105);

(b) a person becomes or ceases to be an employer;

(c) an employer becomes a wholly owned subsidiary of another company which is not an employer under the scheme.

Certain schemes are exempt from the member-nominated trustee and director requirements including, amongst others, schemes which provide only death benefits, schemes with less than two members and relevant small self-administered schemes (the MNT Regulations, regs 4 and 6).

7.5 Funding of final pay benefits

7.5.1 Minimum funding requirement

The Pensions Act 1995, ss 56 to 61, introduces the minimum funding requirement ('MFR'). This is supplemented by the Occupational Pension Schemes (Minimum Funding Requirement and Actuarial Valuations) Regulations 1996 (SI No 1536 as amended by SI 1997 No 786) (the 'MFR Regulations').

The MFR is that the value of the scheme's assets must not be less than its liabilities. The MFR Regulations prescribe the liabilities to be taken into account and how those liabilities and the scheme assets are to be valued. Broadly, schemes will be required to have sufficient assets to provide for pensions in payment either to be bought out with annuities or run off as a closed scheme. For active and deferred members, schemes will be required to provide for a fair cash equivalent transfer value of their accrued rights. Discretionary benefits are disregarded for the purposes of MFR.

Triennial MFR valuations are required. The first must be undertaken within three years of the last actuarial valuation before 6 April 1997. To ensure that MFR is being met, annual actuarial certificates must be obtained between MFR valuations.

Where a MFR valuation reveals a scheme to be between 90 and 100 per cent funded on the MFR basis, the shortfall must be made good over a five-year period. In the event that the scheme is less than 90 per cent funded on the MFR basis the employer must secure that the scheme is brought up to the 90 per cent level within one year. However, these time limits are subject to transitional arrangements under which schemes have up to 5 April 2002 to adjust to MFR. If a valuation before that date shows that MFR is not met, the period over which the shortfall must be made good is extended to 5 April 2007, although if the scheme is less then 90 per cent funded it must become 90 per cent funded by 5 April 2003.

Within 12 weeks of the signing of an MFR valuation, the trustees must produce a schedule of contributions. The schedule must show the respective rates and due dates of all the employers' and members' contributions (other than additional voluntary contributions) over the period which the schedule covers. The standard period is five years. However, where under the transitional arrangements a funding shortfall need not be made good until 5 April 2007 the period is extended to that date. The rates shown must be as agreed between the employer and the trustees and certified by the scheme actuary that (broadly) those rates are adequate to meet the MFR. If the trustees and the employer are unable to agree within 8 weeks of the signing of the MFR valuation, the trustees must set such rates as, in their opinion, are adequate to meet the MFR. Again, those rates must be certified by the actuary.

In the case of a multi-employer scheme, the schedule of contributions should specify the contribution rate and due dates applicable to each employer. All the employers must agree the schedule and any variation of it. Alternatively they may nominate a person to act as their representative for that purpose (MFR Regulations, Sched 5, para 2(1)).

7.5.2   Funding on an 'ongoing concern' basis

MFR, as implied, is a minimum. Its purpose is to ensure that a scheme has sufficient assets to meet certain minimum liabilities in the event of the scheme being wound up. However, unless all the target employees are to be made redundant, a purchaser will be concerned that the liabilities in respect of service up to completion are fully funded on an 'ongoing concern' basis. It is first necessary to identify the past service liabilities and then to consider whether the available assets are sufficient to fund them. Since under a final pay scheme all pensionable service counts for pension based on final pensionable pay at retirement or earlier termination of employment, it is generally accepted that the past service liabilities should be calculated by reference to projected final pensionable pay at retirement or earlier termination of employment (rather than final pensionable pay at completion).

If the past service liabilities were to be based on final pensionable pay at completion the purchaser would be faced with funding not only the pension referable to service after completion but also any increase in the pension referable to service up to completion which is attributable to pay increases after completion. This may result in a significant increase in the contribution rate after completion, whereas generally the contribution rate is fixed at a level which is intended, all other things being equal, to remain reasonably stable throughout the employees' remaining working lives. This is broadly consistent with company accounting requirements (*see* SSAP 24: *Accounting for Pension Costs*).

At the time of the transaction the ultimate final pensionable pay of the employees will not, of course, be known. Likewise, the investment return which will actually be obtained on the current scheme assets will be unknown. To ascertain whether the current assets are likely to be sufficient to fund the past service liabilities it is necessary to make assumptions as to the rate of future pay increases and investment return and also as to other unknowns, such as mortality and the rate of withdrawals from service before retirement. In addition, the value placed on the assets may differ from the market value to avoid the results being distorted by short-term fluctuations in the stock market, which are not really material given the long-term nature of pension liabilities. Allowance may also be made for discretionary benefits which have historically been provided, such as periodic increases to pensions in payment and enhanced early retirement terms. If a practice, albeit discretionary, has been established, the purchaser may find it necessary to maintain it in the interests of good employee relations and, indeed, to terminate it may breach the duty of 'good faith' (*see* p 83).

7.5.3 Funding: target with own final pay scheme

Whether the past service liabilities are fully funded can be ascertained by comparing the respective values of the past service liabilities and the scheme assets. It may be possible to determine the position with reasonable accuracy by extrapolation from the last actuarial valuation of the scheme if that valuation is relatively recent. If reliance is to be placed on the valuation, the purchaser should obtain warranties that the valuation is accurate and that since the date as at which it was made nothing has occurred which would affect adversely the funding of the scheme. It is unlikely that the actuary owes in tort any duty of care to the purchaser unless the valuation was to the actuary's knowledge commissioned for the purpose of being made available to the purchaser (*James McNaughton Paper Group Ltd v Hicks Anderson & Co Ltd* [1991] 2 WLR 641 and *Morgan Crucible Company plc v Hill Samuel & Company Ltd* [1991] 2 WLR 655). Generally, it is preferable from the purchaser's viewpoint if the agreement for sale provides for an actuarial valuation of the scheme to be carried out after completion and for the vendor to make good any deficiency. The agreement should specify the actuarial assumptions and method to be used. Expressions such as 'reasonable assumptions' are too vague to be meaningful. A provision along these lines is better than a funding warranty as it quantifies the vendor's liability and does not come within the ambit of any provision limiting the vendor's liability for breach of warranty.

Whether the vendor agrees to such a provision is a matter for negotiation. If the scheme is in deficit the vendor may argue that the contributions have been paid as recommended by the actuary and that any part of the contributions which are being paid to fund a previously discovered deficiency should, like salaries, be regarded as part of the liabilities of the target being acquired on an 'ongoing concern' basis; furthermore, they will have been reflected in the accounts. Even if it is conceded that a valuation provision should be included, the actuarial assumptions and method are likely to be the subject of much negotiation. A small difference in the assumptions may have a very significant effect. As the financial implications are unlikely to be apparent to the principals, the actuary should be asked to quantify as well as he can on the information available any differences which may become the subject of horse-trading at the end of the day.

The vendor may also argue that any payment to be made to the purchaser in respect of a deficiency should be reduced to allow for the corporation tax relief available to an employer on paying a special contribution to the scheme of an amount equivalent to the deficiency. The adjustment may be made simply by reducing the amount of the payment by the percentage rate of corporation tax.

However, this assumes future taxable profits against which the relief may be set and in any event results in the purchaser suffering a cash flow disadvantage. Therefore, from the purchaser's viewpoint it is preferable if the acquisition agreement provides for the purchaser to account to the vendor for the tax relief on the special contribution as and when it results in a corporation tax deduction. The vendor should ensure that account is taken of a deduction whether it is in the taxable profits of the target or of any member of the group or consortium to which any loss attributable to the payment by the target of the special contribution is surrendered by way of group relief or consortium relief in accordance with the Income and Corporation Taxes Act 1988, ss 402 to 413.

In order to obtain corporation tax relief the special contribution should be paid into the scheme by the employer or former employer of the employees for whom the contribution is paid. Moreover, only a participating employer may, in the normal course, pay a special contribution to a scheme. Also, a special contribution may be paid within the terms of Revenue approval only if it is actuarially justified or it will not result in the scheme holding more than the permitted reserve. Where a special contribution is paid, the employer has an automatic right to relief on that contribution if the scheme is exempt approved (Income and Corporation Taxes Act 1988, s 592). Such relief will, however, be spread over a number of years unless the total of the special contributions paid to the scheme in the chargeable period is an amount less than the greater of £0.5 million and the employer's ordinary annual contributions in that period (PSO Update 16). For this purpose, special contributions which are certified by an actuary as made solely to finance cost of living increases for existing pensioners under the scheme are disregarded. The period of spread is determined solely by the size of the total special contributions paid in that chargeable period as follows:

£0.5 million or over but less than £1 million	2 years
£1 million or over but less than £2 million	3 years
£2 million or over	4 years.

In the event that the employer ceases to trade, or its trade is taken over by another employer, during the period of spread, the special contributions will be reallocated (IR12 (1991) para 5.7).

In considering any adjustment it should also be borne in mind that a deficiency payment will normally be paid by way of adjustment to the consideration with the consequential capital gains tax implications.

The vendor may argue for any surplus to be reflected in the purchase price. This is probably the only way in which the vendor can obtain any benefit from it. In a share acquisition any attempt by the vendor to take over the target company's scheme by being substituted as the principal employer under the scheme and then to expel the target company and its employees is likely to fail *(Re Courage Group's Pension Schemes—see* p 85). This is not, however, an invariable rule. The particular circumstances of a transaction may be such that a substitution could be made (eg where a substantial part of the target's business and workforce is to be transferred to the vendor prior to completion). As the substitution would result in the target company losing the benefit of the surplus (eg in the form of reduced contributions), if under the scheme the substitution may be made only with the consent of the target company, the giving of such consent may amount to financial assistance by the target company within the meaning of the Companies Act 1985, s 151 (*see* Chapter 5).

The extent of any adjustment to the purchase price on account of any surplus is a matter for negotiation. The purchaser should bear in mind:

(a) the tax relief available to an employer on its ordinary contributions to the scheme (Income and Corporation Taxes Act 1988, s 592);

(b) the extent to which the surplus is already reflected in the target's accounts;

(c) the duty of 'good faith' restrains the purchaser's unilateral pursuit of its own interests without a proper regard to those of the members and pensioners by, eg, introducing a large new class of members and not contributing in respect of them so as to run off the surplus (*Hillsdown Holdings PLC v The Pensions Ombudsman and Others* [1996] PLR 427); and

(d) the restrictions (Inland Revenue, statutory and trust) on extracting surplus from a continuing scheme.

Broadly, before any surplus may be paid to the employer the surplus must be used to provide what is known as limited price indexation or 'LPI' for short (Pensions Act 1995, s 37). LPI is increases to pensions when in payment in line with price inflation up to a maximum of 5 per cent in any year. These increases do not, however, have to be provided on any guaranteed minimum pensions or money purchase benefits. Only surplus in excess of 105 per cent of the past service liabilities (after the grant of LPI and any other benefit improvements) may be paid to the employer (Income and Corporation Taxes Act 1988, Sched 22, para 3(3) and the Pension Scheme Surpluses (Valuation) Regulations 1987 (SI No 412), para 10(3)). The assets and liabilities must for this purpose be calculated in accordance with those regulations. Where under the scheme any person other than the trustees has power to distribute funds to the employer, that power vests in the trustees, although if the power was conferred by the scheme on the employer it will be exercisable only with the employer's consent (Pensions Act 1995, s 37). As the employer has no right to the payment of any surplus, it will have to strike a bargain with the trustees whereby, in consideration for the payment of part of the surplus to the employer, it consents to the grant of certain benefit improvements. Such a bargain was approved in *Taylor and Others v Lucas Pension Trust Ltd* [1994] OPLR 29. To secure their co-operation the trustees can be expected to press for generous treatment of employees and pensioners (per Millett J in *Re Courage Group's Pension Schemes* [1987] 1 All ER 528 at 545). Any surplus paid to the employer will be subject to a free-standing tax (currently, 40 per cent) regardless of the profits or losses of the employer (Income and Corporation Taxes Act 1988, s 601).

7.5.4   Funding: group final pay schemes

If the target's employees are members of a group pension scheme of the vendor the Inland Revenue will not usually allow the employees to continue as members of the vendor's scheme on an indefinite basis after completion (*see* p 97). It will, therefore, be necessary to make alternative pension arrangements for the employees. These will usually involve a transfer of assets from the vendor's scheme to a scheme nominated by the purchaser.

The vendor's scheme will usually provide for a partial winding-up on the target company ceasing to participate in it following a share acquisition. Alternatively, the rules may provide for leaving service benefits to be paid. As the employee will not have actually left service, an immediate early retirement pension cannot be paid (see IR12 (1991) para 6.1).

Unless prior to completion of an assets acquisition the purchaser is admitted to participation in the vendor's scheme for an interim period, the employees working in the relevant undertaking will normally become entitled to leaving service benefits under the vendor's scheme on completion (*see* p 84). These may include the option for an employee aged 50 or over to draw an immediate early retirement pension even though he is continuing in active employment. The drawing of such a pension will break continuity of pensionable service for Inland Revenue maximum benefit purposes but will not normally affect whether the earnings cap applies or not (*see* p 107). In most cases the employees will acquire a statutory right to the transfer of the cash equivalent of their benefits to another arrangement (*see* p 104). The trustees may have power to pay more. If they do, they should consider exercising it (*Whishaw v Stephens* [1970] AC 508). Whether they do have such a power and if they do whether the power is exercisable by them alone or only with the consent of the vendor depends upon the particular terms of the vendor's scheme.

Where following an asset acquisition the purchaser participates in the vendor's scheme and subject to any special terms of participation, the same provisions under the vendor's scheme applicable on a target company ceasing to participate in it following a share acquisition will normally apply. Special terms of participation are sometimes included in the deed of adherence by which the purchaser is included in the vendor's scheme. These may, for example, disapply the partial winding-up provision on the purchaser ceasing to participate and instead provide for leaving service benefits. The pension attributable to post-completion employment cannot be paid while the employee continues in the purchaser's employment. Curiously, the Inland Revenue have been known in these circumstances to allow the pension attributable to pre and post-completion employment to be split and for the pension attributable to pre-completion employment, but not that attributable to post-completion employment, to be paid to eligible employees while they are still in the purchaser's employment. The scheme rules are unlikely without amendment to permit the pension to be split in this way. Splitting of the pension would break continuity of pensionable service for Inland Revenue maximum benefit purposes. Again, it would not normally affect whether the earnings cap applies or not.

A partial winding-up involves the segregation of a portion of the scheme assets. The scheme rules will usually provide for the portion to be determined by the trustees or the actuary but sometimes the vendor, as the principal employer under the scheme, will also be involved. The trustees' duty is to act fairly as between the outgoing members and the remaining members, pensioners and deferred pensioners (*Stannard v Fisons Pension Trust Ltd* [1991] IRLR 27, CA). The actuary's duty is similar. In *Re George Newnes Group Pension Fund* [1969] 98 J Inst of Actuaries 251, it was said that the actuary should aim 'to achieve the greatest practicable degree of fairness between the various persons interested', although in the *Fisons* case Dillon LJ said he would 'not place particular emphasis on the use of the superlative'. It is thought that the principal employer may be under a fiduciary duty if the power is vested in it alone but just under a duty of 'good faith' if the power is vested in the trustees but exercisable only with the consent of the principal employer (*see* p 84).

In whomever the power is vested they have a duty to give properly informed consideration to the exercise of the power, and failure to do so will result in any exercise of the power being ineffective (*Kerr v British Leyland (Staff) Trustees Ltd* (1986) 26 March *unreported*, CA). This duty was considered again by the Court of Appeal in the *Fisons* case. Fisons plc sold its agricultural and fertilizer division. The employees continued in the Fisons scheme for a limited period (the 'transitional period') after completion while alternative pension arrangements were made for them. Some eight months before the end of the transitional period the trustees met and provisionally agreed the method of calculating the transfer, although in fact the relevant power did not become exercisable until the transitional period had ended. The method selected was the total service method (*see below*) which reflected the fact that at the time the past service liabilities were not fully funded. Between the trustees making their decision and the transitional period ending, the value of the Fisons scheme increased greatly because of a rise in the stock market. This might have enabled the more generous past service reserve method to be used. The trustees had not been advised of the increased value of the scheme when, at the end of the transitional period and without reconsidering the matter, they authorised the payment of the transfer. Dillon LJ, upholding the decision of the trial judge that the relevant power had not been properly exercised, said:

> To give properly informed consideration to the discretion [the trustees] had to exercise, they needed also to know the relevance of the value of the fund to the problem in hand in relation to actuarial principles and the implications of their decision on future contributions. That information the actuaries could have given them (and in my opinion should have given them since it was the actuaries' duty to put the trustees in a position, so far as the actuaries could, to make a properly informed decision).

There are various methods which may be used to calculate the applicable portion on a partial winding-up, including:

(a)   the *leaving service* method, which involves valuing the past service liabilities based on current final pensionable pay;

(b)   the *past service reserve* method, which involves valuing the past service liabilities allowing for future pay increases;

(c)   the *share of fund* method, which involves dividing all the scheme assets amongst the continuing and leaving members in proportion to the respective values of their benefits; and

(d)   the *total service* (past and future) method, which involves assuming the members affected continue in pensionable service until retirement and contributions continue until then to be paid at the existing rate, the relevant portion being the amount by which the present net value of the benefits at retirement exceeds the present net value of the future contributions.

The past service reserve and share of fund methods were considered in *Re Imperial Foods Limited's Pension Scheme* [1986] 2 All ER 802. Under the Imperial scheme the employees' contributions were fixed and the employers' contributions varied according to what was required to meet the balance of the cost of the benefits. Two subsidiaries were sold and at the time the scheme was in surplus, the value of the scheme assets exceeding the value of the past service liabilities. The scheme rules provided for the segregation of such portion of the fund as the actuary considered appropriate. He used the past service reserve method. It was contended that he should have used the share of fund method, which would have produced a larger amount. The case was decided on the narrow point that the actuary's certificate could not be impeached, as the method used was one which could be used by a competent actuary and there had been no mistake or improper motive. In any event Walton J strongly supported the use of the past service reserve method, which he considered adequately provided for the entitlements and expectations of the outgoing employees. The judge pointed out that under a scheme where the employer pays the balance of the cost and there is no question of discontinuance the position of the members is very much the same whether the scheme is in surplus, strict balance or deficit. He considered the past service reserve method to be appropriate in all three cases (although, in the case of a deficit, it would be necessary to be satisfied as to the strength of the company's covenant to contribute). He rejected the share of fund method as it involves applying part of the surplus (which he referred to as 'temporary surplus funding by the employing company') for the benefit of the outgoing employees, whereas it does not do the same for the continuing employees. While benefits might be provided in future from the surplus, there was no certainty whatsoever that they would be and even if benefits were so provided they would have to be shared with later entrants to the scheme. The argument that, out of fairness to the subsidiaries, surplus should be made available as they had contributed towards it was rejected, as the financial position of the companies was not a relevant consideration and, even if it was, the subsidiaries' contributions had been at the ultimate expense of the parent company.

In the *Fisons* case Staughton LJ commented, *obiter dictum*, that in the *Imperial Foods* case Walton J was of the view that any surplus should be disregarded. Instead he thought the trustees should have regard to, and evaluate the likelihood that, existing employees and pensioners would receive some benefit from the surplus in the future. He also commented that it can be argued that in view of the existence of a surplus the purchaser's scheme should receive the highest figure produced by any of the four methods of calculation, namely share of fund, past service reserve, total service reserve and leaving service. In relation to share of fund he said that he imagined that there were 'a number of different ways in which a fund containing a surplus could be shared between remaining and transferring employees and there might be a good deal of argument as to which, if any, was or were just and equitable'.

It is thought that the views of Staughton LJ and Walton J may not be as far apart as it may at first seem. Walton J observed that in calculating the past service reserve 'the basis adopted was a generous one in that it certainly preserves for the transferring members not only their strict contractual rights but also a considerable surround of likely increases and additional discretionary benefits'. He also observed that benefit improvements were not being considered at the time and even if benefits were to be improved later 'there can be no conceivable reason why [the vendor] should wish to benefit persons who have already left its service'. Therefore, it may perhaps be said that an evaluation had, in fact, been made of the likelihood of the surplus being used to provide benefits in future.

7.6   Shortfall and excess clauses

Given the uncertainty as to the position under the vendor's scheme, the acquisition agreement will normally specify the method and assumptions to be used to calculate the transfer value. An obligation on the vendor to use its best endeavours to procure that the trustees of the vendor's scheme pay the prescribed transfer value probably requires the vendor to do little more than draw the trustees' attention to the acquisition agreement and, perhaps, ensure that they have sufficient funds with which to pay the transfer value. Therefore the purchaser should ensure that the vendor is under an obligation to make good any shortfall in the transfer value paid by the trustees. While any lesser commitment from the vendor may be commercially unacceptable to the purchaser, the vendor should bear in mind that the trustees are required to consider independently the amount to be transferred and, indeed, unless the statutory transfer right is exercised, whether to make a transfer at all. Any assurance from the trustees that they will make the transfer on the proposed basis would not be binding on them as it would be given before the transfer power becomes exercisable on the target ceasing to participate in the vendor's scheme. It may, however, be possible to commit the trustees by a formal alteration to the scheme rules, although this would be unusual.

To reduce its exposure the vendor should require the amount payable to make good any shortfall in the transfer payment to be reduced to allow for any tax relief (*see* p 89) and also for any benefits retained in the vendor's scheme for the employees concerned.

Similarly, to cover the situation where the vendor's scheme trustees decide to pay more than the amount specified in the acquisition agreement, the vendor may seek an excess clause, ie an undertaking from the purchaser to pay to the vendor an amount equal to any excess payment. The purchaser is likely to resist giving any such undertaking. The purchaser will obtain any value from an excess payment only if it will be available in the new scheme to reduce future employer contributions. It will not be available for that purpose if the new scheme is to provide money purchase benefits, as the excess payment will be credited to the members immediately on transfer. Even if the excess payment would be available to reduce future contributions, the immediate value to the purchaser may be limited because of the requirements under SSAP 24. Tax and cash flow considerations should also be taken into account.

From the vendor's viewpoint, a particular advantage of an excess clause is that it provides protection from the target employees claiming that the transfer value should have been greater than that provided for in the acquisition agreement. This the employees can do without any risk as to costs by making a complaint to the Pensions Ombudsman. While the target employees may make such a complaint on their own initiative, the purchaser may put them up to it. It is, therefore, not uncommon for a vendor to seek an undertaking from the purchaser that neither the purchaser nor any member of the purchaser's group will either encourage any of the target employees to claim more or give them any financial assistance in the event of them doing so.

7.7   Transitional period

It is common practice for target employees to continue as active members of the vendor's scheme for a limited period following completion. This is generally to give the purchaser time in which to make alternative pension arrangements for the employees and undertake a communication exercise. With the advent of the Pensions Act 1995 this practice, it is thought, is likely to become less prevalent in future.

7.7.1   Inland Revenue requirements

On the completion of a share acquisition the association between the target company and the principal employer changes. The Inland Revenue should be notified of the change by the submission of form PS 256 within 180 days of the end of the scheme year in which completion occurs. They will, on application, normally allow the target company to continue to participate in the vendor's scheme after completion but not for more than 12 months without good reason. During the period of continued participation new employees of the target company may be admitted to the scheme. Inland Revenue practice is slightly different following an asset acquisition. They will normally allow those employees employed at completion in the relevant undertaking to be members of the vendor's scheme only during the transitional period. Existing and new employees of the purchaser may not join. The Inland Revenue do not require the purchaser formally to adhere to the vendor's scheme, although such adherence will normally be required under the terms of the vendor's scheme and, where applicable, under the contracting-out requirements. Whether the purchaser formally adheres or not, the form PS 274 should be completed and lodged with the Inland Revenue Pension Schemes Office. This must be done within 180 days after the end of the scheme year in which completion of the acquisition occurs. (IR12 (1991) para 21.6 and Retirement Benefits Schemes (Information Powers) Regulations 1995 (SI No 3103), reg 6.)

7.7.2   Contracting-out

If the vendor's scheme is contracted-out for the purposes of the state earnings related pension scheme it will be necessary to ensure that the target's employees are covered by a contracting-out certificate throughout the transitional period. If it is a share acquisition and the target company has its own contracting-out certificate in relation to the scheme this can simply be maintained. Similarly, where the target company is covered by a holding company certificate held by the principal employer for the purposes of the scheme or by the employer who has power to act on behalf of all the employers in the scheme, it can remain covered by that certificate. However, in other circumstances it is not normally possible for the target company to remain on the holding company certificate. Moreover, it would seem that in these circumstances the holding company certificate could not continue for the other employers covered by it as for there to be such a certificate each of the employers in the scheme must be capable of being covered by it. Where there is a holding company certificate, the holding company is treated as the employer for certain contracting-out purposes (eg the supply of information) but not for the purposes of consultation with independent trade unions unless the unions otherwise agree in writing (The Occupational Pension Schemes (Contracting-out) Regulations 1996 (SI No 1172) (the 'Contracting-out Regulations'), reg 12).

In an asset acquisition it is necessary to arrange for the purchaser to obtain its own certificate or to be included on a holding company certificate. Where there is a holding company certificate, the purchaser can be included on it in the same circumstances as a target company can remain on such a certificate following a share acquisition. As part of the process of obtaining such a certificate or, as applicable, becoming covered by a holding company certificate notice must be given to (among others) the target employees covered by the scheme and any independent trade unions recognised to any extent for the purposes of collective bargaining.

At the end of the transitional period the target company or, as applicable, the purchaser should surrender its single company certificate or, as the case may be, be removed from the holding company certificate. This involves the making of a formal election to the Secretary of State. Notice of intention to make such an election must be given in advance to, among others, the employees in respect of whom the election is to be made and any independent trade unions recognised to any extent for the purposes of collective bargaining. Where there are any such unions, the consultation period is three months unless prior to the notice being given the unions consent in writing to a shorter period. If they do or if there are no such unions the consultation period may be limited to one month. The election must, unless the Secretary of State otherwise agrees, be made within three months of the expiry of the consultation period. The Secretary of State also has power where he determines an employment should not continue to be contracted-out to cancel or vary a contracting-out certificate. If he does so, he may also require an employer to give notice to, among others, the employees in relation to whom the employment was contracted-out by virtue of the certificate immediately before its cancellation or variation (Contracting-out Regulations, regs 9 and 47).

7.7.3   Pensions Act 1995

Where in relation to the member-nominated trustee and director requirements alternative arrangements or appropriate rules are in place, the trustees may discontinue them either at the commencement or at the end of the transitional period (*see* p 86).

Generally, the vendor will be concerned that the transitional arrangements do not interrupt the smooth operation of the vendor's scheme. The Pensions Act involves all the participating employers in certain matters, including:

(a) *member-nominated trustees/directors*: various discretions (including the discretion to propose alternative arrangements) are exercisable by the appropriate person, that is, where any employers have notified the trustees in writing that they wish to be consulted as to the nomination of the appropriate person, the person nominated by those employers but otherwise the person nominated by the trustees (MNT Regulations, Sched 3);

(b) *exclusion of non-members being appointed member-nominated trustees and directors*: where any of the employers so requires, a person who is not a member must have the approval of all the employers (as distinct from the appropriate person) to qualify for selection as a member-nominated trustee/director (s 20(5) as amended by the MNT Regulations);

(c) *schedule of contributions*: if the default provisions are not to apply the schedule has to be agreed between the trustees and the persons whom the employers nominate to act as their representative for this purpose or, if no such nomination is made, all the employers (*see* pp 87 and 91);

(d) *statement of investment principles*: the trustees are required to prepare, maintain and from time to time revise such a statement. Before preparing or revising the statement they are required to consult the person nominated for the purpose by all the employers. In the absence of such a nomination, the trustees must consult all the employers unless all the employers notify the trustees that they do not wish to be consulted (s 35) and The Occupational Pension Schemes (Investment) Regulations 1996) (SI No 3127), reg 11.

The vendor may, therefore, wish to ensure that the purchaser or, as applicable, the target company nominates the vendor's nominee for these purposes by including an appropriate provision in the acquisition agreement and/or, where applicable, the deed of adherence.

There are other matters under the Pensions Act which may involve a participating employer. It is not thought that these will have any application in the normal case. They include:

(a) *payment of surplus to the employer*: if the power to pay surplus from an ongoing scheme to the employer is vested in the employer, s 37 provides that the power is vested in the trustees but exercisable only with the consent of the person whom the employers nominate to act as their representative for this purpose or, if no such nomination is made, by all the employers (the Occupational Pension Schemes (Payment to Employers) Regulations 1996 (SI No 2156), reg 13);

(b) *extension of period to make good funding deficiency*: the Occupational Pension Regulatory Authority may extend the period over which a deficiency in minimum funding is to be made good or where there is serious under-funding (ie less than 90 per cent) the funding is to be brought up to 90 per cent on the application by (i) of the trustees, or (ii) all the employers, or (iii) where, as would be the case during a transitional period, all the employers are not connected or associated with each other the employers of at least two-thirds of the active scheme members (MFR Regulations, Sched 5, para 2(3) and (4));

(c) *methods of securing shortfall in case of serious under-funding*: the employer is given certain discretion as to how shortfall is to be secured (eg charge over assets) (MFR Regulations, Sched 4);

(d) *trustees may extend the class of persons who may receive the death benefit*: this power is exercisable only with employer consent (s 68(2)(*a*) and (3));

(e) *modification orders to enable surplus to be paid to the employer or the scheme to be contracted-out*: application to the Occupational Pensions

Regulatory Authority may be made by trustees, any other person who has power to alter the rules or the employer (s 69).

7.7.4   General considerations

The vendor will be concerned to ensure that during any transitional period contributions and a fair share of the administrative expenses are paid in respect of the target employees. The vendor may also seek to include in the acquisition agreement protective provisions against any undue increase in the liabilities under the vendor's scheme in respect of them. The vendor will, eg, be vulnerable if pay increases granted during the transitional period will count for benefits under the vendor's scheme or if enhanced early retirement terms apply in the event of, for example, redundancy.

The purchaser will be concerned with employer liabilities in relation to the vendor's scheme. Such liabilities may arise under the scheme rules (eg trustee indemnity from the employers) or under statute (eg obligation to contribute to a funding deficiency (Pensions Act 1995, s 75)). The purchaser may, therefore, seek an appropriate indemnity from liability other than for the agreed contributions and expenses. The purchaser may also seek protection against the benefits applicable to the target employees under the vendor's scheme being changed.

If any of the target employees leave service during the transitional period a notional profit may accrue to the vendor's scheme, the profit being the amount (if any) by which the transfer value which would have been paid in respect of the employee if he had remained in service and joined the new scheme exceeds the value of the leaving service benefits. In the *Imperial Foods* case Walton J described as 'totally absurd' a proposal that profits of that nature should be transferred to the new scheme since they relate to employees who never have anything to do with the new scheme.

7.8   Exposure after participation ends

7.8.1   Debt on employer

Section 75 of the Pensions Act 1995 provides that if at the *applicable time* the value of the scheme assets is less than the scheme liabilities, the shortfall shall be treated as a debt due from the employer to the trustees. The scheme assets and liabilities are to be valued for this purpose on broadly the same basis for MFR (Occupational Pension Schemes (Deficiency on Winding-Up etc) Regulations 1996 (SI No 3128) (the 'Deficiency Regulations').

The rules of a multi-employer scheme may apportion the liability for ny deficiency among the employers. Otherwise an employer's share of the deficiency is the ration that the scheme liabilities in respect of its employment of employees and former employees bears to the total value of the scheme liabilities in respect of employment with all the employers (GN19: Retirement Benefit Schemes—Winding Up and Scheme Asset Deficiency published by the Institute of Actuaries and the Faculty of Actuaries).

The amount of any deficiency is determined at the *applicable time*. Broadly this is defined in the Deficiency Regulations in relation to multi-employer schemes as meaning:

(a) if the scheme which is wound up, any time between the commencement of winding-up and the last of the employers going into liquidation (within the meaning of the Insolvency Act 1986, s 247(2));

(b) where the scheme is not being wound-up but in relation only to the particular employer concerned:

    (i) immediately before that employer going into liquidation (as above); and

    (ii) immediately before that employer ceasing to employ persons in employment to which the scheme relates but only if at that time one or more of the other employers are continuing to employ such persons.

The *applicable time* in *(b)(ii)* will occur whenever an employer ceases to employ persons of the description (eg full-time) or category (eg works) of employment to which the scheme relates. This may, but will not necessarily be, the same time the employer ceases to participate in the scheme. It could be earlier. The *applicable time* will not, however, occur on the employer ceasing to employ such persons if it is the last employer to employ such persons or if it, together with all the other employers, ceases to employ such persons contemporaneously. In these circumstances, the employer will remain potentially liable under s 75 to pay a share of any debt arising on the scheme's eventual wind-up.

Section 75 does not in terms provide that there must be a debt on employer valuation when an employer ceases to participate in the scheme. Where the current funding status of the scheme is known a view could, perhaps, be taken that such a valuation is not necessary. However, a formal valuation should not be dispensed with lightly. Broadly, an outgoing employer will remain potentially liable to pay a share of any subsequent winding-up debt unless:

(a) no debt was treated as becoming due under s 75 by virtue of the outgoing employer ceasing to employ persons in employment to which the scheme relates; or

(b) such a debt was due and was settled before the *applicable time* brought about by the subsequent winding up of the scheme or the outgoing employer going into liquidation.

The Deficiency Regulations contain transitional provisions which apply to an employer who between 19 December 1996 and 5 April 1997 ceased to employ persons in a description or category of employment to which the scheme relates and at that time the scheme was not being wound up but continued to have active members. In relation to such an employer the *applicable time* is not when it ceased to participate in the scheme but whichever is the earlier of (a) the date at which the first MFR valuation is made and (b) the earliest time a debt is treated under s 75 as beoming due from another employer. In other respects the employer is in a similar position to an employer which ceases to participate in the scheme on or after 6 April 1997. In particular, it will continue to be potentially liable for any deb which arises on the eventual winding up of the scheme unless no debt arises under s 75 at the *applicable time* (as above) in relation to it or any such debt which arises is discharged.

In a share acquisition the contingent liabilities under s 75 cannot be avoided. The target company has primarily liability under the section. It is, therefore, not entirely safe to rely on an indemnity from the vendor. It is important to ensure that any debt arising under s 75 on the target company ceasing to participate in the scheme is ascertained and settled. If it is not, the target company will be at risk of a claim arising when the scheme is eventually wound up. As this may not be for many years, the risk that the vendor will not at that time be in a position to meet any indemnity claim cannot be discounted. In the case of an asset acquisition, the purchaser may prefer not to participate at all.

7.8.2   Sex equality

The Pensions Act 1995, ss 62–66, incorporates in every scheme an equal treatment rule. It is the responsibility of the trustees, as distinct from the employer, to ensure that the rule is complied with. Where, however, a court or tribunal finds that there has been a breach, the employer is required to provide such resources as are necessary, without further members' contributions, to remedy the breach. This applies to any breach of the equal treatment rule in relation to benefits. It also applies to any breach concerning the age or length of service needed to become a scheme member. However, in relation to any other breach concerning the ability to join a scheme the employer cannot be required to provide such resources in respect of any period earlier than 31 May 1995. The liability of an employer in this connection does not terminate on the employer ceasing to participate in the scheme. The relevant limitation periods are discussed on p 116. (The Occupational Pension Schemes (Equal Treatment) Regulations 1995 (SI No 3183).)

7.8.3   Vendor's scheme rules

The purchaser should ensure that there is no continuing liability under any trustee indemnity. Also, the rules may provide that an employer should make good any funding deficiency referable to its employees and former employees on the employer ceasing to participate in the scheme on a more stringent basis than under s 75.

7.8.4 Inland Revenue

The purchaser should ensure that no refund of surplus will subsequently be made to any employer under the vendor's scheme which may prejudice Inland Revenue approval of the new scheme or result in the pensionable service of the target employees under the two schemes not being treated as continuous for the purposes of determining Revenue maximum approvable benefits (IR12 (1991), para 13.35). Broadly, while a scheme is ongoing the Revenue will only allow surplus in excess of 105 per cent of the liabilities (when calculated on the prescribed basis) to be paid to the employer. This does not apply on a winding-up when the scheme rules may provide for any surplus in excess of the discontinuance liabilities to be paid to the employer. To prevent the restriction in relation to ongoing schemes being circumvented by the original scheme being wound up and replaced by another scheme, the Revenue will not approve the new scheme, or at least will not allow the pensionable service completed under the two schemes to be treated as continuous, unless the transfer from the original scheme is at least equal to 105 per cent of the liabilities (when calculated on the prescribed basis). The Revenue may regard any new scheme of the target as a replacement scheme for this purpose. In an open letter dated 9 April 1991 to the National Association of Pension Funds, the Revenue advised that it is not their practice to apply their requirements in this respect where there is no connection between the earlier transfer and the subsequent refund, but, where there *is* a connection, the length of the interval between the two events is unlikely to influence their decision.

7.9 Effecting transfer to new scheme

It is beyond the scope of this book to delve into the technicalities involved in effecting a transfer from the vendor's scheme to the new scheme. It is, however, worth making a few points.

7.9.1 Advising employees of options

An employee must be given written information as to his rights and options under the vendor's scheme. The trustees are required to supply this information as soon as practicable and in any event within 2 months of the employee or the company which was his employer while he was a scheme member notifying the trustees that his pensionable service has ended. The Occupational Pensions Regulatory Authority may impose a civil penalty on the trustees if they fail to supply such information (Occupational Pension Schemes (Preservation of Benefit) Regulations 1991 (SI No 167 as amended by SI 1996 No 2131), reg 27A(1)(*a*)).

7.9.2   Trustees' duty

Where a transfer is to be made pursuant to a discretionary power, the trustees should proceed with caution. The transfer power will be exercisable only for the purpose of providing benefits for the transferring members and other beneficiaries. It will be a fiduciary power to be exercised (or not exercised) according to what the trustees consider to be in the best interests of the members and beneficiaries concerned. The trustees will need to satisfy themselves that the transfer terms available are of sufficient overall benefit to those members and other beneficiaries to provide a better option for them than any others available. The trustees should have regard to both quantum and security. They should also consider the need for special terms and guarantees under the receiving scheme. For example, the trustees may wish to guard against any part of the transfer value being paid to the employer as surplus on winding up. This could occur where the transfer value exceeds the value of the leaving service benefits, as on a winding-up only leaving service benefits need be payable as of right, with the consequence that the excess may be payable to the employer as surplus, subject to the requirements concerning limited price indexation (*see* p 91).

7.9.3   Statutory transfer right

An employee on ceasing to be in pensionable service at least one year before normal pension age acquires a statutory right to a transfer value. If normal pension age is below 60 the employee will acquire such a right so long as he is under normal pension age on ceasing to be in pensionable service. The employee will have a right to request from the trustees a statement of the transfer value. Once produced, the amount will be guaranteed for, broadly, 3 months from the date it is calculated.

The transfer value is the cash equivalent on the date the transfer right is exercised (or on ceasing to be in pensionable service under the vendor's scheme if later) of the benefits which have accrued to or in respect of the employee. The benefits for this purpose will normally be based on current final pensionable pay (taking into account discretionary practices unless the trustees, on actuarial advice, direct otherwise). The transfer value may be reduced in certain circumstances where the scheme is in deficit.

The employee may elect to have the transfer value paid to any new scheme of his employer or, if he prefers, to a personal pension scheme or an annuity policy. If the transfer to the new scheme is made without the statutory right being exercised, that right will also be transferred and will be exercisable against the trustees of the new scheme (Pension Schemes Act 1993, Part IV, Chapter IV and the Occupational Pension Schemes (Transfer Values) Regulations 1996 (SI No 1847)).

7.9.4 Contracting-out

If the vendor's scheme and the new scheme are both contracted-out on a salary-related basis the liability in respect of any GMP and section 9(2B) rights (*see* p 81) may, with the member's consent, be transferred without difficulty. Similarly, no problems arise if the vendor's scheme is contracted-out on a money purchase basis and the new scheme is contracted-out on a salary-related basis. However, unless the regulations are changed problems will arise if the vendor's scheme is contracted-out on a salary-related basis and the new scheme is either contracted-out on a money purchase basis or is not contracted-out at all. If the new scheme is contracted-out on a money purchase basis the entire cash value of the section 9(2B) rights must be applied to provide protected rights. As these are non-commutable and cannot be drawn before age 60, the member will, in respect of section 9(2B) rights, lose any commutation option or option to retire before age 60 which he might have enjoyed under the vendor's scheme. The problem is more acute if the new scheme is not contracted-out. Neither the GMPs nor the section 9(2B) rights can be transferred to it, although the excess of the pre-6 April 1997 benefits over the GMP and any voluntary contributions may be transferred. While for a year or so after April 1997 these problems are likely to be manageable as the section 9(2B) rights will be relatively small it will become increasingly difficult to provide members after an acquisition with continuous pensionable service in these circumstances. Alternatives will have to be considered (eg applying the amount which would otherwise have been transferred to enhance the members' benefits in the vendor's scheme) (the Protected Rights (Transfer Payment) Regulations 1996 (SI No 1461), regs 3 and 4 and the Contracting-out (Transfer and Transfer Payment) Regulations 1996 (SI No 1462), regs 3, 5, 8 and 10 and the Personal and Occupational Pension Schemes (Protected Rights) Regulations 1996 (SI No 1537), reg 3(*b*)).

7.9.5 Transfers without consent

The vendor's scheme rules may authorise the trustees to effect the transfer to the new scheme without the employee's consent in certain circumstances. Under the Occupational Pension Schemes (Preservation of Benefit) Regulations 1991 (SI No 167 as amended by SI 1993 No 1822 and SI 1996 No 2131) a transfer may be made without the employee's consent only in certain prescribed circumstances. In particular, it is necessary for an actuary to certify to the trustees of the transferring scheme that the transfer credits to be acquired for each member under the new scheme are, broadly, no less favourable than the rights transferred based, where applicable, on projected final pensionable earnings. Where there is an established custom of additional benefits or increases being awarded on a discretionary basis, the actuary must also certify that there is good cause to believe that the discretionary benefits or increases under the new scheme will, broadly, be no less favourable. If the rights granted under the new scheme are more favourable than the rights under the transferring scheme, allowance may be made for this when determining whether the discretionary benefits are as favourable.

If the vendor's scheme and the new scheme are both contracted-out on a salary-related basis, the liability for GMPs and section 9(2B) rights (*see* p 81) may be transferred to the new scheme without the employees' consent, subject to certain prescribed requirements being met (The Contracting-out (Transfer and Transfer Payment) Regulations 1996 (SI No 1462), regs 4 and 9).

A transfer from a scheme contracted-out on a salary-related basis to one contracted-out on a money purchase basis may be made only with the employees' consent (reg 10). Similarly, employees' consent is always required to a transfer between schemes contracted-out on a money purchase basis (The Protected Rights (Transfer Payment) Regulations 1996 (SI No 1461), reg 3).

Not less than one month before a transfer without the consent of the employees concerned is due to take place the employees must be given information about the proposed transfer and details of the value of the rights to be transferred, including rights to survivors' benefits and rights in respect of death-in-service benefits (the Occupational Pension Schemes (Preservation of Benefit) Regulations 1991 (SI No 167), reg 12(4B) as amended by SI 1996 No 2131).

Whether it is possible to make the transfer without consent or not, the vendor's scheme trustees may wish to protect themselves by requiring consents. In any event, the employees' consents will be required to the deduction from pay of their contributions (if any) to the new scheme unless the deduction is already authorised by their employment contracts (Employment Rights Act 1996, s 13).

7.9.6   Inland Revenue consent

The Inland Revenue Pension Schemes Office should be consulted in advance before a transfer is made in respect of a group of employees. Their specific authority, as such, is not required if both schemes have been formally approved. If either scheme has not been so approved, specific authority is required unless the Revenue has previously approved the payment of transfers to or from that scheme. It is not, however, necessary to obtain specific authority in relation to the new scheme if the vendor's scheme is expressly named in the documents of the new scheme as one from which a transfer may be accepted (IR12 (1991), paras 10.24 and 10.32).

7.9.7   Stamp duty

The Stamp Office practice with regard to the transfer of securities, or the assignment of policies, from the vendor's scheme to the new scheme is to stamp the transfer instrument with the fixed 50p duty as a 'conveyance of any other kind'. The transfer instrument is not a conveyance on sale as the assumption of liabilities by the new scheme trustees is not for monetary consideration and it is a long-standing Stamp Office practice to accept that such an assumption of liability is not a stampable assumption of liabilities for the purposes of the Stamp Act 1891, s 57.

7.9.8   Inland Revenue limits

Unlike a share transaction, an asset acquisition results in a break in employment. Where, however, the employee's position remains essentially unchanged employment before and after completion will be treated as continuous for Inland Revenue maximum approvable benefit purposes. This is subject to two exceptions. First, the employee must not, while employed by the purchaser, draw any benefits to which he is entitled in respect of his employment with the vendor. Secondly, in the case of a controlling director, specific Revenue approval is required, which will be given only if it can be shown that there is continuity of trade. A controlling director is, very broadly, a director who directly or indirectly is interested in 20 per cent or more of the ordinary share capital of the company (IR12 1991, para 7.11 and Appendix I).

In making alternative arrangements care should be taken to ensure that those employees who were not previously subject to the earnings cap do not accidentally become caught by it. The earnings cap which was introduced by the Finance Act 1989 limits the earnings which may be taken into account for the purpose of determining maximum approvable benefits and member contributions. The limit for the tax year 1997/98 is £84,000. It is normally increased each 6 April with prices. Broadly, employees who joined a scheme of the vendor before 1 June 1989 will not be subject to the earnings cap so long as that scheme was in existence before 14 March 1989 and since 1 June 1989 the employee has been in continuous pensionable service under one or other of the vendor's schemes apart from certain permitted breaks, such as secondment and statutory maternity leave. Whether the earnings cap applies or not is not dependent upon a transfer value being paid to the new scheme in respect of the past service benefits under the vendor's scheme. To avoid becoming caught by the earnings cap an employee must, upon ceasing to accrue benefits under the vendor's scheme, become a member of the new scheme although, again, there are certain dispensations for employees then on secondment, statutory maternity leave or the like. Moreover, the disapplication of the cap is automatic only if the new scheme was established before 14 March 1989 and approved before 27 July 1989 and then only if the employee concerned has not previously transferred schemes without the cap applying to him. In other cases it is necessary to apply to the Inland Revenue for the cap to be disapplied. In practice, this will normally be agreed. (IR(12) 1991, Appendix III.)

It is also desirable to ensure that employees who are subject to the pre-17 March 1987 limits in the vendor's scheme continue to be subject to those limits in the new scheme. In particular, these limits permit greater commutation for employees with short service. They will continue automatically if the new scheme was established before 17 March 1987 and approved before 23 July 1987 but, again, only if the employee has not previously transferred schemes. In other cases, an application to the Inland Revenue should be made. It will normally be granted (again, see IR12 1991, Appendix III).

7.9.9   Variation of benefits

A question which sometimes arises is the extent to which pension benefits and contributions may be lawfully varied when the target employees cease to participate in the vendor's scheme. The purchaser may not wish to mirror the vendor's scheme because, for example, the purchaser already has its own scheme or the target has too few employees for a final pay scheme to be a practical proposition. The flexibility available depends upon whether it is a share or asset acquisition and in the case of a share acquisition the terms of the employment contract. The position following an asset acquisition is governed by the Transfer of Undertakings (Protection of Employment) Regulations 1981 and is discussed on p 109. This section is, therefore, concerned with the position following a share acquisition.

It is probably the intention of most employers that the employees should be entitled to no more than to be a member of the scheme subject to the scheme rules from time to time in force. In this way the employer maintains maximum flexibility. A change in the benefits which is made without contravening any of the scheme rules would not, it is thought, constitute a variation of the employment contract. Whether an employer has been successful in maintaining such flexibility can be determined only by examining the terms of the employment contract and any documents which may provide evidence of those terms (eg the explanatory booklet and the written statement of the terms of employment which must be given under the Employment Rights Act 1996, s 1). In particular, it would be necessary to show that the power of amendment was fairly and reasonably brought to the employee's attention.

Even if the employer has successfully maintained the right to vary the pension arrangements, the employer would be subject to a duty of 'good faith' when exercising that right (*see* p 83). Also, the Unfair Contract Terms Act 1977 may, perhaps, apply although this is untested. For it to apply the employment contract must be a customer contract, ie a contract to which one party to the contract (the employer) deals and the other party (the employee) does not deal, or hold himself out as dealing, in the course of business. Business is defined as including a profession. It is not clear, therefore, whether an employee would not, for this purpose, be regarded as dealing in the course of business. If the Act were held to apply, then any right under the employment contract to vary the pension terms cannot be exercised by an employer so as to render its performance substantially different from that which the employee reasonably expected from the contract (s 17).

If a change in the pension arrangements would constitute a variation of the employment contract, the employee's consent should be obtained. Silence does not equal consent. If the employer fails to do so, the employee may be entitled on retirement to claim for his full contractual pension. If consent cannot be obtained, the employer should terminate the existing contract and offer re-employment. This will give rise to the possibility of unfair dismissal and also to the obligation to inform and consult with trade unions or the employee's representatives with a view to reaching agreement. Whether an industrial tribunal would regard the termination of the original contract as unfair dismissal depends upon the particular facts but it is thought that the tribunal would give considerable weight to the need for the variation from a commercial viewpoint (eg unifying employment terms with those of other employees in the purchaser's group). The procedure adopted by the employer in consulting employees over charges will also be critical.

If an employer were to press ahead and make the changes in breach of contract, the question arises whether an employee would be entitled to leave service and claim constructive dismissal and damages. If the scheme was a money purchase arrangement and the employer failed to pay the contractual contributions, the employee would probably be entitled to do so on the basis that failure to pay contractual remuneration is normally a fundamental and repudiatory breach (*Rigby v Ferodo Ltd* [1988] ICR 29, HL). Whether there would be such a breach by the employer simply indicating that it did not intend to provide the employee at retirement with his contractual pension is less certain, although it is thought that this could be an anticipatory breach of contract which would be sufficient to found a constructive dismissal claim.

7.10 Transfer of Undertaking Regulations

The Transfer of Undertakings (Protection of Employment) Regulations 1981 (SI No 1794) ('TUPE') will normally apply on an asset acquisition (*see* p 00). The regulations give effect under UK law to the Acquired Rights Directive, which the UK Government is required under European law to implement. The principle underlying TUPE is that where there is a transfer of a business, employees employed in that business should be transferred along with the business on their existing terms and conditions. The rights and obligations are retroactively and prospectively preserved (reg 5(2)).

TUPE does not, however, apply to so much of the contract of employment or collective agreement as relates to occupational pension schemes or any rights, powers, duties or liabilities under or in connection with any such contract or subsisting by virtue of any such agreement (reg 7). This exemption does not extend to any provisions of an occupational pension scheme which do not relate to old age, invalidity or survivors' benefits. Thus, benefits payable only in the event of, say, redundancy may be outwith the pensions exemption. Otherwise, 'occupational pension scheme' has the same meaning as in the Pension Schemes Act 1993, s 1. It therefore includes most forms of retirement benefits schemes. It does not, however, include personal pension schemes and any liability of the vendor to contribute to such a scheme will transfer to the purchaser under TUPE.

The validity of the pension exemption and, in particular, whether it correctly reflects the corresponding exemption in the Acquired Rights Directive has been tested in the UK courts on a number of occasions. Most recently it was upheld by the High Court in *Adams and Others v Lancashire County Council and BET Catering Services Limited* [1996] PLR 49. An appeal has, however, been lodged.

On the premise that the pension exemption is effective, the question arises whether employees who are transferred without the benefit of their existing pension rights would be entitled to treat themselves as dismissed or otherwise sue for breach of contract. It is thought they can do neither unless the purpose, as distinct from a consequence, of the asset acquisition was to deprive the employees of their pension benefits. This would, it is thought, be a breach of the employer's duty of 'good faith'.

Regulation 5(5) provides that the provisions under TUPE novating the employment contract are:

> without prejudice to any right of an employee arising apart from these Regulations to terminate his contract of employment without notice if a substantial change is made to his working conditions to his detriment; but no such right shall arise by reason only that...the identity of his employer changes unless the employee shows that, in all the circumstances, the change is a significant change and is to his detriment.

Regulation 5(5), therefore, preserves the right of an employee to claim constructive dismissal if a substantial change is made to his working conditions to his detriment. The employee may not, however, do so by reason only of a change in the identity of his employer unless he shows, in all the circumstances, the change is significant and to his detriment.

To claim constructive dismissal there must first be a breach of the contract (*Western Excavating (ECC) Ltd v Sharp* [1978] ICR 221). The vendor would be honouring any contractual pension rights up to the point of transfer. The purchaser may not do so afterwards but it would not be in breach of contract as no contractual pension rights transfer. Moreover, there would not be an anticipatory breach as at no stage is there a breach of contract. In order to succeed, therefore, the employee would, it seems, have to show that by failing to secure, or not using sufficient efforts to secure, equivalent pension rights with the purchaser the vendor was in breach of its duty of 'good faith'. If the employee were successful in bringing such a claim it is unclear whether the liability would fall on the vendor or the purchaser. The pension exemption may mean the liability remains with the vendor. If it were not for the exemption the breach, albeit committed by the vendor, would be, it is thought, treated as committed by the purchaser (reg 5(2)).

Also, if the purchaser does not provide equivalent pension benefits an employee may try to claim constructive dismissal on the basis that there has been a change in the identity of employer to his detriment. It is not, however, thought that the reference to identity of employer is intended to cover the terms of employment which he is prepared to offer. If it did, the reference in reg 5(5) to 'substantial change in his working conditions to his detriment' would be superfluous. In any event, reg 7 excludes from the ambit of regulation so much of the employment contract or collective agreement which relates to occupational pension schemes. It is not thought, therefore, that the claim would succeed.

Finally, the question arises as to what happens to the contractual pension rights if they do not transfer. In respect of past service the vendor must provide leaving service benefits in accordance with the preservation requirements of the Pension Schemes Act 1993. It seems, however, this would be the extent of the vendor's liability in the absence of an obligation, which would be very unusual, under the employment contract in respect of pensions to be earned in respect of employment with a future employer (the *Adams* case referred to above).

7.11   Money purchase schemes

With a typical money purchase scheme, the contributions paid by and on behalf of an employee are invested until he retires, when the accumulated fund is used to buy a pension from an insurance company. As no particular level of benefits is guaranteed the only past service liability which can arise is for outstanding contributions and expenses. Unless there are to be completion accounts, the purchaser should obtain appropriate warranties. The purchaser should ask for details of the payment schedule which the trustees are obliged to maintain (Pensions Act 1995, s 87). The purchaser should also consider whether the likely future pension contributions, when compared with those paid in the past, will have any material effect on profits because, for example, the scheme has only recently been established or the target employees are to be offered membership of a final pay scheme of the purchaser. The purchaser should seek a warranty that there is no commitment (whether legally enforceable or not) to provide any employee with a specific level of benefits. Sometimes a money purchase scheme is used simply as a funding vehicle for providing 'final pay' type benefits. This may be apparent from the scheme rules or explanatory literature but not necessarily so. If a specific level of benefits has been promised, the same funding considerations which arise in relation to final pay schemes should be addressed.

The Deficiency Regulations extend s 75, Pensions Act 1995 (deficiencies in assets) to be extended to money purchase schemes in a modified form (*see* p 100). Broadly, they provide that the section will apply only where the deficiency is attributable to certain criminal offences. A former employer will not be liable so long as there were active members in the scheme after it had ceased to participate.

In some cases pensions are paid out of the scheme instead of securing them with an insurance company. These schemes are subject to the MFR in the same way as final pay schemes (the MFR Regulations, reg 28(1)(*f*)).

Where the target employees participate in a group scheme of the vendor, the purchaser should ensure that all the employees are provided with vested benefits even if they have not qualified for them under the preservation requirements of the Pension Schemes Act 1993 because they have completed less than two years' qualifying service. If the vendor's scheme is contracted-out of the state earnings related scheme the 'protected rights' may be transferred only to another contracted-out scheme. Any unpaid age-related rebate will follow subject to certain conditions (*see* p 82). If the new scheme is not contracted-out the protected rights can be either left behind or transferred to a personal pension scheme. The employees will have a statutory right to have their accumulated funds transferred to a new scheme unless they are over normal pension age or, if that age is 60 or over, within one year of attaining it (*see* p 104). However, it should be noted that under the statutory transfer provisions there does not appear to be any requirement for the vendor's scheme to account for interest or investment return after the transfer option has been exercised so long as the transfer is effected within six months. Also, purchasers should be aware of the hefty penalties which some insurance companies impose when a group of members is transferred.

7.12   Non-approved arrangements

Since the Finance Act 1989 employers may provide pension benefits through non-approved arrangements. These may be funded or unfunded. There are neither any special tax concessions nor limits on benefits. They will nevertheless give rise to similar considerations as approved schemes. One point to watch is the tax position if an employee of the vendor with an unfunded pension is to be employed after completion by the target company or the purchaser. Any transfer of funds between the companies in respect of the accrued pension liability may be treated as income of the employee in the year of assessment in which the transfer is made, even though the employee has neither received nor has any entitlement to the money transferred (Income and Corporation Taxes Act 1988, s 595(1)). The unfunded liabilities should, therefore, be reflected in the consideration.

An employee who ceases to be in pensionable service under a non-approved scheme more than one year before normal pension age (or if that age is below 60 before 60) acquires a right to a cash equivalent transfer value. This appears to be the case whether the scheme is funded or not. The receiving scheme or annuity contract must satisfy certain prescribed requirements. Those which relate to Inland Revenue approval apply only if the transfer is being made from an approved scheme. Hence, it should be possible for an employee to exercise effectively the statutory transfer right. A transfer from a funded scheme may be scaled down if the scheme is in deficit. Although it could, perhaps, be argued that as an unfunded scheme has no assets the cash equivalent can be reduced to zero, the better view is, it is thought, that the entire resources of the employer are available to meet the liability and so no scaling down is permissible. (Pension Schemes Act 1993, ss 93 and 94 and the Occupational Pension Schemes (Transfer Value) Regulations 1996, reg 8(6).)

Benefits may also be provided on a discretionary basis. The amount of damages payable in the event of a breach of warranty that there are no discretionary benefits is uncertain bearing in mind that, by definition, the benefits are determinable at will. The purchaser should therefore seek to provide in the acquisition agreement that, in calculating the loss flowing from any breach of warranty, any discretionary benefits will be treated as payable as of right.

7.13   Personal pension schemes

It is not thought that any particular problems should arise in relation to personal pension schemes. These are, in essence, contractual arrangements made between the employee and the insurance company or other pension provider. The schemes may be used to contract-out of the state earnings related pension scheme: full national insurance contributions are payable; and the Department of Social Security remits to the scheme an amount equivalent to the contracting-out rebate (*see* p 81). The employer may contribute to the scheme and the purchaser should ensure that any such contributions have been timeously paid. A purchaser should also ensure that there are no sex equality problems. In an asset acquisition it should be remembered that the TUPE pension exemption does not extend to personal pension schemes and so the purchaser will assume any liability of the vendor to pay personal pension scheme contributions.

7.14   Sex equality

The law on sex equality has been in a state of flux since 1990 and some issues are unlikely to be resolved for some time. Although this area is beyond the scope of this book, an outline has been included given its importance.

7.14.1   Article 119 of the Treaty of Rome

Article 119 established the principle that men and women should receive equal pay for equal work. On 17 May 1990 the European Court of Justice gave its landmark judgment in the case of *Barber v Guardian Royal Exchange Assurance Company* [1990] 5 ECR 1889. The ECJ ruled that pensions under private occupational pension schemes were 'pay' for the purposes of Art 119. Consequently, pension benefits had to be equal for male and female members doing equal work. In order to limit the retrospective effect of its decision the court also ruled that Art 119 'may not be relied on in order to claim entitlement to a pension with effect from a date prior to that of [the] judgment'.

In the intervening years views differed on the ambit of this judgment on retrospective claims and whether the limit applied at all to schemes which were not contracted-out. It was also unclear whether Art 119 applied to the trustees of occupational pension schemes. On 28 September 1994, the ECJ gave judgment in the case of *Coloroll Pension Trustees Ltd v Russell* [1994] OPLR 179. The *Coloroll* case decided, amongst other things, that:

(a)   Art 119 could be relied upon against the trustees of an occupational pension scheme in addition to the employer.

(b)   It was not necessary for all benefits to be levelled up to comply with Art 119. Consequently, subject to trust law and employment considerations, benefits could be changed to provide for the lower level of benefit as between men and women but only in respect of service after the date of the amendment.

(c)   Equal treatment applied only in respect of pensionable service on and after 17 May 1990.

(d)   There was no difference between treatment in contracted-out and contracted-in schemes.

(e)   It was permissible in the case of final pay schemes to use sex-biased actuarial factors.

(f)   On a transfer of pension rights from one occupational pension scheme to another, the second scheme is obliged, on the member reaching retirement age, to increase the benefits it originally undertook to pay him so as to eliminate the effects contrary to Art 119 of the inadequacy of the transfer value because of the discriminatory treatment suffered under the first scheme.

7.14.2   Part-timer claims

On the same date as the *Coloroll* judgment, the ECJ also gave judgment in two other very significant cases. These were the cases of *Vroege v NCIV Instituut Voor Volkshuisvesting BV and Another* and *Fisscher v Voorhuis Hengelo BV and Another* both reported at [1995] ICR 635. Broadly, these two cases confirmed that where a scheme refused to admit part-time employees this could amount to indirect sex discrimination as first held in *Bilka-Kaufhaus GmbH v Karin Weber von Hartz* [1986] IRLR 317. It should be noted that excluding part-time workers from a scheme is not *per se* indirect sex discrimination. The concept of indirect sex discrimination is difficult; it arises where a provision of a scheme has a disproportionate impact on one sex and cannot be objectively justified.

However, the most significant aspect of these cases was the ruling in relation to temporal limitations. The ECJ determined that claims could be made in respect of periods of employment dating back to 8 April 1976 (being the date the ECJ first held that Art 119 had direct effect (*Defrenne v Société Anonyme Belge de Navigation Aérienne Sabena* [1976] 1 ECR 455). Subject to that, the period in respect of which claims may be made and the time limit for making such claims was to be determined by domestic law with reference to the most closely analogous time limits. The court also held that potential members could not avoid the obligation to pay back payments of employee contributions.

7.14.3 Pensions Act 1995

As discussed on p 102 the Pensions Act 1995, ss 62 to 66, provides that any scheme which does not contain an equal treatment rule shall be treated as including one. An equal treatment rule is one which relates to the terms on which membership of a scheme is offered as well as to the benefits of the scheme. Consequently, it covers both access to (ie the ability to join) a scheme and the benefits under it. Where the equal treatment rule is breached the employer must provide such additional resources as are necessary to remedy that breach (*see* p 102).

For the equal treatment rule to apply:

(a) the employee and an employee or former employee of the other sex must be employed on comparable work (ie like work, work rated as equivalent or work of equal value); and

(b) the two employees must be in the same employment or must be employed by associated employers (ie employers subject directly or indirectly to common control) at the same establishment or at different establishments at which for employees of the relevant class common terms and conditions are observed.

The employee may select any employee of the other sex as a comparator. It is irrelevant that there are employees of the other sex employed on the same terms as the employee making the complaint.

The equal treatment rule, as far as it relates to benefits, is treated as having had effect from 17 May 1990. When the rule applies, if any term relating either to access to the scheme or treatment under it is less favourable to one of the employees than to a comparator of the other sex, the term is treated as modified so as not to be less favourable.

The Pensions Act also offers a statutory defence which is based very broadly on the European concept of objective justification. It provides that the equal treatment rule does not operate if the trustees of the scheme (not the employer) can prove that the different treatment is genuinely due to a material factor which is not the difference of sex but is the material difference between the woman's case and the man's case.

The Pensions Act also provides for various exemptions from the equal treatment rule which very broadly mirror previous European case law. These cover, eg, statutory maternity and family leave provisions, bridging pensions and certain actuarial factors.

The provisions of the Pensions Act in regard to equal treatment are supplemented by the provisions contained in the Occupational Pension Schemes (Equal Treatment) Regulations 1995 (SI No 3183) (the 'Equal Treatment Regulations').

7.14.4   Limitation periods

The limitation periods under the Equal Pay Act 1970 apply to claims under the equal treatment rule. This means that the complainant is not entitled to be awarded any payment by way of arrears of benefits or damages in respect of a time earlier than two years before proceedings are instituted. This applies wherever the proceedings are brought. Therefore, a person wrongly denied membership may claim that he is entitled to be admitted to membership with effect from a date not more than two years before the date on which proceedings are instituted. The limitation applicable to a claim for equal benefits is less clear. It is thought that it applies to instalments of pension which should have been, but have not been, paid (in which case the two-year period does not start to run until retirement). The alternative view is that it applies to the pension which should have been but has not been credited to the member (in which case he may claim no more than two years' back credits). There is, in any event, some doubt as to whether the two-year period is compatible with European law. In *Marshall v Southampton and South West Hampshire Area Health Authority (No 2)* [1993] IRLR 445 the ECJ ruled that a fixed upper limit on awards for compensation for sex discrimination breached European law. However, in *Johnson v Chief Adjudication Officer (No 2)* [1995] IRLR 157 the ECJ held, in a social security context, that limiting backdated compensation was not necessarily inconsistent with European law. The validity of the two-year time limit under the Pensions Act 1995 has been referred to the ECJ.

For High Court claims for breach of contract or breach of statutory duty the time limit is six years from the date on which the breach occurred (the Limitation Act 1980, ss 5 and 9). Claims for non-fraudulent breaches of trust must be brought within six years of the date that the benefit fell into possession (Limitation Act 1980, s 21(3)). Complaints to the Pensions Ombudsman must normally be made within three years of the act or omission complained of or, if the complainant was unaware of the act or omission when it occurred, within three years of the earliest date he knew or ought reasonably to have known of its occurrence (Personal and Occupational Pension Schemes (Pensions Ombudsman) Regulations 1991 (SI No 588)). It may be therefore that where it is not apparent that benefits have not been equalised time would never start to run. Even where it is apparent, it is thought that time would not start to run in relation to any particular benefit payment until it became due.

The Pensions Act provisions on limitation periods take effect only for claims made after 1 January 1996. The position for claims made between 31 May 1995 and 1 January 1996 is governed by the Occupational Pension Schemes (Equal Access to Membership) Amendment Regulations 1995 (SI No 1215). These are in substantially the same terms as the Equal Treatment Regulations. For claims made before 31 May 1995, the position is slightly more complicated. Although there are significant difficulties, the Employment Appeals Tribunal held in the case of *Preston v Wolverhampton Healthcare NHS Trust* [1996] PLR 363 that the applicable time limits were the same as provided by the Equal Treatment Regulations.

7.14.5 Common issues on acquisitions

It is rare for a purchaser not to be confronted with some potential sex equality liabilities. The likelihood and the scope of the problems will be more marked on taking over a scheme. A purchaser should seek indemnity cover against or ensure that the inequalities are addressed in any post-completion shortfall valuation or that any transfer value is calculated on an equalised basis.

There are often difficulties associated with the method used to equalise retirement ages. Occasionally, retirement ages have been equalised in breach of the principle first established in *Smith v Avdel Systems Ltd* [1995] ICR 596 that pre-amendment pensionable service must be calculated with the more favourable retirement age. One of the commonest forms of equalisation is to equalise retirement ages at the higher age after a certain date (the 'equalisation date') and for service between 17 May 1990 (the date of the *Barber* judgment) and the equalisation date, the retirement age is at the lower age. A purchaser should examine the amendment power of the relevant scheme to see whether it is possible to amend the scheme in such a way: sometimes the scheme's amendment power may be very restricted. Further, there is always a risk that the amendment could be held to be ineffective if it appears that the scheme trustees were not acting in the best interests of their beneficiaries or were paying far too much attention to the commercial needs of the employer. In addition, there may be liability in respect of members who transferred out or who originally received their pension before the equalisation took effect.

Even where the schemes have equalised their retirement ages properly, there is still a residual concern in contracted-out salary related schemes over the schemes' guaranteed minimum pension ('GMPs'). The GMPs are in effect a replacement of part of the state pension (*see* p 82). Consequently, they are based on the unequal state retirement ages of 60 for women and 65 for men. It is uncertain whether under European law GMPs need to be equalised. However, it is clear that they must be equalised under the equal treatment rule apart from differences in indexed increases to GMPs in payment (Equal Treatment Regulations, reg 14). Whether this partial exemption is permitted under European law has yet to be determined. Possibly it is having regard to the decision of *Birds Eye Walls Ltd v Roberts* [1993] OPLR 203 which held that the provision of bridging pensions was not unlawful under European law.

A particular concern arises where the scheme is not open to the whole workforce. It is necessary to establish whether those employees who are excluded are being either directly or indirectly discriminated against. Discrimination may arise where the scheme is, say, closed to hourly paid employees even though they are doing work of equal value to the staff employees who are permitted to join the scheme. Indirect discrimination may arise from, eg, minimum working hours or minimum age precondition. Where there has been discrimination regard should be had to the potential future service costs as well as the additional past service liability.

The other common area of concern is often past unequalised transfers particularly where there has been a bulk transfer to or from a scheme on a previous acquisition or disposal. Expert actuarial advice may need to be obtained to quantify the amount of the liability.

7.14.6   Asset acquisitions

The pensions exemption under TUPE, reg 7, (*see* p 109) would appear to be sufficiently broadly drafted to provide that past sex equality liabilities referable to any of the target employees do not pass on an asset acquisition. The case law on the pensions exemption has not concentrated on this area previously. Consequently, a purchaser should still insist on taking an indemnity for any sex equality pension issues. Moreover, the pension exemption would not be effective to hold harmless the purchaser's scheme if an unequalised transfer was taken from the vendor's scheme. Given the very broad definition given to 'employer' by the Pensions Act 1995 and the Equal Treatment Regulations, if a purchaser participates in a vendor's scheme then despite the effect of the pensions exemption the sex equality liabilities may transfer. Further, participation may in itself have the effect that the purchaser has by implication assumed the vendor's pension liabilities.

7.15   Pensions checklist

The pensions checklist set out below will require adaptation to each particular case. It does not purport to be exhaustive but is designed to highlight some of the principal areas of potential concern to a purchaser. It is suggested that enquiries on the items listed should be made at the earliest possible stage, since the information obtained may enable the purchaser and its advisers to form a preliminary view of the state of the scheme or schemes and, in particular, to see if there are any obvious queries as to its funding. The purchaser should normally obtain actuarial advice and the checklist is not in any way suggested to be a substitute for such advice.

The checklist relates to every scheme, contract or arrangement (whether approved or non-approved and whether funded or unfunded) to which the target or any of its subsidiaries is a party and which provides 'relevant benefits' as defined by the Income and Corporation Taxes Act 1988, s 612, for any one or more present or former directors or employees or for their widows, widowers, children or dependants. The details listed below should be obtained in respect of each such scheme separately. Details of any *ex gratia* pensions should also be obtained.

1   Name of scheme

2   Documentation

2.1 Trust deeds and rules (including any amendments).

2.2 If a group scheme, the deed by which the target adhered to it.

2.3 Explanatory literature (including any announcements relating to benefit improvements or other amendments not yet incorporated into the formal documentation).

2.4 Latest actuarial report.

2.5 Latest annual actuarial certificate under the MFR.

2.6 Latest scheme accounts.

2.7 Inland Revenue letter of approval.

2.8 Contracting-out certificate.

2.9 Memorandum and articles of association of any trustee company.

2.10 Insurance policies.

2.11 Registrar of Pension Schemes: form PR1 (90).

3   Scheme assets

3.1 List of scheme assets and their value.

3.2 Details of any self-investment in target or vendor's group.

3.3 Statement of investment principles.

3.4 Investment management agreements.

3.5 Custodian and nominee arrangements.

4   Membership data

4.1 Entry conditions.

4.2 If discretionary, how is that discretion operated in practice?

4.3 List of members showing dates of birth, sex, pensionable service and pensionable earnings.

4.4 List of pensioners and deferred pensioners showing dates of birth, sex and pension entitlement.

5   Benefits
5.1 Discretionary increases to pensions in payment or in deferment over previous ten years.
5.2 Other discretionary practices: redundancy, early retirement, long service bonus etc.
5.3 Any credit of additional pensionable service not fully vested?
5.4 Any backdating of pensionable service on joining the scheme for pension benefits?
5.5 Any benefit augmentations or special terms?
5.6 Do benefits accrue at a uniform rate or does the rate increase with age or length of service?
5.7 Are any employees provided only with life cover?

6   Contributions
6.1 Schedule of contributions.
6.2 Employer's contribution rate over previous three years.
6.3 Are contributions paid in arrears?
6.4 Anticipated future contribution rate.

7   Trustees
7.1 Names of the trustees.
7.2 Member-nominated trustees/directors: appropriate rules/alternative arrangements.
7.3 In whom is the power of appointment and removal vested?
7.4 Who owns the shares in any trustee company?

8   Employers
8.1 Does any employer (other than the target and its subsidiaries) participate in the scheme?

The checklist is, it is hoped, largely self-explanatory, but questions 4 and 5 require a special mention.

With regard to question 4, consideration should be given whether employees excluded from membership may have an 'equal value' or indirect sex discrimination claim.

In question 5 it is important to ascertain full details of the benefits and discretionary practices so that the past service liabilities can be properly quantified. If pensionable service is backdated on joining the scheme there is a contingent liability in respect of current employees who have not yet joined the scheme for which it can reasonably be argued that allowance should be made when determining the past service liabilities.

Chapter 8

Accounting for Acquisitions

The subject of accounting for acquisitions is complex and controversial. Because of the impact which acquisitions can have on reported profits and earnings, the methods of accounting for them are under continual scrutiny and review. The emphasis in this chapter is placed on accounting for acquisition of a corporate target, since it is in that context that the majority of issues arise. The accounting treatment of assets acquisitions is considered at p 132. The purpose of this chapter is to provide an introduction to the basic issues, from a purchaser's point of view. The Accounting Standards Board issued new Financial Reporting Standards in September 1994 (FRS 6 and FRS 7) which have limited much of the discretion open to the purchaser in its accounting treatment of the acquisition. The related topic of accounting for goodwill and intangible assets is the subject of an exposure draft issued in June 1996 which, when implemented, will further affect the position and will have a significant impact on some of the issues described below.

In the context of corporate acquisitions, the problems of share premium account and pre-acquisition profits have caused difficulty for many years. Those interested in the history of the subject should read Christopher Napier and Christopher Noke, 'Premiums and Pre-acquisition Profits: The Legal and Accountancy Professions and Business Combinations' [1991] MLR 810. Those who would like an entertaining and colourful account of the commercial issues should try Terry Smith, *Accounting for Growth* 2nd edn 1996. The problems of share premium account and pre-acquisition profits are related and, before considering the law in detail, it is necessary to understand their practical significance and why they are related. Having struggled to an understanding of the law, the practitioner then has to understand the accounting rules for the treatment of mergers and acquisitions.

8.1 Background issues

The Companies Act 1985, s 130, provides that where a company issues shares at a premium, whether for cash or otherwise, a sum equal to the aggregate amount or value of the premiums on those shares must be transferred to a share premium account. Once the share premium account has been set up, it cannot be used except for making bonus issues and paying certain expenses and may not be reduced without the consent of the court.

Shares are issued at a premium if they are issued for an amount in excess of their nominal value. When one company, the purchaser, acquires the issued share capital of another in exchange for the issue of shares of the purchaser then, on the assumption that the market value of the target's shares exceeds the nominal value of the consideration shares, the question will arise whether the consideration shares have been issued at a premium and, if so, what amount should be transferred to a share premium account. The answer has a direct impact on the value at which the target's shares are brought into the purchaser's accounts. If the effect of s 130 is to oblige the purchaser to set up a share premium account of the difference between the nominal value of the consideration shares and the market value of the target's shares, it also means, in practice, that the purchaser is bound to bring the target's shares into its accounts at that same market value. When a share premium account is established in this way the transaction will be accounted for as an acquisition in the consolidated accounts of the purchaser's group. The emphasis of the approach on consolidation is slightly different, in that the shares issued should be accounted for at their fair value and the most reliable measure of fair value would be the market price of those shares, if they are listed, or a valuation prepared specifically for the purpose, if they are not. This is required both by FRS 7, para 78 and 79 and the Companies Act 1985, Sched 4A, para 9. In practice the value in the consolidated accounts is likely to be the same as that used in the purchaser's own accounts.

While most acquisitions will be accounted for as acquisition following the introduction of FRS 6 it is useful to understand the alternative and why purchasers have, in the past, sought to avoid an acquisition accounting treatment. One reason has been because, on the assumption that the market value of the consideration paid for the target's share capital is greater than the fair value of the identifiable underlying net assets of the target, the difference will show up as goodwill in the consolidated balance sheet of the purchaser's group. Under accounting standards which currently apply, this goodwill must then be written off against reserves (and share premium account is not available for this) or amortised through the profit and loss account, thus reducing reported profits (this treatment of goodwill seems certain to change following publication of Financial Reporting Exposure Draft 12 (*see further below*)).

In addition (and this is why the problem relates to the question of pre-acquisition profits), acquisition accounting restricts the reserves which are shown in the consolidated balance sheet to the reserves of the purchaser and only the post-acquisition reserves of the target, affecting the presentation and strength of the consolidated balance sheet. The requirement under acquisition accounting to adjust the book values of the target's assets to their fair values may also produce an increased charge for depreciation in the consolidated accounts with its consequent impact on reported consolidated profits. The extra reserve produced by accounting for the acquisition on a valuation basis in the purchaser's own accounts (ie taking the target's shares into the books at a valuation) is the share premium account and is not available for dividend, and the related asset ('investment in subsidiary') will be shown at the same value. The fact that the target may have reserves available for dividend will not, of itself, affect the accounts of the purchaser and, if the new subsidiary pays dividends to the purchaser out of reserves which it had at the time of the acquisition, the purchaser will normally have to apply the proceeds to reduce the value of the target's shares in its accounts (although in practice, this will depend on whether the distribution by the target to the purchaser has led to a permanent diminution in the value to the purchaser of its investment in the target). Therefore, although payment of such a dividend may provide the purchaser with cash to fund a dividend of its own it will not, where such a reduction is necessary, increase the purchaser's distributable reserves. The distribution of pre-acquisition profits is considered further below (p 131). The rules relating to the accounting treatment of mergers and acquisitions are contained in the Companies Act 1985, Sched 4A, and in FRS 6 (Acquisitions and Mergers) and FRS 7 (Fair Values in Acquisition Accounting).

Where 'merger accounting' is permitted, the purchaser can bring the target's shares into its accounts at the nominal value of the shares which it issues as consideration without any additional requirement to recognise the premium on those shares. On consolidation, the assets and liabilities of the target will be brought into account at their book value (without any requirement for adjustment to their fair value) and questions of goodwill will not arise nor, obviously, any question of finding a reserve against which it can be written off. When it comes to distribution of pre-acquisition profits by the target, while merger accounting will not itself increase the amount of the distributable reserves in the purchaser there may, nonetheless, be a difference in the effect of receiving dividends from the target: because the target is valued in the purchaser's books only at the nominal value of the purchaser's shares issued as consideration, it is unlikely that the receipt of a dividend from the target (out of its pre-acquisition reserves) will result in a permanent diminution in the value of that investment. The receipt of the target's dividend by the purchaser will instead generally be treated as a realised profit and as there is unlikely to be a need for reduction in the value of the purchaser's investment in the target, will add to the total amount the purchaser then has available to pay by way of dividend (*see further* p 131). The circumstances in which merger accounting is permitted have now been significantly curtailed by FRS 6 with the effect that merger accounting is in practice now available only in the case of a true merger of equals mutually sharing in the risks and benefits of the combined entity.

The simple distinctions between acquisition and merger accounting are blurred by the availability of merger relief in certain cases, where acquisition accounting is required by FRS 6. In these cases the acquisition accounting rules apply on consolidation so that an 'equivalent' reserve to the share premium account has to be set up based on the fair value of the shares issued. However, in the purchaser's own accounts this reserve does not have to be set up so that the investment will have a lower carrying value, potentially allowing the distribution of pre-acquisition profits. Merger relief is explained further below.

8.2   Share premium account

The law relating to share premium account is to be found in cases decided before the introduction of merger relief under the Companies Act 1985, s 13. In *Head (Henry) Ltd v Ropner Holdings Ltd* [1952] Ch 124 a holding company was formed to acquire the shares of two other companies whose share capital was taken by the holding company into its books at a valuation corresponding to that of the assets of the target. The court held that the excess of the valuation over the nominal value of the consideration shares had to be credited to a share premium account. Harman J said (at p 128):

> Apparently, if the shares are issued for a consideration other than cash and the value of the assets acquired is more than the nominal value of the shares issued, you have issued shares at a premium.

This might be thought to be the end of the matter, but, before the decision in *Shearer (Inspector of Taxes) v Bercain Ltd* [1980] 3 All ER 295, there was a body of legal opinion to the effect that it was the directors of the purchaser who placed the fetters on their own wrists. Because the existence or otherwise of the share premium account arising as a result of an acquisition is directly related to the amount at which the target's shares are brought into the holding company's books, it follows, it was said, that it is the directors' decision as to that amount which is vital in determining the question. If the target's shares are brought in at an amount in excess of the nominal amount of the consideration shares, then the excess must indeed be credited to a share premium account; but there is no statutory provision which expressly requires the directors to bring the shares in at a valuation.

In *Craddock v Zevo Finance Co Ltd* [1944] 1 All ER 566 the Court of Appeal was asked to consider, for tax purposes, whether investments acquired by a dealing company in a reconstruction in exchange for the issue of shares should be brought into the purchaser's books at 'cost' (the nominal value of the consideration shares allotted) or at their market value (which was less). It confirmed the correctness of bringing in the investments at cost. Lord Greene MR said (at p 569):

> The propriety of the course adopted is manifest when the uncertainty as to the value of the investments ... is borne in mind. It is, I think, true as a general proposition that, where a company acquires property for fully

paid shares of its own, the price paid by the company is the nominal value of the shares. It is for those who assert the contrary to establish it, as could be done, for example, in the suggested case of a deliberately inflated valuation.

If the target's shares are brought in at an amount equal to the nominal value of the consideration shares it would not be consistent with any ordinary accounting practice to have a share premium account and it was therefore said to follow (because neither s 130 nor any other provision of the Act expressly requires the target's shares to be brought in on a valuation basis) that the section could not require a share premium account where the target's shares were, in fact, brought into the books at cost.

The difficulty with s 130 in the context of acquisitions is the difficulty that lies at the root of accounting for all acquisitions in exchange for the issue of shares. The shares which the purchaser issues as consideration for the acquisition are not, in its hands, money's worth (as Lord Greene pointed out in the *Zevo* case), and in truth, there is no cost to the purchasing company at all. The purchaser suffers an addition to its balance sheet 'liabilities' of the nominal amount of the consideration shares, but this liability is not one which the company can ever be called upon to meet unless it has assets available for the purpose. In a winding up, although the rights attaching to shares may require a division of surplus assets in a certain way, the number of shares in issue does not affect the amount of the assets which are available for distribution among the members.

Shearer (Inspector of Taxes) v Bercain Ltd [1980] 3 All ER 295 placed the matter beyond doubt. In that case an investment holding company acquired shares in two other companies valued at £96,000 in exchange for 4,100 shares of a nominal value of £1 each. It created a share premium account which, after deducting expenses, amounted to £91,717. It then received dividends from the two targets of £36,000, on receipt of which it wrote down the value of its investment in its subsidiaries from £96,000 to £59,950. The Revenue contended that these dividends could have been distributed by the holding company by way of dividend and raised a shortfall assessment. The holding company pleaded that under the relevant taxation legislation, it was subject to a 'restriction imposed by law' preventing distribution, in that it was obliged to create the share premium account and therefore had no distributable reserves. Walton J agreed, following *Head (Henry) Ltd v Ropner Holdings Ltd* and said (at p 301) that the matter would appear 'as plain as a pikestaff'.

8.2.1 Merger relief

The Companies Act 1985, s 131, excludes the application of s 130 where the company issuing the consideration shares

> ... has secured at least a 90 per cent equity holding in another company in pursuance of an arrangement providing for the allotment of equity

shares in the issuing company on terms that the consideration for the shares allotted is to be provided—(*a*) by the issue or transfer to the issuing company of equity shares in that other company, or (*b*) by the cancellation of any such shares not held by the issuing company.

'Arrangement' is defined by s 131(7) to mean 'any arrangement, scheme or arrangement (including an arrangement sanctioned in accordance with ss 425 or 582)'. The exemption also extends to cover shares issued, under the same arrangement, by the purchaser in exchange for the issue or transfer of non-equity shares in the target.

Many share-for-share acquisitions will therefore fall outside the terms of s 130 altogether and it will not be necessary (or indeed possible) to create a share premium account. Section 133 expressly provides that a sum corresponding to any amount representing premiums which, by virtue of s 131, is not included in the company's share premium account can also be disregarded in determining the amount at which any shares or other consideration provided for the shares issued is to be included in the company's balance sheet.

The purchaser is to be regarded as having secured at least a 90 per cent equity holding in the target in pursuance of an arrangement if as a result of any acquisition or cancellation of equity shares in the target in pursuance of that arrangement it holds equity shares in the target (whether all or any of those shares were acquired in pursuance of that arrangement or not) of an aggregate nominal value equal to 90 per cent or more of the nominal value of that company's equity share capital (s 131(4)). If the equity share capital of the target is divided into different classes, the section does not apply unless the requirements are satisfied in relation to each of those classes taken separately (s 131(5)). Equity share capital is defined by s 744 as any issued share capital except any part which, neither as respects dividends nor as respects capital, carries any right to participate beyond a specified amount in a distribution, and 'equity shares' is defined by s 131(7) as meaning shares comprised in equity share capital. Relief extends to consideration shares allotted for non-equity share capital in the target as part of the same arrangement.

8.3   The accounting rules

Before considering the accounting rules and their implications for the purchaser in further detail it is worth keeping in mind that there are four ways in which the acquisition may be accounted for in the purchaser's own accounts and in its consolidated accounts:

(a)   by merger accounting in the consolidated accounts, and taking advantage of merger relief in the purchaser's own accounts;

(b)   by merger accounting in the consolidated accounts, and not taking advantage of merger relief in the purchaser's own accounts (even though, necessarily, merger relief must be available in order that there is merger

accounting in the consolidation);
(c) by acquisition accounting in the consolidated accounts, if the conditions for merger accounting are not available, together with taking advantage of merger relief in the purchaser's accounts, if it is available. This approach is popular and commonly used where, for example, shares are used to fund an acquisition by means of vendor placing (*see* p 237 *et seq*);
(d) by acquisition accounting in the consolidated accounts and not taking advantage of merger relief in the purchaser's own accounts, if the conditions for merger relief are not satisfied

This range of accounting treatment is relevant only when the purchaser uses its shares to fund all or part of the consideration. Plainly the question of share premium does not arise where cash or some other investment is used to fund the acquisition, in which case treatment of the acquisition will always be under the acquisition method.

It is also useful to keep in mind the distinction between the accounting treatment in the purchaser's own accounts and that on consolidation. Share premium and merger relief are issues for the purchaser's own accounts, although their application will have an impact on the consolidated accounts. The accounting treatment in the consolidated accounts needs to be considered separately. In the consolidation, except in the case of a true merger, the acquisition method will be used. If acquisition accounting has been used in the consolidation but in the purchaser's own accounts merger relief is available and has been used there will be a restatement of the value of the consideration to its market value in the consolidated accounts, the difference between nominal value and market value being credited to a non statutory capital reserve against which consolidation goodwill may be offset.

The company accounts of the purchaser are the relevant accounts for deciding the amount the purchaser can declare by way of dividend (and, as explained above, the availability or otherwise of merger relief may affect the use of dividends received out of the target's reserves to fund dividends to the purchaser's shareholders), whereas the value at which the target's assets must be brought into account, the question of whether goodwill arises and the treatment of preacquisition reserves of the target, are all questions relevant to the consolidation. The availability of merger relief means that merger accounting is possible, but in view of the conditions prescribed in FRS 6 it is now of much more limited application.

8.3.1 Merger accounting

The Companies Act 1985, Sched 4A, para 10 sets out the legal conditions for merger accounting in the consolidated accounts. They are:
(a) that at least 90 per cent of the nominal value of the relevant shares in the target is held by or on behalf of the parent and its subsidiary undertakings;
(b) that the proportion referred to in para (*a*) was attained pursuant to an ar-

rangement providing for the issue of equity shares by the parent company or one or more of its subsidiary undertakings;

(c) that the fair value of any other consideration did not exceed 10 per cent of the nominal value of the equity shares issued; and

(d) the adoption of merger accounting accords with generally accepted accounting principles or practice.

For this purpose, 'relevant shares' means those carrying unrestricted rights to participate in distributions and in assets upon a liquidation. The 'generally accepted accounting principles or practice' referred to in (d) above are to be found in FRS 6. In summary this provides that merger accounting is permitted only if:

(a) no party to the business combination is portrayed as either acquirer or acquired;

(b) all parties to the business combination participate in establishing the management structure for the combined entity and in selecting management personnel, such decisions being made on the basis of a consensus between them rather than purely by exercise of voting rights;

(c) the relative sizes of the combining entities are not so disparate that one party dominates the combined entity by virtue of its relative size;

(d) the consideration received by the equity shareholders of each party comprises primarily equity shares in the combined entity, and any non-equity consideration or equity shares carrying diminished voting or distribution rights represent an immaterial proportion of the fair value of the consideration received; equity shares acquired by one party in the two years prior to the merger are to be taken into account for this purpose; and

(e) no equity shareholder of any of the combining entities retains any material interest in the future performance of only part of the combined entity.

Thus to apply merger accounting the purchaser must comply with three sets of rules. It must obtain merger relief under s 131 and must then meet the conditions of Sched 4A, para 10 which themselves require that it complies with FRS 6. Applicability of merger relief does not, however, lead to merger accounting unless the above conditions are satisfied. If they are not, acquisition accounting will apply.

One important point to note is that, where merger accounting is permitted, the consolidated accounts for the period in which the merger took place will show profits and losses of the target for the entire period without any adjustment in respect of that part of the period prior to the merger. Although this will not affect the legal position relating to dividends, it will of course have a significant effect upon the perceived results of the purchaser for the period.

8.3.2   Acquisition accounting

If acquisition accounting is required in a case which qualifies for merger relief then a new, non-statutory reserve will be thrown up in the purchaser's own accounts and on consolidation equal to the difference in the fair value of the consideration paid for the target company and the nominal value of the consideration shares allotted. Because this reserve is not share premium account it is possible to use it for writing off goodwill arising on consolidation.

Where acquisition accounting and share premium account are required it is possible to apply to the court to reduce share premium account. This has the effect of creating a reserve against which goodwill can be written off. See *Re Ratners Group plc* (1988) 4 BCC 293, *Re Thorn EMI* (1988) 4 BCC 698. Such a reduction is subject to approval by special resolution in accordance with Companies Act 1985, s 135 (see s 130(3)), and must be confirmed of the court. A court will sanction a reduction provided it is satisfied that all shareholders are treated 'equitably' in the reduction; that shareholders in general have had the proposals properly explained to them so that they can exercise an informed judgement; that creditors are safeguarded and that the reduction is not without discernable purpose (see *Re Ratners*). The reduction of share premium account will have the effect of creating a distributable reserve equal to the amount of share premium which has been reduced (*Quayle Munro, Petrs* [1994] 1 BCLC 410) and accordingly it is usual practice for the company seeking confirmation of its reduction to give an undertaking to the court placing limitations on the extent to which the reserve will be treated as distributable, for the protection of its existing creditors.

Acquisition accounting requires that on consolidation the fair value of the purchase consideration must be allocated between the underlying net tangible and intangible assets of the target. See Sched 4A, para 9. Further, FRS 7, 'Fair Values in Acquisition Accounting' sets out detailed requirements for determining the fair value of the assets and liabilities of the target. As its title suggests, it is of relevance only in the context of acquisition accounting and applies not only in the preparation of consolidated accounts for inclusion of a target company, but equally to the acquisition of a target *business*.

FRS 7 was introduced in 1994 and is mandatory, like FRS 6, in relation to all accounting periods commencing on or after 23 December 1994. The basic principle of FRS 7 is to ensure that, on acquisition, all the assets and liabilities of the acquired entity (company or business) at the date of their acquisition are recorded at their fair values reflecting their condition at that date, and that all charges to the acquired assets and liabilities that arise afterwards are reported as part of the post-acquisition financial performance of the purchaser's group. Broadly, 'fair value' equates to market value either measured by way of professional valuation, depreciated replacement cost or discounted cash flows. If applying market values leads to an upwards revaluation then it will, naturally, lead to an increased depreciation charge affecting the overall profit to be reported for the target company or business. One of the more significant practical changes resulting from the new standard has been the treatment of post-acquisition restructuring costs, whether they form part of the purchaser's plans for the target at the time of, or after, the acquisition. Unlike previous practice, these costs may not be deducted from the fair value of the assets acquired and will need to be recorded as part of the group's post-acquisition performance. Excluding such costs—which will often have been taken into account by the purchaser in determining the price for the target—will necessarily reduce the amount of goodwill which arises on consolidation to be offset against reserves. This is because goodwill is the difference between the fair value of the cost of acquisition and the fair value of the individual identifiable net assets acquired. The cost of acquisition is determined by reference to the market value of the consideration, together with the expenses of the acquisition. Contingent deferred consideration should be estimated, but adjusted on an annual basis as more information becomes available.

8.3.3   Writing off goodwill

The current accounting rules which provide for the writing off of purchased goodwill (that is to say, goodwill which arises on acquisition, either on consolidation or on the acquisition of an unincorporated business) are found in SSAP 22. The standard requires that purchased goodwill should normally be eliminated from accounts by immediate write-off against reserves (not as a charge in the profit and loss account). An alternative approach of recognising goodwill as an asset and amortising it through the profit and loss account over its useful economic life, in keeping with the accounting treatment of any other capital asset, may also be adopted. These are the accounting rules at the present time. However, this accounting treatment of goodwill has been the subject of considerable discussion, not least because the UK treatment under SSAP 22 has differed from international standards and, it is said, has been utilised to distort the true financial performance of the acquirer. The consequence was the publication by the Accounting Standards Board, after consultation, of FRED 12 ('Goodwill and Intangible Assets') in June 1996, setting out the text of a draft new accounting standard. The treatment of goodwill under FRED 12 does not offer the choice which is possible under the existing standard. It is proposed that purchased goodwill should be recognised as an asset in the balance sheet. Goodwill will then be amortised in the profit and loss account over its useful economic life (usually not more than 20 years). Where goodwill is believed to have a useful economic life of more than 20 years and its value is significant and expected to be capable of continued measurement in future, it should be amortised over that estimated life, or if it is indefinite, not amortised at all. Annual impairment reviews would then be required to establish whether any or further write downs were required.

This new approach will have considerable impact on the accounting for acquisitions. In particular, post acquisition reported profits of the combined group may suffer charges in respect of the goodwill. It seems likely that the acquirer will wish to ensure, so far as possible, that goodwill arising on the acquisition is minimised and this may lead to UK companies deciding that they have to reduce the prices which they are prepared to pay to acquire the target company or business.

One interesting point to consider is what happens, where acquisition accounting is used but merger relief is available, to the non-statutory reserve which exists in such circumstances. Under current accounting principles, this may be used for the immediate writing off of goodwill. The new rules do not allow the reserve to be used in this way (including in respect of the amortisation) and the reserve will sit in the accounts perhaps to be transferred to retained earnings on a disposal of the business concerned. Also, it has to date often been considered desirable to structure acquisitions so as to benefit from the merger relief provisions of s 131, in order that the immediate write-off of goodwill required under existing standards can be effected, but it seems that this reason for structuring the transaction as a share-for-share transaction will no longer be relevant. Nor, obviously, will it be appropriate to apply to the court for reduction of share premium account for such purpose.

8.4 Pre-acquisition profits

The acquisition itself will not affect the ability of the target to pay dividends. If the target pays a dividend to its new holding company out of reserves arising from profits made prior to the acquisition, how is this dividend to be treated in the purchasing company's accounts? It is clearly a receipt of a capital nature and amounts to the partial realisation of a fixed asset.

Where acquisition accounting is used, pre-acquisition profits or losses of the target will be reflected in its assets at the time of the acquisition and, accordingly, distributions to the purchaser out of pre-acquisition profits will be applied in the holding company's accounts to reduce the value of the target's shares. It may not, however, be appropriate to do this where it is unnecessary to provide for a diminution in the stated value of the target. If merger accounting is used it will rarely be necessary to provide for such a diminution. To the extent that it is not necessary to provide for a diminution in value of the shares of the target it appears that the amount of the distribution received will represent a distributable profit in the hands of the purchaser.

The general rule is that any surplus accruing on the realisation of a fixed asset can be distributed by way of a dividend so long as the value of the purchaser's remaining assets is fairly represented by, or in excess of, their book value (see *Lubbock v British Bank of South America* [1892] 2 Ch 198 and *Foster v New Trinidad Lake Asphalt Co* [1901] 1 Ch 208). Whether or not non-revenue profits can be distributed in any particular case is a matter legislated for by the articles of the company concerned, and by the Companies Act 1985, Part VIII. Section 280(3) includes realised capital profits in calculating profits available for distribution, except in the case of investment companies.

The Companies Act 1948, Sched 8, para 15(5), formerly contained a provision which was held, in *Shearer (Inspector of Taxes) v Bercain Ltd*, to prevent the distribution of pre-acquisition profits in any case, by providing that such profits must not be treated as revenue profits in the accounts of the holding company for any purpose. This restriction no longer applies.

In the case where acquisition accounting is used but merger relief is available, and the holding company credits to the investment the distribution paid out of the target's pre-acquisition profits, the question will arise as to whether an equivalent amount of the non-statutory merger reserve can be regarded as realised. This is a point on which there is no authority, although there is a view that the relevant proportion of the reserve is realised only when the investment is sold and cash is received in connection with the sale.

8.5   Accounting for assets acquisitions

An acquisition of business assets, whether funded by shares or cash, will always be accounted for on the acquisition basis. In each case, the target business will be recorded in the acquirer's books at the cost of acquisition. If the acquisition is for cash, the acquisition cost will be the cash price paid. If it is for shares the acquisition cost will be equal to the fair value of those shares, and the difference between the fair value and nominal value will be carried to share premium account.

The identifiable assets and liabilities will be brought into account at their respective fair values, in accordance with FRS 7. Any difference between the fair value of the consideration paid and the fair values of the identifiable assets and liabilities acquired will be goodwill. The goodwill will be written off immediately against reserves (or amortised by an annual charge in the profit and loss account) in accordance with SSAP 22 although, as discussed above, the treatment of such purchased goodwill will change following introduction of new reporting standards as foreshadowed in FRED 12.

The requirement to record assets and liabilities of the target business at their fair value, may require revaluation of the assets acquired and have an impact on depreciation charges and the reported profitability of the target. In this respect, accounting for an asset acquisition gives rise to similar difficulties to those arising on the accounting of a corporate target as an acquisition.

Chapter 9

Investigations and Warranties

The common law rule of *caveat emptor*, although eroded beyond recognition in many fields, retains almost all its old force in relation to the acquisition of private companies and of business assets. Whether the acquisition is of shares or assets, there is limited exception and while there are differences in detail between the two transactions there is little difference in the overall approach to the process of investigation and taking warranties. This Chapter considers the approach of investigation and taking warranties with regard to both types of transaction.

In the case of a share acquisition, the Financial Services Act 1986, s 47 provides that it is a criminal offence for any person to induce or attempt to induce another to enter into an agreement for the acquisition of securities by, *inter alia*, any dishonest concealment of material facts but a civil remedy based on the section will not be awarded by the courts. In *Securities and Investments Board v Pantell SA (No 2)* [1991] 4 All ER 883 Sir Nicholas Browne-Wilkinson VC observed (at p 887) '... the individual investor is given no right of action for contravention of s 47' (the judgment, which concerned other matters has been affirmed by the Court of Appeal). In appropriate cases a civil remedy might be sought by the Securities and Investment Board, but that is unlikely to be of relevance to the private acquisition.

A vendor will not be liable for non-disclosure of relevant information, unless that non-disclosure is itself a misrepresentation or breach of warranty. Nor does any statutory provision imply into a contract for the acquisition of shares any term relating to the target's business. While the Misrepresentation Act 1967, s 3, would limit the operation of clauses designed to exclude liability for misrepresentation, the provisions of the Unfair Contract Terms Act 1977 do not apply to any contract so far as it relates to the creation or transfer of securities (Sched 1, para 1(e)). The ambit of this exception is not as clear as it might be, but it is generally thought that the parties to an acquisition of a corporate target are largely free to make their own bargain, save where liability for fraud is sought to be excluded.

In the case of a business acquisition, the Financial Services Act 1986, s 47 does not apply as the transaction will not typically include investments or the conclusion of investment agreements within the meaning of that Act. Depending on the type of assets to be sold however, terms as to the character and title of those assets may be implied by statute (under the Sale of Goods Act 1979 or the Law of Property (Miscellaneous Provisions) Act 1994 (see Chapter 10)). The Misrepresentation Act 1967, s 3 and the Unfair Contract Terms Act 1977, s 2(2) will apply, generally, to the acquisition so that provisions of the contract which seek to exclude liability for misrepresentation or 'negligence' (ie negligent misstatement) will be ineffective except in so far as such provisions satisfy the requirement of reasonableness in the Unfair Contract Terms Act 1977, s 11(1). Sched 1, paras 1(*a*) and (*b*) of the Unfair Contract Terms Act 1977 provide, however, that this 'reasonableness' requirement in relation to a restriction or exclusion of liability for negligence does not extend to a contract for the acquisition of business assets insofar as it relates to the creation or transfer of an interest in land or of rights or interests in patents, trademarks, copyright, and certain other intellectual property interests.

While the purchaser of business assets will, in consequence of any terms which may be implied by statute, be in a marginally better position compared with the purchaser of shares, relying on such statutory protection alone will not be adequate. To achieve the required degree of comfort in either transaction the purchaser must do what he can by investigation and contractual protection to ensure that, in the case of a share acquisition, the target has no liabilities apart from those of which the purchaser is aware and that, in all cases, shares or assets, the target's assets which are thought to form part of the acquisition are owned by the target/vendor and that there are no other onerous matters affecting the target business which would colour the purchaser's decision to acquire it, or the price at or terms on which it is willing to do so.

The purchaser of business assets is at least theoretically able to select the assets which it wishes to buy and the liabilities which it wishes to assume (see Chapter 10; but see also the statutory novation of employment contracts discussed in Chapter 6). Although commercial considerations may require that, for the sake of maintaining the goodwill of the business, the purchaser accepts the liabilities of the business as they stand, they are taken over by contractual provisions which amount to an indemnity and which can be designed to exclude the liabilities which the purchaser does not want. The target company, on the other hand, cannot so easily be fitted to the Procrustean couch and when acquired, its liabilities remain where they are unless creditors consent to their novation. No contractual provision between the vendor and purchaser can prevent the target company being called to account for those liabilities after completion of the acquisition. Whatever warranties and indemnities the purchaser of a corporate target may take, the target is, and remains, liable to meet its obligations and no warranty or indemnity, however well drafted, will avoid the problem of obtaining reimbursement from a vendor who is unable or unwilling to pay. Even a retention of part of the purchase price as security for the warranties may not be adequate and will not recompense the purchaser for the loss of time involved in solving problems which it did not know it was inheriting.

Because the target company has the capacity to incur contractual, tortious and criminal liabilities, the purchaser's task of ascertaining the precise nature and quality of the assets, liabilities and profit potential of the target is by no means an easy one. Even the business purchaser will find it difficult to identify and define precisely the assets and contractual rights and obligations it wishes to assume and be satisfied they will hold no surprises.

In practice, whatever the nature of transaction, the purchaser will take a broadly similar approach and will seek to protect itself by investigation and by contractual protection.

In theory at least, nothing can afford complete protection and it is certainly true that neither investigation nor contractual protection on its own is satisfactory for the cautious purchaser. In practice, a balance is struck between the two, although much will depend upon the relative strength of the vendor and purchaser. The vendor who has suffered intensive investigations of the target will be less willing to give warranties and if time does not permit exhaustive investigations the purchaser will be more ready to insist upon wide-ranging contractual protection.

This Chapter deals with the usual searches, with accountants' investigations and reports, environmental issues and investigations, with some difficulties relating to the investigation of title to land and, in general terms, with misrepresentation, warranty and indemnity. There is brief discussion of heads of agreement and of the auction sale process at p 183, which is increasingly popular as a method of marketing the target. Taxation is a field apart and it is considered in Chapters 12 and 13.

9.1 Searches

9.1.1 Companies Registry

The purchaser's solicitors will conduct searches against the target company and each of its subsidiaries at the Companies Registration Office as a matter of course and, whether the acquisition is of a target company or of business assets, a search against the vendor is essential.

It is worth making a general comment about such searches. The company search should show an up-to-date copy of the memorandum and articles of association and should reveal the names of the directors and secretary and the names of the shareholders shown in the last annual return, together with any details of subsequent allotments of shares and particulars of any charges given by the target/vendor over its assets as well as giving notice of the appointment of any receiver or liquidator which, in the case of the vendor, will inhibit the directors' ability to sell the target shares or business assets (*see* Chapter 16). The accuracy of the information given on the microfiche search of the register is not, however, guaranteed, because it is compiled by the target itself. To take an example, the file may be incomplete because of failure by the target to register changes in directors. Although this technically renders the officers of the target liable to a default fine, it gives no protection to a purchaser if it discovers after completion that the target has different or more directors than were thought. Neither will the information given necessarily be up to date, even though all relevant statutory provisions have been correctly complied with. For instance, the shareholders may have changed since the last annual return and, save in the case of fresh allotments, there is no obligation to bring the file up to date between returns and, in the case of registrable charges in particular, the period for filing the relevant notification may not have expired (*see further* p 155 with regard to the registration of charges). It follows that, although the company search may provide useful information, it is an extract from a register which may be incorrect or out of date (without any infringement of the Companies Acts) and which affords no statutory protection to the purchaser. Nonetheless, it provides valuable information and should be made both at the outset of the investigation and shortly before signing and completion so as to ensure that there have been no material changes in the information on file registration of new charges or the appointment of a receiver admistrator or liquidator.

9.1.2   Companies Court

The cautious practitioner will, in addition to a search at the Companies Registration Office, make a telephone search of the Companies Court (tel 0171–936 7328) to check that no winding up or administration petitions have been presented against the vendor or, if a corporate sale, the target or its subsidiaries.

9.1.3   Land Charges Registry

If the vendors are individuals eg of a corporate target, it is sensible to make a bankruptcy search at the Land Charges Registry.

9.1.4   Other searches

Where appropriate the purchaser's solicitors may consider searches at other public registries, although in many cases the matters they reveal ought properly be disclosed by the vendor in the course of the purchaser's enquiries and investigations or as disclosures against warranties. Searches may, however, be desirable at the United Kingdom Patent Office, Trade Marks Registry and Designs Registry which will reveal, respectively, the existence of any patents, registered trade marks and registered designs, including any applications that have been filed. If required, details can also be obtained on any assignments that have been recorded, licensees that have been entered or security interests that have been noted on the appropriate registry.

Property searches require special consideration and are discussed at p 155.

One point to note is that it is usual to accept as disclosed the information revealed by a company search as of the date of signing. The disclosure letter may treat as a general disclosure information on other public registers. The purchaser should ensure, where searches are accepted as disclosed, that it has conducted the relevant search and that the general disclosure is limited to the results of the search he has made as at a particular date (*see* the precedent Disclosure Letter at p 623).

9.2 The accountants' investigation

Irrespective of whether the purchaser of the target is a listed company, it is quite usual to instruct a firm of accountants, often the purchaser's auditors, to carry out an investigation into the target's affairs. The objective of such an investigation is to extract financial, commercial and administrative information from the target and to subject that information to close scrutiny so that the purchaser is provided with an expert, independent assessment of the target and its activities.

The advisability of instructing a firm of accountants to carry out an independent investigation of the target's affairs is underlined by a series of decisions which have the effect that it is very unlikely that a purchaser will have any cause of action against those concerned in the preparation of the target's statutory accounts simply because they have been negligently prepared. The class of persons who may rely on a statutory auditor's report having been limited by the courts, more recent decisions have identified circumstances in which auditors may nonetheless be liable and the practice is now for the target's auditors to restrict, where possible, the reliance which may be placed on their statements and where practicable, to seek contractual protection from liabilities which they may otherwise assume where there are areas of uncertainty eg disclosure of audit working papers. Accordingly, the purchaser will often wish to appoint its own reporting accountants—although the recent trend of limiting liability has also affected such appointments.

The leading case and starting point from which to consider the current position is *Caparo Industries v Dickman* [1990] 1 All ER 568, an important redefinition by the House of Lords of the circumstances in which professional advisers will incur tortious liability to third parties for negligently prepared information and advice. The Lords considered the test for the existence of a duty of care propounded by Lord Wilberforce in *Anns v London Borough of Merton* [1978] AC 728, which had two requirements: (1) sufficient proximity between adviser and advisee; and (2) no policy considerations which would negate or limit the existence of the duty. In *Caparo*, the Lords moved away from Lord

Wilberforce's universal test and stressed instead that the correct approach was to examine whether a particular set of circumstances falls within an existing category where a duty has been imposed, with new categories being developed incrementally and by analogy with existing ones rather than by reference to a general test. With specific reference to liability for negligent misstatement, the House of Lords held that the essential elements were the same as for any other tortious liability: foreseeability of damage, proximity and whether it is 'fair, just and reasonable' to impose the duty. However, applying *Hedley Byrne and Co Ltd v Heller and Partners Ltd* [1964] AC 465, the Lords gave specific guidance on the meaning of 'proximity' in the context of liability for negligent misstatement. Lord Oliver (at p 587) identified four factors: (1) the allegedly negligent advice was required for a purpose known to the adviser at the time the advice was given; (2) the adviser knew that the advice would be communicated to the advisee, either individually or as a member of an ascertainable class, for that purpose; (3) the adviser knew that the advisee was likely to act on the advice without further enquiry; and (4) the advisee in fact acted on the advice and suffered loss by so doing.

Caparo was concerned with a take-over offer by Caparo Industries for a public company, Fidelity plc. Caparo claimed that it had launched its offer on the basis of Fidelity's statutory accounts, which had been prepared by Touche Ross. After the offer was successful, Caparo alleged that the accounts had been negligently prepared and that it would not have made the offer had there been an accurate disclosure of Fidelity's financial position. Caparo sued Touche Ross, claiming that the auditors owed them a duty of care, both as potential and actual investors in Fidelity. The Lords rejected Caparo's claim: the accounts had been prepared for the purpose of complying with Fidelity's statutory obligations, and even though it may have been foreseeable that they might be used as the basis for a take-over offer this was not sufficient to impose a duty of care in favour of Caparo.

Cases since *Caparo* have confirmed its restrictive approach to the imposition of liability to third parties for negligent misstatement eg in *James Mc-Naughton Paper Group Ltd v Hicks Anderson and Co* [1991] 1 All ER 134, CA, an accountant who had been asked by a company which was the target of a take-over offer to prepare draft accounts was held to owe no duty of care to the offeror in respect of the accounts. More recently, however, the courts have in a number of decisions, while confirming the approach in *Caparo,* recognised that there will be circumstances in which an auditor will have the necessary degree of proximity to, eg, the bidder, and will have intended that his statements be relied upon so as to have 'assumed responsibility' to the bidder sufficient to incur liability to the bidder for negligent misstatement. In *Morgan Crucible Co plc v Hill Samuel Bank Ltd* [1991] 1 All ER 148, the Court of Appeal held on assumed facts, as a preliminary issue, that it was arguable that an offeror for a public company might have a cause of action in respect of negligent misstatements in the target's defence circulars where the statements were made after the existence of the bidder as a prospective acquirer was known. By contrast, in *Caparo*, the auditor's statement had not been given for the purpose for which the plaintiff had relied upon it. A similar distinction was made in *Galoo Ltd (in liq) v Bright Grahame Murray (a firm)* [1995] 1 All ER 16, which concerned an acquisition of a private company, where the Court of Appeal explained the distinction (at p 37) as follows: 'mere foreseeability that a potential bidder may rely on the audited accounts does not impose on the auditor a duty of care to the bidder, but if the auditor is expressly made aware that a particular identified bidder will rely on the audited accounts or other statements approved by the auditor, and intends that the bidder should so rely, the auditor will be under a duty of care to the bidder for the breach of which he may be liable'. *Galoo* involved an interlocutory application, but the 'assumption of responsibility' approach has been adopted in final hearings eg *ADT v Binder Hamlyn* (1995) December, *unreported*.

In this context further points are worth noting: while a fuller discussion of professionals' liability is beyond the scope of this book, the approach in *Caparo*, and later in *Morgan Crucible* and *Galoo* is being applied in other fields of professional and expert liability. It had (for example) been well established that the statements made in a prospectus could be relied upon by subscribers, but not by purchasers in the aftermarket and, adopting the approach in *Caparo,* this was confirmed in *Al-Nakib Investments (Jersey) Ltd v Longcroft* [1990] 3 All ER 321. More recently however, the courts have accepted as arguable that market practice has changed and that adopting an approach based upon *Morgan Crucible* and *Galoo* it may be possible to say that the necessary degree of intention and proximity can be established so as to found liability to purchasers in the aftermarket for negligent misstatement in a prospectus (see *Possfund Custodian Trustee Ltd v Diamond* [1996] 2 All ER 774, an application to strike out; although note that express provision as to responsibility for prospectuses has since been introduced in the Public Offers of Securities Regulations 1995, reg 13). It follows that professional advisers and experts in all fields will take particular care when giving any confirmation or assurance to the purchaser of the target company or business. Even if the expert is not otherwise responsible for a statement previously made, it may assume responsibility by repeating the statement in circumstances where it is reasonable, and intended, that, eg, a purchaser rely on it. The recent body of cases in the field of professional liability has caused professional advisers, and particularly accountants, to examine carefully their various activities. In the context of acquisitions, there are a number of circumstances, such as access to audit papers or preparation of completion accounts, where the practitioner is likely to come up against this more rigorous approach (*see below*).

In the light of *Caparo* and despite the more recent decisions, a purchaser should not rely on the target's statutory accounts for financial information in the absence of a specific (and clear) assumption of responsibility to the purchaser by the target's auditors; the auditors will seek to avoid such assumption unless there are exceptional circumstances. The same considerations should not arise in relation to an investigation of the target carried out by the purchaser's own accountants who will owe their client a duty of care under the terms of their engagement, subject to any agreed limitations (*see below*).

A full report prepared by reporting accountants in connection with an acquisition is not dissimilar from the type of report required by an issuing house which is sponsoring a company seeking a listing for its securities for the first time. In such a case, the issuing house requires a considerable amount of information regarding the company's affairs, both because it may be taking the risk of underwriting the issue and because of the need to preserve its reputation. However, these two types of investigative report differ from an accountants' report included (where required) in an acquisition circular issued to shareholders in accordance with the rules of the London Stock Exchange or in a prospectus. These latter reports are brief and are required to contain only a summary of the target's accounts covering a specified period, together with the accounting policies on which they have been based and the associated notes. They do not, for example, nor are they required to, include any commentary on how the company's profits were earned, whether it is sufficiently profitable, or what its future prospects might be.

The requirements for circulars relating to acquisitions are contained in the Stock Exchange's *Listing Rules* (the *Yellow Book*), Chapters 10, 11 and 14. It should be noted that certain of the information required by the rules relates to the acquiring company. In classifying an acquisition, and so determining which requirements have to be met, no distinction is generally made between acquisitions for cash and acquisitions for shares or other securities or (with minor exceptions) between acquisitions of shares or of business assets. Where, however, the acquisition would increase the shares of a class already listed by 10 per cent or more or where debt securities of any amount are issued, then full listing particulars are required. An acquisition will generally require, under the *Yellow Book*, presentation of financial information about the target in the form of a comparative table but in exceptional circumstances, a short form accountants' report is required. Guidance on the accountants' role in preparing financial information for inclusion in the circular has been published by the Auditing Practices Board, which issued two exposure drafts as 'Statements of Investment Circular Reporting Standards' (SIRs) in July 1996. SIR 100 ('Investment circulars and the reporting accountant') is proposed as an overarching standard establishing general principles for the work of reporting accountants on all engagements dealing with investment circulars, such as a Super Class 1 circular; the draft gives guidance, among other things, on agreeing the terms of the reporting accountants' engagement, presentation of their reports and comfort letters, whether required under the *Yellow Book* or confirming the extraction of information in the circular. SIR 200 ('Accountants' reports on historical financial information in investment circulars') is the first of a number of similar standards proposed to deal with particular issues, and proposes guidance on the accountants' report required in eg a Super Class 1 circular, where information in the form of a comparative table is not acceptable (*see* p 219).

The requirements of the Stock Exchange concerning financial information about the target are set out in Chapter 12 of the *Yellow Book*. If a report is necessary the accountants are required to express an opinion whether or not the financial information given shows a true and fair view, for the purpose for which it was prepared, of the financial matters set out in it.

A short form report to be contained in the circular is designed to inform the purchaser's shareholders solely about the trading record and asset position of the target. By contrast, an accountants' acquisition report is designed to inform the purchaser's management about the target, so that management is in a position to decide whether the proposed acquisition represents a sound commercial investment.

Because the scope of an acquisition investigation is wide and can cover the whole range of a target's business, the accountants will usually hold an early meeting with the purchaser in order to discuss the scope of the report. At this time the accountants should learn of any particular aspects of the target's business about which the purchaser has already been satisfied, and they should be forewarned of any areas which merit special attention.

If other professional advisers are involved at this stage, it is advisable that they too should be engaged in these discussions so that they can liaise with the accountants and, together, prevent unnecessary duplication of work. For instance, the accountants and the solicitors would normally both expect to enquire into the terms of any leases held by the target, and it is obviously not in the purchaser's interest to retain both these professional advisers to carry out such an examination. On the other hand, the accountants can often assist the solicitors by gathering for them information available from the target's premises. Liaison between professional advisers should also ensure that all relevant areas are covered within the limitations imposed by the purchaser's timetable. The implications of this latter factor are too often overlooked but are most important because time constraints, imposed for one reason or another, undoubtedly limit the depth to which the accountants will be able to probe. It is also helpful for the parties to ensure that a careful note and copies are made of documents and information given by the vendor's advisers in the course of the investigation (whether given to the purchaser, its reporting accountants, or its other advisers), since they will often form the basis of the information to be disclosed in qualification of the contractual warranties. Keeping such a record will reduce dispute over what should or should not be regarded as disclosed at a later date.

Before the accountants start their investigation they should be given clear instructions, in writing, from the purchaser. These instructions should refer specifically to any areas which they are required to examine in depth, such as the impact on the target of the wide-ranging legislation contained in the Financial Services Act 1986, and also to any areas specifically to be excluded from their investigation. The responsibility of the reporting accountant to its client, the purchaser, will be dictated by the terms of its engagement letter and the common law, which will imply a duty of care into the engagement (see eg *Henderson v Merrett Syndicates* [1994] 3 All ER 506). The engagement letter has increasingly become a document for negotiation before appointment of the reporting accountant. It has become commonplace that the letter will propose, in addition to setting out the scope of work, a limit on liability. At the time of writing, a cap on the accountants' liability will typically be proposed at the lesser of: (a) the transaction value; (b) £25 million; or (c) some other figure referable to the particular transaction eg if there is special risk involved. An indemnity for liability otherwise suffered by the firm and its agents and employees as a result of their work (ie if they become joined in some wider proceedings) should also be expected. The limit on liability is subject to the requirement of reasonableness under the Unfair Contract Terms Act 1977 and will typically be expressed not to apply in the event of fraud or dishonesty on the part of the firm. While limiting liability in this way is believed to reflect a concerted approach by the major accountants' firms (and it has been reported that the potentially restrictive effect has been notified to the Office of Fair Trading), practitioners advising the purchaser should note that it is usually the case that the terms of the engagement letter can be negotiated and the practitioner, when presented with such a document for consideration, should review it carefully in each case. It is likely that practice will develop in this area and practitioners would be well advised to check the up-to-date position.

Once engaged, the accountants should seek access to the target. Usually this will have been agreed to by the target during the course of the negotiations and the accountants should make detailed arrangements with the management of the target accordingly. Confidentiality is an important factor and the accountants should be fully aware of the need to respect the wishes of the management of the target, not only because there may be other potential acquiring companies, but also because it may be harmful to the target's business if staff, customers and suppliers become aware of a possible change in ownership.

In general terms, the acquisition report should be designed to present the information which the purchaser requires (within the cost and time scale limitations imposed) at a time when it is of most use to the purchaser in influencing the course which the negotiations will take prior to their finalisation. The accountants should be mindful that a well presented report may be of little use if it is delivered to the purchaser late.

The report will include much financial information which will be historical and will have been audited by the target's auditors. At an early stage, the accountants will require access to the auditors' working papers, both to obtain an insight into the target's business and to establish the degree of reliance that can be placed upon the figures which depict the target's historical performance and which will be the subject of contractual warranties given by the vendors. Of course, the most recent financial information available may not, and probably will not, be audited and the accountants will have to make an assessment of the reliability of the unaudited management accounts. Generally they will do this through an examination of previous trends and by a comparison of previous management accounts with the audited accounts for the corresponding periods. It is important to appreciate that the accountants will not themselves conduct an audit of the target's affairs unless the purchaser's instructions, unusually, require them to do so. The accountants will perform an appraisal of the target's accounts, but will not necessarily verify the target's assets and liabilities independently or make an in-depth examination of the target's systems of internal control.

Access to working papers of the target's auditors has been the subject of recent scrutiny by the profession, where concern has been expressed that such access might lead to the assumption by the auditor of an additional duty of care in respect of the audit beyond that inherent in its statutory responsibility (as described in *Caparo, above* at p 138). In October 1995 the Technical and Practical Auditing Committee of the ICAEW issued guidance on access to audit working papers, including the terms of specimen letters it recommended be obtained from the purchaser and its reporting accountants before access to such papers is given. The specimen provides for a waiver by the purchaser and reporting accountant so that the target's auditor does not assume a liability as a result of giving access to the papers, and for an indemnity to be given by the purchaser, but not its accountants. Practitioners should consider the terms of such waiver letters carefully in the context of the particular case, and propose amendments to the extent they can reasonably be negotiated (although there is reluctance on the part of auditors to depart from the specimen form). In particular, it would be appropriate to ensure that, if the purchaser later had a claim against the vendor under the warranties in the acquisition agreement (ie unrelated to mere disclosure of audit papers) in respect of which the vendor could recover from its auditors, any such liability of the auditors would not then flow back to the purchaser under the indemnity.

Apart from audit papers, much of the information required by the accountants should be readily available in one form or another at the target's principal place of business and can be obtained most easily by the management of the target. Accountants therefore often find it convenient to leave with management a list of the basic information they require for the purpose of their report. This enables them to spend more of their time appraising and interpreting the information obtained than in finding it.

Accountants' acquisition reports can, of course, take a number of different forms, but a report should be tailor-made to suit the particular requirements of the purchaser and the business environment in which the target operates. It may be useful to consider the outline of an acquisition report, an example of which is set out below, in order to provide an indication of the content of a typical report on a small manufacturing target company. Where, on an acquisition of business assets, not all the assets and liabilities of the target business are to be assumed, the report's contents will be modified accordingly.

9.3   Accountants' acquisition report

1   Introduction
This will normally recite the terms of reference under which the report is written; it should set out the scope of the work undertaken and refer to any general caveats relevant to the report as a whole. The prime sources of information should be identified and the reader's attention drawn to material areas not covered by the accountants' examination and to the reasons why these areas have been excluded.

2   History and business
2.1   *History*   A brief history of the target should be set out.
2.2   *Business*   Details of the target's present business with a description of its products, its principal operations and an assessment of its general position within the market in which it operates, within the context of the national economic situation, should be included.
2.3   *Growth*   An indication of the recent growth of the target and of its present size should be given, normally by reference to a brief summary of the net assets and profitability shown in its most recent audited accounts.
2.4   *Premises and locations*   The amount of work done will depend upon the division of work agreed with the solicitors. Certainly brief details of each property, its location and of any professional valuation should be included.

3   Corporate structure
3.1   *Capital structure*   Details of the target's present capital structure and of its present shareholders should be given, with recent changes.
3.2   *Group structure*   If the target comprises more than one company, information about the structure of the target group should be set out together with a description of the relationship between the subsidiaries and the parent company. Minority interests in subsidiaries should also be identified.
3.3   *Memorandum and articles of association*   This section should contain details of any unusual (but relevant) clauses in the target's memorandum and articles of association and details of share rights if relevant to the offer.

4   Management and personnel
4.1   *Directors and senior executives*   Details of the remuneration, including pensions and commissions, of the target's executives should be given, together with information on the terms of any service contracts and on any facilities granted to executives which may form part of their contracts of employment. The executives' qualifications should also be set out, and the accountants should make an assessment of the competence of the man-

agement if this is a part of their brief.

4.2 *Other employees* The number of other employees should be analysed by department and location, and the basis on which they are remunerated should be shown. The facilities available to employees should be described and information given as to any known employee turnover statistics.

4.3 *Pension arrangements* Details of pension arrangements for employees should be given and an assessment made of any unfunded liabilities.

4.4 *Succession and training* The target's policy for management succession should be set out and an assessment made of any problems which the reporting accountants anticipate may arise. Details of the target's policies for staff and trade training schemes and the cost of such schemes should be included.

4.5 *Labour relations* An assessment of the target's labour relations should be made, and any negotiating rights given to unions representing employees should be identified. The reporting accountant may also comment on the likely reaction of executives and employees to a change in ownership of the business.

5   Operations and systems

5.1 *Research and development* The level of, and need for, research and development in the target's business should be discussed together with any future plans for the commitment of manpower to research.

5.2 *Purchasing and sources of supply* A description of the purchasing procedure should be given with an assessment of the effectiveness of the buying department. The principal suppliers to the target should be identified and the dependence upon individual suppliers for goods or services disclosed.

5.3 *Production* The scale of production and the approach of management to present and future production problems should be discussed. The current manufacturing capacity and any bottlenecks should be referred to, as should the age of the plant, its serviceability, and the plans for its renewal and replacement. The degree of dependence on assembly or manufacturing at more than one location and on sub-contractors should be considered.

5.4 *Warehousing* The procedures for receiving, storing and issuing stock should be assessed, and the adequacy and suitability of the warehousing facilities should be commented upon.

5.5 *Marketing, competition and selling* In this section the target's major customers and competitors (which may often include the purchaser) should be mentioned. Details of any significant contracts with customers, of the selling prices and discounts offered by the target, of the sales force (or any appointed agents), of the dependence on export sales and the approach to exports, and of the advertising policy of the target should all be set out.

5.6 *Distribution*   A description should be given of the methods of distribution used, including the use of the target's own vehicle fleet, and whether the fleet is owned or leased. If a number of different transport facilities is used, the extent of the target's dependence on any one facility should be noted.

5.7 *Accounting*   This section should comprise a description and appraisal of the target's accounting systems and management accounting information.

6   Taxation and indemnities

The purpose of this section is to inform the purchaser of the target's outstanding corporation tax liabilities, when its corporation tax liabilities were last agreed with the Inland Revenue, compliance with VAT and PAYE legislation, and whether there are any close company or other tax problems associated with a change in ownership. Reference should be made to any indemnities recommended by the accountants which should be sought from the vendor of the target.

7   Accounting policies

This section should set out the accounting policies of the target in considerable detail so that the accounts can be properly understood. Any unusual accounting policies or any variations from best accounting practice should be highlighted.

8   Turnover and profits

This section should include not only the statutory published profit and loss account information but also a detailed breakdown of overhead expenses. An analysis of margins, variances and ratios covering the previous four- or five-year period should be included with a report on the performance of the target during that period.

9   Assets and liabilities

This section should consist of a complete description of each item in the target's balance sheet. A commentary on contingent liabilities and capital commitments should also be included.

10   Cash flows

A table showing the target's sources and application of funds during the period covered by the report should be summarised in this section.

11   Future prospects

According to the quantity and quality of information prepared by the target, the contents of this section may vary from a general discussion on the target's future, such as the effects of technological changes and trends in customer demand, to a detailed analysis of profit forecasts, cash flow projections and long term forecasts, and an assessment of their probable reliability.

12   Miscellaneous

12.1 *Borrowing facilities*   Details of the target's existing facilities should be shown; the security given and the further security available should also be set out as should a summary of principal banking covenants and compliance by the target with such covenants.

12.2 *Leasing commitments*   A summary of the target's commitments under leasing and hire-purchase agreements should be provided together with the nature and terms of the agreements.

12.3 *Insurance*   Details of the target's major insurance policies and of any deficiencies in insurance cover should be brought to the purchaser's attention.

12.4 *Government legislation*   An assessment of any relevant government enactments or guidelines affecting the target's operations should be included, whether or not the target has contravened such regulations, and whether a change in ownership would affect either the purchaser's or the target's position in relation to these regulations.

13   Summary and conclusions

This section should set out the main points included in the report, especially the matters of which the purchaser should be wary in its negotiations with the target. The report may highlight a number of areas which merit inclusion of specific warranty or indemnity protection in favour of the purchaser in the acquisition agreement.

The report, without summary and conclusions, should be discussed at an early draft stage with the target's management to ensure that all the facts presented in it are correct. This will give the target's management the opportunity to make representations to the accountants if it believes there are serious omissions or misplaced emphases in the report. The reporting accountants can then consider, but may not necessarily agree with, these representations before signing their report and presenting it to the purchaser. On reading the report the purchaser might ask for further work to be carried out; it is more likely that he will accept the report and find it an invaluable aid during the final stages of negotiations with the target's owners or management. A well constructed report also acts as a permanent record of the state of the target's affairs at the time of the purchase.

9.4   Environmental issues and investigations

9.4.1   Environmental issues

The late 1980s and the 1990s has seen the emergence of a body of new legislation, EC and domestic, and new trends in common law focusing on environmental protection and remediation which the purchaser of a company or business will ignore at his peril. Important requirements arising from such legislation include:

Consent	*Legislation*
authorisations for prescribed processes (eg by local authorities for integrated pollution control or air pollution control)	Environmental Protection Act 1990, Part I
consents to discharge effluents directly to water courses or to groundwater	Water Resources Act 1991
consents to discharge effluents to the sewers of a water company	Water Industry Act 1991
waste management licences and the waste management licensing regime for the keeping, treatment, disposal and deposit of controlled waste	Environmental Protection Act 1990, Part II
licences to keep specified hazardous substances on site	Planning (Hazardous Substances) Act 1990
licences for storage and disposal of radioactive materials	Radioactive Substances Act 1993
provisions relating to contaminated land	Environmental Protection Act 1990, Part IIA (as inserted by the Environment Act 1995 and currently expected to be implemented in late 1997)

This development in environmental regulation has inevitably resulted in the inclusion of environmental risk as an issue to consider in the acquisition process. The procedures which have been developed to deal with environmental issues in this context in the United Kingdom are still relatively new. It is, however, possible to identify a number of practices which are regularly used and pitfalls which should be avoided.

In theory, the environmental issues which need to be considered on an acquisition of shares are broader in range than those which are relevant to a purchase of business assets. In practice, however, the distinction is not always made. A purchaser of shares in a target will be concerned by the extent of potential exposure under the principal heads of environmental liability, namely:

(a)   past and current environmental performance of the target itself, which may give or have given rise to third party claims against the target (eg by a neighbour, public interest group or regulatory body);

(b)   past and current operational matters affecting the target, including the quality of its equipment, where failure to comply with the required standards may give rise to sanctions for breach of regulatory controls; and

(c)   the condition of land owned by the target which, if deficient, may give rise to clean up obligations. The clean up liability may, in certain circumstances, fall on the person who owns or occupies the land when the liability crystallizes, regardless of causation.

A purchaser of business assets is interested in the viability of any plant and equipment to be acquired as part of its acquisition and, importantly, the condition of any land which it is taking over (heads (b) and (c) of environmental liability above). It will be less concerned by the liabilities which attach solely to the vendor (under first head (a) above) except in so far as it is likely to inherit a situation which amounts to a nuisance as part of the way in which the business is operated, when it may find itself recommencing the nuisance if it continues to operate the process at the site in a similar way.

As a result, little distinction has, to date, been made in the approach taken to environmental issues arising on a share or business acquisition and for the purposes of this Chapter, environmental investigations and contractual provisions relating to share and business acquisitions are treated similarly. One practical difference which should be noted by a purchaser of business assets, however, is that where the business involves on-going processes or operations, any necessary environmental permits and licences will need to be transferred to the purchaser as the new licence-holder. The conditions for transfer will depend on the nature of the licence, and the legislation under which it is granted. Where the target is a company no new licence will be required (provided the licence is in the target's own name, and not in the name of the vendor's group), but consideration will need to be given to any change of control condition.

An investigation of the target company for environmental exposure will focus on the major potential areas. It should cover:

(a)   the licences which are held by the target and which may be required in order to enable the business to operate lawfully now and in the short term; such as Integrated Pollution Control (IPC), Local Air Pollution Control (LAPC) and waste management (including compliance with the statutory duty of care as to waste)—it should be noted that licences may include upgrading conditions requiring expenditure;

(b)   potential contaminated land liability, including the potential liability of an owner of the land; and

(c)   potential common law liability.

9.4.2   Environmental investigations

In common with other aspects of the investigation into the target business, the earlier the environmental issues can be identified, the greater the opportunity to address any problems to the purchaser's satisfaction.

Basic environmental information may come to light in the responses to the standard information requests. Replies to property enquiries and any other information requests should be considered, as well as considering the environmental issues inherent in the target's sphere of business, to decide whether it is appropriate to commission more specific environmental investigations. Once the disclosure exercise is under way, information which has an environmental aspect may be forthcoming by way of disclosures against employee, property or litigation warranties in addition to disclosures against environmental warranties. As a result, the purchaser and its advisers should ensure the co-ordination of these diverse sources of information.

The vendor may disclose or make available to the purchaser reports of environmental investigations or audits prepared for it in the past. Plainly, any such report will be of considerable assistance to the purchaser in its environmental assessment of the target. However the purchaser should, when assessing such a report, consider whether or not the information is likely to be up to date and whether it is able to rely on the professional opinion of the person who wrote the report, ie whether it would have a remedy, either in contract or in tort, against the consultant who prepared it in the event that it suffers loss as a result of having relied on the report.

There are several points when considering such reports. First, how recently was the report prepared? Environmental reports can become out of date quite rapidly because of the rate of change in environmental regulation and investigation techniques. The effect of intervening change should be borne in mind. Other obvious points are to ensure, where possible, that the instructions or commission to the consultant are available and then to check whether the consultant is experienced in the particular field of investigation and that, if redress is required from him, he will be able to make good any liabilities.

One particular issue is whether, in the absence of any direct contractual relationship, the purchaser would have any cause of action against the author of the report. Unless the report was specifically prepared with reliance by the purchaser in mind, no duty of care may arise in tort. For this reason, reports which are otherwise acceptably up to date and sufficiently detailed are sometimes reissued by consultants and specifically addressed to the purchaser (for which the consultant may well require an additional fee). Alternatively, the purchaser may ask the vendor to warrant the accuracy of the findings and conclusions of the report. (*See above* at p 138 *et seq.*)

In practice, particular consideration needs to be given to the investigation of environmental issues where the target is involved in an environmentally sensitive business or there are doubts over the use to which any land for which the purchaser may inherit a liability may have been put. Under these circumstances, the purchaser will wish to obtain up-to-date information which, if necessary, will give it legal redress in respect of an up-to-date report without the potential problems of reliance referred to above. Typically, specialist environmental consultants will be employed for such purposes.

The most common form of investigation is known as the 'Phase I' investigation (or audit or survey). A Phase I investigation typically involves a walk-through visit to the target's properties and is intended to provide an assessment of environmental housekeeping standards, process control and to identify obvious issues such as the visible presence of asbestos, possible polychlorinated biphenyl (PCB) containing equipment, underground storage tanks, etc. The Phase I investigation will also include a review of publicly available environmental information, most notably local hydrogeological records which give an indication of whether or not there are any sensitive environmental targets in the vicinity, such as drinking water aquifers or high quality rivers. The results of a Phase I investigation may suggest that a more detailed, 'Phase II' investigation should be commissioned on all or some of the target's properties. A Phase II investigation will typically involve the drilling of boreholes and subsequent testing and analysis of soil and groundwater samples.

The Phase I investigation can by its nature only be indicative of the presence or absence of potential environmental problems. A carefully designed Phase II investigation based on a grid of boreholes across the site and/or site border boreholes will give a clearer (but not necessarily full) picture of whether or not the site is actually contaminated and of the mobility of any contaminants. Where it is apparent at the outset of a transaction that there are environmental issues of concern it may be appropriate to move straight to a Phase II investigation or have a consultant design an investigation which is somewhere between Phase I and Phase II. Most reputable consultants are now able to provide a Phase I investigation speedily and commissioning such an investigation is now standard practice in appropriate cases.

Care should be taken with the choice and appointment of consultants and in particular as to the terms of their appointment and their financial status. Financial status will often be provided by the consultant's professional indemnity cover and the purchaser should seek confirmation that such cover is in place. The consultant will often seek to limit his liability to an amount which reflects the limits of his liability insurance. Where the consultant is to carry out intrusive work such as the sinking of boreholes there will be further matters to resolve between consultant and vendor such as access to the site, responsibility for any waste resulting from the work and for damage caused by the consultant.

The identity or range of parties who may rely on the results of the investigation should be specified at the time of the consultant's appointment. In addition to the purchaser, these may include the target and its subsidiaries and any bank or other person providing finance in respect of the acquisition. If the purchaser is contemplating selling on the target, or part of it, arrangements for the consultant to accept liability to the subsequent purchaser are also best made at the time of appointment. It will usually be sufficient for the consultant to address the report directly to the various parties who are to rely on it, thereby assuming a duty of care. If the interest of a person to whom the report is addressed, other than the purchaser, is not immediately apparent it would be wise to clarify their interest, to overcome uncertainty as to the foreseeability of loss to them. The fee paid to the consultant by the person commissioning the report, on terms that it will also be addressed to others, should provide adequate consideration. Because of these points, the lawyers will often be asked to advise on the terms of such appointment letters.

9.4.3   Environmental warranties and indemnities

Investigation will inform the purchaser of problem areas, but will not protect it from financial risk. Consequently the results of investigation may lead to the purchaser, or in some cases the vendor, to seek contractual protection against the risk associated with environmental matters. Potential environmental liability may be seen as reason to adjust the price payable for the target, depending on which of the vendor or purchaser is to bear the risk of later problems or may be an issue to be covered by detailed environmental warranties, or indemnities, or a combination of both.

Many acquisition agreements now contain detailed warranties as to environmental matters such as those set out in the precedent Agreement for Sale (Shares) at p 402 and the Agreement for Sale (Assets) at p 563. Environmental warranties will provide comfort as to the level of information provided and a remedy in damages if they are breached. Typically, however, the warranties will be subject to vendor protection provisions limiting the liability of the vendor, and the effect of disclosures may make them uncertain in scope. In addition, the purchaser will have to prove his loss. It is unlikely, in any event, that a purchaser will obtain meaningful warranties relating to the physical condition of land. As a result, if there is a perceived environmental risk or a statutory clean up obligation in respect of contaminated land, the matter may best be dealt with by specific indemnity, allocating the financial consequences of any such environmental liabilities to the party who has agreed to bear it.

In part for these reasons, there is a tendency towards a more frequent use of indemnities as a means of allocating environmental risk in those situations where it is fact that a higher level of protection is required. The party providing the indemnity will usually wish to narrow down the type of loss covered by the indemnity in order to have a clear understanding of the extent of its potential exposure. Thus, in addition to its maximum liability under the indemnity and its duration, the terms of an indemnity will often include other provisions which would narrow its scope. Over and above the more usual limits on liability a vendor may argue, for example, that it should have no liability if the claim in respect of which the purchaser calls on the indemnity was initiated by a voluntary act on the part of the purchaser post-completion. For example, where the purchaser voluntarily conducts an environmental investigation or where it notifies the regulatory bodies of an environmental breach. Naturally, such points are subject to negotiation.

Commonly, an indemnity is linked to an obligation for one party (usually the purchaser) to effect, after completion, a clean-up of the contamination giving rise to the risk concerned at the expense of, or with a contribution from, the other party. The results of any Phase II investigation carried out prior to completion are, in such circumstances, commonly used as a baseline for such a clean-up or as a means of identifying, for the purpose of the indemnity, which contamination was present at completion and which occurred after (the latter typically being wholly for the purchaser's account). In cases where there is no such 'baseline' information available the parties need to understand, should an indemnity claim subsequently be made, that there may be difficulty identifying the conditions at the date of completion and accordingly, advising who is responsible. As a result, environmental indemnities tend to be lengthy and complex. As liabilities under them can be significant, they may be the subject of protracted negotiations. They are often drafted as a separate deed outside the main agreement.

Another common source of controversy relates to warranties as to compliance with applicable laws, or indemnities against non-compliance with such laws. Not unreasonably, both vendor and purchaser will have in mind the possibility of environmental laws becoming considerably stricter within a relatively short time scale, and the vendor will not wish to be fixed with liability by reference to legal standards stricter than those applicable at the date of completion. General interpretation provisions which extend the definition of applicable laws to modifications or re-enactments of existing legislation should therefore be considered carefully by the vendor. Even in the case of existing environmental legislation, there may be considerable doubt as to how strictly this will be applied and how provisions such as the requirement to use 'best available techniques not entailing excessive cost' (Environmental Protection Act 1990, s 7) may be applied in specific cases. Ultimately, this is something on which the purchaser will have to take a commercial view, assisted by its professional advisers. *See also* the Agreement for Sale (Shares), Note 70 at p 471.

9.5   Difficulties with investigation of title to land

The investigations of title which are conducted on an acquisition of shares and an acquisition of business assets are broadly similar and this section addresses the property investigation in both contexts. The business acquisition involves, of course, a purchase of an interest in land. For this reason the usual investigations give more protection than on a share purchase. The presence of leasehold

interests will give rise to particular issues in the context of a business transaction, and these are considered further in Chapter 10, at p 198.

If the target has significant interests in land or has properties which, although they have little or no market value, are crucial to the continuance of the
target's business, the purchaser's solicitors will either investigate title or ask
for a certificate of title from the vendor's solicitors in addition to seeking the
usual property warranties (*see* Agreement for Sale (Shares)—Warranties,
p 411 and Agreement for Sale (Assets)—Warranties, p 556). In order to give a
certificate of title the vendor's solicitors will themselves first have to carry out
a full up-to-date investigation of title. There may be insufficient time for this.
For reasons of confidentiality the vendor's solicitors may not be able to approach those directors or employees of the target with the greatest knowledge
of the target's property interests. Other factors may lead to restrictions in the
scope of the certificate. In addition, there may be difficulty in persuading the
vendor's solicitors to give a certificate in a form which the purchaser's solicitors consider sufficiently comprehensive to be of value to the purchaser and its
financiers. For these reasons and since an investigation of title carried out by
the purchaser's solicitors will often reveal matters affecting the value of the
property interests, or matters relevant to the running of the target's business
which, not being matters of title, may not be disclosed in a certificate of title,
it is usually helpful to a purchaser to have an investigation carried out by the
purchaser's solicitors.

For all these reasons any such investigation (and, consequently, the giving
of any such certificate) may be considerably hampered. How far do these difficulties affect reliance upon such an investigation or certificate? A complete
account of title investigation is beyond the scope of this book, but the following
notes may be of interest. The tools of the title investigator are searches and inspection of title documents, and these will be considered separately. In addition
to inspection by the purchaser's surveyor, inspection of the property itself by
the title investigator is always desirable but rarely feasible either because it is
simply impractical or for reasons of confidentiality. In addition, the title investigator will raise enquiries and requisitions of the vendor's solicitors. The replies to these should be annexed to the disclosure letter or incorporated by
reference, and the accuracy of those replies warranted (*see* Warranty 2.8
(I)(2)(k) on p 413 and Warranty 2.2(K) on p 558). The purchaser's solicitors
should resist attempts by the vendor's solicitors to circumvent this warranty by
giving replies to the enquiries and requisitions which are qualified, eg 'Not so
far as the vendor is aware, but no warranty is given', or 'The purchaser should
rely on inspection and survey', where, for reasons of confidentiality, this is impractical.

An investigation of title depends to a large extent on the quality and quantity
of information supplied by the vendors the target and their respective directors
and solicitors by way of copies of title deeds (and inspection of the originals)
and in replies to enquiries and requisitions. The purchaser requires protection

against non-disclosure or inadequate disclosure of relevant property matters in that investigation and notwithstanding any investigation of title by the purchaser's solicitors or any certificate of title given by the vendor's solicitors, should require the normal property warranties (see Agreement for Sale (Shares), p 411 and Agreement for Sale (Assets), p 556). The vendor should have nothing to fear from this if it has made full and proper disclosure of property matters since such disclosure will qualify the property warranties to the extent of that disclosure.

The property warranties should be the same in the case of both share and asset acquisitions except that, in the case of a share acquisition, the purchaser will require the additional warranty covering continuing liabilities in respect of properties previously owned by the target company (see Warranty 2.8(I)(3) at p 413). Such continuing liabilities will principally be liabilities as original tenant under leasehold properties or where it was not the original tenant, under the terms of licences to assign and assignments of leasehold properties acquired by the target company at some stage in the past, and subsequently disposed of by it. As the Landlord and Tenant (Covenants) Act only removes such original tenant liability (subject to the provisions of that Act) 1995 under new tenancies granted since 1 January 1996, the date on which the 1995 Act came into force, this additional warranty will be required in all share acquisitions for the foreseeable future except where the target and all its subsidiaries were incorporated or first occupied new leasehold premises after 1 January 1996.

9.5.1   Searches

The intending purchaser or mortgagee of land who searches a statutory register is usually protected by his search. This protection, however, is not afforded if the ownership of the land remains unchanged. As a result, in the protection offered by searches, there is a marked difference between the conventional share and asset transaction.

Companies Registration Office

The Companies Act 1985, s 395 *et seq*, requires registration within twenty-one days of certain types of charges created by companies, but the list of charges required to be registered is by no means exhaustive and does not include, for instance, encumbrances such as leases or contracts for sale. In any event, a clear mortgage register gives no protection to the purchaser of shares. A registrable charge which is not registered is void only against a liquidator or creditor of the company and not against the company itself or its shareholders (see *Independent Automatic Sales Ltd v Knowles & Foster* [1962] 3 All ER 27). When a charge is rendered void against a liquidator or creditor the moneys secured thereby become automatically repayable so that non-registration may even affect the target (and thus the purchaser) adversely. It is also possible that a registrable charge has been granted, but has not yet been registered. Prior to the expiry of the statutory period, it seems that charge would be valid (see *Burston Finance Ltd v Speirway Ltd* [1974] 3 All ER 735).

Local authority searches including Local Land Charges Registry

Non-registration does not affect the enforceability of local land charges but, if a local land charge is not revealed by a search because of non-registration or because of an error by the local authority, compensation may be payable under the Local Land Charges Act 1975. It is, however, payable only to a 'purchaser' which is defined by s 10(3) of the Act as any person who 'for valuable consideration...acquires any interest in land or the proceeds of sale of land...'. Although lessees and mortgagees are specifically included, a purchaser of shares does not fall within the definition and any person searching in this capacity will not obtain a right to compensation.

Land Registry

Under the Land Registration Act 1925, s 20, failure to register a registrable encumbrance will render it void, but only in the case of a disposition of the land in favour of a purchaser for value (including a mortgagee or lessee but, again, not including a purchaser of shares). A search by a person other than a purchaser for value of the land confers no priority period (see the Land Registration (Official Searches) Rules 1993 (SI No 3276), r 10).

Land Charges Department

Again, official searches protect only purchasers of the land itself (Land Charges Act 1972, ss 4 and 11) and compensation for loss arising out of charges registered against estate owners prior to a good root of title will be payable only to such a person (Law of Property Act 1969, s 25). Failure to register such a charge created by the target will not affect its validity as against the target.

Other searches

Although, again, no protection will be conferred on a purchaser of shares, it will be prudent for other searches to be made, whether the acquisition is of shares or assets. For example, mining searches with British Coal for land in past or present mining areas and searches of the relevant county council or London borough under the Commons Registrations Act 1965 for land in all areas.

9.5.2 Inspection of title documents

The title investigator should inspect the title documents in the vendor's, target's or mortgagee's possession and will require their production upon completion of the acquisition (*see* Agreement for Sale (Shares), cl 5.2(D)(3) on p 384 and Agreement for Sale (Assets), cl 6.2 on p 512). How much protection does this afford? The following paragraphs address this question.

Registered land

Inspection of a land or charge certificate held by the vendor, the target or its mortgagee will show that the target is the registered proprietor of the land described. It is worth making a careful check that the target's name corresponds with that entered in the register when the entry was made. Although the Land Registry will accept the inclusion of a company number in the proprietorship register it is not obliged to do so, and name swaps between companies can have the effect of confusing the investigator. Although inspection of the land or charge certificate will yield much information and, coupled with the Land Registry search on form 94C mentioned below, will also assure the purchaser of shares that the Land Registry is not, at that moment, registering a disposition in favour of some other person (as the Registry normally requires land certificates to be deposited with it for that purpose—Land Registration Act 1925, s 64), the mere fact that there are no other encumbrances noted on the register does not mean that they do not exist. For example, overriding interests (see the Land Registration Act 1925, s 3(xvi)) cannot be registered in any event and the purchaser's solicitors should enquire as to the existence of these in their enquiries and requisitions of the vendor's solicitors. Also, the registration of a caution, to protect a contract for sale or an option, does not require the production of the certificate at the Land Registry. In certain circumstances the Land Registry may dispense with production of the certificate (eg registration of a general vesting declaration (Land Registration Rules 1925 (SI No 1093), r 226)). The safest course is to obtain from the target, or direct from the Land Registry (the Land Registration (Open Register) Rules 1991 (SI No 122)) up-to-date office copy entries of the register together with a search in form 94C obtained immediately prior to completion which, while it confers no priority, will reveal any dealings affecting the title which have been lodged for registration at the Land Registry. Because the statutory search procedure does not give any priority to purchasers of shares, even unregistered encumbrances which should have been registered will continue to subsist after the completion of the share acquisition.

However, on an acquisition of business assets the purchaser is able to make a search in form 94A (Whole Property) or 94B (Part of a Property) which confers 30 working days' priority on the purchaser (Land Registration (Official Searches) Rules 1993, r 2(1)), provided that the transfer of the property is completed and validly lodged for registration at the Land Registry within that priority period (r 6, r 7(2)). Any application for registration of any other dealings such as a mortgage or caution lodged during the priority period will be overridden by that transfer.

Unregistered land

Inspection of title deeds to unregistered land will not reveal oral leases, estate contracts or the unregistered land equivalent of overriding interests, neither will it give any protection against the existence of puisne mortgages (registered at the Land Charges Registry or not) or even against previous sales of the property or part not protected by endorsement of a memorandum on the retained title deeds (see *Claridge v Tingey, Re Sea View Gardens, Warden* [1967] 1 WLR 134).

In the context of an acquisition of business assets the purchaser is able to make a land charges search at the Land Charges Registry in form K15 which gives 15 working days' priority to the purchaser, so giving similar protection to that conferred by Land Registry searches in Forms 94A and 94B. The purchaser should not overlook the need, if the property is in an area of compulsory registration of title, to apply for first registration of title to the property within 2 months of completion of the purchase if the property is freehold or, if leasehold, the lease term has more than 21 years unexpired at the date of the assignment (Land Registration Act 1925, s 123(1)).

As in the case of registered land, a check should be made that the target's present name corresponds with that applying at the date of the conveyance, lease or assignment of the land.

In practice on a share transaction, the conveyancing investigator to a large extent relies upon the efficiency of existing mortgagees or other encumbrancers. They will, the investigator hopes, have effected the necessary registrations or secured possession of the title deeds, in order to guard against subsequent dealings with the land by the target which would render their security or encumbrance void. The share purchaser should remember, however, that he is hoping that encumbrancers have donned some visible armour to protect themselves against weapons which are more powerful than those available to him.

9.5.3   Additional issues on an acquisition of business assets

One difference between a share transaction and an assets transaction is the searches that are made by the purchaser in an assets transaction. In an assets transaction, additional protection is available to the purchaser of assets because the acquisition of the target's business assets involves a transfer, or a grant of a lease, of the property itself. The additional protections are explained in section 9.5.2 *above* and the protection available under searches of registered land in Form 94A or 94B and unregistered land in Form K15 to a purchaser of assets (so long as completion takes place and, in the case of registered land the transfer is lodged for registration, within the priority period afforded by the searches) gives a significant advantage over a purchaser of shares. However, the 94A or 94B or K15 searches will have to be made in respect of all of the relevant properties for full protection to be obtained and, where the transaction includes a large number of properties or time is short, this may not be possible. In addition, where there are leasehold properties for which reversioner's licence to assign is required (*see* the Agreement for Sale (Assets), Sched 5, Part II), the assignments or transfers of the leases will often take place after completion of the acquisition and therefore some of the searches (including land registry and land charges) obtained at completion will not confer protection on the purchaser at the time the relevant transfers or assignments take place. If, however, the sale agreement gives the purchaser sufficient control over the properties from completion, the subsequent searches should not give adverse results. A purchaser of assets also has the possibility of compensation from a local authority for non-registration of local land charges or errors in the local searches (as explained *above* p 156).

9.6 Misrepresentation, warranty and indemnity

If a false statement of fact is made by the vendor to the purchaser about the target, what remedies does the purchaser have? Of all the questions with which this book deals, none is more difficult to answer, particularly in a brief space. Despite a number of recent decisions there remain comparatively few decided cases which specifically relate to company acquisitions. However, the basic problem—a false statement followed by a sale—has been one which has occupied the courts for centuries and it is surrounded by such a web of rules and classifications, many of which are only of historical interest, so that any exposition of the modern law, however brief, is bound to reflect its complexity.

Until the decision in *Hedley Byrne & Co Ltd v Heller & Partners Ltd* [1964] AC 465 the law gave no damages for a non-fraudulent misrepresentation which was not a term of the contract between the parties. Not until *Esso Petroleum Co Ltd v Mardon* [1976] 2 WLR 583 (considered on p 164) did it become clear that the rule in *Hedley Byrne*, which gives damages for a negligent misstatement, can apply if the parties to the statement subsequently proceed to contract. The problem, therefore, was to distinguish between 'mere' representations giving no right to damages and representations which did form part of the contract between the parties. In this search the characterisation and classification of the offending statement was all important. Was it a mere recommendation of the object to be sold, a statement of opinion or a statement of fact? If it was a misrepresentation of fact, was it made innocently or fraudulently? Was it part of the contract between the parties (ie a warranty) or was it a collateral contract? It was necessary to answer these questions to determine whether the representee had a remedy at all and, if so, what his remedy was: was it rescission, an indemnity or damages? If damages, were they to be assessed on the tortious or contractual basis? The Misrepresentation Act 1967 caused many of these classifications to become less significant in terms of the net result to the representee. Nevertheless, the Act was grafted on to the law as it stood before 1967 and the classifications are with us still.

9.6.1   Non-contractual misrepresentation

The contract for the acquisition of a private company or of business assets is a unique type of contract. The operative terms are relatively straightforward, providing either for a sale and purchase of shares or dealing with the mechanics for transferring the various assets. However, for the reasons noted on p 134, this simple contract is often accompanied by a long string of representations and warranties relating to the assets, liabilities and obligations of the target business. Because such contracts are normally negotiated between solicitors and are complex and carefully thought-out documents, it is perhaps less likely than in other fields that representations made by the vendor to the purchaser which do not appear in the written contract will be held to have induced the contract and give rise to remedies, although recent case law has reminded the practitioner of the liability which, if not effectively excluded, can attach to the maker of non-contractual misrepresentations.

If a false statement of fact does induce the contract then, whether the misrepresentation was made fraudulently, negligently, or innocently, the purchaser will have the right to rescind the contract even if the misrepresentation has become a term of the contract or the contract has been performed (Misrepresentation Act 1967, s 1). If the representation is true when made, but becomes untrue to the knowledge of the representor and he dishonestly fails to correct it before the conclusion of the contract, the other party can rescind (*British and Commonwealth Holdings v Quadrex Holdings Inc* [1989] QB 842). Rescission will not be possible if the contract has been affirmed by the purchaser; if the purchaser has taken some action since the contract which makes it impossible to put the parties back as they were before (eg if the target's business has ceased or changed substantially); or if any innocent third party would be prejudiced. If the misrepresentation is fraudulent, damages can be claimed in the tort of deceit, and if it is negligent within the meaning of the Misrepresentation Act 1967 (ie if the representor cannot prove that he had reasonable ground to believe and did believe up to the time the contract was made that the facts represented were true—s 2(1)), damages can be claimed under the provisions of s 2(1) of the Act. Section 2(2) of the Act provides that upon an action for rescission the court may declare the contract subsisting and award damages in lieu. The purchaser who is victim of an innocent misrepresentation may therefore, if the court thinks fit, be awarded damages instead of, but not as well as, rescission (including in cases where rescission is no longer available). Although where damages in lieu of rescission under s 2(2) is the only remedy (eg the misrepresentation is neither fraudulent nor negligent and rescission will not be awarded), it is likely that such damages will be lower than an award under s 2(1). The question of damages is considered on p 168.

It is the object of the vendor entering into the Agreements for Sale in Appendices I and II to restrict liability, so far as possible, in respect of 'mere' representations which induce the purchaser to enter into the contract, and to confine the purchaser's remedy to those representations given as warranties in the agreement or contained in the disclosure letter which qualifies the warranties; to the extent it can be agreed, the vendor will also wish to limit the purchaser's remedy to breach of contract in respect of those warranties. The means by which this is to be achieved has been the subject of recent judicial consideration, which is reflected in the Agreements for Sale in Appendices I and II. These provide: that the written agreement for sale is the entire agreement between the parties; that the purchaser acknowledges that it has not entered into the agreement for sale in reliance on any representations other than those contained in the agreement or the disclosure letter and that, except for fraud, the purchaser shall have no remedy for any statement or representation made to him save for a remedy for breach of the statements given as warranties in the sale agreement. The final limb of this clause, in particular, is necessary to give effect to the exclusion of liability for pre-contractual misrepresentation. In *Thomas Witter Ltd v TBP Industries Ltd* [1996] 2 All ER 573 a similar clause, without such final limb which was widely used in sale agreements prior to judgment in that case was held to be ineffective to exclude liability in tort for pre-contractual misrepresentations, notwithstanding that it was in common usage. As Jacob J said (at p 596) it should be 'manifestly made clear that a purchaser has agreed only to have a remedy for breach of warranty', for a term to have that effect and that the vendor '... must bring it home that he is limiting liability for falsehoods he may have told'; a clause designed to achieve this by a 'roundabout route' is unlikely to be effective.

The vendor may seek to limit the purchaser's remedy by providing (in the limiting clause which seeks to exclude liability for misrepresentation) that the purchaser's remedies are confined to *breach of contract* because tortious remedies for pre-contractual misrepresentations which are incorporated in a contract are preserved by Misrepresentation Act 1967, s 1. If the limiting clause were simply to confine the purchaser's remedies to the warranties contained in the contract (which may also be representations and are often expressly described as such) a remedy for breach may lie both in contract and for misrepresentation and the circumstances may also admit, depending on the statement in question, a remedy for negligent misrepresentation. The principal difference in these remedies is the measure of damages which for misrepresentation is, like negligent misstatement, based on the tortious measure; a remedy in misrepresentation in particular carries more favourable rules as to consequential loss (*see below*). In view of the foregoing the position now, following the decision in *Witter*, is that a vendor will seek to provide in the sale agreement (often in the 'entire agreement' clause) that the purchaser's remedies are limited to claims for breach of the contractual warranties, thereby excluding liability for pre-contractual misrepresentations. It may also seek to exclude claims for misrepresentation (and misstatement) in respect of those warranties so as to confine the remedy to one in contract, although such a provision will not always be acceptable to the purchaser and is not easy to justify. Either way, to be effective the contract should state clearly that the purchaser's remedies are so limited and for the reasons explained below, provide that the exclusion will not operate in cases of fraud. Clause 11.2 on p 392 and cl 18.2 on p 525 are each intended to have this effect; and *see also* Note 58 to the Agreement for Sale (Shares) at p 469. It is also desirable that the clause acknowledges that the purchaser has been advised of the effect of such a clause; while in practice such a statement will be no more than evidential value it may assist in demonstrating the reasonableness of the exclusion.

Having limited the purchaser's remedies, it is necessary to consider the Misrepresentation Act 1967, s 3 (as amended by the Unfair Contract Terms Act 1977) which provides that:

> If a contract contains a term which would exclude or restrict—
>
> (a) any liability to which a party to a contract may be subject by reason of any misrepresentation made by him before the contract was made; or
> (b) any remedy available to another party to the contract by reason of such misrepresentation,
>
> that term shall be of no effect except in so far as it satisfies the requirement of reasonableness as stated in section 11(1) of the Unfair Contract Terms Act 1977; and it is for those claiming that the term satisfies that requirement to show that it does.

Section 11(1) provides that the requirement of reasonableness is that the term should have been a fair and reasonable one to be included, having regard to the circumstances which were, or ought reasonably to have been, known to, or in the contemplation of, the parties when the contract was made.

The effect of s 3 on the clause purporting to limit liability for pre-contractual representations was considered by the court in *Witter* (an asset transaction), where, even if the clause under consideration in that case did have the effect of excluding liability for pre-contractual representations, it was held that notwithstanding that (as Jacob J so found) 'skilful and reputable solicitors commonly included clauses (of the type before him) in share purchase agreements', such a clause would be neither fair nor reasonable and as such, was held to be ineffective to exclude liability under s 3. The court's objection was to the scope of the clause, which did not distinguish between different types of mispresentation; the clause was not severable and so it was to be assumed that the vendor sought to exclude liability for all misrepresentations, including those which were fraudulent. Even though the clause was accepted by the party seeking to rely on it as not working in the case of fraud, the judge declined to construe the clause so that it did not apply to a fraudulent misrepresentation. Accordingly, it is now standard practice for the post-*Witter* exclusion clause, designed to exclude liability for pre-contractual representations, expressly to exclude fraud from its ambit. Quite whether there are circumstances in which such a clause, which has the effect of excluding liability for negligent misrepresentation, will be found to be unreasonable is an interesting question. In *Witter* the judge concluded that for recklessness to be treated in a similar way to fraudulent misrepresentation, the recklessness would need to amount to such a disregard of the truth that it should be regarded as reckless; this type of situation is clearly exceptional—one example might be the kind of 'reckless negligence' referred to by Hobhouse LJ in *Downs v Chappell* [1996] 3 All ER 344, when no distinction, for the purpose of apportioning damages between defendants, was made between the vendor's fraud and its accountants' 'reckless negligence'.

It is clear that an 'entire agreement' clause (which purports to state eg that save for the written agreement there are no other representations which will be of effect) cannot be relied upon to exclude liability for pre-contractual misrepresentation (*Goff v Gauthier* (1991) 62 P & CR 388, concerning a conveyance of land; and the observations of Langley J in *Williams v Natural Life Health Foods* [1996] 1 BCLC 288 at p 298, concerning negligent mistatement, since upheld by the Court of Appeal).

It could be said that the provision excluding the vendor's liability for pre-contractual representations is not subject to the Misrepresentation Act 1967, s 3 at all and that liability is not excluded or restricted by the contractual provision, because, as the clause acknowledges, the purchaser has not relied on any other representations. It is unlikely, however, that this argument will find sympathy with the court. In *Cremdean Properties v Nash* (1977) 244 EG 547, at p 551, Bridge LJ indicated that, in his view, exclusion clauses which purported to deny the very existence of a representation did not avoid the effect of s 3.

Section 3 of the 1967 Act should also be borne in mind when considering the vendor protection provisions in the Agreements for Sale eg the provisions requiring notification of claims within a specified period (*see* p 175).

In summary, vendors are well advised to seek to include in the contract a limiting clause to exclude liability for pre-contractual representations reflecting the judgment in *Witter*. The acquisition of shares in the target will probably have been preceded by discussion and correspondence and, it is suggested, it is reasonable to ask the purchaser to specify in the contract those representations upon which reliance is placed and to confine its remedies to such contractual statements. Whether or not its remedies should be confined to breach of contract seems less easy to justify but will, no doubt, be for discussion. The practitioner should, however, take care to explain to the purchaser the effect of such a clause and in particular, discuss with the purchaser whether all material documents, statements and assurances which have been given or made to him in the course of negotiations and on which he relies in his evaluation of the target are indeed warranted in the agreement. This is particularly so in the case of financial information and documents which may have been handed over in preliminary discussions and been the basis of the purchaser's willingness to proceed to the stage of negotiating draft contracts. Provision of this information will often pre-date the lawyers' involvement and they may not otherwise be aware of its existence. The limiting clause may have the effect of precluding the purchaser from a remedy if such information is misleading, unless it is covered by a specific warranty.

9.6.2   Negligent misstatement

Apart from his remedies for misrepresentation and under the 1967 Act, the purchaser may also have a remedy, in tort, if he enters into the contract in reliance upon a negligent misstatement. The rule in *Hedley Byrne & Co Ltd v Heller & Partners Ltd* [1964] AC 465 has been stated thus (Lord Denning MR in *Esso Petroleum Co Ltd v Mardon* [1976] 2 WLR 583, at p 595):

> If a man, who has or professes to have special knowledge or skill, makes a representation by virtue thereof to another—be it advice, information or opinion—with the intention of inducing him to enter into a contract with him, he is under a duty to use reasonable care to see that the representation is correct and that the advice, information or opinion is reliable. If he negligently gives unsound advice or misleading information or expresses an erroneous opinion and thereby induces the other side to enter a contract with him, he is liable in damages.

Liability under the rule in *Hedley Byrne* is not restricted to professional advisers (see dicta of Ormrod LJ in *Esso Petroleum Co Ltd v Mardon*, at p 601 and see, in particular, the recent decision in *Williams v Natural Life Health Foods Ltd* (1996) *unreported*, 5 December, CA, when a managing director incurred personal liability for his negligent mistatement). The above formulation seems wide enough to embrace a misstatement by a vendor whose knowledge of the target will of course be more extensive than the purchaser's. As a practical matter, however, the damages remedy for negligent misrepresentation given by the Misrepresentation Act 1967 probably renders this cause of action redundant (*Esso v Mardon*, at p 602). The difference between such remedies is illustrated by *Howard Marine and Dredging Co Ltd v Ogden (A) & Sons (Excavations) Ltd* [1978] 2 All ER 1134 at p 1144. It would appear that the losses for which the purchaser will be compensated may differ—contrast the decision in *Royscot Trust Ltd v Rogerson* [1991] 3 All ER 294 (on s 2(1)) and the approach of the House of Lords to a negligent valuer's responsibility for losses in *South Australia Asset Management Corp v York Montague Ltd* [1996] 3 All ER 367.

Any provision included in the modern acquisition agreement limiting liability (except for fraud) to claims *in contract* for breach of specified warranties, discussed above (p 161) will, it is suggested, also have the effect of excluding liability for negligent misstatement. The requirement under the Misrepresentation Act 1967, s 3 that such clauses satisfy a test of reasonableness would, it seems, not apply. However, an equivalent requirement will arise under the Unfair Contract Terms Act 1977, s 2(2) except, of course, for the exceptions to that Act for securities, land and intellectual property transactions, in Sched 1.

9.6.3 Contractual misrepresentation

A warranty is a subsidiary contractual term, breach of which will not entitle the innocent party to treat the contract as discharged but which will give rise to a claim for damages.

The warranties included in a contract for the acquisition of a private company or of business assets are, for the most part, statements of fact and, as such, can be classed as representations. If a representation is made during negotiations and then appears in the written agreement, the party relying on it can still claim rescission of the contract if it proves to be false (provided its remedies have not been limited, as described above, p 161). The Misrepresentation Act 1967, s 1, provides that:

> Where a person has entered into a contract after a misrepresentation has been made to him and—
>
> (a) the misrepresentation has become a term of the contract;
>
> ...then, if otherwise he would be entitled to rescind the contract without alleging fraud, he shall be so entitled...

To enable the contract to be rescinded for misrepresentation, however, it seems on the face of the section that the misrepresentation must have been made to the purchaser before the contract was entered into. It can be said that if the representation appears only once in the history of the transaction, and is included in the written contract as a term of it, then the Act does not apply. Although the courts may be reluctant to draw this distinction, it is common practice to safeguard the purchaser by expressly including the right of rescission in the contract, at least for any breach discovered before completion (*see* the Agreement for Sale (Shares), cl 8.8 (p 389)). Where remedies for misrepresentation are also expressly excluded, rescission for breach of contractual warranty will need to be addressed specifically.

The drafting of warranties in an acquisition agreement will depend, in many respects, upon the type of business in which the target is engaged. The purchaser's solicitors will, after consultation with their client and their study of any accountants' report, attempt to obtain assurances with regard to those aspects of the target's business which are important to the purchaser. There are, however, many warranties which are standard for almost any type of acquisition. These general warranties will be aimed, in more or less detail, at ensuring that the latest audited accounts of the target are accurate and that the target has carried on its business in the normal course since the date of the last accounts without incurring any extraordinary liabilities. In addition, the purchaser will want details of other matters such as significant contracts, litigation etc. There is, of course, a distinction between the warranties taken on a share acquisition and those on an acquisition of business assets since the former will need to focus in particular on liabilities, including contingent liabilities, while these will generally be of less significance to the business purchaser except in the unusual case where it has agreed to assume responsibility for all liabilities. A full set of 'standard' warranties is contained in the Agreement for Sale (Shares), Sched 3 (at p 397) and the Agreement for Sale (Assets), Sched 6 (at p 559), which are drafted, respectively, with the trading company or business in mind. It is unlikely that all these warranties will be appropriate to any individual transaction. Taxation is dealt with in Chapter 14. Pensions are covered in Chapter 7, and pension warranties on p 434 and 577.

Apart from 'standard warranties', the need for warranties to address the specific circumstances of the target may be appropriate. When considering the requirement for, and terms of, specific warranties the practitioner advising the purchaser should consider the information available to him about the target and its particular business, including any accountant's report, and discuss with the purchaser potential problem areas. Does the target grant overriding discounts to its customers which will be a liability after completion? Are there specific regulations compliance with which is fundamental to the target's ability to continue to trade? What documents or information does the purchaser, in fact, rely upon in deciding whether to proceed? These and other matters will require consideration and the drafting of any additional warranted statement should also be considered carefully with the desired remedy for breach in mind. A warranty about expected turnover may, for example, either be expressed as a guarantee of that turnover, or may merely take effect as a warranty as to the vendor's opinion, depending on its terms (*see Esso v Mardon, above* (p 164)).

9.6.4   Disclosure

It is the scheme of the Agreements for Sale to oblige the vendors to make disclosures which qualify the warranties by means of one specific disclosure letter, so that it will be possible to say, after completion, what was disclosed and what was not. For an example of the argument that can otherwise result, see *Levison v Farin* [1978] 2 All ER 1149. In that case Gibson J said, at p 1157:

> A protection by disclosure will not normally be achieved by merely making known the means of knowledge which may or do enable the other party to work out certain facts and conclusions.

Purchasers will approach general disclosures with caution. One such example, in the case of a corporate target, is disclosure of board minutes over a period of years, when if time is limited or there are a large number of subsidiaries, an alternative approach might be to confine disclosure to those material subsidiaries or of board minutes covering a more limited period of time. If the disclosed register of members is incomplete, the purchaser should insist it is written up. Entitlement to entry on the register is, after all, what is being acquired. Whether for general or specific disclosure, the principle of disclosure should, however, be that only identifiable documents should be regarded as disclosed and contained in agreed bundles which include for example, disclosed correspondence or due diligence material. Documents or information which might be referred to in other disclosed material should, it is suggested, generally not be regarded as disclosed unless the relevant document is identifiable and ideally, to pre-empt later debate as to the completeness or content of the disclosed document, also included in agreed bundles.

It must be doubted, however, whether clauses such as cl 8.2 of the Agreement for Sale (Shares) or cl 11.2 of the Agreement for Sale (Assets) are completely effective. Where a purchaser has actual knowledge of facts relating to the target it is difficult for him to deny them simply because they were not set out in the disclosure letter. *Eurocopy plc v Teesdale* [1992] BCLC 1067, CA, was an interlocutory decision in an action arising out of a company acquisition in which the agreement for sale contained a clause which sought to preserve the purchaser's rights where he had information relating to the breach of warranty which was not disclosed in the disclosure letter. Eurocopy, the purchaser, alleged an undisclosed breach of warranty, but, despite the terms of the agreement for sale the defence alleged, among other things, that Eurocopy could have no claim because it was aware of the relevant facts, albeit other than through the disclosure letter. Eurocopy applied to have this part of the defence struck out, but was unsuccessful both at first instance and in the Court of Appeal. A recent decision of the Court of Session in Scotland also recognises that warranties are capable of being qualified orally and not merely by the formal written disclosure letter (*Edward Prentice v Scottish Power PLC* (1996)(available on *Lexis*)) although that particular case related to whether sufficient disclosure had been made in an appropriate form so as to entitle the defender to withdraw an option notice that had been served, and no mention was made of the *Eurocopy* decision.

The purchaser will often seek an express warranty from the vendor in respect of the accountants' report, or part of it. This will be resisted by the vendor who will regard the report as a private document prepared for the benefit of the purchaser, and not one in respect of which it should assume liability. A compromise is often for the vendor to warrant specific factual statements, but not the report as a whole. By contrast, whether or not warranted, the vendor will often seek formal disclosure of the contents of the report so as to ensure that all the matters of which they have informed the accountants, and which appear in the report, are regarded as disclosed. This can cause difficulty in practice, because the purchaser may wish to resist showing the vendors the report in its final form. It may be possible to resolve the problem by agreeing that the report is regarded as disclosed even though not seen by the vendors.

One difficulty which sometimes arises on the acquisition of a corporate target is the problem of representations made to the vendors in connection with the warranties. The vendors may ask the directors of the target to check the warranties and to confirm their accuracy or specify what disclosure should be made. Such a confirmation or disclosure, if incorrect, could give rise to a claim for negligent representation which might fall on the target, either because the representation was given on behalf of the target or because the directors are entitled to be indemnified by the target. The purchaser will obviously not wish the target to be liable in this way, and Sched 3, para 2.1(C) to the Agreement for Sale (Shares) (p 398) contains a disclaimer. The point is sometimes approached in a different way, by the vendor agreeing not to pursue claims against employees in relation to information they have provided (or failed to provide) in connection with the warranties and disclosure. On an acquisition of business assets, if there is no such waiver the issue will need to be covered by the indemnity in favour of the vendor in respect of pre-acquisition employee liabilities which might otherwise be inherited (*see* p 520). The precedent Agreements for Sale include waivers by the vendor (*see* p 390 and p 520).

9.6.5   Damages for misrepresentation and breach of warranty

The measure of damages is different in contract and tort. The contractual measure aims to place the plaintiff in the position which he would have enjoyed had the contract not been broken. The plaintiff is therefore entitled to the loss of his bargain. The tortious measure aims to place the successful plaintiff in the position in which he would have been if the tort had not been committed ie in the case of a misrepresentation inducing a contract, as if he had not entered into the contract at all.

If damages are calculated according to the contractual measure, the purchaser is entitled to the difference between the market value of the shares or business assets (as the case may be) as they are, and their value as it would have been if the warranty had been true. Under the tortious measure, on the other hand, the purchaser is entitled to the difference between the market value of the shares or business assets (as the case may be) as they are and the price paid. The practical difference between the two approaches can be simply illustrated using a share acquisition as an example. Suppose a balance sheet warranty is given and the target has a liability which was not, but which should have been, disclosed in the balance sheet; the purchaser of the whole of the target's capital would, under the contractual measure, normally be entitled to recover the amount necessary to discharge the liability. It would not affect the position if the target possessed an unrelated asset, not taken into account in the calculation of the purchase price, which was worth as much as, or more than, the undisclosed liability. However, on the tortious basis, the existence of such an asset would affect the calculation and there would be no damage, if, despite the misrepresentation, the target was worth the price paid. On an acquisition of business assets the approach would be somewhat different since a purchaser, if liable for such an amount, would usually have agreed to assume such liability by way of indemnity, when in practice it will simply offset its warranty claim against its indemnity liability. The distinction between the contractual and tortious bases can be seen in the decision of the House of Lords in *Swingcastle Ltd v Alistair Gibson (a firm)* [1991] 2 All ER 353 where, if the contractual measure had been applied, the purchaser would have been entitled to compensation at a contractual rate of interest of 45 per cent. As it was a case of negligence the tortious measure was applied; the purchaser could not recover more than it would have earned if it had not entered into the transaction and since it could not be shown that it would have earned the contractual rate of interest if it had put its money elsewhere, the interest claim failed.

The foregoing is subject to one very important qualification in the case of a share acquisition. The measure of damages is calculated according to the value of the shares of the target and while the amount of the assets and liabilities of the target will certainly affect the value of those shares, the relationship may be neither simple nor direct. In a case where undisclosed liabilities, or a shortfall in assets, is small in relation to the target's business it may well be that the value of the target's shares is not affected at all. Where the target is bought for its profit earning capacity, and it can be demonstrated that the value of its shares was calculated by reference to earnings, then a shortfall in assets will normally affect the value of the shares only if the profit earning capacity of the target is affected. The purchaser will, however, normally expect to be reimbursed for undisclosed liabilities and shortfalls in assets, except when they arise within negotiated limits, and it is for this reason that the so-called 'pound for pound' clause is frequently found in the agreement for sale (see the Agreement for Sale (Shares), cl 8.4 on p 388. This clause purports to say that, without affecting the purchaser's ability to claim damages on any appropriate basis, the vendors will pay to the purchaser an amount equal to any deficiency or liability of the target which arises from any breach of any of the warranties or which would not have existed or arisen if the warranties had been true. In *George Fischer (Great Britain) Ltd v Multi Construction Ltd* [1995] 1 BCLC 260 it was held that the measure of damages a holding company suffered for breach of contract in respect of loss caused to its subsidiaries was to be on a pound for pound basis, and might seem to render such a clause redundant. However, the point turned on the evidence before the trial judge which, it seems, was not contested and the decision is not considered a basis for changing the practice of the purchaser to seek the pound for pound clause, where it can be negotiated.

The pound for pound clause is a particular feature of a share acquisition, rather than an acquisition of business assets when there is no intermediate shareholding acquired. A draft acquisition agreement presented by the business purchaser will, however, commonly request such a clause which, apart from the purpose for which it is primarily designed, will often clarify a purchaser's entitlement when bringing a claim, precluding lengthy debate over matters such as whether it has suffered loss, and the amount of that loss.

In a case where the value of the shares is calculated by reference to profits and profits have been misstated, the purchaser's damages claim may well be a multiple of the shortfall. Occasionally, such a multiple is stated as liquidated damages. Provided any such clause is a reasonable pre-estimate of the purchaser's loss (eg it reflects the multiple of profits paid by the purchaser as consideration), there is no reason why such a clause should not be effective.

Most of the litigation which has come before the courts relating to contracts for the sale of shares or of business assets has been concerned not with breach of contract but with the tort of deceit following a fraudulent misrepresentation or under statutes which impose liability on company directors for misstatements or omissions in company prospectuses. In these cases the tortious measure applies and the plaintiff is entitled to damages based, broadly speaking, on the difference between the price paid and the value of the shares received, not a measure based on his loss of bargain. These principles have recently been reviewed by the House of Lords in *Smith New Court Securities Ltd v Scrimgeour Vickers (Asset Management) Ltd* [1996] 4 All ER 769 (confirming the approach in *Doyle v Olby (Ironmongers) Ltd* [1969] 2 All ER 119). Damages for non-contractual negligent misrepresentation awarded under the Misrepresentation Act 1967, s 2(1), will be ascertained according to the tortious rules, *F & H Entertainments Ltd v Leisure Enterprises Ltd* (1976) 120 SJ 331, *Alman and Benson v Associated Newspapers Group Ltd* (1980) (*unreported*) and *Cemp Properties (UK) v Dentsply Research and Development Corp* [1991] 34 EG 62; it has been held that the measure under s 2(1) is the measure of damages in tort not for negligence, but for fraudulent misrepresentation, so that all losses are recoverable, provided they are not too remote *(Royscot Trust Ltd v Rogerson* [1991] 3 All ER 294, CA: criticism of this decision was noted, without comment, by the House of Lords in the *Scrimgeour Vickers* case). It seems that damages for innocent misrepresentation awarded in lieu of rescission under s 2(2) should never exceed the sum which would be awarded if the representation was a warranty *(William Sindall PLC v Cambridgeshire County Council* [1994] 1 WLR 1016) and may be limited to an indemnity in respect of obligations arising out of the contract *(Whittington v Seale-Hayne* (1900) 82 LT 49).

Damages are usually measured at the date of breach (usually, the date of acquisition), but this general rule will not be applied inflexibly where to do so would prevent the plaintiff from being fully compensated eg where there is a misrepresentation which continues to operate or where the purchaser is locked into a business *(Smith New Court v Scrimgeour Vickers, above*, and see, on this point, *Downs v Chappell* [1996] 3 All ER 344, CA).

What measure will the courts apply when assessing damages for breach of a contractual representation? In *JEB Fasteners Ltd v Marks Bloom & Co* [1983] 1 All ER 583 the plaintiffs bought a manufacturing company without obtaining warranties. The accounts of the target for its first year of operations were inaccurate and the disappointed plaintiffs sued the accountants. It was held that the defendants had been negligent in the preparation of the accounts, but because the plaintiffs' motive for the acquisition was to obtain the services of the target's two directors the court held that the accounts had not affected the purchaser's judgement to any material degree in deciding to proceed with the acquisition and their claim was therefore dismissed (the case should now be understood in the light of *Caparo Industries v Dickman—see* p 137). At p 587 Donaldson LJ said:

> The plaintiffs did not take the usual precaution of requiring the directors of [the target] to warranty the accuracy of the audited accounts and the fact that there had been no material change in the profitability of the company since the end of the period covered by those accounts. Accordingly they cannot sue the directors for breach of warranty but must rely on a claim against the defendant auditors for negligent misstatement. Furthermore, the measure of damage is different. It is not the difference between the value of the company if the facts had been as stated in the accounts and its actual value, but the loss which the plaintiffs have sustained as a result of acting in reliance on the accuracy of the accounts.

These remarks are, of course, *obiter dicta* but they are a very helpful clarification of a question which had been rendered obscure by the difficult case of *Esso Petroleum Co Ltd v Mardon* [1976] 2 WLR 583. In that case Esso let Mr Mardon a petrol station, representing to him that the potential throughput was likely to reach 200,000 gallons by the third year of operation. That estimate had been made before the requirements of the planning authority were known. In fact, the planning authority had required that the petrol station be built backing on the main road and not facing it so that the gallonage actually achieved was far less. Although the actual configuration of the site was known to Esso at the time they let the site to Mr Mardon, already having made their representation, they did not revise their figure. The representation was made before the Misrepresentation Act 1967 came into force, but the Court of Appeal held that Esso were liable in damages both on the basis of the rule in *Hedley Byrne* and also because what they had said amounted to a contractual warranty. Although they had not guaranteed the throughput, the court held that Esso had by implication warranted that on a careful assessment they had estimated the throughput of the service station at 200,000 gallons in the third year. This warranty was broken because there was no such careful assessment based on the site as finally constructed. The court decided that the measure of damages was the same whether Mr Mardon's claim was founded on *Hedley Byrne* or breach of warranty. In a crucial passage Lord Denning said (at p 595):

Mr Mardon is not to be compensated here for 'loss of a bargain'. He was given no bargain that the throughput would amount to 200,000 gallons a year. He is only to be compensated for having been induced to enter into a contract which turned out to be disastrous for him. Whether it be called breach of warranty or negligent misrepresentation, its effect was not to warrant the throughput, but only to induce him to enter the contract. So the damages in either case are to be measured by the loss he suffered.

The key to *Esso Petroleum Co Ltd v Mardon* seems to be that the warranty found was that reasonable care had been used in making the representation as to the throughput. If this warranty had been true then the representation would not have been made at all and accordingly the plaintiff would not have been induced to enter into the contract. Since the tortious measure would also seek to put the purchaser into the position which he would have enjoyed had he not entered into the contract, it can be seen that in this case the two measures produce the same result.

In calculating the damages for breach of warranty, it will sometimes be necessary to project what would have occurred had the warranty been correct eg if a proper forecast had been made. The *prima facie* assumption in such cases where, for example, an inaccurate forecast has been made, is that an accurate forecast would have reflected what actually occurred (as opposed to what was warranted) and damages would be calculated on that basis—*Lion Nathan Ltd v CC Bottlers Ltd* (1996) *The Times*, 16 May.

In *Esso v Mardon* it was held that if there had been no negligent statement, the purchaser would not have entered into the contract. Although it was not, strictly, an example of a 'no transaction' approach to assessment of damages it seems that the assessment in such a case may nonetheless be affected by the House of Lords' decision in *South Australia Asset Management Corp v York Montague Ltd* [1996] 3 All ER 367, when it was held, *obiter* that the 'no transaction' basis of assessment of damages (which would have led to the negligent valuer being liable for all losses as a result of the plaintiff having entered into a transaction which he would not otherwise have entered into, including losses attributable to a fall in the property market which would have been suffered if there was no negligence) should be abandoned. In cases such as negligent misstatement, where the purchaser's claim is based on a breach of duty of care, it is necessary to ascertain the scope of the duty owed (ie to the purchaser) and the loss arising from breach of that duty in order to determine what loss should be compensated. The *South Australia* principles may be appropriate where the vendor is liable for breach on the tortious basis or where the breach of an express warranty is itself a breach of duty to take care.

It is not always the contractual measure which produces the highest damages for the purchaser. Suppose the purchaser buys a company in circumstances where only limited warranties are given. An example might be a management buy-out, where the existing management team purchases the shares of the target and the vendors refuse to give substantial warranties because, as they claim, the purchasers know more of the business than they do themselves. However, it might be that, in such a case, a warranty would be given as to, for example, the operation of a group pension scheme. If that warranty were misleading, damages on the contractual basis would compensate the purchaser for any corresponding diminution in the value of his shares. Suppose, however, that the purchase was a disastrous one and that there were very substantial undisclosed liabilities. The purchaser does not have the protection of the normal warranties and so therefore cannot claim against the vendors unless he can say that the existence of the warranty about the pension scheme induced him to enter into the contract and that he is therefore liable to be compensated for the damage he has suffered as a result, ie the difference between the price paid and the value received. If the purchaser could show that the statement in question amounted to a tortious misrepresentation (whether a negligent misstatement at common law or a negligent misrepresentation within the 1967 Act) which induced the contract then he could claim damages on the tortious basis; but what if the representation is not negligent, but nevertheless amounts to a contractual warranty as in the example above? Unfortunately there does not appear to be any clear authority and the cautious practitioner acting for a vendor on these occasions will do his best to limit the vendor's liability to the contractual measure. In the United States the law clearly restricts the plaintiff, in these circumstances, from recovering any loss which the defendant can prove with reasonable certainty the plaintiff would have suffered had the contract been performed (see the Second Restatement of Contracts, s 349). For English authorities on the subject see *Cullinane v British 'Rema' Manufacturing Co Ltd* [1954] 1 QB 292, *Lloyd v Stanbury* [1971] 1 WLR 535; *Anglia Television Ltd v Reed* [1972] 1 QB 60 and *C & P Haulage v Middleton* [1983] 3 All ER 94.

Although the above discussion has tended to emphasise the differences between the consequences of assessing damages on the contractual and tortious basis, in most cases the price paid is likely to be equal to the value of the shares as warranted; so the result of applying either measure to any particular breach of warranty is the same and argument does not focus on the practical effect of the difference. In *Levison v Farin* [1978] 2 All ER 1149 the target had made losses in the period between the date of the warranted balance sheet and the date of completion, and the vendors had given a warranty that between the balance sheet date and the completion date there would have been no material adverse change in the overall value of the net assets of the company on the basis of a valuation adopted in the balance sheet allowing for normal trade fluctuations. It was found that the disclosures which the vendors had made were not sufficient to avoid their liability under the warranty and damages were assessed in the amount of the diminution of the net assets of the target in the period between the accounts and completion, less the tax benefit which subsequently accrued to the target, and therefore to the purchaser, from the losses in the period (for which *see* p 313). Gibson J formulated the measure of damages in contractual language, saying (at p 1159) that it was true that the purchaser was entitled to receive the company with the warranty as to net asset value performed as at the date of completion. Given that the purchase price actually paid (the make up of which the judge investigated) was the same as the value of the target as it would have been had the warranty been performed, the application of either the tortious or the contractual basis would have produced the same result. In deducting the tax benefits from the damages Gibson J followed Viscount Haldane LC in *British Westinghouse Electric & Manufacturing Co Ltd v Underground Electric Railways & Co of London Ltd* [1912] AC 673, at p 689:

> When in the course of his business [the plaintiff] has taken action arising out of the transaction, which action has diminished the loss, the effect in actual diminution of the loss he has suffered may be taken into account even though there was no duty on him to act.

In other words, although it was not suggested that the purchaser was under a duty to earn profits against which the tax losses could have been offset, the fact that he had received a benefit was taken into account and was not regarded as too remote.

9.6.6   Vendor protection clauses

The vendor should not be confident that damages recoverable as a result of a misrepresentation or breach of warranty cannot exceed the purchase price, even if the tortious basis of assessing damages is applicable. A purchaser of business assets who does not assume responsibility for all the past liabilities of the business is unlikely to suffer a loss exceeding the price paid but, while the purchaser cannot recover in respect of damage which could have been avoided if he had taken reasonable steps to minimise the loss caused by the breach of warranty, it is suggested that there is no reason to suppose eg that the purchaser of shares must allow the target to be placed in liquidation. If the target owes a liability in circumstances in which the vendor should have disclosed to the purchaser, so that the vendor is in breach of, for example, a balance sheet warranty in not doing so, then, even if the liability exceeds the purchase price, the purchaser may have excellent reasons for providing the target with funds to meet the liability (and claiming reimbursement from the vendors) rather than allowing the target to be placed in insolvent liquidation. Abandoning the target might cause severe damage to the purchaser's commercial reputation or involve the purchaser in loss in respect of guarantees which he had given after completion. Indeed, by the time the liability comes to light the purchaser may well have provided further funds to the target and these will now be required towards meeting the liability. All these matters may involve the vendor in a claim for consequential loss and vendors who wish to limit their liability to the amount of the purchase price should insist upon an express stipulation to this effect in the sale agreement.

It has become practice for the vendor of a private company or of business assets to put forward a large number of provisions for the purpose of limiting its liability to claims by the purchaser and prescribing the circumstances or extent to which claims may be made; such clauses should be reviewed carefully and, it is suggested, be acceptable only to the extent they properly reflect principles of mitigation or eliminate potential double recovery. Taken cumulatively, the provisions will sometimes result in a variety of procedural and other hurdles which will inhibit the bringing of a claim and can be a trap for the unwary. The vendor protection clauses tend to fall within a number of categories, such as the following:

(1) Those which place financial limits on the amount which may be claimed, eg a maximum or 'cap' on liability; exclusion of small claims (on the basis that they are immaterial and a nuisance, although the purchaser should note that where warranties are qualified so that they only cover 'material' matters, such small claims will often already be excluded). It is also common to specify a 'threshold' figure which accumulated claims must exceed before any claim may be brought (when all, or only the excess, may be claimed). There is no hard and fast rule as to the level of these limits, which depend on negotiation, the nature of the business and the extent of the purchaser's anticipated investment.

(2) Those which provide for time limits giving notice for bringing of claims, either within a fixed period, or referable to the production of accounts, eg for the second or third complete financial period after completion. Shortening the limitation period can be particularly useful if the vendor is old, as the existence of a potential liability for breach of warranty can cause difficulties in the administration of an estate. Similarly if a corporate vendor of shares or business assets is to be wound up following the sale, such a limit will enable the winding up to occur sooner than may otherwise be possible. Where the winding-up of a vendor company or of an individual vendor's estate following completion is thought to be likely, the purchaser will often require a substantial retention or deposit out of the purchase price to be used as security for warranty claims. This will protect the purchaser from an immediate distribution of assets occurring after completion, where the vendor believes that no claims will be brought under the agreement and decides it is able to make the distribution. If the vendor makes an improper distribution of assets, the purchaser may well, ultimately, be able to recover but it is plainly preferable to do so out of the security deposit. Apart from a time limit for notifying claims, vendors may also propose that proceedings must be commenced within a specified period after notification. This is not always sensible as this can force a purchaser who considers that he may wish to make a claim to issue a writ before the expiry of the period, exacerbating a situation which could perhaps otherwise have been resolved by negotiation.

(3) Those limitation provisions which provide the vendor with credit for 'hid-

den' assets. The most common example is where the purchaser has acquired the target by reference to a set of warranted accounts which, with hindsight, include either undervalued assets, or overstated liabilities, when the vendor will wish to offset such hidden value against a warranty claim. It is sometimes suggested that such a provision is appropriate only if the subject matter of the over- or undervaluation relates to the purchaser's claim (eg both relate to stock), and then only to the extent of any aggregate over- or undervaluation in the accounts. If the purchaser does agree to such a provision, it may insist that establishing the existence of credits is at the vendor's cost.

(4)   Provisions which clarify the responsibility for loss where it is attributable to a 'voluntary' act of the purchaser which has occurred after completion and which is outside the scope of the business as it is carried on before completion (eg changes in the basis of preparation of accounts).

(5)   Provisions which require that the purchaser first seeks recovery against a third party who is liable in respect of the loss (including an insurer).

(6)   Conduct of claim provisions which give the vendor a right to influence or take over the conduct of claims against third parties when there is a possibility of a claim under the warranties. The purchaser will often be reluctant to allow the vendor conduct of claims, as it will fear that the vendor will not share with it a common interest in the continuing goodwill of the target business.

(7)   Where there are several warrantors, provisions limiting or apportioning their individual liability.

Specimen short form vendor protection provisions which a purchaser may choose to put forward are set out in Agreement for Sale (Shares) Sched 8 para 4 at p 461 and the Agreement for Sale (Assets) Sched 8 para 4 at p 606. More extensive provisions are not uncommon.

The vendor protection provisions in the agreement represent exclusions or restrictions of the vendor's liability and as such they will be construed narrowly. It is also necessary to consider the statutory rules which affect the vendor's ability to exclude or restrict its liability for misrepresentation, under the Misrepresentation Act 1967, s 3. If the purchaser's remedy for misrepresentation is effectively excluded by the clause which limits the vendor's liability to breach in contract (*see* the discussion of *Thomas Witter v TBP Industries above*, p 161) it would seem that the vendor protection provisions, and s 3 will be of relevance to claims in misrepresentation only to the extent that the clauses limit the vendor's liability for fraud which is excluded from the earlier limiting clause (*see* p 162). It is suggested, however, that the cautious practitioner will specify that the vendor protection provisions in the agreement apply not only in respect of breach of warranty, but also in respect of any other statement made, so as to be effective to limit liability, so far as appropriate, in respect of pre-contractual representations and, eg negligent misstatement.

To the extent that the vendor protection provisions are operative as regards misrepresentations, the Misrepresentation Act 1967, s 3 would apply and the limits will be regarded as effective only to the extent they satisfy the requirement of reasonableness (*see* p 162 *above*). While it was not a point before the court in the *Witter* case the judge commented (at p 599) that 'to the extent which the clause prevents a claim based on what in the law of limitation is called 'concealed fraud', it might be unreasonable'. The clause in question required that claims must be brought within a specified period. To meet the point made by the judge, one approach might be to provide that any time limit for notifying claims does not begin to run until the fraud were known. However, a simpler approach is generally taken and such clauses frequently provide simply that the limit would not apply in the case of fraud. Quite how far the observation should be regarded as applying to other vendor protection provisions is unclear. It is well settled that the victim of a fraudulent misrepresentation should be compensated for all his losses, provided they are not too remote, and so the effectiveness of a clause which seeks to limit his compensation would seem vulnerable under s 3. However, other vendor protection provisions (eg those described at (3)–(7) *above*) simply attempt to regulate certain matters in the event of the claim and, it is suggested, in some cases (eg (3)) are not inconsistent with the basis upon which damages would be calculated in the event of a claim for fraud. Provided such clauses do not substantively limit the purchaser's remedy it is suggested they should not be regarded as unreasonable. The Agreement for Sale (Shares) at p 462 and the Agreement for Sale (Assets) at p 606 take the simple approach of disapplying the limitations to the extent of a claim based on fraud, wilful misconduct or wilful concealment. Although the exclusion is probably wider than necessary for the vendor, it reflects in part the purchaser's reluctance for its remedies to be limited in such cases.

The 1967 Act deals with liability for misrepresentation. Quite separately, the vendor protection provisions in all asset acquisition agreements, which also limit liability for breach of contractual warranty and for negligent misrepresentation, should be considered in light of the Unfair Contract Terms Act 1977. Section 3(1) imposes a requirement of reasonableness in respect of a provision in a contract which excludes or restricts liability for a breach of contract, if the purchaser is dealing as consumer or on the vendor's standard terms of business. Where the purchaser has its own advisers and is entering into the transaction on the basis of negotiated acquisition agreement, it seems inconceivable that this provision could apply to an acquisition agreement. Section 2(1) is of greater significance. Section 2(1) imposes the requirement of reasonableness in s 11(1) in respect of any provision which seeks to limit or exclude liability in respect of 'negligence' under the Act, which would include a negligent misstatement of the vendor. It is suggested, however, that provided the exclusions in respect of fraud, discussed above in the context of the Misrepresentation Act 1967, s 3, are incorporated into the vendor protection clauses, s 2(1) of the 1977 Act does not impose any greater restriction. The 'reasonableness' requirement of the Unfair Contract Terms Act 1977 does not, of course, apply to transactions for the transfer of interests in securities, land or certain intellectual property rights; although the ambit of those exclusions to the share or business sale agreement is not wholly clear.

9.6.7   Joint and several liability

Warranties may be given by all the selling shareholders in the sale agreement, by those who are substantial shareholders, or by the directors of the target (or by any combination). When more than one person is liable on the warranties, the purchaser normally requires the liability to be joint and several and to avoid a presumption that they have merely joint liability, this should be expressly stated. The purchaser is then able to bring proceedings against all or any of the warrantors as he wishes and to bring separate actions against each. For further detail about joint and several liability see *The Law Commission Report on Contribution* (1977 Law Com No 79). A recent limited, but valuable, review focused on the liability of professional defendants was undertaken by the Common Law Team of the Law Commission and is contained in its *Feasibility Investigation on Joint and Several Liability* (1996). It will be noted that joint, several, and joint and several obligations have a particular technical meaning which may be of significance in an acquisition from several vendors (see para 17-001 *Chitty on Contracts* 27th edn 1994). Similar principles apply for tortious liability.

Recovery of judgment against one of a number of joint or joint and several warrantors will not prevent proceedings against the others in respect of the same claim, although of course satisfaction of the judgment will discharge the whole liability. The plaintiff who brings successive actions will not, however, be able to recover costs in any action other than the first unless the court is of the opinion that there are reasonable grounds for bringing the action (Civil Liability (Contribution) Act 1978, s 3). If any of the warrantors should die, his personal representatives will be liable jointly and severally with the surviving warrantors. If the purchaser wishes to discharge one joint and several warrantor from his liability, he will take care to preserve his rights against the others. If one joint and several warrantor is effectively discharged (ie by release under seal or by accord and satisfaction) the other warrantors will also be released (*North v Wakefield* (1849) 13 QB 536). If the purchaser wishes to release one warrantor without the others, then unless all agree, the best that can be done is a covenant not to sue the warrantor who is to be released. An intention to preserve claims against others may be implied (*Watts v Aldington* (1993) *unreported*) but should not be assumed. A release which reserves rights against other warrantors will take effect as a covenant not to sue.

If one joint and several warrantor is called upon to pay damages he may claim a contribution from the other warrantors who are liable in respect of the same damage. The right to contribution is governed by the Civil Liability (Contribution) Act 1978. The amount recoverable will be such as may be found by the court to be just and equitable having regard to the extent of the defendant's responsibility for the damage in question and may extend from nothing to a complete indemnity, but if the defendant's liability was limited by contract, he will not be liable to pay a contribution in excess of that limit (s 2). The joint and several warrantor who has made a *bona fide* settlement of the warranty claim can still claim a contribution (s 1(4)). The limitation period is two years from the date of judgment or the date when the compromise was agreed (Limitation Act 1980, s 10). It will be noted that the rights of contribution of those warrantors with whom one warrantor is jointly liable means that a settlement of that warrantor with the purchaser may be only a partial settlement of his overall liability, if the other warrantors are then pursued by the purchaser and seek contribution from him.

If vendors in a share sale accept joint liability on warranties it may be sensible for them to stipulate between themselves that in the event of liability arising they will make payments to ensure that any liability (including costs) is borne in proportion to the number of shares sold by each of them. Agreements for contribution are not affected by the Act (s 7(3)).

Contribution is a matter for the warrantors; of itself it does not affect the rights of the purchaser to recover for breach.

9.6.8   Warranties by the purchaser

Cases arise in which the vendors seek warranties from the purchaser. The normal example is a case where the purchaser is issuing shares as consideration for the acquisition and the vendors intend to retain those shares. Because the acquisition of the purchaser's shares will represent a substantial investment by the vendors, they will seek warranties about the purchaser's affairs. Where the purchaser is listed or its shares are the subject of dealings on the Alternative Investment Market, the warranties can normally be in a much shorter form than those which the purchaser will seek in relation to the target.

The rule in *Houldsworth v City of Glasgow Bank* (1880) 5 App Cas 317 formerly made such warranties ineffective. In that case the plaintiff sought to avoid his liability to make a contribution in the winding up of a company by claiming that he had been induced to take his shares by misrepresentation and, accordingly, that he had a claim as a creditor equivalent to the amount which he was obliged to pay as a contributory. The court held that he could not claim as a creditor in respect of the transaction under which he had become a member. The rule is now set aside by the Companies Act 1985, s 111A which provides that a person is not debarred from obtaining damages or other compensation from a company by reason only of his holding or having held shares in the company. It is conceivable that such warranties can be attacked as an unlawful return of capital but this is unlikely in a normal case.

9.6.9   Indemnity

Liability in respect of misrepresentation arises because of breach of a duty imposed by law or by contract, but liability under an indemnity arises not because of breach but because the parties have stipulated that one shall save another from loss in specified circumstances. Contractual provisions relating to tax are considered in Chapter 14. Indemnities are useful when the vendors have disclosed matters to the purchaser (so that the warranties are thereby robbed of their force) but the purchaser still demands contractual protection against the consequences of the matter in question, but *see* p 334 for a comment on the tax-effectiveness of indemnities. The indemnity is not uncommon as a means of dealing with environmental problems (*see* p 152).

Indemnities are normally strictly construed and liability under them will not go beyond that expressly stipulated. It is therefore common expressly to include liability for interest and costs incurred. Where indemnities are given by more than one person in the agreement for sale the liability is normally assumed jointly and severally. It may be sensible to provide that those giving the indemnity contribute between themselves to ensure that each vendor bears the liability in proportion to any benefit enjoyed by him.

Since indemnities are taken in respect of specific matters, it is perhaps obvious to say that the purchaser should ensure that while the disclosures are expressed to qualify the warranties, they should not qualify the indemnities. It may be appropriate for the indemnity to be subject to the vendor protection provisions, or alternatively that different limitation provisions (eg as the period for notification of claims) should apply, depending on the specific matter which it is designed to address.

9.6.10   Insurance

Insurance against liability under warranties and indemnities is quite often sought, although is more common for warranties given on a share acquisition rather than of assets, as the latter will tend to leave with the vendor risk that it already has rather than create a new risk to insure. Insurers will seek to exclude liability under warranties which look to the future (eg as to recoverability of debts) and, because they are insurers, will be extremely wary in accepting liability under a warranty which relates to the adequacy of other insurance policies (see eg the Agreement for Sale (Shares), Sched 3, para 2.7(F) on p 406 and the Agreement for Sale (Assets), Sched 6 para 2.7(I) on p 573). They will also seek to exclude liability relating to any matter within the warrantors' knowledge at the date of the agreement or, of course, liability arising from fraud or dishonesty on the part of the insured. Tax avoidance schemes are also unpopular.

Although insurers should be consulted at an early stage, they may be wary of committing themselves to provide cover until after contracts have been exchanged and may be reluctant to accept the risk where the purchaser has stipulated that the vendor take out insurance. They may require a report on the contract from their own solicitors (for which the proposers have to pay) before agreeing to cover. The following is a list of points which may be relevant in connection with such a report in connection with a share acquisition and serves as a useful checklist for vendors generally (even when not seeking insurance).

(1) Is there any 'pound for pound' clause? (*see* p 169). The effect of such a clause may be that damages might be claimed by the purchaser in circumstances where the value of the target as a whole is not diminished by the circumstances giving rise to the breach of warranty.

(2) Some of the warranties may be qualified with statements such as 'so far as the vendors are aware'. Does the contract provide that this implies due and careful enquiry by the vendors? (*see* Note 11, p 464). This could mean that the vendors become liable under warranties so qualified, even though they are honestly ignorant of the circumstances giving rise to the liability. Where the phrase is used the vendor will probably not be required to conduct an exhaustive review of all old archives (*William Sindall plc v Cambridgeshire County Council* [1994] 1 WLR 1016). So as to be confident that the vendor is not attributed with the knowledge of its employees who have not been consulted (eg for reasons of confidentiality) any provision which deems the vendor to have made enquiry are best given by reference to an identified list of employees. Where there is such a list, is the vendor deemed to know all that those individuals know or only to make reasonable enquiry of them? Have the named individuals confirmed in writing that they have considered the warranties and made all relevant disclosures? Can that confirmation be relied upon or (as is more common) does it seek to provide that it is given 'without liability'?

(3) If accounts are warranted as 'accurate' the warranty is unlikely to be true, but it is unlikely that any claim would be made unless the deficiency is material. On the other hand, if accounts are warranted as making 'full' provision for all liabilities (including perhaps contingent or unquantified liabilities) then the warranty does not reflect accounting practice. Accounts normally make provisions only for material contingent losses which can be estimated with reasonable accuracy (see Statement of Standard Accounting Practice 18).

(4) A warranty that no liability has been incurred since a balance sheet date 'otherwise than in the normal course of trading' is quite restrictive as it would not cover, for example, replacement or repair of fixed assets or redundancy claims.

(5) Warranties under which plant or equipment is warranted as being in any particular condition or having any particular value are dangerous.

(6) A warranty that debts are recoverable is in the nature of a guarantee.

(7) Warranties relating to management accounts or profit forecasts are dangerous and should be carefully considered. The vendors should be alert to

spot whether or not management accounts or forecasts are warranted in a roundabout way, for example by being annexed to the disclosure letter which is itself warranted as true. The same applies to other documents annexed to the disclosure letter by way of disclosure.

(8)   Any warranty which says that a pension scheme is adequately funded is dangerous.

(9)   A warranty under which insurance is said to be adequate causes underwriters (who are insurers themselves) to be on their guard.

(10) Any warranty which warrants the truth of written or oral information other than information contained in the disclosure letter is worrying.

(11) Are warranties given in absolute terms or are absolute warranties qualified in some way eg as to material matters? Is materiality defined?

(12) 'Sweeper' warranties under which the vendors warrant that all material facts have been disclosed are obviously wide-ranging.

(13) So far as tax warranties are concerned, capital allowances are often claimed; intra-group transactions are quite common and book values are not normally equal to base costs. If warranties covering these points are given without qualification or disclosure, it is likely that insufficient work has been done by the vendors on tax disclosures.

(14) The sale agreement will contain a deed of tax indemnity or other provisions relating to adjustment of the purchase price for tax claims (*see* Chapter 14). Insurers will wish to check that the indemnity is limited to taxation arising before completion; that it is limited to claims falling on the target and does not cover claims against the purchaser arising otherwise than in respect of the target or the shares to be sold; that it excludes claims arising from transactions in the ordinary course of business since the accounts, claims in respect of which provisions have been made which are insufficient only by reason of any increase of rates of taxation or retrospective changes of the law, and claims which would not have arisen but for a voluntary act or transaction of the purchaser. Is credit allowed for overprovisions relating to taxation? Does the indemnity include requirements that notice be given of claims and that the indemnifiers be entitled to require that the target takes steps to minimise the loss? Is there a grossing up clause (*see* Chapter 14)?

(15) The agreement should contain limitations on liability. Is there a minimum claim level (whether in the aggregate or in respect of any particular claim)? Is there a limit on total liability? (*see* p 174). Are there time limits within which claims are to be made? Are there provisions which limit liability to representations contained in the agreement and the disclosure letter? Does the payment of a claim under the indemnity provisions *pro tanto* satisfy a claim under the warranties?

(16) In preparing the disclosure letter, has care been taken to ensure that all items of the disclosure letter are not warranted 'correct', eg management accounts, budgets or forecasts? Is it clear from the agreement that the dis-

closure letter does actually qualify the warranties? Surprisingly, it sometimes is not.

9.7 Heads of agreement

Although not strictly relevant to a discussion of warranties and investigations it is convenient to mention heads of agreement here, since the signing of such a document will often mark the commencement of the detailed investigation. Whether or not heads of agreement are entered into is largely a matter of taste: it is often preferable to proceed with negotiating the formal agreement rather than spend time negotiating heads, particularly where the principal terms are already understood and clearly reflected in correspondence between the parties. On the other hand, heads of agreement will almost always be desirable where the transaction is complex and preliminary discussions have taken place over a protracted period of time and terms are reflected (if at all) in a variety of documents; and it is often helpful to clarify, at the outset, areas which may be contentious or where there may be a gap in the parties' expectations eg the terms of a particular indemnity or of an earnout calculation. Advisers should ensure that any heads of agreement or prior correspondence are stated expressly not to create a binding contract. While English law, unlike some civil law jurisdictions (*see* p 342), does not generally imply terms committing parties to pre-contractual negotiations there is no reason in principle why, if one party makes representations to the other in the course of negotiations about his intentions which are incorrect, knowing the other is likely to act on them to his detriment, the other should not be entitled to a remedy if damage is suffered eg for negligent misstatement or in deceit (*Edgington v Fitzmaurice* [1885] 29 ChD 459).

Occasionally, parties will agree that, while the heads of agreement are generally 'subject to contract', certain of the terms should be binding, such as those concerning the confidentiality of information to be provided in the investigation process, costs (eg in the event of negotiations breaking down) or providing for a period of exclusivity. Provided the latter is expressed in terms of 'lockout' rather than 'lock in' and supported by consideration it will be effective (see *Walford v Miles* [1992] 1 All ER 453, HL; see also *Pitt v PHH Asset Management Ltd* [1993] 4 All ER 961).

9.8 Auction sales

It is appropriate to mention the 'auction sale' approach to sale of a private company or business which has become increasingly popular. A so-called auction is primarily a means of marketing the target, coupled with a controlled sale process. A well-managed auction process can be attractive to a vendor, who finds itself able to achieve the best price for the target and to sell on favourable terms. If the process is not tightly controlled there can be little advantage and considerably more work. The typical auction sale will involve the following:

(1) Preparation and circulation of an information memorandum concerning the company or business to be sold. An auction sale will usually (but not invariably) involve a financial adviser who will be involved in the preparation of the information memorandum. The memorandum will typically be circulated by the financial adviser to prospective purchasers. Where the target is a corporate entity the circulation of the memorandum will be subject to the restrictions on publishing unapproved investment advertisements under the Financial Services Act 1986, s 57 and unless approved, circulation of the memorandum may be made to only a restricted class of person, so as to fall within one of the exemptions from that section (*see* p 27). The exception of particular relevance is that contained in the Financial Services Act 1986 (Investment Advertisements) (Exemptions) Order 1996 (SI No 1536), reg 11 which permits such advertisements to be made to persons who fall within one of the categories set out in that regulation including: persons who are themselves authorised; companies which have (or whose holding company has) more than 20 members and called up share capital or net assets of more than £500,000; and certain substantial trusts. The exemption will permit the advertisement to be distributed to most listed companies, financial advisers and many institutional investors. Section 57 will not generally apply to circulation of an information memorandum in connection with a sale of business assets (unless the assets include investments within the meaning of Sched 1 to the Act).

(2) Assembling a 'data room'. The data room will be assembled by the vendor and its advisers and will comprise comprehensive information covering all aspects of the target's business, which will form the basis of the purchaser's investigation and of subsequent disclosure by the vendor against any warranties that are given. It is usual to prepare ground rules for use of the data room—eg access, copying, the manner in which further information requests should be handled and so forth—with the intention that each prospective purchaser has the same information available to it. The data room, for reasons of confidentiality, will generally be 'off site' and commonly at the lawyers' offices.

(3) Once initial interest in response to the information memorandum is known, the vendor will circulate a timetable and 'rules of the game' to prospective purchasers. The process will generally involve submission of indicative bids (usually after a preliminary data room investigation). The resulting short list of prospective purchasers will then be invited to make firm bids on the basis of a draft contract which has been prepared by the vendor's lawyers (unlike the usual process, where it is the purchaser who prepares the draft) and to give their proposals for its amendment and after having conducted a full data room investigation.

(4) The vendor will then select (usually only one) preferred bidder, when a period of exclusivity is agreed, during which the final terms are negotiated and settled and contracts entered into.

The key to a successful auction sale for a vendor is good preparation and tight control of the process. For example, if new disclosures were to emerge at the preferred bidder stage, it will undermine the purchaser's confidence in the data room information, and the purchaser will often then feel able to raise new issues or modify its bid.

A purchaser should be wary of an auction sale, noting that the principle of *caveat emptor* applies to the transaction and that non-disclosure does not, of itself, amount to a misrepresentation (unless, of course, it can be said to be in breach of a contractual warranty). Since it will usually be required to negotiate the vendor's draft contract, this may place it at a significant disadvantage since its own contract will usually have been more beneficial than that proposed by the other side.

The timetable for comment and for investigation is often extremely tight and the purchaser is well advised to plan ahead and to assemble a well-briefed team. It should examine the contract and the data room with considerable care and, notwithstanding its desire to acquire the target, not hesitate in seeking further information or adequate protection in the sale agreement. Of course, it will not wish to lose the opportunity to purchase but should avoid being railroaded by a vendor anxious to promote the possibility of competing interest in the target, so as to maximise price and minimise debate over the contract terms. A vendor should, naturally, ensure that the purchaser is not misled as to the existence of other bidders *(see Smith New Court v Scrimgeour Vickers, above)*.

Chapter 10

Transferring Shares and Business Assets from Vendor to Purchaser

This chapter considers the mechanics of transferring a corporate target from the vendor to the purchaser and the transfer of business assets from a vendor which may or may not be incorporated.

10.1 Title Covenants

Whether the transaction involves shares or assets, it will be usual to specify that the asset(s) to be bought and sold are owned by the vendor and will be acquired by the purchaser free from all liens, charges, equitable interests and other encumbrances, except to the extent of any interests which are specifically identified. In addition, both vendor and purchaser will consider whether it is appropriate that the shares or assets are sold with *full title guarantee*, or with *limited title guarantee*, in order to import into the transaction the implied covenants for title contained in Part I of the Law of Property (Miscellaneous Provisions) Act 1994. Instead of the previous statutory keywords (beneficial owner, settlor, trustee, mortgagee and personal representative) which, under the Law of Property Act 1925, s 76, implied certain covenants, there are now only these two key phrases which may be applied to dispositions of real and personal property and choses in action. Their use is not limited by the capacity of the vendor—any type of owner may sell with full title guarantee or limited title guarantee.

A detailed discussion of the covenants for title implied by the 1994 Act is beyond the scope of this book. It is useful, however, to summarise the covenants applicable on a sale of shares or business assets and their relationship to other provisions of the acquisition agreement.

Full title guarantee

A vendor who sells with full title guarantee covenants that:

(a)   right to dispose: the vendor has the right to dispose of the shares/business assets;

(b)   further assurance: the vendor will at its own cost do all that it reasonably can to give the purchaser the title it purports to give;

(c)   charges and encumbrances: the vendor is disposing of the property free from:

(i)   all charges and encumbrances (whether monetary or not); and

(ii)   all other rights exercisable by third parties,

other than any charges, encumbrances or rights which that person does not and could not reasonably be expected to know about;

(d)   real property covenants: in addition, if the transaction is a sale of business assets which includes a freehold or leasehold interest in land, further covenants are implied. The implied covenant for further assurance will mean that all reasonable assistance will be given to effect registration (or first registration) of title to the property; that the disposition (unless otherwise provided) is of the whole of the interest in the property (if registered) or of the unexpired term of the lease or of the freehold (if of unregistered interests). It is also implied in the sale of a leasehold interest that the lease is subsisting and that there is no subsisting breach of condition or tenant's obligations nor anything which would render the lease liable to forfeiture.

These covenants are given subject to the statutory qualifications, referred to below.

Limited title guarantee

The vendor who sells with limited title guarantee covenants in the terms referred to at (a), (b) and (d) above. As regards charges and encumbrances, however, the implied terms are more limited in that the vendor covenants that:

(c)   it has not since the last disposition for value:

(i)   charged or encumbered the property by means of any charge or encumbrance which subsists at the time of sale, or granted third party rights in relation to the property which so subsist; or

(ii)   suffered the property to be so charged or encumbered or subjected to such rights

and that (in either case) it is not aware that anyone else has done so since the last disposition for value

Whether the vendor sells with full title guarantee or limited title guarantee, the Act provides statutory qualifications and the vendor will not be liable in respect of:

(a)   any particular matter to which the disposition is expressly made subject; or

(b)   anything else which, at the time of the disposition, is within the actual knowledge of the purchaser or is a necessary consequence of facts then within his actual knowledge. For this purpose, the 'deemed notice' provisions of the Law of Property Act 1925, s 198 are disregarded.

The covenants contained in the 1994 Act are imported only if the statutory phrases *full title guarantee* or *limited title guarantee* are used. Furthermore, it is possible to amend the covenants. There are therefore three possible ways of importing covenants for title into a transaction:

(a) importing covenants in the form in which they are set out in the statute;
(b) importing the covenants in a modified form, which can be done by deleting, modifying, or adding new wording; and
(c) including express covenants for title in place of the implied covenants. While rare in conveyancing transactions, this approach is more common in sales and purchases of shares or business assets (sometimes coupled with the use of the implied covenants in addition).

It is also possible to incorporate no covenants for title at all, whether express or implied. This is frequently seen in sales by insolvency practitioners (*see* Chapter 16).

The covenants for title implied by the 1994 Act are in addition to terms implied by any other statute. For example, on an acquisition of business assets any fixed assets and stock to be acquired will generally be goods within the meaning of the Sale of Goods Act 1979 and accordingly there will be an implied term as to title in respect of those items under s 12 of that Act (which, by virtue of the Unfair Contract Terms Act 1977, s 6, cannot be excluded).

The purchaser acquiring shares or business assets will always require assurance that the shares or business assets to be acquired are owned by the vendor and will not be subject to encumbrances or rights in favour of others. This assurance may be achieved either by taking express warranties to this effect (*see* eg Agreement for Sale (Shares), Sched 3, para 2.1(B), at p 398 and Agreement for Sale (Assets), Sched 6 para 2.7(B), at p 569) or by providing that the shares or assets are sold with full title guarantee or limited title guarantee in the statutory, or an amended, form. However in all cases the purchaser should consider what modification is made to the covenants or what additional warranties or assurances should be taken, in view of the qualifications to the covenants implied by the 1994 Act, which are limited by reference to matters within the actual or constructive knowledge of the purchaser (*see* eg the Agreements for Sale, at p 387 and p 518). It is for this reason that the precedent Agreements for Sale use the statutory keywords and extend the covenants. If reliance is placed solely on contractual warranties, the purchaser should note that such warranties are generally subject to disclosure and limits on the amount of and time for bringing claims in respect of them (*see* the Agreement for Sale (Shares), Sched 8 at p 461 and the Agreement for Sale (Assets), Sched 8 at p 606). As a result it is appropriate that any express and implied warranties and covenants as to title are to have similar effect and if reliance is to be placed on express warranties alone the purchaser should consider excepting those which deal with title and encumbrances from the limitations and from general disclosures.

10.2   Share acquisition

A share acquisition is, in terms of the transfer itself, a simple transaction. The process involves an agreement to sell the shares in the target and transfer takes place by executing a stock transfer form which is delivered, together with the relative share certificate, to the purchaser at completion. Subject to the company's articles of association, which should always be checked at an early stage in the preparations and be complied with (and which may, for example, prohibit registration of transfers to certain persons or require that the shares be offered first to other shareholders on a pre-emptive basis), the shares will be lodged with the target at completion, and the target's board should then instruct that the transfer be registered, when the purchaser will be entered in the register of members in respect of the shares transferred to it (*see* the precedent completion board minutes at p 631). Under Companies Act 1985, s 183(1) it is not lawful for a company to register a transfer unless a proper instrument of transfer has been delivered to it or the transfer is exempt. A proper instrument of transfer is any transfer which complies with the requirements of the Stock Transfer Act 1963, which applies to fully paid shares; in other cases the provisions for transfer in the target's articles should be observed. Registration of a transfer in respect of the shares will be effective to transfer the legal title to the shares. Unless exempt under the Stamp Duty (Exempt Instruments) Regulations 1987 (SI No 516) the transfer will require stamping (at the rate of 50p per £100 or part thereof) and it is unlawful to register an unstamped transfer—*see* Chapter 12, p 281. Beneficial ownership may be transferred by contract, but the company's register of members will not reflect beneficial interests, merely legal interests. Stamp duty reserve tax (also effective at the rate of 0.5 per cent of the value of the consideration) will be payable on the contract in respect of the transfer of beneficial ownership (*see* p 282).

Upon registration of the transfer the purchaser becomes a member of the company and able to exercise its rights as such. It is entitled to delivery of a certificate, which is *prima facie* evidence of its title to the shares, within two months thereafter (Companies Act 1985, ss 185 and 186). If the purchaser has acquired control of the target, including its board, registration should be a straightforward process. If for some reason the purchaser does not have control of the board and the directors have discretion not to register transfers there may (occasionally) be difficulty, although the directors may refuse to register a transfer only in the proper exercise of their powers and not on personal grounds. The purchaser, as transferee, will normally be the beneficial owner in such circumstances but before becoming registered the owner must exercise its rights through the vendor who remains registered in respect of the shares. It is for this reason that the vendor's power of attorney is taken at completion to cover the period before stamping and registration (*see* the Agreement for Sale (Shares) cl 5.2(A)(3) and the form of power of attorney on p 635). On payment of the price in full it seems that the purchaser will be recognised as having that right in any event, but not where part payment only is made (eg where there is deferred consideration) *(Musselwhite v CH Musselwhite & Son Limited* [1962] Ch 964). It may be possible, where directors refuse to register a transfer, for the purchaser to exercise rights (ie by directing the vendor) to change the articles in an appropriate way or by removing the directors and appointing its own representatives in order that it can then be registered as shareholder.

10.3   Asset acquisition

The formalities for transferring ownership of an incorporated target are simplified by virtue of the fact that it is necessary only to transfer the target's shares in order to transfer the target, with its assets and liabilities.

An asset acquisition is, legally, a more complex transaction because, unlike a share acquisition, the assets are not neatly packaged in the target company and it is instead necessary to identify and transfer each asset, or category of asset, that forms part of the business which the purchaser is to acquire. The sale agreement will need to specify, and provide for transfer of, all such assets (*see*, for example, the extensive definitions in the Agreement for Sale (Assets), cl 2.1 on p 509). The purchaser will not usually assume responsibility for all liabilities of the vendor in respect of the business, although if the parties intend that the purchaser is to be responsible for some such liabilities, the manner in which responsibility is to be assumed will be dealt with by the contract. However, while the general principle is that the purchaser will not assume responsibility for the vendor's liabilities this will not always be so easy in practice. Some assets, when transferred to the purchaser, will carry with them responsibility for certain liabilities that, in order that the purchaser acquires full benefit of what is to be acquired, it must also discharge or become responsible for associated liabilities. One obvious example is the assignee of a leasehold interest in land who will, upon assignment, become liable under any provision in the lease to make good dilapidations even where the dilapidations have occurred prior to the purchaser's occupation. Another is the statutory novation of employees' contracts (*see* Chapter 6). In both examples, the legal responsibility will fall to the purchaser. Separately, however, the purchaser may in practice find itself sorting out problems which relate to the vendor's period of ownership and for which the vendor is legally liable, in order to preserve the goodwill of the business acquired. The contract for sale will need to allocate responsibility for any such liability as between vendor and purchaser and provide the purchaser with recourse to the vendor in such circumstances.

The following sections consider, in outline, the treatment of the different categories of assets which may form part of the acquisition, the treatment of liabilities and other procedural matters which commonly require attention in the contract, although reference should also be made to other chapters (3, 12) and to the Agreement for Sale (Assets) on p 501. Some of the points will be of equal significance in a share acquisition and where relevant, this is noted.

A typical agreement for the sale of business assets contains a surprising, often initially confusing, number of definitions, particularly when contrasted with an agreement for the sale of shares. Agreements adopt this format in an attempt to identify, as precisely as practicable, the different types of assets which are to be acquired; although agreements will also commonly provide that the purchaser is to acquire anything else which is used in or for the benefit of the business, it is rare for the parties to leave it at that. As a result, particular care and attention should be taken with the definitions. Having defined what is to be acquired it is relatively common to specify, usually for the avoidance of doubt, that certain assets or liabilities are to be excluded from the sale, such as shares in a subsidiary of a vendor which is otherwise selling all its assets, or the entitlement to repayment of loans made to other companies in the vendor's group, which there is rarely any point in transferring to the purchaser.

10.3.1 Current assets

The acquisition may include current assets of the vendor attributable to the target business. Current assets include stock and work-in-progress (eg partly finished goods or, if the business involves the provision of services, where work has commenced in relation to the services, but is not invoiced at the date of completion) *see* the Agreement for Sale (Assets), Sched 1 at p 529.

Cash and cash equivalents

Whether or not the acquisition includes cash and cheques drawn in favour of the vendor in relation to the business to be sold (to the extent they are not 'book debts' - *see below*) is a matter for agreement. Generally, cash and cash equivalent amounts will be excluded since there is little point in the purchaser paying the vendor in cash for what is, or is in effect, cash. Instead the vendor will normally retain cash and cash-equivalent balances, if necessary with a corresponding adjustment to the consideration payable by the purchaser. Note that the sale of cash on deposit at the bank (rather than on current account) will carry a charge to stamp duty of 1 per cent, although the simple way to avoid such a charge is to move the cash from deposit to current account prior to sale.

While cash and its equivalent will normally be excluded from the assets to be sold, the purchaser will need to think carefully about the effect of excluding such assets on the overall transaction. For example, if the vendor's book debts due to it in relation to the target business are to be acquired by the purchaser, but the vendor is to retain cash balances, it is obvious that the structure could encourage the vendor to accelerate collection of book debts prior to completion in order to maximise the cash balances at the time of completion (which it then retains), reducing the value of the assets (in the form of book debts) which the purchaser acquires. If the purchaser is also to assume responsibility for trade creditors the position is exacerbated: it would be possible for the vendor to maximise the cash position not only by accelerating the collection of debts but also by delaying payment of creditors. Apart from its effect on price and value of the assets acquired, the purchaser will be concerned that aggressive management of cash balances by the vendor will be detrimental to the relationships the target business has with its suppliers and customers, because it will inherit those relationships at completion. The Agreement for Sale (Assets), at cl 11.5, p 518 attempts to prohibit the vendor from taking such detrimental action although in practice, it will often be difficult to monitor and if there is breach, difficult to assess the damage. Apart from the impact on customer/supplier relations, the purchaser should, however, ensure that to the extent the vendor is able to manage the assets to be handed over at completion to his advantage, the purchaser is adequately protected by an adjustment in price. Preparation of a completion balance sheet, with the price payable by the purchaser being adjusted by reference to net assets actually acquired will protect the purchaser. Alternatively a more limited exercise, to equal effect, will involve the price payable being calculated by reference to the variable assets to be acquired (eg stock and other current assets; book debts if relevant).

Stock and work-in-progress

The business assets to be acquired will typically include stock and work-in-progress. If the target business is involved in the manufacture of any products or in any production processes, its stock will comprise raw materials, finished goods and partially finished items, or work-in-progress. A target engaged in the provision of services will typically include its work-in-progress among the business assets to be sold, representing the purchaser's entitlement to invoice for such services after completion, where part of the work done has occurred prior to completion. The price payable for stock and work-in-progress is typically left open for adjustment based on the actual value of stock/work-in-progress as at the date of completion, possibly as part of a wider completion audit (an approach adopted in the precedent agreement at p 529).

The sale agreement will include arrangements for stocktaking and valuation of work-in-progress as at the transfer date and the basis for valuation of stock (*see* eg Agreement for Sale (Assets), p 535). Here, also, it is important to consider the interplay between different assets, their effect on price and the impact on the business to be acquired by the purchaser. An example (of equal relevance to a share acquisition which involves the preparation of completion accounts) is where the agreement for sale might specify that finished goods are to be valued at their list price, whereas unfinished goods or work-in-progress are to be valued at the lower of cost and net realisable value. If the consideration payable by the purchaser is to be calculated by reference to the value of current assets at the date of completion, a vendor may choose to speed up production so as to maximise the amount of finished stock, which will be valued at a higher price compared to work-in-progress at completion. This may have several undesirable consequences for the purchaser. It would increase the overall consideration payable (because the purchaser is paying for finished stock, valued to include profit); if production has been accelerated, quality may be impaired; if the products have a short shelf life (eg food), then the purchaser will not wish to pay for surplus stock as at the time of completion which becomes out of date before it can be sold. As a result, it is not uncommon for the purchaser to place a limit on the value of stock it is willing to acquire or to provide, where short dated stock (for example) is of potential concern, that such stock should, if in volumes materially in excess of the normal seasonal stock levels, be treated as having a nil or reduced value.

Stock will not, of course, always be physically located on the target's premises. Stock may be stored on premises owned by a third party (eg bulk raw materials or stock held by suppliers) or may be held by customers on a sale or return basis. The stocktaking procedures in relation to stock not physically located on the vendor's premises should ensure that any third party in possession or control of such stock confirms that it is held unincumbered by any security interest, such as a lien or retention of title or rights of set-off. Such a confirmation is particularly relevant where the third party has dealings with the vendor otherwise than in relation to the target business. In such a case it may not be sufficient to discharge amounts owing in respect of the target business in order to acquire unincumbered title to the stock: other amounts might also require settlement in order that the stock is free from any such interests (of course, covenants and warranties as to unincumbered title will be relevant in this context, *see p* 187).

Implied terms

The business assets will almost certainly include 'goods' within the meaning of the Sale of Goods Act 1979, s 61(1). Both stock and fixed assets are likely to be goods for such purpose, and certain terms may be implied into the sale under ss 13–15 of that Act. In particular, under s 14(2), it will be an implied term that the goods supplied are of satisfactory quality, if the sale of the goods is 'in the course of a business'. It is not entirely clear that the sale of a business as a going concern will be regarded as a transaction subject to the Act in all circumstances. Whether or not it applies, the vendor will generally seek to exclude implied terms under the 1979 Act, the purchaser instead relying on express contractual warranties. Any such exclusion is effective only insofar as it satisfies the requirement of reasonableness under the Unfair Contract Terms Act 1977, s 6(3). Such implied terms cannot, of course, be excluded if the purchaser is dealing as a consumer (s 6(2)), although that is thought to be most unlikely in a fully negotiated acquisition where the purchaser is advised. The extent to which a purchaser's remedies may otherwise be excluded is considered further at p 161.

10.3.2 Book debts: treatment of trade debtors and trade creditors

Book debts represent those amounts which are due to the vendor in relation to the business, and will include the vendor's entitlement to be paid in respect of amounts invoiced for goods or services supplied, as well as entitlements to rebate (eg volume purchase rebates from suppliers). Book debts may also include prepayments as at the time of completion, for example where the vendor has paid in advance for certain services (eg rentals) although these may be approached separately (*see below*). Clearly, there is a relationship between book debts payable and book debts actually paid (which have become cash or cheques drawn in favour of the vendor), and the contract should be drafted to avoid overlap. As noted, clarity is particularly important where cash is excluded from the sale, but book debts are not.

Treatment of book debts varies from transaction to transaction. A simple asset transaction (eg not involving the whole of the vendor's business) will usually involve treating the book debts in the same way as cash balances, and provide that the vendor retains them. In a more complicated, comprehensive, transaction it is not unusual that they are acquired by the purchaser, who takes over the business as if it were a share acquisition (when responsibility for discharging some or all liabilities, particularly trade creditors, may also be assumed by the purchaser). Whatever the circumstances it is appropriate to consider treatment of book debts (which typically represent trade debtors) in conjunction with treatment of trade creditors of the business as they are broadly similar in type, reflecting on the one hand the company's entitlement to receive payment for its goods or services and on the other its obligation to pay for those received from others. Together they represent the liquidity of the business and, if responsibility for creditors is separated from the entitlement to receive payment from debtors, payment of the creditors would have to be funded from some other source.

There are essentially three approaches to the treatment of book debts and trade creditors on the acquisition of business assets:
(a) vendor retains ownership of and collects book debts, also retaining responsibility for payment of trade creditors;
(b) vendor retains ownership of book debts but the purchaser collects them on the vendor's behalf as its agent. Out of the amounts collected the purchaser discharges trade creditors outstanding at the date of completion as agent for the vendor, but such creditors remain the responsibility of the vendor (eg if book debts collected are insufficient to discharge them) and the purchaser will hand over any surplus of amounts received in excess of

amounts due to trade creditors; or

(c)   purchaser acquires title to the book debts and also assumes responsibility (by giving an indemnity to the vendor) for discharging trade creditors.

The first approach is most relevant where only part of the business assets are acquired. The second and third approaches are most suitable for the type of acquisition of business assets contemplated by this book—of substantially the whole of a business as a going concern—as they involve least disruption to the business and relations with customers and suppliers. Apart from stamp duty considerations (*see below*) transfer of ownership of debts would probably be more common although in order that the purchaser acquires legal title to the book debts a written notice of the assignment under the Law of Property Act 1925, s 136 would need to be given and the debtor would not otherwise be bound in respect of the purchaser's interest until it receives notice of it. However, the second approach is probably most common and it is that approach which is adopted in the Agreement for Sale (Assets), at p 515. It will be seen that, whichever approach is selected, the person (vendor or purchaser) who has control over the income of the business (the book debts) also has the practical responsibility to discharge its outgoings (eg trade creditors). 'Trade creditors' is a term susceptible to interpretation, and the purchaser should specify clearly in the agreement what 'trade creditors' it agrees to discharge.

There are a number of factors which dictate the approach most appropriate for any particular transaction. These fall broadly into the categories of: stamp duty; security for discharge of the creditors of the business and goodwill; treatment of bad debts; and practicality.

Stamp duty

Transfer of ownership of book debts to the purchaser is usually unattractive because the document under which the book debts are transferred will be stampable at the rate of 1 per cent of the *gross* value of the book debts transferred (note that the assumption of responsibility for creditors does not result in 'netting off' creditors against debtors for stamp duty purposes), *see further* p 288. However, in some cases there may be no practicable alternative to transferring to the purchaser the gross value of the book debts if, for example, the vendor needs to be paid in cash in full at the time of completion, in order that it can procure the discharge of any security over the business assets (in such cases, the purchaser will usually require that the contract includes a mechanism for adjusting the price paid to take account of any bad debts and will wish to take security for any amount which it might become entitled to on such price adjustment). Notwithstanding stamp duty charges, an acquisition of business assets which involves transferring essentially the whole of the business sometimes involves transferring ownership of debtors to the purchaser. This is particularly so where, as is not uncommon, the transaction started life as a share acquisition but for some reason it is decided that a sale of assets should occur, on a basis 'as if' a share transaction. In such cases, execution of documentation outside the jurisdiction may be appropriate to avoid stamp duty (*see further* p 291).

Security and goodwill

If the vendor is to retain responsibility for discharging trade creditors and other liabilities of the business, the purchaser will wish to ensure that there is a mechanism in place to ensure that the vendor does indeed fulfil those obligations. After completion there may be no particular commercial advantage to the vendor settling debts of the business quickly. Customers and suppliers of the target business will not necessarily draw a distinction between the vendor's and the purchaser's ownership of the business and a delay or failure to discharge trade creditors or other liabilities on the part of the vendor may adversely affect the business and goodwill acquired by the purchaser. Equally, where the book debts remain the property of the vendor the purchaser will be keen to ensure that the vendor's debt collection techniques do not adversely affect the purchaser's relations with customers of the business. One practical approach, if the purchaser is not to acquire the debts, is for the purchaser to have control over the vendor's collection of debts and discharge of creditors by an arrangement under which the purchaser collects debts and uses amounts received on behalf of the vendor to discharge creditors of the business first, only then paying over the surplus (in effect, the second approach described above). In such circumstances the agreement will need to address issues such as which debts (eg pre- or post-completion) are to be regarded as having been paid when monies are received and what effort the purchaser is expected to take to ensure collection of debts (*see* the Agreement for Sale (Assets), at p 515).

One other point is the discharge of liabilities apart from trade creditors. Where any failure on the part of the vendor to discharge other creditors will affect the purchaser's business, the purchaser may provide in the sale agreement that it is able to pay those sums on behalf of the vendor and then set off such payment against the vendor's money (eg surplus trade debts) which passes through its hands.

Bad debts

If the purchaser acquires ownership of the debts, and pays for them at their face value, it will take on the risk of bad debts. In such a case the purchaser will wish to ensure that the contract contains an appropriate mechanism for adjusting the price paid for bad debts, usually by providing that the vendor repays an amount equal to the bad debt and the vendor then assumes the right to collect that debt. Alternatively, the amount the purchaser pays at the outset will be reduced by an agreed provision for bad debts and it will be a matter for agreement whether it is obliged to account to the vendor for any surplus. The issue of bad debts obviously also arises in a share transaction, where the point will commonly be addressed either by warranty or by completion accounts adjustment.

Practicality

If the purchaser acquires the business from the vendor as a going concern and is to occupy the premises previously occupied by the vendor in relation to the business, it is obvious that for a period at least after completion, those who owe the vendor in relation to the business will continue to make payment at the business premises, even though they are now occupied by the purchaser. Similarly, there will be a transitional period when creditors of the vendor in relation to the business will continue to seek payment from the vendor at (what is then) the purchaser's premises, when the vendor is no longer in occupation. On a purely practical level, if the purchaser takes over physical occupation of the vendor's premises, there is sense in the purchaser being responsible for receipt and payment of debtors and creditors—although the practical point will never be determinative in itself. If the vendor retains ownership of the book debts (even if the purchaser receives them as his agent for discharge of the business) he will usually wish to make sure that any money received by the purchaser is held on trust for the vendor and ideally in a separate account, in order to reduce the risk to the vendor of any insolvency of the purchaser.

10.3.3   Prepayments and accruals

Where completion accounts are prepared, these will recognise apportionments of prepayments made by the vendor and accrued liabilities (eg in respect of employee remuneration, utilities etc) which the purchaser will often as a matter of convenience discharge. If there are no completion accounts to be prepared, vendor and purchaser will provide in the agreement for sale for an apportionment statement to be drawn up within a short period after completion. As with any acquisition, the purchaser will wish to ensure that the statement is drawn up on a basis that takes proper account of holiday pay liabilities, excess mileage charges, dilapidations and other similar amounts which may not accrue evenly and for which responsibility is transferred to the purchaser and the vendor also will wish to ensure that it receives proper credit for any prepayments, overriding discounts and other amounts which benefit the purchaser but which are referable in part to its own period of ownership.

10.3.4   Freehold and leasehold property

The agreement will need to specify and provide for the transfer of the property interests of the vendor in relation to the business. As there is legislation and established practice which affects the sale and purchase of property it is usual to include separate provisions relating to the property assets (*see* the Agreement for Sale (Assets), Sched 3 and 5 on pp 531 and 538). The following paragraphs consider the property provisions in the agreement for sale and the particular difficulty of landlord's consents in respect of leasehold property.

Property provisions in the agreement for sale

A contract for the sale or other disposition of an interest in land can only be made in writing signed by or on behalf of each party and only by incorporating all the terms which the parties have expressly agreed, either in one document or, where contracts are exchanged, in each. The terms may be set out in it or be incorporated by reference to some other document (Law of Property (Miscellaneous Provisions) Act 1989, s 2). Note that if terms are contained in side letter rather than in the contract, the whole contract for sale of the property, not merely the terms in the side letter, may be unenforceable.

In many respects, the properties can be sold on the same basis as on a conventional sale of property including the incorporation of the National Conditions of Sale (20th edn) with appropriate amendments, although it is also necessary to fit the sale of the property assets into the structure of the whole transaction. For example, on a conventional sale of property the insurance risk usually passes to the purchaser on exchange of contracts but this may not be the case on a sale of business assets where completion falls after exchange. The treatment of apportionments may also differ (*see above*).

The property sale provisions in the precedent Agreement for Sale (Assets) (at p 538 *et seq*) are contained in Sched 5 Parts I (freehold), II (leasehold) and III (creation of new leasehold interests, where the vendor is retaining any of its existing freehold or leasehold interests and simply granting a lease or underlease to the purchaser). Not all will apply to every transaction and appropriate amendments to Sched 5 should be made.

In all cases there will be provisions making it clear what each property is sold and each new lease is granted subject to (ie in the case of registered land, matters recorded in the registered title). It will usually be the case that the purchaser will have investigated title prior to exchange (*see p* 153) and the agreement will state that the purchaser is deemed to have accepted that title. Unlike a conventional property transaction it is not usual to leave title investigation to the interval between exchange and completion. The commercial aspects of the transaction will assume investigations are complete at exchange, or covered by warranty. The property provisions in the sale agreement will also deal with those matters for incorporation in the transfer or assignment, such as covenants to be given between the parties, the exclusion of the vendor's liability for breach of covenant in respect of repair (in the case of leasehold property) and variations to the covenants implied by the Law of Property (Miscellaneous Provisions) Act 1994 (*see p* 187).

Leasehold consents

For freeholds and long leasehold properties (eg 999 year leases where no landlord or third party consents are required for the transfer of the property) the relevant properties may be transferred to the purchaser on completion of the acquisition and the normal registration at the Land Registry will be made after completion.

For other leasehold properties the position is more difficult. In these cases the consent of the landlord (and sometimes also a superior landlord) is almost invariably required under the terms of the lease before any assignment or underletting to the purchaser can be made.

Timing difficulties are common. Confidentiality requirements of the vendor will often dictate that no application may be made to the relevant landlord for consent before exchange. The interval between exchange and completion (if any) is rarely sufficient to obtain relevant consents. As a result, it is usual to set out in some detail a mechanism to deal with the issue and the framework within which the vendor and purchaser may operate pending consent. Such a framework is set out in the Agreement for Sale (Assets), Sched 5, Parts II and III. A full commentary on such provisions is beyond the scope of this chapter. However, the following points are noteworthy.

As landlord's consent will often not be obtained by completion, it is usual to include provisions to cover the period between completion and obtaining consent, when the property can be transferred to the purchaser. The purchaser will wish to take over and run the business from completion of the acquisition and the agreement will provide for occupation by the purchaser, who is obliged to perform the covenants and other obligations on the part of the tenant under the lease and indemnify the vendor against any breach (Sched 5, Part II, para 10). It will not normally be appropriate for the purchaser to pay rent direct to the landlord since the purchaser will not be recognised as tenant by the landlord. The vendor should continue to pay rent, subject to the purchaser paying to the vendor a licence fee equal to the rent in advance of the normal rent payment dates. Note that a landlord is entitled to object to this arrangement since the vendor will be in breach of the covenant in the lease against parting with possession and there is a risk of the landlord taking action (eg forfeiture or injunction) against the vendor as tenant or the purchaser as unlawful occupier.

Also, the agreement should set out the arrangements for applying for landlord's consent, covering matters such as who is to make the application, what financial and other information about the purchaser is to be submitted to the landlord and whether guarantees are to be offered (Sched 5, Part II, para 6). It may prove more difficult to satisfy a landlord about the covenant of the purchaser if it is a newly formed company without a trading history, in which case other comfort will generally be required. If landlord's consent has not been obtained within a fixed period then it is usual to provide that application be made to the court for a declaration that the landlord is unreasonably withholding consent (Sched 5, Part II, para 6.7). Contemporaneously with, or as an alternative to, such an application the agreement may provide for the grant to the purchaser of an underlease in which case application will have to be made again to the landlord for its consent to the grant of the underlease, with equivalent provisions for an application for a court declaration. However, it will usually be more difficult for a landlord to object to the grant of an underlease to the purchaser than to an assignment to the purchaser since the landlord will retain the vendor as tenant. On the issue of refusal of consent to an assignment or the granting of an underlease *see* Stephen Tromans: *Commercial Leases* 2nd edn (Sweet & Maxwell, 1996) at p 183 *et seq*.

If landlord's consent to assignment or underlease is not obtained, even upon a court application, within any time limits set by the agreement the purchaser may, exceptionally, decide to take an assignment in breach of the terms of the lease. The parties will need to give very careful consideration to such a course of action since it will involve an assignment in breach of covenant for which the landlord will have remedies in circumstances where the landlord has already indicated he will not accept the purchaser as tenant. This is particularly important in relation to leases to which the Landlord and Tenant (Covenants) Act 1995 applies (broadly, those granted on or after 1 January 1996), because the mechanism by which the tenant is automatically released from his covenants on assignment does not operate where the tenant has assigned the lease in breach of covenant. Alternatively, the parties may decide that if the landlord's consent cannot be obtained then the relevant property should be excluded from the transaction and revert to the vendor. Since this will typically be some time after completion of the business acquisition it is obviously unattractive, but whether it is practicable will depend on the nature and significance of the property to the business.

As will be apparent, a great deal of care needs to be taken to identify the best approach to leasehold properties. The precedent Agreement for Sale (Assets) deals with the more usual approaches; alternative approaches may, of course, be appropriate to the circumstances of a particular transaction.

10.3.5 Fixed assets

Fixed assets are those tangible assets owned by the vendor and used in the target business to generate turnover and profit. Strictly, they include freehold and leasehold property as well as plant and machinery. A distinction is usually drawn between freehold and leasehold property interests and other fixed assets, since the terms of sale of interests in land will take into account normal conveyancing practices (*see above*).

The precedent agreement (at p 506) draws a distinction between 'immovable' fixed assets and 'movable' fixed assets. Such a distinction is not always made, or may not be relevant to the particular circumstances of the transaction, but reflects the possibility that certain fixed assets may have become affixed to, and are part of, the premises whereas others are separable and title will pass by delivery (*see also* cl 9.1(B) at p 515, which provides for severance). Movable fixed assets, such as vehicles or office equipment or computers, where title passes by delivery will not be subject to stamp duty. Immovable fixtures and fittings which form part of the premises will be stampable as part of the interests in land transferred (*see further* p 288).

Fixed assets used in the business may be owned by the vendor, or may be the subject of hire purchase, conditional sale or leasing agreements. These assets are excluded in the Agreement for Sale (Assets) from the definition of 'fixed assets' and instead it is provided that the vendor's interest in such assets are transferred to the purchaser by transfer of the contractual arrangements relating to them (*see p 209 below*). Although not strictly relevant to a discussion of fixed assets, it is worth noting the distinction which is drawn between an operating lease or contract hire arrangements under which, typically, higher rentals are paid and the economic interest in the asset is retained with the lessor, and a finance lease or hire purchase arrangement, where the economic risk and reward in respect of the asset rests with the lessee and the lease is merely an arrangement to finance the acquisition or use of the assets in question. The distinction is relevant where completion accounts are to be prepared and in particular where the purpose of those accounts is to adjust the purchase price by reference, *inter alia*, to the value of fixed assets acquired. Assets held under finance leases will, for accounting purposes, be treated as capital assets of the vendor. Assets subject to an operating lease would not appear in the balance sheet as a fixed asset. Thus for completion accounts purposes, where the net assets will be compared with net assets at an earlier date as shown in audited accounts, fixed assets to be included in the calculation of assets at completion should usually include assets subject to finance and hire purchase agreements, so as to ensure the accounts compare like with like. Rules for preparation of completion accounts should be checked with the purchaser's accountants.

Transfer of fixed assets does not typically require documentation. Certain assets will, however, require specific attention eg vehicles, where the contract should ensure that registration documents are delivered in order that the purchaser may notify DVLC of the change of ownership. The Agreement for Sale (Assets) provides for delivery of all relevant documents (cl 6.2(D) at p 512).

Fixed assets will, of course, include computer hardware, discussed further below (p 207).

10.3.6   Intellectual property

Even where the target business does not own or use registered intellectual property such as patents, trade marks or design rights it will be a rare acquisition of business assets which does not involve the transfer of some form of intellectual property interests to the purchaser. For example, businesses will generally have a copyright interest in their manuals and brochures. The precedent agreement (at p 506) offers a comprehensive description of such intellectual property interests.

Completion of the agreement will transfer title to intellectual property interests which are not registered, although it is not uncommon for the purchaser to require that a 'catch-all' assignment of unregistered intellectual property is delivered at completion. Registered intellectual property rights are by comparison easier to deal with because the registration system allows both the rights themselves and the proprietor to be easily identified. It should be remembered, however, that intellectual property rights are territorial and that registered rights are likely to be registered in each jurisdiction in which they are used. Non-registrable rights, such as copyright, unregistered design right and know-how, can be more difficult to identify and consequently protect and transfer.

The formalities for transferring intellectual property rights differ depending upon the right to be transferred. It is normal practice for separate transfer documents to be executed for each type of intellectual property right to be transferred. This is particularly important for registered rights as the transfer document will need to be presented to the appropriate registry. It will also be necessary to execute separate assignments for each country in which the rights are registered. It may be necessary, if the number of overseas registrations (for example) is too great, to rely on further assurance clauses for the execution of such documents. In such cases it is desirable to take a security power of attorney under the Powers of Attorney Act 1974, s 4 in order that the purchaser is able to ensure that such registrations occur. The appropriate United Kingdom Registry will require evidence that the transfer is duly stamped or that stamp duty is not due (*see further* p 289).

The following paragraphs deal with the common intellectual property rights: patents, trade marks, design rights, copyright and know-how.

Patents

Patents, applications for patents and rights under patents are all transferable under the Patents Act 1977, s 30. The 1977 Act provides that the transfer shall be by way of assignment which must be in writing and must be signed by both the vendor and the purchaser. In addition to the main acquisition agreement, it is normal for the vendor and purchaser to execute a separate form of patent assignment as this will need to be duly stamped and registered with the Patent Office in the United Kingdom and perhaps with registries outside the United Kingdom and avoids the need to register the entire acquisition agreement with the Patent Office. *See further* p 289 concerning the current approach of the Inland Revenue and Patent Office to the question of whether an assignment is duly stamped.

One form of assignment can be used to encompass existing patents, applications for patents and rights under patents (*see* the precedent assignment at Appendix X, p 659). Certain issues should be addressed expressly in the assignment eg the right to sue for previous infringements and to seek all available remedies. The assignment of an application must include the right to be registered as the owner of the patent. The purchaser should also require a further assurance undertaking as it will often require assistance in providing information or executing further documents for submission to the Patent Office. Also, the purchaser cannot sue for infringement until it has been registered as the new proprietor and in the interim will require the vendor to commence and pursue infringement actions on its behalf.

The purchaser should register the assignment as soon as possible after stamping. A subsequent purchaser from the vendor of the same rights will not necessarily be bound by the sale to the original purchaser if he had no actual knowledge of the first assignment or if no application had been made to register the first assignment with the Patent Office at the time of the second sale (it is possible to apply for registration before syamp duty has been paid, registration being conditional on payment). Also, if an infringement occurs after transfer of title, then under the Patents Act 1977, s 68 damages cannot be given for the period before the assignment is registered, unless it is registered within six months or the court or the comptroller is satisfied that registration was not practicable within that time.

Trade marks

Registered trade marks are transmissible by assignment under the Trade Marks Act 1994, s 24. A registered trade mark is transmissible either in connection with the goodwill of a business or independently. Trade mark assignments must be in writing but need be signed only by the assignor (vendor/proprietor). Unregistered trade marks are assignable either together with and at the same time as registered trade marks or separately provided that they are assigned with the goodwill of the business. A precedent assignment is included at Appendix XI, p 661.

As with patents it is important for the purchaser to register the assignment at the Trade Marks Registry in the United Kingdom as soon as possible. Under the Trade Marks Act 1994, s 25 until an application has been made for registration of the new proprietor as the owner of the mark, the transaction is ineffective as against a person acquiring a conflicting interest in or under the mark in ignorance of it. Also, as with patents, if an infringement occurs after transfer of title, damages or an account of profits cannot be given for the period before the assignment is registered unless the application for registration is made within six months or the court is satisfied that registration was not practicable within that period.

Design rights

Registered designs are assigned in writing and, like trade marks, the assignment need be signed only by the vendor. Only the registered proprietor of a design can sue for infringement and therefore the purchaser should ensure the assignment is registered at the Patent Office in the United Kingdom.

Section 19(3B) of the Registered Designs Act 1949 (as amended), provides that any assignment of a registered design is deemed automatically to assign the associated design right (where the proprietor of the registered design is also the design right owner) unless it is expressly excluded. Despite the wording of this provision it is questionable whether the associated design right can be split from the registered design as s 19(3A) of the 1949 Act provides that an interest in the registered design will not be registered unless the person entitled to that interest is also entitled to a corresponding interest in the design right. As a practical matter therefore, it appears that the design right can probably not be separated from the associated registered design. The provisions for transferring an unregistered design right are the same as for copyright (*see below*). One important point to note is that an assignment of an unregistered design right will be deemed also to assign any registered design that exists.

Copyright

Copyright is transmissible by assignment which, to be effective, must be in writing and signed by or on behalf of the assignor (Copyright, Designs and Patents Act 1988, s 90). One interesting aspect of copyright, when compared to other intellectual property rights, is that it is divisible and that an assignment may be partial. For instance, an author of a work may assign separately the right to copy the work and produce it as a cinema film or a theatre production.

As a practical matter a purchaser should always obtain a formal assignment of copyright rather than rely on the acquisition agreement. When drafting a copyright assignment it is important to identify accurately the copyright to be assigned. The purchaser is often advised to seek a general assignment of all of the vendor's copyright which also identifies specific known examples (this approach is taken in the precedent assignment at Appendix XII, p 665). The vendor will be keen to ensure that this approach does not encompass any copyright it is retaining for use in any retained business.

Know-how

Know-how (including trade secrets and confidential information) is not, strictly speaking, capable of assignment as it is not a property right *per se*. Know-how is the accumulated experience of the vendor and its employees in relation to a particular business. As know-how cannot be assigned formally, a purchaser should seek to obtain the exclusive benefit of the know-how by preventing others from using it and ensuring that all tangible records are within its possession. The purchaser should therefore seek disclosure of all relevant know-how, remembering that some know-how will transfer through the transfer of employees and so it should be checked that employment terms contain adequate confidentiality and restrictive covenant provisions. The purchaser's main protection comes through the use of restrictive covenants (*see* the Agreement for Sale (Assets) cl 10 at p 516 and *see further* Chapter 4).

Intellectual property agreements and licences

The preceding paragraphs deal with the assignment to the purchaser of intellectual property interests of the target business which are owned by the vendor. Alternatively, the vendor may enjoy the right under the terms of a licence granted in its favour. If rights are licensed to the vendor, the purchaser should ensure that the benefit of the licences will be assigned to it. This may require the consent of the licensor. The provisions described below, in relation to contracts, will represent a framework for the assignment of licences to the purchaser. If the right to use intellectual property is fundamental to the business the purchaser should consider whether such consent should be obtained prior to exchange of contracts or as a condition precedent to completion of the acquisition.

The purchaser should also inspect the terms of agreements under which the vendor has licensed its own technology or other intellectual property rights of the business to a third party. Sale of the right (eg trade mark or patent) as part of the business assets may, on occasion, be fettered (eg requiring consent of the licensee) if significant licences have been granted.

Shared rights

It is not uncommon for a transaction to produce a situation where both the vendor and purchaser wish to make use of the same intellectual property rights in their respective businesses. In such a situation it will be necessary to decide how the interest in the rights in question can be shared between the parties. The common approach is for the parties to agree who, as between themselves, should own the right and who should have the benefit of a non-exclusive, and possibly royalty-free, licence to use the intellectual property right. As a practical matter the licensee should ensure that his continued use of the right is adequately protected through the terms of the licence. Often the owner of the right will have primary responsibility for maintaining and renewing the right and ensuring that appropriate action is taken against those that infringe the right.

10.3.7 Goodwill

Goodwill is an intangible asset which represents the ability of the target business to generate a return from its identifiable assets. In accounting terms, goodwill represents the difference in value between the aggregate value of the individual identifiable net assets and their 'market' value—that is to say the price a third party might be willing to pay for them.

It is usual for the agreement for the sale of business assets to provide for the purchaser to acquire the goodwill of the business in addition to the tangible assets of the vendor in relation to the business. Goodwill manifests itself in the form of reputation, name, market position, the quality of customer lists and customer relations, staff relations and a variety of other intangible assets. Acquisition of goodwill is particularly important where intellectual property (notably trade marks) is to be transferred, (*see further* the discussion of intellectual property *above*). The purchaser will wish to acquire goodwill so that, if the purchaser has a claim against the vendor for breach of warranty or for some other breach of the acquisition agreement, it may be compensated not only for tangible loss, but also for the damage caused to the goodwill of the business and other intangibles acquired. It will also be important in the context of enforcing a restrictive covenant or an intellectual property right. Save for goodwill transferred with trade marks, goodwill will be transferred by completion of the agreement for sale, although it is often also the subject of a separate, express assignment. To mitigate an immediate charge to stamp duty it is common to execute the agreement and any assignment of goodwill outside the United Kingdom. *See further* Chapter 12 at p 291.

10.3.8 Computer hardware and software

Virtually all businesses will operate computer equipment and software. The extent and complexity of these operations will be governed by the nature of the business and the size of the organisation operating it. Whether or not the purchaser acquires the vendor's computer systems or merely requires the data (ie having its own systems to which data can be transferred and which are otherwise sufficient to support the business) will depend on the circumstances. Usually, the acquisition will involve the parties agreeing to transfer some computer assets or software rights.

Hardware

The vendor is likely to have some equipment that it owns (which will transfer as part of the fixed assets) and some which it leases or is the subject of hire purchase or conditional sale arrangements. Transfer of hardware subject to any such contractual arrangements will be subject to the provisions in the sale agreement for the transfer of contracts (*see below*). The support and maintenance of the equipment will probably be the subject of a separate contractual arrangement which would be transferred in a similar way. Computers and peripherals may be linked together in a network. The cabling which facilitates this form of network will often be owned outright by the vendor and will consequently transfer as part of the fixed assets. In some instances, particularly where more sophisticated and expensive ISDN and fibre optic cabling is used, the vendor may have the benefit of separate maintenance arrangements and ordinarily these too will be subject to the provisions in the agreement for the transfer of contracts (*see below*). Fixed communications routes will usually be owned by a third party such as a telecommunications provider and be subject to separate contractual arrangements, which may similarly require transfer to the purchaser.

Software

Computer software will be the subject of copyright, as it is considered a literary work. Consequently the right to use computer software cannot usually be assigned to the purchaser without the consent of the copyright owner. The formalities for transferring copyright are dealt with above and the approach described there will be appropriate where the vendor itself owns all rights in computer software which is to be transferred. This is relatively uncommon except perhaps, where the software has been developed by an employee when it should be checked, for avoidance of doubt, that the rights belong to the employer, not the employee. However, it is more likely that some, or possibly all, of the software used by the vendor will be used under licence from a third party proprietor. The vendor's ability to transfer the benefit of such a licence will depend upon its terms, which in turn may depend upon whether the software is bespoke specialised software (eg developed specifically for the target business) or off-the-shelf PC software. The approach to assignment of the benefit of such licences will be the same as that for other contracts, described below. Users of software often take out software support agreements with either the original supplier or a third party support organisation. These too will be subject to the provisions described below dealing with the transfer of the benefit of contracts.

Shared facilities

Particular difficulties arise when the business to be acquired has been part of a group where there are group computing functions (eg accounting). The main computing resources are likely to be retained by the group. If the purchaser needs to put in place its own independent arrangements for the target business this will often take some time and can involve considerable expense and in the short term it may be a practical necessity for the purchaser to continue to receive computing services for the target business from the vendor (such an arrangement is also common on the sale of a corporate target). The formal arrangements which will need to be put in place should detail amongst other things the levels of service and support that will be available for the duration of the arrangements. Where the software is licensed from third parties the vendor will need to procure the right to use that software on behalf of the purchaser in respect of the target business. Not surprisingly, the software licensor may seek to extract an additional licence fee in respect of the newly separated user. To ensure appropriate maintenance can be carried out on the software both the vendor and the newly separated target business will need access to the underlying source code. This may require amendment to software escrow arrangements (if any).

Data protection

One consequence of using computers and storing personal records electronically is data protection. If the acquisition involves the transfer of data which is subject to a data protection registration then the purchaser will need to put in place its own registration. It is possible to apply for registration prior to transfer of the data in order to avoid breaching any of the data protection principles or the provisions of the Data Protection Act 1984 and if the purchaser is not already registered (or its registration does not encompass the information to be transferred to it) it should obtain registration prior to completion. (Note that a broader regime for data protection is contemplated by the EU Directive on data protection, although it is not required to be implemented by member states until October 1998).

10.3.9 Contracts

A vendor will have in place a variety of contractual arrangements in relation to the target business, some or all of which will pass to the purchaser as part of the acquisition. The purchaser will wish to take on those contractual arrangements which are necessary for it to be able to operate the target business independently from the vendor. Contractual arrangements will range from the supply of utilities through to the supply, distribution and sales arrangements of the vendor in relation to the business, and will include any leasing or hire purchase arrangements applicable to fixed assets as well as intellectual property and software licensing arrangements. The vendor's financing arrangements are also part of its contractual matrix, although it is rare for these to transfer to a purchaser of business assets.

Which contracts the purchaser will take on as part of the acquisition will be for negotiation and will depend on the circumstances. If the purchaser has no other similar business itself, it may agree to take on the whole of the vendor's outstanding contractual arrangements in relation to the target business. If the purchaser has an existing business which it is combining with the target business, there may be contracts (eg supply and distribution arrangements) in which it has no interest because it already has its own arrangements in place. In such a case the purchaser may prefer not to take on certain contracts, although leaving them behind with the vendor may cause practical difficulties as the vendor will need to negotiate their termination, possibly with payment of compensation to the other contracting party. Whether the purchaser is to take all or only some of the contracts, it should endeavour to specify clearly those it does agree to assume, preferably by listing all such contracts or, at the very least, the most important arrangements. If only some contracts are to be taken on, the concern will be that important contracts will be left behind. If all contracts are assumed, the purchaser may inadvertently agree to take on responsibility for contracts it does not want. In either case, the warranties in the sale agreement will need to support the purchaser's approach. In the first instance, the warranties should provide that the 'Contracts' (ie those to be assumed) include all material contracts relating to the business (*see* the Agreement for Sale (Assets), warranty 2.8(A)(4) on p 574) and in each case the warranties will need to assure the purchaser that it is not acquiring 'onerous' contracts (*see* warranty 2.8(A)(6) on p 574). The purchaser should consider whether contracts it agrees to take on should include outstanding offers or tenders and the definitions should say so (usually, they will). It will note that contracts may be oral and that terms may not always be clear where they are reflected in a course of dealing or competing 'standard terms'. Again, it will be important that the warranties require disclosure of material terms, whether written or not.

In theory, the transfer of contractual arrangements from vendor to purchaser could be fraught with difficulties; contracts may not be freely assignable and it will be noted that only the benefit, not the burden, of a contract is assignable. In practice, problems arise relatively infrequently and the most common problem is the counterparty to a non-assignable contract or licence seeking to extract a fee, or to renegotiate terms, for its consent to assignment and allowing the purchaser to continue to benefit from the contractual right or licence. This is particularly so in the case of computer licensing arrangements (*see p 207 above*) and occasionally, asset leasing arrangements. Where such contracts exist, the purchaser should consider whether it is willing to proceed to completion without such consent having been obtained. If the purchaser does accept some risk of problems with consents, it is wise nonetheless for the parties to provide for the possibility that the counterparty may seek a fee for its consent to assignment and certainly be clear who will be responsible for paying any such sum (eg the vendor). Alternatively it may be appropriate to hold back part of the consideration until consent is obtained, although in the case of important contracts a mere adjustment to the consideration if consent is not given will be inadequate if the business cannot function without the benefit of the right in question: for example, consent to the transfer of trade mark licences may be fundamental if the trade marks are central to the business to be acquired. Making completion conditional on consents will be the only practical solution in such cases.

In practice the purchaser will identify those contracts which are of particular significance to the ongoing business and consider whether consent to assignment or novation (if required) should be obtained prior to, or as a condition of, completion. Even if consent is not required the purchaser may decide that, where a key contract is terminable at will or on a short period of notice, that it is desirable to seek the counterparty's agreement that the contract will not be terminated after the business has changed hands. Where a formal assignment is not obtained the purchaser will rely on the relevant provisions in the agreement for sale providing for the benefit of contracts to be transferred to him.

The following paragraphs consider first, issues associated with the assignment of the benefit of the contracts, and second, the manner in which the purchaser will take on the burden of performing the outstanding contracts. In practice, of course, most contracts will comprise an amalgam of benefit and burden and both issues will be relevant.

Benefit

The benefit, but not the burden, of a contract may be assigned. Whether or not the benefit of a particular contract may be assigned will depend on its nature and terms. A contract which is 'personal' in nature, or which involves personal confidence where the identity of (eg) the transferor (vendor) is important, cannot be assigned so that the other contracting party becomes bound to the transferee/purchaser without its consent. A contract of employment is one example of such a contract although the transfer of such contracts is subject to the provisions of the Transfer of Undertakings (Protection of Employment) Regulations 1981 (*see* Chapter 6).

Contracts containing an express prohibition on assignment are similarly incapable of binding the other contracting party to any purported assignment between vendor and purchaser (*Linden Gardens Trust Ltd v Lenesta Sludge Disposals Ltd* [1994] 1 AC 85, HL) and assignment in breach of contract. Where a contract is expressly or impliedly non-assignable, assignment without consent will not confer any rights on the purchaser against the other contracting party, although it will not affect the rights between transferor and transferee and if the transferor has contracted to assign the benefit of a contract to the transferee it will be in breach if it fails to do so. If assignment is not permitted it may be possible for the vendor to sub-contract rights under the contract to the purchaser. However, it should be noted that contracts which prohibit assignment will very often also expressly prohibit sub-contracting, for example where the contract concerned is a licence to use intellectual property.

Whether or not formal consent to the assignment is required, it is usual to give notice of change of ownership of the business and, in consequence, of assignment of the benefit of contracts. The purchaser will notify customers and suppliers at completion (the sale agreement will often require that such a notice is to be agreed with the vendor (*see* the Agreement for Sale (Assets), cl 17.1, on p 524). It is prudent that the purchaser gives such notice. The mere fact that the purchaser, rather than the vendor, owns the business after completion will not always be effective notice, since the purchaser will often carry on the business in the same name and using the same employees as used by the vendor. It should be noted that the purchaser cannot acquire a better right against the other party to the contract than the vendor and will take subject to rights that counterparty has against the vendor arising out of the same contract. If, however, the counterparty has rights against the vendor arising out of some arrangement other than the assigned contract it cannot set up those rights as a defence against the purchaser in relation to its obligations under the assigned contract once it has received notice of the assignment. Written notice of assignment under Law of Property Act 1925, s 136(1) will give effect to the assignment of the benefit of the contract at law and entitle the purchaser to bring action against the other contracting party in its own name.

Burden

The burden of a contract cannot be assigned and the vendor will need to ensure that the sale agreement contains an effective mechanism for the purchaser to take on and perform the vendor's obligations, failing which it is likely to find itself in breach of its obligations to perform the contract—having sold the business to the purchaser it is unlikely itself to have the assets or employees to perform the contract. There are (limited) exceptions to this rule: an assignee of the benefit of a contract is in effect bound by the burden where the performance or observance of a burden or restriction is a condition of receiving the benefit of the contract, and certain obligations may fall within the so-called 'pure' principle of benefit and burden. In such case the purchaser would be obliged to discharge the burden or, if it fails to do so, forgo the benefit. Such contracts are exceptional and whether or not a contract can be analysed in this way depends on whether the obligation is truly conditional to the benefit or whether it is an independent obligation which the parties agree is one by which the purchaser will be bound *(Tito v Waddell (No 2)* [1977] Ch 106). The transfer of the burden to the purchaser in this way is the exception and in practice the vendor will wish to ensure that the agreement for sale requires that the purchaser observes the restrictions and performs the obligations in a contract so that the vendor will not be liable for any breach by the purchaser and, to the extent possible, will also require the purchaser to become bound to the other party.

The simplest way of transferring contractual rights and responsibilities to the purchaser is by novation of the contract, whereby the purchaser becomes directly responsible to the other contracting party in the place of the vendor, who is wholly or partly released. Novation plainly requires the agreement of the other party to release the vendor and in practice a formal novation is rare. Instead the purchaser will simply perform the contract after completion in accordance with the terms of the sale agreement and the analysis of the transfer will depend on the circumstances. As the purchaser and the other contracting party will continue to have dealings it may be possible to infer consent to the arrangement, or even to a novation. However, because the burden of contracts cannot be assigned to the purchaser and as alternatives where the benefit of a contract is non-assignable, it is standard practice to include in the agreement for sale alternatives if assignment or novation, both of which require the consent of the other contracting party, is ineffective to transfer rights and responsibilities to the purchaser. These typically provide, eg, that the vendor sub-contracts performance of the contract to the purchaser, with the vendor holding the benefit of the contract on trust for the purchaser. The purchaser indemnifies the vendor for any breaches of contract as a result of the purchaser's performance after completion. Such vicarious performance is an effective solution for many contracts where there is to be transferred to the purchaser the burden of performance. However, whether sub-contracting, or vicarious performance, of a contract is possible is subject to similar considerations to those which apply on assignment of contract.

If novation, assignment or sub-contracting, or vicarious performance is not possible, then the agreement for sale will often contemplate that the purchaser will perform the contract at the vendor's direction and hold the benefit of the contract for the purchaser, with appropriate indemnities which provide that the risk and reward in respect of that arrangement for the period after completion falls on the purchaser. Whether this will be permitted will depend on the contract. In practice, such a provision would obviously mean that the vendor would need to use the purchaser's or some other staff in order to effect such performance. The parties will wish to take care that any such arrangement will not effectively breach the contract.

The Agreement for Sale (Assets), cl 7.2 at p 513 contains mechanisms to deal with the transfer of contracts. Where there is risk of breach, it may be necessary to modify or expand the provisions.

10.3.10   Employees

See Chapter 6 for a consideration of the transfer of employees in the context of an acquisition of business assets and Chapter 7 in relation to pensions.

10.3.11   Third party rights

The Agreement for Sale (Assets) at p 508 includes 'third party rights' among the assets to be acquired by the purchaser, being rights of the vendor against third parties arising out of the conduct of the business. The object is to transfer to the purchaser the benefit of any warranty or other claims that are associated with, and which it may need to pursue in relation to, the assets that it acquires. The definition needs to be carefully drafted so as to transfer to the purchaser any benefit of any rights that are associated with the assets (and any liabilities) which it acquires (or agrees to assume) but so that it does not acquire a right against a third party to bring an action in relation to a matter where the economic risk in relation to that matter has been left with the vendor.

10.3.12   Release of charges

A search at Companies Registration Office will have been conducted against the vendor at an early stage (*see* Chapter 9 at p 135). The search will reveal those mortgages and charges registered against the vendor under Companies Act 1985, s 395. The practitioner should ensure that any such mortgages and charges are released at completion or, in the case of a floating charge, that satisfactory evidence from the charge holder that it has not crystallised is delivered. Although the search may not reveal any charges which have recently been created and which may still be registered, the prudent practitioner will refresh the searches immediately prior to completion.

10.3.13   Taxation

As an almost invariable rule an acquisition of business assets will be on terms that the vendor retains responsibility for its own taxation liability in relation to the target business, and the purchaser does not assume any responsibility for that tax liability. Equally, unless otherwise agreed the purchaser will not acquire benefit of the right to claim any tax reliefs or rebates that the vendor may be entitled to in relation to the business. The taxation treatment of an acquisition of business assets is considered in Chapter 12.

10.3.14   Liabilities (other than trade creditors)

As a general rule, an acquisition of business assets will not involve the purchaser agreeing to assume responsibility for discharging the liabilities of the vendor in relation to the business. Indeed, the fact that the liabilities of the business remain the responsibility of the vendor as a matter of law is often a driving force behind the choice of an assets rather than a share structure, particularly where there is some doubt over the financial substance of the vendor and its ability to meet responsibilities it would assume on a share sale (eg under warranties and indemnities). Accordingly, the agreement for sale will typically include a clause providing that the vendor will be responsible for, and will discharge, all liabilities of the business that relate to the period prior to completion, and not uncommonly a clause under which the purchaser agrees with the vendor to be responsible for debts and liabilities that are attributable to the period after completion. For the sake of completeness, there is typically provision for the vendor to indemnify the purchaser in relation to any liability the purchaser suffers in respect of the period prior to completion and vice versa. A particular difficulty emerges for the purchaser where, as a practical matter, it is not responsible for and has not assumed responsibility for liabilities of the business for the period prior to completion, yet in order to preserve the goodwill of the business that it has acquired, it is minded to settle claims and disputes with its customers. This is particularly so where there is an ongoing arrangement with customers and the customer seeks to offset a pre-completion claim that it has against the vendor, against its liability to pay the purchaser for a supply made after completion; even though the purchaser is not liable for the vendor's default the practical situation is that the purchaser may not be able to ignore the dispute if there is a risk to its relations with the customer. The purchaser will seek to make it clear in the agreement for sale that if it needs to discharge such liabilities in order to preserve good business relations with its customers, it should be able to do so and then recover from the vendor under the indemnity clauses. It is a matter for negotiation whether the vendor will agree to this.

A different problem arises for the vendor, where it is bound to discharge liabilities of the business in relation to the period prior to completion, but has no means of doing so. For example, if it has made supplies in relation to which it has given warranties prior to completion and the goods supplied are defective, it may have no means of remedying defects after completion (having sold the business) other than with the help of the purchaser. In such circumstances, it is not uncommon for the agreement for sale to provide that the purchaser will assist in discharging the vendor's liability under third party warranty claims (eg by remedying the defect or replacing the item in question) at the vendor's cost. It is usual to specify the terms, including a time limit, on which the purchaser will assist.

10.3.15   Risk and insurance

The benefits of contracts of insurance are generally not capable of assignment without the consent of the insurer. It is unusual for the purchaser to take over the vendor's insurances and instead the business and assets will generally be added to the purchaser's own insurances, or it will take out new policies.

On an acquisition of business assets, risk in the assets transferred will typically transfer to the purchaser on the effective date of the business transfer. Where signing, completion and the effective date are simultaneous, this is straightforward. Where completion and transfer of risk falls after exchange, then the position is more complicated because it is necessary to determine who is on risk in the intervening period and to ensure that the necessary insurance cover is, or continues, in place. While the purchaser will usually have an insurable interest so as to enable it to take out its own insurances from exchange the exact position depends on who is to bear the economic risk of uninsured losses between signing and completion. There is little point in duplicating cover where the vendor's insurances are adequate and what commonly happens in practice is that the purchaser's interest is noted on the vendor's policies, and the vendor is under an obligation to maintain the policies until completion when the assets will become covered by the purchaser's own, or new, policies. Where there are already outstanding insurance claims eg in respect of assets which are to be transferred to the purchaser, the parties will need to decide whether the benefit of the claims (eg the proceeds) should accrue to the purchaser or whether it simply pays less for the asset, with the vendor retaining its rights to pursue the outstanding claim.

Whatever route is proposed, parties seeking to preserve the benefit of insurance should ensure that the benefits of the insurance and the liabilities for which it provides cover are at all times vested in the same person, failing which the insured may have no insurable interest, and the policy would lapse.

The insurance position is more complicated where the purchaser assumes responsibilities for liabilities which are themselves insured. In such case the purchaser should ensure that the responsibility it takes on is after recovery under the vendor's insurances, to the extent relevant.

10.3.16   Records

The purchaser should ensure that he specifies in the sale agreement that he is acquiring all the records of the vendor in relation to the business and the assets acquired. If only part of the vendor's business is sold, the vendor will wish to retain many of the records. Statutory books such as the register of members and minute books will be retained by the vendor in any event. Otherwise, the purchaser will require all documents of title, customer lists, staff records (to the extent they are not required by law to be retained by the vendor) accounting records, computer records, PAYE, national insurance records and any other records, documents and information necessary to enable the purchaser to run the business. VAT records will be transferred automatically with the business where it is transferred as a going concern (Value Added Tax Act 1994, s 49) unless the vendor successfully claims that it should retain these (*see further* p 291). Subject to necessity and mutual obligations of confidentiality, the agreement should contain rights of access to the other party to records handed over or retained. *See* the Agreement for Sale, cl 9.2(B) at p 513.

10.3.17   Stationery and trade names

It is fairly typical for promotional and other material to be handed over at completion and used up by the purchaser within an agreed period but, even if the purchaser is to use the same business/company name as the vendor, the purchaser will need to ensure that with effect from completion it identifies its own details on any letterhead of the vendor (which will show the incorporation details of the vendor in accordance with Companies Act 1985, s 349). It will be particularly important that the purchaser's own (new) VAT number appears on any invoices which are delivered from completion, even if as a practical matter it uses up the vendor's supply of invoices in relation to the business.

Supplies of packaging for goods should also, as far as practicable, evidence that the purchaser, not the vendor, has supplied any goods. It is an offence under the Trade Descriptions Act 1968 to apply a misdescription in relation to the sale of goods, which would include using packaging which refers to the vendor (rather than the purchaser) as manufacturer (one solution which can assist in such circumstances is to effect a name swap at completion). In practice, difficulties can usually be sorted out with the local Trading Standards Office if the issue is of serious concern (eg there is a large volume of packaging which it will take time to use up). Obviously it is unsatisfactory to discard large volumes of stationery or packaging unless it cannot be avoided. If that is the only solution, the purchaser will wish to make sure that he does not pay for it as part of the stock.

Chapter 11

Acquisitions by a Listed Company

The requirements of the London Stock Exchange are set out in *The Admission of Securities to Listing* (the *Yellow Book*). The *Yellow Book* contains the listing rules made under Part IV of the Financial Services Act 1986, and reflects five EC directives: the Admission Directive, the Listing Particulars Directive, the Interim Reports Directive, the Major Shareholding Directive and the Public Offers Directive. These directives lay down, among other things, minimum requirements for the admission of securities to listing; the content, scrutiny and publication of listing particulars as a condition of admission to listing; the continuing obligations of issuers after admission and the requirements for publication of a prospectus when transferable securities are offered to the public.

The directives make provision for the competent authority in each member state to impose additional requirements for these purposes. The London Stock Exchange is the competent authority appointed under the Financial Services Act 1986. The Exchange has delegated most of its functions as competent authority to the Quotations Committee and the Listings Department.

The requirements concerning acquisitions or realisations of assets by listed companies and their subsidiaries arise from the continuing obligations which a listed company owes to its shareholders and which are set out in the *Yellow Book*, Chapters 9 to 16. The requirements relating to transactions involving acquisitions and realisations by a company any class of whose securities are listed are set out in Chapter 10 of the *Yellow Book* and in the case of transactions with related parties, Chapter 11. Additional requirements apply for special categories of listed companies, such as property and scientific research-based companies (*Yellow Book*, Chapters 18–21). The summary given in this Chapter concentrates on the requirements in relation to the purchaser. The regulations apply to the acquisition and disposal of assets of all kinds, but, in the context of this book, the comment in this Chapter is limited to the acquisition of companies and businesses. This Chapter does not consider in any detail the requirement for full listing particulars. It should be noted, however, that listing particulars will be required if shares are to be issued which will increase shares of a class already listed by 10 per cent or more, or if listed debt securities of any amount are to be issued and in certain circumstances eg where listing particulars or where reports on any matter are required (such as working capital), the purchaser will require a sponsor to advise in connection with the transaction. If the company is applying for listing of its securities which are to be offered to the public in the United Kingdom for the first time a prospectus is required under the Financial Services Act 1986, s 144(2) although for this purpose, the content and procedures are essentially the same as for publication of listing particulars (*Yellow Book*, para 5.1(d); as to unlisted securities *see further* p 250). In other cases where additional shares are to be issued, in connection with an acquisition a notice is required under Rule 5.28 of the *Yellow Book*. The circular, if required, will normally suffice. Listing particulars may be included within any circular which is required to be published. The *Yellow Book* contains extensive rules regarding the content of listing particulars, which are beyond the scope of this book.

11.1   Classes of acquisition

Transactions are divided into four classes for the purpose of the listing rules: 'Super Class 1' and Classes 2 and 3, each of which are classified according to their relative size; in addition 'related party' transactions fall within the scope of the Exchange's requirements. If the acquisition is Super Class 1 it will be necessary for the purchaser to make an announcement to the Companies Announcements Office of the Exchange (CAO), to send a circular to shareholders, and to obtain approval of the transaction by the passing of an ordinary resolution in general meeting (para 10.37). A Class 2 transaction requires an announcement, but no circular or meeting, and a Class 3 transaction does not require announcement or circular unless all or part of the consideration is to be satisfied by the issue of securities for which listing is being sought, in which case an announcement must be made (para 10.29). Deciding into which class the acquisition falls involves a comparison between the purchaser and the target, whereas related party transactions are those which involve a 'related party'. Related parties are: a past (eg within the previous 12 months) or present director or a past or present substantial shareholder (*see further* p 232) and if the transaction is with a related party it will generally be necessary to obtain shareholder approval. If the transaction is so large as to amount to a reverse takeover, shareholder approval of the purchaser will normally be required and the purchaser will normally be treated as a new applicant for listing (*see further* p 231).

11.1.1   Super Class 1

Transactions are classified by their size and by reference to the percentage ratios referred to in Chapter 10, para 10.5 of the *Yellow Book*. The transaction will be Super Class 1 where any of the following comparisons gives rise to a percentage ratio of 25 per cent or more:

(a) *assets:* the net assets the subject of the transaction divided by the net assets of the purchaser. Net assets of the purchaser means the aggregate of its share capital and reserves (excluding minority interests). Where the transaction involves the acquisition of an interest in an undertaking (as defined in Companies Act 1985, s 259(1)) which gives rise to consolidation of the target, the 'net assets the subject of the transaction' means the value of 100 per cent of the target's net assets even if a lesser interest is acquired. If the transaction would not give rise to consolidation then, if it is an asset acquisition the 'net assets the subject of the transaction' is taken to be equal to the consideration or, if greater, the book value of the assets. The Exchange may require adjustments to the calculation of net assets to be acquired in certain circumstances, for example to ascribe value to an indemnity arrangement (*see* p 236) or to exclude liabilities which form part of the consideration;

(b) *profits:* the profits attributable to the net assets the subject of the transaction divided by the profits of the purchaser. Profits are calculated after deducting all charges except taxation and extraordinary items. As under the assets comparison, where the target is an undertaking which will be consolidated, 100 per cent of its profits are included in the calculation, whether or not a lesser interest is to be acquired;

(c) *consideration to assets:* the consideration divided by the net assets of the purchaser. Consideration in the form of securities is calculated by reference to their aggregate market value before the announcement. The consideration will generally be the amount to be paid but the Exchange may require other amounts to be treated as part of the consideration, for example, where the purchaser has agreed to discharge liabilities of the vendor. If part of the consideration is to be deferred (for example as an 'earn out'), the maximum amount must be used in the calculation and if there is no maximum, the transaction will normally be treated as Super Class 1, irrespective of the classification into which it would otherwise fall;

(d) *consideration to market capitalisation:* the consideration divided by the aggregate market value of all the equity shares of the purchaser (calculated by reference to their value at the close of business on the last day immediately preceding the announcement);

(e) *gross capital:* the gross capital of the target company or business divided by the gross capital of the purchaser. 'Gross' capital for this purpose is calculated by aggregating the shares and debt securities of the purchaser at their aggregate market value before the announcement if available or otherwise at their nominal value, all other liabilities (other than current liabilities and including for this purpose minority interests and deferred taxation), and the excess of current liabilities over current assets. Gross capital of the target is calculated similarly, save that the value of the consideration payable is taken instead of the share and debt capital at market value, and there is also added, in the case of a corporate target, the value of any of its shares and debt securities not acquired.

If the transaction is Super Class 1 only because of the 'consideration to assets' comparison it will be treated as Class 2 if all other comparisons give, in each case, a percentage ratio for the transaction of 22.5 per cent or less or, in the case of an acquisition where at least 90 per cent of the consideration is in the form of equity shares, 25 per cent or less (para 10.22). The Exchange will need to be kept informed if the percentage ratios change after first discussions with the Exchange and before announcement. The usual procedure for clearing class tests with the Exchange is for the company's advisers to submit, at an early stage, a formal letter setting out the class test calculations and requesting confirmation from the Exchange. Note that the class test letter must be updated and resubmitted at the date of approval of any circular.

For comparison purposes net assets and profits are based on the latest published audited consolidated accounts or a published preliminary statement of annual results if the purchaser has, or will have by the time terms of the transaction are agreed, published such a statement. Half-year results may be included if the purchaser publishes a balance sheet with its half-year results, provided it confirms in writing to the Exchange that the balance sheet has been prepared in accordance with the Company's accounting policies and practices, and that the results have been reviewed by the Company's auditors whose findings have been discussed with its audit committee (para 10.19). Net assets may be adjusted to take account of transactions since the latest accounts or half-year results for which information has already been published.

The Exchange may require the transaction to be aggregated with other transactions in the previous 12 months, for the purpose of classification. This will usually occur only if it is entered into with the same or a series of connected parties, if it relates to an acquisition of securities in the same target or, together, such acquisitions lead to the purchaser having substantial involvement in a business activity which did not previously form part of its business activities. In such a case the latest transaction may be treated as falling within Super Class 1 even though, alone, it may not do so (paras 10.25 and 10.26).

There are special rules for property companies and mineral companies and if the transaction involves the acquisition by any listed company of an unlisted property company, valuations will be required (Chapter 18).

11.1.2 Class 2

A Class 2 transaction is one where the relevant percentage ratios amount to 5 per cent or more but each of which is less than 25 per cent.

11.1.3 Class 3

A Class 3 transaction is one where the percentage ratios are less than 5 per cent.

11.1.4 Reverse takeover

A reverse takeover will arise where any of the comparisons give rise to a percentage ratio of 100 per cent or more or would result in a fundamental change in the business of the listed company or a change in board or voting control of the purchaser. However, the Exchange will allow the transaction to be treated as Super Class 1 if the target is of a similar size to the purchaser and in a similar line of business, if the enlarged group is suitable for listing and if there will be no change of board or voting control (para 10.21).

If the transaction does not fall within this exception and will give rise to a reverse takeover, the Exchange will, upon announcement, suspend the listing of the company's securities. A Super Class 1 circular, requiring approval of the purchaser's shareholders in general meeting, will be required and listing particulars must be prepared and published as if the company was a new applicant, with certain modification. If the transaction is approved and proceeds, the old listing will be cancelled and a new listing must be sought for the combined group and following the publication of listing particulars, the listing will normally be restored.

11.1.5 Announcements

An announcement to the Company Announcements Office will be required in any case where all or part of the consideration for the acquisition is satisfied by the issue of securities of the purchaser for which listing is being sought. Otherwise, an announcement will be required only if the transaction is Super Class 1 or Class 2 or a related party transaction.

Announcements should be provided to the CAO for release to the market, and should include the following information:
(a) particulars of the target, including its name;
(b) a description of the business carried on;
(c) the consideration, explaining how this is being satisfied, including the terms of any arrangements for deferred consideration;
(d) the value of the net assets of the target which are the subject of the transaction;
(e) the net profits attributable to the target;
(f) the benefits which are expected to accrue to the purchaser as a result of the

transaction;

(g)   details of any service contracts of proposed directors of the purchaser.

When an announcement is not required but the purchaser wishes to make one, the announcement should include either details of the consideration or the value of the assets being acquired. Any announcement about the transaction, however small, which does not state the value of the consideration or indicate the size of the transaction may mislead shareholders.

An announcement should be made without delay after terms have been agreed (usually upon exchange of contracts). The listed company has a general obligation to notify major new developments which are not public knowledge and which may lead to a substantial movement in share price, subject to exceptions for transactions in the course of negotiation where the information is restricted to defined classes of individual or certain bodies (eg the MMC) who are made aware of its confidentiality. If there are leaks or there is the possibility of a false market a warning announcement will be appropriate (paras 9.1–9.5).

11.1.6   Circulars

A circular to shareholders will be required if the transaction is Super Class 1 or is with a related party. The content requirements differ depending on which of these categories the transaction falls within and, so far as they relate to acquisition circulars (as opposed to a circular involving the issue of securities), are set out below. An important point to note is that a Super Class 1 circular requires an indebtedness statement and a working capital statement which must in each case cover the target company. These take time to produce and the timetable for the transaction should take them into account—in particular the working capital statement must be accompanied by a letter from the sponsor (para 2.14) who will also need to be satisfied as to the availability of working capital. The indebtedness statement must be given as at a date not earlier than 42 days prior to publication of the circular. Companies will usually wish that the date coincides with their normal (eg month end) reporting cycles. In addition to the *Yellow Book* contents requirements, Super Class 1 and related party circulars will contain a notice of meeting and Super Class 1 circulars will often contain an open offer to shareholders where the consideration for the acquisition is shares (*see* p 241).

The Department's formal approval to the final form of a Super Class 1 circular is required in advance, and drafts of the circular should be submitted as soon as possible through the company's brokers. The same applies to related party transaction circulars. Class 2 or 3 announcements do not require prior approval. Where securities are being issued as consideration for an acquisition, listing will not normally be granted until the circular has been published (para 7.2).

To obtain the Exchange's formal approval, a number of documents may be required, as specified by the *Yellow Book* (*see* para 14.2) including, for example, letters from the sponsor in relation to a Super Class 1 transaction that no accountant's report is required (if that is so), and as to sufficiency of working capital and, where shares are to be issued without the publication of a prospectus, a letter from the issuer to the Exchange with confirmation to the effect that no prospectus is required (para 7.7(b)). Three copies of the circular and related documents must be submitted to the Exchange at least 14 days prior to the intended publication date (para 14.3). The company's brokers (or sponsor, if one is required; para. 2.3) will usually submit the documents, which may subsequently be amended and resubmitted. Although not always practicable, it is desirable that the document submitted to the Exchange is as near to its final form as possible so as to avoid last minute issues arising with the Exchange.

11.2   Contents of Super Class 1 circular

1   Information about the acquisition and general Super Class 1 requirements

1.1 *Particulars of the transaction and the target's business*   Particulars of the transaction, including the name of the target company or business, a description of the business carried on by, or using, the net assets which are the subject of the transaction, the value of those net assets and the profits attributable to them (para 10.37 and 10.38(a); para 10.31(a)(b)(d)(e)).

1.2 *Consideration*   Particulars of the consideration and how it is being satisfied, including the terms of any arrangements for deferred consideration (para 10.31 (c)). Where shares are issued in connection with the acquisition, a statement of the aggregate value of the consideration (para 6.C.22(a)). A statement that application has been made to the Exchange for any consideration shares to be admitted to the Official List, setting out details of the relevant shares (para 6.B.1). An indication of whether or not all the shares to be issued have been marketed or are available to the public in whole or in part in connection with any application for listing (para 6.B.2).

1.3 *Comparative table or accountants' report*   If the acquisition is of a target company and will lead to consolidation, a comparative table covering the target company and its subsidiary undertakings is required which must be extracted, without material adjustment, from appropriate audited accounts for the last three completed financial periods (paras 10.38(c), 12.9 and 12.17). Alternatively, an accountants' report covering the target group and its subsidiary undertakings will be required if there has been material change to the target group structure or to its business within the period, including by acquisition, or if there has been material change in its accounting policies, or if material adjustment to the audited accounts of the target is required to achieve consistency with the purchaser's audited accounts. An accountants' report will also be required if the target has no, or qualified, auditors' reports for the period, or if the Exchange requires it (para 12.19). The accountants' report should cover the last three completed financial periods, be prepared by qualified independent accountants and must contain their opinion as to whether or not their report gives a true and fair view of the financial matters contained in it for the purpose of the acquisition, as well as any reservations and reasons for qualification (para 12.14). Any statements of adjustments must be prepared and signed by the accountants and submitted to the Exchange. In the case of an asset acquisition, the financial information to be given will be as agreed with the Exchange, and the purchaser must, in its circular, confirm that its directors consider that the value to the purchaser justifies the price paid (para 10.38(d); para 12.13).

1.4   *Effect of the acquisition*   The effect of the acquisition on the purchaser including any benefits which are expected to accrue to the purchaser as a result (para. 10.31(f)) and the effect also on the earnings and assets and liabilities of the purchaser's group. The latter may take the form of a *pro forma* statement of net assets (para 10.38(f)).

1.5   *Directors' responsibility statement*   The directors of the purchaser must make a declaration that they take responsibility for the information contained in the Super Class 1 circular in the form prescribed by the Exchange, with appropriate modifications (para 10.38(e)).

1.6   *Experts' consents*   Where a statement or report attributed to a person as an expert is included in the circular a statement that it is included, in the form and context in which it is included, with the consent of that person (para 14.1(d)). The term 'expert' does not include a person simply providing financial advice to the company who is referred to in the directors' statement of recommendation.

1.7   *Profit forecasts*   If the purchaser has published a profit forecast or estimate for any period for which the results have not yet been published a forecast or estimate must be included in the relevant circular and reported on by the auditors or reporting accountants and the sponsor. A form of words which expressly or by implication states a maximum or minimum for the likely level of profit, or contains data from which a calculation may be made, is a profit forecast. In certain circumstances, a dividend forecast may amount to a profit forecast (paras 12.21–12.27)

2   Information about the listed company and its capital

2.1   *Name and address*   The name, registered office and, if different, head office of the purchaser (para 6.C.1).

2.2   *Documents on display* (para 6.C.7)   A statement that for a period of not less than 14 days from the date of the circular or for the duration of any offer of shares (if any) to which the circular relates, if longer, at a named place in or near the City of London or such other place in the United Kingdom as the Exchange may agree, the following documents (or copies thereof), where applicable, may be inspected:

(a) the memorandum and articles of association of the purchaser;

(b) any trust deed of the purchaser and any of its subsidiary undertakings which is referred to in the circular;

(c) each material contract entered into by any member of the purchaser's group within the two years immediately preceding publication of the circular (as required by para. 6.C.20). Material contracts exclude those outside the ordinary course of business and practice tends to be to regard contracts involving amounts equal to 3–5 per cent or more of assets or profits (depending on the nature of the contract) as material, as well as any which, by their terms, are unusual. In addition, the service contracts of each existing or proposed director (as required by para. 6.F.12). In the case of any contract not reduced into writing, a memorandum giving full particulars thereof;

(d) if the acquisition involves an issue of shares by the purchaser the documents describing the relevant terms and conditions of the transaction, together, where appropriate, with any opening balance sheet, if the purchaser has not prepared its own or consolidated annual accounts (as appropriate);

(e) all reports, letters, and other documents, balance sheets, valuations and statements by any expert any part of which is included or referred to in the circular;

(f) written statements signed by the auditors or accountants setting out the adjustments made by them in arriving at the figures shown in any accountants' report included in the circular and giving the reasons therefor; and

(g) the audited accounts of the purchaser (or, in the case of a group, its consolidated audited accounts) for each of the two financial years preceding the publication of the circular including, in the case of a company incorporated in the United Kingdom, all notes, reports or information required by the Companies Act.

Where any of the documents are not in the English language, full translations or, if so agreed with the Exchange, a summary translation, must be available for inspection (para 6.C.8).

2.3 *Major interests in shares* In so far as is known to the purchaser, the name of any person other than a director who, directly or indirectly, is interested in 3 per cent or more of its capital, together with the amount of each such person's interest or, if there are no such persons, an appropriate negative statement. If the acquisition involves an issue of shares the information should be given in relation to the share capital both as existing and as enlarged (para 6.C.16 and para 10.42). Note that the disclosure requirement is wider than the notification requirements of the Companies Act 1985, s 198.

2.4 *Material contracts* A summary of the principal contents of each material contract (not being a contract entered into in the ordinary course of business) entered into by any member of the purchaser's group within the two years immediately preceding the publication of the circular, including particulars of dates, parties, terms and conditions, any consideration passing to or from the purchaser or any other member of its group, unless such contracts have been available for inspection in the last two years in which case it will be sufficient to refer to them collectively as being available for inspection (*see* para 2.2(c) *above*). Such information should also be given, in a separate statement, in respect of the target group (para 6.C.20 and para 10.41(a)).

3   Information about the group's activities

3.1 *Litigation*   Information on any legal or arbitration proceedings (including any such proceedings which are pending or threatened of which the purchaser is aware) which may have or have had in the recent past (covering at least the previous 12 months) a significant effect on the purchaser's group's financial position or an appropriate negative statement. Such information should also be given, in a separate statement, in respect of the target group (para 6.D.8 and para 10.41(a)).

4   Information about the purchaser's assets and liabilities, financial position and profits and losses

4.1 *Significant changes since last accounts*   A description of any significant change in the financial or trading position of the purchaser's group which has occurred since the end of the last financial period for which either audited financial statements or interim financial statements have been published, or an appropriate negative statement. Such information should also be given, in a separate statement, in respect of the target group (para 6.E.8 and para 10.41(a)).

4.2 *Statement of indebtedness*   Details on a consolidated basis as at the most recent practicable date (which must be stated and which in the absence of exceptional circumstances must not be more than 42 days prior to the date of publication of the circular) of the following, if material:

(a)   the total amount of any loan capital outstanding in all members of the group, and loan capital created but unissued, and term loans, distinguishing between loans guaranteed, unguaranteed, secured (whether the security is provided by the purchaser or by third parties), and unsecured;

(b)   the total amount of all other borrowings and indebtedness in the nature of borrowing of the group, distinguishing between guaranteed, unguaranteed, secured and unsecured borrowings and debts, including bank overdrafts, liabilities under acceptances (other than normal trade bills) or acceptance credits, hire purchase commitments and obligations under finance leases; and

(c)   the total amount of any contingent liabilities or guarantees of the group.

An appropriate negative statement must be given in each case where relevant, in the absence of any loan capital, borrowings, indebtedness and contingent liabilities described above. As a general rule, no account should be taken of liabilities or guarantees between undertakings within the same group; a statement to that effect should be made if necessary. Such information should also be given in respect of the target group and included in a single statement for the purchaser's group on the basis that the acquisition has taken place (para 6.E.15 and para 10.41(b)).

4.3 *Working capital* A statement by the purchaser that in its opinion the working capital available to the purchaser's group is sufficient for its present requirements, or, if not and the purchaser has securities already listed, how it is proposed to provide the additional working capital thought by the purchaser to be necessary. Such information should also be given in respect of the target group and included in a single statement for the purchaser's group on the basis that the acquisition has taken place. Where a working capital statement is given by the purchaser its sponsor must also report to the Exchange in writing that it has written confirmation from the purchaser that the working capital available to the group is sufficient for its present requirements, that the sponsor is satisfied that such confirmation has been given after due and careful enquiry by the purchaser and that the persons or institutions providing finance have stated in writing that the relevant financing facilities exist (paras 6.E.16 and 10.41(c), paras 3.10 and 3.11 and para 2.14).

5 Information about the management

5.1 *Directors' interests in shares* If, as will generally be the case, the purchaser is a company subject to the Companies Act 1985, interests (distinguishing between beneficial and non-beneficial interests) relating to securities which:

(a) have been notified by each director to the purchaser pursuant to the Companies Act 1985, s 324 or 328;

(b) are required pursuant to s 325 of the Act to be entered in the register referred to therein; or

(c) are interests of a connected person of a director which would, if the connected person were a director, be required to be disclosed under (a) or (b) above, and the existence of which is known to or could with reasonable diligence be ascertained by that director;

or an appropriate negative statement (para 6.F.4). In the case of a purchaser which is a company not subject to the Companies Act 1985, the interests of each director including any connected person, the existence of which is known to or could with reasonable diligence be ascertained by that director, whether or not held through another party, in the share capital of the purchaser together with any options in respect of such capital should be stated (para 6.F.5). In any case, if the acquisition involves an issue of shares the information should be given in relation to the share capital both as existing and as enlarged (para 10.42).

5.2 *Directors' interests in transactions*   All relevant particulars regarding the nature and extent of any interests of directors of the purchaser in transactions which are or were unusual in their nature or conditions or significant to the business of the purchaser's group, and which were effected by the purchaser:

(a)   during the current or immediately preceding financial year; or

(b)   during an earlier financial year and which remain in any respect outstanding or unperformed;

or an appropriate negative statement (para 6.F.6).

5.3 *Directors' service contracts*   Details of existing or proposed directors' service contracts (excluding contracts previously made available for inspection in accordance with para 16.9 and not subsequently varied), such details to include name of employing company, date of contract, unexpired term and details of any notice periods, full particulars of the directors' remuneration including salary and other benefits, commission or profit sharing arrangements, provision for compensation on early termination of contract and other details necessary to determine the liability on early termination of the contract. An appropriate negative statement should be given where relevant (para 6.F.12 and para 10.31(g)).

5.4 *Emoluments*   Where shares are to be issued in connection with the acquisition and the total emoluments receivable by the directors of the purchaser will be varied in consequence of the transaction, full particulars of the variation; if there will be no variation, a statement to that effect (para 6.C.22(b)).

6   Information about the recent development and prospects of the group

6.1 *Group prospects*   Unless otherwise agreed by the Exchange in exceptional circumstances, information on the purchaser's group's prospects for at least the current financial year. Such information must relate to the financial and trading prospects of the group together with any material information which may be relevant to it, including all special trade factors or risks (if any) which are not mentioned elsewhere in the circular and which are unlikely to be known or anticipated by the general public and which could materially affect the profits. Such information should also be given in respect of the target group and included in a single statement for the enlarged group on the basis that the transaction has taken place (para 6.G.1(b) and para 10.41(c)).

6.2 *Profit forecasts*   Where a profit forecast or estimate appears (para 12.22), the principal assumptions upon which the purchaser has based its forecast or estimate must be stated. The forecast or estimate must be examined and reported on by the reporting accountants or auditors whose report must be set out in the circular; there must also be set out a report from the sponsor confirming that it has satisfied itself that the forecast has been made after due and careful enquiry by the directors (para 6.G.2 and para 2.15; *see also* para 1.7 *above*).

7   Contents of all circulars

Chapter 14 (para 14.1) contains general requirements for the content of any circular:

(a)   it must provide a clear and adequate explanation of its subject matter;

(b)   if voting is required, it must contain all information necessary to allow shareholders to make a properly informed decision, and contain a heading drawing attention to the importance of the document and advise shareholders who are in any doubt as to what action to take to consult appropriate independent advisers. The circular must also contain a recommendation from the directors as to the voting action shareholders should take, indicating whether or not the proposal described in the circular is, in the opinion of the directors, in the best interests of the shareholders as a whole;

(c)   it must state that where all the shares have been sold or transferred by the addressee, the circular and any other relevant document should be passed to the person through whom the sale was effected for onward transmission;

(d)   where the circular relates to a transaction in connection with which shares are to be listed, a statement that application has been or will be made for the shares to be admitted to the Official List and, if known, statements as to: the commencement date of dealings, the ranking of new shares for dividend, whether they rank *pari passu* with existing listed securities, the nature of documents of title, the proposed date of issue and the treatment of any fractions.

11.3   Related party transactions and contents of related party circulars

If the acquisition by the purchaser is from, or involves, a related party, it will generally require shareholder approval under Chapter 11 of the *Yellow Book*. Exceptions apply to transactions of a revenue nature in the ordinary course of business. Other exceptions can be found in para 11.7 of the *Yellow Book*. Those which are of most relevance in the context of an acquisition are: where the related party is involved in the underwriting (para 11.7(g)); or where the acquisition is a small transaction (para 11.7(b)). A small transaction is one where the percentage ratios arising under the comparisons described on p 221 is 0.25 per cent or less. If on only one comparison the percentage ratio is greater than 0.25 per cent and all others are less than 5 per cent no shareholder consent will be required if the purchaser notifies the Exchange of details of the transaction, provides written confirmation from an independent adviser that the terms of the transaction are fair and reasonable so far as the shareholders of the purchaser are concerned and undertakes to the Exchange to provide details of the transaction in its next published annual accounts. Transactions with the same, or associated, related parties must be aggregated (if not otherwise approved) and shareholder consent will be required in respect of the latest if it would be Class 2 or larger transaction.

A related party of the purchaser will be:-

(a) a substantial shareholder, being any person who is or was within the 12 months preceding the transaction entitled to exercise or control 10 per cent or more of the voting rights at general meetings of the purchaser or any of its parent, subsidiary, or fellow subsidiary undertakings;

(b) a director or shadow director of the purchaser or of any of its parent, subsidiary or fellow subsidiary undertakings, or a person who was within 12 months of the date preceding the transaction such a director or shadow director; or

(c) an associate of any person under (a) or (b) above. The associates of an individual are his spouse or child, the trustees of certain family trusts, and companies in which he or they exercise control over 30 per cent or more of the votes at general meetings or have the right to appoint or remove directors who hold the majority of voting rights at board meetings. Interests of more than one director will be aggregated for the purpose of determining whether such a company is a related party. An associate of a corporate substantial shareholder means its parent, subsidiary and fellow subsidiary undertakings, any company whose directors are accustomed to act in accordance with the substantial shareholder's directions or instructions and any company in which it or they, together, exercise control (determined in the manner described above for an individual).

If the purchaser proposes to enter into a transaction with a related party then it must make an announcement, which must include the information described above for a Super Class 1 transaction (*see* p 221)), giving also the name of the related party and details of the nature and extent of the related party's interest in the transaction. The purchaser must, in addition, send a circular to its shareholders (para 11.4). Approval of the acquisition by the purchaser's shareholders must be given either before it has been entered into or, if the acquisition is conditional upon approval, prior to completion. The purchaser must ensure that the related party abstains from voting on the relevant resolution (para 11.10(f)). If a meeting is called to approve the transaction and a party to it then becomes a related party, the Exchange will normally require that the related party abstains from voting on the resolution and that a further circular is dispatched for receipt by shareholders prior to the meeting containing that information required in a related party circular but which was not set out in the circular convening the meeting.

The variation or novation of an existing agreement with a related party will require shareholders' approval under Chapter 11 of the *Yellow Book* even though the person concerned was not a related party at the time of the original transaction. This is of particular relevance where shareholders of the target are also (and remain) directors of the target after acquisition. If the terms of any earn out or payment of deferred consideration is modified, the related party implications should be considered. It may be possible to agree with the Exchange that the variation is to be regarded as a small transaction (*see* p 231 *above*).

The contents requirements of a related party circular are as follows:

1 Information about the acquisition and general related party requirements

1.1 *Fairness of the transaction* A statement by the directors (other than any director who is, or an associate of whom is, a related party or who is a director of a related party in respect of the transaction) that the transaction is fair and reasonable so far as the shareholders of the purchaser are concerned and that the directors have been so advised by an independent adviser acceptable to the Exchange (para 11.10(e)).

1.2 *Valuations* An independent valuation is required in respect of the purchase of an asset, including a target company (para 11.10(d)).

1.3 *Interests in the transaction and abstention from voting* Full particulars of the transaction, including the name of the related party concerned and of the nature and extent of the interest of such party in the transaction (para 11.10(c)). Where applicable, a statement that the related party will abstain and has undertaken to take all reasonable steps to ensure that its associates will abstain, from voting at the meeting (para 11.10(f)).

1.4 *Experts' consents* Where a statement or report attributed to a person as an expert is included in the circular a statement that it is included, in the form and context in which it is included, with the consent of that person is required (para 11.10(i)). The term 'expert' does not include a person simply providing financial advice to the company who is referred to in the directors' statement of recommendation.

1.5 *Aggregation* Where relevant, details of any other transactions entered into by the purchaser's group with the same related party or its associates which have not been approved by shareholders. This will apply only where the transactions in the aggregate within a 12 month period would be classified as a Class 2 transaction or greater (para 11.10(h) and para 11.9).

2 Information about the listed company and its capital

2.1 *Name and address* The name, registered office and, if different, head office of the purchaser (para 6.C.1).

2.2 *Documents on display* (para 6.C.7) A statement that for a period of not less than 14 days from the date of the circular or for the duration of any offer of shares (if any) to which the circular relates, if longer, at a named place in or near the City of London or such other place in the United Kingdom as the Exchange may agree, the following documents (or copies thereof), where applicable, may be inspected:

(a) the memorandum and articles of association of the purchaser;

(b) any trust deed of the purchaser and any of its subsidiary undertakings which is referred to in the circular;

(c) each material contract entered into by any member of the purchaser's group within the two years immediately preceding publication of the circular (as required by para 6.C.20) and the service contracts of each existing or proposed director (as required by para 6.F.12) or, in the case of any contract not reduced into writing, a memorandum giving full particulars thereof (*see also* para 2.2(c) on p 226 *above*);

(d) if the acquisition involves an issue of shares by the purchaser the documents describing the relevant terms and conditions of the trans-action, together, where appropriate, with any opening balance sheet, if the purchaser has not prepared its own or consolidated annual accounts (as appropriate);

(e) all reports, letters, and other documents, balance sheets, valuations and statements by any expert any part of which is included or re-ferred to in the circular;

(f) written statements signed by the auditors or accountants setting out the adjustments made by them in arriving at the figures shown in any accountants' report included in the circular and giving the reasons therefor; and

(g) the audited accounts of the purchaser (or, in the case of a group, its consolidated audited accounts) for each of the two financial years preceding the publication of the circular including, in the case of a company incorporated in the United Kingdom, all notes, reports or information required by the Companies Act.

Where any of the documents are not in the English language, full transla-tions must be available for inspection unless the availability of summary translations is agreed with the Exchange (para 6.C.8).

2.3 *Major interests in shares*   In so far as is known to the purchaser, the name of any person other than a director who, directly or indirectly, is in-terested in 3 per cent or more of its capital, together with the amount of each such persons' interest or, if there are no such persons, an appropriate negative statement (para 6.C.16). Note that the disclosure requirement is wider than the notification requirement of the Companies Act 1985, s 198.

2.4 *Material contracts*   A summary of the principal contents of each materi-al contract (not being a contract entered into in the ordinary course of business) entered into by any member of the purchaser's group within the two years immediately preceding the publication of the circular, including particulars of dates, parties, terms and conditions, any consideration pass-ing to or from the purchaser or any other member of its group, unless such contracts have been available for inspection in the last two years in which case it will be sufficient to refer to them collectively as being available for inspection (*see* para 2.2(c) *above*) (para 6.C.20).

2.5 *Consideration   and   effect   of   the   transaction   on   directors' emoluments*   Where shares are issued in connection with the acquisition a statement of the aggregate value of the consideration for the transaction and how it is to be satisfied; and if the total emoluments receivable by the directors of the purchaser will be varied in consequence of the transaction, full particulars of the variation; if there will be no variation, a statement to that effect (para 6.C.22).

3   Information about the purchaser's assets and liabilities, financial position and profits and losses

3.1 *Significant changes since last accounts*   A description of any significant change in the financial or trading position of the purchaser's group which has occurred since the end of the last financial period for which either audited financial statements or interim financial statements have been published, or an appropriate negative statement (para 6.E.8).

4   Information about the management

The following information will be required where the related party is a director or an associate of a director of the purchaser or any of its parent, subsidiary or fellow subsidiary undertakings.

4.1 *Directors' interests in shares*   If, as will generally be the case, the purchaser is a company subject to the Companies Act 1985, interests (distinguishing between beneficial and non-beneficial interests) relating to securities which:

(a)   have been notified by each director to the purchaser pursuant to the Companies Act 1985, s 324 or 328;

(b)   are required pursuant to s 325 of that Act to be entered in the register referred to therein; or

(c)   are interests of a connected person of a director which would, if the connected person were a director, be required to be disclosed under (a) or (b) above, and the existence of which is known to or could with reasonable diligence be ascertained by that director;

or an appropriate negative statement (para 6.F.4). In the case of a purchaser which is a company not subject to the Companies Act 1985, the interests of each director, including any connected person, the existence of which is known to or could with reasonable diligence be ascertained by that director, whether or not held through another party, in the share capital of the purchaser together with any options in respect of such capital should be stated (para 6.F.5).

4.2 *Directors' interests in transactions*   All relevant particulars regarding the nature and extent of any interests of directors of the purchaser in transactions which are or were unusual in their nature or conditions or significant to the business of the purchaser's group, and which were effected by the purchaser:

(a)   during the current or immediately preceding financial year; or

(b)   during an earlier financial year and remain in any respect outstanding or unperformed;

or an appropriate negative statement (para 6.F.6).

4.3 *Directors' service contracts*   Details of existing or proposed directors' service contracts (excluding contracts previously made available for inspection in accordance with para 16.9 and not subsequently varied), such details to include name of employing company, date of contract, unexpired term and details of any notice periods, full particulars of the directors' remuneration including salary and other benefits, commission or profit sharing arrangements, provision for compensation on early termination of contract and other details necessary to determine the liability on early termination of the contract. A negative statement should be given if appropriate (para 6.F.12 and 10.31(g)).

5   Contents of all circulars

Chapter 14 (para 14.1) contains general requirements for the content of any circular:

(a) it must provide a clear and adequate explanation of its subject matter;

(b) if voting is required, it must contain all information necessary to allow shareholders to make a properly informed decision, and contain a heading drawing attention to the importance of the document and advise shareholders who are in any doubt as to what action to take to consult appropriate independent advisers. The circular must also contain a recommendation from the directors as to the voting action shareholders should take, indicating whether or not the proposal described in the circular is, in the opinion of the directors, in the best interests of the shareholders as a whole;

(c) it must state that where all the shares have been sold or transferred by the addressee, the circular and any other relevant document should be passed to the person through whom the sale was effected for onward transmission;

(d) where the circular relates to a transaction in connection with which shares are to be listed, a statement that application has been or will be made for the shares to be admitted to the Official List and, if known, statements as to: the commencement date of dealings, the ranking of new shares for dividend, whether they rank *pari passu* with existing listed securities, the nature of documents of title, the proposed date of issue and the treatment of any fractions.

11.4   Indemnities and similar arrangements

Advisers to a listed company should be aware of the provisions of paragraph 10.24 of the *Yellow Book* which treats automatically as a Super Class 1 transaction any exceptional agreement or arrangement under which a listed company agrees to discharge any liabilities for costs, expenses, commissions or losses incurred by that other party (whether or not contingent) and which is either unlimited or where the maximum liability is equal to or exceeds 25 per cent of the average of the company's profits for the last three financial years, such profits being calculated in the same way as for transaction classification purposes, above (but treating any losses as profits of 'nil').

The provisions of paragraph 10.24 are wide and would be of potential application to acquisitions. However, it is specifically provided that indemnities such as those customarily given in connection with sale and purchase agreements or to underwriters or placing agents in an underwriting or placing agreement, and indemnities given to advisers against liabilities to third parties arising out of providing advisory services are not 'exceptional'. In most cases, it will be clear that the provision will be of no application. The exception, however, applies only to indemnities of a type 'customarily given'. In cases of doubt the Exchange should be consulted.

11.5   Shareholders' approval

The approval of shareholders to the transaction will normally be required if the transaction is Super Class 1 or is a related party transaction, or in the case of a reverse takeover.

If shareholders' approval is required it will be necessary to make completion of the acquisition subject to shareholders' approval. In these cases the circular giving the required information will be sent to shareholders before completion of the acquisition and will include a notice of meeting and a proxy card complying with the Exchange's requirements. See Chapter 14 of the *Yellow Book* which sets out general requirements for the content of circulars.

Shareholders' approval will also be required if it is necessary to increase the authorised share capital of the purchaser to make the acquisition and to give the directors the necessary authority to allot shares. (*See further* Chapter 2.) A large overhang of shares available for issue will usually require an explanation in the circular of the company's plans to use such excess headroom.

11.6   Using shares to fund an acquisition

When a listed company makes an acquisition it frequently wishes to use its own shares to fund the price. The vendors may be willing to accept some shares in the purchaser as consideration, but more often than not they require cash. There are essentially two methods of using shares in the London market to raise cash for an acquisition: the rights issue and the placing. Which method is used will depend upon a number of considerations, and market reaction will often be the most important, but the following part of this Chapter deals with a number of points which arise under the heads of timing, accounting, stamp duty, and the listing condition.

Using shares to fund a business acquisition is rare. However, it is a possibility where there is a rights issue or cash placing or where the transaction is structured as a share transaction. Additional comment concerning business acquisitions is dealt with separately at the end of this Chapter (p 251).

As used in this chapter, a 'rights issue' means an offer to existing shareholders of new shares for cash *pro rata* to their existing shareholdings on renounceable provisional letters of allotment, while a 'placing' means an offer (not on renounceable letters) of new shares to selected persons or 'placees' (often institutional investors but who may include individuals or companies and may also include existing shareholders). A placing may be a 'vendor placing' in which the new shares are (traditionally) allotted to the vendors as consideration for the acquisition and then sold by them to the placees to raise any cash consideration which they require (a modified structure to save SDRT is described on p 244). Alternatively, a placing may be a 'cash placing' in which the new shares are placed directly for cash which is used to pay the vendors. Although the legal and accounting results are different, the net economic effect to the vendors of these two types of placing, vendor or cash, is the same. It is common practice, at least in the case of a large placing, to offer some or all of the shares to be placed to existing shareholders in an 'open offer', with all or some of the placees taking those shares which the existing shareholders do not want. This type of offering does not, however, turn the issue into a rights issue as it does not involve the issue of a negotiable document in respect of the existing shareholder's entitlement. The Association of British Insurers has said that its members will expect a listed company proposing to issue its shares as vendor consideration to make an offer of those shares to existing shareholders where the issue amounts to more than 10 per cent of the purchaser's existing capital or involves a discount of more than 5 per cent on the market price of the consideration shares (*see* Chapter 2). This 5 per cent discount is determined by reference to the market price immediately prior to announcing the transaction, which can be a practical problem. Where the market is volatile it takes time to prepare the documents for an open offer so there may be a delay between announcement and posting. Save in exceptional circumstances, the Stock Exchange will not permit an open offer where the discount to market price is more than 10 per cent, when compared with the middle market price at the time of announcement (para 4.26, *Yellow Book*).

It is obvious that a rights issue and a cash placing can be used to raise more money than is needed for the acquisition, while the vendor placing will raise only the purchase price. On the other hand the rights issue is not suitable where the objective is solely to fund a small acquisition as the issue involves a fairly major market operation. There are a number of variants on the basic theme of rights issue or placing, including the so-called 'vendor rights issue' where the consideration shares are allotted to the vendors and then offered to the purchaser's shareholders on an underwritten basis. A recent development involves 'bookbuilding', an underwriting technique which is commonly used in an international equity offering. Under the conventional vendor placing, the price at which the underwriter agrees to acquire the purchaser's shares is set by agreement between purchaser and underwriter immediately prior to announcement, and the bank or broker who has agreed to act as underwriter (ie to procure placees) will seek to sell the shares to placees immediately upon announcement, failing which he will be committed to purchase them himself. Obviously, this exercise follows investigation by the underwriter as to the likely interest in the issue and in recent years it has been increasingly common to conduct a formal, confidential, pre-marketing exercise.

Bookbuilding involves a more formal, public, marketing in which formal expressions of interest to purchase within an indicative price range are sought, following which the price is set. Bookbuilding is said to offer the opportunity for the purchaser to achieve a better price for its shares although on a vendor placing, as its shares are already quoted, this opportunity is probably more limited than in an initial public offering. A bookbuilt vendor placing is unlikely to be undertaken under current practice in all but the largest vendor placings; if a firm commitment to sell the target is made at the time of announcement, there may be a risk that the vendor will receive shares rather than cash, as it is not guaranteed a price for its shares in the bookbuilding process. The commissions typically payable in a bookbuild exercise are higher (around 5 per cent), although the risk to the underwriter—who does not commit himself until the end of the marketing exercise—would appear to be less.

11.6.1   Timing

Timing is important for a number of reasons and in a number of ways. The vendors will want the cash consideration at completion and, normally, as quickly as possible. The timing of the announcement of the issue is not subject to official control, following the general consent issued under the Control of Borrowing Order 1958 (SI No 1208) in 1989 which exempts any transaction from the order, except transactions by local authorities. In practice, the London Stock Exchange is consulted.

Issues in the London market to fund acquisitions are normally underwritten. That is to say they are not announced until a securities house has entered into a commitment to take the securities (although see the comments on bookbuilding, *above*). On a rights issue, the underwriting will be in the classic form and underwriters will agree to take those rights shares not taken up by existing shareholders which cannot be sold in the market at or above the offer price. In the case of a placing the bank (or broker) involved will agree to find purchasers of the new shares from the vendors or, in the case of a cash placing, subscribers for the new shares to be allotted by the company direct to the placees. The period commencing with the date of this commitment, normally on the announcement of the issue, and ending on the date when the shares are finally taken up is the underwriting period and underwriters will receive a fee according to its length. A typical fee structure might be 2 per cent of the amount of the issue for the first thirty days of the underwriting period and one-eighth of 1 per cent for every week or part of a week thereafter. With this in mind, the purchaser will wish to keep the underwriting period as short as possible. At the time of this edition underwriting commission structures have come under pressure in light of review by the competition authorities; change seems likely and in November 1996 two rights issues (by Stakis plc and More Group plc) adopted what has been hailed as a more flexible structure by inviting sub-underwriters to tender for a proportion of the shares to be allocated at lower commission levels. It remains to be seen whether such tender arrangements will become standard practice; the development of more competitive commission structures seems certain, however.

Rights isse

Where the sole or main purpose of a rights issue is to fund an acquisition, it is likely in practice that a meeting of the purchaser's shareholders will be required to approve the acquisition (if it is Super Class 1, *see* p 220) or to increase share capital and grant the directors authority to allot under the Companies Act 1985, s 80 (*see* p 8). The resolutions to carry these matters into effect are ordinary resolutions and fourteen clear days' notice will be required, although the articles of the purchaser should be checked. The acquisition agreement will be conditional on these matters and on the admission of the new shares to the Official List of the London Stock Exchange. Because the provisional allotment letters are negotiable documents they cannot in practice be issued until the conditions of the issue have been satisfied, so the steps are: sign the acquisition agreement, announce and post circular to shareholders, wait fourteen clear days, hold shareholders' meeting, complete acquisition (having borrowed the money to do so), post provisional allotment letters, wait twenty-one days, collect proceeds, repay borrowings. However, the purchaser may not be able, or willing to borrow to bridge the gap between the date of posting of the provisional allotment letters and the date upon which the proceeds of the rights issue are received. This will be particularly so if the underwriting remains in any respect liable to be rescinded, such as in the event of *force majeure*, although in practice the purchaser will negotiate hard to avoid such a term. If the purchaser cannot fund the cash required as consideration for the acquisition until the proceeds of the rights issue are received, it may require that completion is delayed for a further three weeks when, rescission apart, the proceeds should be received.

Statutory rights issue

In order to keep the underwriting period to a minimum it is obviously important to ensure that a rights issue does not require a s 89 disapplication. The scheme of s 89 *et seq* is not to require a disapplication if there is an offer to existing shareholders which complies with the statutory procedure, but there are a number of points to watch. First, a statutory offer must remain open for twenty-one clear days which does not start until the offer is made. Where the offer is sent by post it is deemed to be made at the time at which the letter would be delivered in the ordinary course of post (s 90(2)). This poses obvious difficulties in the case of foreign shareholders, and indeed the impossibility of knowing when a letter would be delivered to them in the ordinary course of post makes it imperative to find another way of communicating the offer to them. This problem is compounded by the fact that certain jurisdictions, such as the United States and Canada, have securities laws which prohibit the making of offers in those jurisdictions without regulatory filings. Luckily, s 90(5) provides that where a holder has no registered address in the United Kingdom, the offer may be made by publishing it in the *London Gazette*. It is the practice therefore to make the offer to overseas shareholders by these means but, in addition, to send the documents for convenience unless prohibited from doing so by the local law.

Another point to watch in the statutory procedure is the treatment of fractions. It is the normal practice to aggregate fractions and sell them in the market, but s 89 provides that the offer must be made to shareholders in proportions which are 'as nearly as practicable' equal to the shares held by them. Where the computer will do it, this seems to require allocations to be rounded up and down as appropriate. The sale in the market of the shares resulting from the aggregation of fractions amounts to a cash issue, but this will normally be covered by the general '5 per cent' disapplication obtained at the purchaser's latest annual general meeting.

In practice, almost all listed companies will have disapplied s 89 at their last annual general meeting for a 'rights issue' thus permitting an issue of ordinary shares which does not accord strictly with the statutory requirements. Where a new class of shares (eg convertible preference shares) is used to fund the issue, however, existing authorities may not apply and a new authority will be required.

Vendor placing with open offer

In the case of a placing the underwriting period is shorter, even where some or all of the new shares are offered to existing shareholders. Such an offer need not be made on renounceable documents and can therefore take place during the notice period for the meeting, although the Stock Exchange requires the offer to be kept open for 15 *business* days. The steps are: sign the acquisition agreement, announce and post circular to shareholders containing offer, wait 15 business days (which will include the 14 clear days, not confined to business days, required as notice of the meeting), hold shareholders' meeting, complete the acquisition and placing simultaneously (if the timing of receipt of cleared funds permits it).

If the acquisition is not conditional upon shareholder approval or on any other condition (eg OFT clearance) but it is still necessary to make the open offer to shareholders under the ABI guidelines then a number of interesting points arise. The vendor will probably insist on being paid on completion and will not wish completion to be delayed or made conditional upon receipt of funds from the placing. The bank (or broker) will place the shares, but as they are placed subject to clawback, the final identity of those who are to take them will not be known until the expiry of the open offer, 15 business days later. The bank can effect this transaction either by acquiring the shares from the vendors as principal and selling them on or, to save stamp duty (SDRT may be chargeable, *see* p 244), placing them as agent for the vendor. The key point however is that the bank will have parted with the money at the beginning of the period and if something goes wrong, will end up bearing the risk.

In the case of a conditional acquisition contract the bank can protect itself in the placing agreement against unexpected events occurring prior to completion but once the money has passed the risks clearly become greater. Thus, for example, where shares are allotted on a renounceable basis to the vendor, if one of the vendors then becomes bankrupt or enters into liquidation during the period between the date on which the money is paid and the date on which the shares are finally allocated, the bank will wish to ensure that the agency arrangements remain binding and incorporate appropriate powers of attorney to permit it to allocate the shares to the purchasing shareholders or placees. Subject to the rules about voidable transactions (*see* Chapter 16), which are unlikely to apply, there will be no problem here if the bank has purchased the shares as principal, but the agency relationship does require careful study if it is to withstand a liquidation. Quite where the beneficial interest in the consideration shares has gone during this period following *J Sainsbury v O'Connor* (*see* p 300) is an interesting academic question. So long as the arrangements are such that the beneficial interest in the shares either never was in the vendors, or has left them before the bankruptcy or liquidation, it is unlikely that the transaction will be upset.

Consideration should be given to the position if a placee were to default. If the contract is entered into with the vendors (with the bank acting as agent) can the bank then sue the placee? If it does so in the name of the vendor, what loss has the vendor suffered, when he has already been paid? The answer is to impose a direct collateral obligation by the placee to the bank that it will pay the price on time and include provisions in the agency agreement which, in the event of default, permit the bank to sell the shares in the market and to claim against the defaulting placee under its direct obligation, and keep the proceeds.

What if the placees claim rescission on the grounds of some misrepresentation in the circular or listing particulars? In the case where the contract is conditional the bank will not be at risk because it will have the right to rescind the placing agreement if there is such a misstatement, and it will never become liable to subscribe for the shares or pay the vendors, as the case may be. Where it has already paid however, it will be unable to recover from the vendors and will be exposed because it cannot recover from the placees either. The purchaser will give warranties and indemnities in the placing agreement which ought to give the bank a right of recovery against the purchaser if it is unable to recover from its placees. Whether or not the Bank can take security for the warranties and indemnities in these circumstances without the purchaser giving unlawful financial assistance under Companies Act 1985, s 151 is an interesting question, following the decision in *Barclays Bank plc and others v British & Commonwealth Holdings plc* [1996] 1 BCLC 1 and the giving of such security may well suggest that the company is doing more than inducing the beneficiary of such security to participate in the transaction (*see* p 45).

Cash placing

In the case of a cash placing it may be necessary to pass a special resolution to disapply pre-emption rights of existing shareholders under Companies Act 1985, s 89 (*see* p 8). This requirement will extend the notice period to twenty-one clear days and therefore increase the underwriting period. Most listed companies pass a general disapplication of s 89 at their annual general meetings, but this will normally cover new shares only up to 5 per cent of their issued capital (or a 'rights issue', statutory or non-statutory, *see above*), in accordance with the guidelines published by the Association of British Insurers, and this annual 5 per cent disapplication is unlikely to be sufficient to fund a major acquisition. This is one of the reasons for the popularity of the vendor placing.

11.6.2   Accounting

An issue of shares for cash, whether as a rights issue or as a placing will involve a share premium account of the difference between the net price and the nominal value of the shares. These matters are discussed in Chapter 8. The acquisition will be accounted for on an acquisition basis and, if the price paid exceeds the fair value of the assets of the target, goodwill will arise on consolidation, which cannot be written off against share premium account. It will normally be possible, however, to reduce capital by writing down the share premium account in order to establish a reserve against which, under current accounting principles (but soon to change), goodwill arising on consolidation may be written off (*see* p 130). This will involve a special resolution which must be sanctioned by the court. The purchaser will not wish to extend the underwriting period by including the special resolution as one of the matters to be dealt with at the extraordinary general meeting convened to approve the acquisition, but it is possible to convene a separate extraordinary general meeting by notice included in the same circular.

In a vendor placing it will normally be possible to obtain merger relief under the Companies Act 1985, s 131. The difference between the nominal value and the fair value of the consideration shares will show up as a non-statutory reserve. Under current accounting principles it would be usual for goodwill arising on consolidation to be written off immediately against such reserves. *See,* however, Chapter 8 for the proposals for changing the accounting treatment of purchased goodwill. While, under the proposed new rules, the availability of merger relief is likely to become of reduced significance, the Companies Act 1985, s 89 advantages over a cash placing will ensure that the vendor placing remains a popular financing technique.

11.6.3   Stamp duty

The stamp duty costs of the acquisition itself will not be increased by a rights issue or a cash placing. However in the case of a vendor placing further securities are involved, namely the purchaser's shares issued to fund the acquisition. A traditional vendor placing will involve the allotment of the purchaser's shares to the vendors on renounceable documents, and a further transaction in securities on the sale of those shares by the vendors to the placees. This transaction will be subject to stamp duty reserve tax (*see* p 281) which it has now become commonplace to avoid by structuring the vendor placing so that the vendors are entitled to receive cash rather than shares; the cash is provided by the purchaser allotting the consideration shares direct to the placees. The vendors agree in the sale agreement that the consideration for shares in the target is expressed to be the allotment and issue of the consideration shares to persons nominated by the bank arranging the placing, and the purchaser undertakes to procure payment by the bank to the vendors, equal to the cash raised by the placing of the shares. As the vendors have no entitlement to the consideration shares, there is no agreement to transfer chargeable securities from vendor to placee and hence no SDRT (and no stamp duty). The key question is whether the other advantages of a vendor placing are available, namely whether the issue of the purchaser's shares amounts to an issue of shares for non-cash consideration for the purposes of Companies Act 1985, s 89; whether merger relief under s 131 is available; and whether there is an exemption from valuation under s 103. While care should be taken that these provisions operate properly in any particular case, practitioners seem to agree that the structure can have all these advantages (although the matter is not free from doubt). Under those sections, the relief will apply where the allotment of the purchaser's shares is on terms that the consideration for the shares allotted is to be provided by eg the transfer to the purchaser of shares in the target (or, under s 89(4), such shares are paid up otherwise than in cash, within the meaning of s 738). However, there is no requirement under any of the sections that the purchaser's shares be allotted to the vendor. One point to watch in the structure is the purchaser's agreement to procure payment by the placee. If it were expressed as a guarantee or indemnity, the arrangement would contravene the prohibition on giving financial assistance, contained in the Companies Act 1985, s 151 unless (which is doubted) it could be said that it was not 'financial assistance' within the wider, non-technical, meaning of that expression (*see* Chapter 5). The Agreement for Sale (Shares), at p 375 and the vendor placing agreement (p 637) are prepared on the SDRT saving basis. Adopting this structure for the placing also has the incidental advantage that, as the shares never pass through the hands of the vendors, the difficulties which can arise under an unconditional placing with open offer, described above, are avoided (*see* p 241).

In a case where the bank arranging the placing acts as a principal and agrees to buy the shares from the vendor and sell them on to the placees there will be a double charge to SDRT unless the transaction is within the Finance Act 1986, s 89A. Section 89A will exempt the agreement to sell to the issuing house if:

(a) the agreement is part of an arrangement, entered into as part of its business, under which it is to offer the securities for sale to the public;
(b) the agreement is conditional on admission of the securities to listing;
(c) the consideration under the agreement is the same as the price at which the issuing house is to offer the securities for sale; and
(d) the issuing house sells the securities in accordance with the arrangement referred to in (a).

There can be doubts about the applicability of s 89A in many cases, either because the securities are not offered to 'the public' but to a small class of persons or because part of the placing takes place after the listing has become effective, so that the agreement to place is not in fact conditional upon listing. However, if the bank acts as agent for the vendors in placing the shares rather than as principal one charge to SDRT is avoided; if the SDRT saving structure described above is adopted both charges are avoided.

A vendor placing may also add to the stamp duty costs of the acquisition itself. Cases arise in which the target owes substantial sums to the vendor. Such a debt may exist before the acquisition or may be created as a result of the payment of a substantial pre-sale dividend (*see* p 268). In this case the purchaser is normally required to pay for the shares and to put the target in funds to repay the indebtedness resulting from the declaration of the dividend. In order to raise the money to repay the indebtedness by means of a vendor placing it will be necessary to capitalise the debt owing from target to vendor in the form of equity share capital. Procuring the repayment of indebtedness by the target does not usually involve a stamp duty charge (*see* p 280), but purchasing share capital does, although the Stamp Office has been known to argue that an undertaking by the purchaser to procure repayment of the target's indebtedness falls within Stamp Act 1891, s 57; it is submitted such an argument is weak, when considering the wording of s 57. Accordingly, funding the repayment of debt by a vendor placing will increase the cost of the acquisition to the purchaser by 0.5 per cent of the value of the debt which has to be capitalised.

11.6.4 The listing condition

Even after the Exchange has granted permission for the admission of the new shares to the Official List, the admission of the shares to listing will not become effective until the decision of the Exchange to admit the shares to listing is announced by dissemination on the electronic systems used by the Exchange to communicate with its member firms or, exceptionally, posted on a notice board at the Exchange (see *Yellow Book* para. 7.1). Announcement of admission will not be made until after the shares have been allotted. There has been only one case in which the listing did not become effective after the permission had been granted, but underwriters will invariably insist that their commitment is conditional upon the listing becoming effective.

This gives rise to practical difficulties. In the case of a vendor placing the purchaser cannot allot the consideration shares until completion of the acquisition, but the vendors will not complete until they get their cash and the placees will not pay until the listing is effective. The normal procedure is for the Exchange to make the announcement of admission to listing after they have been notified of the allotment, but vendors are understandably reluctant to part with the target and then wait until they are paid. In that case they bear the risk of something happening which means that the notice is not posted. Such an event is almost inconceivable, but the consequences are severe, and a vendor who requires cash will not run any risk, however slight, of ending up with unlisted shares in a purchaser with a problem.

The normal way out of this conundrum is to go through all the completion procedures but for the parties' solicitors to hold the completion documents in escrow subject to the announcement of admission to listing. The consideration shares are allotted subject to completion, the Exchange is informed of the allotment and makes the announcement, whereupon the acquisition automatically completes simultaneously with admission. In a case where there is a delay between contract and completion it is necessary for the acquisition agreement (as well as the placing agreement) to provide that completion is conditional not merely on the grant of permission for the admission of the consideration shares to the Official List, but upon the listing becoming effective. The escrow is often informal, but is sometimes evidenced by an escrow letter.

Much the same procedures can be applied in the case of a cash placing, but the considerations in a rights issue are somewhat different. The underwriters will still insist on their commitment being subject to admission to listing becoming effective, but the announcement of listing will not be made until after the provisional letters of allotment have been despatched. It will not normally be desirable for the letters of allotment to be expressed as being subject to completion of the acquisition as the rights letters are negotiable and of value, but on the other hand, where the purpose of the issue is to raise the purchase price, shareholders are entitled to be assured that the acquisition has been completed. In such a case it would create a major problem if the issue went ahead without the acquisition but equally, there is clearly a major problem for the purchaser if the acquisition were to go ahead without the issue. As the rights issue proceeds will not be available for some weeks after all the conditions of the acquisition have been satisfied the acquisition will normally be completed with borrowed funds. If something goes wrong between completion of the acquisition and the announcement of admission to listing the purchaser could be left with a new subsidiary and a large overdraft.

There used to be a useful section in the Companies Act 1985 and its predecessors (s 86) which provided that where a prospectus stated that an application had been made for listing and the listing was not granted the allotment was void. This section was repealed and not replaced by anything in the Financial Services Act 1986. The result is that, in the event of a failure to announce the admission of shares to listing, the allotment is still valid. As the announcement has not been made when the rights letters are despatched, it is good practice to include a statement in the provisional letters of allotment, that they will lapse if the announcement is not made. This degree of conditionality does not cause a problem because the condition will normally have been satisfied by the time the letters have been received. It is possible to take advantage of this by completing the acquisition in escrow, in the same way as described above for a vendor placing, then mailing the letters, and then releasing the documents from escrow when the announcement of admission to listing is made. Then, if the announcement is not made, the allotment letters lapse, the underwriters are off the hook and the acquisition does not complete. In this case, of course, it is necessary for the acquisition agreement to be conditional upon the admission to listing becoming effective.

11.7   The Alternative Investment Market

On 31 December 1996 the Unlisted Securities Market ceased to exist. Former USM companies sought a full listing on the Official List of the Exchange, sought admission to trading on the Alternative Investment Market, or 'AIM', (or elsewhere) or otherwise ceased to have a marketing arrangement in relation to their shares.

A company whose securities are admitted to trading on AIM is subject to the rules set out in Part 16 of the *Rules of the Stock Exchange* (different from the *Yellow Book*). The rules are binding on AIM companies by virtue of the undertaking contained in their application for admission to AIM. No information is required to be published on admission of new shares for a company which already has its shares admitted to trading on AIM unless a prospectus is required under the Public Offer of Securities Regulations 1995 (SI No 1537) when, in addition to the information required by those regulations, certain additional information is required under the *Rules*. Where an admission document is required, it must state on its first page that application for admission has been or will be made to AIM and 'it is emphasised that no application is being made for admission ... to the Official List. AIM is a market primarily for emerging or smaller companies. The rules ... are less demanding than those of the Official List ...'. An AIM company must also comply with continuing obligations as regards the publication of information through the Company Announcement Office on a similar basis, but also considerably less onerous, as those which apply to a listed company.

The AIM *Rules* include requirements in relation to transactions by the AIM company or its subsidiary undertakings, excluding revenue transactions in the ordinary course of business (or share issue or financing transactions unrelated to an acquisition or disposal of a fixed asset). An AIM company has obligations with regard to 'substantial transactions' and certain transactions with a related party (defined in the same way as for a listed company (*see* p 233)). The following addresses acquisitions in which the AIM company is purchaser, although similar provisions would apply were it vendor. A substantial transaction is one where the calculation on any of the following comparisons gives rise to a percentage ratio of 10 per cent or more:

(a) *assets:* the net assets the subject of the transaction divided by the net assets of the purchaser. As with a listed purchaser, if the acquisition gives rise to consolidation of a target company, 100 per cent of the target's assets should be included, whatever the interest to be acquired; in other cases the target's net assets are taken to be the consideration, or in the case of a business acquisition the book value of those assets, if greater. The net assets of the purchaser are the aggregate of its share capital and reserves as stated, in most instances, in its last published audited accounts or later preliminary statement of annual results (if the preliminary statement has been notified to the CAO);

(b) *profits:* the profits attributable to the net assets the subject of the transaction divided by the profits of the issuer. Profits are calculated after deducting all charges except taxation and extraordinary items and are as stated, in most instances, in the last published audited accounts or later preliminary statement of annual results (if the preliminary statement has been notified to the CAO). In the case of an acquisition which leads to consolidation, 100 per cent of the target's profits are included, irrespective of the interest which is acquired;

(c) *consideration to assets:* the consideration divided by net assets of the purchaser. The consideration is the amount paid to the vendors and if the consideration includes listed or AIM shares, their value is taken at their aggregate market value. Deferred consideration should be included at the maximum amount payable;

(d) *consideration to market capitalisation:* the consideration divided by the aggregate market value of all the equity shares of the purchaser.

Even if the single transaction does not exceed the requisite percentage ratio, transactions completed during the twelve months prior to the date of the latest transaction must be aggregated with that transaction if they are with the same, or connected, persons; if they involve one particular company; or if together they lead to substantial involvement in a new business activity.

A substantial transaction, determined by the comparisons set out above, will give rise to an obligation to notify the Companies Announcement Office of the Exchange. A transaction with a related party will require notification if, under any of the above comparisons, the calculation gives rise to a percentage ratio of 5 per cent or more. If any of the comparisons give rise to an anomalous result, the Exchange may disregard the result and substitute other relevant indicators of size, although not, it seems, in the case of a related party transaction. Where the transaction by the AIM company requires notification, either as a substantial transaction or as a transaction with a related party, six copies of the announcement should be sent to the CAO. The announcement should include the following details (para 16.22 of the *Rules*):

(a)   particulars of the transaction, including the name of the target company or business;
(b)   a description of the business carried on by, or using, the net assets which are the subject of the transaction;
(c)   the consideration, and how it is being satisfied (including the terms of any arrangements for deferred consideration);
(d)   the value of the net assets which are the subject of the transaction;
(e)   the profits attributable to the net assets which are the subject of the transaction;
(f)   the effect of the transaction on the issuer including any benefits which are expected to accrue to the purchaser as a result of the transaction;
(g)   details of any service contracts of proposed directors of the purchaser; and
(h)   any other information necessary to enable investors to evaluate the effect of the transaction on the purchaser.

In addition, if the transaction is with a related party, the announcement must include the name of the related party and details of the nature and extent of his interest in the transaction and, at least seven days prior to the transaction being entered into, the purchaser must send a copy of the announcement to its shareholders and, if any percentage ratio exceeds 0.25 per cent, details of it must be included in the purchaser's next annual accounts, whether already notified or not. In practice, it may be appropriate to enter into the transaction on a conditional basis and then despatch the notice to shareholders at least seven days prior to completion. The condition could be, for example, the purchaser not having received any material objection from its shareholders to the acquisition—although it will be a matter for discussion with its nominated adviser what will happen if there is such an objection. The AIM *Rules* do not prohibit the transaction from proceeding.

A reverse takeover by an AIM company, being an acquisition or series of acquisitions in a 12 month period which exceed 100 per cent in any of the above percentage ratios (or which would result in a fundamental change in its business or in board or voting control) will result in a suspension of trading and the purchaser must send an explanatory circular to shareholders and seek their prior approval in general meeting (upon which the transaction must be conditional). If shareholder approval is given, the issuer's admission to trading on AIM will be discontinued and it must reapply for admission.

11.8   Using unlisted shares to fund an acquisition

If an AIM company decides to use its shares to fund an acquisition it may decide to use any of the rights issue or placing procedures outlined above (*see* p 237). The commentary set out above for a listed company will be of broadly similar application to the transaction. In addition, however, a prospectus may be required under the Public Offer of Securities Regulations 1995, which replaced the prospectus regime of Part III of the Companies Act 1985 for almost all purposes and gives effect to the EC Public Offer Directive. The POS Regulations apply to any investment which is not admitted to the Official List or the subject of an application to the Official List and which falls within Sched 1, paras 1, 2, 4 or 5 of the Financial Services Act 1986. Shares and debentures (or loan notes) fall within its ambit. An AIM company, or other unlisted purchaser, must ensure that the offer falls within one or more of the other exemptions, or publish a prospectus.

Under the POS Regulations, a person is to be regarded as offering securities if, 'as principal, he makes an offer which, if accepted, would give rise to a contract for the issue or sale of the securities by him or by another person with whom he has made arrangements for the issue or sale of the securities' or he invites a person to make such an offer (reg 5). When securities are offered to the public in the United Kingdom for the first time the offeror must publish a prospectus. Under reg 6 an offer made to any section of the public, whether selected as members or debenture holders of a body corporate, is to be regarded as made to the public.

It will be seen that the allotment of an unlisted purchaser's shares as consideration for the acquisition might involve an offer to the public within the meaning of the Regulations, whether it is a simple share for share transaction or (where a market—eg AIM—exists for the shares) when the funding of cash consideration is by way of vendor placing or other market operation.

In practice, the simple share for share exchange will almost always be exempt from the requirement to produce a prospectus by virtue of reg 7(2)(*b*), which provides an exemption where the securities are offered to no more than 50 persons. If there are more than 50 vendors it may in any event be preferable to structure the acquisition as a takeover offer in which case the exemption in reg 7(2)(*k*) would apply. Where the purchaser's shares are offered to placees in an underwriting, such an arrangement should be capable of exemption either because they are offered to no more than 50 persons or because the offer is made to persons sufficiently knowledgeable to understand the risks (reg 7(2)(d)) or is in connection with a *bona fide* invitation to enter into an underwriting agreement with respect to those securities (reg 7(2)(*e*)).

An issue of unlisted shares as consideration for an acquisition may involve the publication of an investment advertisement under the Financial Services Act, s 57. As such, any such investment must be exempt, or approved, in accordance with that Act (*see further* Chapter 3).

11.9 Using shares to fund an acquisition of business assets

It is possible to fund an acquisition of business assets by an issue of the purchaser's shares, usually where the funding is structured as a cash placing or rights issue. If these funding mechanisms are used there is no practical consequence which follows from the proceeds being used for the acquisition of assets rather than shares.

The vendor placing structure for a direct acquisition of assets is rare. While the exception from the statutory pre-emption rights by virtue of the Companies Act 1985, s 89(4) will apply to an issue of shares in consideration for assets other than shares, merger relief under s 131 would not be available and the premium arising on issue of the purchaser's shares must be added to the share premium account. Any difference between the fair value of the consideration and the fair value of the identifiable assets of the business acquired will be accounted for as goodwill which (under current accounting rules—although it is proposed that they change) will require writing off; the share premium account is not available for such purpose (*see further* Chapter 8).

Most particularly, the Companies Act 1985, s 103(1) would require a valuation of the business assets. That section provides that a public company shall not allot shares as fully or partly paid up in cash unless the consideration is independently valued (under s 108), a report with respect to the value has been sent to the company (within 6 months prior to the allotment), and a copy of the report has been sent to the allottee (s 103(2)). The exception for share acquisition in s 103(3) would not apply (*see further* p 26).

Occasionally, a business acquisition will be structured as a share transaction in order that it can be financed by way of vendor placing, attracting merger relief and avoiding the requirement for a valuation under s 103. The simplest approach is for the business to be hived into a separate 'newco' by the vendor, and for the purchaser to buy that company in the normal way. However, the taxation consequences of such a hive down will need to be looked at carefully—in particular from the capital gains tax point of view, the assets will have transferred from the original company into newco on a no gain, no loss basis. When newco leaves the vendor's ownership a capital gains tax charge will arise under the Taxation of Chargeable Gains Act 1992, s 179, on the difference between market value of the relevant asset at the date of transfer and its historic capital gains base cost, as increased by indexation allowance. Stamp duty and capital allowances will also require consideration (*see further* Chapter 13 and 16).

Chapter 12

Taxation of the Transaction (Shares and Business Assets)

Almost every aspect of taxation can apply, in some way, to the acquisition of a private company or of business assets. Detailed discussion of all possible revenue considerations is outside the scope of this book, and the purpose of this Chapter and Chapter 13, which deals with the taxation position of the target company is to mention (in more or less detail) matters which often arise in practice.

12.1 Structuring the transaction

One of the initial decisions the purchaser and the vendor will have to take is whether it is the shares in the target company or its assets which are to be sold. There are a number of advantages and disadvantages to each course of action, and what benefits one party may, of course, be unattractive to the other.

The main taxation issues which arise (and are addressed in detail in the following sections of this chapter) are:

(1) On an asset sale, the purchaser may be able to obtain capital allowances for certain of the assets acquired. The vendor (that is, the target), however, may suffer claw-back or balancing charges in respect of any capital allowances it has previously claimed itself. Where the target is sold, its capital allowance position is unaffected.

(2) An asset sale provides opportunities for capital gains tax roll-over relief under the Taxation of Chargeable Gains Act 1992, s 152. The target may be able to roll-over its gains on the disposal of qualifying assets into other assets bought by it or another company in its group within the relevant period, while the purchaser may be able to use its acquisition to shelter gains realised by it or another company in its group. On a share sale relief will be available only to vendors who receive shares or loan stock in the circumstances set out in the Taxation of Chargeable Gains Act 1992, s 135.

(3) On a share sale, the base cost for capital gains tax purposes to the target of its assets is unaffected (unless the Taxation of Chargeable Gains Act 1992, s 179 applies). A purchaser who acquires assets may obtain a higher base cost. This will also increase the amount of indexation allowance available on a future disposal of the assets. However, the tax liability of the target may be greater on an asset sale than the vendors would suffer on a share sale, and the vendors may incur further taxation in extracting the proceeds of sale from the target.

(4) On an asset sale, the purchaser may obtain a deduction as a trading expense for corporation tax purposes for the cost of any trading stock acquired. The target will include such amount as part of its trading income.

(5) In some instances, an asset sale may produce a stamp duty saving, perhaps if the assets consist mainly of chattels which pass by delivery. On the other hand *ad valorem* stamp duty on a transfer of shares is charged on the consideration at the rate of 50p per £100 or part, while the rate of stamp duty on the consideration for other property is £1 per £100 or part. The amount of any liabilities of the target which are assumed by the purchaser on an asset sale form part of the consideration (Stamp Act 1891, s 57). Thus the stampable consideration may be much greater, and subject to stamp duty at a higher rate, on an asset purchase than on a share purchase.

(6) Value added tax will not be chargeable on a sale of assets (except perhaps in respect of certain property interests) provided the acquisition amounts to a transfer of a going concern within the Value Added Tax (Special Provisions) Order 1995 (SI No 1268), art 5. If the target is required to charge value added tax, the purchaser will have to consider the extent to which it will be able to recover this as input tax. The transfer of shares, on the other hand, is exempt from value added tax.

The considerations to be taken into account are by no means limited to taxation matters.

However, this Chapter limits its consideration to the taxation treatment of the participants to the transaction. On the sale of a corporate target it is the vendor's tax position which is the focus of most tax planning and, save for stamp duty, taxation of the purchaser is not generally considered. Taxation considerations for both parties to the acquisition of business assets is then considered. The structure of this Chapter is, accordingly:

(12.2) Taxation of the vendors of a corporate target (*see below*);

(12.3) Stamp duty and stamp duty reserve tax considerations for the purchaser (p 280);

(12.4) Taxation issues for the parties to an acquisition of business assets (p 283).

12.2 Taxation of the vendors of a corporate target

This part of the Chapter is concerned with tax payable by the vendors. It does not deal with the taxation treatment of any reconstruction or reorganisation which may be undertaken as a preparatory step to any sale. Nor is there any detailed examination of the tax planning opportunities available to the vendors. Readers should, however, note that the unification of income tax and capital gains tax rates and March 1982 rebasing for capital gains tax purposes introduced by the Finance Act 1988 overturned much conventional wisdom as to the optimum method of structuring a transaction and every transaction should be approached afresh. Consideration is now commonly given to proposals which formerly would have seemed heretical, such as constituting part of the consideration as dividends or remuneration. Indeed, it can be easier to shelter income, through pension scheme payments or investments in enterprise investment scheme companies and enterprise zone properties, than it is to shelter capital gains from tax in the absence of retirement relief or a share for share exchange. The Finance Act 1988 changes had an equally dramatic effect on anti-avoidance legislation, most of which is framed with a view to preventing the conversion of income into capital. Nevertheless, some of those provisions are still of concern in some cases and will, of course, be of renewed importance if a differential between income and capital gains tax rates is reintroduced.

Tax will normally be payable on any gain made by the vendors on the sale of their shares in the target. Where the gain is not part of a trade an individual will, subject to any exemption or special charge which may be applicable, pay capital gains tax on the gain. Companies will pay corporation tax on the gain whether or not it forms part of their trade, but, if it does not form part of their trade, the tax will normally be assessed under the same rules as apply to capital gains tax. Corporation tax on capital gains is currently payable at the rate of 33 per cent (unless the small companies rate of 23 per cent is available), while for an individual capital gains tax is payable at the individual's marginal rate of income tax (currently the lower rate of 20 per cent, the basic rate of 23 per cent or the higher rate of 40 per cent) although under the Taxation of Chargeable Gains Act 1992, s 3 exemption is granted, to individuals only, on the first £6,500 of total chargeable gains (less allowable losses) in the year of assessment. For the purposes of computing the gain an indexation allowance is granted for both individuals and companies by the Taxation of Chargeable Gains Act 1992, ss 53–57. It should be noted that the indexation allowance can no longer be used to create or increase a capital loss.

The indexation allowance is calculated from March 1982, or the date of acquisition if later, on the acquisition cost (subject to any rebasing election under the Taxation of Chargeable Gains Act 1992, s 35(5)) or, if greater, the market value of the asset on 31 March 1982 if held at that date. Expenditure allowable under the Taxation of Chargeable Gains Act 1992, s 38 also qualifies for indexation. Acquisition costs have generally been rebased to 31 March 1982, although special provisions apply to ensure that neither chargeable gains nor allowable losses are thereby increased (see Taxation of Chargeable Gains Act 1992, s 35). While the rate of tax applied will be the same, an individual vendor will generally, because of the availability of the indexation allowance and re-basing to 31 March 1982 (and, in appropriate cases, retirement relief), be concerned to obtain a capital gains tax rather than an income tax treatment (but see pre-sale dividends below).

Several matters which should be considered when advising vendors are outlined below, classified as follows:

(12.2.1) the non-resident individual vendor;
(12.2.2) the use of trusts and non-resident companies;
(12.2.3) reinvestment relief;
(12.2.4) transfer of assets on retirement;
(12.2.5) consideration payable by instalments;
(12.2.6) share-for-share exchanges;
(12.2.7) pre-sale dividends;
(12.2.8) sale of debts;
(12.2.9) the Income and Corporation Taxes Act 1988, s 703;
(12.2.10) the Income and Corporation Taxes Act 1988, s 776; and
(12.2.11) the Income and Corporation Taxes Act 1988, ss 765 and 765A.

12.2.1   The non-resident individual vendor

An individual is chargeable to capital gains tax if he is resident or ordinarily resident in the United Kingdom. It is beyond the scope of this book to examine in detail what constitutes 'residence' or 'ordinary residence' or to deal with the complicated cases which arise in connection with visitors to the United Kingdom. It is worth, however, making a few points.

(1)   In order to escape liability for capital gains tax it is normally necessary to be neither resident nor ordinarily resident in the United Kingdom, nor carrying on a trade, profession or vocation through a branch or agency in the United Kingdom with which the shareholding is connected, for the whole of the year of assessment in which the disposal is made. In the case of the sale of shares in a private company, the disposal will be made when an unconditional contract is entered into for the disposal, or, if there is no unconditional contract, on the date of completion. If an individual is ordinarily resident in the United Kingdom, he will not escape capital gains tax simply by departing for the whole of the year of assessment in which the gain is made and then subsequently returning. If he has an intention to return, even if he is physically absent through the whole of the year, he will still be 'ordinarily resident'.

(2)   Where a vendor intends to live abroad permanently, it can be worth ensuring that the gain does not arise in a year of assessment for any part of which he has been resident in the United Kingdom. There are, however,

valuable extra-statutory concessions. If a person claims that he has ceased to be resident and ordinarily resident in the United Kingdom, and can produce some evidence of this (eg that he has sold his house here and set up a permanent home abroad), his claim is usually admitted provisionally with effect from the date following his departure. Normally, this provisional ruling is confirmed after he has remained abroad for a period which includes a complete tax year and during which any visits to this country have not exceeded three months in aggregate. If, however, he cannot produce sufficient evidence, the decision on his claim will be postponed for three years and will then be made by reference to what actually happened in that period. During the three intervening years, his tax liability is computed provisionally on the basis that he remains resident in the United Kingdom. His liability is adjusted, if necessary, when the final decision is made at the end of three years. When a person leaves the United Kingdom and is treated on his departure as not resident and not ordinarily resident in the United Kingdom he is not charged to capital gains tax on gains accruing to him on disposals made after the date of his departure (see Extra-Statutory Concession D2 and the Inland Revenue booklet IR20(1996) *Residents' and Non-residents' Liability to Tax in the United Kingdom*, para 9.3). The Revenue is not obliged to apply the Extra-Statutory Concession if there is any tax avoidance motive and, particularly where the intention to dispose of the shares is formed while the vendor is still resident in the United Kingdom, its use should be approached with care (see *R v IRC, ex p, Fulford-Dobson* [1987] STC 344).

(3) Special provisions may apply to non-residents who carry on a trade, profession or vocation in the United Kingdom through a branch or agency or who are dual resident companies (*see*, for instance, Taxation of Chargeable Gains Act 1992, ss 10, 25 and 185).

(4) The non-resident vendor may, of course, have a liability to tax in his own country of residence. However, under a number of the double taxation conventions to which the United Kingdom is party, a gain realised by a resident of the other party to the convention is exempted from tax by that party if, under the convention, the United Kingdom is entitled to charge the gain to taxation, notwithstanding that, under the United Kingdom's domestic law, the gain is not chargeable because the person who realised it is neither resident nor ordinarily resident in the United Kingdom, nor carrying on a trade, profession or vocation through a branch or agency. It is therefore possible to escape tax entirely.

12.2.2 The use of trusts and non-resident companies

As capital gains tax is charged at the vendor's income tax rate, the proceeds of a disposal of shares by an individual in a private company may well be subject to capital gains tax at the rate of 40 per cent. This liability can be mitigated by, prior to the disposal, transferring the shares to a United Kingdom resident settlement which, although entitled to an annual exemption equivalent to only one-half of the exempt amount available to an individual, will be liable to tax at the basic rate only, or, in the case of discretionary and accumulation and maintenance settlements, at the rate of 34 per cent. Gifting shares to a settlement will not, provided the requirements of the Taxation of Chargeable Gains Act 1992, s 165 are met, crystallise a chargeable gain if the shares in question are unquoted shares in a 'trading company' or in the 'holding company' of a 'trading group' or if the company is the transferor's 'personal company' (*see* p 261). In these circumstances, the transferor on making an appropriate claim will avoid the liability to tax. On the subsequent sale of the shares by the trustees of the settlement, the gain arising will be calculated using the acquisition cost of the shares to the transferor. Advantage can be taken of the settlement's lower rate of tax only if the transferor and his spouse are excluded from benefiting under the settlement. If they are not so excluded then gains realised by the trustees will be taxed as the gains of the transferor (see Taxation of Chargeable Gains Act 1992, s 77).

Non-resident trusts have for many years provided United Kingdom resident vendors with a means of mitigating capital gains tax. Because the holdover relief under the Taxation of Chargeable Gains Act 1992, s 165 described above is not available on a gift to a person resident outside the United Kingdom or to a company controlled by persons resident outside the United Kingdom, to be most effective forward planning has been essential, in order to transfer shares into a non-resident trust before any significant increase in value accrues. Nevertheless, the use of a non-resident trust and holdover relief under s 165 can be combined by gifting the shares in the target company to a company in which up to 49 per cent of the share capital is held by non-resident trustees. The transferee company is subsequently sold to the purchaser, so that a significant proportion of the proceeds of sale accrue to the non-resident trustees.

The advantages afforded by non-resident trusts was much restricted by the Taxation of Chargeable Gains Act 1992 ss 80–98 and Sched 5 (introduced by the Finance Act 1991) but their use remains a possible option, in particular where the settlor is domiciled outside the United Kingdom or does not retain an interest in the property of the trust. It is worth noting that 'professional trustees' resident in the United Kingdom are treated as non-resident where the settlor was not resident, ordinarily resident or domiciled in the United Kingdom at the time of the settlement (Taxation of Chargeable Gains Act 1992, s 69).

Under the Taxation of Chargeable Gains Act 1992, s 10 gains accruing to a non-resident company which, if it were UK resident, would be a close company, are apportioned among the participators (ie shareholders and certain loan creditors). Credit is given for the capital gains tax paid when a distribution, either as a dividend, or on liquidation, is made to the participator within the following two years.

12.2.3 Reinvestment relief

The 1993 Finance Act and subsequent Finance Acts have significantly reduced the capital gains tax burdens for entrepreneurs by the introduction of an entirely new relief known as reinvestment relief and extending the scope of retirement relief (as described more fully at p 260). The legislation is contained in the Taxation of Chargeable Gains Act 1992, ss 164A–164N. The effect of reinvestment relief is that any individual who makes capital gains over and above his annual exempt amount can defer payment of the tax indefinitely by investing the gain in shares in unquoted companies.

The relief as originally introduced provided roll-over relief in respect of disposals of personal company shares, but has now been extended such that any chargeable gain including the disposal of shares and of business assets of an unincorporated entity realised by an individual and most trustees can be rolled over into the cost of the qualifying investment, being the acquisition of eligible shares in a qualifying company. The reinvestor must make a qualifying investment within a period, referred to as the qualifying period, which begins 12 months before the disposal and ends three years after the disposal of the original asset; the Revenue has a discretion to extend the period.

The relief must be claimed. The mechanics are that a reduction is made both in the proceeds of the disposal and in the acquisition cost of the qualifying investment. The amount of the gain which can be rolled over is the smallest of:

(a) the amount of the chargeable gain accruing from the disposal of the original asset;

(b) the actual amount paid for the qualifying investment;

(c) the market value of the qualifying investments if acquired otherwise than by way of arm's length (eg, in the case of a connected party transaction); and

(d) the amount specified in the claim.

Where claimed, the relief is claimed before retirement relief (Taxation of Chargeable Gains Act 1992, s 164BA). A vendor can, however, ensure the application of retirement relief in appropriate cases either by not claiming reinvestment relief or by restricting the amount claimed to such amount as allows the operation of retirement relief.

Conditions applying to the qualifying company

A 'qualifying company' is an unquoted company which exists wholly or mainly for the purpose of carrying on one or more 'qualifying trades' or whose business is that of being a holding company of one or more qualifying subsidiaries or whose business consists entirely of carrying on one or more qualifying trades *and* the holding of shares in one or more qualifying subsidiaries.

In order to constitute a qualifying subsidiary, that company must be in a capital gains group of which the holding company is the principal company ie, the holding company must not itself be a 75 per cent subsidiary of another company and must itself be entitled to 75 per cent of the ordinary share capital of each qualifying subsidiary and to more than 50 per cent of its profits and assets on a winding-up. Each qualifying subsidiary must also be a company within one of the various descriptions in the Taxation of Chargeable Gains Act 1992, s 164G(5). Again, the most relevant description will usually be that the qualifying subsidiary exists wholly for the purpose of carrying on a qualifying trade.

Qualifying trade

The trade must be conducted on a commercial basis and with a view to the realisation of profits. The trade or a substantial part of it must not consist of one or more of a list of forbidden activities which include dealing in land, banking and financial services, leasing and legal and accountancy services (Taxation of Chargeable Gains Act 1992, s 164I). Since 29 November 1994, property development and farming constitute qualifying trades.

Eligible shares

These are defined as ordinary shares in a company which do not carry any present or future preferential rights to dividends or assets on a winding-up or any present or future preferential right to be redeemed.

There are numerous anti-avoidance provisions designed to prevent the reinvestor recovering directly or indirectly all or part of the cost of his qualifying investment (the Taxation of Chargeable Gains Act 1992, s 164L). There are also provisions for the clawback of relief, for example if within a certain period the shares cease to be eligible shares or the reinvestor ceases to be resident or ordinarily resident in the UK. A detailed discussion of these two areas is outside the scope of this book.

12.2.4   Transfer of assets on retirement

The Taxation of Chargeable Gains Act 1992, s 163 and Sched 6, grants valuable relief from capital gains tax to the owner of a family business selling after reaching 'retirement age' (now 50) or who has been forced to retire earlier through ill health. The first £250,000 of gains and half the next £750,000 of gains will be free of capital gains tax if they arise on a 'material disposal of business assets' by a person who has reached the age of 50 or who has retired through ill health before that age (s 163(1)). A 'disposal of business assets' includes both the sale of assets of an unincorporated business and a sale of shares (s 163(2)(*c*)).

Changes to retirement relief in the Finance Act 1993 substantially widened the availability of retirement relief in relation to a material disposal of shares or securities. Previously, retirement relief had been available only if the individual made a material disposal of shares or securities in the individual's family company. The term family company meant a company in which either not less than 25 per cent of the voting rights were exercisable by the individual or not less than 5 per cent were exercisable by the individual and more than 50 per cent exercisable by the individual or his family. This requirement has been replaced with the requirement that the company now be the individual's personal company ie, a company as to which not less than 5 per cent of the voting rights are exercisable by the individual.

In addition, following the Finance Act 1993, a disposal of shares or securities may be a material disposal if the individual was or had been a full-time working officer or employee which expression, in essence, requires the individual to work full-time in a technical or managerial capacity.

The provisions are complex and will need to be reviewed in each case. The qualifying conditions applying to the company and applying to the disposal are summarised below.

Conditions applying to the company

A disposal of business assets is 'material' if throughout a period of one year ending with the 'operative date' the vendor either owns the business then owned by the company *or* the company is the vendor's personal company of which the vendor is a full time working officer or employee and the company is either a trading company or the holding company of a trading group (s 163(5)).

A 'personal company' in relation to an individual means a company in which the voting rights are exercisable as to not less than 5 per cent by the individual. A 'trading company' is defined as any company whose business consists wholly or mainly of the carrying on of a trade or trades. The holding company of a trading group also qualifies for relief; a 'trading group' is defined to mean a group of companies (being the parent and its 51 per cent subsidiaries) the business of whose members taken together consists wholly or mainly of the carrying on of a trade or trades.

A 'full time working officer or employee' is defined as an officer or employee who is required to devote substantially the whole of his time in a managerial or technical capacity to the service of the company or, as the case may be, the companies in the group taken together.

Qualifying conditions for disposal

The conditions relating to the company need to be fulfilled in relation to each vendor who seeks relief and if the period ending with the 'operative date' on which they are fulfilled exceeds ten years the full relief is obtained. For the purposes of calculating this period separate periods during which the vendor carried on a business may be aggregated provided that not more than two years elapse between any two qualifying periods. If the conditions are fulfilled in respect of a shorter period than ten years (with a minimum of one year) relief is reduced *pro rata*.

For the purposes of the relief the 'operative date' is the date of the disposal or, if earlier, either the date on which the company ceased trading (provided the vendor had reached the age of 50 or retired through ill health prior to such cessation) or the date on which the vendor retired as a full time working employee or officer. If the operative date is the date of retirement the company must continue to qualify as a family company carrying on a trade and the vendor must continue as an employee or officer of the company to devote at least ten hours per week to the service of the company (or of the group) in a technical or managerial capacity until the date of sale or cessation of trade.

The amount of the gain available for relief will be restricted by reference to the chargeable business assets of the company (or the group) at the time of the disposal. Relief is given on that part of the gain which bears the same proportion to the total gain as the value of the 'chargeable business assets' bears to the value of the 'chargeable assets' of the target (or the group). Every asset is a chargeable asset except those on the disposal of which no chargeable gain would arise (Sched 6, para 7(3)). Examples of a non-chargeable asset would be tangible moveable property of less than £6,000 and debts. 'Chargeable business assets' means assets (including goodwill but not including investments) which are assets used for the purposes of a trade carried on by the company or by a member of the group. Special rules apply in the case of groups to exclude investments in subsidiaries from the definition of chargeable assets and to apportion the value of assets in subsidiaries which are not wholly owned.

A number of detailed rules exist making provision for disposals by trustees, for aggregating several disposals and in relation to assets which have been owned by the vendor's spouse.

A vendor who has obtained relief under the Taxation of Chargeable Gains Act 1992, s 135, on an exchange of shares in the target for shares in the purchaser will not be entitled to retirement relief on a disposal of the consideration shares (unless they qualify for relief in their own right) even though a disposal of shares in the target would have been eligible for relief. The Taxation of Chargeable Gains Act 1992, Sched 6, para 2, allows such a vendor to elect within two years of a share for share exchange (or of any reorganisation of capital falling within the Taxation of Chargeable Gains Act 1992, s 126) for the provisions of s 127 not to apply to the exchange. The exchange will therefore be treated as a disposal for capital gains tax purposes and retirement relief will be available if the other conditions for relief are fulfilled.

12.2.5   Consideration payable by instalments

It is often the case that some part of the consideration payable for the acquisition of a private company will be payable after completion. Examples include where part of the consideration is retained as security for warranties or where the consideration is based on profits yet to be earned. In these cases it is necessary to consider the impact of capital gains tax upon the arrangements which are proposed.

It is the normal rule (Taxation of Chargeable Gains Act 1992, s 48) that capital gains tax is payable on the disposal by reference to the total consideration receivable. Consideration is brought into account without a discount for postponement of the right to receive any part of it and, in the first instance, without regard to a risk of any part being irrecoverable or to the right to receive it being contingent. The Taxation of Chargeable Gains Act 1992, s 49(1)(*c*) specifically provides that no allowance will be made for any contingent liability in respect of a warranty or representation made on the disposal by way of sale of any property other than land, although, if the contingent liability becomes enforceable, adjustments are made. A retention as security for warranties will not therefore normally affect the capital gains tax computation.

The Taxation of Chargeable Gains Act 1992, s 280 applies where consideration is payable by instalments over a period exceeding eighteen months beginning not earlier than the time when the disposal is made. Liability to tax may be deferred if the vendor satisfies the Board of Inland Revenue that he would otherwise suffer undue hardship. The Board may allow the tax to be paid by instalments over a period not exceeding eight years and ending not later than the time at which the last of the instalments of consideration is payable. The vendor has to show hardship and it seems that this will normally be shown if he cannot pay the tax out of the resources made available to him by the transaction. The section applies only where the consideration is truly payable by instalments. For instance, if the consideration is paid by means of a 'vendor placing' and the vendor then deposits part of the consideration with the purchaser, even though that part of the consideration might be returnable only at some future date, the consideration does not appear to be payable by instalments within the meaning of the section.

Where consideration is calculated by reference to profits earned after completion (sometimes called an 'earn out'), or is otherwise indeterminate in amount, the computation is more difficult. In these cases the practice of the Revenue is to value the contingent right to receive the consideration and to charge tax by reference to the aggregate of the consideration actually received and the value of the contingent right. The contingent right is itself a chargeable asset and in *Marren (Inspector of Taxes) v Ingles* (1980) 54 TC 76 it was held that this right was disposed of when the vendor received the future consideration, thus giving rise (in that case) to a further chargeable gain. The Taxation of Chargeable Gains Act 1992, s 22(1), provides that there is a disposal of assets by their owner where any capital sum is derived from assets, even though no asset is acquired by the person paying the capital sum. It was argued on behalf of the taxpayer that this subsection was confined to cases where no asset was acquired by the person paying the capital sum and, of course, in cases relating to deferred consideration an asset (ie the shares in the target) is so acquired even though it is acquired before the final consideration is paid. The House of Lords rejected this argument, holding that the section applies whether or not assets are acquired by the person paying the capital sum. See also *Marson (Inspector of Taxes) v Marriage* (1979) 54 TC 59. It has been suggested that, if there is a limit on the total consideration payable, or if the amount to be paid is definite although payable at an indeterminate time, it may be that *Marren v Ingles* does not apply, and s 48 does, so that tax is to be calculated by reference to the full amount, not the value of the contingent right. This area is one of some uncertainty and although some clarification has been given where the deferred consideration consists solely of shares or debentures (*see below*), in many cases the treatment will depend on the view taken by the vendor's Inspector of Taxes.

A further consequence of *Marren v Ingles* is that deferral of the charge to capital gains tax by means of roll-over relief (*see* 'share for share' exchanges *below*) will, in strict law, not be available to the extent that the consideration shares are to be issued at some future date, since the contingent right to an allotment of shares does not amount to an issue of shares within the Taxation of Chargeable Gains Act 1992, s 135.

In order to avoid the problems arising from *Marren v Ingles*, it became common to issue shares or other securities of the purchaser to which special rights attached, in place of a simple covenant to pay. These securities were issued to the vendors at completion and carried rights to ensure that their value fell to be determined by reference to the earn out formula. Similar arrangements involving the retention by or issue to the vendors of special shares in the target carrying a right to a dividend or to be repurchased by the target on the basis of the earn out formula have also been used.

The Revenue agreed in Extra-Statutory Concession D27 (*see* Finance Act 1997, s 89, inserting a new s 138A into the Taxation of Chargeable Gains Act 1992) that where, under the sale agreement, a right is created to an unascertainable amount (whether or not subject to a maximum) which is to be satisfied wholly by the issue of shares or debentures, the Revenue will, if the vendor so elects, treat that right as a security for capital gains tax purposes, so that roll-over relief will be available. In those circumstances, therefore, there is no longer any need for such special shares or securities. If, however, the deferred consideration is to be satisfied or may be satisfied in cash, then the value of the right to the deferred consideration will be brought into the capital gains tax computation and the Taxation of Chargeable Gains Act 1992, s 138A will not apply.

12.2.6   Share for share exchanges

Where the consideration for the acquisition is the issue of shares or debentures by a purchaser company, capital gains tax otherwise payable on the sale of shares in the target may be deferred. The relevant provisions are contained in the Taxation of Chargeable Gains Act 1992, ss 126–138.

In order to obtain roll-over relief it is necessary that at least one of the following circumstances exists:

(a) the purchaser holds, or in consequence of the exchange will hold, more than one quarter of the ordinary share capital of the target. 'Ordinary share capital' is defined for this purpose (by the Income and Corporation Taxes Act 1988, s 832(1)) as 'all the issued share capital (by whatever name called) of the company, other than capital the holders of which have a right to a dividend at a fixed rate but have no other right to share in the profits of the company'; or

(b) the exchange takes place as the result of a general offer made to members of the target or any class of them (with or without exceptions for persons connected with the purchaser), the offer being made in the first instance on a condition such that if it were satisfied the purchaser would have control of the target; or

(c) purchaser holds, or in consequence of the exchange will hold, the greater part of the voting power in the target.

Circumstance (c) was introduced by the Finance (No 2) Act 1992, s 35 in order to bring the provisions of the Taxation of Chargeable Gains Act 1992, s 135 into compliance with the EC Directive on Cross-Border Mergers (90/434/EEC). However, it applies also to purely domestic transactions.

The consideration shares or debentures must be issued to the vendors. For the purposes of the Taxation of Chargeable Gains Act 1992, s 135 'issue' includes 'allot' (Taxation of Chargeable Gains Act 1992, s 288(5)) and consideration shares or debentures may therefore be issued on renounceable letters of allotment without prejudicing the availability of relief although, of course, any subsequent renunciation will result in a disposal of the shares for capital gains tax purposes.

The Taxation of Chargeable Gains Act 1992, s 137 imposes an overriding condition on the application of roll-over or hold-over relief in these circumstances. The condition is that the exchange is effected for *bona fide* commercial reasons and does not form part of a scheme or arrangements of which the main purpose, or one of the main purposes, is avoidance of liability to capital gains tax or corporation tax. This condition, however, does not affect relief available to any vendor who (together with persons connected with him) does not hold more than 5 per cent of, or of any class of, the shares in or debentures of the target. It is open either to the purchaser or to the target to apply for clearance and, if the Board of Inland Revenue notifies the applicant that it is satisfied that the exchange will be effected for *bona fide* commercial reasons and will not form part of any such scheme or arrangements, the condition is deemed satisfied. If the overriding condition imposed by s 137 operates to defeat roll-over relief, the section provides that tax assessed on vendors and not paid within six months from the date when it is payable is recoverable within two years from any other person who holds all or any part of the consideration shares or debentures that were issued to the vendor and who acquired them without there having been a chargeable disposal for capital gains tax purposes or who acquired them from the vendor in the circumstances referred to in the Taxation of Chargeable Gains Act 1992, s 58(1) (disposals between spouses), or s 171(1) (disposals between members of a group of companies).

On a subsequent disposal of the new holding the calculation of the tax payable can be complex, particularly where only part of the new holding is disposed of and the shares in the target were originally acquired at different dates and at different prices. The basic rules are to be found in the Taxation of Chargeable Gains Act 1992, ss 104–109 and (in relation to shares held on 6 April 1965) Sched 2, para 4.

Vendors who have reached retirement age and who wish to avail themselves of the reliefs conferred by the Taxation of Chargeable Gains Act 1992, s 163 should consider carefully before they sell the shares in their personal company in exchange for shares in the purchaser so as to obtain roll-over relief, as the retirement relief will not be applicable to the sale (as there is no disposal) and may not be available on a subsequent disposal of the consideration shares, if these do not themselves qualify for relief. In these circumstances, the vendor may elect that roll-over relief should not apply.

If the provisions of the Taxation of Chargeable Gains Act 1992, s 135 apply, no disposal is treated as occurring. Consequently no tax is payable on the exchange and the new shares or debentures are treated in the hands of the vendors as if they had been acquired at the time when, and for the consideration for which, the shares in the target were acquired; in other words the gain (or loss) accrued at the time of the exchange is 'rolled over' into the consideration shares or debentures.

This treatment is modified where the consideration debentures are 'qualifying corporate bonds' within the meaning of the Taxation of Chargeable Gains Act 1992, s 117, broadly, any sterling denominated, non-convertible company debenture, whether or not it is quoted on a stock exchange. Instead the consideration debentures are treated as acquired at the date of the exchange for a consideration equal to the market value of the shares in the target. The gain (or loss) on the shares in the target is calculated but is 'held over' and does not accrue until a subsequent disposal of the consideration debentures (Taxation of Chargeable Gains Act 1992, s 116(10)).

The tax treatment of the qualifying corporate bond is further modified depending on whether the holder is a corporate or non-corporate. In the case of corporates, the Finance Act 1996, s 80 *ff* (Loan Relationships) assesses all profits and losses arising from a loan relationship for corporation tax purposes as income. Profits are treated as either Schedule D Case I or Case III depending on whether or not the loan relationship is for the purpose of the company's trade (referred to as trading or non-trading credits), and similarly for losses (referred to as trading or non-trading debits).

Non-corporates

Any gain or loss on a qualifying corporate bond is outside the scope of capital gains tax (Taxation of Chargeable Gains Act 1992, s 115(1)), including any loss attributable to the indexation allowance. Accordingly, if the purchaser subsequently proves unable to redeem the consideration debentures, the vendor not only has a non-allowable capital loss but the held-over gain will be brought into charge in full. Provisions contained in the Taxation of Chargeable Gains Act 1992, s 254 give loss relief on the same basis as is available on a qualifying loans to traders (Taxation of Chargeable Gains Act 1992, s 253). However, it is not clear that s 254 will be available in the circumstances of all exchanges because of the restrictions on relief in s 253(1) which require the borrower (ie the purchaser) to use the money lent (ie the nominal amount of the consideration debentures) for the purposes of its trade or to lend it to another group company which so uses it. This requirement is obviously not met in every case. The vendors may therefore wish the terms of the consideration debentures to be such that they are not qualifying corporate bonds. This is possible in a number of ways for non-corporates, eg by providing an option for redemption in a foreign currency other than at the rate of exchange prevailing at redemption (see s 117(2)). Care must be taken that the consideration debentures are not 'relevant discounted securities' for the purposes of the Finance Act 1996, Sched 13 as these are automatically qualifying corporate bonds (s 117(2AA)).

Corporates

As in the case of non-corporates, the consideration debentures, if qualifying corporate bonds, are treated as acquired at the date of exchange for a consideration equal to the market value of the shares in the target and the gain or loss 'held over' until a subsequent disposal of the consideration debenture. Any profit or loss to the corporate holder of the debenture will be taxed or relieved on an accruals basis as a non-trading credit or debit.

The only way of structuring a debt instrument for a corporate holder so that it is not a qualifying corporate bond, such that any profits or gains (other than interest) are taxed as capital, is to have a genuine conversion mechanism into shares. Since the introduction of the foreign exchange legislation in the Finance Act 1993, and now the loan relationships legislation in the Finance Act 1996, a debt held by a corporate which has a settlement currency other than sterling is treated as a qualifying corporate bond and is exempt from capital gains (see Taxation of Chargeable Gains Act 1992 s 117(A1) (as inserted by

Finance Act 1996, Sched 14, para 61)). Profits and losses are taxed on an income basis.

12.2.7   Pre-sale dividends

If the target has significant distributable reserves, a United Kingdom resident corporate vendor will be able to reduce its capital gain on the sale of the target by procuring the payment of a dividend by the target prior to the sale. In the hands of a United Kingdom resident company such a dividend is free of corporation tax (Income and Corporation Taxes Act 1988, s 208) and such a payment allows the purchase price of the target to be reduced while the vendor still receives the same total consideration, including the dividend. Because the purchase price of the target's shares is reduced, the capital gain is, of course, lower. The Taxation of Chargeable Gains Act 1992, ss 30–34 reduce the scope for avoidance of tax on capital gains by companies on disposal of subsidiaries by treating the consideration for the disposal as increased by such amount as may be just and reasonable where the value of the shares are materially reduced and a tax-free benefit is conferred, unless it is shown that avoidance of tax was not the main purpose or one of the main purposes of the scheme or arrangements in question. A payment of a dividend to a company in the same group is not caught by these provisions save to the extent that it is attributable to profits realised by the target as a result of certain tax free disposals of assets. A pre-sale dividend paid out of the target's 'normal' profits and reserves remains effective. A pre-sale dividend cannot be used to create a capital loss (Taxation of Chargeable Gains Act 1992, s 177).

A pre-sale dividend may be paid under the terms of a group income election under the Income and Corporation Taxes Act 1988, s 247 (*see* p 301) and so no liability to advance corporation tax (ACT) will arise. Both purchaser and vendor will wish to satisfy themselves that a valid group election is in force at the date of payment of the dividend. The group election ceases to apply when the purchaser ceases to be the beneficial owner of the target (s 248(4)) so that where the parties wish to make the payment under a group election it will be necessary to pay the dividend prior to exchange of contracts. For group relief purposes, 'arrangements' for the transfer of beneficial ownership can affect the ability of purchaser and target to surrender group relief (Income and Corporation Taxes Act 1988, s 410: *see* p 304), but these provisions do not apply to group income elections and accordingly the election will remain in force while the beneficial ownership of the target is with the purchaser notwithstanding that arrangements exist for its sale, unless these amount to 'option arrangements' within the Income and Corporation Taxes Act 1988, Sched 18, para 5B such that, by application of the provisions of Sched 18, the target is no longer a 51 per cent subsidiary of the vendor. The Revenue state in Statement of Practice 3/93, para 8 that there may be 'option arrangements' if for an example an offer for shares in the target, whether formally made or not, is allowed to remain open for an appreciable period so that the potential purchaser is allowed to choose the amount to create a bargain. The agreement not to seek another purchaser while negotiations proceed could amount to a fetter on the vendor's beneficial ownership of the target within *Wood Preservation Ltd v Prior* [1969] 1 WLR 1077, although see also *O'Connor (Inspector of Taxes) v J Sainsbury plc* [1991] STC 318 where the existence of options granted to a third party over shares in a subsidiary did not cause the taxpayer company to cease to be their beneficial owner.

The purchaser who agrees to a pre-sale dividend paid under a group income election will wish to be sure that the target is not going to become liable to pay ACT in respect of the dividend and will, for safety's sake, also wish to ensure that the terms of the sale agreement give the target an effective indemnity against that liability if it should arise.

In some circumstances it may be desirable to make the dividend payment outside the group election. This will be the case where the vendor can use the ACT to frank its own dividend (Income and Corporation Taxes Act 1988, s 239) and if the purchase price is adjusted to allow for the interest cost of the ACT payment over the period prior to its recovery by the target the result can be satisfactory for both parties. However, the provisions of the Income and Corporation Taxes Act 1988, ss 245–245B, which prevent the set-off of ACT where there is a change in ownership of the company and certain other circumstances exist, must be borne in mind (*see* p 318). Section 247 provides that it is for the target to choose whether or not to pay the dividend within the group election and on the face of the section it seems that the choice must be made while the group election remains in force.

In practice, the target may not have sufficient funds to pay the dividend and therefore it will be necessary for the vendor to lend an equivalent amount to fund the payment. The sale agreement will provide that, at completion, the purchaser must put the target in funds to repay this loan. Because the purchase price will have been reduced by the amount of the dividend, this will not involve any additional cash outlay on the purchaser's part (and may indeed reduce the liability to stamp duty on the acquisition). Where the parties wish to make the payment under a group election then of course it is necessary that the dividend is 'received' while the election remains in force, and if no money is to pass (because the dividend is immediately to be re-lent) then the question will arise whether the mere crediting of accounts is a sufficient receipt. On the authority of *Garforth (Inspector of Taxes) v Newsmith Stainless Ltd* (1978) 52 TC 522, the crediting of an account is probably sufficient, but it is prudent to ensure that cheques are passed from target to vendor and vice versa, and cashed. The Companies Act 1985, s 153(3), specifically provides that a distribution by way of dividend is not prohibited by s 151 which prohibits financial assistance by the target in connection with the sale of its own shares (*see* p 51).

A pre-sale dividend may also prove beneficial for individual vendors, for whom the ACT paid in respect of the dividend represents a lower rate income tax credit. The current rate of ACT is 20 per cent. As a £80 dividend carries with it a £20 tax credit (at current rates of tax), further tax of £20 need be paid to satisfy liability to higher rate income tax at 40 per cent, thus giving an effective tax rate of 25 per cent (£20 out of £80) on the cash dividend. Of course, no group election is available for individual vendors so this route will be of use only if the target can utilise any ACT payable on the dividend. This may well be the case as privately owned companies tend not to have paid significant dividends so that mainstream corporation tax paid by the target in past years will be available against which ACT can be recovered (Income and Corporation Taxes Act 1988, s 239(3)).

The practitioner should also give some thought as to whether the pre-sale dividend is caught by the provisions of the Finance Act 1997, Sched 7. The effect of Sched 7, broadly, is to treat certain qualifying distributions, like pre-sale dividends, which are linked to a transaction in securities as a foreign income dividend ('FID') for tax purposes with the effect preventing non-taxpayers, such as pensions funds and non resident companies with the benefit of a double tax treaty, from reclaiming in cash from the Revenue all or part of the tax credit attaching to the dividend. The main impact of Sched 7 for the purchaser is likely to be in the situation where the target has a subsidiary which pays a pre-sale dividend outside a group income election (*see* p 268) such that ACT will become payable, in order to frank a pre-sale dividend by the target to the vendor. If, under Sched 7, the target's dividend to the vendor is treated as a FID, the dividend from its subsidiary cannot be used to frank the FID. Both the subsidiary and target would in these circumstances pay ACT. Although this additional ACT should eventually be recoverable, a purchaser should ensure that its tax indemnity covers the ACT liability and any related costs.

Because these transactions involve the payment of an abnormal dividend in connection with a transaction in securities the practitioner will consider whether or not the Income and Corporation Taxes Act 1988, s 703, is in point. If time permits the parties may well seek a clearance under s 707 but it is suggested that the section ought not apply. A pre-sale dividend has the effect of turning capital into income rather than the reverse, and represents an extraction of profit from the target which could have taken place at any time while the target belonged to the vendor. It is a curious effect of the structural changes to income and capital gains taxation introduced by the Finance Act 1988 that it is now in certain circumstances less tax efficient to receive capital rather than income— the mischief that s 703 was designed to prevent!

As a matter of company law, it will be necessary to consider the provisions of the Companies Act 1985, Part VIII, to ascertain the distributable reserves of the target. Under s 270, the distribution must be justified by reference to the company's accounts and in some cases it may be necessary to prepare interim accounts. Last, but not least, the duties of the directors of the target must be considered. It is, of course, their duty to act in the interests of the target and in some cases it may be appropriate for them to seek assurances from the vendors or the purchaser that the target will have sufficient working capital following payment of the dividend.

12.2.8 Sale of debts

It is not uncommon for the target to owe debts to the vendors. Normally, these can be dealt with by the purchaser placing the target, at completion, in funds to repay the debt but, if the debts are too substantial for the target to bear the cost of repaying or refinancing them, the only practical solution may be for the vendors to assign the debts to the purchaser. In such a case, it is likely that the target's business has not been successful and such assignments commonly occur as part of a transaction which realises a capital gains tax loss for the vendors. Since the introduction of the new loan relationships legislation in the Finance Act 1996 different rules will apply depending on whether the sale of debt is by a corporate or non-corporate.

Corporates

The tax treatment of debts owed by the target to a corporate vendor requires further consideration in the light of the new loan relationship legislation introduced by the Finance Act 1996. The treatment is considered under the separate headings of assignment, waiver of loan and capitalisation.

(1) *Assignment* This approach has the attraction of removing the debt from the vendor's group so that post-acquisition it remains outstanding between members of the purchaser's group including the target. The vendor does not receive relief for any undervalue at which the debt is assigned (Finance Act 1996, Sched 9 para 6). However, if the debt is acquired by the purchaser, at a discount ie, for less than full value, the purchasing company may in certain circumstances be taxed on the full amount of the discount. Section 85 of the Finance Act 1996 in conjunction with Sched 9 paras 5 and 6, provides that taxable profits of the holder of the debt are computed on a basis that assumes that all amounts owed to it will be paid in full (Sched 9 para 11 may also be in point). If the face value of the loan remains in excess of the amount paid for it on acquisition, the taxable profit of the purchasing company could include the difference between face value and the amount paid even if the loan is waived by the purchaser rather than repaid by the target. Such a reduction in the face value of the loan eg, by the purchasing company waiving all or part of the loan owed to it could in certain circumstances give rise to a tax charge in the target company, as explained below ('waiver of loan').

(2) *Waiver of Loan* No tax charge arises in the target company (the debtor company) on the release of a debt where the creditor company and debtor company are obliged to use the authorised accruals basis of accounting pursuant to the Finance Act 1996 s 87 (see the Finance Act 1996, Sched 9 para 5(3)). The creditor and debtor company are obliged to use the accru-

als basis where they are connected (see the Finance Act 1996, s 87). Control for these purposes is defined in Taxes Act 1988, s 416 and includes possessing the greater part of the share capital. There is no deduction for the creditor company in respect of any part of the amount released (Sched 9 paras 5 and 6).

There remains the possibility of a tax charge arising in the target company if Income and Corporation Taxes Act 1988, s 94 is in point. If the target company has obtained a tax deduction for the debt (eg, it represents the unpaid purchase price of trading stock) a tax charge will arise. Before the debt is released, it is advisable that the circumstances in which the debt arose are established.

(3) *Capitalisation*   Capitalisation of the debt will not give rise to a taxable profit in the target company, although it is unlikely that the vendor will obtain a capital gains base cost equal to the amount of the indebtedness (*see below*).

Subject to the Income and Corporation Taxes Act 1988, s 94 point, it will therefore be preferable either for the vendor to release all or part of the loan before exchange of contracts or capitalise the debt. Any acquisition of the debt for less than face value could give rise to an unexpected tax liability in the purchasing company.

Non-corporates

Any loss which non-corporate vendors realise on a sale of the debt will not normally be allowable for tax purposes since a debt, unless it is a debt on a security, is not a chargeable asset in the hands of the original creditor. The relief in respect of loans to traders contained in the Taxation of Chargeable Gains Act 1992, s 253 may be of assistance, but it is quite limited in scope. In particular, it does not apply where the borrower and lender are companies in the same group (s 253(3)(*c*)) or where the lender assigns the loan (s 253(3)(*b*)).

Can the corporate or non-corporate vendors convert the debts, before the sale, into securities, so as to realise a capital gains tax loss when they sell? At least part of the answer is given by *Harrison v Nairn Williamson Ltd* (1977) 51 TC 135.

In that case the taxpayer company received a holding of preferred shares in a subsidiary company in replacement of a holding of loan stock worth considerably less than its nominal value. In computing its allowable loss arising on a subsequent sale of the preferred shares, the taxpayer company claimed to bring into account the full amount paid for the subscription of the loan stock. It was held, however, that the predecessor provision to what is now the Taxation of Chargeable Gains Act 1992, s 17 applied to the acquisition of the loan stock by the taxpayer company because it was acquired 'otherwise than by way of a bargain made at arm's length'. Accordingly, the acquisition cost of the loan stock (and hence the preferred shares) was its market value at the date of its subscription and the allowable loss was restricted to the difference between the market value and the sale consideration.

It was argued for the taxpayer company that the provision did not apply, because there was no 'disposal' of the loan stock by the target, only an acquisition by the taxpayer company, but the Court of Appeal did not agree. In any event s 17 as it now stands clearly applies in such a case unless the consideration is of an amount or value lower than the market value of the asset. This last condition stops the market value rule applying to give a higher base cost than the actual consideration in these cases.

It follows that debt reconstructions of this nature made shortly before a sale are unlikely to have the effect of making losses on debts allowable in full for capital gains tax purposes. The same will apply if new shares were issued as a rights issue, providing funds to repay the debt (see *IRC v Burmah Oil Co Ltd* (1981) 54 TC 200 and the Taxation of Chargeable Gains Act 1992, s 128(2)). The question of what is or is not a reorganisation of share capital within the Taxation of Chargeable Gains Act 1992, s 127 was considered in *Dunstan (Inspector of Taxes) v Young, Austen and Young Ltd* [1989] STC 69.

If the vendor waives debts due from the target, the vendor should take care to apportion part of the sale consideration to the waiver. If all the consideration is attributed to the shares, the vendor may find he has translated what should be a capital loss into a capital gain. In *Aberdeen Construction Group Ltd v IRC* (1978) 52 TC 281 the taxpayer company narrowly avoided such a fate. See also *Booth (EV) (Holdings) Ltd v Buckwell (Inspector of Taxes)* (1980) 53 TC 425 and *Spectros International plc v Madden* [1997] STC 114 where the vendor was bound by the allocation of consideration stipulated in the sale agreement although a different allocation would have produced a more favourable result.

12.2.9   The Income and Corporation Taxes Act 1988, section 703

The Income and Corporation Taxes Act 1988, s 703 and succeeding sections are concerned, as the headnote to Part XVII of the Act states, with 'tax avoidance'. The sections provide the Revenue with powers enabling them to serve notices cancelling income tax advantages arising from a very wide range of transactions involving securities, although it appears that s 703, when originally enacted as the Finance Act 1960, s 28, was intended only to provide the Revenue with power to counteract 'dividend stripping'.

It is instructive to remember what dividend stripping was. If a company had large revenue reserves and the owner of shares in the company was in a position to have these paid out by way of dividend, he would wish to avoid income tax on the dividend. He would therefore sell the shares 'cum dividend', receiving a purchase price equal to the value of the securities including the potential dividend. The purchase price would not be subject to income tax but would be chargeable only to any relevant capital gains tax in his hands (before 1965, of course, there was no capital gains tax). The purchaser would be a person or company who would not suffer the same rate of tax on the dividend and, once the dividend had been declared to the purchaser, the purchaser would then sell the shares back to the original owner at their 'ex dividend' price. If the purchaser of shares was, for instance, a dealer in securities, the loss which the purchaser made on selling the shares back to the original owner at a low price would be allowable for income tax purposes and be available to offset the tax chargeable on the large dividend he had received in the meantime. Payment of the dividend therefore caused the purchaser no tax disadvantage, whereas the original owner had converted the dividend into capital and obtained a tax advantage.

The powers conferred on the Revenue by s 703 to counteract dividend stripping have been used to counteract a wide range of tax advantages deriving from the sale of private companies. In order for the Revenue to be able to serve a s 703 notice the following conditions have to be satisfied (s 703(1)):

(a)   one of the circumstances mentioned in s 704 must have occurred;
(b)   there must be a transaction in securities;
(c)   in consequence of the transaction the taxpayer must be in a position to obtain, or have obtained, a tax advantage;
(d)   the taxpayer must be unable to show that the transaction or transactions were carried out either for *bona fide* commercial reasons or in the ordinary course of making or managing investments and that none of them had as their main object, or one of their main objects, to enable tax advantages to be obtained.

Two cases in point which illustrate the potential application of the section to private company acquisitions are those of *IRC v Cleary* (1967) 44 TC 399 and *IRC v Brown* (1971) 47 TC 217. The facts in the *Cleary* and *Brown* cases were broadly the same. In each case, the taxpayer had arranged for the sale of the shares owned by him or her in one company to another company controlled by the taxpayer and his or her associates. Were it not for the section, the taxpayer would have been charged only to any applicable capital gains tax on the sale. In both cases, however, the taxpayer paid income tax on the consideration received (for the quantum of the tax advantage see *Bird v IRC* [1988] 2 WLR 1237, HL).

In order to understand the cases, it is necessary to analyse them in the light of the conditions for the application of the section given above.

Condition (a)

Had any of the circumstances mentioned in s 704 occurred? In both cases the part of s 704 which was relevant was s 704D which states the relevant circumstances in effect as follows:

(1)   That in connection with the *distribution* of *profits* of a company to which this paragraph applies, the person in question so receives [a consideration which either—
        (i)   is, or represents the value of, assets which are (or apart from any-

thing done by the company in question would have been) available for distribution by way of dividend, or
(ii) is received in respect of future receipts of the company, or
(iii) is, or represents the value of, trading stock of the company,

and the person in question so receives the consideration that he does not pay or bear tax on it as income].

(2) The companies to which this paragraph applies are—
(a) any company under the control of not more than five persons; and
(b) any other company which does not satisfy the conditions that its shares or stocks or some class thereof (disregarding debenture stock, preferred shares or preferred stock), are listed in the Official List of the Stock Exchange, and are dealt in on the Stock Exchange regularly or from time to time,

so, however, that this paragraph does not apply to a company under the control of one or more companies to which this paragraph does not apply.

Reading s 704D in the light of nature it is impossible to conceive that it applies to the circumstances of the *Brown* and *Cleary* cases, but the words shown in (author's) italics are given extended and artificial meanings by s 709(3) which provides that, in s 704:
(a) references to profits include references to income reserves or other assets,
(b) references to distribution include references to transfer or realisation (including application in discharge of liabilities).

It is therefore possible to render the opening words of s 704D so that they read: 'That in connection with the *transfer* of *assets* of a company to which this paragraph applies'.

In both the *Brown* and *Cleary* cases the purchaser company was one to which the paragraph applied and it had transferred assets (ie it had paid cash) to the taxpayer.

In the *Cleary* case the purchaser company had sufficient reserves and cash to pay a dividend of an amount equal to the purchase price and it was therefore held that the consideration was 'assets which are (or apart from anything done by the company in question would have been) available for distribution by way of dividend'. In the *Brown* case the company had sufficient standing to the credit of its profit and loss account to pay a dividend equal to the cash element of the consideration, but its current liabilities exceeded its current assets by £3,000. It therefore had to borrow the amount of the cash consideration from a bank. Megarry J took the view, affirmed on appeal, that as the company had reserves available for distribution there was no legal impropriety in its borrowing the money to effect that distribution. The money once borrowed was, therefore, 'assets available for distribution'. Even though a prudent or cautious financier might not have paid a dividend in such circumstances, it was legally possible and that was sufficient.

Condition (b)

In neither case was there any difficulty on this point. The sale of shares in a company is obviously a transaction in securities (which in any event is defined to include a sale by s 709).

Condition (c)

Did the taxpayer obtain a tax advantage? In *IRC v Parker* (1966) 43 TC 396 Lord Wilberforce indicated that a taxpayer obtains a tax advantage if he receives something which is not subject to income tax but which, if he had received it in another way, would have been. In both the *Brown* and *Cleary* cases, if the purchaser company had declared a dividend, the taxpayer would have received it. It did not declare a dividend but used its assets to pay the consideration for the shares acquired from the taxpayer. In both cases, therefore, the taxpayer received cash as consideration for shares when, if it had been received by way of dividend, it would have been subject to income tax. The tax advantage was therefore obtained. (See also *Anysz v IRC* and *Manolescue v IRC* (1977) 53 TC 601 and *Williams v IRC* (1980) 54 TC 257.)

Condition (d)

In neither case was the taxpayer able to show that the transactions were carried out for *bona fide* commercial reasons and that none of them had, as their main objects, to enable tax advantages to be obtained. In the *Brown* case Russell LJ said (on appeal—(1971) 47 TC 217, at p 239) that:

> [The] evidence amounts to no more than saying that the taxpayer and his wife wanted some money and entered into the transaction to get it. Now it seems to me that you do not show that a transaction of sale of securities for full consideration to a company already owned by yourself is a transaction to be entered into for *bona fide* commercial reasons merely by saying that it is such a sale transaction and that you wanted the money.

In considering the application of s 703 to acquisitions, the potential application of s 704C should not be overlooked. This section applies if the taxpayer receives a consideration which represents the value of assets which are (or would have been) available for distribution as dividend, 'in consequence of a transaction whereby any other person...receives...an abnormal amount by way of dividend'. In *Emery v IRC* [1984] 54 TC 607 the target owned valuable properties which it sold for a profit of £244,000. The taxpayer then sold his shares in the target to an investment company for £223,409 payable by instalments and subsequently sold his right to receive those instalments to a wholly owned subsidiary of the purchaser for the same price. The target then paid a dividend of £260,500 to the purchaser. It was held that the vendor had received the consideration in consequence of an operation whereby the purchaser received an abnormal dividend and accordingly the consideration was treated as income.

In *IRC v Garvin* [1981] STC 344 the facts were similar but there the House of Lords held that there was no sufficient connecting link between the sale of the shares in the target and the declaration of the dividend. The fact that the purchaser acquired the whole of the share capital of a target with substantial undistributed profit did not by itself form sufficient ground for holding that such acquisition was the cause of the subsequent distribution of those profits by the target. The court held that the word 'whereby' in s 704 imported some causal connection between the transactions and the subsequent receipt of the abnormal dividend. In that case the Revenue attempted also to bring s 704D into play, by contending that the consideration was received 'in connection with the distribution of the profits' of a company to which s 704D applied. The targets were under the control of five or fewer persons at the time they were sold, but there was no evidence that they were so controlled at the date of the distribution. The court held that the relevant date was the day of the distribution of profits and accordingly that s 704D did not apply.

It is fair to say that in both these and the *Brown* and *Cleary* cases there was an element of tax avoidance. In each case the vendors entered into a series of transactions with a view to obtaining as capital that which could more easily have been obtained as dividend. If an acquisition has this result then it must be prudent to utilise the clearance procedure given in s 707. In the *Brown* case Megarry J said:

> Having provided reasonable safeguards for the *bona fide* or ordinary transaction, I do not think that the legislature has given any indication of intending to use kid gloves in these cases.

In the light of the Finance Act 1988 changes to the taxation of income and capital gains, the potential for obtaining a tax advantage (condition *(c)*) is reduced and so the importance of this section has been diminished. However, the rebasing to 1982, the indexation allowance, the individual's annual exemption and the possibility of deferral of the charge to tax through roll-over or other reliefs may make a capital gains tax treatment preferable, so that the prudent practitioner will continue to give consideration to the section.

12.2.10   The Income and Corporation Taxes Act 1988, section 776

This section attempts to counter tax avoidance by the realisation of gains in a capital form on a disposal of land which, if realised in another way, might be assessed as trading income. The section can have the effect of taxing as income under Case VI of Schedule D capital gains realised on the sale of shares in a company.

The section applies (s 776(2)):

(a)   if land or any property deriving its value from land has been acquired for the sole or main object of realising a gain from disposing of the land; or

(b)   if land is held as trading stock; or

(c)   if land is developed with the sole or main object of realising a gain from disposing of the land when developed.

It is necessary that the land should be situated in the United Kingdom (s 776(14)).

If a gain of a capital nature is obtained from the disposal of the land either by the person holding or developing the land or by any connected person (as defined by the Income and Corporation Taxes Act 1988, s 839) or, indirectly, by any person who is a party to any arrangement as respects the land which enables a gain to be realised, the gain may be taxed as income. The section does not require that there should be any tax avoidance motive for the transaction (*Page v Lowther* [1983] 61 Ch D).

The section is very widely drafted. In particular s 776(4) provides that land is disposed of if, by any one or more transactions or by any arrangement or scheme, whether concerning the land or property deriving its value from land, the property in the land or control over the land is effectually disposed of. Accordingly, the sale of a land owning company or a company which controls a land owning company could fall within the section.

Under s 776(10) there is an exemption in respect of a disposal of shares in a company which holds land as trading stock or a company which owns directly or indirectly 90 per cent or more of the ordinary share capital of another company which holds land as trading stock, provided all the land so held is disposed of in the normal course of its trade by the company which held it and so as to procure that all opportunity of profit in respect of the land arises to that company. This exemption does not extend to 'arrangements' or 'schemes' for realising gains by indirect methods or by a series of transactions, which are caught by s 776(2)(ii).

Although there is a procedure under s 776(11) for obtaining a clearance, this is rarely used, since the Revenue have proved reluctant to confirm such clearance, so that application merely serves to put the Revenue on notice. See eg *Chilcott v IRC* (1982) 57 TC 446, and *Sugarwhite v Budd (Inspector of Taxes)* [1988] STC 533. Indeed, very few assessments have been raised under this section because most taxpayers likely to be caught opt for assessment under Schedule D Case I as a trading venture (see *Kirkham v Williams* [1991] STC 532).

12.2.11 The Income and Corporation Taxes Act 1988, sections 765 and 765A

The origins of the Income and Corporation Taxes Act 1988, s 765 lie in foreign exchange control. It has proved a useful anti-avoidance measure in addition and so survived the 1979 abolition of foreign exchange control. Section 765 makes unlawful without prior consent of HM Treasury certain transactions undertaken or permitted by a company resident in the United Kingdom in relation to a non-resident company over which it has control. The United Kingdom resident company may not cause or permit the non-resident company to create or issue any shares or debentures nor (except for the purposes of enabling a person to be qualified to act as a director) may it transfer to any person, or cause or permit to be transferred to any person, any shares or debentures of the non-resident company, being shares or debentures which it owns or in which it has an interest. Contravention of the section is a criminal offence, and consideration must accordingly be given by a corporate vendor to its possible application where the target company is a non-resident company or, where the target is resident in the United Kingdom, debt owed by non-resident subsidiaries of the target company to the vendor or other companies in the vendor's group is to be assigned to the purchaser.

Provided that the purchaser and the vendor are not connected persons within the meaning of the Income and Corporation Taxes Act 1988, s 839, a sale of shares or debentures of a non-resident company will normally fall within one of the published general consents (contained in The Treasury General Consents 1988). The transfer must be for full consideration paid to the vendor and no arrangements must exist as a consequence of which the vendor or a person connected with the vendor might become entitled to, or to any interest in, any of the shares or debentures transferred.

If there is no relevant general consent, special consent must be sought from HM Treasury (who are advised by the Inland Revenue) unless the transaction is exempted from s 765 by the s 765A.

The Directive of the Council of the European Communities dated 24 June 1988 (88/361/EEC) which took effect from 1 July 1990 requires there to be free movement of capital between residents of Member States. Accordingly, the Income and Corporation Taxes Act 1988, s 765A prevents s 765 from applying to all such transactions carried out on or after that date. Transactions will be within the scope of the Directive only if they involve the transfer of capital between persons resident in different Member States. However, if the transaction, were it to be subject to s 765, would require special consent of HM Treasury, s 765A requires the United Kingdom resident company to report it to the Inland Revenue within six months of the transaction being carried out. The information specified under the Movements of Capital (Required Information) Regulations 1990 (SI No 1671) must be provided. This is substantially the same information as would be required in an application for special consent.

No complete definition of 'movement of capital' is given in the Directive, but it is clear that this must be widely construed. The Directive also requires residence to be determined by reference to exchange control regulations. A number of Member States including the United Kingdom no longer have such regulations and the United Kingdom will adopt the test of residence for tax purposes in those cases. The views of HM Treasury and the Inland Revenue on the operation of the Directive and s 765A are set out in the Inland Revenue Statement of Practice SP2/92.

12.3   Stamp duty and stamp duty reserve tax considerations for the purchaser

Since the last edition of this book the introduction of TAURUS and the proposed abolition of stamp duty and stamp duty reserve tax in relation to all property other than land has been abandoned. On 1 July 1996 CREST, the electronic system for uncertified securities was introduced. Stamp duty is no longer an issue for sales of securities within the CREST system, although stamp duty reserve tax at the rate of 50p per £100 (or part) (eg 0.5 per cent) is generally payable. Stamp duty (and in theory stamp duty reserve tax) remain very much in point on private company acquisitions. Liabilities to these taxes may also arise where the cash consideration for the purchase is raised through a vendor placing (*see* p 238).

Stamp duty is chargeable under the head 'conveyance or transfer on sale' on transfers of registered shares from vendor to purchaser. Unless stock transfer forms are presented for stamping within 30 days a penalty is payable, and the company secretary will be liable to a £10 fine under the Stamp Act 1891, s 17, if he registers a transfer which is not duly stamped. The exemptions which apply to transfers of property certified at £60,000 or less do not apply to share transfers. Duty is payable by the purchaser and is chargeable at the rate of 50p per £100 (or part) of the consideration.

Loan capital is generally exempt from stamp duties. However, where the purchaser agrees to pay to the vendor the amount of any indebtedness which is due from the target to the vendor, the amount of the indebtedness repaid may be treated as consideration for the shares in the target (see Stamp Act 1891, s 57). An undertaking by the purchaser instead to procure repayment by the target will not be regarded by the Stamp Office as falling within s 57, unless it is plain that the target does not have sufficient resources to make payment. In such circumstances, the indebtedness could be reconstituted as loan capital and assigned to the purchaser against payment of the amount involved.

Duty is charged on so much of the consideration as is ascertainable at the date the transfer is stamped. The consideration is ascertainable if the information exists from which it may be calculated. Thus, where the consideration is, for example, to be determined following the preparation of completion accounts, the transfer should be presented for stamping within the thirty day period and the duty paid subsequently, once the amount of the consideration has been determined. Where the consideration is unascertainable, the 'contingency principle' may operate, whereby all contingencies are ignored. Accordingly, if there is a specified maximum amount of consideration or, in the absence of a maximum, a minimum amount, this will be treated as the consideration payable and the duty calculated accordingly.

The contingency principle applies in 'earn out deals' where part of the consideration given for the purchase of shares is deferred and becomes payable only if profit targets are met. The level of future profits is unascertainable, and so this consideration should not be liable to duty, but if it is subject to a maximum (or minimum) amount stamp duty will become payable on the transfer of the shares to the purchaser by reference to that maximum (or minimum). Should the profit targets not be met, so that the full consideration does not become payable, the stamp duty cannot be reclaimed.

Where the deferred consideration is to be satisfied in shares, it is possible to argue that part of the consideration received by the vendors is the right to the future allotment. This right is a chose in action (see *Marren (Inspector of Taxes) v Ingles* (1980) 54 TC 76) and as such is not dutiable consideration at all. However, in many cases the purchaser will retain the option to satisfy the deferred consideration in cash, and this may be regarded by the Stamp Office as sufficient to make the transfer stampable in respect of the deferred consideration as well.

Part IV of the Finance Act 1986 introduced a new tax, the stamp duty reserve tax, which is chargeable where there is an agreement to transfer 'chargeable securities'. The charge to tax arises on the date the agreement is made (or if a conditional agreement on the date the condition is satisfied) and is chargeable at the rate of 0.5 per cent of the consideration (Finance Act 1986, s 87 as amended by Finance Act 1996, s 188). The tax is due and payable on the last day of the month following that in which the agreement was made (Stamp Duty Reserve Tax Regulations 1986 (SI No 1711), reg 3). Where the agreement is completed later, but within six years, repayment of the stamp duty reserve tax may be obtained if the duly stamped instrument of transfer is presented to the Stamp Office. Despite its name, stamp duty reserve tax is a tax distinct from stamp duty and unlike stamp duty it is directly assessable.

'Chargeable securities' are defined by the Finance Act 1986, s 99(3) to include stocks, shares, loan capital and units under a unit trust scheme, but the definition does not include shares in companies incorporated outside the United Kingdom (unless recorded in a register kept in the United Kingdom), bearer shares or most forms of loan capital. Renounceable letters of allotment are, however, subject to the tax (Finance Act 1986, s 88(2)).

Although the charge to stamp duty reserve tax is potentially of very wide scope, it will not, in practice, usually be of concern in relation to the acquisition of shares in a private company because the purchaser will wish to complete the purchase and registration of the shares in its name. An exception may occur where a purchaser company intends that on completion the shares in the target should be transferred into the beneficial ownership of another company within the purchaser's group. Unless the acquisition agreement contains provision for the purchaser to substitute the other company to complete the agreement, a direct transfer of the shares from the vendor to the purchaser's subsidiary must not be taken, as there is no relief from stamp duty reserve tax equivalent to that from stamp duty afforded by the Finance Act 1930, s 42 (*see below*). Instead, in order to avoid stamp duty reserve tax on the acquisition agreement, it is necessary for there to be two transfers, first, from the vendor to the purchaser and, secondly, from the purchaser to its associated company. Relief under the Finance Act 1930, s 42 may then be claimed in respect of the latter transfer, and the acquisition agreement will not be subject to stamp duty reserve tax, as it will have been duly completed by a stamped instrument.

It became a common practice over the past few years, until the Budget in November 1996, to mitigate stamp duty on the sale of shares in the target by reorganising the existing share capital of the target before sale into worthless deferred sterling shares and issuing new shares denominated in a foreign currency and represented by share warrants to bearer (see Companies Act 1985, s 188) which carry all the value of the company and which are handed over so as to give effect to the transfer of title at completion of the acquisition. This approach to stamp duty saving was rendered ineffective by the anti-avoidance legislation introduced in the Finance Act 1997.

Capital duty was formerly payable upon certain increases in the capital of a company and was therefore relevant to company acquisitions where the consideration took the form of an issue of shares in the purchasing company. Capital duty was introduced by Part V of the Finance Act 1973 on the entry of the United Kingdom into the European Community in compliance with Council Directive 69/335/EEC of 17 July 1969, the provisions of which ceased to be mandatory from 1985. Capital duty was repealed in the United Kingdom by the Finance Act 1988, s 141 with effect from midnight on 15 March 1988. Where exemption from capital duty under the provisions of the Finance Act 1973, Sched 19, para 10 had been provisionally obtained prior to that date, the relief will be confirmed provided that the circumstances in which the relief may be lost had not arisen at that date. Despite the repeal of capital duty, it remains necessary to comply with the requirements of the Companies Act 1985, s 88 and to make returns of allotments to the Registrar of Companies together, where appropriate, with the duly stamped contract or written particulars where the contract is not reduced to writing.

As part of the reform of stamp duties in 1986 which included the introduction of stamp duty reserve tax and the reduction of the rate of stamp duty chargeable on transfers of registered shares, various reliefs from stamp duty, as well as from capital duty, available where the consideration for the acquisition was or included the issue of shares in the purchasing company were repealed.

Exemption from stamp duty may be available if the vendor and the purchaser are companies associated within the meaning of the Finance Act 1930, s 42. To meet this requirement, the vendor or the purchaser must be directly or indirectly the beneficial owner of not less than 75 per cent of the ordinary share capital of the other, or not less than 75 per cent of the ordinary share capital (formerly the requirement was in both cases 90 per cent of the issued share capital) of each of the vendor and the purchaser must be directly or indirectly in the beneficial ownership of a third company. Ordinary share capital is defined as for corporation tax purposes and means all issued share capital other than share capital which carries the right to a dividend at a fixed rate and which has no other right to share in the profits of the company. It is apparent that this exemption may be available in the case of the reorganisation of a group of companies, but is unlikely to apply to an acquisition of a company at arm's length.

Relief from stamp duty is also available for certain reconstructions or reorganisations falling within the provisions of the Finance Act 1986, ss 75, 76 and 77 and in respect of transfers by way of gift (see Finance Act 1985, s 82 and the Stamp Duty (Exempt Instruments) Regulations 1987 (SI No 516)), but consideration of these lies outside the scope of this book.

12.4   Taxation issues for the parties to an acquisition of business assets

This part of the Chapter addresses tax issues to be considered on the sale of business assets by a United Kingdom resident company to an unconnected purchaser who will continue to use those business assets in the United Kingdom to carry on the same business. Where the vendor and purchaser are connected additional tax considerations, not addressed in this chapter, will apply. The matters covered in this Chapter are:

12.4.1   apportionment of price;
12.4.2   stamp duty;
12.4.3   PAYE and national insurance;
12.4.4   VAT; and
12.4.5   inheritance tax.

Where a purchaser acquires the share capital of a target company, all the liabilities of that company stay with it. However, where the purchaser buys the assets of the company's business then, except where the assets acquired are subject to existing third party rights (such as a mortgage), the purchaser will acquire the assets free from all liabilities, except to the extent it agrees to assume them. Accordingly, the assets will be acquired free from liabilities to tax and any tax charge that has arisen in respect of the vendor company's activities prior to completion will remain for the account of the vendor. Exceptions to this basic principle are discussed below at p 292.

12.4.1   Apportionment of price

An assets acquisition will generally involve the acquisition of several different categories of asset. It is necessary for both vendor and purchaser to ascertain how much is to be paid for each particular asset or category of assets and apportion the overall consideration accordingly. If the consideration is not apportioned in the agreement it will nonetheless need to be agreed later with the Inland Revenue. The Revenue will not permit the vendor to use one apportionment and the purchaser to use another.

It is usually in the interests of both vendor and purchaser to make sure that the other party is contractually bound, in the contract of sale, to the apportionment of price. The price apportionment can have a significant impact on the post tax effect of the transaction for both vendor and purchaser but despite this it is a matter which is often considered only at a late stage in negotiation. Difficulty arises because the vendor will generally want to receive the purchase price, so far as possible, in a non taxable form while the purchaser will generally want to pay it in a way which maximises his tax deduction: the two approaches are generally inconsistent. One further advantage of agreeing an allocation of price in the agreement is that a *bona fide* agreed apportionment will also bind the Inland Revenue (*Stanton (Inspector of Taxes) v Drayton Commercial Investment Co Limited* [1981] STC 525).

The Agreement for Sale (Assets), cl 3.1 sets out an apportionment of the price for each category of asset. The following paragraphs consider the position of both vendor and purchaser and their respective approaches to allocation of the purchase price. It is assumed both vendor and purchaser are UK resident companies.

Position of vendor

The vendor's preference will be to apportion the price so as to achieve a tax treatment of the consideration in the following order of priority:
(a)   non-taxable;
(b)   subject to immediate relief;
(c)   taxable.

Non-taxable   Receipts may be non-taxable for a number of reasons. There are no hard and fast rules because this will largely depend on the vendor's own current tax position. For example, the consideration for any particular category of asset may be non-taxable because of trading or capital losses, or because the cost or tax written down value of the asset is equal to or exceeds the value of the consideration received for it.

A vendor will not normally want the consideration for stock to be increased above cost price as this would give rise to a taxable income receipt. However, if the vendor has carried forward trading losses then it may wish to allocate as high a price as possible to items giving a revenue profit, such as trading stock, to utilise those trading losses (Income and Corporation Taxes Act 1988, s 393A) and direct consideration away from other assets which will carry a tax charge on sale. This approach will be particularly relevant if the vendor is to cease trading as a consequence of the disposal, since trading losses will otherwise be lost forever, subject to carrying back the losses for three years (*see* p 313).

Alternatively, the vendor may have capital losses carried forward which can be set against capital gains arising on the sale, in which case it will wish to allocate as much consideration as possible to the relevant capital assets. If the consideration received from an asset is equal to the base cost of that asset, as increased by indexation allowance, no tax is payable. The base cost of an asset may, however, have been reduced as a result of various claims for relief made by the company, such as rollover relief, where the capital gain of one asset has been rolled over into the acquisition cost of the asset which is among the business assets to be sold (Taxation of Chargeable Gains Act 1992, ss 152–160 and *see further below*); another example is where compensation or insurance proceeds have been received in respect of the asset being sold and a claim has been made to roll over the insurance proceeds into, and diminishing, the base cost of the asset rather than treating the receipt of the insurance proceeds as a part disposal for capital gains purposes (Taxation of Chargeable Gains Act 1992, s 23).

It is likely that included among the business assets to be sold there will be capital assets in respect of which the vendor has claimed capital allowances, which are available in respect of certain capital assets which depreciate. Depreciation is not a tax deductible item, even though it is recorded as an expense in the profit and loss account of the company. Instead, the company may claim capital allowances, amounting to a statutory tax deduction for 'wear and tear'. There are several different categories of capital allowance, but the most important in the context of an acquisition of business assets is the category of capital allowances in respect of plant and machinery. Subject to certain exceptions, expenditure on plant and machinery is, for tax purposes, not looked at individually for each asset but rather all such expenditure is aggregated and forms a 'pool' of expenditure. Any consideration received on the disposal of assets from the pool of plant and machinery is deducted from the value of the pool. The amount standing to the value of the pool at the end of the year qualifies for a writing down allowance equal to 25 per cent of the value of that pool.

If disposal proceeds for the accounting period exceed the tax written down value of the pool (as increased by acquisitions) a tax charge arises ('balancing charge'), which is treated as a trading receipt in respect of the accounting period in which it is incurred, normally the period in which the trade is discontinued eg in the context of a sale of business assets by the vendor, on completion (Capital Allowances Act 1990, ss 73 and 144).

It may be that the plant and machinery is sold for less than the value attributable to it in the tax computations, ie disposal proceeds are lower than tax written down value. In such a case, there is an excess of unallowed expenditure over disposal value on the discontinuance, and a 'balancing allowance' arises. A balancing allowance is deductible against all profits as a trading expense of the year in which it is incurred (Capital Allowances Act 1990, ss 72 and 144).

Immediate relief   If the purchase price cannot be received in a non-taxable form, the vendor's next preference will be to allocate the consideration to an asset for which relief, such as rollover relief, is available. Rollover relief is available where a capital gain is made on the sale of goodwill, land, buildings, and fixed plant used for the purposes of trade and various other assets (Taxation of Chargeable Gains Act 1992, s 155). The relief allows the capital gain to be sheltered if an amount equivalent to the proceeds attributable to the sale (not the proceeds of sale equal to the capital gain, but the *whole* proceeds) are reinvested, within the period commencing one year before the sale and ending three years after the sale, in other assets which would qualify for roll-over relief on disposal. For example, the capital gain arising on the sale of goodwill could be reinvested on a purchase of new trading premises. Roll-over relief may be claimed not only by the vendor but by other trading companies in the vendor's group.

Where the vendor is selling trade marks, thought should be given to apportioning consideration to the trade mark (which is usually of minimal value) and the goodwill attaching to it (which is where the value usually lies). This will enable the capital gain on the goodwill element to be rolled over into other qualifying capital assets.

Taxable   The least attractive option for the vendor is to allocate the consideration to a taxable item, such as disposal of trading stock at above book value where there are no tax reliefs available to shelter the liability.

It is worth noting that gains realised on the disposal of patents are taxed as income (under Schedule D Case VI) but generally, the charge to tax is spread over six years (Income and Corporation Taxes Act 1988, s 524) during which period other income reliefs against which the charge can be offset may, of course, arise.

Position of purchaser

The purchaser's preference as to allocation of the consideration will be to achieve a tax treatment in the following order of priority:
(a)   revenue deduction;
(b)   capital allowances or roll-over relief;
(c)   capital expenditure.

The purchaser will also wish to consider the stamp duty implications of apportionment (*see* p 287).

Revenue deduction   To achieve its primary aim of a revenue deduction, the purchaser will want to allocate as high a price as possible to stock and work-in-progress. This will have the effect of reducing the purchaser's tax charge on trading profits going forward. An obvious adverse consequence of this approach for the vendor is that the higher the proceeds allocated to trading stock, the larger the (usually, taxable) trading receipt for the vendor.

Rollover relief or capital allowances   The purchaser's next preference will be to claim either roll-over relief expenditure (ie apportioning as high a price as possible to capital assets) to shelter a past or anticipated future gain or to claim capital allowances on the expenditure. The most common form of assets qualifying for capital allowances and which usually constitute at least part of the business acquired by the purchaser are industrial buildings, plant and machinery, patents and know-how. It should be noted that the Revenue has introduced anti-avoidance legislation, effective from 24 July 1996, which restricts the opportunities previously afforded to a purchaser to claim capital allowances on plant and machinery expenditure in excess of original cost incurred in respect of the asset.

There are special capital allowance rules relating to both patents and know-how. The rules applicable to know-how deserve particular consideration. If know-how is sold as part of a business transfer, the sale and purchase is treated as a sale and purchase of goodwill (Income and Corporation Taxes Act 1988, s 531(2)). The receipt is, therefore, taxable in the vendor's hands as a capital gain which can be rolled over to another capital asset, and the acquisition of know-how is treated as the acquisition of a capital asset by the purchaser into which a capital gain can be rolled over. It is, however possible at the joint election of both vendor and purchaser for this tax treatment to be disapplied. In such a case the consideration received by the vendor on disposal of the know-how is treated as an income receipt taxable under Schedule D Case VI against which only current year trading losses of the trade can be offset, as opposed to trading losses carried forward from earlier accounting periods. The effect of the joint election in relation to know-how is that the purchaser can claim tax depreciation in the form of capital allowances on its expenditure (Income and Corporation Taxes Act 1988, s 531(3)). Otherwise such expenditure would not be deductible for tax purposes but would merely form part of the capital gains base cost of the goodwill acquired (*see further below*).

Capital expenditure   If the consideration paid by the purchaser is treated as capital expenditure the only tax benefit is that such expenditure will form part of the capital gains base cost of the relevant asset(s). If the asset acquired has an expected life of less than 50 years then that base cost will in any event waste away since it is treated as a depreciating asset for capital gains purposes. Even if the base cost does not waste away, a base cost is only of use to the purchaser if, having acquired the asset, it decides to sell it on, or has a capital gain which is capable of being rolled-over into the base cost of the new asset.

Conclusions

The appropriate apportionment for debtors and creditors is usually fairly clear as these are cash or cash equivalent. The apportionment of consideration to stock, capital assets such as goodwill and assets qualifying for capital allowances will have tax implications for both the vendor and the purchaser and the apportionment of the purchase price is, as described, capable of materially affecting the economic effect of the transaction to vendor or purchaser.

12.4.2   Stamp duty

The apportionment of consideration has an additional consequence for the purchaser with regard to United Kingdom stamp duty which is payable on the instrument of transfer in respect of certain categories of asset.

If the business to be transferred comprises any of the following assets the documents which give effect to the transfer are liable to stamp duty apportioned, in each case at an *ad valorem* rate of £1 per £100 (or part thereof) of the consideration in respect of that asset:
(a)   freehold land and assignment of leasehold interests
(b)   fixtures
(c)   goodwill
(d)   benefit of contracts
(e)   work-in-progress relating to a specific contract
(f)   debtors
(g)   patents
(h)   trade marks

The transfer of know-how is not stampable (as it is not property for stamp duty purposes) nor is an assignment/grant of the benefit of a licence to use intellectual property (eg patents or trade marks), unless the licence is exclusive and irrevocable. If this is the case the assignment is stampable as if it were a conveyance on sale and any periodical payment under the licence, up to an amount payable over 20 years, is treated as if it were a premium to the extent that the payment is ascertainable at the date of execution of the document (Stamp Act 1891, s 56). If the amount of the licence fee payable is subject to future levels of turnover so that neither a minimum nor maximum fee can be ascertained at the date the licence is entered into, no stamp duty will be payable. Care would be needed in drafting the licence to achieve this result; avoiding stamp duty should not be allowed to outweigh commercial considerations.

Stamp duty is payable on documents. The contract for sale and purchase of the business assets is a stampable document (Stamp Act 1891, s 59). Stamp duty is calculated on the gross value of the assets purchased, not the net value (eg after deducting any associated liabilities). Accordingly, the assumption by the purchaser of any liabilities of the target business will be regarded as forming part of the consideration for stamp duty purposes as if a cash sum equal to the liabilities assumed had been paid (Stamp Act 1891, s 57). In addition to the contract for sale, any conveyance or transfer executed pursuant to it is stampable. If, however, a legal estate in land forms part of the assets to be transferred, the conveyance only, and not the contract for sale, is stampable as regards that asset (Stamp Act 1891, s 59(1)). It should be noted that fixtures and fittings are land for both general law and for stamp duty purposes. No stamp duty is payable on the sale of the moveable property (chattels) since title to such assets passes by delivery not by way of document.

With regard to assets other than land, provided that a conveyance, transfer or assignment is made in conformity with the agreement within six months after the execution of the contract or agreement (or such longer period as the Revenue may think reasonable) and duly stamped as regards the relevant asset(s), Stamp Act 189,1 s 59(5) provides that the contract shall be deemed to be duly stamped.

Jurisdiction

The Stamp Act 1891, s 14(4) provides some guidance as to the territorial limits of stamp duty. Although to some extent stamp duty is a voluntary tax, one of the principal reasons for stamping a document is that, under s 14(4), it cannot be used in evidence in civil proceedings unless it is 'duly stamped'. Documents transferring property (real, personal or intellectual) which is physically situate in the United Kingdom are always stampable whether or not executed in the UK. The liability to stamp duty arises on execution. If the document is simply executed outside the United Kingdom, it is not 'duly stamped' for the purposes of s 14(4). The document may however be stamped within 30 days of being brought into the United Kingdom for the first time, without penalty (Stamp Act 1891, s 15(2)(*a*)) (although as to patents and trademarks *see below*).

Any document relating to any matter or thing to be done in the United Kingdom is also liable to stamp duty. For example a document transferring title to a property in France, expressed to be governed by French law, from one English company to another English company in consideration of the issue of shares, was held to be stampable, on the basis that it related to property situated in the United Kingdom (the shares issued in the transferee company) and a thing to be done in the United Kingdom (the issue and registration of those shares) (*I R Comrs v Maple & Co (Paris) Ltd* [1908] AC 22). It should also be noted that a stampable document executed in the United Kingdom is within the charge to United Kingdom stamp duty even though it relates to assets or things to be done outside the United Kingdom. In such a case it is unlikely, however, that any sanction will apply for any failure to stamp. For example, it is unlikely that an overseas share registrar would raise any objection to registering the transfer of shares in an overseas company, which was executed in the United Kingdom, because of the absence of a United Kingdom stamp.

Any document assigning land in the United Kingdom or trade marks or patents registered at the Patent Office or Trade Marks Registry will be liable to stamp duty. The assignment cannot be registered unless duly stamped. Prior to the recent decision in *Parinv (Hatfield) Ltd v IRC* [1996] STC 933, if such a document was executed outside the United Kingdom, the Registrar took the view that the liability was deferred and did not arise until 30 days after the document was first brought into the United Kingdom. The assignment was therefore 'duly stamped' while it remained outside the United Kingdom, and could be registered without production of the original. However, following the *Parinv* case the Inland Revenue has advised the Patent Office that an assignment of UK intellectual property, even if executed and held offshore, is liable to stamp duty from the date of execution of the assignment. Accordingly the Patent Office has been instructed by the Revenue not to register an offshore assignment on which stamp duty is payable unless it has been paid. The decision in *Parinv* is under appeal at the date of this book. Until finally determined, it may be wise for practitioners to continue to advise the execution and holding of intellectual property assignments outside the jurisdiction in order to defer (sometimes indefinitely) the duty, until the purchaser wishes to register the assignment.

In the case of trade marks and patents relative to jurisdictions wholly outside the United Kingdom a liability will arise only if the assignment is executed in the United Kingdom, although in such a case there is unlikely to be any adverse consequence from not stamping the document.

Sanctions for not stamping

Any person who registers in any roll or registers a document at HM Land Registry which is insufficiently stamped is liable to a fine (Stamp Act 1891, s 17). The current penalty is £10. Trade mark registrars, company secretaries and others whose duty it is to maintain the relevant register are entitled to refuse to register the document and cannot be compelled to register a document which is insufficiently stamped (*R v Registrar of Joint Stock Companies* (1888) 21 QBD 131). Failure to stamp does not invalidate the document and if it is registered, despite Stamp Act 1891, s 17, the registration is valid (*Brown v Root McDermott Fabricators Ltd* [1996] STC 483). The fine is a civil, not a criminal, penalty.

Under the Stamp Act 1891, s 14 an unstamped document cannot be used in evidence before a court or tribunal, other than in criminal proceedings. As a practical matter therefore, stamping of the relevant document may be necessary if it is required as evidence in any proceedings to enforce the provisions of the relevant document (eg a covenant or indemnity) or to claim damages for breach (eg for breach of warranty). If the document has not been properly stamped then the duty and any penalties for failure to stamp will have to be paid before it can be used in court. Penalties are the liability of the purchaser (Stamp Act 1891, s 15(2)(*d*)) (for example in respect of the assignment of goodwill) as is the duty payable on the contract for sale (Stamp Act 1891, s 59(1)). As a practical matter if the vendor is seeking to enforce a provision of the agreement (eg deferred consideration) rather than seek enforcement of the purchaser's obligation to stamp, he will pay the duty and add the cost to his claim. A vendor may consider seeking an undertaking from the purchaser's solicitors (if he can get it) that the contract will be duly stamped.

Stamp duty mitigation

If the consideration paid for stampable assets, ignoring any goods or chattels, is less than £60,000 a certificate of value can be included into each stampable document stating that the consideration payable in respect of the relevant assets is below such level. In such case there is no need to present the document to the Revenue or pay stamp duty (Finance Act 1958, s 34(4) and Finance Act 1963, s 55). Most business acquisitions will, however, involve consideration in excess of £60,000, bearing in mind that stamp duty is calculated on the gross, not net, value of the assets purchased.

Stamp duty is payable at the rate of £1 per £100 (or part) on debts owed to the business which are assigned to the purchaser. It is common, as a result, to exclude debts from the sale altogether and to adjust the purchase price either leaving the vendor to collect the debts itself or for the purchaser to collect the debts as agent for the vendor (commonly also using the proceeds to discharge trade creditors). The effect may, of course, be to reduce the value of stampable assets below the £60,000 threshold in which case a certificate of value can be included in the document and no stamp duty will be payable.

A further way to mitigate stamp duty is by 'offer and acceptance'. This involves one party, the vendor, making a written offer which is accepted by conduct (eg payment by the purchaser). Care must be taken, however, to ensure that no memorandum of the sale is made as this will be stampable. Mitigation by offer and acceptance cannot be used to avoid stamp duty in respect of the transfer of land interests or other assets where a written document is required to transfer title which will need to be stamped in order to effect registration of title (in the case of land) at the Land Registry.

The amount of stamp duty may merit considering execution and retention of the sale contract and relevant conveyances, transfers and assignments required to give effect to it outside the United Kingdom with a right to call for assignments as and when necessary. Where documents must be brought into the jurisdiction, eg for enforcement, the duty payable will at least have been deferred without penalty (although for intellectual property assignments, see the discussion of *Parinv* at p 289 *above*). It is appropriate in such a case for the purchaser to have a right to call for an assignment or transfer of the specific asset where production of the assignment or transfer is required in the United Kingdom rather than all similar assets of that type so that even where stamp duty is payable, it is also minimised and the amount payable is restricted to the asset to be brought onshore. To ensure that the vendor does execute assignments after completion, the purchaser should take a security power of attorney under Powers of Attorney Act 1974, s 4. Where execution and retention of documents offshore is arranged, the parties should check carefully any tax, including transfer tax, implications of the local jurisdiction. France, for instance, has prohibitive transfer taxes (*see* p 339). Consider also, which documents should be retained outside the jurisdiction: certainly, all those which evidence the terms of the transaction should be retained outside.

If documents (other than those which need to be stamped for registering title in the United Kingdom) executed outside the United Kingdom are required as evidence in English proceedings to enforce their terms, bringing them into the jurisdiction will trigger a charge to duty. This consequence can be minimised by separating out those provisions of the agreements which are more likely to be the subject of claims and placing them in a separate document. Warranties, indemnities and covenants, including restrictive covenants, are obvious candidates for such treatment. It should be possible to draft the documentation in such a way so as to ensure that if, for example, the warranty agreement only is required to be produced in the proceedings, the documents transferring title remain outside the jurisdiction.

More sophisticated methods of eliminating a charge to stamp duty are possible. One example is to take advantage of the intra-group stamp duty relief contained in Finance Act 1930, s 42. A stamp duty group created between a corporate vendor and a corporate purchaser (neither of which need to be UK resident) may be established so that the vendor holds 75 per cent or more of the ordinary share capital (as defined for the purposes of Income and Corporation Taxes Act 1988, s 832) in a new company (such shares having negligible voting/dividend rights) and the purchaser holds 25 per cent of the ordinary share capital of the company (its shareholding subscribed at a premium sufficient to enable it to pay the purchase price). The new company then acquires the assets from the vendor while they form a stamp duty group. The vendor's shareholding (which is of negligible value) is either subsequently acquired by the purchaser, redeemed for a nominal sum by the new company or diluted so as to be wholly insignificant. Care will be needed to ensure that the structure does not fall foul of the anti-avoidance provisions of Finance Act 1967, s 27. It may also have corporation tax consequences as it will prevent the new company from being grouped with the purchaser.

12.4.3   Other taxes

There are certain exceptions in the area of taxation to the principle that on an assets transaction the liabilities remain with the vendor and these are considered below.

PAYE/National Insurance

Income Tax (Employment) Regulations 1993, reg 80 provides that the purchaser of a business does not become liable for the payment of any tax which was deductible from any emoluments paid to the employees before the change (in ownership of the business) took place. Thus, unless the purchaser specifically assumes pre-completion PAYE and National Insurance liabilities of the vendor, such liabilities will remain with the vendor. Under reg 80 the business is not, on sale, treated as having come to an end for PAYE purposes and no forms P45 are issued to employees. The purchaser will nonetheless require the up-to-date PAYE records for each employee as well as P11D records (record of benefits). If the information provided to the purchaser is incorrect, there is a risk that the purchaser will under-deduct tax. If the purchaser is under-deducting tax on emoluments paid because he has been given incorrect information as to PAYE codings by the vendor such liability for the under-deduction will fall on the purchaser not the vendor, as the liability for PAYE arises when emoluments are paid (Income and Corporation Taxes Act 1988, s 203 and 203A) and for national insurance when earnings are received (Social Security Contributions and Benefits Act 1992, s 6). There are special rules for determining when emoluments are paid for PAYE purposes (see Income and Corporation Taxes Act 1988, s 203A).

As a result, it is essential that the purchaser obtain accurate and up-to-date PAYE and National Insurance records and should also seek a warranty as to the state of the records (see the Agreement for Sale (Assets) at p 566).

VAT

The general rule is that the sale of goods by a VAT registered business is a taxable supply and attracts VAT at the standard rate (currently 17.5 per cent). Some items might be liable to tax at the zero rate but these are most likely to be items of stock eg food, books, newspapers. However, almost invariably the sale of business assets will be a 'transfer of business as a going concern' for the purposes of Value Added Tax (Special Provisions) Order 1995, (SI No 1268) art 5 and will be regarded as neither a supply of goods or services for VAT purposes and where a collection of assets are sold by one person to another Customs and Excise will usually accept that the transaction has involved a transfer of a business.

A vendor will wish to ensure that the price is expressed to be *exclusive* of VAT so that in the event that VAT is chargeable, it is payable in addition to the price. If the contract is silent VAT will be assumed to be inclusive (Value Added Tax Act 1994, s 19) and if it is subsequently the case that VAT should have been charged, the vendor will be liable to account for it with no recourse to the purchaser apart possibly from arguing that this was not the parties' intention in preparing the agreement and at worst, if this is resisted, claiming that the contract ought to be rectified. In any event, it is obvious that advisers will not be thanked for allowing a 17.5 per cent price reduction and the point should always be noted.

If VAT is chargeable, the vendor must produce a VAT invoice. The VAT invoice is the purchaser's evidence that VAT has been accounted for by the vendor and of the purchaser's entitlement to recover VAT from Customs and Excise.

A considerable number of VAT Tribunal decisions concern the provisions of Value Added Tax (Special Provisions) Order 1995, art 5. Most of these are concerned with the purchaser who has paid VAT and then been denied the right to recover the VAT. Article 5 is not a relief to be claimed; if the conditions for its application are met it is mandatory. The text of art 5 is as follows:

(1) Subject to paragraph (2) below, there shall be treated as neither a supply of goods nor a supply of services the following supplies by a person of assets of his business—

   (a) their supply to a person to whom he transfers his business as a going concern where—

      (i)   the assets are to be used by the transferee in carrying on the same kind of business, whether or not as part of any existing business, as that carried on by the transferor, and

      (ii) in a case where the transferor is a taxable person, the transferee is already, or immediately becomes as a result of the transfer, a taxable person or a person defined as such in section 2(2) of the [Manx Act];

   (b) their supply to a person to whom he transfers part of his business as a going concern where—

      (i)   that part is capable of separate operation,

      (ii) the assets are to be used by the transferee in carrying on the same kind of business, whether or not as part of any existing business, as that carried on by the transferor in relation to that part, and

      (iii) in a case where the transferor is a taxable person, the transferee is already, or immediately becomes as a result of the transfer, a taxable person or a person defined as such in section 2(2) of the [Manx Act].

(2) A supply of assets shall not be treated as neither a supply of goods nor a supply of services by virtue of paragraph (1) above to the extent that it consists of—

   (a) a grant which would, but for an election which the transferor has made, fall within item 1 of Group 1 of Sched 9 to the Value Added Tax 1994; or

   (b) a grant of fee simple which falls within paragraph (a) of item 1 of Group 1 of Sched 9 to the Value Added Tax Act 1994,

unless the transferee has made an election in relation to the land concerned which has effect on the relevant date and has given any written notification of the election required by paragraph 3(6) of the Sched 10 to the Value Added Tax Act 1994 no later than the relevant date.

(3) In paragraph (2) of this article—

'election' means an election having effect under paragraph 2 of Sched 10 to the Value Added Tax Act 1994;

'relevant date' means the date upon which the grant would have been treated as having been made or, if there is more than one such date, the earliest of them;

'transferor' and 'transferee' include a relevant associate of either respectively as defined in paragraph 3(7) of Sched 10 to the Value Added Tax Act 1994.

It will be noted that to fall within art 5 the transferee must be a taxable person (para (1)(*a*)(ii)). A taxable person for this purpose means not only a person who is registered for VAT but also one who is liable to be registered for VAT, eg by virtue of the transfer and the supplies he will be making in consequence of that transfer. The transferee must intend to carry on the same kind of business as the transferor. While the wording of art 5 (para(1)(*a*)(i)) seems to require a specific intention, the test applied by the court is not whether the purchaser would, but whether he could, carry on the same kind of business as the vendor (*CCE v Dearwood Ltd* [1986] STC 327 QBD).

Where part of an existing business is transferred the same rules apply, with an additional requirement that the part of the business transferred is capable of independent operation (art 5(1)(*b*)).

The cases tend to indicate that in the view of HM Customs and Excise, virtually anything can be a 'transfer of business as a going concern' and so fall within the article. Even though the prescribed practice for determining whether a particular transfer falls within art 5 is set out in Customs leaflet 700/9/96 there is inconsistency of practice between local Customs offices and it is generally advisable that a ruling from Customs and Excise be sought confirming that the transfer falls within art 5 (or not). For the ruling to be binding the application must disclose all material facts *(Matrix Securities Ltd v IRC* [1994] STC 272).

If land (freehold or leasehold) is one of the assets transferred as part of the asset acquisition, as is commonly the case, there are further complications. If the vendor has waived his exemption in respect of the supply of his land pursuant to Value Added Tax Act 1994, Sched 10, para 2, or the land to be transferred includes the freehold of a new commercial building or civil engineering work (ie the practical completion of which was within the three years prior to the transfer) then notwithstanding the other provisions of art 5, VAT will still be chargeable unless the purchaser has both waived his exemption in respect of those buildings and notified Customs and Excise that he wishes to do so prior to completion of the sale (see VAT (Special Provisions) Order 1995 (SI No 1268), art 5(2) and (3)).

On a transfer of a business as a going concern the purchaser may apply to take over the vendor's VAT registration number. It is not generally advisable to do so, as the purchaser will also assume responsibility for the vendor's VAT liabilities including those attributable to errors in record keeping and returns. The assumption of the vendors' VAT registration number is rare except, for example, on incorporation of a partnership. Where the registration is taken over, full VAT warranties should be obtained (*see* Agreement for Sale (Assets), p 566).

When art 5 applies, Value Added Tax Act 1994, s 49 requires that VAT records must be transferred to the purchaser unless Customs and Excise agree to their retention by the vendor. Customs and Excise are becoming more reluctant to agree to their retention by the vendor and will wish to be convinced that there are genuine commercial needs for the vendor to hold on to the records. Where those records are incorporated into and form part of the VAT records of another business which are retained by the vendor, and it is impracticable to separate the records, it is usually possible to demonstrate such a case.

A further VAT matter to be considered is adjustments under the capital goods scheme. This scheme adjusts the recovery of VAT where a business has purchased land or buildings costing more than £250,000 or computer hardware over £50,000. It applies to purchases made after 1 April 1990. The amount of VAT recovered on the initial purchase is adjusted over a five year period (in the case of computer hardware) or ten year period (in the case of land and buildings). Broadly, the scheme provides that if the asset is put to more exempt use for VAT purposes during the period, for example because the business expands into credit broking and uses its computer hardware for this purpose, then the company is obliged to repay part or all of the VAT it initially recovered on acquisition of the asset (because at the time of acquisition the business was making taxable supplies only for VAT purposes). On the other hand, if the asset is put to a use during the period which would, if so used at the time of acquisition, entitle it to recover more VAT, the business will recover additional VAT (subject to a maximum of the amount of VAT initially incurred on the acquisition of the asset). When a business is transferred as a going concern the purchaser takes over the responsibility for the ensuing adjustments over five or ten years. Accordingly a purchaser will need to know the remaining number of intervals applicable to goods subject to the capital goods scheme, the total VAT originally incurred on the acquisition and the percentage of VAT which was claimed during the first interval. A suggested clause is set out in the Agreement for Sale (Assets) at p 523.

The sale and purchase agreement should also contain provisions covering any VAT deferment accounts. When goods are imported from outside the European Community VAT must be paid at the point of importation on the value of the goods imported. A VAT deferment account enables payment to be postponed. Provision of the VAT deferment account number to the supplier allows the goods to be imported and Customs will then collect the duty within the month via a direct debit from a bank account. The bank account has to be supported by a bank guarantee in favour of Customs and Excise. It is important when acting for a vendor to ensure that employees or agents of the business realise that the old VAT deferment account number must not be used and that where necessary, guarantees are reduced or cancelled. The purchaser must make his own VAT deferment account arrangements.

Inheritance Tax

Inheritance tax could be relevant on a business acquisition in two respects. These matters are addressed by warranty in the Agreement for Sale (Assets) (p 566).

The first relates to the power of sale that a transferee of any property has, by virtue of Inheritance Tax Act 1984, s 212, to enable him to pay inheritance tax for which he is liable. For the purpose of paying the IHT a person liable for IHT (other than as transferor) has power to sell or mortgage the property to which the IHT is attributable. This power is available whether or not the property is still vested in that person (eg if the property has been transferred to another person). Thus if the vendor company has been the donee of a gift which becomes chargeable to IHT because the doner dies within seven years of making the gift and it sells the asset to the purchaser, the powers under Inheritance Tax Act 1984, s 212 may arise. A suggested warranty is set out at the Agreement for Sale (Assets) at p 566.

The second is the Inland Revenue charge under Inheritance Tax Act 1984, s 237 which gives the Inland Revenue a statutory charge on property, the transfer of which has given rise to a charge for inheritance tax but the tax in respect of which remains unpaid. This could, for example, also arise where an individual has gifted an asset to the vendor company and dies within seven years of the gift when the gift becomes a chargeable transfer for IHT purposes. To the extent IHT is not paid an Inland Revenue charge will attach to the asset transferred (even if the asset is no longer owned by the original donee). If the purchaser has no notice of the charge, it will attach to the consideration paid to the vendor rather than to the asset. In the case of land interests a purchaser will, however, have notice of the charge. With unregistered land, the charge will be registered against the land as a Class D(I) land charge at the Land Registry. In relation to registered land, the Inland Revenue completes a form submitted to the relevant District Land Registry and a notice of a liability tax is entered on the proprietorship register, so putting the purchaser on notice of the IHT liability.

Chapter 13

Taxation of the Corporate Target

This Chapter deals in outline with some of the aspects of the target company's affairs which, in practice, often arise in connection with acquisitions. It deals exclusively with the tax affairs of the target company. A business forming part of a company which is wholly tax resident in the United Kingdom is not a separate entity for tax purposes and so is not addressed. Taxation of vendor and purchaser in relation to an acquisition of business assets is addressed in Chapter 12.

The matters covered by this chapter are:

(13.1) the target in a group;
(13,2) tax losses;
(13.3) management expenses;
(13.4) advance corporation tax carry forward;
(13.5) advance corporation tax carry back;
(13.6) other anti-avoidance measures;
(13.7) the close company target;
(13.8) value added tax;
(13.9) inheritance tax;
(13.10) *Ramsay* and *Furniss v Dawson*.

It will be seen that tax problems and considerations can arise not only because of the target's past transactions but also because of the acquisition itself, which can give rise to tax charges on the target or loss of reliefs or allowances.

13.1   The target in a group

The target may be a member of a group for tax purposes if it has subsidiaries or if it is itself a subsidiary of another company. It may be, of course, that the target has subsidiaries and is itself a subsidiary. In such a case the acquisition will carve a sub-group out of a larger group. Different provisions of the Taxes Acts apply to different types of subsidiary. The statutes describe subsidiaries as '51 per cent subsidiaries', '75 per cent subsidiaries' or, occasionally, '90 per cent subsidiaries'. The relevant definitions are contained in the Income and Corporation Taxes Act 1988, s 838, and in the sections referred to below. The basic rules are that a company is a 51 per cent subsidiary of another if and so long as more than 50 per cent of its 'ordinary share capital' is owned directly or indirectly by that other, and a company is a 75 per cent subsidiary of another if and so long as not less than 75 per cent of its ordinary share capital is owned directly or indirectly by that other; however, it will be a 90 per cent subsidiary only if the other company owns not less than 90 per cent of its ordinary share capital *directly*. It is obvious from this that a company which is a 75 per cent subsidiary will always be a 51 per cent subsidiary and a company which is a 90 per cent subsidiary will be both a 75 per cent subsidiary and a 51 per cent subsidiary. However, if company A owns 100 per cent of the ordinary share capital of company B which in turn owns 100 per cent of the ordinary share capital of company C, company C will not be a 90 per cent subsidiary of company A (although it will be both a 75 per cent and a 51 per cent subsidiary of company A and a 90 per cent subsidiary of company B).

References to ownership are to beneficial ownership. There are circumstances short of an outright disposal in which beneficial ownership of an asset may be lost. Beneficial ownership is a wider concept than equitable ownership. It is possible for a person to cease to have beneficial ownership of an asset without it passing to another person, eg on entering into a conditional contract for sale (see *Wood Preservation Ltd v Prior* [1969] 1 WLR 1077). This question was most recently examined in *J Sainsbury plc v O'Connor (Inspector of Taxes)* [1991] STC 318, itself a group relief case although the decision is of much wider application. Sainsbury held 75 per cent of the issued share capital of a joint venture company but of this holding 5 per cent was the subject of put and call options on terms such that any increase or decrease in value of the 5 per cent holding would not accrue to Sainsbury but to its joint venture partner. The Court of Appeal applied (as it was bound to do) its earlier decision in *Wood Preservation Ltd* but provided some further explanation of that case's ratio. It held that the test to be applied was whether the nature and extent of the rights retained by Sainsbury left it with more than the bare legal shell of ownership. On the facts, despite the commercial effect of the option arrangements, this was so.

References to indirect ownership are to ownership through another body corporate. Where all subsidiaries in a chain are wholly owned the top company indirectly owns all the share capital of the bottom company, but where some companies in the chain are only partially owned s 838 contains provisions for ascertaining the percentage owned by one company of another. The provisions are complex but they work out as might be expected. The definition of 'ordinary share capital' in the Income and Corporation Taxes Act 1988, s 832(1) is not, however, quite as might be expected. It means 'all the share capital (by whatever name called) of the company, other than capital the holders of which have a right to a dividend at a fixed rate but have no other right to share in the profits of the company'.

In addition to the rules in s 838, the tests in the Income and Corporation Taxes Act 1988, Sched 18 will generally have to be applied. These apportion the profits of a company available for distribution and its assets available for distribution on a notional winding up among 'equity holders' in the company. An equity holder is any person who holds 'ordinary shares' (any shares other than fixed rate preference shares) or who is a loan creditor of the company in respect of a loan which is not a 'normal commercial loan' (see Sched 18, para 1(5)). A company will not be treated as a subsidiary of another company unless the latter is entitled under these tests to the appropriate percentage of the first company's income and assets. Option arrangements are taken into account when considering the percentage entitlement to income and assets (Income and Corporation Taxes Act 1988 Sched 18 paras 5B to 5E). For example, in the case of para 5B the percentage of income and assets on a winding-up is recomputed on the assumption that the outstanding option rights are exercised. If this produces a lower percentage than the basic Sched 18 rules, the lower percentage applies.

If the target is a member of a group many tax consequences ensue. The main points which may be significant in the context of an acquisition are dealt with below and these relate to: group income; group relief; surrender of advance corporation tax (ACT); and tax on capital gains.

13.1.1   Group income

Under the Income and Corporation Taxes Act 1988, s 247, a United Kingdom resident company which is a 51 per cent subsidiary of another United Kingdom resident company may pay dividends, annual payments or interest to that other company or to that other's 51 per cent subsidiaries without paying ACT in respect of the dividends or deducting tax at source from the annual payments or interest under the Income and Corporation Taxes Act 1988, s 349(1) or (2). Payments so made are called 'group income'. In order that a company may avail itself of this privilege the paying company and the receiving company must make a joint election to the inspector. The election comes into force three months after it is made (or earlier if the inspector is satisfied that it is validly made) but ceases to have effect if the companies become no longer entitled to make it. It follows from this that any purchaser will wish to ensure that any dividends or other group income paid or received by the target before completion and which were paid gross because of an election under the section were validly so paid. Under s 247(6) the inspector is empowered to make assessments or adjustments in the event that a company purports to make a payment gross under an election but the election is invalid.

If a target is a 51 per cent subsidiary of another company before the acquisition and proposes to pay a dividend within a group income election before it is acquired, the dividend should be paid before any arrangements are entered into which might fetter the vendor's beneficial ownership (see *Wood Preservation Ltd v Prior* [1969] 1 WLR 1077 and *O'Connor (Inspector of Taxes) v J Sainsbury plc* [1991] STC 318) and certainly before contracts are exchanged, as references to ownership of share capital in the context of subsidiaries are to beneficial ownership and the target will therefore cease to be a 51 per cent subsidiary of the vendor at the latest when contracts are exchanged for the sale of the target's share capital. If there is an interval between contract and completion, the vendor will probably remain the registered shareholder and thus remain entitled to receive any dividend paid during that period (subject to the terms of the acquisition agreement). After the *Sainsbury* case, if the contract is conditional and the vendor remains entitled to the underlying dividends and voting rights of the target and to its profits and assets on a winding-up it is possible for the vendor to retain beneficial ownership of the shares in the target such that dividends can continue to be paid inside a group income election. This is particularly the case if the contract is conditional on matters outside the purchaser's control. Further considerations applicable in the case of pre-sale dividends paid in the context of an acquisition are discussed at p 268.

For group income purposes a company is not a 51 per cent subsidiary of another ('the parent company') if, in tracing a chain of indirect ownership, one of the owners in the chain is not resident in the United Kingdom or holds the shares as trading stock (see s 247(8)). Additionally, the parent company must be beneficially entitled to more than 50 per cent of any profits available for distribution to equity holders of the subsidiary company and to more than 50 per cent of any assets of the subsidiary company available for distribution to its equity holders on a winding-up, applying for these purposes the tests in the Income and Corporation Taxes Act 1988, Sched 18.

The group income provisions also apply where a company is a trading company or a holding company owned by a consortium (see s 247(9)).

13.1.2   Group relief

Under the Income and Corporation Taxes Act 1988, s 402 group relief applies between companies resident in the United Kingdom if one is a 75 per cent subsidiary of another or if both are 75 per cent subsidiaries of a third. The ownership chain is broken if it passes through a company not resident in the United Kingdom (although this may not now be correct depending on the outcome of the *ICI v Colmer* [1993] 4 All ER 705 case on which, at the time of updating this chapter, a decision from the European Court of Justice is awaited) or if shares are held as trading stock (see the Income and Corporation Taxes Act 1988, s 413(3) and (5)). Section 413(7)–(10) strikes at certain artificial arrangements.

If a company which is a member of such a group has incurred trading losses in an accounting period or has certain other amounts eligible for relief from corporation tax arising in that period, it may surrender the amounts to another company within the group which can utilise them to relieve its own tax liability in respect of a 'corresponding accounting period'. Group relief can also be surrendered by companies owned by a consortium to the members of the consortium (and members of the same group as those consortium members) and vice versa (s 402(3)). Under 'pay and file' introduced for accounting periods ending after 30 September 1993 a claim for group relief (or for withdrawal of group relief) must be made before the later of two years from the end of the period to which it relates and the time the assessment for that period has become final and conclusive (Income and Corporation Taxes Act 1988 Sched 17A para 2), subject to a longstop date of six years from the end of the period to which the claim relates (Sched 17A, para 3). The Inland Revenue have a discretion to extend these time limits (see Statement of Practice 11/93).

A claim for group relief need not be for the full amount available for claim but must be quantified (Income and Corporation Taxes Act 1988 Sched 17A paras 7 and 8).

Consent to the surrender of losses must be given by the surrendering company. Where the vendor sells a 75 per cent subsidiary from which it intends to claim group relief arising in previous accounting periods it should be a term of the sale agreement that the surrendering company will consent to the surrender.

The claimant company may pay the surrendering company for the relief. It is provided by s 402(6) that payments for group relief are not to be taken into account for corporation tax purposes, either in respect of the claimant company or the surrendering company. Any payments for group relief have to be made 'in pursuance of an agreement' between the claimant company and the surrendering company and must not exceed the amount of the relief surrendered. The amount paid is usually approximately equal to the corporation tax which would otherwise be paid so that, in effect, instead of paying tax to the Inland Revenue the claimant company pays an equivalent amount to the surrendering company.

If the target itself is a company owning 75 per cent subsidiaries, it may well have been the claimant company or surrendering company in respect of group relief, but when it is sold still owning its subsidiaries then, so long as the target is not itself a subsidiary of any other company or is not owned by, or by a member of, a consortium, the purchaser in effect buys the complete group and all the group relief arrangements will pass under the purchaser's control. The purchaser will be concerned to see, or to take a warranty to the effect, that all group relief surrenders and payments within the target group have been properly made, but at least the group relief arrangements will not have to be disentangled.

More difficult problems arise when the target is itself a 75 per cent subsidiary of another company or is owned by a consortium. In a case where the target has been surrendering or claiming group relief from companies which are not to be acquired at the same time as the acquisition of the target, it is necessary, at the time of the acquisition, to give some thought to the group relief arrangements, both in respect of accounting periods completed before the acquisition and in respect of the accounting period current at the date of acquisition.

It is probable that the group relief arrangements in respect of some accounting periods completed before acquisition will not have been finalised because the tax computations remain to be agreed or submitted. If the target is a loss maker, it may well be necessary or desirable, after the acquisition has been completed, for the vendor to receive and pay for group relief in respect of accounting periods completed before the acquisition. In such a case the vendor will be anxious to ensure that it is able to obtain the benefit of the target's losses and the purchaser will wish to ensure that the target will be paid for them (and vice versa if the target is a profit maker obtaining the benefit of group relief surrendered to it by companies in the vendor group). In either case it will be necessary to have a written group relief agreement requiring the target or its subsidiaries to surrender the losses and to make arrangements for liaison between vendor and purchaser with regard to the corporation tax computations. It was settled by *Chapman (AW) Ltd v Hennessey* (1981) 55 TC 516 that it is possible to make surrenders of group relief after the target has left the group.

Group relief in respect of the accounting period current at the time of the acquisition tends to be complicated. There is provision in the Income and Corporation Taxes Act 1988, s 409 for apportionment of group relief when companies join or leave a group during an accounting period but the Income and Corporation Taxes Act 1988, s 410 provides that if in any accounting period arrangements are in existence by virtue of which, at some time during or after the expiry of that accounting period, a company could leave a group, there can be no group relief between the company and the members of the group which it proposes to leave. It should be noted that the section applies whether the company is a surrendering company or a claimant company. The section (certainly in its form prior to consolidation of the Income and Corporation Taxes Act 1988) could be interpreted as providing that, if any such arrangements exist, the company shall be deemed never to have been a member of the previous group for group relief purposes, but this was confirmed as incorrect in *Shepherd (Inspector of Taxes) v Law Land plc* [1990] STC 795. Prior to that decision, the Inland Revenue's practice had been to apply the section back to the beginning of the accounting period during which the 'arrangements' came into existence but the taxpayer successfully argued that relief is deprived only from the actual date on which 'arrangements' came into existence.

'Arrangements' is a deliberately loose term and arrangements can come into existence before contracts are in fact exchanged. Previously, it was often advantageous to the vendor if the target changed its accounting date so that an accounting period ended just before the arrangements arose (although pinning down the date when the arrangements arose can be difficult). In the light of the *Law Land* decision, this is no longer strictly necessary but may afford certainty. Under s 409, the purchaser group will have the benefit of group relief involving the target only on and after the date upon which the beneficial ownership of the target's share capital passes (profits and losses are apportioned on a time basis unless this would be unreasonable or unjust). An accounting period should not, however, be changed too lightly as there may well be many tax consequences that flow from such a change, beside the need to prepare audited accounts for the shortened period. The object of s 410 seems to be to prevent companies with large losses arising or due to arise in an accounting period (caused perhaps by capital allowances) joining an unconnected group or acquiring an unconnected company, surrendering their losses and separating again under pre-existing 'arrangements'. It should also be noted that the provisions apply to a company remaining within the selling group if the company which is sold has succeeded to its trade. Packaging a trade in a company for subsequent sale may therefore affect group relief between the company to which the trade formerly belonged and the other members of the group.

For a discussion of the meaning of the word 'arrangements' in this context and the wide meaning given to it see *Pilkington Bros Ltd v IRC* [1981] STC 219 and more recently *Scottish and Universal Newspapers v Fisher* [1996] SCD 311, a Special Commissioners decision where the term 'arrangements' was construed more narrowly. See also Inland Revenue Statement of Practice SP3/93.

For a note on group relief and financial assistance under the Companies Act 1985, s 151, *see* p 63.

13.1.3 Surrender of advance corporation tax

Under the Income and Corporation Taxes Act 1988, s 240, a company resident in the United Kingdom can surrender ACT paid in respect of dividends to its resident 51 per cent subsidiaries provided they are 51 per cent subsidiaries throughout the accounting period in which the dividends were paid. The rules about following the ownership chain are the same as for group relief (*see* p 302) and the provisions of the Income and Corporation Taxes Act 1988, Sched 18 are also applied by s 240(11)(*b*) to determine whether a company is a 51 per cent subsidiary.

The Finance Act 1996 Sched 25 inserts a new Sched 13A into the Income and Corporation Taxes Act dealing with the surrender of ACT and provides a statutory footing for the withdrawal of claims for the surrender of ACT. The claim for the surrender of ACT must be made by the surrendering company within the period of six years from the end of the relevant accounting period of the surrendering company. The withdrawal of any surrender can only be made with the consent of the subsidiary concerned. The Revenue have announced that this provision will not take effect at the earliest until accounting periods ending in 1999. Until such time the surrender of ACT and withdrawal of ACT surrenders will continue on an informal basis.

A company may wish to surrender ACT if it cannot use it for set-off against its own liability to mainstream corporation tax. Under the Income and Corporation Taxes Act 1988, s 239(2), the amount of ACT which can be set against a company's liability for mainstream corporation tax in any accounting period is limited to ACT which would have been payable on a distribution made at the end of that period, being a distribution which, together with the ACT payable in respect of it, is equal to the company's income and capital gains charged to corporation tax for that period. If a company has paid distributions in an accounting period which, when grossed up, exceed its chargeable profits, the excess is called surplus ACT and can be set off against tax in other accounting periods. Under s 239(3) surplus ACT can be carried back to accounting periods beginning in the previous six years if a claim is made to that effect within two years after the end of the accounting period (see *Procter & Gamble Ltd v Taylerson (Inspector of Taxes)* [1988] STC 854) and under s 239(4) it can be carried forward indefinitely, but surrendering ACT under s 240 can enable it to be used by a subsidiary in a current accounting period. It should be noted that a surrender under s 240 can be made in respect of any ACT and not just surplus ACT.

ACT surrendered to a subsidiary is treated as if it were ACT paid by that subsidiary subject to certain limitations. If it is surplus to the subsidiary's own requirements it cannot be carried back (although it is treated as the first amount to be set off against mainstream corporation tax, leaving the subsidiary's own ACT free to be carried back) and s 240(5) provides that ACT surrendered to a subsidiary may not be set off against that subsidiary's mainstream corporation tax for any accounting period in which, or in any part of which, it was not a subsidiary of the surrendering company.

Section 240(11) prevents ACT surrenders between the target and the selling group in an accounting period during which arrangements are in existence for the target to leave the group. The section also strikes at certain artificial arrangements and is the ACT equivalent of the group relief anti-avoidance provisions contained in the Income and Corporation Taxes Act 1988, ss 410 and 413.

It is common for payments to be made by subsidiaries to surrendering companies in return for ACT surrendered. Such payments are treated in the same way as payments for group relief, and are not taken into account for tax purposes in calculating the profits or losses of the paying or receiving company (s 240(8)).

Where the target is a parent company and is not itself a subsidiary, the purchaser will be concerned to see that any ACT surrenders have been properly made, so that the target group's corporation tax computations have been correctly prepared. If the target is a subsidiary and has received the benefit of surrender of ACT from a parent which is not being purchased, the purchaser will wish to ensure that the target has not paid for, and will not become liable to pay for, any ACT which becomes irrecoverable under s 240(5) when the target leaves the vendor group.

A number of anti-avoidance measures directed at the sale of subsidiaries with surplus ACT were introduced into the Income and Corporation Taxes Act 1988 by the Finance Act 1989. These are considered on p 318.

13.1.4 Surrender of tax refunds under 'pay and file'

A detailed description of 'pay and file' which came into operation in respect of accounting periods ending on or after 1 October 1993 is beyond the scope of this book. Briefly, pay and file requires companies to pay their corporation tax liabilities on or before the due date for payment (ie nine months after the end of the relevant accounting period). This may result in additional amounts becoming due (together with interest) or an entitlement to a tax refund (attracting interest at a lesser rate). The Finance Act 1989, s 102 permits a company in a group to surrender its right to a refund to another company which has a liability to additional tax, thus reducing the interest charge. The companies must be members of the same group throughout the relevant accounting period and remain so at the date the claim is made. Any payment made between the companies in respect of the surrender will, like payments for group relief and ACT, be outside the scope of corporation tax.

For the purposes of determining whether two companies are members of the same group the provisions relating to group relief are applied. It is not clear that this is sufficient to import s 410, since one of the conditions of that section operating is that one company should have amounts which it would be entitled to surrender by way of group relief. Section 413(7) and Sched 18 will apply for the purposes of determining whether the relevant company is a 75 per cent subsidiary.

13.1.5 Tax on capital gains

Groups for the purposes of corporation tax on chargeable gains are defined under the Taxation of Chargeable Gains Act 1992, s 170. A company ('the principal company of the group') and all its 75 per cent subsidiaries form a group. If any of those subsidiaries have 75 per cent subsidiaries, the group includes them and their 75 per cent subsidiaries, and so on, but a group does not include any company (other than the principal company of the group) that is not an 'effective 51 per cent subsidiary' of the principal company of the group. A company is an effective 51 per cent subsidiary of another company if that other company is beneficially entitled to more than 50 per cent of any profits available for distribution to equity holders of the subsidiary and to more than 50 per cent of any assets available for distribution to equity holders on a winding up. For this purpose, the tests in Sched 18 apply, with slight modifications (see the Taxation of Chargeable Gains Act 1992, s 170(8)).

A company cannot be the principal company of a group if it is itself a 75 per cent subsidiary of another company, unless it is prevented from being a member of the same group as the other company because it is not an effective 51 per cent subsidiary of the principal company of the group to which the other company belongs. A company cannot be a member of more than one group, and s 170(6) contains rules for determining to which of two or more potential groups a company belongs.

The rules for determining a capital gains tax group are less restrictive than those for other corporation tax purposes, because a member of a group is not required to be a 75 per cent subsidiary of the principal company of the group, provided it is an effective 51 per cent subsidiary of it and is a 75 per cent subsidiary of that company. Further, although all the members of the group must be United Kingdom resident companies, it is permitted to trace ownership through companies resident outside the United Kingdom and to take account of shares held as trading stock.

As a general point, the provisions now considered will not cause great difficulty where the target is a parent company (sold with its subsidiaries intact) but is not and has not been a 75 per cent subsidiary of any other company. If, however, the target is or has been a 75 per cent subsidiary (whether or not it has subsidiaries itself) the provisions may give rise to unexpected liabilities.

Tax recoverable from other group members

Under the Taxation of Chargeable Gains Act 1992, s 190, if a chargeable gain accrues to a company which at the time is a member of the group and the company fails to pay its corporation tax assessed for that accounting period within six months of the due date, if the tax so assessed included any amount in respect of chargeable gains, an amount of that tax not exceeding corporation tax on the amount of that gain may be recovered from a company which was at the time when the gain accrued the principal company of the group and any other company which, within the two year period preceding the gain, was a member of the group and owned the asset disposed of or any part of it (or, where the asset in question was an interest or right in or over another asset, owned either asset or any part of either asset).

It should be noted that what can be recovered is corporation tax on the amount of the gain, so it seems that any allowable capital losses available to the company which should have paid the tax and which might have reduced the tax payable need not be brought into account when assessing the other group company.

It will be seen, therefore, that if the target is the principal company of a group, it may be made liable for its subsidiary's chargeable gains even if the subsidiary in question is not a subsidiary of the target at the time of the acquisition. Moreover, if the target owned an asset which was disposed of to another member of the group (perhaps the vendor) before the acquisition of the target, the target can be made liable after the acquisition to account for tax on chargeable gains payable by a company with which it has then no relationship. Section 190(3) provides that the company paying tax assessed under s 190(1) can recover an equal amount from other group companies, but the purchaser is likely to want an express indemnity from the vendor.

A number of other provisions, notably those relating to the migration of companies and the taxation of gains of non-resident companies, also allow tax to be recovered from other companies in the same group.

Intra-group transfers

Under the Taxation of Chargeable Gains Act 1992, s 171 transfers of chargeable assets within a group do not give rise to any immediate charge to tax. The section provides that both parties to the transfer are treated as if the asset were acquired for a consideration of such amount as would secure that on the transferor's disposal, neither a gain nor a loss would accrue. In other words, the consideration is assumed to be the disposing company's base value including any indexation allowance (Taxation of Chargeable Gains Act 1992, s 56(2)). To take a simple example, suppose that company B acquires an asset at a cost of £10,000 which subsequently increases in value to £20,000. Company B is then acquired by company A and becomes its 75 per cent subsidiary. A transfer of that asset from company B to company A will be deemed to be made at the price (ignoring indexation allowance) of £10,000 irrespective of the asset's worth and of what company A actually pays company B for it. Suppose company A pays the market value, ie £20,000. When company A sells the asset to a third party at a price of £30,000 the chargeable gain would be £20,000 (ie £30,000 less £10,000) even though company A has actually paid £20,000 for the asset.

By s 171(2) certain disposals fall outside the terms of the section. Examples are the disposal of a debt and the disposal of an interest in shares in a company in consideration for a capital distribution. This means that the liquidation of a subsidiary will involve a chargeable disposal of its shares by the parent (see the Taxation of Chargeable Gains Act 1992, s 122).

Section 171 also does not apply where the transaction is treated by the Taxation of Chargeable Gains Act 1992, ss 127 and 135 as not involving a disposal (s 171(3)). This is an important provision and ensures that where, for example, shares in a subsidiary are hived down to a second subsidiary on a share for share basis, that second subsidiary acquires those shares at current market value while the consideration shares received by the parent in the share for share exchange will have the original base cost of the shares transferred. These statutory provisions reverse the decision in *Westcott (Inspector of Taxes) v Woolcombers Ltd* [1987] STC 600, and see also *NAP Holdings UK Ltd v Whittles (Inspector of Taxes)* [1994] STC 979.

Section 171 is obviously useful, as assets can be transferred within a group of companies without incurring an immediate liability to tax on any chargeable gains, but in the context of an acquisition it can cause problems. The section may mean, for instance, that an asset owned by the target has a lower base value for tax purposes than its actual cost. If the target has acquired that asset from a company which was in the same group at the time of the acquisition, on any subsequent disposal of that asset outside the group the purchaser may be aggrieved to find that the target's tax bill is higher than he thought (*see the example given above*). A general warranty is therefore taken to cover this point (the Agreement for Sale, Sched 4, warranty 2.6(F) at p 424).

The section may also, in conjunction with the 'value shifting' provisions of the Taxation of Chargeable Gains Act 1992, ss 30 to 34, affect the liability to capital gains tax arising on the disposal of shares in a subsidiary from which assets have been transferred.

Companies leaving a group

In the early days of capital gains tax it was possible to make use of what is now s 171 to avoid the charge to corporation tax on capital gains by means of what became known as 'the envelope trick'. If company Y owned an asset which had grown substantially in value it could transfer that asset to a new 75 per cent subsidiary, X, formed for the purpose in exchange for the issue of shares by X. The shares of X were deemed acquired by Y at their current market value (ie the actual value of the asset at the time of the transfer), but s 171 applied to the transfer of the asset. Y could then sell the shares of X to a purchaser so that dominion over the asset passed without any charge to tax on capital gains. X was the 'envelope' in which the asset was placed before it was sold.

To prevent this form of tax avoidance what is now the Taxation of Chargeable Gains Act 1992, s 179 was enacted. A more recent scheme along similar lines was stopped by the introduction of s 179(2A) and (2B). Section 179 provides that if company X, called 'the chargeable company' by the section, leaves a group owning an asset which it has acquired within the last six years from company Y which was at the time of the acquisition a member of the group which X is leaving, X is treated as if, at the time of the acquisition from Y, it had sold and immediately reacquired the asset at its market value. Where the target ceased to be a member of the group in an accounting period ending before 1 October 1993 the chargeable gain or loss was treated as accruing at the time at which the intra-group transfer of the asset took place (Taxation of Chargeable Gains Act 1992, s 178(3)). Where the target ceases to be a member of the group in an accounting period ending after 30 September 1993 (ie, after pay and file) the chargeable gain or loss is treated as accruing at the later of:

(a)   the beginning of the accounting period in which, or at the end of which, the target company leaves the group; or

(b)   the date on which the target company actually acquired the asset from a fellow group member.

It can be seen, therefore, that a liability under Taxation of Chargeable Gains Act 1992, s 179 arises much later than under its predecessor section applicable in respect of pre pay and file accounting periods. This now leaves it open to the vendor to argue that it can shelter all or some of the s 179 liability by way of group relief out of current year losses on a time apportionment basis unless this is unreasonable or unjust.

It should be noted that the provisions of the Taxation of Chargeable Gains Act 1992, s 35 and Sched 3 which allow for the rebasing of acquisition costs to the market value as at 31 March 1982, will not apply where X acquired the asset from Y prior to 6 April 1988. Instead, where the asset was acquired by the group on or before 31 March 1982, the gain that would otherwise be chargeable under s 179 is to be reduced by one-half (Taxation of Chargeable Gains Act 1992, s 36 and Sched 4).

The section also applies if, at the time when X leaves the group, it does not itself own the asset in question, but the asset is owned by an 'associated company' of X which is also leaving the group. For the purposes of the section, two or more companies are associated companies if, by themselves, they would form a group (s 179(8)). The section does not apply, however, if X and Y both leave the group together and are associated companies (s 179(2)).

The section applies not only to the original asset which X acquired but also to any replacement asset if any gain on the asset has been rolled over into that replacement asset under the Taxation of Chargeable Gains Act 1992, ss 152 to 158.

References to companies ceasing to be a member of a group are construed in accordance with the Taxation of Chargeable Gains Act 1992, s 170(10) which provides that a group remains the same group so long as the same company remains the principal company of the group and, if at any time the principal company of a group becomes a member of another group, the group of which it was the principal company before that time is regarded as the same as that other group. However, it would be possible for a member of the first group not to become a member of the other group if, although a 75 per cent subsidiary, it is not an effective 51 per cent subsidiary of the principal company of the other group. In those circumstances, s 179 will not apply, unless during the following six years the company ceases to be a 75 per cent subsidiary and an effective 51 per cent subsidiary of one or more members of the other group and it or another company at that time in the same group as it holds the asset or a replacement asset (s 179(5) to (7)). A company does not cease to be a member of a group for the purposes of s 179 if it ceases to be a member of a group in consequence of another member of the group ceasing to exist (s 179(1) as amended by the Finance (No 2) Act 1992, s 25).

Section 179 is difficult to construe. Assume a group which looks like this:

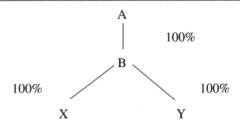

The following permutations (among others) are possible.

(1) If X is the target, X will leave the A group (all the companies) and the section will therefore apply to any asset which X owns at the time of the acquisition and which was acquired from any of the other companies within the six year period. If Y sold the asset to X, it will not help if Y is bought by the same purchaser at the same time. X and Y are not associated companies because, by themselves, they do not form a group.

(2) If B is the target and is sold with its subsidiaries intact, B, X and Y will leave the A group. *Prima facie* the section will apply, again, to any asset which X owns and has acquired within the six year period from any of the other companies, but if the asset has been acquired by X from B or Y it seems that the section will not in fact apply, because of s 179(2). Two or more associated companies (B, X and Y) are ceasing to be members of a group (the A group) at the same time and the section does not have effect as respects an acquisition by one from another of those associated companies. B, X and Y are associated because, by themselves, they form a group. If X has acquired the asset from A then, of course, the section will apply.

(3) If B is the target and X owns the asset which it has acquired from B, which in turn acquired it from A within the six year period, although the acquisition by X from B is not in point (because of s 179(2)) the section will still apply to B as the chargeable company because B is leaving the group having acquired the asset from A and 'an associated company' (X) is also leaving the group owning the asset. B and X are associated because by themselves they form a group. However, if A sold the asset to Y rather than B and Y sold it to X, will the section still apply when B, X and Y leave the group? It will not apply to X because its acquisition from Y is taken outside the charge by s 179(2). Y no longer owns the asset, so the section will apply to Y only if the asset is now owned by a company which is Y's 'associated company' and which is also leaving the group. It is possible to argue that X is not associated with Y because by themselves they do not form a group, although they do if B is added. This is an odd result and one that presumably was not intended by the draftsman. Where a sub-group leaves a larger group it is clear for the purposes of the exemption in s 179(2) that each of the members of the sub-group is associated with each other member, but it is not clear that the same result is obtained

from construing the reference to 'associated company' in s 179(3).

(4) If A is the target, no company will leave any group and the section will not apply.

(5) It should be noted that the section applies if X leaves a group owning an asset which it acquired from another company which was a member of that group at the time of the acquisition of the asset. The section does not in fact say that X has to be a member of the same group at the time the asset was acquired, although this is clearly the intention. Suppose that X and Y were quite unrelated at the time of the acquisition of the asset by X from Y but subsequently B acquired X's share capital so that X became a member of the B group. If X is the target and is sold by B within the period of six years from the date of X's acquisition of the asset from Y, the section appears to apply because X is ceasing to be a member of the B group and, at the time of the acquisition of the asset, Y was a member of the B group. Normally, of course, this will not matter because the section only supposes the asset to have been sold and reacquired at market value at the time of the acquisition, and if X and Y were unrelated the sale was probably at market value, so that X's base value will be high and no further tax will be payable. It is possible, however, that X acquired the asset at an undervalue (eg pursuant to an option granted some time before) and in that case the section would appear to produce a charge to tax even though s 171 had never applied to the asset in question.

Under s 179(11) tax assessed on the chargeable company can be recovered, if it is not paid within six months, from any company which was the principal company of the group which the chargeable company left (or which is the principal company at the date on which the tax became payable) and also from any company which owned the asset in question on the date for payment of the tax or when the chargeable company ceased to be a member of the group. It is difficult to believe that this provision is as wide as it appears. If X leaves the group owning the asset and then sells it at arm's length to an unrelated third party and X is subsequently assessed for tax under s 179, it seems from the section that if the third party is a company it can be charged to tax. Innocent purchasers will hardly regard as sufficient the right to indemnity from X which is conferred by s 179(11).

13.2 Tax losses

If a company has incurred a loss in carrying on a trade, it may claim to have the loss set off for tax purposes against profits, of whatever description (including chargeable gains), made in the accounting period in which the loss is sustained or, if the company was then carrying on the trade, of preceding accounting periods falling wholly or partly within the three years previous to that accounting period (Income and Corporation Taxes Act 1988, s 393A). In respect of a loss incurred in accounting periods ended before 1 April 1991, the loss may be carried back to accounting periods falling wholly or partly within a period equal to the length of the accounting period in which the loss is incurred and set against profits of whatever description (including chargeable gains) (Income and Corporation Taxes Act 1988, s 393(2)).

Alternatively, the company may carry forward the loss against any trading income from the same trade in succeeding accounting periods until the loss is exhausted (Income and Corporation Taxes Act 1988, s 393). If a target has trading losses otherwise eligible for carry forward, the purchaser will wish to know whether the change in ownership of the target's shares will affect the availability of these losses for set-off against future profits made by the target. The Income and Corporation Taxes Act 1988, s 768, which is considered below, has the effect of preventing such a carry forward in many cases. In relation to changes of ownership occurring on or after 14 June 1991, the Income and Corporation Taxes Act 1988, s 768A will in the same circumstances prevent a carry back of losses under s 393A. Sections 768 and 768A are in addition to, and not in substitution for, a considerable body of authority on this question.

Although the acquisition of shares in the target will not itself affect the target's trade, the target's business may change following the acquisition as its affairs come under new control. In each case it is a question of fact whether or not the old trade has been discontinued and a new trade has been commenced. If this has occurred, any losses incurred in the old trade are not available for carry forward against the profits of the new, because the new trade is not 'the trade' within the meaning of s 393.

Before the enactment (originally in the Finance Act 1969) of what is now s 768, many cases came before the courts which concerned changes in a target's business at the same time as the acquisition of its shares.

In *Ingram (JG) & Son Ltd v Callaghan (Inspector of Taxes)* (1968) 45 TC 151 the target's trade consisted of manufacturing rubber goods. For a period of nine months the company ceased to manufacture rubber goods but sold similar products made of plastic which had been made by another company. At the end of this nine month period the target was acquired by the purchaser and thereafter manufactured and sold similar products but now made of plastic. It was held on appeal that the target's trade had been permanently discontinued and a new trade set up. Losses made in the manufacture of rubber goods were therefore not available to be carried forward to be set off against the profits of the manufacture of the plastic goods.

In *Gordon and Blair Ltd v IRC* (1962) 40 TC 358 the target was a brewer. Shortly before the acquisition it had ceased to brew its own beer and entered into arrangements with the eventual purchaser to the effect that the purchaser would brew the beer which was then sold by the target under the target's brand name. It was held that the target's former trade had ceased when it ceased to brew beer and a new trade had been commenced. Similar cases relating to changes in a trade prior to or following an acquisition are *Tryka Ltd v Newall*

(Inspector of Taxes) (1963) 41 TC 146 and *Seaman (Inspector of Taxes) v Tucketts Ltd* (1963) 41 TC 422.

In all the cases cited above it was held, on the facts, that the changes in the target's trade had amounted to a discontinuance, but it is not every change in the nature of a trade which amounts to a discontinuance and therefore means that losses cannot be carried forward. The expansion of an existing trade is not necessarily regarded as a new trade and a trade may be suspended for some time and then revived. In *Robroyston Brickworks Ltd v IRC* (1976) 51 TC 230 the target manufactured and sold bricks and had been making losses for a number of years. In March 1968 the target ceased brick production and by August 1968, when the purchaser acquired it, had sold off its entire stock of bricks and its plant and machinery, paid off its creditors and gradually dispensed with the services of the remaining employees. Following the acquisition the target commenced manufacturing bricks at the purchaser's brickworks. The Court of Session held that the target's trade had only been suspended and that accordingly losses accrued prior to the transfer of the trade from one works to another were available to be set off against future profits. Cases such as this are now likely to be caught by s 768.

Section 768(1) has the effect of disallowing carry forward if:

(*a*) within any period of three years there is both a change in the ownership of the company and (either earlier or later in that period, or at the same time) a major change in the nature or conduct of a trade carried on by the company, or

(*b*) at any time after the scale of the activities in a trade carried on by a company has become small or negligible, and before any considerable revival of the trade, there is a change in the ownership of the company.

By s 768(4) 'major change in the nature or conduct of a trade' includes:

(*a*) a major change in the type of property dealt in, or services or facilities provided, in the trade; or

(*b*) a major change in customers, outlets or markets of the trade.

Section 768 applies even if the change is the result of a gradual process which began outside the period of three years referred to in s 768(1).

As a result, events which might not formerly have been held to amount to the discontinuance of one trade and the setting up of another will, if coupled with a change of ownership, prevent losses being carried forward. In *Willis (Inspector of Taxes) v Peeters Picture Frames Ltd* (1983) 56 TC 436, it was held that whether a change is 'major' is a question of fact and degree for the Commissioners and it seems that the word will not be construed literally, ie as relating to more than one half of the type of property dealt in or of the customers, outlets or markets. It is also necessary to consider whether the events amount to a change in the trade (*Purchase (Inspector of Taxes) v Tesco Stores Ltd* (1984) 58 TC 46).

The Inland Revenue have given some guidance, in Statement of Practice SP10/91, updated on 22 April 1996, on the circumstances in which a 'major change in the nature or conduct of a trade' may occur. Generally, a major change will not be regarded as having occurred when a company makes changes to increase its efficiency or keep pace with developing technology or management techniques. Likewise, rationalisation of a product range by withdrawing unprofitable items and, perhaps, replacing them with new products of a kind related to those already being produced will not cause the section to have effect.

Section 768(1)(*b*) deals with cases (such as the *Robroyston* case cited above) in which the target's trade has been suspended and its shares acquired during the period when the trade was suspended. Although suspension of a trade does not necessarily amount to a discontinuance, losses will not be available for carry forward in cases caught by the section.

The section contains machinery for enabling the inspector to ascertain the beneficial ownership of shares in the company for the purposes of ascertaining whether or not a change in the ownership of the company has taken place.

Section 769 defines a 'change of ownership'. The definition is wide and certainly includes an acquisition of a controlling interest by a single purchaser. When the purchaser is already a shareholder in the target, however, it is worth checking the rules carefully, because not every sale and purchase of shares between shareholders results in a change of ownership. If the target is a 75 per cent subsidiary of another company (applying for this purpose the tests in the Income and Corporation Taxes Act 1988, Sched 18) and continues to be so after a change in the direct ownership of the target, that change of ownership is disregarded (s 769(5)). In other words, the transfer within a group of shares in a subsidiary will not normally trigger the section. However, the sale of the parent company will mean a change of ownership of all of its 75 per cent subsidiaries (s 769(6)).

Capital allowances available to a trading company are treated as trading expenses (Capital Allowances Act 1990, s 144). If they go to increase the trading loss, ss 768 and 768A will apply to prevent their carry forward in the same way as the sections apply to other trading losses. Neither s 393 nor s 768 restrict the purchaser taking advantage of any capital allowances unclaimed at the date of sale. It may therefore be advantageous to disclaim such allowances for periods prior to completion and to claim them in later periods when they can be used to reduce profits of the target or, by way of group relief, of the purchaser or other companies in the purchaser's group.

As noted above, trading losses may to a limited extent be set off against chargeable gains, but there is no reciprocal treatment, so that allowable capital losses may be carried forward only to be set off against chargeable gains.

13.3 Management expenses

Prior to 29 November 1994 an investment company's (eg a holding company of a group) excess management expenses and charges on income (plus unused capital allowances) could be carried forward without any of the equivalent restrictions in s 768 for carry forward of trading losses applying, although there was the possible application of the *Ramsey* principle (described in more detail at p 328) applying to prevent the utilisation of such losses. It was, therefore, advantageous for purchasing groups to acquire companies with excess management expenses with a view to routing investment income and assets pregnant with gains through them. From 29 November 1994 the carry forward of excess expenses is restricted (under Income and Corporation Taxes Act 1988, s 768B) on a change of ownership of the company if after the change:

(a) there is a significant increase in the company's capital; or

(b) within the period of six years beginning three years before the change there is a major change in the nature or conduct of the business carried on by the company; or

(c) the change in ownership occurs at any time after the scale of the activities in the business carried on by the company has become small or negligible and before any considerable revival in the business.

Statement of Practice 10/91 (as updated) provides guidance on the circumstances in which there is a major change in the nature or conduct of the business. In particular, the Revenue state that it will not matter whether the change occurs at a particular point in time or is the result of a gradual process. For example, the Statement provides that there would be a major change in the nature of the business where an investment company switches from investing in quoted shares to investing in real property for rent.

A further restriction in relation to the availability of carried forward expenses of management of investment companies is s 768C which provides that on a change of ownership and irrespective of increases in capital or major change to the nature of the business excess management expenses cannot be carried forward and set against chargeable gains on assets acquired intra-group under Taxation of Chargeable Gains Act, s 171 within three years after such change of ownership.

Section 769 defines a change in ownership and is described more fully at p 316.

As a general point it should be noted that trading losses, management expenses, charges on income and capital allowances are capable of being surrendered under group relief arrangements only in respect of the accounting period in which they are incurred (Income and Corporation Taxes Act 1988, s 403). The purchaser acquiring a target with losses accrued in completed accounting periods can therefore utilise these losses only against profits or gains made in the target itself (or its subsidiaries in the relevant accounting periods). Only losses accruing in future accounting periods will be available for group relief within the purchaser group. The Income and Corporation Taxes Act 1988, s 409 deals with the treatment of the accounting period current at the date of acquisition (*see* p 304). Capital losses are not available for group relief at all.

13.4 Advance corporation tax carry forward

Surplus ACT can, under the Income and Corporation Taxes Act 1988, s 239(4), be carried forward indefinitely to be set off against a company's liability to mainstream corporation tax (*see* p 305). A target which was once profitable but has ceased to be so, or which has significant foreign source income received subject to foreign withholding taxes so that its mainstream corporation tax liability is reduced, may therefore have a large amount of surplus ACT capable of being carried forward and set off against its mainstream corporation tax in future accounting periods. This can be attractive for a purchaser if the purchaser expects to be able to arrange for the target to increase its United Kingdom taxable profits (eg by diverting business from another member of the purchaser group) as the purchaser will then have the benefit of the target's surplus ACT. The Income and Corporation Taxes Act 1988, s 245, however, prevents the carry forward of surplus ACT in similar circumstances as the Income and Corporation Taxes Act 1988, s 768 prevents the carry forward of tax losses (ie change of ownership coupled with a major change in the trade or a revival of the trade).

If s 245 applies, the date of the change of ownership is deemed to start a new accounting period and there is no carry forward into that and subsequent accounting periods. Section 768 applies only to trading companies, but, as surplus ACT can arise in investment companies, s 245 applies to them as well and defines 'major change in the nature or conduct of a trade or business' as including a change whereby the company ceases to be a trading company and becomes an investment company or vice versa and, if the company is an investment company, a major change in the nature of the investments held by the company. The Inland Revenue Statement of Practice SP10/91 (as updated) (*see* p 318) is relevant to s 245 as well as to s 768, s 768A, and s 768B Income and Corporation Taxes Act 1988, described more fully on p 315.

13.5 Advance corporation tax carry back

Section 245 applies to ACT which the company is treated as having paid by virtue of the Income and Corporation Taxes Act 1988, s 240 (surrender of ACT to a subsidiary) as it applies to ACT which it has actually paid. Further, the Income and Corporation Taxes Act 1988, s 245A prevents the carry forward of surrendered ACT where there is a major change in the nature or conduct of a trade or business of the company which surrendered the ACT within the period commencing three years before the change of ownership and ending three years after the change of ownership.

It used also to be possible for the purchaser to turn the target company's surplus ACT to advantage by transferring, prior to their disposal to a third party purchaser, assets intended for sale to the target company. As a consequence of the Taxation of Chargeable Gains Act 1992, s 171 the gain on disposal would be realised by the target and the tax on the gain could be offset by the surplus ACT. The Income and Corporation Taxes Act 1988, s 245B now restricts the carried forward ACT available to the target company where such an intra-group transfer followed by a disposal occurs within three years after the change in ownership of the target company.

Legislation introduced in the Finance Act 1993 prevents the carry back of ACT in circumstances where a once profitable company with ACT carry back capacity is acquired by a group with surplus ACT. On acquisition profitable companies would be transferred under the target company and dividends paid to it under a group income election. The target would then pay dividends outside a group income election and carry back the ACT to previous accounting periods (see *Pigott (Inspector of Taxes) v Staines Investment Co Ltd* [1995] STC 114). Section 245(3A) provides that where there is a change in ownership on or after 16 March 1993 and within a three year period either side there is also a major change in the nature of the trade or business of the company, the company will not be able to carry back ACT in respect of dividends paid after the change in ownership to accounting periods beginning before the change in ownership. For these purposes the accounting period in which the change of ownership takes place is divided into two separate accounting periods.

13.6   Other anti-avoidance measures

There are many anti-avoidance measures which may be relevant to the target, which have been described elsewhere in this or the preceding Chapter. However, there are two other pieces of anti-avoidance legislation worthy of note. First, Income and Corporation Taxes Act 1988, s 767A was introduced to prevent the use of company purchase schemes to avoid payment of corporation tax. Typically, this would involve the vendor selling a company with tax liabilities to a purchaser having first stripped the company of all its assets by way of an intra-group transfer. This would leave the Revenue trying to recover tax from an insolvent company. Section 767A provides that where a company changes ownership and fails to pay its corporation tax liability for any accounting period beginning before the date of change which remains unpaid 6 months after the date it has been assessed then the Revenue can in certain circumstances recover the unpaid tax from any person who controlled the company during the three years before the change or from any company also controlled by that person at any time during the three years before the change.

The target company could, therefore, be assessed for tax under s 767A in relation to unpaid tax liabilities of other companies previously owned by the vendor. The purchaser should ensure that the tax indemnity covers any liability
which might arise under s 767A. In addition, the vendor may also wish to take
a counter-indemnity from the purchaser since the circumstances in s 767A
could apply by reason of the actions or inaction of the purchaser, and an assessment made on the vendor in respect of any unpaid tax which was provided for
in the last set of audited or completion accounts. It is usual on a share sale for
the purchaser to pay the tax which has been provided for in the most recent audited accounts of the target or the tax provided in the completion accounts. The
provision will have been taken into account in reducing the purchase price paid
by the purchaser. Accordingly, to the extent tax has been provided for in the
most recent accounts prior to completion the purchaser cannot make a claim
under the tax indemnity and will be required to satisfy such liability from its
own resources (see the Tax Deed , cl 2.3(A) on p 488).

Second, Taxation of Chargeable Gains Act 1992, Sched 7A introduced
complex provisions to prevent the use of bought in capital loss companies. Pri-
or to such legislation, there had been a revival in the use of bought in capital
loss companies following the case of *Shepherd v Lyntress Ltd* [1989] STC 617,
which held that the Revenue could not successfully attack such schemes under
Ramsay/Furniss v Dawson principles if properly carried out. The effect of
Sched 7A is broadly to ringfence the capital losses in the target/target group
such that they cannot be used to shelter gains on assets transferred to the target
group by the purchaser's group after acquisition. Sched 7A applies not only to
capital losses realised by the target group prior to acquisition but also broadly
to capital losses crystallised on the disposal of assets after completion in respect of assets which were held by the target group on the date the purchaser
acquired the target's shares.

The capital losses in the target company and its own group of associated
companies at the time of entry into the purchaser's group are available in limited circumstances, namely against:

(a) gains arising in the accounting period of the loss, but before entry into the
     purchaser's group;

(b) gains arising on assets held by the target company or an associated com-
     pany before entry into the purchaser's group; and

(c) gains arising on assets acquired post entry from outside the group being
     assets not used or held otherwise than for the purposes of a trade carried
     on by the loss company throughout the time from entry to the disposal of
     the asset on which the gain was realised.

Again, there are special rules (similar to those relating to the carry forward
of trading losses) disallowing the use of such losses in relation to (c) above
where there is a major change in the nature or conduct of the trade (Sched 7A
para 8 and SP10/91). The legislation is extremely complicated and a detailed

analysis is beyond the scope of this book. However, the effect of the legislation is that bought-in capital losses are usually of very little value to the purchaser.

13.7   The close company target

A company controlled by a few individuals has the potential to become a tax avoidance vehicle. A number of provisions have been enacted to counter this, of which the most notorious were those relating to shortfall apportionment, now repealed by the Finance Act 1989 and replaced by a simpler regime which applies to close companies whose income consists mainly of passive investment income ('close investment-holding companies'). What follows is intended as a brief summary of the close company legislation.

13.7.1   Close companies

Most resident targets will be close unless they are part of a listed group. Close companies are defined by the Income and Corporation Taxes Act 1988, s 414, and the target will be close if it is United Kingdom resident and satisfies either the 'control test' in s 414(1) or the 'apportionment test' in s 414(2). By virtue of s 414(5), however, the target will not be close if it is controlled by a United Kingdom resident 'open' company (ie a company which is not close).

Under the control test, the target is close if it is under the control of five or fewer participators or of any number of participators who are directors. The words 'control', 'participator' and 'director' are given extended meanings by ss 416 and 417 which prevent most attempts to 'open' a company which would otherwise be close.

A person is taken to have 'control' of a company if he 'exercises or is able to exercise or is entitled to acquire' control, whether direct or indirect, over the company's affairs, and in particular a person is taken to have control if he possesses or is entitled to acquire:

(a)   the majority of the share capital or issued share capital of the company or of the voting power in the company; or

(b)   such part of the issued share capital as would entitle him to the greater part of the income if it were distributed; or

(c)   rights which entitle him to receive the greater part of the assets of the company on a winding up.

Where two or more persons together satisfy any of the conditions of control they are taken to have control of the target, so that if it is possible to point to any five or fewer participators (or any number of participators who are directors) who together have control, the target will be close. For this purpose rights or powers of nominees or 'associates' (relatives, partners, co-trustees and co-beneficiaries) are attributed to participators. 'Participator' is so defined that almost any person who could have control over or an interest in a company's affairs (alone or together with others) falls within the definition. In particular it includes those who possess or are entitled to acquire share capital or voting rights in the target; any loan creditor of the target (widely defined but excluding banks lending in the ordinary course of business—s 417(9)); any person who possesses or is entitled to acquire a right to receive or participate in distributions etc; and any person who is entitled to secure that income or assets will be applied directly or indirectly for his benefit (s 417(1)).

'Director' includes any person occupying the position of director by whatever name called, any person in accordance with whose directions or instructions the directors are accustomed to act and any person who is a manager and owns or controls alone or with associates 20 per cent or more of the ordinary share capital of the target (s 417(5)).

The target satisfies the apportionment test if five or fewer participators or any number of participators who are directors would, in the event of the winding-up of the company, be entitled to receive the greater part of the assets of the company which would then be available for distribution to participators, or would be so entitled if the rights of any loan creditor were disregarded. For the purpose of this test, any participator which is a company is itself assumed to be wound up.

This book deals with companies whose controllers are few enough to enable negotiations for an acquisition to be carried on with them individually. In such a case, if the target is resident, the definitions are cast so widely that it is almost bound to be close unless it is controlled by a company which is not a close company. If a parent company of a group is close, all its subsidiaries will normally be close, but if the parent company of a group is open (otherwise than by reason of foreign residence), the companies which it controls (directly or indirectly) will escape closeness via s 414(5). In practice, if the target is open, it is most likely to be open because the ultimate holding company of the group of which it forms part has shares listed on the London Stock Exchange and falls within s 415, which takes most listed companies out of the net of closeness.

In deciding whether or not a target is close, the trail does not stop at these shores. If the target is controlled directly or indirectly by non-residents, it is necessary to look at their structure to decide whether or not they would be close if they were resident, as under s 414(6) foreign companies which would be close if resident here are treated as close in determining the status of resident companies which they control.

13.7.2 Close investment-holding companies

A close company is a close investment-holding company in any accounting period unless throughout that period it exists wholly or mainly for the purpose of carrying on a trade or trades on a commercial basis or one or more of the other activities listed in the Income and Corporation Taxes Act 1988, s 13A(2).

Broadly, only a company which makes portfolio investments will be a close investment-holding company.

A close investment-holding company is not eligible for the small companies' rate of corporation tax (Income and Corporation Taxes Act 1988, s 13). A shareholder may have his entitlement to be paid the amount of the tax credit attaching to distributions made by the company restricted, if it appears to the Inspector that arrangements exist (such as a dividend waiver) whereby he is enabled to claim such an amount, or a greater amount than would otherwise have been the case, unless the company's ordinary share capital consists of only one class of shares and no person waived his entitlement to any dividend or failed to receive any dividend in the relevant accounting period (Income and Corporation Taxes Act 1988, s 231(3A) and (3B)).

13.7.3 Shortfall apportionment

The provisions which previously provided for the apportionment of undistributed close company income were repealed for accounting periods beginning after 31 March 1989. In the majority of close company acquisitions such liabilities will have been identified and settled. Where, however, these provisions are thought relevant, previous editions of this book contain a fuller discussion.

13.7.4 Loans to participators

Under the Income and Corporation Taxes Act 1988, s 419, a loan by a close company to an individual participator (including 'associates', certain companies and participators in any company controlling the lender) can give rise to a liability on the lender to make a payment equivalent to ACT on the amount of the loan. The payment is not in fact ACT and does not, therefore, fall to be set off in computing the lender's liability to mainstream corporation tax.

The section extends to cover cases where the participator incurs a debt to the close company or a debt due from the participator to a third party is assigned to the close company. Debts which participators incur for the supply by the close company of goods or services in the ordinary course of trade are not included unless the credit given exceeds six months or is longer than that normally given to the company's customers. The section does not apply to loans made in the ordinary course of a business carried on by the close company which includes the lending of money, and there are limited exemptions for full time employees or directors who do not have a 'material interest' in the close company (5 per cent: see Income and Corporation Taxes Act 1988, s 168(11)). Outright misappropriation of the company's funds cannot be regarded as an act of the company and is therefore not a loan or advance for this purpose (*Stephens (Inspector of Taxes) v Pittas (T) Ltd* [1983] STC 576).

By s 419(4) relief is given where the loan is subsequently repaid, although if payment of tax has not been made under s 419 the Revenue will normally seek payment of interest on any such amount for the period from the date on which payment should have been made to the date relief becomes available.

The due date for payment of the tax has been amended by Finance Act 1996, s 173. Under pay and file the due date for payment was 14 days after the end of the company's accounting period. The company itself had the obligation to report the loan and pay the tax. The date for payment is now 9 months after the end of the company's accounting period (ie it is aligned with the due date for corporation tax on the company's profits). Where the loan is now repaid prior to the due date for paying the tax on the loan, no tax will become chargeable. The amendments apply to loans made in accounting periods ending on or after 31 March 1996.

Under s 421 an individual can incur a charge to higher rate tax if the company releases or writes off the loan (but will be treated as having paid tax at the lower rate of 20 per cent ie the notional ACT paid by the company). Section 422 applies the provisions to loans made by companies which are controlled by close companies but which are not themselves close, eg because they are non-resident. Section 419 will then apply as if the loan had been made by the close company itself.

Where the participator is a director or employee of the target the provisions of the Income and Corporation Taxes Act 1988, s 160 (beneficial loan arrangements) may also be relevant.

If the target is close, the purchaser will require a warranty to the effect that no such loans have been made by the target or by companies controlled by the target (*see* the Agreement for Sale (Shares) p 422).

13.7.5   Payments treated as distributions

Under the Income and Corporation Taxes Act 1988, s 418(2), expenditure incurred by a close company in providing for a participator's living or other accommodation, entertainment, domestic or other services or 'other benefits or facilities of whatever nature' is treated as a distribution by the company. Unlike s 419, this does not apply to benefits provided for individuals who are taxed on benefits in kind in any event (directors or employees earning more than £8,500) and does not apply to provision for relatives of any pension or gratuity given on death or retirement of a director or employee.

If the target is close the purchaser will require a warranty to the effect that the target is not liable to be treated as having made a distribution within this section as a result of any event prior to completion, as otherwise ACT on the deemed distribution can become payable by the target (*see* the Agreement for Sale (Shares) p 422).

13.7.6   Inheritance tax apportionment

Under the Inheritance Tax Act 1984, ss 94 and 202, a close company is liable to pay inheritance tax in respect of transfers of value made by it. The section provides for apportionment among the participators according to their respective rights and interests in the company immediately before the transfer and if the company does not pay the tax, the persons to whom amounts are apportioned are liable to pay. If the target is itself a participator in a close company it can become liable to apportioned inheritance tax under s 202(2) even though its liability may (if the target is close) be sub-apportioned among the target's own participators by virtue of s 94(2). Purchasers will therefore normally require a warranty or indemnity covering liability under s 202.

13.8   Value added tax

In most cases the target will be liable to register for VAT and either will have a VAT registration in its own name or benefit from a group registration under the Value Added Tax Act 1994, s 43. If a group registration is not in force the purchaser's main concern will be that the accounts show full provision for any VAT liability and that in respect of transactions in the current accounting period all VAT has been properly accounted for. It is also prudent to take specific warranties against certain VAT matters. For instance, the purchaser will wish to know if the target has made any election to waive exemption under the Value Added Tax Act 1994, Sched 10, para 2, or is authorised to use any special method for attribution of input tax. If the target has received a default surcharge liability notice under the Value Added Tax Act 1994, s 59 or a serious misdeclaration penalty under the Value Added Tax Act 1994, s 63, it may indicate poor accounting systems. Such matters are provided for in the Agreement for Sale (Shares), Sched 4, warranty 2.12 (p 424).

If a group registration is in force additional considerations arise. The effect of a group registration is to enable all companies within the scope of that registration (and not all the companies in a group need be included) to make supplies from one to the other without accounting for VAT (Value Added Tax Act 1994, s 43(1)). The representative member is liable to account to or recover from Customs and Excise all VAT payable by or due to the group, but all the members of the group will be liable jointly and severally for any VAT due from the representative member. If the target and its subsidiaries include all the companies within the group registration then the purchaser will probably wish to continue with that registration and may in due course wish to include the acquired companies within its own group registration. If, on the other hand, the group registration includes companies in the vendor's group which the purchaser is not acquiring, the terms of the group registration will need to be amended. Whether the purchaser takes over the group registration will depend in part upon whether the representative member is included in the target and its subsidiaries or whether it is a company retained by the vendor. Agreement will have to be reached between the parties and arrangements made either to separate out the group members and apply for a new group registration for the target and its subsidiaries or for inclusion of the target and its subsidiaries in the purchaser's group registration. The Tax Deed entered into pursuant to the Agreement for Sale (Shares) (p 484), will cover any liability falling on the target or its subsidiaries for VAT attributable to any other member of the vendor's group registration.

The tax indemnity, in conjunction with the tax warranties, will need to cover the charge to tax under Value Added Tax Act 1994, Sched 9A. This will apply only if the target company is or was a member of the vendor's VAT group. Schedule 9A has particular application to 'entry' and 'exit' schemes. Both schemes involve companies joining and leaving VAT groups at appropriate stages to recover VAT which would otherwise be irrecoverable. An entry scheme might, for example, involve a company wishing to lease goods or services on which it cannot recover the VAT. A special purpose company ('LeaseCo') could be incorporated outside the VAT group, acquire the relevant goods/services and recover in full the associated VAT cost. It would then join the VAT group and ensure that a greater part of the payments are made while the two companies are members of the same VAT group, such that the supply is disregarded for VAT purposes and the irrecoverable VAT cost is avoided.

An exit scheme might, for example, involve a LeaseCo which wishes to lease goods from another member of the group, but where the group may not be able to recover the VAT incurred on the acquisition of the assets (because for example it makes exempt supplies for VAT purposes, such as a bank, which makes exempt supplies of financial services). The company to which the asset is to be leased would make a substantial pre-payment to the LeaseCo while the two are in the same VAT group. LeaseCo would leave the VAT group, buy in the goods and services, recovering the VAT in full and lease the asset to its former VAT group member, for a new nominal sum, which would attract only a small amount of irrecoverable VAT.

Schedule 9A enables Customs and Excise to counteract such schemes so that either the relevant companies involved are deemed to be or not to be (as the case may require) members of the same VAT group. Any direction can affect both future transactions as well as past transactions. VAT due is recovered by assessing the person served with the direction. A direction can be served in respect of past transactions only if a specified part of the scheme (which is a 'relevant event' for the purposes of the legislation) took place after 28 November 1995. Where a VAT scheme has been completed prior to completion of the acquisition the scheme and any liability arising from it should be caught under the normal provisions of the tax indemnity. However, there could be situations where a scheme has been commenced prior to completion but which the purchaser could inadvertently complete after completion of the acquisition. One particular point to note in this regard is that a 'relevant event' includes the leaving or joining of a VAT group. A prudent purchaser should ensure that it has a specific indemnity covering such matters (*see* the Tax Deed at p 486).

13.9 Inheritance tax

Under the Inheritance Tax Act 1984, s 1, inheritance tax is charged on the value transferred by a 'chargeable transfer'. Section 3 of that Act defines a 'transfer of value' as (subject to certain exceptions) any disposition made by 'a person' which brings about a reduction in the value of that person's 'estate'. Section 2(1) defines a chargeable transfer as 'any transfer of value which is made by an *individual* [other than] an exempt transfer'. Consequently, although a company, being a person and having an estate, can make a transfer of value, no company can make a chargeable transfer. It follows that inheritance tax problems relating to the acquisition of companies at arm's length are mercifully few. However, a company can be liable to pay inheritance tax in the following exceptional circumstances:

(1)   Under the Inheritance Tax Act 1984, s 202 (apportionment in the case of close companies: *see* p 324).

(2)   Any company (whether open or close) may, like any other person, be liable to inheritance tax in respect of a chargeable transfer by virtue of the Inheritance Tax Act 1984, ss 199 to 201, in any of the capacities listed in those sections (other than those of transferor and settlor). Generally speaking, it is unlikely that any liability will arise unless the target has been involved in tax avoidance schemes. The liability may arise:

(*a*)   if the target is a transferee of value;

(*b*)   if at any time after the transfer in question there is vested (eg by gift) in the target (beneficially or not) property to the value of which any inheritance tax is attributable or if the target is beneficially entitled to an interest in possession in such property (the liability will not arise if the target has obtained the property as purchaser or derives title from a purchaser, unless the property is subject to an Inland Revenue charge);

(*c*)   if property (or income from it) which has become comprised in a settlement as a result of a chargeable transfer is applied for the benefit of the target;

(*d*)   if a transfer has been made under the settled property provisions, and:

(i)   if the target is trustee of a settlement;

(ii)   if the target is entitled (whether beneficially or not) to an interest in possession in settled property; or

(iii)   if any settled property is applied for the benefit of the target at or after the time of the transfer in question; or

(*e*)   in the case of a transfer on death:

(i)   if the target is a personal representative of a deceased person;

(ii)   if the target is trustee of a settlement in which was comprised property to the value of which inheritance tax is attributable; or

(iii) if property (or income from it) which was comprised in a settlement at the time of the transfer in question, is applied for the
benefit of the target.

The terms 'trustee' and 'personal representative' include anyone who has
acted in relation to the property so as to become liable as executor or trustee.

It may be noted that, where a close company is entitled to an interest in possession in settled property, the participators in the company are treated by the
Inheritance Tax Act 1984, s 101 as the persons beneficially entitled to that interest according to their respective rights and interests in the company. This is
illustrated by *Powell-Cotton v IRC* [1992] STC 625.

In addition to an indemnity against liability under ss 199 to 201 the purchaser should also seek protection against diminution in the value of the target's assets through the imposition of the Inland Revenue charge for unpaid tax under
the Inheritance Tax Act 1984, s 237.

There is also the question of any adjustment to the burden of inheritance tax.
There is, of course, nothing to prevent the parties to any transaction agreeing
how the burden of tax is to be borne. Moreover, ss 211 and 212 may give other
persons rights against the target in this respect. In particular:

(*a*) under s 211(3) where personal representatives have paid inheritance tax
arising on a death and an Inland Revenue charge is imposed on any property, the personal representatives may in certain circumstances require repayment to them of the tax by the person in whom the property is vested;
and

(*b*) by virtue of s 212(1) and subject to certain exceptions, where a person is
liable for inheritance tax attributable to the value of any property, he has
the power, whether or not the property is vested in him, to raise the
amount of the tax (either for payment or recoupment) by a sale or mortgage of, or terminable charge on, the property.

A purchaser may therefore wish to seek protection against any diminution
of the assets of the target through any claims against the target in respect of adjustment of the burden of inheritance tax and in particular against any claims
arising under ss 211 and 212.

13.10 *Ramsay* and *Furniss v Dawson*

The 'emerging principle' or 'new approach' in *Ramsay (WT) Ltd v IRC* (1981)
54 TC 101 and *Furniss (Inspector of Taxes) v Dawson* (1984) 55 TC 324 has
created uncertainty in a number of areas which affect the purchase of private
companies. It is a principle of statutory construction which requires an intervening transaction with no commercial purpose inserted for tax avoidance reasons into a composite transaction to be disregarded so that the same tax
consequences are to be taken to follow from the composite transaction as
would follow in the absence of the intervening transaction. It cannot create a

liability simply because of the existence of a tax avoidance motive where that liability would not otherwise exist (*Countess Fitzwilliam v IRC* [1992] STC 185). It is not a general anti-avoidance measure. The principle may affect the transaction itself and the taxation of the target both before and after the acquisition.

The limits of the principle have to some degree been resolved through the further cases which have now been decided by the House of Lords (notably *Craven v White, IRC v Bowater Property Developments Ltd, Baylis v Gregory* [1988] 3 WLR 423 and *Ensign Tankers (Leasing) Ltd v Stokes (Inspector of Taxes)* [1992] STC 226). Its limitations were further defined in *IRC v McGuckian* [1994] STC 888, a Northern Ireland case where the court refused to apply *Furniss v Dawson* principles in relation to an assignment of rights to receive dividends the main object of which was to mitigate the taxpayer's liability to income tax. One of the main reasons for refusing to apply such principles was that although the assignment was obviously an artificial device, it was the whole substance of the transaction which need to be looked at and if the court were to strike it down it would be perilously close to holding that every transaction entered into solely to reduce or avoid liability to taxation should be treated as having no real effect (see also *Pigott (Inspector of Taxes) v Staines Investment Co Ltd* [1995] STC 114).

The extent to which the principle applies to stamp duty and to value added tax remains uncertain (*Ingram* v *IRC* [1985] STC 848 and *Raceshine Ltd v Commissioners & Customs & Excise* MAN/91/1135, respectively). Some practical guidance to the circumstances in which the Revenue had indicated the principle would be sought to be applied prior to these decisions can be found in the correspondence with the Revenue in 1985 published by the Institute of Chartered Accountants in England and Wales (TR588).

Furniss v Dawson was, of course, itself a case relating to the acquisition of a private company. In cases where the parties are seeking to avoid tax the principle may apply to disregard steps inserted into the transaction for no commercial purpose other than the avoidance of tax. Purchasers will be concerned to know whether the target has been involved in any transactions to which the principle might apply and a warranty should be sought (see the Agreement for Sale (Shares), Sched 4, warranty 2.5(D) (p 423). Vendors may wish to give this warranty 'to the best of their knowledge and belief' rather than accepting absolute liability.

Chapter 14

Taxation: Warranties and Indemnities

Warranties and indemnities on taxation matters will predominantly arise in the context of a share acquisition since an acquisition of business assets will not involve the purchaser becoming responsible for the vendor's tax liabilities. Accordingly, the primary focus of this chapter is the private company acquisition and a discussion of taxation warranties and indemnities. The taxation treatment of all warranties and indemnities (eg other than tax) is also considered. Acquisitions of business assets are briefly discussed at p 336.

14.1 Share acquisitions

No consistent and logical treatment of tax in agreements for the sale of private companies has yet evolved. Given the complex and arbitrary nature of the legislation concerned, it is doubtful if it ever will.

Even though an accountants' investigation may have been commissioned, the purchaser is likely to require assurances in one form or another:
(a) that the target has complied with all appropriate tax legislation;
(b) that the latest accounts contain proper provision for taxation;
(c) that there are no surprises (perhaps in the form of disguised base values);
(d) that the target has not been involved in any of the transactions which anti-avoidance legislation or case law has rendered dangerous;
(e) that the target has all the reliefs and allowances which should be available to it; and
(f) that the target is not going to be visited with liability to pay tax assessed on others (eg liability under the Taxation of Chargeable Gains Act 1992, ss 190 and 191 to pay tax in respect of chargeable gains incurred by other group members).

The purchaser's advisers will therefore wish to obtain warranties and indemnities from the vendors to cover all these eventualities. Faced with the bewildering array of potential liabilities it is possible to overreact. In a famous phrase Lord Davey remarked that 'every grocer's shop takes power to bridge the mighty Zambezi'. Those acquiring grocer's shops today are more inclined to suspect the proprietor of having issued quoted Eurobonds or having dual resident status. It is a foolhardy purchaser, however, who does not seek to obtain as much information and protection as he reasonably can in respect of the taxation of the target. What form should this protection take? In relation to some taxation matters, warranties are clearly appropriate and in relation to others an indemnity is more suitable, but in many cases the selection of warranty or indemnity (or both) to cover a potential liability is largely a matter of taste.

Warranties should be taken with regard to the taxation attributes of the target's assets as indemnities may not be appropriate. The accounts will show the assets at a valuation. Is this valuation the same as the base value for the purpose of corporation tax on chargeable gains? There may be many reasons why it is not so and a simple example arises in connection with the replacement of business assets. Suppose the target has at some time in the past disposed of a branch office for £200,000 realising a capital gain of £100,000. It has not become chargeable to tax on this gain, because the whole of the consideration has been used to purchase a new office for £200,000. Under the provisions of the Taxation of Chargeable Gains Act 1992, s 152 the gain is 'rolled over' and the acquisition cost of the new offices is deemed to be not £200,000 but £100,000 so that upon the sale of the new offices for £300,000 a chargeable gain of £200,000 (not £100,000) will arise. This fact is not disclosed in negotiations and when the target comes to dispose of the office in due course the purchaser is aggrieved. He looks to his indemnities but finds they do not relate to gains made by the target after completion. Why indeed should the vendors indemnify the target against tax on gains made after completion when they will not have the benefit of these gains? The purchaser is, however, objecting to the fact that he was not aware of the amount of the contingent liability to tax which was inherent in the asset in question. A warranty that the base cost was the same as the value attributed to the office in the accounts would have given him a remedy against the vendors.

Warranties are also appropriate where the purchaser wishes to be assured that the target has or has not taken any particular action. A warranty that all taxation returns have been made accurately and on time and that all taxation has been properly and punctually paid is of obvious value. The purchaser will not wish to be involved with back duty claims with the Inland Revenue or with PAYE or VAT audits, even in relation to quite small sums. The loss of management time can be substantial, particularly if key employees of the target leave as a result of the acquisition so that the facts have to be mastered by incoming staff. It may be said that the purchaser is adequately protected if the target is indemnified by the vendors against the tax due and against penalties, costs and interest relating to taxation, but in practice this is not the case. A more satisfactory result may well be achieved by asking for a warranty; if the vendors have knowledge of a dispute they are unlikely to deceive the purchaser by giving a false warranty (indeed if they do, they should consider their liability under the Financial Services Act 1986, s 47) and it is usually better for the purchaser to force a disclosure so that he knows the worst before the acquisition and can make appropriate arrangements (including perhaps a specific indemnity) to enable him to deal with the problem.

An indemnity is appropriate where the target is liable to pay tax arising from the income or gains of others. As explained above, under the Taxation of Chargeable Gains Act 1992, s 190, the target may be made liable for chargeable gains realised by other members of the same group. A warranty that no such chargeable gains had occurred would not normally be acceptable by itself. The purchaser is not, in fact, concerned to see that the primary liability has not arisen; he is concerned to ensure that the target is properly indemnified against the liability. Indemnities are also useful when obtaining protection against liability under anti-avoidance sections. It is often simpler to take an indemnity rather than to attempt to draft a warranty. Of course, if it is likely that the target has entered into tax avoidance transactions then warranties may be appropriate as well, as they may bring out disclosures.

In many cases, however, it will be a matter of taste whether a warranty or an indemnity is taken and the choice of warranties (in addition to the general indemnity) included in the Agreement for Sale (Shares) at p 419 is to that extent arbitrary. Neither does the selection pretend to be exhaustive or mandatory in all cases. The choice of what protection to demand must be left to the individual practitioner in the circumstances of the particular transaction with which he or she is concerned. For example, no specialised type of company (eg an insurance company) is considered.

14.1.1 Tax warranties

Examples of tax warranties are given in the Agreement for Sale (Shares), Sched 4. One basic warranty is that the provisions in the latest audited accounts are adequate. The warranties relate to: general taxation matters (2.1(A) to (G)); distributions and payments (2.2(A) to (F)); losses (2.3(A) to (C)); close companies (2.4); anti-avoidance (2.5(A) to (D)); capital assets (2.6(A) to (L)); claims, elections and clearances (2.7(A) to (C)); miscellaneous (2.8(A) to (E)); loan relationships (2.9(A) to (G); taxation of employees and agents (2.10(A) to (F)); stamp duties (2.11(A) to (B)); VAT (2.12 (A) to (B)) and inheritance tax and gifts (2.13). It is unlikely that all the warranties will be appropriate in any particular transaction. Certain of the warranties will apply only where the vendors are individuals (2.8(E)) and others where the vendor is a company ((2.2(B)) and (C)).

One problem in formulating suggestions is the question of how specific to make the warranties. Is it, for instance, satisfactory to take a simple warranty that the target has properly operated the PAYE system? Or is it desirable to go further and ask for a warranty that tax has been properly deducted from, for example, all payments as compensation for loss of office (Income and Corporation Taxes Act 1988, s 148) and in respect of certain benefits in kind (eg Income and Corporation Taxes Act 1988, s 143 (cash vouchers))? Apart from the comfort of seeing the likely problem areas written down in the agreement, the advantage of being specific is that it focuses the minds of the vendors on the point in question and may lead to a disclosure. Most practitioners acting for purchasers will yield to the temptation to use general words and then go to the specific 'without prejudice to the generality of the foregoing'.

The drafting problem of general and specific wording also arises because one warranty tends to overlap with another. For instance, it is normal to take a warranty that the latest audited accounts contain full provision for all tax liabilities. This general warranty will overlap with many other specific warranties (eg that all claims for group relief have been properly made) but the advantage of the specific warranty remains. An element of repetition is inevitable.

14.1.2 Tax indemnity

The established method of giving tax indemnities has been for the vendor to indemnify the target itself by a deed given at completion containing perhaps both a general indemnity and specific indemnities, although specific indemnities are now less commonly required. On occasion the indemnities will be found in the sale contract, which will indemnify the purchaser against any depletion or diminution in the assets of the target. However, for the reasons discussed below, whether it appears in the sale agreement or a separate deed, it has become usual for the benefit of a deed of indemnity or any tax covenant in the sale agreement to include the purchaser, so that payments made by the vendor to the purchaser in respect of tax liabilities of the target may fall to be treated for tax purposes as adjustments to the purchase price. The Tax Deed (p 488) to be entered into pursuant to the Agreement for Sale (Shares) adopts this approach. In some instances, the process can be taken to its logical conclusion by excluding the target altogether from the benefit of the indemnity, but there are usually other reasons (eg privity of contract) why the company should remain a party to the deed.

The Tax Deed, cl 2.1 (at p 487) contains a general indemnity designed to cover any liability incurred before completion which is not reflected in the latest audited accounts of the target, excluding liabilities incurred in the ordinary course of business since the date of those accounts. It also contains specific indemnities against certain liabilities which may arise after completion (*see eg* cl 2.1(D) at p 487). The vendor will seek to add further exclusions as appropriate to the circumstances of the particular transaction.

14.1.3 Tax treatment of payments under warranties and indemnities

The following discussion applies to payments made by the vendor for any breach of warranty or any indemnity payment, not merely payments under taxation warranties and indemnities.

If the vendor is called upon to make any payment to the purchaser or the target under the warranties or indemnities he will wish to be satisfied that any payment goes to reduce the consideration which he is treated as having received for the purposes of computing any capital gain. In respect of payments under the warranties statutory provision is made in the Taxation of Chargeable Gains Act 1992, s 49(1)(*c*) which provides that:

> In the first instance no allowance shall be made…for any contingent liability in respect of a warranty or representation made on a disposal by way of sale or lease of any property other than land.

The section goes on to provide that if any contingency subsequently becomes enforceable the capital gains tax computation will be adjusted accordingly. Where the disposal is for cash this will result in a repayment of tax or a discharge of any outstanding liability. The section applies equally where the consideration is one to which the Taxation of Chargeable Gains Act 1992, s 138 applies where no actual tax will have become payable as a result of the sale. In these circumstances any payment under the warranties will serve to increase the base cost of the consideration shares on any ultimate disposal (see Extra Statutory Concession D52). In either event the purchaser's position, ie his overall acquisition cost of the target, will be adjusted correspondingly.

In the case of indemnities the position is less clear. Indemnities may be given to the target although provision may be made for the sums so indemnified to be paid to the purchaser (particularly in the case of a sale of less than a 100 per cent interest in the target). In the past the Revenue seem to have allowed any payments under the indemnities made to the target as a deduction against the vendor's consideration for the purposes of calculating the capital gain. The position is far from clear and it may nevertheless be open to the purchaser to argue that the fact that the company has received indemnities against specific matters cannot affect the position or reduce the amount which is treated as having been paid for the acquisition of the shares in the target.

Whatever the position of the vendor, it is, however, generally accepted that a right of indemnity enforceable by the target against the vendor is an asset for capital gains tax purposes falling within the Taxation of Chargeable Gains Act 1992, s 22 so that any amount received by the target will be subject to tax. This results from the decision in *Zim Properties Ltd v Procter* (1984) 58 TC 371 (and see also Inland Revenue Extra Statutory Concession D33) that a right to bring an action to seek to enforce a claim that was neither frivolous nor vexatious, where the right could be turned to account by negotiating a compromise yielding a capital sum, constituted an asset for the purposes of capital gains tax. Where the right of action is acquired on or after 10 March 1981 (when what is now the Taxation of Chargeable Gains Act 1992, s 17 came into effect), and its holder (as will generally be the case) gave no consideration to acquire it, it will be treated as acquired without cost. The result of this is that the target's net of tax receipt from an indemnity payment would be reduced and in order to provide a full indemnity the payment would need to be increased. A vendor will, not unnaturally, be unwilling to gross up for tax any payment made to the target under an indemnity and the prudent vendor should, indeed, refuse to give any indemnity which has that effect. Since any payment made to the purchaser in respect of a tax liability of the target would seem not to be subject to tax in the purchaser's hands (although it would correspondingly reduce the purchaser's acquisition cost for the target's shares) the Tax Deed, cl 2.2 (at p 488) provides for the vendor instead to make payments to the purchaser by way of reduction in the consideration in respect of relevant taxation claims. If such payments are subject to tax in the purchaser's hands (which it is not thought to be the case) then it is submitted that it is appropriate for these to be grossed up and cl 6 on p 492 has this effect.

Cases arise in which provision must be made for a non-tax liability which is expected to fall on the target but which is unquantified at the time of the sale. As a condition of the sale the purchaser may insist that the target receives an indemnity against this payment, but if this liability is itself deductible in calculating the target's liability to tax, then it may be more satisfactory for the vendor to agree to make payment, as in respect of tax liabilities, direct to the purchaser. Not only will this have the effect of ensuring that this amount is deducted for the purposes of calculating the vendor's capital gains tax bill, but, because the target retains the benefit of the tax deduction, the payment from vendor to purchaser can be calculated by reference to the net, after tax, diminution in the target's assets.

14.2   Asset acquisitions

Since tax liabilities are not usually transferred to the purchaser on an acquisition of business assets, the warranties required are usually much more limited than on a share sale and would normally be restricted to matters such as PAYE and VAT (*see further* Chapter 12 at p 292). A payment by the vendor to the purchaser under a warranty claim will usually represent an adjustment to the consideration. The parties should address in the business sale agreement which asset any such adjustment should apply to; usually it would represent an adjustment (decrease) to the amount paid for goodwill.

Chapter 15

Europe

Notwithstanding the substantial number of cross-border acquisitions that have been carried out in recent years, European acquisitions continue to be the subject of a number of legal difficulties and there are significant differences in the laws and regulations applicable to acquisitions in different European countries. These differences are being reduced to a certain extent, in the case of EC Member States at least, as a result of the EC harmonisation programme. However, the harmonisation of company law and the regulations governing take-overs is not the panacea it might appear to be. The principal legislative instruments employed by the EC in this area are Directives. These are binding on Member States as to the result to be achieved within a stated period, but it is left to national governments to decide on the method by which they are transformed into national law. As a result, there are often significant differences between the measures enacted to implement Directives in individual Member States. In addition, the measures proposed by the European Commission to level the playing field for take-overs across the European Union would apply only to public companies or, in the case of the proposed 13th Directive on take-overs and other general bids, only to listed companies, and not to the acquisition of private companies or unincorporated businesses. Furthermore, the field of acquisitions, especially those involving public take-overs, is one in which national business culture and practices play a role which is at least as important as the strict legal requirements. The differences between the regimes governing acquisitions in the various countries of Europe, in many cases, have more to do with differing attitudes towards ownership and control of business entities, than differences in technical legal requirements.

This chapter gives an outline of some of the most significant legal considerations which are likely to be relevant in the case of an acquisition by a United Kingdom company of a target company or business incorporated in another European jurisdiction. It is not a substitute for local advice in relation to any particular transaction or its implementation, but it may be helpful in drawing attention to potential problem areas in order that they can be considered and, if

337

necessary, taken into account in the planning of the acquisition at an early stage. Where the target is a company, the considerations mentioned in this chapter will in general be applicable to the acquisition of a target which is legally the equivalent in the jurisdiction concerned of an unquoted public company, as well as a target which is the local equivalent of a private company in the United Kingdom. Acquisitions of unincorporated business entities can take many varied forms, and this chapter offers an introduction to some of the issues which affect the transfer of different categories of asset in different jurisdictions.

In addition to the direct acquisition of a target company or business incorporated or located in another European jurisdiction, the acquisition by a United Kingdom company of a United Kingdom target with European subsidiaries or shareholders may require compliance with the laws and regulations of the jurisdiction in which those subsidiaries or shareholders are located. The conduct of acquisitions of unquoted companies (whether the equivalent of a private company in the United Kingdom or a plc) is not generally the subject of specific regulation in Europe, in contrast to the United Kingdom where the rules of the City Code apply to acquisitions of all public companies resident in the United Kingdom, the Channel Islands or the Isle of Man (whether listed or not) and to some private companies. There are, however, some exceptions. For example, in Belgium, the Banking Commission regulates all acquisitions of companies whose shares are regarded as being in public hands, in Germany, the voluntary Ubernahme-Kodex applies to offers for AGs which have agreed to abide by the Kodex, and in Portugal, public offers for all companies whose shares have at any time been held by the general public are subject to special rules.

15.1   General considerations

Share acquisitions are, in general, much more common than acquisitions of business assets in Europe. Share acquisitions tend to be simpler transactions than transactions involving the transfer of individual assets and liabilities and generally involve lower transfer taxes. A share acquisition is less likely to involve the need to obtain consents from third parties (although changes of control may require consents, for example, under financing, licence or joint venture agreements), whereas third parties who have contracts with the target are likely to need to consent to the transfer of assets and liabilities by the target in order for the transfer to be effective. However, there may in some cases be tax advantages in structuring the transaction as an acquisition of business assets; for example, the purchaser's base cost of assets on a subsequent disposal will be higher. On the other hand, on a sale of assets, there may be differences of view on the allocation of the purchase price. For example, allocating a large part of the purchase price to goodwill could result in a large chargeable gain for the vendor. It is possible in some countries to avoid this result by allocating some of the purchase price as consideration for a non-competition covenant from the vendor, which can subsequently be written down for tax purposes. Asset acquisitions in some jurisdictions will, however, carry very high transfer taxes. In France, for example, a sale of business assets results in a transfer tax of up to 11.4 per cent payable by the purchaser (in addition to any taxes payable by the vendor on profits of sale) depending on the value of the assets transferred, whereas the equivalent tax on a transfer of shares ranges up to 4.8 per cent.

In the case of a share acquisition, whereas the purchaser will acquire the target with all its liabilities in addition to its assets, if the purchaser buys assets, it may expect the position to be equivalent to that applicable in the United Kingdom and that it will be able to choose which assets it acquires and avoid assuming the target's liabilities, which may be difficult to quantify. This rule is not universal, however. In the case of assets acquisitions in Germany, if the purchaser acquires all or substantially all the business assets of the vendor company, it will also become jointly and severally liable for all the vendor company's debts and obligations, by operation of law. In France, a sale of a business as a going concern ('Fonds de Commerce') will not include the transfer of the liabilities of the business, unless otherwise agreed by the parties. However, in this type of transaction, French law provides specific protection for the creditors of the business. The creditors may require, upon publication of notice of the sale, that their debts are paid out of the purchase price. In view of this requirement, the price paid for a Fonds de Commerce is generally placed in an escrow account until the expiry of the period during which the creditors may require repayment. Failure to publicise the sale in the required manner will result in the creditors of the business retaining the right to require the purchaser to discharge their debts.

A further method by which an acquisition can be effected is by way of statutory or legal merger. To effect a legal merger, the purchaser must use a company incorporated in the jurisdiction of incorporation of the target. The detailed formalities of legal mergers vary from country to country but, in general, legal mergers are normally achieved either by the absorption of the target, or the contribution of its assets and liabilities, into the acquisition vehicle, with shareholders in the target receiving shares in the acquisition vehicle, or the merger of the target with the acquisition vehicle into a new company set up for the purpose, with the shareholders in each of the merged companies receiving shares in the new company. In each case, the assets of the companies involved must be valued by an accountant, who may be required to be independent, and the terms of the merger must be set out in a formal merger agreement which must be put to shareholders and approved by resolution requiring (depending on the jurisdiction and the type of company concerned) a majority of two-thirds or 75 per cent in favour. However, acquisition by legal merger is relatively rare. In some countries, such as France and the Netherlands, this is due to the tax treatment of the operation and, in others, it is due to the degree of the formalities involved and to the time required to complete the merger. For example, in Italy, Norway, Portugal and Spain, a waiting period, ranging from one to three months, must normally elapse after the passing of the necessary shareholders' resolutions, before completion. In some countries, creditors have rights to require that their debts are either guaranteed or secured prior to the merger becoming effective.

In the case of a share acquisition, the contract will be made between the purchaser and the shareholders of the target. Most companies in Europe are privately held and, in many cases, will be held by a limited number of members of the same family. Alternatively, the target may be a subsidiary of another company. In most cases, therefore, the number of shareholders will be small and it will be possible for the purchaser to acquire the target by means of a private contract between itself and each of the selling shareholders. This contract will normally contain warranties, indemnities and undertakings concerning the target, its assets and liabilities and its business in favour of the purchaser, and is likely to afford the purchaser the greatest level of protection. Traditionally, acquisition agreements in European jurisdictions have been a great deal shorter and simpler than would be normal in the United Kingdom. While this is changing and longer Anglo-Saxon forms are now being used more widely, presenting the vendors with a standard United Kingdom-style draft acquisition agreement could in some cases be counter-productive, especially in the case of an acquisition of a small family-held target.

If the number of selling shareholders is large, it may be logistically impracticable to arrange for all the selling shareholders to become parties to a single agreement, particularly if this is to contain extensive warranties and other protections in favour of the purchaser. It may therefore be necessary to send out a circular to the target's shareholders. In this case, it will be necessary to investigate the relevant local regulations applicable to the distribution of circulars. The rules governing the information to be made available to prospective investors, and imposing liability if that information is incomplete or misleading, will be relevant. Additional rules may be applicable if the consideration payable by the purchaser includes shares or other securities. As mentioned in Chapter 3, under English law, a circular offer to shareholders of a target is likely to constitute an investment advertisement within the meaning of the Financial Services Act 1986, s 57 and, if so, subject to certain exceptions, may not be issued unless it is issued by an authorised person, or unless its contents have been approved by an authorised person (*see further* p 27).

The governing law of the acquisition agreement is a matter of major importance which should be decided at an early stage. It may be thought that the law of the jurisdiction of incorporation of the target or where its business is carried on and its assets are located will be the most suitable. However, the legal rules affecting the validity and enforceability of the provisions of the acquisition agreement, the remedies available for breaches of warranty and the limitation periods within which claims may be brought vary in each jurisdiction. It is not safe to proceed on the basis that these rules will be more or less the same as those applicable under English law. For example, in Germany, in the absence of express agreement to the contrary, a limitation period for warranty claims of six months will be applicable. It may be the case that, in the absence of specific provision, damages for breach of warranty will not be payable after completion of the acquisition. The implications of the choice of law will need to be carefully reviewed. Even if English law is chosen to govern the acquisition agreement, where the target is incorporated in another European jurisdiction, local law will remain relevant to the target's constitution, its business dealings and its tax position and will still need to be investigated and, if possible, warranted by the vendors.

Where the target is not a single company held by a single holding company, or a single business, but several companies or businesses located in a number of countries, it may be helpful in avoiding conflicts of laws to split the documentation, so that reorganisations and transfers in each country are dealt with in an agreement between a local buyer and a local seller, governed by the local law of that country, with the series of local agreements being overlayed with a master agreement between vendor and purchaser. If this approach is adopted, care needs to be taken to include appropriate conditions in each individual country agreement to ensure that the parties are not obliged to complete the transaction in circumstances where completion of the transfer of shares or assets in some countries is delayed. Timing considerations and the legal steps necessary to convey title to certain kinds of assets in the various jurisdictions should be addressed at an early stage, since they may cause practical difficulties or require the involvement of third parties (such as a notary).

15.2 Heads of agreement

Once agreement in principle has been reached between the vendors and the purchaser on the basic terms and structure of the acquisition, the parties may wish to record these terms in writing, as an intermediate step, before the conclusion of the formal acquisition agreement. It may be felt that heads of agreement will serve to reinforce the commitment of the parties to the transaction and to identify and avoid any possible misunderstandings between the parties as to the major terms. In the United Kingdom, heads of agreement (which may also be called a letter of intent or memorandum of understanding) are normally non-binding. One reason is that settling heads of agreement which create legal rights and obligations is time consuming and the time is generally better spent in negotiating the definitive acquisition agreement. Furthermore, one party may find particular terms in heads of agreement invoked against it by the other party insisting at a later stage in the negotiations that those terms, which may have been only briefly described in the heads, be included in the definitive agreement in a form which accords with the other party's interpretation.

When contemplating heads of agreement in connection with the acquisition of a target in Europe, however, United Kingdom purchasers should proceed with caution. The laws of a number of countries in Europe (for example, Belgium, France, Germany and Luxembourg) impose on parties to negotiations the obligation to negotiate in good faith and not to break off negotiations except for good reason. This is directly contrary to the position under English law, as set forth by Lord Ackner in the case of *Walford v Miles* [1992] 2 WLR 174, when he said:

> The concept of a duty to carry on negotiations in good faith is inherently repugnant to the adversarial position of the parties when involved in negotiations. Each party to the negotiations is entitled to pursue his (or her) own interest, so long as he avoids making misrepresentations...A duty to negotiate in good faith is as unworkable in practice as it is inherently inconsistent with the position of a negotiating party.

In a number of European jurisdictions, a party that breaks off negotiations, after having reached agreement in principle with another party, may find itself liable to pay damages to that other party. In some jurisdictions, actions for specific performance may be possible. This can be the case even if heads of agreement are expressed to be 'subject to contract', which should be sufficient to avoid the creation of legal relations under English law, or are qualified in some other similar manner. While, in these jurisdictions, the obligation to negotiate in good faith is not dependent on the conclusion of heads of agreement, the signature of heads of agreement will be evidence that agreement in principle has in fact been reached.

While such agreements are not enforceable under English law, in some European jurisdictions, it is possible to supplement the duty to negotiate in good faith by concluding a 'lock-in' agreement, incorporating a positive duty on the parties to negotiate. It is also possible to enter into a legally binding 'lock-out' agreement with the vendor giving the purchaser a period of exclusivity within which to agree the acquisition (as, indeed, is the case under English law). In the event of breach by the vendor of such an agreement, specific performance or injunctive relief may be available. However, outside the United Kingdom the purchaser's remedies may be confined to damages (which are often difficult to quantify), or to the reimbursement of its costs.

15.3   Investigation of the target

The scope of the investigation to be carried out by the purchaser and its advisers will need to be agreed with the vendors. Although the First Company Law Directive, which has generally been implemented by all EC Member States, sets basic standards for information to be publicly filed by companies with commercial registries, most of the information which a purchaser will wish to review before proceeding formally with the acquisition will not be available from public sources. Such information as is publicly filed may well be out of date. One particular point to clarify at the outset is the nature and accuracy of information filed on public registers. In a number of jurisdictions (including Germany and the Netherlands), the public register of information on companies is not required to record all charges over the company's assets. Charges over land may be filed at land registries but not, for example, floating charges over book debts etc. Of course, protection can be taken by warranty, but whether warranties will provide a satisfactory remedy to a purchaser will depend on the financial standing of the person giving them. Some vendors, particularly the owners of small and medium-sized family controlled companies, may be unwilling to disclose details of the target's business until they are certain that the purchaser will buy the company. This is especially so if the purchaser could be regarded as a competitor.

A balance has to be struck between the competing interests of information and confidentiality. For example, it is normal practice for a purchaser or its accountants and lawyers to be allowed access to information on the target's business, provided that the purchaser and its advisers sign an agreement to keep the information thus disclosed strictly confidential. As with any acquisition in the United Kingdom, the smaller the amount of information made available to the purchaser, the greater the protection the purchaser should seek from the vendors by means of warranties. The purchaser may also seek to defer payment of part of the consideration in these circumstances or place part of the consideration in escrow in order to satisfy post-completion price adjustments or warranty claims. As regards accounts of the target which the purchaser may obtain, the Fourth Company Law Directive includes rules as to the format and content of company accounts (including a requirement that such accounts must be audited and show a 'true and fair view of the company's assets, liabilities, profits, losses and financial position'). However, the Directive does not deal with accounting standards and practices. These vary substantially between the countries of Europe and, in a number of countries, the content of a company's published accounts is influenced by the objective of producing information for tax authorities and not with a view to showing the company's real profitability. Such information will therefore need to be interpreted with particular care.

15.4 Foreign investment control and industry controls

An acquisition in Europe may be restricted by rules on foreign ownership which apply generally, or which are applicable to the particular industry in which the target operates. In addition, in some countries, there are special rules applicable to the ownership of particular types of asset eg land. For example, in Switzerland, a law known as the 'lex Friedrich' regulates the acquisition of certain companies holding Swiss land and also restricts the direct foreign acquisition of Swiss land. Furthermore, certain types of industry are often subject to close regulation which affects acquisitions by any purchaser, whether domestic or foreign. Examples include banking, financial services and insurance, defence, the media and utilities (water, gas, electricity etc). The precise forms of these regulations vary widely, and may require the purchaser to obtain prior consent before the acquisition will be permitted, or may allow the acquisition to be made without specific consent, but leave the target open to having its authorisation or licence to operate in the relevant sector revoked as a result of the change of control. It will also be important to review the target's corporate constitution to establish whether it contains restrictions on the acquisition of shares by foreigners (such restrictions have only recently been abolished in Finland and Sweden) or the percentage of voting rights that may be exercised by foreigners.

The manner in which the controls on acquisitions by foreigners and industry controls are implemented in practice is generally much more important than their mere existence and may be dependent on the political climate in the country concerned at the time. In the United Kingdom, for example, the government could have effectively blocked the take-over of Jaguar plc by Ford in 1989 through the exercise of the powers attached to the 'golden share' issued to the Secretary of State at the time of Jaguar's privatisation. However, in keeping with the government's free market approach, these powers were not invoked. Similarly with the sale by British Aerospace of the Rover Group, the country's last British-owned volume car manufacturer, to BMW in 1994, but again the government made no move to block that sale.

In many countries, approval or exemption is readily available in relation to most industries. In other cases (eg banking and the media), in several countries, it is unlikely that a cross-border acquisition of a major company would be permitted in normal circumstances, even where legislation does not specifically restrict acquisitions by foreigners. Indeed, in the case of some industries (eg defence), governmental and municipal contracts, or the licences which are required to carry on specific operations or to sell certain products, are so important that the authorities have considerable influence even in cases where they lack specific legal powers to regulate a particular transaction. The EC has recognised that some activities are so sensitive that Member States should be permitted to exercise controls, even as regards acquisitions by EC resident investors, on the grounds of ensuring public security, plurality of the media, prudential rules for financial institutions and any other 'legitimate interest' accepted by the European Commission.

15.5 Merger control

The largest acquisitions are subject to control at European level under the EC Merger Regulation, which operates to exclude the jurisdiction of local merger control authorities. However, the Commission has discretion, in certain circumstances, to pass jurisdiction back to the relevant national merger control authorities, which exercise control in relation to transactions the parties to which do not satisfy the turnover thresholds set out in the Merger Regulations. For a fuller discussion of relevant competition law considerations, *see* Chapter 4. In the context of an acquisition by a United Kingdom purchaser of a target in another European jurisdiction, the effect of merger control legislation on the proposed acquisition should be considered in each country in which the target carries on business, and not only in the jurisdiction of incorporation of the target. In the case of a transaction not falling under the European Commission's jurisdiction under the Merger Regulation, it may be necessary to deal with competition authorities in several countries, each with their own requirements, timetables and language. On a practical level, it is highly likely that, if material competition issues do exist in more than one jurisdiction, consideration will need to be given to the practicality and desirability of proceeding with the acquisitions separately, or one without the other.

15.6   Employee considerations

Although, in the case of a share acquisition, there will be no change in the identity of the employer of the employees of the target, and therefore no effect on the contracts of employment of the target's employees, the position is more complicated in the case of an assets acquisition. In the United Kingdom, the Transfer of Undertakings (Protection of Employment) Regulations 1981 will apply, in effect, to secure the automatic transfer of the relevant employees. Since these Regulations are derived from the Acquired Rights Directive (77/187/EEC), similar legislation should be in force in each EC Member State. However, the precise way in which the local legislation operates will differ.

Even in the case of an acquisition of shares, employment legislation in the countries in which the target carries on business will be relevant to the ongoing business of the target. Employment legislation should be investigated, particularly if the purchaser intends to reorganise the business of the target and implement redundancies following completion of the acquisition, since the protective effect of employment legislation in some jurisdictions can be onerous. Minimum wage legislation is in force in most EC Member States, and maximum working hours legislation came into force in all those countries with effect from 23 November 1996, the implementation date of the Working Time Directive (93/104/EEC). Collective agreements with trade unions may be relevant, and may impose duties to inform and consult with recognised trade unions or works councils in relation to proposed reductions in manning levels.

In a number of countries, employees of companies beyond a certain size have the right to board representation or to be consulted on the appointment of board members. The following are some examples. In the Netherlands, official authorisation is required in most cases to terminate a contract of employment. Written application for authorisation must be made to the regional director of the employment bureau covering the location where the employee normally works. This authorisation must be requested prior to any notice of termination being given. Where an employer in Germany is considering individual redundancies, he must consider whether redundancy could be avoided by short time working, reducing overtime, internal transfers or other measures, most of which require consultation with the company's works council. Employers must ensure that employees dismissed are those least affected 'socially', which means taking into account length of service, age, family status, number and income of dependants, health, occupational disability, membership of a protected group and prospects in the labour market. In Italy, many executives are protected from unfair dismissal by binding industry agreements. Dismissal of an executive without 'just cause' or 'justified motive' or without following the correct procedures, may leave an employer liable to penalties, which are often severe. These agreements allow an executive to appeal against termination to a college of arbitration. Failure to observe the procedures renders the termination null and void. In practice, except in cases of serious misconduct, an executive is highly likely to appeal against termination.

Immigration rules and work permit requirements should also be considered if the purchaser plans to transfer key personnel to run the target's business after completion of the acquisition. In some countries, legislation requires that a certain proportion of the directors of local companies must be local residents or nationals.

15.7   Taxation

Tax rates vary among the countries of Europe to such an extent that they may exercise a considerable influence on the price at which a purchaser is prepared to proceed with an acquisition. Although the European Commission has from time to time expressed the desire to co-ordinate and approximate national policies on all aspects of direct corporate taxation, it is generally recognised that the goal of harmonisation of the bases and rates of taxation across the Member States to provide overall tax neutrality will be difficult to achieve. The EC has, however, adopted a number of Directives which will have consequences for cross-border acquisitions, two of which are referred to below. The level of pre-tax return from investment in one country which is required to produce the same post-tax return for a parent company in another country will vary according to the country of incorporation of the purchaser and of the target, and the discrepancies can be surprisingly large.

Any acquisition raises significant tax considerations. In relation to the acquisition by a United Kingdom purchaser of a United Kingdom resident target, these are dealt with in Chapter 12. Where the target is resident in another country, the problems are compounded by the interaction of different tax regimes. Tax considerations will influence the choice of the entity which legally acquires the shares in the target (eg the purchaser itself, a domestic vehicle resident in the purchaser's own jurisdiction, or a special acquisition vehicle incorporated in the target's jurisdiction, or in a 'tax haven'). These will relate primarily to the method of funding, but there may be other factors, such as the desire to accumulate dividends from the target in the foreign jurisdiction to avoid withholding tax (although in the EC, as a result of the Parent/Subsidiary Companies Directive on withholding tax (90/435/EEC), profits of a subsidiary resident in one Member State distributed to a parent company resident in another are exempt from withholding tax), and the ability to benefit from reliefs which may apply in the target's jurisdiction. If the business to be acquired includes patents, trademarks or other assets which attract royalties, the vendor's tax position may now be assisted by the EC Directive on Cross-Border Mergers (90/434/EEC) which requires Member States to permit deferral of any tax charge on a disposal in particular circumstances, even where the purchaser is incorporated in another Member State.

If a special locally incorporated acquisition vehicle is used, this can be funded either by capital from the parent or by debt, either from third parties or from the parent. Consideration will need to be given to the treatment of dividend flows on any capital and the treatment of any interest paid, including its deductibility. An advantage of a locally incorporated acquisition vehicle is that, very often, interest expenses can be offset against the profits of the target, thus reducing the overall rate of tax in the target's jurisdiction. However, thin capitalisation rules may apply to restrict the amount of interest for which tax relief can be obtained.

An acquisition of a company in Europe will almost certainly involve foreign currency and, for a United Kingdom purchaser, there is therefore the possibility of a foreign currency exposure against sterling. The taxation of any foreign currency exposure will be dealt with under the exchange gains and losses legislation in the Finance Act 1993. The legislation is complex but, broadly speaking, gains and losses arising as a result of currency fluctuations on certain assets and liabilities in respect of trading transactions are treated as trading receipts or allowable trading expenditure. In respect of non-trading transactions, gains are taxed as non-trading income under Schedule D Case VI. Losses are relieved by offset against any of the company's profits of the accounting period, by group relief, carried back to earlier accounting periods, or carried forward to the next accounting period (Finance Act 1996, s 83). Gains and losses are charged to and relieved from tax as they accrue over the life of the asset or liability. The legislation applies to all companies (subject to limited exclusions) including non-resident companies.

Where a United Kingdom parent company borrows in a foreign currency to purchase an overseas subsidiary, the borrowing will be a qualifying liability and the shares in the overseas subsidiary will be a non-qualifying asset for the purposes of the relevant tax legislation (Finance Act 1993). Normally, any exchange gain or loss on the borrowing would be required to be brought into account on an accruals basis in each year, and no capital gain or loss would be realised on the shares until they are sold, when a realised capital gain or loss would crystallise.

Any currency fluctuation on the borrowing would be taxed under the non-trading gains and losses rules in Finance Act 1993, s 129. The reader should be aware of the possibility of the parent company making a matching election in these circumstances to avoid the mismatch between the taxation of the asset on realisation and the liability on a yearly accrual basis. The matching rules are to be found in the Exchange Gains and Losses (Alternative Method, etc) Regulations 1994 (SI No 3227). The effect of a valid matching election is that the exchange gains and losses on the borrowing will not be taxed under the Finance Act 1993, ss 129–131, but will instead be treated as a chargeable gain or allowable loss for capital gains purposes when the asset is disposed of (reg 10(6)).

As can be seen from the above, the taxation of exchange gains and losses is a difficult area which should be approached with particular care. At the time this book goes to press, it remains too early to comment on the consequences of introducing the 'Euro' as a currency for foreign acquisitions.

Where there is an immediate intention to dispose of a significant part of the target's assets in order to repay borrowings, care will need to be taken to ensure that any proceeds of sale from the local jurisdiction can be remitted without tax penalty back to the entity that incurred the borrowing. In addition to tax charges, there may be company law, exchange control and other regulatory constraints on the remittance of profits.

Where the purchaser wishes to pay for the acquisition with an issue of shares to the vendors, there may be tax advantages for the target's shareholders in being issued with shares in a company incorporated in the target's jurisdiction, in addition to shares in the purchaser, which are then paired with the shares in the purchaser. The paired shares are sometimes known as 'stapled stock'. In simple terms, paired shares are a method by which the shareholders in the target in another jurisdiction can receive shares in the purchaser, but be treated for tax purposes largely as if the purchaser was resident for tax purposes in their own country, and so avoid the possibility of a withholding tax on dividends or other tax charge in the purchaser's jurisdiction, and perhaps also benefit from imputation tax credits.

It is worth checking what local stamp duty or equivalent tax is payable on the transfer of assets. A number of European countries are more expensive than the United Kingdom in this respect, especially on the transfer of real property. Asset transfer taxes in France, as noted above, can be prohibitive.

15.8 Conclusion

The legal and regulatory systems of the countries of Europe which impinge on the planning and execution of acquisitions differ substantially. They can constitute a major trap for an unwary purchaser who assumes that the rules that will apply will be the same as those in the United Kingdom. In addition, on a practical level, the logistical problems that will be encountered in a cross-border acquisition will almost invariably be greater than those involved in a purely domestic transaction. Identifying problems of this kind early on can enable them to be avoided or overcome, when confronting them for the first time at a later stage in the transaction could lead to the deal being derailed.

Any prospective purchaser contemplating an acquisition in Europe should seek advice on the local law and practice applicable to the particular transaction in question at the outset. Legal issues in the jurisdiction of the target and local practices may well affect the basic structure of the acquisition, as well as the conduct of the negotiations and the form of the final agreement itself.

Chapter 16

Insolvency

Special considerations apply in the case of insolvency, for example where the target company is insolvent (but its underlying business is thought to be viable) or where the vendor of the target company or of business assets is insolvent. For the purpose of this chapter, a distinction is drawn between the case where an insolvency procedure (whether receivership, administration, liquidation or bankruptcy) has commenced, and that where such a procedure has not yet begun but is, or may be, imminent. In the first case, where either shares in the target or some or all of the insolvent target's assets are among the assets to be realised in the vendor's receivership or liquidation, the primary considerations for the purchaser are the validity of the transaction, the ability of the vendor to deliver good title to the shares in the target and the warranty and other protections he is able to achieve. In the second case, the sale may be liable to avoidance or adjustment under the provisions of the Insolvency Act 1986 and the ability to recover for breaches of warranty and other post-completion payments from the vendor will be cast into doubt. This chapter deals mainly with the insolvency of a corporate vendor proposing to sell its own assets in the context of its own insolvency situation, or the shares in a subsidiary target which is ring-fenced from its parent's problems.

Receivership and insolvency sales, while involving largely the same techniques as any acquisition transaction, are *sui generis* and this chapter seeks to highlight some of the wider issues without a separate discussion of each type of transaction. It is also worth noting that, directly or indirectly, virtually all transactions in this area will be of assets, because of the general rule that the purchaser does not on an asset acquisition become exposed to the associated liabilities (save in particular cases eg employees).

16.1   Shares or assets?

A fundamental question where the target or vendor is in financial difficulties is whether to purchase shares or its assets. While, normally, the purchaser of a

351

company will protect itself from hidden liabilities by investigation it will nonetheless rely heavily on warranties and indemnities from the vendor and the vendor's ability to meet its liabilities under them and occasionally also by taking
security (eg retention or deposit). However, where a receiver, administrator or
liquidator has already been appointed it is very unlikely, in practice, that warranties will be given as the well-advised office-holder will wish to minimise
any personal liability in respect of the sale; even if warranties are (rarely) given
they will invariably be without recourse to the office-holder such that the purchaser would have a claim only against an insolvent vendor. Where the context
of the acquisition is that the vendor's group is in financial difficulties but no
appointment of a receiver, administrator or liquidator has yet occurred, the position will seem better since warranties will be available in the normal way, but
the purchaser should bear in mind that his ability to recover his loss in the event
of the vendor's subsequent insolvency is likely to be limited, so that in practice
there is little difference to the two situations.

If warranties are unavailable or of questionable value, a share acquisition
will be a risky transaction to a purchaser. It will not be protected from liabilities
which have not been revealed by his own investigations and even if the target's
business is sound he will have no way of knowing whether the target has been
effectively ring-fenced from liabilities of other members of the vendor's group.

If the receivership, administration or liquidation has already commenced
against the vendor, the purchaser will almost invariably try to purchase assets,
rather than shares. If an insolvency procedure has commenced against the target company, the transaction will invariably be of assets. The advantage of an
assets sale is that the purchaser is then less dependent on warranties, since he
will not inherit liabilities other than those he agrees to assume, and his primary
concern will be to verify the value of the assets and to ensure that he will receive good title to them, free from any charges or other rights in favour of any
other person. These are matters which, to a large extent, he will be able to verify by his own investigation and his need for warranties will be much diminished. The principal exception to the rule that on the acquisition of assets, a
purchaser will not inherit liabilities, will arise where the business is sold as a
going concern. In such a case its employees, with their accrued rights, will generally transfer automatically to the purchaser by virtue of the Transfer of Undertakings (Protection of Employment) Regulations 1981 (*see* Chapter 6).

The one exception to the general rule that shares will not be acquired is the
hive-down to a new company, where shares are then acquired. The hive-down
involves establishing a fire-break from the vendor's liabilities by an asset transfer into a new company. The purchaser will in such case reduce the risk associated with the purchase of shares as the business of the company in
receivership or liquidation is then contained in a new subsidiary with a view to
its sale. The hive down of a business to a new subsidiary is commonly chosen
to make more saleable those parts of a company in receivership which are
capable of continuing as a going concern (*see further below*).

Even where there has been no hive down there may be occasions, nevertheless, when a purchaser decides to proceed with a share acquisition despite the lack of warranty protection. One situation might be where there is value in the target itself which cannot be transferred on an asset sale. For example, the target may have valuable licences under which the rights are not transferable (and will not terminate on change of control). This is rare. If a share acquisition is to proceed, the purchaser will place particular emphasis on conducting a detailed investigation of the target to satisfy himself, as far as possible, that there are no problems. The purchaser should ensure he has access to key management and is able to satisfy himself as to the extent of their knowledge. He may consider seeking formal representations from management, if it seems appropriate. It is highly desirable that he is able to approach third parties, such as customers, suppliers, bankers, and others with whom the target has important relationships.

Another practical precaution for the purchaser is in the negotiation of the acquisition agreement, where the best protection he may be able to achieve is a retention, either in an escrow account or as deferred consideration, of as much of the consideration as possible (indeed, such an approach is also desirable on an asset sale). However, since the receiver, liquidator or administrator will wish to realise assets as rapidly as possible, such a proposal may well be unwelcome. If consideration can be withheld, it will be necessary to negotiate an appropriate basis upon which the escrow is released or the deferred consideration payable, which will often be by reference to a closing balance sheet or post-acquisition profits (or, if it is assets which are to be acquired, the settlement of all retention of title claims). Alternatively, it may be appropriate to provide that the money is released if no claims relating to the period prior to the purchaser's ownership are made within an agreed period after completion. Such an arrangement can be structured to be similar in effect to a warranty. Where an escrow arrangement is established the purchaser should ensure that express rights of set-off for any claim by the purchaser against the deferred consideration are set out in the agreement to minimise reliance on any implied right, which will be less clear. While the statutory rights of set-off on liquidation are fairly wide it should be noted that to the extent that contractual rights of set-off exceed the statutory rules they will be invalid in the event of the vendor's liquidation (Insolvency Rules 1986, r 4.90). Difficulties may arise when seeking to establish the applicability of statutory set-off under r 4.90 and it may be preferable to express the vendor's entitlement to receive money from the escrow fund as a condition, rather than an asset against which the purchaser has a right of set-off. See Wood, *English and International Set-Off* (1989) and also the commentary to the Insolvency Act 1986, s 323 (the equivalent provision in personal bankruptcy) in *Muir Hunter on Personal Insolvency* (Sweet & Maxwell 1988).

16.2 Hive down

In a hive down, the insolvent, or near insolvent, vendor will transfer those parts of its business to be sold to one or more newly incorporated subsidiaries (a newco) in consideration either for the issue of shares in newco, or for a debt left outstanding from newco to the parent which is discharged by the purchaser on the subsequent sale of newco. A key feature is that newco will not inherit the liabilities of the parent except to the extent specifically assumed in the transfer, and so a purchaser will acquire the newco shares free of such liabilities. However, if the transfer is being made as part of a formal insolvency procedure, the liquidator, receiver or administrator will transfer to newco only such title to the assets as the parent has; if the assets transferred to newco are subject to encumbrances or other charges, the purchaser will need to make arrangements, in its subsequent purchase of newco, for release of those encumbrances or must otherwise satisfy himself as to the burden they represent. It will be usual for the liquidator, receiver or administrator to exclude personal liability on the sale, and also to exclude liability of the parent under any implied warranties (for instance, he will not sell with any title guarantee, and will seek to exclude implied terms under the Law of Property (Miscellaneous Provisions) Act 1994 and to the extent relevant (and possible) the Sale of Goods Act 1979 (*see* Chapter 10).

A particular attraction of a hive down to a newco, rather than the direct purchase of the assets themselves, is the ability to transfer past trading losses of the parent with the business, to offset against newco's future profits. The transfer of losses to newco arises by virtue of the Income and Corporation Taxes Act 1988, s 343, which treats newco as succeeding to the parent's trade without any discontinuance of the trade occurring, provided that at any time within two years after the hive down at least a 75 per cent interest in the trade is owned by the same persons as such an interest belonged to at some time within a year before the hive down. This condition will be met provided that at least 75 per cent of the issued share capital of newco is beneficially owned by the parent when the hive down occurs. It will not be met if the parent has already gone into liquidation, since a company in liquidation ceases to be the beneficial owner of its assets. Making arrangements for the sale of newco prior to the hive down may also result in the parent ceasing to be the beneficial owner of its assets and deprive the parties of relief under s 343; the possible effect of any such arrangements on beneficial ownership should thus be considered (*Wood Preservation Ltd v Prior* [1969] 1 WLR 1077 and *O'Connor (Inspector of Taxes) v J Sainsbury plc* [1991] STC 318 (*see* p 300)). After liquidation has commenced, since relief under s 343 is not available, there will be no tax advantage of a hive down over selling the assets themselves.

Even where s 343 relief applies, the parent's trading losses are not automatically available in full to newco; they will be reduced under s 343(4) by the excess of 'relevant liabilities' retained by the parent over the market value of its 'relevant assets' (see Income and Corporation Taxes Act 1988, s 344(5)–(12)). Section 343 also requires newco to assume the capital allowance position of the parent, which may not be to newco's advantage. Further, relief from stamp duty under the Finance Act 1930, s 42 on the transfer of dutiable assets to new-co will generally not be available by reason of the Finance Act 1967, s 27(3). Therefore, stamp duty is likely to be a further cost of hive down as well as being payable on the sale of newco shares (*see* Chapter 12 on the stamp duty costs of an assets acquisition). On the sale of newco, a charge to corporation tax on chargeable gains in respect of capital assets transferred to it from the parent may be incurred by newco under the Taxation of Chargeable Gains Act 1992, s 179 (*see* p 310). A prospective purchaser of the parent's business must therefore consider carefully whether the availability of tax losses afforded by a hive down will be outweighed by any tax disadvantages.

The purchaser will wish to see how the employees of the business have been dealt with. Generally speaking, on the sale of a business as a going concern, the Transfer of Undertakings (Protection of Employment) Regulations 1981, reg 5 will operate to transfer automatically to the purchaser contracts of employment of all employees employed immediately before the transfer. Regulation 4, however, was designed to permit a liquidator, receiver or administrator to hive down an undertaking or part of an undertaking to newco which can then be sold to the purchaser free of employee liabilities. Regulation 4 operated by postponing the date of the first transfer (the hiving down to newco of the undertaking or part) to the date of the second transfer (the disposal of newco or newco's business). If employees were dismissed between the first transfer and the second transfer by the receiver or the administrator they were not employed immediately before the date of the second transfer and so liability did not pass to newco or the purchaser. In *Litster v Forth Dry Dock and Engineering Company Ltd* [1990] 1 AC 546, the House of Lords decided that the transferee should acquire liability not only for the claims of employees employed immediately before a transfer, but also for the claims of those employees who would have been employed immediately before a transfer if they had not been dismissed prior to the transfer for a reason connected with the transfer where that reason was not an economic, technical or organisational reason involving changes in the work force. While reg 4 was not discussed in *Litster*, the effect of that decision appears to be to make reg 4 ineffective. This is because a dismissal of employees between the first transfer (the hive down of the business to newco) and the second transfer (the sale of that business to the purchaser) will almost always be for a reason connected with the transfer which will not be an economic, technical or organisational reason involving changes in the work force, with the consequence that the ultimate transferee of the business will be liable for the claims by these employees.

The economic need to dismiss the workforce in order to achieve a sale of the business is not an economic, technical or organisational reason for these purposes (*Wheeler v Patel and J Goulding Group of Companies* [1987] IRLR

211). Regulation 8 provides that a dismissal for a reason connected with the transfer is automatically unfair unless it is for an economic, organisational or technical reason involving a change in the workforce. The remedies available to unfairly dismissed employees are described in Chapter 6.

In other respects, the hivedown to newco is no more than a particular type of asset sale and raises equivalent issues to a direct acquisition of assets from the insolvent company. Many of the various practical issues described in Chapter 10 are relevant although the purchaser will have limited opportunity to build in the normal protections. All the usual difficulties common to such a transaction can arise; if the business depends on contractual arrangements, those contracts will need to be assigned, novated or sub-contracted to newco and it will be necessary to check that the contractual terms permit this. If the parent is already insolvent, novation or entry into new contracts will be the preferred approach although where there are a large number of contracts, this can be a practical problem; usually, however, this will be arranged promptly because of the importance of maintaining good relations with customers and suppliers during such a difficult period. Similarly, trade mark, patent, software and other licences will need to be transferred and their transferability will be a matter which the purchaser must investigate. It will also be necessary to deal specifically with the different assets comprised in the hive down; in common with any assets transfer, difficulties may be experienced in the assignment of leasehold premises, where any necessary landlord's consent to the assignment is withheld or delayed and issues of guarantee or security will arise. The purchaser of newco will also wish to review the hive-down documentation to see what has been transferred to newco and what arrangements have been put in place for the collection of book debts (which will invariably be retained by the vendor) and to ensure use of any assets that newco will need to carry on business has been properly addressed. These may include freehold premises, plant and machinery, or property held under finance or hire purchase contracts. Furthermore, while the terms of the hive down may exclude any liability to creditors, if these include important suppliers, the purchaser will wish to know that any delay in payment will not affect continuity of supply since he might otherwise find himself paying the creditor to preserve the business. One other particular area of difference between the solvent and 'insolvent' asset transfer is in the area of retention of title claims, which most commonly arises in receivership sales. Such claims will usually be discharged in the ordinary course of business in the solvent transaction but in the insolvency situation, rights of the unpaid seller will invariably be asserted. Insolvency practitioners tend to take a pragmatic approach when dealing with retention of title claims and can be expected to accept responsibility for settling them. If goods subject to retention of title claims are sold by a receiver he may be liable for conversion or under the Torts (Interference with Goods) Act 1977. As a result he will normally take care to ensure that they are dealt with properly. This is one—often the only—exception to the *caveat emptor* approach to receivership sales.

16.3 Practical points: where an insolvency procedure has already commenced against the vendor

It is normal practice when embarking upon a company acquisition to conduct a search against the vendor and target at the Companies Registry (*see* p 135). A company search and searches of the central register of winding-up and administration petitions at the Companies Court should also be conducted against the vendor (telephone 0171 936 7328). Although in practice the purchaser will usually know whether he is dealing with a company against which some insolvency procedure has commenced (*see below*), the results of these searches may alert the purchaser to the presentation of a petition for winding-up or administration of the vendor, the appointment of a receiver or other matters (such as charges over the assets of the vendor) where special considerations will be relevant.

Equally, where the vendors include private individuals, a search of the Land Charges Registry should be made to determine whether any bankruptcy petition or order has been registered against any vendor.

There are different types of insolvency procedure which may affect the vendor and each has slightly different implications for the purchaser. The law in this area is extensive and the following is intended as a summary only.

16.3.1 Receivers

A receiver may be appointed under a fixed charge given by the company over some or all of its assets. The receiver may be appointed either by the charge-holders under the charge, or by the court, or may be appointed by a mortgagee in exercise of his powers under the Law of Property Act 1925, s 101.

The receiver's appointment, authority and powers will vary depending upon whichever of the foregoing is the basis of his appointment. This section concentrates on the considerations for a purchaser dealing with a receiver appointed in respect of a corporate vendor under powers contained in a debenture secured by a fixed charge. Such a receiver is generally appointed in respect of specific assets and where there is no floating charge, unlike an administrative receiver who will be appointed under a floating charge in respect of the whole, or substantially the whole, of the company's property and has power to carry on the company's business in the exercise of his functions. The considerations relevant to receivers appointed under a fixed charge are also applicable to administrative receivers, although the additional statutory provisions applicable to administrative receivers are considered below (p 361).

A receiver appointed by the court is an officer of the court and his powers are derived from the order appointing him. He is personally liable on contracts entered into by him and while he is entitled to an indemnity out of the assets of the company, to the extent they are sufficient, for liabilities incurred in the proper performance of his duties, he will be most unwilling to incur any such liability under warranties given on the sale of any assets. The appointment takes effect from the date of the order appointing him, and upon his appointment the powers of the company and its directors are entirely in abeyance in respect of the property put in his possession or under his control.

A receiver appointed under the terms of a debenture must be appointed in the manner set out in the debenture; if he is to execute any deed as agent of the company (such as a transfer of shares in the target where the target's articles require transfers to be by deed or other conveyances or assignments eg of land or patents) then he must be appointed by deed.

Much more common than a court-appointed receiver is the receiver appointed by the debenture holder under the terms of the debenture held by him with security over the company's assets. In such case, the receiver's powers will be derived from the terms of the debenture, which will generally be extensive. The debenture will usually appoint the receiver as the agent of the *company* in respect of the assets which are the subject of the charge, although the company cannot terminate the agency, and while the receiver owes certain duties to the company, he has a primary responsibility to the debenture holder who appointed him. The receiver's appointment by the debenture holder suspends, during the period of receivership, the powers of the directors over the assets in respect of which the receiver has been appointed so far as is requisite to enable the receiver to discharge his functions.

Where a receiver is appointed, any person wishing to deal with the company in receivership in relation to those assets should expect, therefore, to deal with the receiver and not with the directors, although he will need to satisfy himself as to the authority of the receiver to act and his powers (*see below*). A receiver appointed by a debenture holder under the terms of the debenture takes office from the time at which the instrument appointing the receiver is received by him, provided he accepts the appointment by the end of the next business day (Insolvency Act 1986, s 33). The Insolvency Rules 1986, Pt 3, Chapter 1 set out the requirements for confirmation of the fact and time of his acceptance, and its publication.

Where the shares in the target are one of the assets to be sold in the receivership, the purchaser will wish to satisfy himself that he will receive good title to the assets. The power of a court-appointed receiver to sell will be derived from his appointment, and the court order should be checked to ensure that he is duly empowered to make such a sale. If he is not or if it is a requirement that the court sanctions such a transaction, any agreement should be conditional upon such sanction.

The authority of the receiver to act is more difficult where he is appointed under the powers contained in the debenture and it will be necessary to make careful checks to ensure that he is properly authorised. It will be necessary to check the instrument setting out his powers, and whether any formalities for his appointment have been complied with; if he is expressed to act as agent of the company, his powers will be subject to the same limitations as those of the company. There are a number of circumstances which could render invalid the appointment of a receiver or the exercise of his powers. These will include:

(a) where the debenture pursuant to which he is appointed is illegal or unenforceable (if, for example, it constituted the giving of unlawful financial assistance by the company (*see* Chapter 5), or had not been duly executed, or had not been duly registered under the Companies Act 1985, s 395);

(b) where the conditions under the debenture enabling the debenture holder to appoint him have not arisen, or been duly complied with;

(c) where any formalities for his appointment set out in the debenture have not been complied with. For example, if joint receivers are appointed, does the debenture permit this, and are they able to act severally?

(d) where the powers conferred on him by the debenture do not extend to the act or acts he purports to take. Unlike an administrative receiver, a receiver appointed under a fixed charge does not by virtue of his office have any powers expressly conferred on him (except to the extent that the Law of Property Act 1925, s 109 applies); and

(e) where winding-up has commenced against the company (this will terminate his agency on behalf of the company, but not his appointment (*see* p 362).

It will not be possible for a purchaser dealing with such a receiver to investigate all these matters fully. However, it should be possible to make the following checks:

(a) conduct a company search against the vendor to check for registration of the charge and any winding-up or administration petition or order;

(b) obtain a copy of the debenture and seek evidence of compliance with any unusual requirements; and

(c) obtain copies of the receiver's appointment and his acceptance under s 33.

Where there is any apparent irregularity, the purchaser should satisfy himself that it will not invalidate the appointment. Indeed, since a receiver who purports to act in the absence of proper authority may incur significant liability both to the company, and to persons with whom he deals, the well-advised receiver can be expected to have satisfied himself as to these matters.

Despite these checks, it is possible that the appointment might not be valid. If the charge is void *ab initio* (for example, improperly executed), then it would seem that the receiver will never have had the requisite authority to act. While any want of authority will generally be capable of ratification by the company, in the absence of such ratification the remedy of a purchaser acting in good faith and without notice of such defect will be rather unsatisfactory, being a claim for damages in an action against the company and/or receiver for breach of warranty of authority (see *Bowstead on the Law of Agency*, 16th edn (1996)).

A receiver appointed under powers contained in an instrument is personally liable on contracts entered into by him in the performance of his functions, except so far as the contract otherwise provides (s 37). It is normal practice for a receiver to exclude his personal liability in a contract for disposal of the shares or other assets in the target. While this will not affect the liability of the company on whose behalf he is acting as agent, he will be reluctant for the company to give warranties on the sale since he will not wish to expose the company and possibly himself to claims in damages.

In addition to checking the authority of the receiver, the purchaser will wish to ensure that any transfer of the target's shares to him will be free of any other security. If the vendor's assets, including the target's shares, are subject to other charges, then it will be necessary to examine whether the receiver is able to deliver title to the shares free of such security. If the receiver's appointment is under a debenture secured by mortgage made by deed, with security ranking in priority to all other security, then it will be possible for the shares to be delivered to the purchaser free from other charges ranking behind that charge, by the debenture holder selling as mortgagee and exercising his power of sale under the Law of Property Act 1925, s 101(1). In such a case, it will be the debenture holder, not the receiver acting as agent for the company, who will execute the transfer (if the company or its agent, the receiver, executes the transfer, releases from subsequent charges must be obtained). However, if there exists security ranking in priority to the security of the debenture under which the receiver has been appointed, statute cannot be invoked to overreach such interests (unlike an administrative receiver who may apply to court for such purpose). Where prior charges cannot be overreached, it will be necessary to obtain a release of the shares from such charges by the chargeholder.

In all cases, the purchaser will also need to give consideration as to the manner in which the shares are to be transferred; a legal charge of the shares will have been effected by registering the shares in the name of the chargee, who must transfer the shares; alternatively, a chargee's interest may be protected by deposit of the share certificate and a stock transfer executed in blank (as to the transferee). Simple completion of the executed transfer will usually suffice to effect the transfer.

Apart from the provisions of the Insolvency Act 1986 dealing with transactions at an undervalue and preferences (*see* p 368), a purchaser will generally be concerned only as to the authority of the receiver to act, and not any neglect by the receiver in the exercise of his powers. A receiver appointed by debenture holders owes a duty of care to the company in respect of whose assets he has been appointed, and if he fails to exercise reasonable care in the circumstances to obtain the best value for the assets commensurate with the time available, he will be liable for any loss suffered by the company or any guarantor of the relevant debt (see *Standard Chartered Bank Ltd v Walker* [1982] 1 WLR 1410, and *American Express International Banking Corp v Hurley* [1985] 3 All ER 564). Breach of this duty of care will, therefore, give rise to a right to damages against the receiver, but will not affect the purchaser whose transaction will not, for this reason alone, be invalidated.

Different considerations apply where the receiver or debenture holder sells the assets to himself (when it is clear that it is liable to be set aside, irrespective of the merits of sale) or where he has an interest in the purchaser, where it seems that a 'fair dealing' rule applies. See the judgment of the Privy Council in *Tse Kwong Lam v Wong Chit Sen* [1983] 1 WLR 1394 (concerning sale by a mortgagee) and *Watts v Midland Bank plc* [1986] BCLC 15 concerning an application for interlocutory relief on a sale by receiver). In the *Watts* case it was suggested (at p 23) that such a fair dealing rule would apply where the sale by the receiver to a purchaser in which the solicitor acting for the receiver was financially interested. 'Financially interested' is presumably not limited to a shareholding, and it would be prudent to assume that the principle may apply if the debenture holder under whose debenture the receiver was appointed is also a significant provider of finance to the purchaser.

16.3.2   Administrative receivers

An administrative receiver is a special category of receiver with powers and obligations defined by statute (Insolvency Act 1986, s 42 *et seq*). A very broad distinction between an administrative receiver and other receivers is that the administrative receiver will have been appointed under a floating charge (which may include fixed charges) over substantially the whole of a company's assets, whereas other receivers will be appointed under a fixed charge for the purpose of realising specific assets only, or by the court. Unlike a receiver appointed under a fixed charge, however, an administrative receiver must be a licensd insolvency practitioner.

Generally speaking, therefore, receivers appointed under a floating charge will be administrative receivers, and provisions of the Insolvency Act discussed below will apply in addition to those provisions of general application (under 'Receivers' *above*, p 357).

A receiver will be an administrative receiver if he is 'a receiver or manager of the whole (or substantially the whole) of a company's property appointed by or on behalf of the holders of debentures of the company secured by a charge which, as created, was a floating charge, or by such a charge and one or more other securities' (s 29(2)). An administrative receiver may therefore be appointed if the floating charge has crystallised, or where the charge comprises both floating and fixed security. Appointment of an administrative receiver does not prevent another receiver being appointed in respect of specific assets, or the liquidation of the company. It will, however, be a bar to the appointment of an administrator, unless the security by virtue of which the receiver is appointed can be challenged (s 9(3)).

The administrative receiver is deemed to be the company's agent unless and until the company goes into liquidation. However, he is personally liable on any contract entered into by him in the carrying out of his functions, unless the contract otherwise provides (s 44). This mirrors the position of a receiver appointed under a fixed charge. An administrative receiver, therefore, will also be unwilling to give warranties on sale, both in his own capacity and as agent for the company.

A purchaser dealing with an administrative receiver will need to make virtually the same enquiries as to the validity of his appointment and his powers to act as he would if dealing with a receiver appointed under a fixed charge (*see* p 359), although the Insolvency Act will provide additional protection. Section 232 provides that the acts of an administrator, administrative receiver, liquidator or provisional liquidator of a company are valid notwithstanding any defect in his appointment, nomination or qualifications. Although s 232 will prevent defects in formalities associated with his appointment from invalidating his acts, it is thought that it will not validate his acts if the debenture under which he was appointed is void (see *Morris v Kanssen* [1946] AC 459, concerning a predecessor to the section). A purchaser should therefore satisfy himself of the administrative receiver's appointment, where there is any apparent reason to doubt the validity of the debenture under which he has been appointed.

An administrative receiver, in addition to the powers contained in the debenture appointing him, has wide powers conferred on him by statute: the debenture by virtue of which he was appointed is deemed, by s 42(1), to include (except in so far as they are inconsistent with any of the provisions of the debenture) the powers set out in Sched 1 to the Act. These powers are extensive and include a power of sale (para 2). Although it is unlikely, it would be prudent for the purchaser dealing with an administrative receiver to check the debenture to ensure that it does not limit the exercise of his powers; however, a purchaser will derive considerable assistance from s 42(3), which provides that a person dealing with the administrative receiver in good faith and for value is not concerned to inquire whether the receiver is acting within his powers.

An administrative receiver is able to transfer the target's shares to the purchaser free from any other security interests: as with a receiver appointed under a fixed charge, any charges whose security ranks after the charge securing the debenture under which the administrative receiver was appointed may be overreached by the debenture holder exercising his power of sale under the Law of Property Act 1925, s 101(1). It is also possible, however, for an administrative receiver to dispose of assets free of charges which rank ahead of his charge, since the Insolvency Act 1986, s 43(1) permits the court, on an application by the administrative receiver, to authorise him to dispose of the property as if it were not subject to the security. For such an order to be made, the section provides that the court is to be satisfied that 'the disposal...would be likely to promote a more advantageous realisation of the company's assets than would otherwise be effected'. The section may be invoked only to enable disposal of assets free from prior security (see s 43(2)); if holders of subsequent security refuse to give a release of their charge, the sale may have to be made by the mortgagee under his statutory power.

An existing appointment of a receiver or administrative receiver will not prevent the winding-up of the company nor does winding-up prevent the appointment of a receiver or administrative receiver. The making of a winding-up order will terminate any such receiver's agency on behalf of the company. However, termination of the receiver's agency to bind the company does not affect the exercise of powers given by the debenture and the Act to hold and dispose of the property charged (*Sowman v Samuel (David) Trust Ltd* [1978] 1 WLR 22). Commencement of winding-up in respect of the vendor, therefore, will not prevent a receiver or administrative receiver from transferring title to shares which are charged by the debenture under which he was appointed. Winding-up will, however, usually terminate any power of attorney granted to the receiver under the debenture. Notwithstanding this, a receiver may for the reasons already given still dispose of assets subject to the charge under which he was appointed without the liquidator's consent or involvement.

16.3.3   Administrators

Administration was designed as a means of rehabilitation of insolvent but viable businesses. The administrator is appointed by the court to manage the business and property of the company and to achieve the statutory purpose for which he is appointed (eg the survival of the company in whole or in part as a going concern or a more advantageous realisation of the company's assets than would be effected on winding-up (Insolvency Act 1986, s 8(3)). Generally speaking, where an administrative receiver has already been appointed, an administrator may not be appointed by the court (s 9(3)). The appointment of administrator and administrative receiver are mutually exclusive and any appointment of an administrator, being made with the consent of the administrative receiver's appointor, will require the administrative receiver to vacate office. If the administrator requires it, any receiver appointed in respect of specific assets must also vacate office (s 11(2)). Similarly, administration is inconsistent with liquidation, and after presentation of a petition for administration, any winding-up order may not be made or resolution passed until the petition is heard or dismissed. An administration order will result in dismissal of a winding-up petition.

Administration has far-reaching consequences for a company and its creditors; while the administration order is in force no steps may be taken to enforce security over the company's property, nor may other proceedings be commenced or continued against the company, in either case without the consent of the administrator or the leave of the court (s 11(3)). A purchaser would thus be prevented from bringing proceedings for warranty or other claims arising on a previous acquisition during the period of the administration.

The appointment of an administrator must, within 14 days of the order appointing him, be notified to the Registrar of Companies (s 21(2)). Business correspondence will show evidence of his appointment (s 12(1)). Since the application for the appointment of an administrator is by order of the court, a search of the central index of administration petitions at the Companies Court (*see* p 357) may reveal the existence of his appointment at an earlier date than a search of the Companies Registry.

Section 232 applies in respect of the appointment of an administrator, and a person dealing with an administrator need not enquire into the validity of his appointment. The administrator, following his appointment, has very wide powers to do all such things as may be necessary for the management of the affairs, business and property of the company, and including the powers set out in Sched 1 to the Act (s 14) which are also conferred on an administrative receiver. The administrator is deemed to act as the company's agent (s 14(5)), and powers of the company or its directors are limited during the period of the administration. The purchaser dealing with the administrator in relation to the target's shares is protected by s 14(6), which provides that a person dealing with an administrator in good faith for value is not concerned to inquire whether the administrator is acting within his powers.

The administrator must draw up proposals for achieving the purpose of the administration and put these before the company's creditors at a meeting to be held within three months of his appointment (s 23); he is obliged to act in accordance with such proposals, as modified with creditors' approval from time to time. This does not mean he cannot act prior to the creditors' meeting; he has a general power to act (s 14(1)) and he may apply to court for directions to act prior to the meeting (ss 14(3) and 17(2)). Notwithstanding the protection afforded him by s 14(6), the purchaser should consider whether the administrator is acting within his powers and, where the sale is to occur prior to the creditors' meeting, whether the sale should be made with, or conditional upon, court approval.

An administrator is able to dispose of the company's property free from the security of any person in that property. Where the property of the company is subject to security which, as created, was a floating charge, he may dispose of the property free from the security without consent (s 15(1)) (notwithstanding crystallisation of the security). In the case of any other security, the administrator must seek an order of the court to sell the property to the purchaser free from the security (s 15(2)). Where such an order is sought on the sale of shares in the target which are subject to a legal charge, it will be necessary to ensure that shares registered in the name of the chargee can be transferred (which may entail an appropriate direction to that effect in the court order).

16.3.4 Liquidators

A liquidator is appointed for the winding-up of a company. Winding-up may either be voluntary or compulsory. A voluntary winding-up commences when the resolution to wind up the company is passed, and a compulsory winding-up is deemed to commence when a petition for a winding-up order is presented. This section principally addresses compulsory winding-up.

A compulsory winding-up will occur following an order of the court. If a winding-up order is granted then, provided no resolution for winding-up has previously been passed, the winding-up is deemed to commence on the date upon which the winding-up petition was presented, not the date upon which the order was made (Insolvency Act 1986, s 129). A purchaser who is dealing with a vendor against whom a winding-up petition has been presented should be aware of the effect of s 127 which provides that any disposition of the company's property after the commencement of the winding-up is, unless the court otherwise orders, void. This will be the case even if the disposition is unarguably to the benefit of the company, although in such a case a court would no doubt validate the transaction. The backdating effect of s 129 in relation to the commencement of a winding-up will therefore mean that, in the absence of any court approval, a purchaser should not contract to purchase the target's shares after presentation of the petition. Problems could arise under s 127 where contracts for the purchase of the target shares have been exchanged, but not completed. If the contract is conditional or voidable by the company, waiver of conditions or confirmation of the contract might constitute a disposition of property under s 127, and similarly if the terms of the contract are varied. In practice it may be prudent to seek the court's approval for completion (which will be obtained in advance of the winding-up), although where the contract is plainly specifically enforceable and there is no possible defence, this would seem to be unnecessary (see *Re French's Wine Bar Ltd* [1987] BCLC 499). Section 127 does not apply to invalidate a disposition of the company's property by a receiver (*Sowman v Samuel (David) Trust* [1978] 1 WLR 22). Of course, the above assumes that the purchaser wishes to proceed notwithstanding the vendor's insolvency. If he does not, then he must look to his contract to see if he may rescind. There is no general rule that the insolvency of one party renders the contract unenforceable or offers grounds for rescission.

Upon the appointment of a liquidator, the control of the company's affairs passes out of the hands of the directors, who cease to have authority. The powers of the liquidator will depend on whether the liquidation is voluntary or compulsory. In a compulsory winding-up, the liquidator has the powers set out in the Insolvency Act 1986, Sched 4 which may be exercised with the sanction of the court or liquidation committee (if they fall within Pt I or II) or without it (if within Pt III). So far as the sale of any subsidiary or business by the vendor in liquidation is concerned, Sched 4 para 6 empowers the liquidator, without sanction (in a voluntary liquidation), to sell any of the company's property by public auction or private contract. Paragraph 7 confers authority for the execution of documents and use of the company's seal. The court's sanction will be required if the sale also involves, say, a compromise with creditors.

A purchaser dealing with the liquidator of a vendor does not need to inquire into the formal validity of the liquidator's appointment (s 232). It is nevertheless important to distinguish between a voluntary or compulsory liquidation. If the liquidation is a creditors' voluntary liquidation, the liquidator may exercise his powers only prior to the first creditors' meeting required to be held as part of the insolvency procedure, with the sanction of the court (s 166). Therefore, although it is unlikely that any sale of a subsidiary would take place prior to that meeting, it will be important to check that procedural requirements have been complied with or, where appropriate, any variation in the procedure has been properly sanctioned by the court. If the liquidation is compulsory or a members' voluntary liquidation, the liquidator is under no such restriction (although it should be noted that a provisional liquidator's ability to act may be limited by the court order appointing him (s 135(5)).

16.3.5   Bankruptcy of individual vendors

The bankruptcy of an individual commences on the date on which the bankruptcy order is made, and continues until it is discharged (s 278). Following the bankruptcy order, the Official Receiver takes office and a trustee in bankruptcy will be appointed, although this may take place several weeks after the bankruptcy order is made. Upon the trustee's appointment, the bankrupt's estate vests in the trustee. In the case of shares in a company owned by the bankrupt, s 306(2) provides that this vesting will occur without any transfer, although the target's articles may contain provisions for the registration of shares in the name of the trustee, and for transfers by the bankrupt or his trustee. The trustee's powers derive from s 314 and Sched 5 to the Act. Schedule 5, para 9, confers on the trustee the power to sell any part of the property for the time being comprised in the bankrupt's estate, without requiring any permission from the bankrupt's creditors or the court. If the sale involves payment of deferred consideration, however, it will require the permission of the court or creditors' committee (being a power falling within Pt I of Sched 5 (para 3)) and it may be prudent to make the contract for the acquisition conditional upon that permission; although s 314(3) provides protection for a person dealing in good faith and for value and where such court or creditors' permission is required, he is not concerned to enquire whether any such permission is given.

Where the vendor is an individual who has a bankruptcy petition outstanding against him, the purchaser should be aware that if a bankruptcy order is subsequently made, any disposition of property by the bankrupt in the period commencing on the date on which the petition was presented, and ending on the vesting of the bankrupt's estate in his trustee (on the trustee's appointment) is void, except where it is made with the consent of the court or is subsequently ratified by the court (s 284). The retrospective effect of s 284 is similar to that applicable to the compulsory winding-up of a company, under s 127 (*see* p 365). Unlike s 127, however, s 284(4) provides relief for persons dealing with an individual against whom a bankruptcy petition is pending 'in respect of any property or payment which he received before the bankruptcy in good faith, for value and without notice that the petition had been presented'. Unlike a petition for winding-up of a company, a petition in bankruptcy need not be advertised prior to the hearing, although notice of the petition must be sent for registration as a land charge. In consequence, a purchaser is likely in practice to have the benefit of the section, where his land charges search does not reveal the petition, and he is not otherwise aware of it.

16.4   Vendor's subsequent insolvency

Where the purchaser becomes aware that the corporate vendor from whom he has acquired a target company or business assets has gone into liquidation, he should review the acquisition document, and decide whether or not he has grounds for claims against the vendor. Any claims should be submitted to the liquidator and, so far as possible, quantified, although the amount he is ultimately able to prove in the liquidation will be governed by the Insolvency Act and the Insolvency Rules. Unless he has taken security, a purchaser would be an unsecured creditor of the vendor in respect of any losses, and for this reason any claims may not be paid in full if indeed there is any amount available for distribution to unsecured creditors. For this reason it is always desirable to ensure that any retention of part of the purchase consideration as security for warranty and other claims remains the purchaser's, not the vendor's, money or if the latter, that the purchaser has a first ranking security over it.

However, where the vendor has claims against the purchaser, for instance in respect of the purchaser's failure to pay any deferred consideration, the purchaser will wish, so far as possible, to be able to offset his liability against any claim he has against the vendor. After the commencement of liquidation the purchaser's right to exercise set-off will be governed by the Insolvency Rules 1986, r 4.90. In summary, this provides that mandatory set-off will operate where, before the company goes into liquidation, there have been mutual credits, mutual debts or other mutual dealings between the company and the creditor proving in the liquidation.

While this provision is wide, if the contractual set-off exceeds this principle of mutuality, then the contractual right to that extent it cannot be exercised. Even if the contract does not provide for set-off, a purchaser may be able to assert set-off upon liquidation if there exists the mutuality required by the rule; in a normal case, warranty claims should be capable of being set off against deferred consideration. Insolvency set-off may operate only for a provable debt; to the extent the purchaser's claim exceeds the amount for which set-off may operate, he must prove in the liquidation in the usual way.

Where the vendor has gone into administration or liquidation after the target has been acquired by the purchaser, the acquisition of the target by the purchaser may be liable to adjustment—for example, if the acquisition of the target was a transaction at an undervalue or was a preference given by the insolvent vendor under the Insolvency Act, ss 238–41 (or, in the case of bankruptcy of an individual vendor, ss 339–42).

An acquisition of a target company or of business assets, if entered into in good faith and on an arm's length basis between unconnected parties, is unlikely to be the subject of attack under these provisions.

16.4.1   Transactions at an undervalue (section 238)

Where a company goes into administration or liquidation, the administrator or liquidator is able to apply to the court for the adjustment of certain prior transactions at an undervalue.

Section 238 of the Insolvency Act 1986 is concerned with transactions which occurred in the period of two years prior to the date on which the petition for the administration order was presented, or the date of commencement of the winding-up (being, in the case of compulsory winding-up, the date of presentation of the winding-up petition). Transactions at risk under the section are those which, in summary, involved a gift by the company or where it received no consideration, or consideration having a monetary value significantly less than that given by the company (s 238(4)). If, however, it can be shown that at the time of entering into the transaction in question, the company was able to pay its debts (within the meaning of s 123) and did not become unable to pay its debts in consequence of the transaction, then the transaction will not be liable to adjustment as a transaction at an undervalue (s 240(2)). Difficulty arises where there is a 'connection' between the vendor and purchaser, when an inability to pay debts is presumed, and it will be for the parties to show otherwise. 'Transaction' includes a gift, agreement or arrangement (s 436).

There is a distinction to be drawn between cases of poor judgement by the vendor or where, with hindsight, the price paid by a purchaser proved to be a bargain, and cases where there has been an improper transfer of assets. This is recognised by s 238(5) which provides a defence where the conditions for a transaction at an undervalue otherwise apply and the court is 'satisfied that (a) the company which entered into the transaction did so in good faith and for the purpose of carrying on its business, and (b) that at the time it did so there were reasonable grounds for believing that the transaction would benefit the company'. It should be noted that for the defence under s 238 to be available, the company must have acted in good faith. The fact that the purchaser alone acted in good faith will not prevent any adjustment of the transaction nor will it prevent an order being made against the purchaser (although s 241(2) places limits on the orders to be made against innocent third parties, it seems that a purchaser, since it is party to the transaction, cannot benefit from them).

In cases of doubt as to good faith on the part of the company, and particularly where there is a presumption of insolvency by reason of a connection between vendor and purchaser, it would be prudent for the purchaser to insist that the vendor provides him with a comprehensive board minute evidencing, so far as is possible, satisfaction of the criteria in s 238(5) ('connection' between vendor and purchaser is discussed below (p 370)).

If the grounds are established to the court's satisfaction, then it may make such order as it may think fit to restore the position of the company to that which it would have been in if the company had not entered into the transaction. The court has a very wide discretion in the type of order it may make for this purpose, and s 241 gives specific authority to the court to order that the property be restored to the vendor, that money be paid or repaid or security be given or released, not only against the immediate parties to the transaction, but also by third parties (subject to s 241(2)).

In addition to the s 238 provisions, where it can be shown that the company entered into a transaction at an undervalue for the purpose of putting assets beyond the reach of his creditors, s 423 permits a court to make orders which may result in the transaction being unwound. Unlike s 239, the provisions relating to transactions defrauding creditors can apply irrespective of insolvency and are not limited to transactions within the two-year period prior to administration or liquidation; in principle, therefore, a purchaser proposing an acquisition from any vendor, irrespective of his solvency, should be alert to the section, although it will generally be where there is an impending insolvency that the matter will fall to be considered. An arm's length transaction should not, of course, fall within the section. In addition to an administrator or liquidator, the person who is, or is capable of being, prejudiced by the transaction may bring an application under s 423 to adjust or unwind it.

16.4.2 Preferences (section 239)

An administrator or liquidator may apply to the court for an order to adjust a transaction if the company has by that transaction given a preference within the period of six months prior to the commencement of its winding-up or date of presentation of the petition for administration. Where the preference is given to a person who is connected with the company, however, this period is extended to two years (*see below*).

Under Insolvency Act 1986, s 239(4) a preference is given by a company to a person if that person is one of the company's creditors, or a surety or guarantor for any of the company's debts or liabilities, and the company does or permits to be done anything which has the effect of putting that person into a position which, in the event of the company going into insolvent liquidation, will be better than the position he would have been in if that thing had not been done. A transaction may not be attacked as a preference unless at the time, or in consequence of the transaction, the company was unable to pay its debts (s 240(2)). For a preference to be attacked, the administrator or liquidator must show that the company was influenced by a desire to improve the position in an insolvent liquidation of the person to whom it has given the preference. This is a significant change from the old law concerning voidable preferences, where it was necessary to show a dominant intention to prefer. In *Re M C Bacon Ltd* [1990] BCLC 324, Millet J makes it plain that s 239(5) contains a completely different test. He says (at p 336) '[sub-section (5)]...requires only that the desire should have influenced the decision. That requirement is satisfied if it was one of the factors which operated on the minds of those who made the decision. It need not have been the only factor or even the decisive one'. Where there is a connection between the parties (other than by reason of the person preferred being an employee), it is presumed that the company giving the preference was influenced in doing so by a desire to improve the recipient's position in an insolvent liquidation (s 239(6)) and the burden of proof is on the parties to show it was not so influenced.

As noted above, in an arm's length transaction between unconnected parties the giving of preferences will not usually arise. It will be prudent to examine questions of preference, however, when there are (apart from the acquisition of the target) dealings between the vendor and purchaser or where the purchaser is 'connected' with the vendor. A simple example of where a preference might arise in the context of an acquisition of the target is where the vendor is indebted to the purchaser, and the target is transferred to the purchaser as part of an arrangement for the reduction of that indebtedness.

The application of s 239 is significantly extended where the vendor and purchaser are connected. Where there is a connection (other than by reason of the person preferred being an employee) the period prior to administration or liquidation during which preferences can be attacked is extended from six months to two years and the company's intent to give the preference is presumed. It should be noted that the inability of a company to pay its debts, which is a precondition to adjustment of a transaction at an undervalue under s 238, is presumed under that section where the parties are connected.

Connected' is defined by s 249, and a person is connected with a company for the purpose of giving a preference if he is a director or shadow director of the company, or an associate of any such person, or if he is an associate of the company. 'Associate' is widely defined by s 435 and includes, as may be expected, husbands, wives, relatives, partners, directors and companies under such a person's control. In addition, however, by s 435(4), employees and employers are included as associates—significantly extending the scope of the section. Careful consideration should be given as to whether any such a connection exists, and if it is possible to eliminate such a connection, it will be helpful to do so to reduce the risk of attack under ss 238 and 239.

In a management buy-out, the 'connected person' test will often be met if the purchasing management group includes directors of the vendor (but will be less problem if the group comprises exclusively the vendor's employees, or directors of the target only). For example, a release of directors' loan accounts could be liable to attack as a preference and the burden would be on the parties to show that it was not.

16.4.3 Individual vendors

Where the vendor is an individual the Insolvency Act 1986, ss 339–42 contain similar provisions enabling transactions at an undervalue and preferences prior to a personal bankruptcy to be adjusted. One significant difference in the case of an individual, however, is that the relevant time at which a transaction at an undervalue may be attacked is five years prior to presentation of the bankruptcy petition, provided he was insolvent at the time (if he was solvent, it may still be attacked, but the period is reduced to two years).

16.5 Preservation of company name

Taking on directors of companies in the vendor's group which have gone into insolvent liquidation could adversely affect the continued use of the target's name. The so-called 'phoenix company' provision in the Insolvency Act 1986, s 216, contains a restriction designed to prevent directors whose company goes into insolvent liquidation from thereafter setting up in business under a similar name. The section will be of concern to a purchaser only where it acquires, with the target, individuals who were also formerly directors of any vendor company which has gone into insolvent liquidation within 12 months after such an individual ceased to be a director. It should be noted that the subsequent insolvent liquidation of such a company, after the purchaser has acquired the target, may result in the application of the section. Where s 216 applies, such individuals cannot be directors of or involved in the promotion, formation or management of any company known by a name by which the company in liquidation was known in the 12 months prior to its liquidation, or a name so similar to such a name so as to suggest an association with that company (s 216(2)). There are exceptions to the prohibition on re-use of such a company name. For example, if the purchaser acquires a target with a name which, though suggesting an association with the name of the insolvent company, has been the target's name throughout the relevant period, then the prohibition resulting from employment of the ex-directors will not apply (Insolvency Rules 1986, r 4.230).

Section 216 will be of particular relevance in the case where a management group, comprising directors of the company in liquidation, is formed to purchase the target. Where directors of vendor group companies are part of the management group, the parties should also be alert to the provisions of the Companies Act 1985, s 320, requiring shareholder approval (*see* p 25).

Appendices

Introduction

The forms of agreement set out in the following appendices are as follows:

(a)   a form of agreement for use when purchasing shares (Appendix I, p 375);

(b)   a form of tax deed to accompany the agreement for the purchase of shares (Appendix II, p 483); and

(c)   a form of agreement for use when purchasing business assets (Appendix III, p 501)

together with a number of ancillary documents in Appendices IV to XIII.

The agreements are not so much precedent agreements as collections of useful clauses. It would be rare indeed to find all the provisions of these agreements incorporated in a contract for the sale of a private company or of business assets. Practitioners should regard them as a library of provisions from which to select rather than agreements to be used as they stand.

The Agreement for Sale (Shares), and the tax deed are intended for general use, whether purchasing from individual vendors or from a corporate vendor. While there are differences between each type of agreement which it is sought to highlight by italicised wording or note, the particular requirements will depend on the circumstances of the transaction concerned. As such, the draftsman will need to consider the applicability of each of the clauses to suit the transaction in hand. The agreement contemplates a target with subsidiaries, and will therefore require amendment if there are none. Amendments will also be required if the consideration in paid wholly in cash. Where the consideration is shares in the purchaser, an additional engrossment should be signed for filing at the Companies Registration Office (Companies Act 1985, s 88).

The Agreement for Sale (Assets), in particular, is likely to require modification to suit the circumstances since the composition of an assets transaction—what is to be acquired and what is not to be acquired—encompasses a very broad range of transactions from the acquisition of a few assets and goodwill to an acquisition of what is, in effect, the whole of a company's assets, undertakings and liabilities. No single precedent can hope to suit every circumstance. Indeed, the agreement is itself in some respects inconsistent (eg in its exclusion of liabilities but its preparation, nonetheless, of completion accounts in which liabilities and book debts are reflected) in an attempt to reflect as broad a range of alternatives to the draftsman as is practicable. Also, the property provisions in Sched 5 will not all be appropriate in any particular circumstances.

With each edition of this work the precedent agreements grow longer, one reason being the inclusion of additional warranties. Unfortunately it does not seem possible to prevent this. The fact is that a specific warranty forces the vendor to address the issue and, perhaps, to produce a disclosure while more general wording (which would produce a shorter agreement) does not. Also, there are whether the acquisition is of shares or assets, a number of variants to dealing with the pension arrangements of the target and, rather than attempt to suggest the component parts, it is thought simplest to include examples of the various schedules in full, despite the repetition that is necessarily involved in that approach.

The precedents set out in the following Appendices are intended for use by solicitors. The reader will note the copyright restrictions and limiations of liability set out on the copyright page at the beginning of the book.

Appendix I

Agreement for Sale (Shares)

Contents

THIS AGREEMENT is dated the [   ] day of [   ] 19[   ] and made

BETWEEN:

(1) [1][   ] PLC *a company registered in England under number*
     [   ] *whose registered office is at [   ] (the 'Vendor'); and*

(2) [   ] PLC a company registered in England under number [   ]
     whose registered office is at [   ](the 'Purchaser').[2]

WHEREAS:

The Vendor wishes to sell and the Purchaser wishes to acquire the entire issued share
capital of [   ] Limited on and subject to the terms of this Agreement.

NOW IT IS HEREBY AGREED as follows:

1 Interpretation

1.1 Definitions

In this Agreement where the context admits:

'Affiliate' means, in respect of any body corporate, a body corporate which is its
subsidiary or holding company, or a company which is a subsidiary of that holding
company, and each such company;

'Audited Accounts'[3] means the audited [consolidated] balance sheet of the Company [and the Subsidiaries] made up as at the Balance Sheet Date and the audited
[consolidated] profit and loss account of the Vendor and the Subsidiaries in respect of the financial year ending on the Balance Sheet Date including, in each
case, the notes thereto and the directors' report and auditors' report; true copies of
all of which are annexed to the Disclosure Letter;

'Balance Sheet Date' means [   ] 19[   ];

'Bank' means [Purchaser's merchant bank—relevant if there is a placing];

'Business Day' means a day (other than a Saturday or Sunday) on which banks are
open for ordinary banking business in London;

'Company' means [   ] Limited a company registered in England under number [   ] and incorporated on [   ] 19[   ] as a private
company limited by shares under the Companies Act(s) [   ];

'Companies Acts' means statutes from time to time in force concerning companies
including (without limitation) the Companies Act 1985, the Companies Act 1989,
Part V of the Criminal Justice Act 1993 and the Companies Consolidation (Consequential Provisions) Act 1985;

'Completion'[4] means completion of the sale and purchase of the Sale Shares in accordance with Clause 5 (Completion);

'Completion Date' means [   ], but if the Conditions have not been satisfied or waived on or before such date, 'Completion Date' shall mean such other
date as the parties may agree but, in any event, not later than [   ];

'Conditions' means the conditions set out in Sub-Clause 4.1 (Conditions);

'Consideration Shares' means ordinary shares of [   ] each in the Purchaser credited as fully paid;

'Directors' means the persons named in Part II of Schedule 1 (The Vendors and the Company) and in Schedule 2 (The Subsidiaries) as directors of the Company and the Subsidiaries and 'The Continuing Directors' means the persons named in those Schedules as continuing directors following Completion;

'Disclosure Letter'[5] means the letter dated the date hereof written and delivered by or on behalf of the Vendor to the Purchaser in agreed terms;

'Encumbrance' includes any interest or equity of any person (including any right to acquire, option or right of pre-emption) or any mortgage, charge, pledge, lien, assignment, hypothecation, security interest (including any created by law), title retention or other security agreement or arrangement or a rental, hire purchase, credit sale or other agreement for payment on deferred terms;

'Management Accounts'[6] means the [consolidated] management accounts of the Company [and the Subsidiaries] for the period from the Balance Sheet Date to [   ] 19[   ] true copies of which are annexed to the Disclosure Letter;

'Placing Agreement'[7] means an agreement in agreed terms proposed to be entered into simultaneously with this Agreement between the Purchaser and the Bank providing for the placing of the Consideration Shares;

'Properties' means the properties particulars of which are set out in Schedule 7 (Particulars of Properties);

'Provisional Consideration' has the meaning given in Schedule 5 (Adjustment of Consideration);

['Purchaser's Group' means the Purchaser and each of its Affiliates];

'Restricted Business' has the meaning given in Sub-Clause 7.1 (Restricted Business);

'Sale Shares' means the shares to be bought and sold pursuant to Clause 2.1 (Sale of Shares) being all the issued shares in the capital of the Company;

'Subsidiaries'[8] means the bodies corporate, details of which arc set out in Schedule 2 (The Subsidiaries);

'Tax Deed'[9] means the deed of indemnity in agreed terms relating to taxation, to be executed and delivered at Completion;

'Vendor's Group' means the Vendor and each of its Affiliates other than the Company and the Subsidiaries; and

'Warranties'[10] means the warranties and representations set out in Paragraph 2 of Schedule 3 (Warranties and Representations), in Paragraph 2 of Schedule 4 (Taxation Warranties and Representations) and in Paragraph [4/8/2] of Schedule 6 (Pensions).

1.2   Construction of Certain References

In this Agreement, where the context admits:

(A)   words and phrases the definitions of which are contained or referred to in Part XXVI of the Companies Act 1985 shall be construed as having the meanings thereby attributed to them;

(B) references to statutory provisions shall be construed as references to those provisions as amended or re-enacted or as their application is modified by other provisions from time to time and shall include references to any provisions of which they are re-enactments (whether with or without modification);

(C) where any statement is qualified by the expression 'so far as the Vendor is aware' or 'to the best of the Vendor's knowledge and belief' or any similar expression, that statement shall be deemed to include an additional statement that it has been made after due and careful enquiry;[11]

(D) references to Clauses and Schedules are references to Clauses and schedules of and to this Agreement, references to Sub-Clauses or Paragraphs are, unless otherwise stated, references to Sub-Clauses of the Clause or paragraphs of the Schedule in which the reference appears, and references to this Agreement include the Schedules;

(E) references to any document being in 'agreed terms' or in 'agreed form' are to that document in the form signed or initialled by or on behalf of the parties for identification; and

(F) references to the Vendors include a reference to each of them.

[1.3 Joint and Several Liabilities[12]

All warranties, representations, indemnities, covenants, agreements and obligations given or entered into by more than one person in this Agreement are given or entered into jointly and severally.]

1.4 Headings

The headings and sub-headings are inserted for convenience only and shall not affect the construction of this Agreement.

1.5 Schedules

Each of the Schedules shall have effect as if set out herein.

2 Sale of Shares

2.1 Sale and Purchase

Subject to the terms of this Agreement, the Vendor with full title guarantee[13] shall sell and the Purchaser shall purchase, free from all encumbrances and together with all rights now or hereafter attaching thereto the entire issued share capital of the Company [comprising [   ] [ordinary] shares of £[   ] each] *[and in respect of each individual Vendor the number of Sale Shares set opposite his name in the second column of Part 1 of Schedule 1.]*

2.2 No Sale of Part Only

Neither the Purchaser nor the Vendor shall be obliged to complete the purchase of any of the Sale Shares unless the purchase of all the Sale Shares is completed simultaneously.

2.3 *Waiver of Pre-emption Rights*

Each of the Vendors hereby waives any pre-emption rights he may have relating to the Sale Shares, whether conferred by the Company's Articles of Association or otherwise.

3 Consideration

3.1 Amount [Consideration Shares]

The total consideration for the Sale Shares shall be the sum of £[   ], but subject to adjustment as provided in Schedules 5 and 6 and in the Tax Deed.

[The total consideration for the Sale Shares shall be the allotment to the Vendor of [   ] Consideration Shares].

3.2 Placing[14]

The total consideration for the Sale Shares shall be the allotment and issue of such number of Consideration Shares as will result in net proceeds of not less than £[   ] to persons nominated by the Bank (or failing the procurement and nomination of such persons by the Bank, and to the extent it does not so procure and nominate such persons, to the Bank) and the procurement of the payment of £[   ] by or on behalf of the Bank to the Vendor, payment to be made as provided in Clause 5.3 (Purchaser's Obligations).

3.3 Dividends Etc

The Consideration Shares shall rank *pari passu* and as a single class with the ordinary shares of [   ] each in the Purchaser in issue at the date of this Agreement, and shall carry the right to receive in full all dividends and other distributions declared, made or paid after the date of this Agreement [save that they shall not carry the right to participate in the [interim] [final] dividend of the Purchaser for the year ending [   ] 19[   ] [declared on [   ]].[15]

4 Conditions[16]

4.1 Conditions

Completion is conditional upon:

[(A) the passing at a duly convened and held general meeting of the Vendor/Purchaser/
[   ] of a resolution in the agreed form to approve the [acquisition/sale] of the Sale Shares and other arrangements on the terms of this Agreement;[17]
(B) the passing at a duly convened and held general meeting of the Purchaser of a resolution [in an agreed form] to [increase the Purchaser's authorised share capital so that it is at least sufficient to allot [   ] Consideration Shares] [grant the directors of the Purchaser authority to allot [   ] Consideration Shares] [to disapply pre-emption rights to permit a cash placing] [to alter the Purchaser's articles of association eg the borrowing limit; create new class of Consideration Shares] [to approve the arrangements in this agreement];[17]
(C) the agreement by the London Stock Exchange to admit the Consideration Shares to the Official List ('Admission') subject (if applicable) only to allotment and listing and the Admission having become fully effective as evidenced by the making of an announcement in respect thereof under paragraph 7.1 of the listing rules issued by the London Stock Exchange;[18]
(D) the Placing Agreement being entered into and becoming, in accordance with its terms, unconditional in all respects (other than in respect of any condition relating to the Completion of this Agreement) or (with the consent of the Purchaser) such conditions having been waived and the Placing Agreement not having lapsed or been terminated by the Bank in accordance with its terms;[19] and

(E)[20] the Office of Fair Trading indicating in terms satisfactory to the Purchaser that the Secretary of State for Trade and Industry in the exercise of his powers under the Fair Trading Act 1973 does not intend to refer the acquisition contemplated by this Agreement or any matter arising therefrom or relating thereto to the Monopolies and Mergers Commission;[21]

and/or

the European Commission indicating in terms satisfactory to the Purchaser that the acquisition contemplated by this Agreement or any matter arising therefrom or relating thereto does not fall within the scope of Council Regulation (EEC) 4064/89 or in the alternative that it does not intend either to initiate proceedings under Art 6(1)(c) thereof or to make a referral to a competent authority under Art 9(1) thereof;[21]

and in the event that the above conditions shall not have been satisfied [or waived by the Purchaser] on or before [   ] 19[   ] this Agreement shall lapse and no party shall make any claim against any other in respect hereof, save for any antecedent breach (including any breach of Sub-Clause 4.2 (Satisfaction)).

[4.2 Satisfaction

The Purchaser shall use its reasonable endeavours to procure the satisfaction of the Conditions set out in Sub-Clauses 4.1((B)–(E). The Vendor shall use its reasonable endeavours to satisfy or procure the satisfaction of all other of the Conditions and shall notify the Purchaser immediately upon the satisfaction of all such Conditions. The Vendor[22] undertakes to and agrees with the Purchaser that the directors of [name relevant company] will post a circular to shareholders on or before [   ] recommending its shareholders to vote in favour of the resolutions referred to in Sub-Clause 4.1(A) stating that the directors have considered all aspects of the sale and are of the opinion that it is in the best interests of the shareholders of [name relevant company].]

4.3   Waiver

The Purchaser may waive in whole or in part all or any of [the Conditions] [list relevant conditions] or extend the period in which [the Conditions] [list relevant conditions] are to be satisfied.

5   Completion

5.1   Date and Place of Completion

Completion shall take place on the Completion Date at the offices of [   ] at [am/pm].

5.2   Vendor's Obligations[23]

On Completion the Vendor shall:

(A)   deliver to the Purchaser:
   (1)   duly executed transfers of the Sale Shares by the registered holders thereof in favour of the Purchaser or its nominees together with the relative share certificates;
   (2)   such waivers or consents as the Purchaser may require[24] to enable the Purchaser or its nominees to be registered as holders of the Sale Shares; and
   (3)   powers of attorney in an agreed form;[25]
(B)   procure that the Directors (other than the Continuing Directors) and the secretary or secretaries of the Company and the Subsidiaries retire from all their offices and

employments with the Company and the Subsidiaries, each delivering to the Purchaser a deed (in the agreed terms) made out in favour of the Company and/or the Subsidiaries acknowledging that he has no claim outstanding for compensation or otherwise and without any payment under the Employment Rights Act 1996;[26]

(C) procure the resignation of the auditors of the Company and the Subsidiaries in accordance with s 293 of the Companies Act 1985, accompanied by a written statement pursuant to s 394 of that Act that there are no circumstances connected with their resignation which should be brought to the notice of the members or creditors of each such company and that no fees are due to them and deliver such resignation and statement to the Purchaser;[27]

(D) deliver to the Purchaser as agent for the Company and the Subsidiaries:

(1) all the statutory and other books (duly written up to date) of the Company and each of the Subsidiaries and its/their certificate(s) of incorporation, any certificates of incorporation on change of name and common seal(s);[28]

(2) certificates in respect of all issued shares in the capital of each of the Subsidiaries and transfers of all shares in any Subsidiary not held by the Company in favour of such persons as the Purchaser shall direct;[29]

(3) the title deeds to the Properties[30] [other than in respect to those Properties:

(a) which are disclosed in the Disclosure Letter as being charged and the title deeds as being held by the chargee; and

(b) for which a certificate of title is to be produced as referred to in Sub-Clause (4)];

(4) a certificate from [   ] in agreed terms as to the title of the Company or the Subsidiaries to [the Properties];[31] and

(5) (or procure the delivery of) service agreements, in the agreed terms, between [   ] and the Company, [each] executed by [   ];[32]

(E) deliver the Tax Deed duly executed by [   ];

(F) procure a board meeting of the Company and of each of the Subsidiaries to be held at which there shall be:

(1) passed a resolution to register, in the case of the Company, the transfers of the Sale Shares and, in the case of the Subsidiaries, the share transfers referred to in Sub-Clause (D)(2) and (subject only to due stamping)[33] to register, in the register of members, each transferee as the holder of the shares concerned;

(2) appointed as directors and/or secretary such persons as the Purchaser may nominate [such appointments to take effect [   ]];

(3) tendered and accepted the resignations and acknowledgements of the directors and secretary referred to in Sub-Clause (B) [each such acceptance to take effect at the close of the meeting];

(4) revoked all existing authorities to banks and new authorities shall be given to such banks and on such terms as the Purchaser may direct;

(5) changed the situation of the registered office and (subject to the Companies Acts) the accounting reference date, each as the Purchaser may direct; and

(6) tendered and accepted the resignation of the auditors and appointing [   ] as new auditors of each of the Company and the Subsidiaries; and

(7) approved and entered into service agreements, in the agreed terms, between [   ] and the Company];

(G) deliver to the Purchaser, certified as correct by the secretary of the relevant company, the minutes of each such board meeting;

(H) procure the discharge of all guarantees and like obligations given by the Company or any of the Subsidiaries in respect of the obligations of [any other person] (and including the guarantees and obligations stipulated to be discharged at Completion in the Disclosure Letter), such discharge to be given in the agreed terms;[34] and

(I) [other][35]

5.3 Purchaser's Obligations

On Completion the Purchaser shall:

(A) [pay] [satisfy] the consideration for the Sale Shares as provided by Clause 3 [and procure the payment referred to in Sub-Clause 3.2 (Placing)] [any payment in cash to be made] by way of banker's draft drawn on a [City of London] branch of a clearing bank and made payable to the Vendor [or as it may direct]; [and]

(B) deposit the sum of £[   ] on the terms of Sub-Clause 8.9 (Application of Deposit);][and

(C) any others.]

5.4 Failure to Complete[36]

If in any respect the obligations of the Vendor or Purchaser are not complied with on the Completion Date the party not in default may:

(A) defer Completion to a date not more than 28 days after the Completion Date (and so that the provisions of this Sub-Clause 5.4, apart from this item, shall apply to Completion as so deferred); or

(B) proceed to Completion so far as practicable (without prejudice to its rights hereunder); or

(C) rescind this Agreement.

6 Purchaser's Right of Access[37]

6.1 From the date hereof the Purchaser and any persons authorised by it, upon reasonable notice [and subject to such confidentiality undertakings as the Vendor may reasonably require] shall be allowed full access to all the premises, books and records of the Company and the Subsidiaries, and the Vendor shall supply or procure the supply of any information reasonably required by the Purchaser relating to the Company, the Subsidiaries and their respective affairs.

7 Restriction *of Vendor['s Group]* [38]

7.1 Restricted Business[39]

In this Clause, 'Restricted Business' means [business activities] within [country or area] and which directly or indirectly competes with the business of the Company or any of the Subsidiaries carried on at the date of this Agreement.

7.2 Covenants

The Vendor undertakes with the Purchaser (as trustee for itself and the Company) and its successors in title that it will not *and that it will procure that none of its Affiliates will:*

(A) for the period of [   ][39] after the date of this Agreement, either on its own account or in conjunction with or on behalf of any person, firm or company, carry on or be engaged, concerned or interested (directly or indirectly and whether as principal, shareholder, director, employee, agent, consultant, partner or otherwise) in carrying on any Restricted Business (other than as a holder of less than 5 per cent of any class of shares or debentures listed on the London Stock Exchange or any other recognised stock exchange);

(B)   for the period of   ]^{39} after the date of this Agreement, either on its own account or in conjunction with or on behalf of any person, firm or company, solicit or endeavour to entice away from the Company or any of the Subsidiaries any person who at the date of this Agreement is (or who within a period of one year prior to the date of this Agreement has been) a director, officer, manager, employee or servant of the Company or any of the Subsidiaries whether or not such person would commit a breach of contract by reason of leaving service or office;

(C)   for the period of [   ]^{39} after the date of this Agreement, either on its own account or in conjunction with or on behalf of any person, firm or company, in connection with any Restricted Business deal with, solicit the custom of or endeavour to entice away from the Company or any of the Subsidiaries any person who at the date of this Agreement is (or who within a period of one year prior to the date of this Agreement has been) a customer of the Company or any of the Subsidiaries whether or not such person would commit a breach of contract by reason of transferring business;

(D)   for the period of [   ]^{39} after the date of this Agreement, either on its own account or in conjunction with or on behalf of any person, firm or company, in connection with any Restricted Business endeavour to entice away from the Company or any of the Subsidiaries any person who at the date of this Agreement is (or who within a period of one year prior to the date of this Agreement has been) a supplier of the Company or any of the Subsidiaries whether or not such person would commit a breach of contract by reason of transferring business;^{40} and

(E)   at any time after the date of this Agreement, directly or indirectly use or attempt to use in the course of any business on its own account or in conjunction with or on behalf of any person, firm or company, any trade or service mark, trade name, design or logo (whether registered or not and including the Listed Intellectual Property referred to in Schedule 3) used in the business of the Company or any of the Subsidiaries or any other name, logo, trade or service mark or design which is or might be confusingly similar thereto [exceptions for group logos etc].

7.3   Vendor to Procure Compliance

The Vendor undertakes to take all such steps as shall from time to time be necessary to ensure compliance with the terms of Sub-Clause 7.2 above by employees and agents of the Vendor or any of its Affiliates.

7.4   Separate Covenants

Each of the undertakings in Sub-Clauses 7.2 and 7.3 shall be construed as a separate and independent undertaking and if one or more of the undertakings is held to be void or unenforceable, the validity of the remaining undertakings shall not be affected.

7.5   Reasonableness

The Vendor agrees that the restrictions and undertakings contained in Sub-Clauses 7.2 and 7.3 are reasonable and necessary for the protection of the Purchaser's legitimate interests in the goodwill of the Company and the Subsidiaries, but if any such restriction or undertaking shall be found to be void or voidable but would be valid and enforceable if some part or parts of the restriction or undertaking were deleted, such restriction or undertaking shall apply with such modification as may be necessary to make it valid and enforceable.^{41}

7.6   Void or Unenforceable Restrictions

Without prejudice to Sub-Clause 7.5, if any restriction or undertaking is found by any court or other competent authority to be void or unenforceable the parties shall negotiate in good faith to replace such void or unenforceable restriction or undertaking with a valid provision which, as far as possible, has the same legal and commercial effect as that which it replaces.

7.7   Registration[42]

Any provision of this Agreement, or of any agreement or arrangement of which it forms part, by virtue of which such agreement or arrangement is subject to registration under the Restrictive Trade Practices Act 1976 shall take effect only the day after particulars of such agreement or arrangement have been duly furnished to the Director General of Fair Trading pursuant to s 24 of that Act.

7.8   Confidential Information Concerning the Company

The Vendor shall not and shall procure that *no other member of the Vendor's Group* nor any officer or employee of the Vendor *or any member of the Vendor's Group* shall make use of or divulge to any third party (other than to the Vendor's professional advisers for the purpose of this Agreement in which case the Vendor shall use all reasonable endeavours to procure that such advisers keep such information confidential on terms equivalent to this Clause) any confidential information relating to the Company and the Subsidiaries save only:

(A)   insofar as the same has become public knowledge otherwise than, directly or indirectly, through the Vendor's breach of this Sub-Clause 7.8 or the failure of the officers, employees or professional advisers referred to above to keep the same confidential; or

(B)   to the extent required by law or by any supervisory or regulatory body.

8   Warranties and Deposit

8.1   General

The Vendor[s][43] hereby [*jointly and severally*][12] warrant[s] and represent[s] to the Purchaser in the terms of the Warranties and acknowledge and accept that the Purchaser is entering into this Agreement in reliance upon each of the Warranties.

8.2   Purchaser's knowledge

The Warranties are given subject to matters fairly disclosed in this Agreement or in the Disclosure Letter, but no other information relating to the Company or the Subsidiaries of which the Purchaser has knowledge (actual or constructive) shall prejudice any claim made by the Purchaser under the Warranties or operate to reduce any amount recoverable.[44] The provisions of s 6(2) of the Law of Property (Miscellaneous Provisions) Act 1994 are hereby excluded.[45]

8.3   Warranties to be independent

Each of the Warranties shall be separate and independent and, save as expressly provided, shall not be limited by reference to any other Warranty or anything in this Agreement.

8.4   Damages[46]

Without restricting the rights of the Purchaser or the ability of the Purchaser to claim damages on any basis in the event that any of the Warranties is broken or proves to be untrue or misleading, the Vendor hereby covenants to pay, on demand, to the Purchaser:

(A)   the amount necessary to put the Company and each of the Subsidiaries into the position which would have existed if the Warranties had not been broken and had been true and not misleading; and

(B)   all costs and expenses incurred by the Purchaser, the Company or the Subsidiaries, directly or indirectly, as a result of such breach.

8.5   Pending Completion[47]

The Vendor shall procure that (save only as may be necessary to give effect to this Agreement) neither the Vendor *nor any member of the Vendor's Group* nor the Company nor any of the Subsidiaries shall do, allow or procure any act or omission before Completion which would constitute a breach of any of the Warranties if they were given at any and all times from the date hereof down to Completion or which would make any of the Warranties inaccurate or misleading if they were so given. In particular, the Vendor shall procure that paragraphs 2.7(A)(1) to 2.7(A)(9) of Schedule 3 (Warranties) shall be complied with at all times from the date hereof down to Completion.[48]

[8.6   Liaison on Conduct of Business[47;49]

The Vendor shall in addition and without limiting Sub-Clause 8.5 (Pending Completion) procure that, from the date of this Agreement until Completion, the business of the Company and the Subsidiaries is carried on in the usual and normal course and that none of the Company or the Subsidiaries shall enter into any contract or commitment or do anything which, in any such case, is either out of the ordinary and usual course of its business or of a material nature without the prior consent in writing of the Purchaser. In particular, but without limiting the foregoing, the Vendor shall procure that from the date of this Agreement until Completion, save with the prior consent in writing of the Purchaser, none of the Company or the Subsidiaries shall:

(A)   make any alteration to its memorandum or articles of association or any other document or agreement establishing, evidencing or relating to its constitution or operation;

(B)   alter the nature or scope of its business;

(C)   manage its business otherwise than in accordance with its business and trading policies and practice to date as disclosed to the Purchaser, except as may be necessary to comply with any legislative changes;

(D)   enter into any agreement or arrangement or permit any action whereby another company becomes its subsidiary or subsidiary undertaking;

(E)   enter into any transaction other than on arm's length terms and for full and proper consideration;

(F)   acquire or enter into any agreement to acquire (whether by one transaction or by a series of transactions) the whole or a substantial or material part of the business, undertaking or assets of any other person;

(G)   dispose of or enter into any agreement to dispose of (whether by one transaction or by a series of transactions) the whole or any substantial or material part of its business, undertaking or assets;

(H)   incur or agree to incur any capital expenditure with a value in excess of £[   ];

(I) take or agree to take any loans, borrowings or other form of funding or financial facility or assistance, or enter into or agree to enter into any foreign exchange contracts, interest rate swaps, collars, guarantees or agreements or other interest rate instruments;

(J) grant or agree to grant any loans or other financial facilities or assistance to or any guarantees or indemnities for the benefit of any person or create or allow to subsist any mortgage, charge or other encumbrance over the whole or any part of its undertaking, property or assets;

(K) enter into or agree to enter into any joint venture, partnership or agreement or arrangement for the sharing of profits or assets;

(L) enter into or agree to enter into any death, retirement, profit sharing, bonus, share option, share incentive or other scheme for the benefit of any of its officers or employees or make any variation (including, but without limitation, any increase in the rates of contribution) to any such existing scheme or effect any key man insurance;

(M) commence, compromise or discontinue any legal or arbitration proceedings (other than routine debt collection);

(N) prematurely repay or prepay any loans, borrowings or other financial facilities or assistance made available to it;

(O) terminate the employment or office of any of its directors, officers or senior employees (here meaning an employee whose present gross annual remuneration exceeds £[   ]) or appoint any new director, officer or senior employee or consultant or materially alter the terms of employment or engagement of any director, senior employee or consultant;

(P) declare, make or pay any dividend or distribution (whether of capital or of profits);

(Q) make or agree to any amendment, variation, deletion, addition, renewal or extension to or of, or terminate or give any notice or intimation of termination of, or breach or fail to comply with the terms of any contract or arrangement having a value of greater than £[   ];[50]

(R) pay or agree to pay any remuneration, fee or other sum to any Vendor, any person connected with [(as such expression is defined in Schedule 3)] or controlled by any Vendor (other than remuneration properly accrued due or reimbursement of business expenses properly incurred, in each case as disclosed in the Disclosure Letter).]

8.7 Further Disclosure by Vendor[47]

The Vendor [without prejudice to Sub-Clause 8.6 (Liaison on Conduct of Business)] shall forthwith disclose in writing to the Purchaser any matter or thing which may arise or become known to the Vendor after the date hereof and before Completion which is inconsistent with any of the Warranties or which might make any of them inaccurate or misleading if they were given at any and all times from the date hereof down to Completion or which is material to be known to a purchaser for value of the Sale Shares.

8.8 Rescission[47]

In the event of any matter or thing that is mentioned in Sub-Clause 8.5 becoming known to the Purchaser before Completion or in the event of it becoming apparent on or before Completion that the Vendor is in [material][51] breach of any of the Warranties or any other term of this Agreement, the Purchaser may at its option either:

(A) rescind this Agreement by notice in writing to the Vendor; or

(B) proceed to Completion but without prejudice to its right to claim for breach of this Agreement or such Warranties.

8.9   Application of Deposit[52]

Subject to Sub-Clauses 8.10 (Interest) and 8.11 (Release), the Purchaser may apply all or part of the deposit referred to in Clause 5.3(B) (Purchaser's Obligations) (the 'Deposit') in recouping any amount lawfully due to it under or by reason of any breach of the terms of this Agreement or the Tax Deed and any amount so applied shall *pro tanto* satisfy the liability concerned.]

8.10   Interest[53]

The Deposit shall be deposited by the Purchaser with bankers selected by it and any interest earned shall accrue to and form part of the Deposit and such interest (net of any tax required by law to be deducted therefrom) shall, accordingly, belong to the Vendor subject to the provisions of this Agreement.

8.11   Release[54]

In the event that the Purchaser shall not have notified the Vendor in writing of any claim under this Agreement before [   ] 19[   ] the Deposit shall be released to the Vendor's solicitors [   ] whose receipt shall be an absolute discharge. If the Purchaser shall have so notified any such claim, it shall use its best endeavours to quantify the amount claimed and any balance shall be so released on that date. Upon final determination of the total amount (if any) falling to be applied by the Purchaser under this Sub-Clause, any balance of the Deposit shall be released to the Vendor's solicitors provided that no amount shall be released before [   ] 19 [   ].

8.12   Waiver of Claims

The Vendor undertakes to the Purchaser that it will not make or pursue any claim which it has or may have against the Company, the Subsidiaries or any of the Employees (as such term is defined in Schedule 3 (Warranties), para 2.11(B)(1)) in respect of or arising out of the Warranties or any information supplied by them to or on behalf of the Vendor or its professional advisers or agents on or prior to the date hereof.

9   Confidentiality

9.1   Confidentiality[55]

Subject to Sub-Clause 9.2 (Permitted Disclosures) and to Clause 10 (Announcements) and without prejudice to Sub-Clause 7.8 (Confidential Information Concerning the Company), each party:

(A)   shall treat as strictly confidential information obtained or received by it as a result of entering into or performing its obligations under this Agreement and relating to the negotiations concerning, or the provisions or subject matter of, this Agreement or the other party ('confidential information'); and

(B)   shall not, except with the prior written consent of the other party (which shall not be unreasonably withheld or delayed), publish or otherwise disclose to any person any confidential information.

9.2   Permitted Disclosures

Sub-Clause 9.1 (Confidentiality) shall not apply if and to the extent that [the party proposing to make such disclosure can demonstrate that]:

(A)   such disclosure is required by law or by any securities exchange or regulatory or governmental body having jurisdiction over it (including the London Stock Exchange, the Panel on Take-overs and Mergers or the Serious Fraud Office) and whether or not the requirement has the force of law;

(B) the confidential information was lawfully in its possession prior to its disclosure by the other party (as evidenced by written records) and had not been obtained from that other party; or

(C) the confidential information has come into the public domain other than through its fault or the fault of any person to whom the confidential information has been disclosed.

9.3 Continuance of Restrictions

The restrictions contained in this Clause on the part of the Vendor shall survive Completion.

10 Announcements

10.1 Restriction[56]

Subject to Sub-Clause 10.2 (Permitted Announcements), neither the Vendor nor the Purchaser shall make any announcement, whether to the public, to the customers or suppliers of the Company, or to all or any of the employees of the Company, concerning the subject matter of this Agreement without the prior written approval of the other (which shall not be unreasonably withheld or delayed).

10.2 Permitted Announcements

Sub-Clause 10.1 (Restriction) shall not apply if and to the extent that such announcement is required by law or by any securities exchange or regulatory or governmental body having jurisdiction over it (including the London Stock Exchange, The Panel on Take-overs and Mergers and the Serious Fraud Office) and whether or not the requirement has the force of law and provided that any such announcement shall be made only after consultation with the other party.

10.3 Continuance of Restrictions

The restrictions contained in this Clause on the part of the Vendor shall survive Completion.

11 Provisions Relating to this Agreement

11.1 Assignment[57]

This Agreement shall be binding upon and inure for the benefit of the successors of the parties but shall not be assignable, save that the Purchaser may at any time assign all or any part of its rights and benefits under this Agreement, including the Warranties and any cause of action arising under or in respect of any of them, to any transferee of the share capital of the Company or of any of the Subsidiaries, or to any Affiliate of the Purchaser who may enforce them as if he had also been named in this Agreement as the Purchaser.

11.2 Whole Agreement[58]

(A) This Agreement, together with any documents referred to in it, constitutes the whole agreement between the parties relating to its subject matter and supersedes and extinguishes any prior drafts, agreements, undertakings, representations, war-

ranties, assurances and arrangements of any nature, whether in writing or oral, relating to such subject matter.

[(B) The Purchaser acknowledges that it has not been induced to enter into this Agreement by any representation, warranty, promise or assurance by the Vendor or any
other person save for those contained in this Agreement and in the Disclosure Letter. The Purchaser agrees that (except in respect of fraud) it shall have no right or
remedy in respect of any other representation, warranty, promise or assurance save
for those contained in this Agreement. The Purchaser acknowledges that its legal
advisers have explained to it the effect of this Sub-Clause 11.2(B).][58]

(C) No variation of this Agreement shall be effective unless made in writing and
signed by each of the parties.[59]

11.3 Agreement Survives Completion

The Warranties and all other provisions of this Agreement in so far as the same shall not
have been performed at Completion, shall remain in full force and effect notwithstanding Completion.

11.4 Rights etc Cumulative and Other Matters

(A) The rights, powers, privileges and remedies provided in this Agreement are cumulative and are not exclusive of any rights, powers, privileges or remedies provided
by law or otherwise.

(B) No failure to exercise nor any delay in exercising any right, power, privilege or
remedy under this Agreement shall in any way impair or affect the exercise thereof
or operate as a waiver thereof in whole or in part.

(C) No single or partial exercise of any right, power, privilege or remedy under this
Agreement shall prevent any further or other exercise thereof or the exercise of
any other right, power, privilege or remedy.

[11.5 Release of One Vendor[60]

*The Purchaser may release or compromise the liability of any of the Vendors hereunder
without affecting the liability of the other Vendors.*]

11.6 Further Assurance

At any time after the date hereof the Vendor shall, at the request and cost of the Purchaser, execute or procure the execution of such documents and do or procure the doing
of such acts and things as the Purchaser may reasonably require for the purpose of vesting the Sale Shares in the Purchaser or its nominees and giving to the Purchaser the full
benefit of all the provisions of this Agreement.

11.7 Invalidity

If any provision of this Agreement shall be held to be illegal, void, invalid or unenforceable under the laws of any jurisdiction, the legality, validity and enforceability of the
remainder of this Agreement in that jurisdiction shall not be affected, and the legality,
validity and enforceability of the whole of this Agreement in any other jurisdiction shall
not be affected.

[11.8 Payment to the Vendor

[Any payment falling to be made to the Vendor under any provision of this Agreement
may be made to the Vendor's solicitors, [   ], whose receipt shall be an absolute discharge.]

11.9 Counterparts

This Agreement may be executed in any number of counterparts, which shall together constitute one Agreement. Any party may enter into this Agreement by signing any such counterpart.

11.10 Costs

Each party shall bear its own costs arising out of or in connection with the preparation, negotiation and implementation of this Agreement save that if this Agreement is lawfully rescinded by the Purchaser the Vendor shall pay to the Purchaser its accountancy legal and [   ] costs in relation to the investigation of the Company prior to the date hereof and the preparation and negotiation of this Agreement [up to an aggregate limit of £[   ] (inclusive of VAT).]

11.11 Notices[61]

(A) Any notice or other communication required to be given under this Agreement or in connection with the matters contemplated by it shall, except where otherwise specifically provided, be in writing in the English language and shall be addressed as provided in Sub-Clause (B) and may be:
  (1) personally delivered, in which case it shall be deemed to have been given upon delivery at the relevant address; or
  (2) if within the United Kingdom, sent by first class pre-paid post, in which case it shall be deemed to have been given two Business Days after the date of posting; or
  (3) [if from or to any place outside the United Kingdom, sent by pre-paid priority airmail, in which case it shall be deemed to have been given seven Business Days after the date of posting; or]
  (4) sent by fax, in which case it shall be deemed to have been given when despatched, subject to confirmation of uninterrupted transmission by a transmission report[, or sent by telex, in which case it shall be deemed to have been given when despatched, provided the recipient's answer back code is duly received by the sender at the start and end of the message,] provided that any notice despatched by fax [or telex] after 17.00 hours (at the place where such fax [or telex] is to be received) on any day shall be deemed to have been received at [08.00] on the next Business Day.
(B) The addresses and other details of the parties referred to in Sub-Clause (A) are, subject to Sub-Clause (C):

Name:

[For the attention of:]

Address:

Fax number:

[Telex number:]

(C) Any party to this Agreement may notify the other parties of any change to its address or other details specified in Sub-Clause (B), provided that such notification shall be effective only on the date specified in such notice or five Business Days after the notice is given, whichever is later[.][, and provided also that any new address shall be in the United Kingdom.]

12 Law and Jurisdiction

12.1 English Law

This Agreement shall be governed by, and construed in accordance with, English law.

12.2 Jurisdiction[62]

In relation to any legal action or proceedings to enforce this Agreement or arising out of or in connection with this Agreement ('proceedings') each of the parties irrevocably submits to the jurisdiction of the English courts and waives any objection to proceedings in such courts on the grounds of venue or on the grounds that the proceedings have been brought in an inconvenient forum.

[12.3 Process Agent[63]

The Vendor appoints [   ] of [   ] as its process agent to receive on its behalf service of process in any proceedings in England. Service upon the process agent shall be good service upon the Vendor whether or not it is forwarded to and received by the Vendor. If for any reason the process agent ceases to be able to act as process agent, or no longer has an address in England, the Vendor irrevocably agrees to appoint a substitute process agent with an address in England acceptable to the Purchaser and to deliver to the Purchaser a copy of the substitute process agent's acceptance of that appointment within 30 days. In the event that the Vendor fails to appoints a substitute process agent, it shall be effective service for the Purchaser to serve the process upon the last known address in England of the last known process agent for the Vendor notified to the Purchaser, notwithstanding that such process agent is no longer found at such address or has ceased to act.]

AS WITNESS the hands of the duly authorised representatives of the parties on the date first before written.

SCHEDULE 1

THE VENDORS AND THE COMPANY

PART I:

Vendor   *No Sale Shares*

PART II:

Name:

Number:

Registered Office:

Authorised Capital:

Issued Capital:

Directors and other
directorships:

Secretary:

Accounting Reference Date:

Auditors:

Continuing Directors:

SCHEDULE 2

THE SUBSIDIARIES

[PART I]

Name:

Number:

Registered Office:

Authorised Capital:

Issued Capital:

Registered Shareholders:

Beneficial owner of
issued capital:

Directors and other
directorships:

Secretary:

Accounting Reference Date:

Auditors:

Continuing Directors:

[Repeat for each Subsidiary ie Part II, Part III...]

SCHEDULE 3

WARRANTIES AND REPRESENTATIONS[64]

1　Interpretation

1.1　In this Schedule, where the context admits:

'Computer Systems' means the Hardware, Software and Data;[65]

'Data' means any data or information used by or for the benefit of the Company at any time and stored electronically at any time;

'Hardware' means any computer equipment used by or for the benefit of the Company at any time including, without limitation, PCs, mainframes, screens, terminals, keyboards, disks, printers, cabling, associated and peripheral electronic equipment but excluding all Software;

'Intellectual Property' means patents, trade marks, service marks, rights (registered or unregistered) in any designs; applications for any of the foregoing; trade or business names; copyright [(including rights in computer software) and topography rights; know-how; secret formulae and processes; lists of suppliers and customers and other confidential and proprietary knowledge and information; rights protecting goodwill and reputation; database rights and rights under licences and consents in relation to such things and all rights or forms of protection of a similar nature to any of the foregoing or having equivalent effect anywhere in the world];[66]

'Intellectual Property Agreements' means agreements or arrangements relating in any way whether wholly or partly to Intellectual Property;

'Listed Intellectual Property' means the intellectual property referred to in the list annexed to the Disclosure Letter;

'Listed Intellectual Property Agreements' means the Intellectual Property Agreements set out in the list annexed to the Disclosure Letter;

'Software' means any set of instructions for execution by microprocessor used by or for the benefit of the Company at any time irrespective of application, language or medium;

[any question whether a person is connected with another shall be determined in accordance with Income and Corporation Taxes Act 1988, s 839 (subject to the deletion of the words from 'Except' to 'arrangements' in sub-section (4) thereof) which shall apply in relation to this Schedule as it applies in relation to that Act;][67]

references to the 'Company' include each of the Subsidiaries; and

reference to any Act, statutory instrument, regulation, bye-law or other requirement of English law and to any English legal term for any action, remedy, method of judicial proceeding, legal document, legal status, court, official or any legal concept or thing shall in respect of any jurisdiction other than England be deemed to include that which most nearly approximates in that jurisdiction to the English legal term.

Where, in this Schedule, a term is defined in and for the purposes of a particular paragraph or Sub-Paragraph the relevant definition shall apply, where the context admits, for all other purposes of this Schedule.

2   Warranties and Representations[68]

The Vendor[s] hereby *jointly and severally* warrant[s] and represent[s][68] to and for the benefit of the Purchaser in the following terms.

2.1   The Company and the Vendor[69]

(A)   *Capacity*   The Vendor has full power and authority to enter into and perform this Agreement, may execute and deliver this Agreement and perform its obligations under this Agreement without requiring or obtaining the consent of its shareholders or of any other person, authority or body and this Agreement constitutes valid and binding obligations on the Vendor in accordance with its terms.

(B)   *Ownership of Sale Shares*   The Vendor is the registered and sole beneficial owner of the Sale Shares free from any encumbrances.

(C)   *Liabilities Owing to or by Vendor*   There is not outstanding any indebtedness or other liability (actual or contingent) owing by the Company *to any member of the Vendor's Group* or to any Director or any person connected with any of them, nor is there any indebtedness owing to the Company by any such person, [and no promise or representation has been made to the Vendor in connection with the Warranties or the Disclosure Letter in respect of which the Company or any of the Subsidiaries might be liable].

(D)   *Competing Interests*   No member of the Vendor's Group nor any person connected with any such member has any interest, direct or indirect, in any business other than that now carried on by the Company which is or is likely to be or become competitive with the business or any proposed business of the Company [save as the registered holder or beneficial owner of not more than 5 per cent of any class of securities of any company which is listed in the Official List of The London Stock Exchange Limited or dealt in on the Alternative Investment Market].

2.2   The Company's Constitution

(A)   *Share Capital*   The Sale Shares comprise the whole of the issued and allotted share capital of the Company and Schedule 2 contains true particulars of the authorised and issued share capital of the Subsidiaries and all the shares there shown as issued are in issue fully paid and are beneficially owned and registered as set out therein free from any encumbrances.

(B)   *Options etc*   No person has the right (whether exercisable now or in the future and whether contingent or not) to call for the allotment, issue, sale, transfer or conversion of any share or loan capital of the Company under any option or other agreement (including conversion rights and rights of pre-emption).

(C)   *Memorandum and Articles*   The copy of the memorandum and articles of association of the Company annexed to the Disclosure Letter is true and complete and has embodied therein or annexed thereto a copy of every resolution or agreement as is required by law to be embodied in or annexed to it, and sets out completely the rights and restrictions attaching to each class of authorised share capital of the Company.

(D)   *Company Resolutions*   Neither the Company nor any class of its members has passed any resolution (other than resolutions relating to business at annual general meetings which was not special business).

2.3 The Company and its Investments

(A) *Particulars of the Company and Subsidiaries* The particulars of the Company and the Subsidiaries set out in Schedules 1 and 2 are true and complete and the Company has no other subsidiary.

(B) *Investments, Associations and Branches* The Company:

(1) is not the holder or beneficial owner of, and has not agreed to acquire, any class of the share or other capital of any other company or corporation (whether incorporated in the United Kingdom or elsewhere) other than of the Subsidiaries;

(2) is not, and has not agreed to become, a member of any partnership, joint venture, consortium or other unincorporated association, body or undertaking in which it is to participate with any other in any business or investment; and

(3) has no branch, agency or place of business outside England and no permanent establishment (as that expression is defined in the relevant double taxation relief orders current at the date of this Agreement) outside the United Kingdom.

[(C) *City Code* During the ten years prior to the date of this Agreement, the Company has not:

(1) had at any time any equity share capital listed on the London Stock Exchange;

(2) had any dealings in its equity share capital advertised in a newspaper on a regular basis for a continuous period of at least six months;

(3) had at any time any equity share capital subject to a marketing arrangement as described in s 163(2)(*b*) of the Companies Act 1985, being (by way of example) subject to dealings on the Unlisted Securities Market or Alternative Investment Market; or

(4) filed a prospectus, with the Registrar of Companies, for the issue of any equity share capital.]

2.4 The Company and the Law

(A) *Compliance with Laws*[70] The Company has conducted its business in all material respects in accordance with all applicable laws and regulations of the United Kingdom and any relevant foreign country or authority and there is no order, decree or judgment of any court or any governmental or other competent authority or agency of the United Kingdom or any foreign country outstanding against the Company or any person for whose acts the Company is vicariously liable which may have a material adverse effect upon the assets or business of the Company.

(B) *Licences etc*

(1) All necessary [and/or desirable] licences, consents, permits, approvals and authorisations (public and private) have been obtained by the Company to enable the Company to carry on its business effectively in the places and in the manner in which such business is now carried on and all such licences, consents, permits, approvals and authorisations are in full force and effect and are not limited in duration or subject to onerous conditions.

(2) All reports, returns and information required by law or as a condition of any licence, consent, permit, approval or other authorisation to be made or given to any person or authority in connection with the Company's business have been made or given to the appropriate person or authority.

(3) The utilisation of any of the assets of the Company or the carrying on of any aspect of the Company's business or any business now being carried on at any of the Properties is not in breach of any of the terms and conditions of

any of such licences, consents, permits, approvals and authorisations and so
far as the Vendor is aware there is no circumstance which indicates that any
such licence, consent, permit, approval or authorisation is likely to be suspended, cancelled or revoked or why any of them should expire within a
period of [one year] from the date of this Agreement.

(4)   At and after Completion there will be no restriction on the right of the Company to carry on its business which does not now apply to the Company.

(C)   *Breach of Statutory Provisions*   Neither the Company, nor any of its officers,
agents or employees (during the course of their duties in relation to the Company)
have committed, or omitted to do, any act or thing the commission or omission of
which is, or could be, in contravention of any Act, Order, Regulation, or the like
in the United Kingdom or elsewhere which is punishable by fine or other penalty
and no notice or communication has been received with respect to any alleged, actual or potential violation of or failure to comply with such Act, Order, Regulation
or the like or any other law or legal requirement.

(D)   *Litigation*

(1)   Neither the Company nor any its officers or agents nor any of its employees
is engaged in or the subject of any litigation, arbitration, administrative or
criminal proceedings[71] whether as plaintiff, defendant or otherwise, [which
adversely affects or is likely to have an adverse effect on the Company's
business and/or the ability of the Company or any purchaser to carry on the
Company's business in the same manner and to the same extent as previously carried on.]

(2)   No litigation or arbitration or administrative or criminal proceedings are
pending or threatened or expected by or against the Company or any such
officer, agent or employee; and so far as the Vendor is aware there are no
facts or circumstances likely to give rise to any such litigation or arbitration
or administrative or criminal proceedings.

(3)   The Company *nor any member of the Vendor's Group* (nor any officer or
employee thereof) has not been a party to any undertaking or assurance given
to any court or governmental agency or the subject of any injunction which
is still in force.

(E)   *Fair Trading*

(1)   No agreement, practice or arrangement carried on by the Company or to
which the Company is or has [in the   ] prior to the date of this
Agreement been a party:

(a)   is or ought to be or ought to have been registered in accordance with
the provisions of the Restrictive Trade Practices Acts 1976 and 1977
or contravenes the provisions of the Resale Prices Act 1976 or is or has
been the subject of any enquiry, complaint, investigation or proceeding
under any of those Acts; or

(b)   is or has been the subject of an enquiry, complaint, investigation, reference or report under the Fair Trading Act 1973 (or any previous legislation relating to monopolies or mergers) or the Competition Act
1980 or constitutes an anti-competitive practice within the meaning of
the 1980 Act; or

(c)   infringes Art 85 of the Treaty of Rome establishing the European Economic Community or constitutes an abuse of dominant position contrary to Art 86 of the said Treaty or infringes any regulation or other
enactment made under Art 87 and/or Art 235 of the said Treaty or is or
has been the subject of any enquiry, complaint, investigation or proceeding in respect thereof; or

(d) has been notified to the Directorate General of Competition of the Commission of the European Communities and/or to the EFTA Surveillance Authority; or

(e) is by virtue of its terms or by virtue of any practice for the time being carried on in connection therewith a 'Consumer Trade Practice' within the meaning of s 13 of the Fair Trading Act 1973 and susceptible to or under reference to the Consumer Protection Advisory Committee or the subject matter of a report to the Secretary of State or the subject matter of an Order by the Secretary of State under the provisions of Part II of that Act; or

(f) infringes any other competition, restrictive trade practice, anti-trust, fair trading or consumer protection law or legislation applicable in any jurisdiction in which the Company has assets or carries on or intends to carry on business or in which the activities of the Company may have an effect.

(2) The Company has not given any assurance or undertaking to the Restrictive Practices Court or the Director General of Fair Trading or the Secretary of State for Trade and Industry, the European Commission, the EFTA Surveillance Authority or the Court of Justice of the European Communities or to any other court, person or body and is not subject to or in default or contravention of any Article, Act, decision, regulation, order or other instrument or undertaking relating to any matter referred to in this Sub-Paragraph 2.4(E).

(F) (1) None of the activities of the Company as currently conducted could give rise to the imposition of any anti-dumping duty or other sanction under any trade regulation legislation in respect of any products manufactured by the Company or in which the Company trades.

(2) No anti-dumping duty or other sanction under any trade regulation legislation is or has been in force in any area in which the Company carries on or intends to carry on business in respect of products manufactured by the Company or in which the Company trades.

(3) No undertaking has been given by the Company to any governmental authority under any anti-dumping or other trade regulation legislation.

(G) (1) The Company is not and has not been in receipt of any aid which could be construed as falling within Art 92(1) of the Treaty of Rome other than:

(a) aid in operation at the date of UK Accession to the Community which is treated as existing aid pursuant to Art 93(1); or

(b) aid or any alteration to existing aid falling within Art 92(3) which has been duly notified to the European Commission pursuant to Art 93(3) and approved by the European Commission.

(2) The Company is not aware of any pending or threatened investigation, complaint, action or decision in relation to the receipt or alleged receipt by it of any aid or alleged aid.

(H) *Product Liability*

(1) There is no claim in respect of Product Liability (as hereinafter defined) outstanding or threatened against or expected by the Company in relation to its business and so far as the Vendor is aware there are no circumstances which are likely to give rise to any such claim. For this purpose 'Product Liability' means a liability arising out of death, personal injury or damage to property caused by a defective product or defective services sold supplied or provided by the Company in the course of its business on or prior to the date hereof.

(2) The Company has not manufactured, sold or supplied any product or service which:

(a)   is, was or will become, in any material respect, faulty or defective; or

(b)   does not comply in any material respect with any warranty or representation, express or implied, made by or on behalf of the Company in respect of it or with all laws, regulations, standards and requirements
applicable to it; and/or

(c)   was sold or supplied on terms that the Company accepts an obligation
to service or repair or replace such products after delivery.

(3)   The Company has not received a prohibition notice, a notice to warn or a suspension notice under the Consumer Protection Act 1987 in relation to any of
its products.

(I)   *Environmental*[72]

(1)   *Definitions*   For the purpose of this Sub-Paragraph, the following terms
shall have the following meanings:

'Environment' means all or any of the media of air, water and land (wherever
occurring) and in relation to the media of air and water includes without limitation the air and water within buildings and the air and water within other
natural or man-made structures above or below ground;

'Environmental Law' means all or any applicable EC, national or local law
or regulation arising through statute, subordinate legislation, or common law
or any relevant code of practice, guidance, note, standard or other advisory
material issued by any competent authority relating to Environmental Matters and in relation to Sub-Paragraph (2)(e) below, includes Part IIA of the
Environmental Protection Act 1990 whether or not in force;

'Environmental Liability or Liabilities' means all costs, expenses, liabilities,
claims, damages, penalties or fines arising from:

(a)   any legal requirement, direction, notice, order or obligation served or
imposed by any competent authority or court of competent jurisdiction
under Environmental Law; or

(b)   the carrying out of any investigatory, monitoring, precautionary, remedial or engineering works (whether on the Properties or elsewhere)
which are necessary to avoid the issue, service or imposition of any notice, requirement or obligation by any competent authority or court of
competent jurisdiction under Environmental Law; or

(c)   the carrying out of any investigatory, monitoring, precautionary, remedial or engineering works (whether on the Properties or elsewhere)
which are necessary in order to ensure the continued operation of the
business of the Company or the protection of the goodwill of the business of the Company and otherwise taking into account the interests of
the business of the Company; or

(d)   the repair, replacement or rebuilding of any part of the Properties or
any disruption of the business caused or necessitated by the carrying
out of any investigatory, monitoring, precautionary, remedial or engineering works (whether on the Properties or elsewhere) in connection
with Environmental Matters;

including in each case all reasonable legal, consulting, monitoring, laboratory and other professional fees and other reasonable costs and expenses associated therewith;

'Environmental Matters' means the pollution of the Environment, the protection of the Environment and human health, health and safety of employees in the work place, the protection of natural amenity, production, the

disposal, release, use, storage, spillage, deposit, escape, discharge, leak, emission, recovery, transport of, or radiation from any Hazardous Material or Waste;

'Environmental Permits' means the permits, licences, consents or authorisations required under Environmental Law in relation to the carrying on of the business of the Company or the occupation or use of the Properties;

'Hazardous Material' means any pollutant, or any hazardous, toxic, radioactive, noxious, corrosive or caustic substance whether in solid, liquid or gaseous form;

'Waste' includes any unwanted or surplus substance irrespective of whether it is capable of being recycled or recovered.

(2) *Environmental Matters*
- (a) The Company has complied at all times with Environmental Law.
- (b) All Environmental Permits have been lawfully obtained and are in full force and effect and the Company has complied at all times with all conditions and limitations in all Environmental Permits.
- (c) The Vendor is not aware of any circumstances which would make it impossible or difficult for the Company to comply with the conditions or limitations in any Environmental Permits in the future and the Company has received no communication revoking, suspending, modifying or varying any of the Environmental Permits and is not aware of any circumstances which might give rise to any such communication being received.
- (d) The Company is not engaged in any litigation, arbitration, administrative or criminal proceedings or negotiations with any person or body relating to any Environmental Liability and no litigation, arbitration, administrative or criminal proceedings or negotiations with any person or body relating to any actual or potential Environmental Liability are pending, threatened or envisaged by or against the Company.
- (e) The Company has not received at any time any communication failure to comply with which would constitute a breach of Environmental Law or compliance with which could be secured by further proceedings under Environmental Law or which relates in any way to any actual or potential Environmental Liability on the part of the Company and the Vendor is not aware of any circumstances, including without limitation the existence of any contractual obligation on the part of the Company, which might give rise to any such communication being received.

(J) *Inducements* So far as the Vendor is aware no officer, agent or employee of the Company has paid any bribe (monetary or otherwise) or used any of the Company's assets unlawfully to obtain an advantage for any person.

2.5 The Company's and Vendor's Solvency

(A) *Winding Up* No order has been made, petition presented or resolution passed for the winding up of the Company or the Vendor and no meeting has been convened for the purpose of winding up the Company or the Vendor. The Company has not been a party to any transaction which could be avoided in a winding up.

(B) *Administration and Receivership* No steps have been taken for the appointment of an administrator or receiver (including an administrative receiver) of all or any part of the Company's assets.

(C) *Compositions*   The Company has not made or proposed any arrangement or composition with its creditors or any class of its creditors.

(D) *Insolvency*[73]   The Company is not insolvent, is not unable to pay its debts within the meaning of the insolvency legislation applicable to the Company and has not stopped paying its debts as they fall due.

(E) *Unsatisfied Judgments*   No distress, execution or other process been levied against the Company or action taken to repossess goods in the Company's possession [which has not been satisfied in full]. No unsatisfied judgment is outstanding against the Company.

(F) *Floating Charges*   No floating charge created by the Company has crystallised and, so far as the Vendor is aware, there are no circumstances likely to cause such a floating charge to crystallise.

(G) *Analogous Events*   No event analogous to any of the foregoing has occurred in or outside England.

2.6   The Company's Accounts and Records

(A) *Books and records*   All accounts, books, ledgers, financial and other records of whatsoever kind ('Records') of the Company:
   (1) have been fully, properly and accurately maintained on a consistent basis and will at Completion be up to date and are in the possession and control of the Company and contain true, complete and accurate records of all matters required by law to be entered therein;
   (2) do not contain or reflect any material inaccuracies or discrepancies; and
   (3) give and reflect a true and fair view of the financial, contractual and trading position of the Company and of its fixed and current assets and liabilities (actual and contingent) and debtors and creditors (as appropriate) and all other matters which ought or would normally be expected to appear therein
   and no notice or allegation that any of the records is incorrect or should be rectified has been received.

(B) *Accounts*   The Audited Accounts:[74]
   (1) were prepared in accordance with the requirements of all relevant statutes and accounting practices generally accepted in the United Kingdom at the time they were audited and commonly adopted by companies carrying on business similar to the Company's;
   (2) show a true and fair view[75] of the assets and liabilities of the Company as at, and the profits of the Company for the accounting reference period ended on, the Balance Sheet Date;
   (3) are not affected by any unusual or non-recurring items;
   (4) in the case of consolidated financial statements, show a true and fair view of the state of affairs of the Company and the Subsidiaries as a whole; and
   (5) apply bases and policies of accounting which have been consistently applied in the audited financial statements of the Company and, in the case of the Company and the Subsidiaries, in the audited consolidated financial statements for the three accounting reference periods ending on the Balance Sheet Date.

(C) *Provision for Liabilities*   Full[76] provision has been made in the Audited Accounts for all actual liabilities of the Company outstanding at the Balance Sheet Date and proper provision (or note) in accordance with generally accepted accounting principles in the United Kingdom at the time they were audited has been made therein for all other liabilities of the Company then outstanding whether contingent, quantified, disputed or not including (without limitation) the cost of any work or material for which payment has been received or credit taken, any future loss which may arise in connection with uncompleted contracts and any claims against the Company in respect of completed contracts.

(D) *Valuation of Stock and Work in Progress*[77]

(1) For the purposes of the Audited Accounts all stock in trade was valued at the lower of cost and net realisable value and all work in progress was valued on a basis excluding profit, including proper provision for losses which are or could reasonably be anticipated.

(2) None of the stock in trade of the Company is obsolete, redundant (being out of fashion or demand), slow moving or likely to realise less than its book value.

(3) The respective amounts of raw materials, work in progress, finished goods, packaging and promotional material held or on order by the Company are appropriate and normal for its present level of business.

(E) *Management Accounts*[78] The Management Accounts have been carefully prepared in accordance with accounting policies consistent with those used in preparing the Audited Accounts[79] and on a basis consistent with the management accounts prepared in the preceding [year]. The cumulative profits, assets and liabilities of the Company stated in the Management Accounts [have not been materially misstated and are not materially inaccurate] and the Vendor does not consider the Management Accounts misleading.

(F) *Returns* The Company has complied with the provisions of the Companies Acts and all returns, particulars, resolutions and other documents required under any legislation to be delivered on behalf of the Company to the Registrar of Companies or to any other authority whatsoever have been properly made and delivered. All such documents delivered to the Registrar of Companies or to any other authority whatsoever, whether or not required by law, were true and accurate when so delivered and the Company has not received notification of the levy of any fine or penalty for non-compliance by the Company or any director of the Company.

2.7 The Company's Business and the Effect of Sale

(A) *Business Since the Balance Sheet Date*[80] Since the Balance Sheet Date:

(1) the Company has carried on its business in the ordinary and usual course so as to maintain it as a going concern and without any interruption or alteration in the nature, scope or manner of its business;

(2) there has been no material deterioration in the financial position, prospects or turnover of the Company;[81]

(3) there has been no significant event or occurrence (including, but not limited to the loss of any significant customer or supplier) which has had or may following Completion have a material adverse affect on the Company's business or its value, profitability or prospects;[81]

(4) the Company has not borrowed or raised any money or taken any form of financial facility (whether pursuant to a factoring arrangement or otherwise);

(5) the Company has paid its creditors in accordance with their respective credit terms or (if not) within the time periods usually applicable to such creditors and save as disclosed there are no debts outstanding by the Company which have been due for more than four weeks;

(6) there has been no unusual change in the Company's stock in trade [or work in progress];

(7) the Company has not entered into, or agreed to enter into, [any capital commitments] [any commitment to acquire or dispose of on capital account any asset of a value in excess of £[   ] or any commitment involving expenditure by it on capital account];

(8)   no share or loan capital has been issued or agreed to be issued by the Company; and

(9)   no distribution of capital or income has been declared, made or paid in respect of any share capital of the Company and (excluding fluctuations in overdrawn current accounts with bankers) no loan or share capital of the Company has been repaid in whole or part or has become liable to be repaid in whole or part.

(B)   *Working Capital*   Having regard to existing bank and other facilities, the Company has sufficient working capital for the purposes of continuing to carry on its business in its present form and at its present level of turnover for the foreseeable future and for the purposes of performing in accordance with their respective terms all orders, projects and contractual obligations which have been placed with, or undertaken by, the Company.[82]

(C)   *Commission*   No one is entitled to receive from the Company any finder's fee, brokerage, or other commission in connection with this Agreement or the sale and purchase of shares in the Company.

(D)   *Consequence of Share Acquisition by the Purchaser*   The acquisition of the Sale Shares by the Purchaser or compliance with the terms of this Agreement will not:

(1)   cause the Company to lose the benefit of any right or privilege it presently enjoys or relieve any person of any obligation to the Company (whether contractual or otherwise) or enable any person to determine any such obligation or any contractual right or benefit enjoyed by the Company or to exercise any right whether under an agreement with the Company or otherwise;

(2)   result in any present or future indebtedness of the Company becoming due or capable of being declared due and payable prior to its stated maturity;

(3)   give rise to or cause to become exercisable any right of pre-emption;

(4)   result in a breach of, or constitute a default under any provision of the memorandum or articles of association of the Company;

(5)   result in a breach of, or constitute a default under any order, judgment or decree of any court or government agency by which the Company is bound or subject; or

(6)   result in a breach of, or constitute a default under the terms, conditions or provisions of any agreement, understanding, arrangement or instrument (including, but not limited to, any of the Company's contracts)

and, to the best of the knowledge and belief of the Vendor, the Company's relationships with clients, customers, suppliers and employees will not be adversely affected thereby and the Vendor is not aware of any circumstances (whether or not connected with the Purchaser and/or the sale of the Sale Shares hereunder) indicating that, nor has it been informed or is otherwise aware that, any person who now has business dealings with the Company would or might cease to do so from and after Completion.[83]

(E)   *Grants*   [The Company has not applied for or received any financial assistance from any supranational, national or local authority or government agency.]
[Full particulars of all grants received from any supranational, national or local authority or government agency (and all applications for any such) [and in respect of which there remains any obligation to repay all or part thereof] are given in the Disclosure Letter and there are no circumstances (including the sale of the Sale Shares) which might lead to the whole or part of any such grant or other financial assistance becoming repayable or forfeited].

(F)   *Insurances*[84]

(1)   Full particulars of all the insurance policies (including, without limitation, the limit and basis of cover under each policy and the amount of the applica-

ble excess) in which the Company has an interest (the 'Company's Insurances') are given in the Disclosure Letter. The Company's Insurances afford the Company adequate cover against fire and such other risks as companies carrying on a similar business to the Company commonly cover by insurance and in particular:

    (a)   the assets of the Company are insured in their full replacement value;

    (b)   the Computer Systems are insured for all foreseeable risks to their full replacement value, together with incidental expenses, including, without limitation, costs and expenses of data recovery and reconstruction; and

    (c)   the Company is now, and has at all material times been, fully covered against accident, damage, injury, third party loss (including Product Liability), loss of profits and other risks normally insured against by companies carrying on a similar business.

  (2)   All the Company's Insurances are in full force and effect and will be maintained in full force without alteration pending Completion, there are no circumstances which might lead to any liability under any of the Company's Insurances being avoided by the insurers or the premiums being increased. In relation to the Company's Insurances, there are no special or unusual terms, restrictions or rates of premium and all premiums have been paid on time. There is no claim outstanding under any of the Company's Insurances nor is the Vendor aware of any circumstances likely to give rise to a claim nor (if the Vendor was to renew the Company's Insurances) is the Vendor aware of any circumstances as to why the insurers would refuse to renew them.

(G)   *Trading Name*   The Company does not trade under any name other than its corporate name and any other name given in the Disclosure Letter.

(H)   *Trade Associations*   Full particulars of all trade or business associations of which the Company is a member are set out in the Disclosure Letter, and the Company is now and has been at all material times in compliance in all material respects with the regulations or guidelines laid down by any such trade or business association and all reports, comments and recommendations made by any such association [during the six years prior to the date of this Agreement] are annexed to the Disclosure Letter.

(I)   *Terms of Business*   True and complete copies of the standard terms upon which the Company carries on business or provides goods or services to any person are annexed to the Disclosure Letter and the Company does not provide and has not provided any goods or services to any person on terms which differ from its standard terms as annexed.

2.8   The Company's Assets

(A)   *Net Asset Value*[85]   The value of the net tangible assets of the Company at [the date of this Agreement] [Completion] determined in accordance with the same accounting policies as those applied in the Audited Accounts (and on the basis that each fixed asset is valued at a figure no greater than the value attributed to it in the Audited Accounts or, in the case of any fixed asset acquired by the Company after the Balance Sheet Date, at a figure no greater than cost) [is not] [will not be] less than the value of the net tangible assets of the Company at the Balance Sheet Date as shown in the Audited Accounts.

(B)   *Assets and Charges*[86]

  (1)   Except for current assets disposed of by the Company in the ordinary course of its business, the Company is the owner legally and beneficially of and has

good marketable title to all assets included in the Audited Accounts and all assets which have been acquired by the Company since the Balance Sheet Date and no encumbrance is outstanding nor is there any agreement or commitment to give or create or allow any encumbrance over or in respect of the whole or any part of the Company's assets, undertaking, goodwill or uncalled capital and no claim has been made by any person that he is entitled to any such encumbrance.

(2)   Since the Balance Sheet Date, save for disposals in the ordinary course of its business, the assets of the Company have been in the possession of, or under the control of, the Company.

(3)   No asset is shared by the Company with any other person and the Company does not depend for its business upon any assets, premises, facilities or services owned or supplied *by other members of the Vendor's Group/a person connected with the Vendor.*

(4)   No charge in favour of the Company is void or voidable for want of registration.

(C)   *Debts*[87]   [Save to the extent of the provision or reserve therefor contained or reflected in the Completion Accounts,] any debts owed to the Company as recorded in the Company's books and records are good and collectable in the ordinary course of business and will realise their full face value within three months of Completion. The rights of the Company in respect of such debts are valid and enforceable and are not subject to any defence, right of set-off or counter-claim, withholding or other deduction and no act has been done or omission permitted whereby any of them has ceased or might cease to be valid and enforceable in whole or in part. No amount included in the Audited Accounts as owing to the Company at the Balance Sheet Date has been released for an amount less than the value at which it was included in the Audited Accounts or is now regarded by the Vendor as irrecoverable in whole or in part. The Company has not factored or discounted any of its debts or other receivables or agreed to do so.

(D)   *Title Retention*   The Company has not acquired or agreed to acquire any material asset on terms that property therein does not pass until full payment is made.

(E)   *Condition of Stock*   The Company's stock in trade is in good condition, meets all relevant statutory, regulatory and industry accepted standards or contractual specifications and is capable of being sold by the Company in the ordinary course of its business in accordance with its current price list without discount, rebate or allowance to a purchaser.

(F)   *Plant*   All plant and machinery, including fixed plant and machinery, vehicles, Computer Systems and other equipment used in, or in connection with, the business of the Company:

(1)   is in good repair and condition and in satisfactory working order and has been regularly and properly serviced and maintained and none is dangerous, inefficient, obsolete or in need of renewal or replacement;

(2)   is capable, and will (subject to fair wear and tear) be capable, over the period of time during which it will be written down to a nil value in the accounts of the Company, of doing the work for which it was designed or purchased; and

(3)   is not surplus to the Company's current or proposed requirements.

(G)   *Intellectual Property Rights*

(1)   The Company is the sole legal and beneficial owner [free from encumbrances] of the Listed Intellectual Property and (where such property is capable of registration) the registered proprietor thereof and (save for copyrights and unregistered design rights not included in the Listed Intellectual Property) owns no other Intellectual Property.[88]

(2) Save as may appear from the Listed Intellectual Property Agreements no person has been authorised to make any use whatsoever of any Intellectual Property owned by the Company.

(3) Save as may appear from the Listed Intellectual Property Agreements all the Intellectual Property used by the Company is owned by it and it does not use any Intellectual Property in respect of which any third party has any right, title or interest.[89]

(4) All the Intellectual Property rights owned or used by the Company are valid and enforceable [and [so far as the Vendor is aware] nothing has been done, omitted or permitted whereby any of them has ceased or might cease to be valid and enforceable].[90]

(5) None of the processes or products of the Company infringes any Intellectual Property or any right of any other person relating to Intellectual Property or involves the unlicensed use of confidential information disclosed to the Company by any person in circumstances which might entitle that person to make a claim against the Company.[91]

(6) None of the Listed Intellectual Property is being used, claimed, applied for, opposed or attacked by any person.

(7) The Vendor is not aware of any infringement of the Listed Intellectual Property or of any rights relating to it by any person.

(8) There are no outstanding claims against the Company for infringement of any Intellectual Property or of any rights relating to it used (or which have been used) by the Company and [during the last three years] no such claims have been settled by the giving of any undertakings which remain in force. The Company has not received any actual or threatened claim that any of the Listed Intellectual Property Rights is invalid [nor is the Company aware of any reason why any patents should be amended].

(9) Confidential information and know-how used by the Company is kept strictly confidential [and the Company operates and fully complies with procedures which maintain such confidentiality. The Vendor is not aware of any such confidentiality having been breached.] The Company has not disclosed (except in the ordinary course of its business) any of its know-how, trade secrets or list of customers to any other person.[92]

(10) All application and renewal fees, costs, charges, taxes [and other steps] required for the maintenance [or protection] of the Listed Intellectual Property have been duly paid on time [or taken] and none of such rights are subject to any existing challenge or attack by a third party or competent authority [and there are no outstanding patent office or trade marks registry deadlines which expire within three months of Completion.]

(11) The Listed Intellectual Property Agreements are all the Intellectual Property agreements to which the Company is a party and each of them is valid and binding and the Company is not in breach of any of the provisions of such agreements.

(12) The Vendor has, if required to do so under the Data Protection Act 1984, duly registered as a data user in respect of the business carried on by the Company and has complied with the data protection principles as set out in that Act.

(13) [93][All current advertising, marketing and sales promotions by the Company comply with all applicable codes of practice and self-regulatory schemes. The Company has not been disciplined under any scheme or code in respect of any such advertising, marketing or sales promotion and no complaint has

been made against it in respect thereof and there are no outstanding complaints or disciplinary proceedings against the Company in respect thereof.[94]

(14) All persons retained or employed by the Company who, in the course of their work for the Company will or might reasonably be expected to bring into existence Intellectual Property or things protected by Intellectual Property are, so far as is reasonably practicable, individually bound by agreements with the Company whereby all Intellectual Property which such persons may bring into existence during their work for the Company vests in the Company and all such agreements contain terms which, so far as is reasonably practicable, prevent such persons disclosing any confidential information about the Company and its business.

(15) None of the Intellectual Property owned or used by the Company is subject to compulsory licensing or the granting of any licences of right nor, so far as the Company is aware, will it become so by operation of law.

(H) *Computer Systems*

(1) The Hardware has been satisfactorily maintained and supported and has the benefit of an appropriate maintenance and support agreement terminable by the contractor by not less than 24 months' notice.

(2) The Hardware and Software have adequate capability and capacity for the projected requirements of the Company for not less than four years following Completion for the processing and other functions required to be performed for the purposes of the business of the Company.

(3) Disaster recovery plans are in effect and are adequate to ensure that the Hardware, Software and Data can be replaced or substituted without material disruption to the business of the Company.

(4) In the event that any person providing maintenance or support services for the Hardware, Software and Data ceases or is unable to do so, the Company has all necessary rights and information to procure the carrying out of such services by employees or by a third party without undue expense or delay.

(5) The Company has sufficient technically competent and trained employees to ensure proper handling, operation, monitoring and use of its computer systems.

(6) The Company has adequate procedures to ensure internal and external security of the Hardware, Software and Data, including (without limitation) procedures for preventing unauthorised access, preventing the introduction of a virus, taking and storing on-site and off-site back-up copies of Software and Data.

(7) Where any of the records of the Company are stored electronically, the Company is the owner of all hardware and software licences necessary to enable it to keep, copy, maintain and use such records in the course of its business and does not share any hardware or software relating to the records with any person.

(8) The Company has all the rights necessary (including rights over the source code) to obtain, without undue expense or delay, modified versions of the Software which are required at any time to improve in any regard the operation and/or efficiency of the Software.

(9) The Company owns, and is in possession and control of, original copies of all the manuals, guides, instruction books and technical documents (including any corrections and updates) required to operate effectively the Hardware and the Software.

(10) The Hardware and Software have never unduly interrupted or hindered the running or operation of the Company's business, and have no defects in operation which so affect the Company's business.

(I) *Properties*[95]

   (1) *Title to Properties*

     (a) The particulars of the Properties shown in Schedule 7 (Properties) are true and correct. Except as shown the Company has no other interest in land and does not occupy any other property and has not entered into any agreement to acquire or dispose of any land or premises or any interest therein which has not been completed.

     (b) The owner of each Property shown in Schedule 7 (Properties) is solely legally and beneficially entitled to and has good and marketable title to and exclusive occupation of each Property.

     (c) Each Property is held free from any mortgage or charge (whether legal or equitable, fixed or floating), encumbrance, lease, sub-lease, tenancy, licence or right of occupation, rent charge, exception, reservation, easement, quasi-easement or privilege (or agreement for any of the same) in favour of a third party.

     (d) The lease, sub-lease, tenancy or agreement for any of the same under which any of the Properties are held is valid and subsisting against all persons, including any person in whom any superior estate or interest is vested.

     (e) There are appurtenant to each Property all rights and easements necessary for its current use and enjoyment (without restriction as to time or otherwise) and the access for each of the Properties is over roads adopted by the local authority and maintained at public expense.

     (f) The Company has not entered into any positive covenants or personal obligations nor does it have any personal rights under which it has any subsisting liability (whether actual or contingent).

   (2) *Matters affecting Properties*

     (a) No Property or any part thereof is affected by any of the following matters or is to the knowledge of the Vendor likely to become so affected:

       (i) any outstanding dispute, notice or complaint or any exception, reservation, right, covenant, restriction or condition which is of an unusual nature or which affects or might in the future affect the use of any of the Properties for the purpose for which it is now used (the 'current use') or which affects or might in the future affect the value of the Properties;

       (ii) any notice, order, demand, requirement or proposal of which the owner has notice or of which the Vendor is aware made or issued by or on behalf of any government or statutory authority, department or body for acquisition, clearance, demolition or closing, the carrying out of any work upon any building, the modification of any planning permission, the discontinuance of any use or the imposition of any building or improvement line, the alteration of any road or footpath or which otherwise affects any of the Properties or their current use or value;

       (iii) any compensation received as a result of any refusal of any application for planning consent or the imposition of any restrictions in relation to any planning consent;

       (iv) any commutation or agreement for the commutation of rent or payment of rent in advance of the due dates of payment thereof;

(v)   any outstanding claim or liability (contingent or otherwise) whether under the Planning Acts (as defined in the Town and Country Planning Act 1990) or otherwise;

(vi)   any outgoings except uniform business rates and water rates; or

(vii)   the requirement of consent from any third party to the charging of the Properties or any of them.

(b)   Each of the Properties is in a good state of repair and condition and fit for the current use and no deleterious material (including without limit high alumina cement, woodwool, calcium chloride, sea dredged aggregates or asbestos material) was used in the construction, alteration or repair thereof or of any of them and there are no development works, redevelopment works or fitting out works outstanding in respect of any of the Properties.

(c)   All restrictions, conditions and covenants (including any imposed by or pursuant to any lease, sub-lease, tenancy or agreement for any of the same and whether the Company is the landlord or tenant thereunder and any arising in relation to any superior title) affecting any of the Properties have been observed and performed and no notice of any breach of any of the same has been received or is to the Vendor's knowledge likely to be received.

(d)   The current use of the Properties and all machinery and equipment therein and the conduct of any business therein complies in all respects with all relevant statutes and regulations including without prejudice to the generality of the foregoing the Factories Act 1961, the Offices Shops and Railway Premises Act 1963, the Fire Precautions Act 1971, the Health and Safety at Work etc, Act 1974, the Betting, Gaming and Lotteries Act 1963 and with all rules, regulations and delegated legislation thereunder and all necessary licences and consents required thereunder have been obtained.

(e)   There are no restrictive covenants or provisions, legislation or orders, charges, restrictions, agreements, conditions or other matters which preclude or limit the current use of any of the Properties and the current user is the permitted user under the provisions of the Planning Acts (including without limit s 52 of the Town and Country Planning Act 1971; s 106 of the Town and Country Planning Act 1990; or s 278 of the Highways Act 1980) and regulations made thereunder and is in accordance with the requirements of the Local Authorities and all restrictions, conditions and covenants imposed by or pursuant to the Planning Acts have been observed and performed and no agreements have been entered into with any public authority or statutory authority in respect of any of the Properties whether pursuant to the Planning Acts or otherwise.

(f)   All necessary planning permissions, listed building consents, bye-law consents, building regulation consents and other permissions and approvals (whether or not required by statute) for the construction, extension and alteration of the Properties have been obtained and complied with, and none of those permissions, consents and approvals has been given on a temporary or personal basis nor does it require the removal at any time of the works so authorised.

(g)   Any necessary or appropriate action to protect the interests of the Company has been taken under the Landlord and Tenant Act 1954 and in relation to rent review provisions in relation to any lease, sub-lease, tenancy or agreement for any of the same and whether the Company is the landlord or the tenant thereunder and all appropriate time limits have been complied with and no rent reviews are outstanding at the date hereof or exercisable prior to Completion.

(h) In relation to any lease, sub-lease, tenancy or agreement for any of the same under which the Company is the landlord:

    (i) the rents collected by the Company have not exceeded the sums lawfully recoverable;

    (ii) no forfeiture proceedings have been taken or are contemplated;

    (iii) no notice has been served by the Company which is still outstanding;

    (iv) no works have been carried out which could give rise to a claim against the Company for compensation or which would have to be disregarded on any rent review;

    (v) all consents and conditions contained therein have been observed and performed to date; and

    (vi) brief details of such leases, sub-leases, tenancies or agreements for any of the same are set out in Schedule 7 and such details are true and correct.

(i) None of the Properties is used for any purpose other than the use specified for each Property in Schedule 7.

(j) Where the interest of the Company in a Property is leasehold, there is no right for the landlord to determine the lease except in the event of non-payment of rent or other breach of covenant by the tenant.

(k) All replies by or on behalf of the Vendor or the Company to enquiries relating to any of the Properties made by or on behalf of the Purchaser were when given and are now true and correct.

(3) *Outstanding Property Liabilities* Except in relation to the Properties, the Company has no liabilities (actual or contingent) arising out of the conveyance, transfer, lease, tenancy, licence, agreement or other document relating to land or premises or an interest in land or premises, including, without limitation, leasehold premises assigned or otherwise disposed of.

2.9 The Company's Contracts

(A) *No Other Contracts* There are not in force in relation to the Company's business, assets or undertaking any agreements, undertakings, understandings, arrangements or other engagements, whether written or oral to which the Vendor *or any member of the Vendor's Group* is a party or has the benefit of or is otherwise subject, the benefit of which would be required to be assigned to or otherwise vested in the Company to enable the Company to carry on its business and/or to enjoy all the rights and privileges attaching thereto and/or to any of its assets and undertaking in the same manner and scope and to the same extent and on the same basis as the Company has carried on business or enjoyed such rights prior to the date hereof.

(B) *The Company's Contracts* Each of the Company's contracts are valid and binding and no notice of termination of any such contract has been received or served by the Company and the Vendor is not aware of the invalidity of, or of any grounds for determination, rescission, avoidance or repudiation of any such contracts.

(C) *Contractual Arrangements* The Company is not a party to or subject to any agreement, transaction, obligation, commitment, understanding, arrangement or liability which:

(1) is of [six] months or greater duration or is incapable of complete performance in accordance with its terms within six months after the date on which it was entered into or undertaken or is otherwise of a length that is greater than is customary in businesses of a similar nature to that of the Company's; or

(2) is known by the Vendor or by the Company to be likely to result in a loss to the Company on completion of performance; or

(3) cannot readily be fulfilled or performed by the Company on time and without undue or unusual expenditure of money and effort; or

(4) involves or is likely to involve obligations, restrictions, expenditure or receipts of an unusual, onerous or exceptional nature; or

(5) is a contract for services (other than contracts for the supply of electricity or normal office services); or

(6) requires the Company to pay any commission, finder's fee, royalty or the like; or

(7) involves liabilities which may fluctuate in accordance with an index or rate of currency exchange; or

(8) is a contract for the supply of assets to the Company on hire, lease, hire purchase, conditional sale, credit or deferred payment terms; or

(9) is dependent on the guarantee or covenant of or security provided by any other person;

(10) in any way restricts the Company's freedom to carry on the whole or any part of its business in any part of the world in such manner as it thinks fit; or

(11) is a contract for the sale of shares or assets which contains warranties or indemnities under which the Company still has a remaining liability or obligation; or

(12) can be terminated as a result of any change in the underlying ownership or control of the Company, or would be materially affected by such change; or

(13) is in any way otherwise than in the ordinary course of the Company's business.

(D) *Substantial or significant contracts*   No contract, agreement, transaction, obligation, commitment, understanding, arrangement or liability entered into by the Company and now outstanding or unperformed involves any of the following:

(1) obligations on the part of the Company which will cause or are likely to cause the Company to incur expenditure or an obligation to pay money in excess of £[   ];

(2) obligations on the part of the Company to purchase any specified minimum quantity or any specified minimum percentage of its total requirement for [   ] or other stock in trade from any one supplier;

(3) the supply by the Company of [   ] or other products or services whether by way of lease or outright sale or otherwise to any one customer such that the value of such supplies exceeds or is likely to exceed [5 per cent] of the total turnover of the Company in the financial year ending [   ] 19[   ] or in any subsequent year.

(E) *Defaults*

(1) Neither the Company nor any other party to any agreement with the Company is in default thereunder, and the Company is not aware of any invalidity or grounds for termination, avoidance, rescission or repudiation of any agreement to which the Company is a party which, in any such case, would be material[96] in the context of the financial or trading position of the Company nor (so far as the Vendor is aware) are there any circumstances likely to give rise to any such event.

(2) Full details of any customers (or any persons to whom the Company in the course of business has supplied goods and services in the twelve months ending on the date hereof) who have defaulted (or who are believed by the Company to be likely to default) [in any material respect] in the payment when due of any monies to the Company are specified in the Disclosure Letter.

(F) *Sureties* Neither the Vendor *nor any member of the Vendor's Group* nor any third party has given any guarantee of or security for, any overdraft loan, loan facility or off-balance sheet financing granted to the Company nor has the Company given any guarantee of or security for any overdraft loan, loan facility or off-balance sheet financing granted to the Vendor *or any member of the Vendor's Group* and there is not now outstanding in respect of the Company any guarantee or warranty or agreement for indemnity or for suretyship given by or for the accommodation of the Company or in respect of the Company's business.

(G) *Powers of Attorney* No powers of attorney given by the Company (other than to the holder of an encumbrance solely to facilitate its enforcement) are now in force. No person, as agent or otherwise, is entitled or authorised to bind or commit the Company to any obligation not in the ordinary course of the Company's business, and the Vendor is not aware of any person purporting to do so.

(H) *Insider Contracts*
(1) There is not outstanding, and there has not at any time during the last six years been outstanding, any agreement or arrangement to which the Company is a party and in which
(a) the Vendor;
(b) *any member of the Vendor's Group;*
(c) any person beneficially interested in the Company's share capital;
(d) any Director; or
(e) any person connected with any of them
is or has been interested, whether directly or indirectly.
(2) The Company is not a party to, nor have its profits or financial position during such period been affected by, any agreement or arrangement which is not entirely of an arm's length nature.
(3) All costs incurred by the Company have been charged to the Company and not borne by *any other member of the Vendor's Group.*

(I) *Debts* There are no debts owing by or to the Company other than debts which have arisen in the ordinary course of business, nor has the Company lent any money which has not been repaid.

(J) *Options and Guarantees* The Company is not a party to any option or pre-emption right, or a party to nor has it given any guarantee, suretyship, comfort letter or any other obligation (whatever called) to pay, provide funds or take action in the event of default in the payment of any indebtedness of any other person or in the performance of any obligation of any other person.

(K) *Tenders, etc* No offer, tender, or the like is outstanding which is capable of being converted into an obligation of the Company by an acceptance or other act of some other person [and the Company is not in negotiations with, nor has it put proposals forward or entered into discussions with any customer or supplier for the renewal of any existing business or acquisition of any new business].[97]

(L) *Documents* All title deeds and agreements to which the Company is a party and other documents owned by or which ought to be in the possession or control of the Company are in the possession or control of the Company and are properly stamped and are free from any encumbrance.

2.10   The Company and its Bankers

(A)   *Borrowings*   The total amount borrowed by the Company from its bankers does not exceed its facilities and the total amount borrowed by the Company from whatsoever source does not exceed any limitation on its borrowing contained in its articles of association, or in any debenture or loan stock deed or other instrument.

(B)   *Continuance of Facilities*   Full and accurate details of all overdrafts, loans or other financial facilities outstanding or available to the Company are given in the Disclosure Letter and true and correct copies of all documents relating thereto are annexed to the Disclosure Letter and neither the Vendor nor the Company has done anything whereby the continuance of any such facilities in full force and effect might be affected or prejudiced.

(C)   *Off-balance Sheet Financing*   The Company has not engaged in any borrowing or financing not required to be reflected in the Audited Accounts.

(D)   *Bank Accounts*   Full and accurate particulars of all the bank and deposit accounts of the Company and of the credit or debit balances on such accounts as at a date (the 'Statement Date') not more than seven days before the date of this Agreement are given in the Disclosure Letter. Since the Statement Date there have been no payments out of any such accounts except for routine payments in the ordinary course of the Company's business and the balances on such accounts are not now substantially different from the balances shown as at the Statement Date.

2.11   The Company and its Employees

(A)   *Directors*   Schedules 1 and 2 show the full names and offices held by each person who is a director of the Company and no other person is a director or shadow director of the Company.

(B)   *Particulars of Employees*[98]

(1)   The individuals, details of which are given in or annexed to the Disclosure Letter (the 'Employees') are all employed by the Company at the date of this Agreement and notice of termination will not be given by the Company on or before Completion. There are no other individuals employed at the date of this Agreement in the Company wheresoever. There will be no other individuals employed at the date of Completion by the Company wheresoever.

(2)   All contracts of service of any of the Employees are terminable on not more than three months' notice without compensation (other than compensation payable in accordance with the Employment Rights Act 1996).

(3)   The particulars shown in the Disclosure Letter show true and complete details of ages and lengths of continuous service of all of the Employees and by reference to each of the Employees remuneration payable and other benefits provided or which the Company is bound to provide (whether now or in the future) to each category of the Employees at Completion or any person connected with any such person and (without limiting the generality of the foregoing) include particulars of all profit sharing, incentive, bonus, commission arrangements and any other benefit to which any such category of the Employees is entitled or which is regularly provided or made available to them (including details of their notice period and their entitlement to holiday) in any case whether legally binding on the Company or not.

(4)   There are no subsisting contracts for the provision by any person of any consultancy services to the Company.

(5)   None of the Employees has given notice terminating his contract of employment.

(6) None of the Employees is under notice of dismissal or has any outstanding dispute with the Company in connection with or arising from his employment nor is there any liability outstanding to such persons except for remuneration or other benefits accruing due and no such remuneration or other benefit which has fallen due for payment has not been paid.

(7) During the period of six months ending with the execution of this Agreement the Company has not directly or indirectly terminated the employment of any person employed in or by the Company.

(8) None of the Employees belongs or has belonged at any material time to an independent trade union recognised by the Company.

(9) There are no employee representatives representing all or any of the Employees.

(10) The Vendor has complied with all of its statutory obligations to inform and consult appropriate representatives as required by law.

(11) There is no plan, scheme, commitment, custom, or practice relating to redundancy affecting any of the Employees more generous than the statutory redundancy requirements.

(12) All plans for the provision of benefits to the Employees comply in all respects with all relevant statutes, regulations or other laws and all necessary consents in relation to such plans have been obtained and all governmental filings in relation to such plans have been made.

(13) There are no loans owed by any of the Employees to the Company.

(14) Since [the last review date/the Balance Sheet Date,] no change has been made in (i) the rate of remuneration, or the emoluments or pension benefits or other contractual benefits, of any officer of the Company or any of the Employees or (ii) the terms of engagement of any such officer or any of the Employees.

(15) Except for the Pension Scheme[s] defined in Schedule 6 the Company is not under any present or future liability to pay to any of the Employees or to any other person who has been in any manner connected with the Company any pension, superannuation allowance, death benefit, retirement gratuity or like benefit or to contribute to any life assurance scheme, medical insurance scheme, or permanent health scheme and the Company has not made any such payments or contributions on a voluntary basis nor is it proposing to do so.

(16) There are no training schemes, arrangements or proposals whether past or present in respect of which a levy may henceforth become payable by the Company under the Industrial Training Act 1982 (as amended by the Employment Act 1989) and pending Completion no such schemes, arrangements or proposals will be established or undertaken.

(17) There is no outstanding undischarged liability to pay to any governmental or regulatory authority in any jurisdiction any contribution, taxation or other duty arising in connection with the employment or engagement of any of the Employees.

(18) None of the Employees will become entitled by virtue of their contract of service to any enhancement in or improvement to their remuneration, benefits or terms and conditions of service only by reason of completion of the sale and purchase under or pursuant to this Agreement.

(19) The Company has not in the last twelve months, entered into any informal or formal agreement to amend or change the terms and conditions of employment of any of the Employees (whether such amendment or change is to take effect prior to or after Completion).

(C) *Service Contracts*   There is not outstanding any contract of service between the Company and any of its directors, officers or employees which is not terminable by the Company without compensation (other than any compensation payable by statute) on not more than three months' notice given at any time.

(D) *Disputes with Employees*   There is no:

   (1)   outstanding or threatened claim by any person who is now or has been an employee of the Company or any dispute outstanding with any of the said persons or with any unions or any other body representing all or any of them in relation to their employment by the Company or of any circumstances likely to give rise to any such dispute;

   (2)   industrial action involving any employee, whether official or unofficial, currently occurring or threatened; or

   (3)   industrial relations matter which has been referred to ACAS or any similar governmental agency in the applicable jurisdiction for advice, conciliation or arbitration.

2.12 Miscellaneous

(A) *Circular*   The information contained in:

   (1)   the proof circular to shareholders of the Purchaser in agreed terms (incorporating listing particulars) and

   (2)   the draft press announcement in agreed terms,

   insofar as it relates to the Company and the Vendor, is true and accurate in all material respects, is in accordance with the facts and is not misleading.

(B) *Sale Memorandum*   All information contained or referred to in the sale memorandum (including any annexure thereto) (the 'Sale Memorandum') attached to the Disclosure Letter is accurate in all respects and the Vendor is not aware of any other fact or matter which renders any such information misleading or which might reasonably affect the willingness of a purchaser to acquire the Sale Shares on the terms, including price, of this Agreement. All forecasts, estimates and expressions of opinion, intention or expectation expressed in the Sale Memorandum are reasonably based and are fair and honest in all respects and have been made after due and careful enquiry.

(C) *All Material Matters Disclosed*   All information contained or referred to in this Agreement (including the Schedules and the documents in agreed terms) and in the Disclosure Letter or in any annexure thereto or which has otherwise been disclosed by or on behalf of the Vendor to the Purchaser [or its advisers/others] on or prior to the date hereof is true and accurate in all [material] respects and the Vendor is not aware of any other fact or matter which renders any such information misleading because of any omission, ambiguity or for any other reason.[99] The Vendor has disclosed to the Purchaser all information and facts relating to the Company and its business, assets and undertaking (including financial information) which are or may be material for disclosure to a purchaser of the Company on the terms of this Agreement and all information and facts so disclosed are true and accurate in all [material] respects.[100]

SCHEDULE 4

TAXATION WARRANTIES AND REPRESENTATIONS

1 Interpretation

1.1 In this Schedule, where the context admits:

'Taxation' and 'Tax' includes (without limitation) corporation tax, advance corporation tax, the charge under s 419 of the Taxes Act 1988, income tax, capital gains tax, the charge under s 601(2) of the Taxes Act 1988, value added tax, excise duties, the charge to tax under Sched 9A of the Value Added Tax Act 1994, customs and other import duties, inheritance tax, stamp duty, stamp duty reserve tax, capital duties, national insurance contributions, local authority council taxes, petroleum revenue tax, foreign taxation and duties, *amounts payable in consideration for the surrender of group relief or advance corporation tax or refunds pursuant to s 102 of the Finance Act 1989* and any payment whatsoever which the Company may be or become bound to make to any person as a result of the operation of any enactment relating to any such taxes or duties and all penalties, charges and interest relating to any of the foregoing or resulting from a failure to comply with the provisions of any enactment relating to taxation;

'Taxes Act 1988' means Income and Corporation Taxes Act 1988;

'TCGA 1992' means the Taxation of Chargeable Gains Act 1992;

'Value Added Tax' and 'VAT' mean value added tax as provided for in the Value Added Tax Act 1994 and legislation supplemental thereto or replacing, modifying or consolidating it;

references to income or profits or gains earned, accrued or received shall include income or profits or gains treated as earned, accrued or received for the purposes of any legislation; and

references to the 'Company' include each of the Subsidiaries.

2 Taxation Warranties and Representations[68]

The Vendor hereby warrants and represents[68] to and for the benefit of the Purchaser in the following terms.

2.1 General Taxation Matters

(A) *Residence* The Company is and always has been resident for taxation purposes only in the jurisdiction in which it is incorporated.

(B) *Tax Provisions* Full provision or reserve has been made in the Audited Accounts for all taxation liable to be assessed on the Company or for which it is accountable in respect of income, profits or gains earned, accrued or received on or before the Balance Sheet Date or any event on or before the Balance Sheet Date including distributions made down to such date or provided for in the Audited Accounts and full provision has been made in the Audited Accounts for deferred taxation calculated in accordance with generally accepted accounting principles.

(C) *Returns* The Company has properly and punctually made all returns and provided all information required for taxation purposes and none of such returns is disputed by the Inland Revenue or any other authority concerned (in the United Kingdom or elsewhere) and the Vendor is not aware that any dispute is likely, or that any event has occurred which would or might give rise to a payment under the Tax Deed.

(D) *Payment of Tax*   The Company has duly and punctually paid all taxation which it has become liable to pay and is under no liability to pay any penalty or interest in connection with any claim for taxation and has not paid any tax which it was and is not properly due to pay.

(E) *Audits*   The Company has not in the last six years received any visit or inspection from any taxation authority.

(F) Transferred Tax Refunds[101]   The Disclosure Letter contains particulars of all arrangements and agreements relating to the transfer of tax refunds to which the Company is or has been a party; and

    (1) all claims by the Company for the transfer of tax refunds were when made and are now valid and have been or will be allowed by way of discharging the liability of the recipient company to pay any corporation tax;

    (2) the Company has not made nor is liable to make any payment under any such arrangement save in consideration for the transfer of tax refunds allowable to the Company by way of discharge from liability to corporation tax and equivalent to the taxation for which the Company would have been liable would it not have been for the transfers;

    (3) the Company has received all payments due to it under any such arrangement or agreement or transfer of tax refunds made by it and no such payment is likely to be repaid; and

    (4) save in respect of this Agreement, there have not been in existence in relation to the Company any such arrangements as are referred to in s 410 of the Taxes Act 1988.

(G) *Special Arrangements and Concessions*

    (1) Full details of any special arrangements and concessions (including, without limitation, any arrangements and concessions relating to the taxation of foreign exchange gains and losses and/or financial instruments and/or loan relationships) which relate to or affect the Company and which have been made with any tax authority or relied upon by the Company, in either case within the last [six] years, are set out in the Disclosure Letter.

    (2) The Company has not taken any action which has had, or might have, the result of prejudicing or disturbing any such special arrangement or concession.

2.2 Distributions and Payments

(A) *Distributions*

    (1) No distribution within the meaning of ss 209, 210 and 212 of the Taxes Act 1988 has been made by the Company except dividends shown in its audited accounts nor is the Company bound to make any such distribution.

    (2) No securities (within the meaning of s 254(1) of the Taxes Act 1988) issued by the Company and remaining in issue at the date hereof were issued in such circumstances that the interest payable thereon falls to be treated as a distribution under s 209(2)(e)(iii) of the Taxes Act 1988.

    (3) The Company has not made or received any distribution which is an exempt distribution within s 213 of the Taxes Act 1988.

    (4) The Company has not received any capital distribution to which the provisions of s 189 of the TCGA 1992 could apply.

    (5) The Company has not used any credit, relief or set off that may be disallowed pursuant to s 237 of the Taxes Act 1988.

    (6) The Company has not issued any share capital, nor granted options or rights to any person which entitles that person to require the issue of any share capital to which the provision of s 249 of the Taxes Act 1988 could apply.

    (7) The Company has not since 8 October 1996:

(a) treated as franked investment income any qualifying distribution received which would fall to be treated as if it were a foreign income dividend pursuant to the provisions of Schedule 7 of the Finance Act 1997; or

(b) made any qualifying distribution which would fall to be treated as a foreign income dividend pursuant to the provisions of Schedule 7 of the Finance Act 1997.

(B) Group Income[101] *[The Disclosure Letter contains particulars of all elections made by the Company under s 247 of the Taxes Act 1988 and the Company has not paid any dividend without paying advance corporation tax or made any payment without deduction of income tax in the circumstances specified in sub-section (6) of that section. In respect of each such election the conditions of s 247 of the Taxes Act 1988 have at all times been and continue to be satisfied.] [The Company is not and has never been a member of a group of companies for the purposes of any taxation.]*

(C) Surrender of Advance Corporation Tax[101] *The Disclosure Letter contains particulars of all arrangements and agreements to which the Company is or has been a party relating to the surrender of advance corporation tax made or received by the Company under s 240 of the Taxes Act 1988 and:*

(1) the Company has not paid nor is liable to pay any amount in excess of the advance corporation tax surrendered to it nor for the benefit of any advance corporation tax which is or may become incapable of set off against the Company's liability to corporation tax;

(2) the Company has received all payments due to it under any such arrangement or agreement for all surrenders of advance corporation tax made by it; and

(3) save in respect of this Agreement, there have not been in existence in relation to the Company any such arrangements as are referred to in s 240(11) of the Taxes Act 1988.

(D) *ACT carry forward*   There has been no major change in the business of the Company within the meaning of s 245 of the Taxes Act 1988.

(E) *Payments under deduction*   All payments by the Company to any person which ought to have been made under deduction of tax have been so made and the Company has (if required by law to do so) provided certificates of deduction to such person and accounted to the Inland Revenue for the tax so deducted.

(F) *Payments and Disallowances*   No rents, interest, annual payments or other sums of an income nature paid or payable by the Company or which the Company is under an obligation to pay in the future are wholly or partially disallowable as deductions or charges in computing profits for the purposes of corporation tax by reason of the provisions of ss 74, 125, 338, 577, 577A, 779 to 784, and 787 of the Taxes Act 1988 or otherwise.

2.3   Losses

(A) *Group Relief*   The Disclosure Letter contains particulars of all arrangements and agreements relating to group relief to which the Company is or has been a party and:

(1) all claims by the Company for group relief were when made and are now valid and have been or will be allowed by way of relief from corporation tax;

(2) the Company has not made nor is liable to make any payment under any such arrangement or agreement save in consideration for the surrender of group relief allowable to the Company by way of relief from corporation tax and

equivalent to the taxation for which the Company would have been liable had it not been for the surrender;

(3)   the Company has received all payments due to it under any such arrangement or agreement for surrender of group relief made by it and no such payment is liable to be repaid;

(4)   the Company is not a dual resident investing company within the meaning of s 404 of the Taxes Act 1988; and

(5)   save in respect of this Agreement, there have not been in existence in relation to the Company any such arrangements as are referred to in s 410 of the Taxes Act 1988.

(B)   *Tax Losses*   There has not within the three years preceding the date hereof been a major change in the business of the Company within the meaning of s 768 of the Taxes Act 1988.

(C)   *Investment Company Deductions*[102]

Either

(1)   [There has not been a change in ownership of the Company within the meaning of s 769 of the Taxes Act 1988 in the period commencing three years before the Balance Sheet Date or in respect of any accounting period commencing prior to that date the corporation tax computations for which have yet to be agreed under s 54 of the Taxes Management Act 1970.]

Or

(1)   [In respect of the change[s] of ownership, full details of which are contained in the Disclosure Letter, there has not been:

(a)   since any such change, any significant increase in the amount of Company's capital for the purposes of s 768(B)(1) of the Taxes Act 1988;

(b)   any change in the nature or conduct of the business carried on by the Company within the period beginning three years before such change to three years thereafter;

(c)   any acquisition of an asset to which s 171 of the TCGA 1992 applied after the change of ownership together with a disposal or part disposal of that asset within the period commencing with the change in ownership and ending three years thereafter;

and at the time of the change of ownership the business carried on by the Company was not small or negligible.

2.4   Close Companies

(A)   *Close Company*[103]

(1)   [The Company is] [The Company is not and has not been within the last six years] a close company.

(2)   No distribution within s 418 of the Taxes Act 1988 has been made by the Company.

(3)   The Company has not made (and will not be deemed to have made) any loan or advance to a participator or an associate of a participator so as to become liable to make any payment under s 419 of the Taxes Act 1988.

(4)   The Company has in respect of accounting periods beginning on or before 31 March 1989 supplied to the inspector such information and particulars as are necessary to make full and accurate disclosure of all facts and considerations material to be known by him to enable him to make intimations pursuant to Sched 19, para 16 of the Taxes Act 1988 that he does not intend to make apportionments in respect of the Company for any accounting period ending on or before the Balance Sheet Date and the Company has received such intimations.

(5) No apportionment pursuant to s 423 and Sched 19 of the Taxes Act 1988 has ever been made or could be made against the Company.

(6) In respect of accounting periods beginning on or before 31 March 1989 the Company has at all times been a 'trading company' or a 'member of a trading group' as defined in Sched 19, para 7 of the Taxes Act 1988.

(7) The Company is not, and has not since 31 March 1989 been, a close investment holding company within the meaning of s 13A of the Taxes Act 1988.

(8) The Company has not expended or applied any sum liable to be regarded as income available for distribution pursuant to Sched 19, para 8 of the Taxes Act 1988 (first business loans) and is not bound (contingently or otherwise) to expend or apply any such sum.

2.5 Anti-Avoidance

(A) *Section 765 of the Taxes Act 1988* The Company has not without the prior consent of the Treasury been a party to any transaction for which consent under s 765 of the Taxes Act 1988 was required. Where such consent would have been required but for the provisions of s 765A(1) of the Taxes Act 1988, the Company has complied in full with the requirements of The Movements of Capital (Required Information) Regulations 1990 and a copy of the notification required pursuant thereto is annexed to the Disclosure Letter.

(B) *Loans to Overseas Affiliates* Prior to the end of the first accounting period after 29 March 1996 the Company was not owed any amount by any associated company resident outside the United Kingdom which is a qualifying debt for the purposes of ss 61 to 66 of the Finance Act 1993.

(C) *Controlled Foreign Companies*
(1) [The Disclosure Letter contains full details of the Company's] [The Company has no] interest in the share capital of any company not resident in the United Kingdom for taxation purposes (or which is treated for the purposes of any double taxation convention as not being so resident) which is controlled by persons resident in the United Kingdom for taxation purposes and in which the Company has 10 per cent or more of the voting rights (a 'controlled foreign company').[104]

(2) No enquiries have been made or intimated by the Inland Revenue in respect of any controlled foreign company.

(3) No direction has been made by the Board of Inland Revenue under s 747 of the Taxes Act 1988 in respect of any controlled foreign company.

(4) Section 748(1) Taxes Act 1988 applies to each controlled foreign company.

(D) *Anti-Avoidance*
(1) The Company has not at any time entered into or been a party to a transaction or series of transactions either
(a) containing steps inserted without any commercial or business purpose; or
(b) being transactions to which any of the following provisions could apply:
ss 703, 729, 730, 737, 739, 770, 774, 776, 779, 780, 781 or 786 Taxes Act 1988 or Sched 9, para 13 of the Finance Act 1996
without in the appropriate cases, having received clearance in respect thereof from the Inland Revenue.

(2) The Company has never been requested to furnish information pursuant to notices served under ss 745 or 778 of the Taxes Act 1988.

2.6   Capital Assets

(A)   *Base Values*
    (1)   The Disclosure Letter contains full and accurate particulars of:
        (a)   the extent to which the book value of an asset or a particular class of assets as shown in the Audited Accounts is in excess of either:
            (i)   the amount falling to be deducted under s 38 of the TCGA 1992 from the consideration receivable on a disposal of that asset; or
            (ii)   the balance of the qualifying expenditure attributable to that asset or pool of assets, as the case may be, brought forward into the accounting period in which Completion will occur and save to the extent disclosed, no such excess exists; and
        (b)   the extent to which provision for taxation in respect of such excess has been made in the Audited Accounts.
    (2)   No election under s 35 of the TCGA 1992 is in effect in relation to the Company and full particulars are given in the Disclosure Letter of the first relevant disposal for the purposes of the said s 35.
    (3)   The Disclosure Letter contains full and accurate particulars of all assets held by the Company on or after 6 April 1988 in respect of which relief is or would be available under Sched 4 of the TCGA 1992 upon disposal.

(B)   *Roll-over Relief*   The Disclosure Letter contains full and accurate particulars of all claims made by the Company under ss 152 to 156, s 158, ss 242 to 245, s 247 or s 248 of the TCGA 1992 and no such claim or other claim has been made by any other person (in particular pursuant to s 165 or s 175 TCGA 1992) which affects or could affect the amount or value of the consideration for the acquisition of any asset by the Company taken into account in calculating liability to corporation tax on chargeable gains on a subsequent disposal.

(C)   *Pre-entry Losses*   The Disclosure Letter contains details of all pre-entry losses falling within of Sched 7A, para 1(2)(a) of the TCGA 1992 which have, or will have, accrued to the Company prior to Completion and details of all assets which, if disposed of on Completion, would give rise to an allowable loss.

(D)   *Depreciatory Transactions*   No loss which might accrue on the disposal by the Company of any share in or security of any company is liable to be reduced by virtue of any depreciatory transaction within the meaning of s 176 and s 177 of the TCGA 1992 nor is any expenditure on any share or security liable to be reduced under s 125 of the TCGA 1992.

(E)   *Value Shifting*   The Company does not hold, and has not held, any shares upon the disposal of which ss 31 or 32 of the TCGA 1992 could apply.

(F)   *Connected Party and Intra Group Transactions*
    (1)   The Company has not disposed of or acquired any asset to or from any person connected with it within s 839 of the Taxes Act 1988 or in circumstances such that the provision of s 17 of the TCGA 1992 could apply to such disposal or acquisition.
    (2)   The Company has not acquired any asset (past or present) from any other company then belonging to the same group of companies as the Company within the meaning of s 170(2) to (14) of the TCGA 1992.
    (3)   The Company has not made, and is not entitled to make, a claim pursuant to s 172 of the TCGA 1992.

(G)   *Group Reconstructions*   The Company has not been party to any scheme of reconstruction or reorganisation to which the provisions of s 139 of the TCGA 1992, s 703 of the Taxes Act 1988 or to which s 343 of the Taxes Act 1988 could apply.

(H)   *Chargeable Debts*   In respect of the period ended 31 March 1996 no gain chargeable to corporation tax will accrue to the Company on the disposal of any debt owing to the Company not being a debt on a security or on the disposal of any corporate bond not being a qualifying corporate bond.

(I) *Chargeable Policies* The Company has not acquired benefits under any policy of assurance otherwise than as original beneficial owner.

(J) *Gains Accruing to Non-resident Companies or Trusts* There has not accrued any gain in respect of which the Company may be liable to corporation tax on chargeable gains by virtue of the provisions of s 13 or s 87 of the TCGA 1992.

(K) *Indexation: Groups and Associated Companies* In respect of the period ended 31 March 1996 the Company did not own any debts or shares to which the provisions of s 182 to s 184 of the TCGA 1992 could apply.

(L) *Company Migration*
   (1) The Company is not a dual resident company for the purposes of s 139(3) or s 160 or s 188 of the TCGA 1992.
   (2) There are no circumstances pursuant to which the Company may become liable to tax pursuant to s 185 (Deemed disposal of assets on company ceasing to be resident in UK), s 186 (Deemed disposal of assets on company ceasing to be liable to UK tax), s 187 (Postponement of charge on deemed disposal) of the TCGA 1992 or s 132 (Liability of other persons for unpaid tax) Finance Act 1988 or s 191 of the TCGA 1992 (Non-payment of tax by non-resident companies).

2.7 Claims, Elections and Clearances

(A) *Claims by the Company* The Company has made no claim under any of the following:
   (1) section 279 of the TCGA 1992 (assets situated outside the United Kingdom);
   (2) section 24(2) of the TCGA 1992 (assets of negligible value);
   (3) section 280 of the TCGA 1992 (tax on chargeable gains payable by instalments);
   (4) sections 242 and 243 of the Taxes Act 1988 (surplus franked investment income); or
   (5) section 584 of the Taxes Act 1988 (unremittable income arising outside the United Kingdom).

(B) *Elections* The Disclosure Letter contains full particulars of all elections made by the Company under the following provisions:
   (1) sections 524, 527 and 534 of the Taxes Act 1988 (lump sum receipts for patents and copyright);
   (2) section 37 of the Capital Allowances Act 1990 (short life assets); and
   (3) section 11 of the Capital Allowances Act 1990 (leasehold interests).

(C) *Clearances* There are annexed to the Disclosure Letter copies of all correspondence relating to applications for clearance under any enactment relating to taxation. All facts and circumstances material to such applications for clearance were disclosed in such applications.

2.8 Miscellaneous

(A) *Assessment of Tax on Lessees* No notice pursuant to s 23 Taxes Act 1988 has been served on the Company.

(B) *Leaseholds* The Company is not liable to taxation under the provisions of ss 34, 35 and 36 Taxes Act 1988 nor does it own any leasehold interest to which the said s 35 may apply.

(C) *Foreign Exchange Gains and Losses*

(1)   No exchange gain or loss of the Company has been calculated in accordance with Sched 15 of the Finance Act 1993 and regulations made thereunder.

(2)   The Disclosure Letter contains full details of all claims to defer unrealised exchange gains made by the Company pursuant to s 139 of the Finance Act 1993.

(3)   The Disclosure Letter contains details of all debts to which the provisions of Chapter II of Part II Finance Act 1993 do not apply by virtue of reg 3 of the Exchange Gains and Losses (Transitional Provisions) Regulations 1994.

(4)   The Company has not received any direction as referred to in s 136(1)(*d*) or s 136A(7)(*b*) of the Finance Act 1993.

(D)   *Financial Instruments*

(1)   The Company has not entered into any transactions for which the provisions of s 165, s 166 and s 167 of the Finance Act 1994 could apply.

(2)   The Disclosure Letter contains full details of all qualifying contracts with non resident persons for the purposes of s 168 of the Finance Act 1994.

(E)   Incorporation of Partnership/Acquisition of Unincorporated Business
In respect of the [agreement]:

(1)   the Vendors and the Company have jointly made elections pursuant to the Capital Allowances Act 1990, ss 77 or 158;

(2)   all capital assets were transferred at market value and no claim for relief under TCGA 1992, s 165 has been or will be made;

(3)   stock and work in progress were transferred at the lower of cost or net realisable value;

(4)   for the purposes of value added tax, the transfer of assets was neither a supply of goods nor services; and

(5)   stamp duty has been properly paid on the [agreement] and on all documents executed pursuant thereto.

2.9   Loan Relationships

(A)   The Company applies an authorised accruals method of accounting (as that term is defined in s 85 of the Finance Act 1996) in respect of all loan relationships (as that term is defined in s 81 of the Finance Act 1996) to which it is a party.

(B)   The Disclosure Letter contains full and accurate particulars of any loan relationship to which the Company is a party, whether as debtor or creditor, where any other party to that loan relationship is connected with the Company for the purposes of Chapter II of Part IV of the Finance Act 1996.

(C)   The Disclosure Letter contains full and accurate particulars of any loan relationship to which the Company is a party and to which s 92 or s 93 of the Finance Act 1996 applies.

(D)   The Disclosure Letter contains full and accurate particulars of any debtor relationship (as that term is defined in s 103 of the Finance Act 1996) of the Company which relates to a relevant discounted security (as that term is defined in Sched 13, para 3 of the Finance Act 1996) to which Sched 9, para 17 or para 18 of the Finance Act 1996 applies.

(E)   The Company has not entered into any transaction to which Sched 9, para 11(1) of the Finance Act 1996 applies.

(F)   The Company has not been, and is not entitled to be, released from any liability which arises under a debtor relationship of that Company.

(G)   The Disclosure Letter contains full and accurate particulars of (i) any loan relationship to which the Company is a party, whether as debtor or creditor, to which Sched 15, para 8 of the Finance Act 1996 has applied or will apply on the occurrence of a relevant event (as defined in para 8(2)) in respect thereof; (ii) in each case, the amount of any deemed chargeable gain or deemed allowable loss which has arisen or will arise in consequence of that relevant event; and (iii) any election made pursuant to Sched 15, para 9 of the Finance Act 1996.

2.10 Taxation of Employees and Agents

(A) *PAYE* The Company has properly operated the Pay As You Earn system deducting tax as required by law from all payments to or treated as made to employees and ex-employees of the Company and punctually accounted to the Inland Revenue for all tax so deducted and all returns required pursuant to s 203 of the Taxes Act 1988 and regulations made thereunder have been punctually made and are accurate and complete in all respects.

(B) *Dispensations and PAYE Audits* The Disclosure Letter contains full details of all dispensations obtained by the Company and all details of any visit from the Audit Office of the Inland Revenue within the last six years including full details of any settlement made pursuant thereto.

(C) *Benefits for Employees*

   (1) The Company has not made any payment to or provided any benefit for any officer or employee or ex-officer or ex-employee of the Company which is not allowable as a deduction in calculating the profits of the Company for taxation purposes.

   (2) The Company has not issued any shares in the circumstances described in s 138(1) of the Taxes Act 1988 and has complied with s 139(5) of the Taxes Act 1988.

   (3) The Company has not issued any shares in the circumstances described in s 77(1) and has complied with s 85 of the Finance Act 1988.

   (4) The Company has not made any payment to which s 313 of the Taxes Act 1988 applies.

(D) *Slave Companies* Any payment made to or for the direct or indirect benefit of any person who is or might be regarded by any taxation authority as an employee of the Company is made to such person direct and is not made to any company or other entity associated with that person.

(E) *Sub-Contractors*[105] [The Company is not and never has been either a contractor or a sub-contractor for the purposes of Chapter IV Part XIII of the Taxes Act 1988.]

   [The Company has properly operated the sub-contractors' scheme deducting tax as required by law from all payments made to sub-contractors of the Company and punctually accounted to the Inland Revenue for all tax so deducted.]

(F) *National Insurance* The Company has paid all national insurance contributions for which it is liable and has kept proper books and records relating to the same and has not been a party to any scheme or arrangement to avoid any liability to account for primary or secondary national insurance contributions.

2.11 Stamp Duties

(A) *Stamp Duty* The Company has duly paid or has procured to be paid all stamp duty on documents to which it is a party or in which it is interested and which are liable to stamp duty.

(B) *Stamp Duty Reserve Tax* The Company has made all returns and paid all stamp duty reserve tax in respect of any transaction in securities to which it has been a party or in respect of which it is liable to account for stamp duty reserve tax.

2.12 Value Added Tax

(A) The Company has complied with all statutory provisions and regulations relating to value added tax and has duly paid or provided for all amounts of value added tax for which the Company is liable.

(B) (1) All supplies made by the Company are taxable supplies and the Company is not and will not be denied credit for any input tax by reason of the operation of s 26 Value Added Tax Act 1994 and regulations made thereunder.

(2) All input tax for which the Company has claimed credit has been paid by the Company in respect of supplies made to it relating to goods or services used or to be used for the purpose of the Company's business.

(3) The Company is not and has not been, for value added tax purposes a member of any group of companies (other than that comprising the Company and the Subsidiaries alone) and no act or transaction has been effected in consequence whereof the Company is or may be held liable for any value added tax chargeable against some other company except where that other company is a Subsidiary.

(4) No supplies have been made to the Company to which the provisions of s 8 of the Value Added Tax Act 1994 might apply.

(5) The Company has not committed any offence contrary to s 60 or s 72 of the Value Added Tax Act 1994, nor has it received any penalty liability notice pursuant to s 64(3), surcharge liability notice pursuant to s 59, or written warning issued pursuant to s 76(2) of that Act.

(6) The Company has not been and is not liable to be registered for value added tax otherwise than pursuant to the provisions of Sched 1, para 1 of the Value Added Tax Act 1994.

(7) The Company has not been required to give security under Sched 11, para 4 of the Value Added Tax Act 1994.

(8) The Disclosure Letter contains details and copies of all elections, together with the relevant notification, made by the Company pursuant to Sched 10, para 2 of the Value Added Tax Act 1994.

(9) The Company is not and has not since 1 August 1989 been in relation to any land, building or civil engineering work a developer within the meaning of Sched 10, para 5(5) of the Value Added Tax Act 1994.

(10) The Company has not paid and is not liable to pay any interest pursuant to s 74 of the Value Added Tax Act 1994.

(11) The Disclosure Letter contains full details of any assets of the Company to which the provisions of Part XV of the Value Added Tax Regulations 1995 (the Capital Goods Scheme) apply and in particular:

(a) the identity (including in the case of leasehold property, the term of years), date of acquisition and cost of the asset; and

(b) the proportion of input tax for which credit has been claimed (either provisionally or finally in a tax year and stating which).

2.13 Inheritance Tax and Gifts[106]

(A) *Powers of Sale for Inheritance Tax Purposes*   There are not in existence any circumstances whereby any such power as is mentioned in s 212 Inheritance Tax Act 1984 could be exercised in relation to any shares in, securities of, or assets of, the Company.

(B) *Gifts*

(1) The Company is not liable to be assessed to corporation tax on chargeable

gains or to inheritance tax as donor or donee of any gift or transferor or transferee of value.

(2) The Company has not been a party to associated operations in relation to a transfer of value within the meaning of s 268 of the Inheritance Tax Act 1984.

(3) No Inland Revenue charge (as defined in s 237 of the Inheritance Tax Act 1984) is outstanding over any asset of the Company or in relation to any shares in the capital of the Company.

(4) The Company has not received any asset as mentioned in s 282 of the TCGA 1992.

SCHEDULE 5

ADJUSTMENT OF CONSIDERATION[107]

1 Interpretation

In this Schedule, where the context admits:

'the Audited Accounts' and 'the Balance Sheet Date' and any other defined term used in this Schedule shall have the same meanings as in the Agreement and the Schedules;

'Completion Accounts' means the accounts prepared in accordance with para and agreed or determined in accordance with Sub-Paragraph 4;

'Net Tangible Assets' means the aggregate value of all fixed and current assets (excluding goodwill, patents, trade marks and other intangible assets)[108] minus the aggregate value of all liabilities and provisions (in accordance with Sched 4, para 89 of of the Companies Act 1985 [and SSAP 18 in respect of contingent liabilities]) and excluding any reserves or capital created by the upward revaluation of assets subsequent to the Balance Sheet Date;

'the Provisional Consideration' means the consideration for the Sale Shares of £[   ] stated in Sub-Clause 2.1 (Amount [Consideration Shares]);

'the Purchaser's Accountants' means [   ];

'SSAP' means Statement of Standard Accounting Practice in force at the date hereof; and

'the Vendor's Accountants' means [   ].

2 Completion Accounts

2.1 Preparation

The Purchaser shall as soon as practicable, and in any event within [42] days after Completion, procure that accounts for the Company and the Subsidiaries shall be prepared in accordance with this Schedule and the parties shall use their best endeavours to secure compliance with this Schedule by their respective accountants. The Vendor shall promptly supply all such information and provide access to all such records and personnel as the Purchaser shall reasonably require for such purpose.

2.2 Description

The Completion Accounts shall consist of a consolidated balance sheet[109] of the Company and the Subsidiaries as at the close of business on the date of Completion [and a consolidated profit and loss account[110] of the Company and the Subsidiaries in respect of the period from the day following the Balance Sheet Date to the date of Completion (both dates inclusive)] [and which shall be substantially in the form of the *pro forma* accounts in the agreed terms].[111]

2.3 General Requirements

Subject to the specific requirements of Sub-Paragraph 2.4 which shall take priority over the general requirements set out below, the Completion Accounts shall:

(A) make full provision for all actual, future and contingent liabilities of the Company and the Subsidiaries as at the date of Completion;

(B) be prepared under the historic cost convention and in accordance with the requirements of all relevant statutes and generally accepted accounting practices and principles, SSAPs and Financial Reporting Standards;[112]

(C) [show a true and fair view of the state of affairs of the Company and the Subsidiaries at the date of Completion [and the profits (or loss) of the Company and the Subsidiaries for the period from the Balance Sheet Date to the date of Completion];]

(D) [apply and adopt the same bases and policies of accounting as applied or adopted for the purposes of the Audited Accounts.][113]

2.4 Specific Requirements[114]

In preparing the Completion Accounts:

(A) no value shall be attributed to goodwill or any other intangible asset;

(B) other fixed assets shall be included at the value at which they were included in the Audited Accounts, (or, if acquired after the Balance Sheet Date, their cost) on a *pro rata* basis at the rates used in the Audited Accounts and, in each case, less provisions for damage or impairment [on the same basis used in preparing the Audited Accounts];[115]

(C) stock shall be determined in accordance with Paragraph 3 (Stock Valuation) and valued [on the same basis as used in the Audited Accounts (details of which are described in the Disclosure Letter)] and full provision will be made for unusable, unsaleable, slow moving or deteriorated stocks;[116]

(D) no value shall be attributed to any assets (including in particular any prepayment or debt) except to the extent that (following Completion) the Company or a Subsidiary will have the benefit of the same;

(E) full provision shall be made for rebates or discounts that will fall due and fees and commissions that will become payable after Completion in either case in respect of sales or other transactions that took place before Completion;[117]

(F) full provision shall be made for any liability arising as a result of the change of control of the Company on Completion;

(G) [to the extent that it is not capable of being set off against the liability of the Company for corporation tax for the current financial year or any previous financial year, full provision shall be made for the advance corporation tax payable on any distribution declared or paid before Completion];

(H) full provision shall be made in respect of the cost of making good dilapidations and/or wants of repair on or to the Properties;[118]

(I) [full provision shall be made in respect of all payments in favour of [   ] and [   ] in their capacity as directors or employees or former directors or employees;][119]

(J) full provision shall be made for any debts due in the ordinary course of trading outstanding and uncollected at Completion for a period of more than 60 days past the due date and proper provision or reserve shall be made for all other bad or doubtful debts included in the Completion Accounts;

(K) full provision shall be made for any repairs or other servicing required in relation to any vehicles or other plant and machinery;

(L) [full provision shall be made for liabilities disclosed in the Disclosure Letter];[120]

(M) provision shall be made for deferred tax in accordance [with normal accounting principles]; and

(N) [specify any other particular requirements—these should be checked (where applicable) with the Purchaser's accountants].[121]

3   Stock Valuation

For the purposes of the preparation of the Completion Accounts, the value of stock shall be ascertained in accordance with the provisions of this Paragraph.

(A)   The Vendor and the Purchaser shall cause a stocktaking to be made on the Completion Date of all the stock insofar as it then belongs to the Company and the Subsidiaries.

(B)   Unless otherwise agreed by the parties such stocktaking shall consist of a physical check of the amount, quality and condition of all such stock situated on the Properties at the Completion Date and an inspection of the books and records and contractual documentation (of the Company and the Subsidiaries) for all stock not so situated together with confirmation from the person or persons having physical possession of such stock of the extent of any interest in or encumbrance claimed over such stock (if any).

(C)   When such stocktaking has been completed the stock shall be valued by the Purchaser in accordance with Paragraph 2.4(C) and included in the Completion Accounts.

4   Procedure[122]

4.1   Submission of Draft

(A)   As soon as the Completion Accounts shall have been prepared, the Purchaser shall send a copy to the Vendor together with such working papers used in connection with the preparation of the same as it considers necessary or appropriate to understand and agree the Completion Accounts and shall in addition, at the same time, send to the Vendor its calculation of the Net Tangible Assets.

(B)   Unless the Vendor shall within 21 days of receipt of the Completion Accounts (and associated papers and calculation as provided in Sub-Paragraph (A)) serve a notice in writing on the Purchaser that it objects to the Completion Accounts (identifying the reason for any objection and the amount(s) or item(s) in the Completion Accounts and/or calculation which is/are in dispute) (such notification being, for the purposes of this Paragraph 4, an 'Objection Notice') the Vendor shall be deemed to have agreed to the Completion Accounts and the Purchaser's calculation of the Net Tangible Assets for all purposes of this Agreement.

4.2   Agreement of Draft

If, within the period referred to in Sub-Paragraph 4.1(B), the Vendor shall give the Purchaser an Objection Notice then the Purchaser and the Vendor shall use their best endeavours to reach agreement upon adjustments to the draft and the value of Net Tangible Assets.

4.3   Independent Accountant[123]

In the event that the Vendor and the Purchaser are unable to reach agreement within 28 days following service of the Objection Notice, either the Vendor or the Purchaser shall be entitled to refer the matter or matters in dispute to an independent firm of chartered accountants agreed upon between them or (failing agreement) to be selected (at the instance of either party) by the President for the time being of the Institute of Chartered Accountants for England and Wales. Such independent firm of chartered accountants shall act as experts not as arbitrators and shall determine the matter or matters in dispute and whose decision shall, save in the event of fraud or manifest error, be binding. The costs of the independent firm of accountants shall be borne by the Vendor and the Purchaser [equally or in such other proportions as the said accountants shall direct].

4.4 Report

If the Vendor accepts, or is deemed to accept, that the said draft complies with Paragraph 2 the Purchaser['s Accountants] shall sign a report to the effect that the Completion Accounts comply with Paragraph 2 and any Completion Accounts so reported on, or (if Sub-Paragraph 4.3 shall apply) the final draft of the Completion Accounts as determined by the independent accountant, shall be the Completion Accounts for the purposes of this Agreement and shall be final and binding on the parties.

4.5 Information and Explanations

The Purchaser and the Purchaser's Accountants shall provide such information and explanations relating to the draft Completion Accounts and their preparation as the Vendor's Accountants, or any independent chartered accountant appointed pursuant to Paragraph 4.3, shall reasonably require.

5 Adjustment of Consideration

5.1 Increase or Reduction

When the Completion Accounts have become binding, the Provisional Consideration shall forthwith:

(A) be increased by the amount (if any) by which the Net Tangible Assets of the Company and the Subsidiaries as at the date of Completion as shown by the Completion Accounts are greater than the Net Tangible Assets of the Company and the Subsidiaries as at the Balance Sheet Date as shown by the Audited Accounts[124] namely [£   ]; or (as the case may be)

(B) be reduced by the amount (if any) by which the Net Tangible Assets of the Company and the Subsidiaries as at the date of Completion as shown by the Completion Accounts are less than the Net Tangible Assets of the Company and the Subsidiaries as at the Balance Sheet Date as shown by the Audited Accounts[124] namely [£   ].

5.2 Payment

Any increase or reduction in the Provisional Consideration shall be paid by the Purchaser or the Vendor (as appropriate) within 14 days after the Completion Accounts have become binding as aforesaid and any amount not paid when due shall carry interest (accrued daily and compounded monthly) at the rate of [   ] per cent per annum above the base rate of [   ] Bank PLC from time to time from the due date until the date of actual payment (as well after judgment as before).

6 Interaction with Other Provisions[125]

[Subject to the due performance of Paragraph 5, if the Purchaser shall have any claim against the Vendor under this Agreement in respect of any liability or deficiency which is taken into account in the Completion Accounts the amount of such liability or deficiency so taken into account shall be deducted from the amount of the Purchaser's claim but, save as aforesaid, preparation and acceptance of the Completion Accounts by the Purchaser shall be without prejudice to any claim which the Purchaser may have against the Vendor under or in respect of any breach of this Agreement.]

SCHEDULE 6

PENSIONS

[A   Company has own final salary scheme]

1   Interpretation

1.1   Definitions

In this Schedule, where the context admits:

'Actuarial Assumptions' means the actuarial assumptions and method set out in a letter in agreed terms dated [   ] from the Vendor's Actuary to the Purchaser's Actuary;

'Actuary' means a Fellow of the Institute of Actuaries or of the Faculty of Actuaries or of any successor body of such Institute or Faculty;

'Company' means the Company and the Subsidiaries or such one or more of them as the context requires;

'Pension Scheme' means [the retirement benefits scheme known as [   ] which was established by a deed dated [   ] (or the trustees from time to time of that scheme as the context requires);] [Scheme A [,] [and Scheme B] [and Scheme C] (or such one or [other] [more] of them as the context requires);]

'Purchaser's Actuary' means [   ] (or such other Actuary as the Purchaser may appoint for the purposes of this Schedule);

'Relevant Employee' means any past or present employee of the Company or of any predecessor to all or part of its business;

['Scheme A' means the retirement benefits scheme known as [   ] which was established by a trust deed dated [   ] (or the trustees from time to time of that scheme as the context requires);]

['Scheme B' means the retirement benefits scheme known as [   ] which was established by a trust deed dated [   ] (or the trustees from time to time of that scheme as the context requires);]

['Scheme C' means the retirement benefits scheme known as [   ] which was established by a trust deed dated [   ] (or the trustees from time to time of that scheme as the context requires);]

'Shortfall' means the amount (if any), determined in accordance with the Actuarial Assumptions, by which the capital value at Completion of the benefits which are then payable, or prospectively or contingently payable, under the Pension Scheme exceeds the value at Completion of the then assets of the Pension Scheme. For the purposes of this definition:

(A)   when calculating the value of the assets of the Pension Scheme no account shall be taken of:

    (1)   any debts of the Company to the Pension Scheme,[126] or

    (2)   any contributions payable to the Pension Scheme after Completion,

    but subject thereto the assets shall be valued in accordance with the Actuarial Assumptions;[127]

(B)   when calculating the liabilities of the Pension Scheme no account shall be taken of any benefits in respect of service after the Completion Date occurs but allowance shall be made in accordance with the Actuarial Assumptions for:

    (1)   projected increases in earnings up to the assumed date of cessation of

pensionable service;[128] and

(2)   increases to pensions in payment or in deferment;

(C)   when calculating the liabilities of the Pension Scheme allowance shall also be made in accordance with the Actuarial Assumptions for any refund of contributions and any benefits in pension form payable in the event of death whilst in service but, save where death occurs before Completion, no account shall be taken of any other lump sum death-in-service benefits;

(D)   any improvement to the benefits under the Pension Scheme which has been announced before Completion shall be deemed to have been duly effected under the Pension Scheme and to have come into force before Completion; and

(E)   the Pension Scheme shall be deemed to be under an overriding obligation to provide benefits [(including guaranteed minimum pensions within the meaning of the Pension Schemes Act 1993)] which are attributable to any period of employment after 16 May 1990 on a basis which does not discriminate between men and women and without reducing the benefits of either sex;[129]

'Vendor's Actuary' means [   ] (or such other Actuary as may be appointed by the Vendor for the purposes of this Schedule).

1.2   Employees

References in this Schedule to employees includes directors.

[1.3   Schedule Applies Separately to Each Pension Scheme

Paragraphs 2 and 3, and for the purposes of those Paragraphs, Paragraph 1, apply separately to each Pension Scheme.][130]

2   Calculation of Shortfall[131]

2.1   Data

The Vendor and the Purchaser shall each use all reasonable endeavours to procure that all such information as the Vendor's Actuary or the Purchaser's Actuary or any independent Actuary appointed under Sub-Paragraph 2.3 may reasonably request for the purposes of this Schedule is supplied promptly to such Actuary and that all such information is complete and accurate in all respects.

2.2   Agreement of Shortfall

The Purchaser's Actuary shall determine the amount (if any) of the Shortfall and shall submit his findings in writing to the Vendor's Actuary for agreement. If the Vendor's Actuary and the Purchaser's Actuary agree the amount (if any) of the Shortfall, the Vendor shall procure that the Vendor's Actuary and the Purchaser shall procure that the Purchaser's Actuary jointly certify that amount as the Shortfall.

2.3   Dispute

If the Vendor's Actuary and the Purchaser's Actuary fail to agree the amount (if any) of the Shortfall within two months from the date the Purchaser's Actuary first submits his findings to the Vendor's Actuary in accordance with Sub-Paragraph 2.2, the matter may, at the option of either the Vendor or the Purchaser, be referred to an independent Actuary to be agreed between the Vendor and the Purchaser or, in default of agreement within 14 days from the first nomination of an Actuary by one party to the other, to be appointed by the President for the time being of The Institute of Actuaries (or any successor body) on the application of either the Vendor or the Purchaser. The certificate of the independent Actuary as to the amount (if any) of the Shortfall shall, save in the event of fraud or manifest error, be final and binding on the parties and, in so certifying, the independent Actuary shall be deemed to be acting as an expert and not as an arbitrator.[132] His costs shall be borne by the Vendor and the Purchaser [equally or in such other proportions as he shall direct.]

3   Payment of Shortfall

3.1   The Vendor shall within a period of 14 days commencing on and including the date the amount (if any) of the Shortfall is certified as aforesaid pay, by way of adjustment so far as possible to the consideration for the Sale Shares,[133] to the Purchaser (or to a third party, as the Purchaser may direct) a sum in cash equal to the amount shown in the certificate as being the Shortfall[134] together with interest thereon (accruing daily and compounded monthly) from and including the date upon which Completion occurs to but excluding the date final payment is made in accordance with this Paragraph (as well after judgment as before). Such interest shall be at the Agreed Rate up to and including the last day in the aforesaid 14-day period and thereafter at the Agreed Rate plus [   ] per cent per annum. In this Paragraph 'Agreed Rate' means the base rate from time to time of [   ] Bank PLC plus [   ] per cent per annum.

4   Warranties and Representations[68;135]

4.1   The Vendor hereby warrants and represents[68] to and for the benefit of the Purchaser in the following terms:

(A)   *No Other Arrangements*   Save for the Pension Scheme the Company is not a party to nor participates in nor contributes to any scheme, agreement or arrangement (whether legally enforceable or not) for the provision of any pension, retirement, death, incapacity, sickness, disability, accident or other like benefits (including the payment after cessation of employment with the Company of medical expenses) for any Relevant Employee or for the widow, widower, child or dependant of any Relevant Employee.

(B)   *No Assurances etc*   Neither the Company *nor any member of the Vendor's Group*:

    (1)   has given any undertaking or assurance (whether legally enforceable or not) as to the continuance, introduction, improvement or increase of any benefit of a kind described in Sub-Paragraph 4.1(A) above, or

    (2)   is paying or has in the last two years paid any such benefit,

to (in either case) any Relevant Employee or to any widow, widower, child or dependant of any Relevant Employee.

(C)   *All Details Disclosed*   All material details relating to the Pension Scheme are contained in or annexed to the Disclosure Letter including, but without limitation, the following:

    (1)   true and complete copies of the following documents referable to the Pension Scheme, *viz*:

        (a)   all deeds, rules and other governing documents;

        (b)   all announcements, booklets and the like of current effect;

        (c)   the latest completed actuarial valuation report and any document (including any draft) containing the results or preliminary results of any subsequent actuarial valuation;

        (d)   the latest completed audited accounts and any subsequent accounts or draft accounts;

      (e)   all investment management, custodian, administration and other agreements to which the Pension Scheme is a party;

      (f)   all insurance policies (if any) and annuity contracts (if any) and all proposals (if any) to effect any such policies or contracts which are with any insurer for consideration;

      (g)   an accurate list of all active members, deferred members and pensioners with such data as is necessary to establish their respective entitlements under the Pension Scheme;

      (h)   an accurate list with the names and addresses of the trustees;

      (i)   the memorandum and articles of association of any trustee which is a company and a list with the names and addresses of the directors and secretary of that company;

      (j)   interna; dispute resolution procedure, schedule of contributions and statement of investment principles for the purposes of the Pensions Act 1995;[136]

(2)   details of the arrangements made or being considered or confirmation that none have been made or are being considered to comply with ss 16 to 2, of the Pensions Act 1995;[137]

(3)   details of the investments and other assets of the Pension Scheme;

(4)   details of all amendments (if any) to the Pension Scheme which have been announced or are proposed but which have not yet been formally made;

(5)   details of all discretionary increases (if any) to pensions in payment or in deferment under the Pension Scheme which have been granted in the ten years prior to the date of this Agreement or which are under consideration;

(6)   details of all discretionary practices (if any) which may have led any person to expect additional benefits in a given set of circumstances (by way of example, but without limitation, on retirement at the behest of the Company or in the event of redundancy); and

(7)   details of the rate at which and basis upon which the Company currently contributes to the Pension Scheme, any change to that rate and/or basis which is proposed or which is under consideration and all contributions paid to the Pension Scheme by the Company in the three years prior to the date of this Agreement.

(D) *Membership*   Every person who has at any time had the right to join, or apply to join, the Pension Scheme has been properly advised of that right. No Relevant Employee has been excluded from membership of the Pension Scheme or from any of the benefits thereunder in contravention of Art 119 of the Treaty of Rome, the Pensions Act 1995 or other applicable laws or requirements or the provisions of the Pension Scheme or otherwise.[138]

(E) *No Pay Restructuring*   There has not in the last four years been any restructuring of the earnings of all or any members or prospective members of the Pension Scheme (by way of example, but without limitation, consolidation of bonuses into basic pay).[139]

(F) *Transfer Payments*   No transfer value has been paid (directly or indirectly) to the Pension Scheme from another arrangement for any member of the Pension Scheme under which any benefits referable to that member contravened Art 119 of the Treaty of Rome, s 62 of the Pensions Act 1995 or other applicable law or requirement.[140]

(G) *Death Benefits Insured*   All benefits (other than any refund of members' contributions with interest where appropriate) payable under the Pension Scheme on the death of any person while in employment to which the Pension Scheme relates are insured fully under a policy with an insurance company of good repute and there are no grounds on which that company might avoid liability under that policy.

(H) *Contributions and Expenses*   Contributions to the Pension Scheme are not paid in arrear and all contributions and other amounts which have fallen due for payment have been paid. No fee, charge or expense relating to or in connection with the Pension Scheme has been incurred but not paid. If any such fee, charge or expense has been paid by any person other than the Pension Scheme, the Pension Scheme has reimbursed that person if and to the extent that the Pension Scheme is or may become liable so to do.

(I) *Augmentation*   No power under the Pension Scheme has been exercised in relation to any employee of the Company or, since the date as at which the last actuarial valuation of the Pension Scheme to be completed prior to the date of this Agreement was undertaken, in respect of any other person:

(1) to provide terms of membership of the Pension Scheme (whether as to benefits or contributions) which are different from those generally applicable to the members of the Pension Scheme; or

(2) to provide any benefits which would not but for the exercise of that power have been payable under the Pension Scheme; or

(3) to augment any benefits under the Pension Scheme.

(J) *Company's Obligations*   The Company:

(1) has observed and performed those provisions of the Pension Scheme which apply to it; [and]

(2) may (without the consent of any person or further payment) terminate its liability to contribute to the Pension Scheme at any time subject only to giving such notice (if any) as is expressly provided for in the documentation containing the current provisions governing the Pension Scheme[141] [.][; and

(3) has at all material times held or been named in a contracting-out certificate (within the meaning of s 7(1), Pension Schemes Act 1993) referable to the Pension Scheme.]

(K) *No Other Employer*   The Company is the only employer for the time being participating in the Pension Scheme. No employer which has previously participated in the Pension Scheme has any claim under the Pension Scheme and in respect of any such employer the period of participation has been terminated and benefits have been provided in accordance with the provisions of the Pension Scheme.

(L) *Administration*   All documentation and records in respect of the Pension Scheme are up to date and so far as the Vendor is aware complete and accurate in all material respects.

(M) *Investments*   None of the assets of the Pension Scheme:

(1) is invested in any description of employer-related investments (within the meaning of s 40 of the Pensions Act 1995); or

(2) save for deposits with banks, building societies and other financial institutions and save for any instrument creating or acknowledging an indebtedness listed on any recognised stock exchange of repute, is loaned to any person; or

(3) is subject to any encumbrance or agreement or commitment to give or create any encumbrance.

(N) *Compliance*   The Pension Scheme:

(1) is an exempt approved scheme (within the meaning of s 592(1) of the Income and Corporation Taxes Act 1988);

(2) has properly and punctually accounted to the Board of Inland Revenue for all and any tax for which the Pension Scheme is liable or accountable;

    (3)   is not liable to taxation on any income from or capital gains on any of the funds which are or have been held for the purposes of the Pension Scheme;[142] and

    (4)   has at all times complied with and been administered in accordance with all applicable laws, regulations and requirements (including those of the Board of Inland Revenue and of trust law);

(O) *Actuarial*[143] The report dated [   ] of [   ] on the actuarial valuation of the Pension Scheme as at [   ] (the 'Valuation Date') (a true copy of the report being annexed to the Disclosure Letter) shows a true and fair view of the respective actuarial values of the assets and liabilities of the Pension Scheme at the Valuation Date on the basis of the actuarial assumptions and method detailed in that report. Since the Valuation Date nothing has occurred, been done or been omitted to be done which may affect materially the level of funding of the benefits under the Pension Scheme.

(P) *Disputes* None of the Pension Scheme, the Company *or any member of the Vendor's Group* is engaged or involved in any proceedings which relate to or are in connection with the Pension Scheme or the benefits thereunder and no such proceedings are pending or threatened and so far as the Vendor is aware there are no facts likely to give rise to any such proceedings. In this Sub-Paragraph 'proceedings' includes any litigation or arbitration and also includes any investigation or determination by the Pensions Ombudsman or the Occupational Pensions Advisory Service and any complaint under any internal dispute resolution procedure established in connection with the Pension Scheme.

(Q) *Indemnities* In relation to the Pension Scheme or funds which are or have been held for the purposes thereof neither the Company nor the trustees or administrator of the Pension Scheme has given an indemnity or guarantee to any person (other than in the case of the Company any general indemnity in favour of the trustees or administrator under the documentation governing the Pension Scheme).

5 Damages for Breach of Pension Warranties[144]

5.1 In determining the damages flowing from any breach of Warranties contained in Paragraph 4, the Company shall be deemed to be under a liability:

(A) to provide and to continue to provide any benefit of a kind referred to in that Paragraph which is now provided or has been announced or is proposed; and

(B) to maintain and to continue to maintain (without benefits being reduced) the Pension Scheme and any other arrangements of a kind described in that Paragraph which are now in existence or are proposed and any discretionary practices of a kind referred to in that Paragraph which have hitherto been carried on.

SCHEDULE 6

PENSIONS

[B   Company participates in group final salary scheme]

1   Interpretation

1.1   Definitions

In this Schedule, where the context admits:

'Actuarial Assumptions' means the actuarial assumptions and method set out in the Actuary's Letter;

'Actuary' means a Fellow of The Institute of Actuaries or of The Faculty of Actuaries or of any successor body to such Institute or Faculty;

'Actuary's Letter' means a letter in agreed terms dated [   ] from the Vendor's Actuary to the Purchaser's Actuary;

'Adjusted Transfer Value' means [the Transfer Value multiplied by the Investment Adjustment from and including the Membership Transfer Date to and including the Payment Date;][145]

'Basic Amount' means an amount, determined in accordance with the Actuarial Assumptions, equal to the capital value at the Completion Date of the benefits which are payable under the Pension Scheme to or in respect of the Transferring Employees, such benefits being calculated as if the Company were to continue participating in the Pension Scheme indefinitely.[146] For the purposes of this definition:

(A)   benefits include any benefits which are contingently or prospectively payable;

(B)   when calculating the value of the benefits payable under the Pension Scheme no account shall be taken of any benefits in respect of service after the Completion Date but allowance shall be made in accordance with the Actuarial Assumptions for:

(1)   projected increases in earnings up to the assumed date of cessation of pensionable service;[147] and

(2)   increases to pensions in payment or in deferment;

(C)   when calculating the value of the benefits payable under the Pension Scheme allowance shall also be made in accordance with the Actuarial Assumptions for any refund of contributions and any benefits in pension form payable in the event of death whilst in service but, save where death occurs on or before the Completion Date, no account shall be taken of any other lump sum death-in-service benefits;

(D)   any improvement to the benefits under the Pension Scheme which has been announced before Completion shall be deemed to have been duly effected under the Pension Scheme and to have come into force before Completion; and

(E)   the Pension Scheme shall be deemed to be under an overriding obligation in respect of members who are, or but for being absent from work would have been, in pensionable service at Completion to provide benefits (including guaranteed minimum benefits) in respect of service after 16 May 1990 on a basis which does not discriminate between men and women and without reducing the benefits of either sex;[148]

'Company' means the Company and the Subsidiaries or such one or more of them as the context requires;

'Contracting-out Benefits' means guaranteed minimum pensions, section 9(2B) rights and protected rights (or such of them as are applicable);[149]

'Interest' means, in respect of any period and any principal sum, an amount of interest (accruing daily and compounded monthly) at a rate equal to the base rate from time to time of [   ] Bank PLC plus [   ] per cent per annum;

'Interim Period' means the period from Completion to but excluding the Membership Transfer Date;

['Investment Adjustment' means, in relation to any period, one plus, when expressed as a fraction, the rate of investment return (whether positive or negative) during that period on a notional portfolio comprising [   ] per cent in the FT-SE Actuaries All-Share Total Return Index and [   ] per cent in the FT- Actuaries British Government Fixed Interest Over 15 Year Index (as published in the *Financial Times*) with allowance for income to be reinvested at monthly intervals. For the purposes of this definition the notional return shall be measured by taking the respective figures on the indices published for the close of business on the last business day preceding the commencement of the relevant period and for the close of business on the last business day preceding the day upon which that period ends;][150]

['Life Assurance Employee' at any time means a person who at that time is both an employee of the Company and covered by the Pension Scheme for certain death-in-service benefits but is not a Pensionable Employee;]

'Membership Transfer Date' means the first day of the first calendar month to commence after the date which is [   ] months after the Completion Date (or such earlier date as the Purchaser may by not less than one month's notice in writing to the Vendor specify or such later date as the Vendor and the Purchaser may agree in writing) except that if for any reason the Company is unable to participate in the Pension Scheme in accordance with Sub-Paragraph 3.1 until the date which would (apart from this exception) be the Membership Transfer Date then the 'Membership Transfer Date' means the day next following the date upon which the Company ceases so to participate in the Pension Scheme;[151]

'Payment Conditions'[152] means:

(A)   if the Purchaser's Scheme is a retirement benefits scheme, the Purchaser notifying the Vendor in writing that[:

(1)]   the Purchaser's Scheme is an exempt approved scheme or that the Board of Inland Revenue has confirmed that the Purchaser's Scheme may accept a transfer payment from the Pension Scheme; [and

(2)   where the employment of the Transferring Employees is to be contracted-out by reference to the Purchaser's Scheme, the Purchaser's Scheme may accept transfer values in respect of Contracting-out Benefits in accordance with the contracting-out requirements of the Pension Schemes Act 1993 and any applicable regulations made thereunder;]

(B)   if the Purchaser's Scheme is a personal pension scheme, the Purchaser's Scheme is approved under Chapter IV, Part XIV of the Income and Corporation Taxes Act 1988 and if the Transferring Employees have Contracted-out Benefits under the Pension Scheme it is an appropriate scheme;

'Payment Date' means the earlier of:

(A)   the date upon which the Adjusted Transfer Value is paid in accordance with Sub-Paragraph 5.2; and

(B)   the date which is 14 days after the later of:

(1)   the date upon which the amount of the Transfer Value is certified in accordance with Sub-Paragraph 5.1 or 7, as the case may be; and

(2)   the date upon which the Payment Conditions are first satisfied;

'Pension Scheme' means [the retirement benefits scheme known as [   ] which was established by a deed dated [   ] (or the trustees from time to time of that scheme, as the context requires);] [Scheme A [,] [and] [Scheme B] [and Scheme C] (or such one or [other] [more] of them as the context requires;]

'Pensionable Employee' at any time means a person who at that time is both an employee of the Company and is, or apart from being absent from work would be, in pensionable service under the Pension Scheme;

'Purchaser's Actuary' means [   ] (or such other Actuary as the Purchaser may appoint for the purposes of this Schedule);

'Purchaser's Scheme' means the scheme or schemes nominated by or at the instance of the Purchaser pursuant to Sub-Paragraph 4.1 (or the trustees or managers thereof as the context requires);

'Relevant Employee' means any present or past employee of the Company or of any predecessor to all or any part of its business;

['Scheme A' means the retirement benefits scheme known as [   ] which was established by a trust deed dated [   ] (or the trustees from time to time of that scheme as the context requires);]

['Scheme B' means the retirement benefits scheme known as [   ] which was established by a trust deed dated [   ] (or the trustees from time to time of that scheme as the context requires);]

['Scheme C' means the retirement benefits scheme known as [   ] which was established by a trust deed dated [   ] (or the trustees from time to time of that scheme as the context requires);]

'Transferring Employee' means a person who:

(A)   immediately prior to the Membership Transfer Date is a Pensionable Employee;

(B)   accepts the offer of membership of the Purchaser's Scheme to be made pursuant to Sub-Paragraph 4.2; and

(C)   consents in writing on or before the date which is [   ] days after the Membership Transfer Date (or before such other date as the Vendor and the Purchaser shall agree) to a transfer payment being made in respect of him to the Purchaser's Scheme from the Pension Scheme;[153]

'Transfer Value' means an amount equal to the sum of:

(A)   the Basic Amount multiplied by the Investment Adjustment for the period from and including the day next following the Completion Date to and including the Membership Transfer Date; plus

(B)   the aggregate contributions paid in respect of the Interim Period to the Pension Scheme by or in respect of the Transferring Employees [(other than, in relation to any Transferring Employee, any such contributions paid whilst he was a Life Assurance Employee)] less [   ] in respect of the cost of insuring the death-in-service benefits in respect of the Transferring Employees together with Interest on the balance from the date of payment of each such contribution to the Membership Transfer Date;

reduced, but only if [the Purchaser's Scheme is a retirement benefits scheme and] the employment of the Transferring Employees is not to be contracted-out by reference to the Purchaser's Scheme, by an amount equal to the sum (determined by applying the Actuarial Assumptions *mutatis mutandis*) of:

(1)   the amount on the day next before the Membership Transfer Date of any protected rights of the Transferring Employees under the Pension Scheme; minus

(2) the discounted value on the day before the Membership Transfer Date of any age-related payment payable in respect of the Transferring Employees on or after the Membership Transfer Date in respect of any period before that date; plus

(3) the capital value on the date next before the Membership Transfer Date of the guaranteed minimum pensions and section 9(2B) rights payable under the Pension Scheme to or in respect of the Transferring Employees;[154]

'Vendor's Actuary' means [   ] (or such other Actuary as the Vendor may appoint for the purposes of this Schedule).

1.2 Statutory Terms

In this Schedule, where the context admits, 'exempt approved scheme', 'personal pension scheme' and 'retirement benefits scheme' have the same meanings as in the Income and Corporation Taxes Act 1988; 'appropriate scheme', 'contracted-out', 'contracted-out scheme', 'contracting-out certificate', 'guaranteed minimum', 'guaranteed minimum pension' and 'protected rights' shall have the same meanings as in the Pension Schemes Act 1993, 'active members', 'age-related payment' and 'section 9(2B) rights' have the same meanings as in the Occupational Pension Schemes (Contracting-out) Regulations 1996 and 'schedule of contributions' has the same meaning as in the Pensions Act 1995.

1.3 Employees

References in this Schedule to employees includes directors.

1.4 Indices

Where in this Schedule or in the Actuary's Letter there is a reference to any index on a particular date and the index for that date is not published or otherwise ascertainable the index for that date shall be determined by the Vendor's Actuary and agreed by the Purchaser's Actuary, or in default of such agreement within one month of the Vendor or the Purchaser giving notice to the other that a dispute has arisen, determined by an independent Actuary pursuant to Paragraph 7.

1.5 Separate Application

Paragraphs 2 to 7 (inclusive) and for the purposes of those Paragraphs, Paragraph 1, applies separately to each Pension Scheme. Where more than one scheme is nominated as the Purchaser's Scheme pursuant to Sub-Paragraph 4.1, those Paragraphs shall, where the context so requires, also apply separately to each of those schemes and the Transferring Employees referable to that scheme. No more than one such scheme may for the purposes of this Schedule be referable to any particular Transferring Employee. If apart from this provision more than one such scheme would be referable to a Transferring Employee, the Purchaser shall notify the Vendor as to which such scheme is to be treated as referable to him.[155]

1.6 Purchaser's Group Reorganisation

If during the Interim Period any of the Pensionable Employees are transferred from the employment of the Company to another company within, or otherwise connected with, the Purchaser's Group (the 'New Employer'), the Vendor shall, at the request of the Purchaser, use all reasonable endeavours to procure that the New Employer is duly admitted to participation in the Pension Scheme with effect from the date of such transfer or if more than one such transfer occurs with effect from the date of the first such transfer. If for any reason the New Employer is not duly admitted to participation in the Pension Scheme then in respect of the employees transferred to it the day next following the date of such transfer shall be the Membership Transfer Date in relation to those employees and this Schedule shall take effect accordingly. Subject to the New Employer being so admitted, the New Employer and the Company shall be treated as one for the purposes of Paragraphs 1 to 7 (inclusive).[156]

2 Data

2.1 Data to be Supplied

The Vendor and the Purchaser shall each use all reasonable endeavours to procure that all such information as the Vendor's Actuary or the Purchaser's Actuary or any independent Actuary appointed under Paragraph 7 may reasonably request for the purposes of this Schedule is supplied promptly to such Actuary.

2.2 Non-availability of Data

If any information requested by an Actuary is not (whatever the reason) made available by the date which is 42 days after the date the request is made, he may make reasonable assumptions as to the information requested and any assumptions so made by an independent Actuary appointed under Paragraph 7 shall (in the absence of manifest error) be treated as facts for any and all of the purposes of this Schedule.

2.3 Data Accuracy Warranty

The Vendor hereby warrants to the Purchaser for itself and as trustee and agent for the Purchaser's Group and the Purchaser's Scheme that all such information which it or any member of the Vendor's Group or the Pension Scheme provides or procures to be provided for any purpose relevant to this Schedule shall be true, complete and accurate in all material respects as at the date the information is required for the purpose of this Schedule and shall contain no omission material to the calculation of the Transfer Value or material to any other calculation or determination for the purposes of this Schedule.

3 The Pension Scheme

3.1 Vendor's Undertakings

The Vendor undertakes to the Purchaser for its own benefit and as trustee and agent for the Company:

(A) to procure that subject to the consent of the Board of Inland Revenue being obtained (which consent the Vendor shall use all reasonable endeavours to procure) the Company is permitted to participate in the Pension Scheme throughout the period which would (apart from the exception to the definition of 'Membership Transfer Date') be the Interim Period;

(B) to procure that until after payment has been made in full in accordance with Paragraph 5 no power or discretion under the Pension Scheme is exercised in a way which would or might affect the Company and/or all or any of its employees save with the consent of the Purchaser;

(C) to use all reasonable endeavours to procure that none of the employees or former employees of the Company is discriminated against in the exercise of any discretionary power (including, without limitation, the grant of discretionary pension increases) under the Pension Scheme;

(D) to procure that if the Purchaser's Scheme is a retirement benefits scheme no payment is made by the Pension Scheme which would or might result in the Purchaser's Scheme not obtaining approval under or, as the case may be, ceasing to be approved under the Income and Corporation Taxes Act 1988, s 591 or in the pensionable service completed by a Transferring Employee under the Pension Scheme not being treated as continuous with the pensionable service completed by him under the Purchaser's Scheme for the purpose of determining the maximum benefits which may be paid under the Purchaser's Scheme without prejudicing the obtaining of approval of or, as the case may be, the approval of the Purchaser's Scheme as aforesaid;[157]

(E) to indemnify and to keep indemnified and to hold harmless on a continuing basis the Company against all and any liability to make any payment to or in connection with the Pension Scheme (including, but without limitation, the amount (if any) the Actuary to the Pension Scheme certifies pursuant to Sub-Paragraph 3.4) other than to pay contributions pursuant to Sub-Paragraph 3.2(A);[158] and

(F) to procure that the Pension Scheme is maintained in full force and effect and does not cease to have active members until after the Company has ceased to participate in the Pension Scheme.

3.2 Purchaser's Undertakings

The Purchaser shall procure that the Company:

(A) pays or procures to be paid to the Pension Scheme the employer contributions which accrue to the Pension Scheme during the Interim Period in respect of the Pensionable Employees [and the Life Assurance Employees] from time to time, such contributions to be deemed to be payable at [the same rate as is in force at the date of this Agreement] [the same rate as is generally payable from time to time by other employers participating in the Pension Scheme] [an annual rate of:
   (1) in relation to a Pensionable Employee, [   ] per cent of [   ] from time to time;
   (2) in relation to a Life Assurance Employee, [   ] per cent of [   ] from time to time];
   plus the contributions (if any) payable during the Interim Period by the Pensionable Employees; and

(B) complies in all other respects with the provisions of the Pension Scheme during the Interim Period.[159]

[3.3 Contracting-out in Interim Period

The Vendor and the Purchaser undertake to co-operate with each other with a view to procuring that the employment of the Pensionable Employees is contracted-out by reference to the Pension Scheme at all applicable times during the Interim Period.][160]

3.4 Statutory Debt

The Vendor shall procure that as soon as reasonably practicable after the Membership Transfer Date (and in any event within three months from that date) the Actuary to the Pension Scheme shall in accordance with all applicable statutory requirements and professional guidance, either certify in writing:

(A) the amount which is due from the Company to the Pension Scheme pursuant to s 75 of the Pensions Act 1995; or

(B) that no such amount is due.

The obligation on the Vendor contained in this Sub-Paragraph 3.4 above shall include, if necessary to comply with the prevailing statutory requirements and professional guidance then applicable, procuring that the Pension Scheme carries out a minimum funding valuation for the purposes of s 57(1)(*a*) of the Pensions Act 1995.[161]

4   The Purchaser's Scheme

4.1   Purchaser to Provide Scheme

For the purposes of this Schedule the Purchaser shall nominate or procure the nomination of one or more [of the following:

(A)] retirement benefits schemes which are, or which are designed to be capable of being, exempt approved schemes[.][;

(B)   personal pension schemes which are approved under Chapter IV, Part XIV of the Income and Corporation Taxes Act 1988.]

4.2   Purchaser to Offer Membership[162]

The Purchaser shall procure that those of the employees of the Company on the Membership Transfer Date who were Pensionable Employees immediately prior to that date are offered membership of the Purchaser's Scheme.

4.3   Final Salary Past Service Credit

The Purchaser shall procure that on payment being made in full in accordance with Sub-Paragraphs 5.2 and 5.3 the Transferring Employees [(other than the MP Employees as defined in Sub-Paragraph 4.4)][163] are credited with benefits under the Purchaser's Scheme in respect of service prior to the Membership Transfer Date which are, in the opinion of the Purchaser's Actuary, substantially no less favourable overall than the benefits which would have been payable under the Pension Scheme in respect of such service had the Company continued to participate in the Pension Scheme on an indefinite basis but disregarding any changes to the benefits under the Pension Scheme on or after the Completion Date and having due regard to whether a transfer is made from the Pension Scheme to the Purchaser's Scheme in respect of the Contracting-out Benefits under the Pension Scheme of the Transferring Employees. The benefits so credited shall be payable in accordance with and subject to the terms and conditions of the Purchaser's Scheme including (but without limitation) the powers of amendment and discontinuance.

[4.4   Money Purchase Alternative

The Purchaser may (at its option) provide benefits under this Paragraph for such (or all) of the Transferring Employees as the Purchaser determines (the 'MP Employees') in lieu of the benefits which would otherwise be provided pursuant to Sub-Paragraph 4.3. For each of the MP Employees the Purchaser shall on payment being made in full in accordance with Sub-Paragraphs 5.2 and 5.3 procure that an amount equal to that part of the Adjusted Transfer Value as is referable to the MP Employee is credited to an account under the Purchaser's Scheme designated to the MP Employee and that amount adjusted for investment return (positive or negative) less relevant expenses shall (subject to any applicable requirements for approval of the Purchaser's Scheme by the Board of the Inland Revenue) be applied to provide money purchase benefits for or in respect of the MP Employee and his service before the Membership Transfer Date.]

5   Payment of Transfer Value

5.1   Calculation

Immediately following the Membership Transfer Date the Vendor shall procure that the Vendor's Actuary calculates the amount of the Transfer Value and submits his findings in writing to the Purchaser's Actuary. If the Purchaser's Actuary agrees the amount of the Transfer Value, the Vendor shall procure that the Vendor's Actuary and the Purchaser shall procure that the Purchaser's Actuary jointly certify that amount as the Transfer Value. If, however, the Vendor's Actuary and the Purchaser's Actuary fail to agree within two months from the date upon which the Vendor's Actuary first submits his findings to the Purchaser's Actuary as aforesaid, the matter may, at the option of either the Vendor or the Purchaser, be referred to an independent Actuary pursuant to Paragraph 7.

5.2 Payment

The Vendor shall use all reasonable endeavours to procure that the Pension Scheme transfers to the Purchaser's Scheme on the Payment Date the Adjusted Transfer Value in cash (or if the Vendor and the Purchaser so agree transfers assets equal in value to the Adjusted Transfer Value).[164]

5.3 Shortfall[165]

If the sum (if any) duly transferred from the Pension Scheme to the Purchaser's Scheme in respect of the Transferring Employees on the Payment Date is less than the Adjusted Transfer Value (the amount of the difference being referred to in this Paragraph as the 'Shortfall'), the Vendor shall forthwith pay, by way of adjustment so far as possible to the consideration for the Sale Shares,[166] to the Purchaser (or to a third party as the Purchaser may direct) an amount in cash equal to the Shortfall together with interest thereon (accruing daily and compounded monthly) from and including the Payment Date to but excluding the date upon which final payment is made in accordance with this Paragraph (as well after judgment as before). Such interest to be at the base rate from time to time of [   ] Bank PLC plus [   ] per cent per annum.[167]

5.4 Payment on Account

If the Purchaser so requests, the Vendor shall use its best endeavours to procure that as soon as practicable after receiving such request (but not before the Membership Transfer Date) a payment on account of the amount payable pursuant to Sub-Paragraph 5.2 is made to the Purchaser's Scheme. Such payment shall be equal to [   ] per cent of the amount which the Vendor's Actuary, in consultation with the Purchaser's Actuary, reasonably estimates to be the amount of the Adjusted Transfer Value. In the event of a payment on account being made in accordance with this Paragraph, the Pension Scheme shall be deemed to have transferred on the Payment Date to the Purchaser's Scheme (in addition to the amount (if any) actually transferred on the Payment Date) an amount equal to the payment made in accordance with this Paragraph [multiplied by the Investment Adjustment for the period from and including the day next following that upon which that payment is made to and including the Payment Date.]

5.5 Apportioning Adjusted Transfer Value

The Vendor shall if the Purchaser so requests arrange for the Purchaser's Scheme to be notified in writing in respect of each Transferring Employee:

(1) the amount of the Adjusted Transfer Value referable to him;

(2) the amount of the part (if any) of the Adjusted Transfer Value which is the cash equivalent of his accrued rights to guaranteed minimum pensions;

(3) the amount of the part (if any) of the Adjusted Transfer Value which is the cash equivalent of his section 9(2B) rights; and

(4)   the amount of the part (if any) of the Adjusted Transfer Value which is the cash equivalent of his protected rights;

where such cash equivalents shall be calculated and verified in a manner consistent with s 97 of the Pension Schemes Act 1993.

6   Additional Voluntary Contributions

6.1   For the purpose of the foregoing provisions of this Schedule there shall be disregarded:

(A)   any benefits under the Pension Scheme which are attributable to additional voluntary contributions made to it by the members of the Pension Scheme and in respect of which the members are not entitled to benefits based on their final pensionable earnings (however defined);
(B)   any such contributions; and
(C)   any transfer in respect of any such benefits or contributions.

The Vendor shall, nevertheless, use all reasonable endeavours to procure that the Pension Scheme transfers to the Purchaser's Scheme on the Payment Date for the benefit of the Transferring Employees all such funds and assets of the Pension Scheme which represent any such contributions made by the Transferring Employees and the investment return on them.

7   Disputes

7.1   Any dispute between the Vendor's Actuary and the Purchaser's Actuary concerning the amount of the Transfer Value or any other matter to be agreed between them in accordance with this Schedule may, at the option of either the Vendor or the Purchaser, be referred to an independent Actuary to be appointed by agreement between the Vendor and the Purchaser or, in default of agreement within 14 days from the first nomination of an Actuary by one party to the other, by the President for the time being of The Institute of Actuaries (or of any successor body) on the application of either the Vendor or the Purchaser. The independent Actuary shall act as an expert and not as an arbitrator.[168] His decision shall, save in the event of fraud or manifest error, be final and binding on the parties and his costs shall be borne by the Vendor and the Purchaser [equally or in such other proportions as he shall direct].

8   Warranties and Representations[68;169]

8.1   The Vendor hereby warrants and represents[68] to and for the benefit of the Purchaser in the following terms:

(A)   *No Other Arrangements*   Save for the Pension Scheme the Company is not a party to nor participates in nor contributes to any scheme, agreement or arrangement (whether legally enforceable or not) for the provision of any pension, retirement, death, incapacity, sickness, disability, accident or other like benefits (including the payment after cessation of employment with the Company of medical expenses) for any Relevant Employee or for the widow, widower, child or dependant of any Relevant Employee.
(B)   *No Assurances etc*   Neither the Company nor any member of the Vendor's Group:
    (1)   has given any undertaking or assurance (whether legally enforceable or not) as to the continuance, introduction, improvement or increase of any benefit of a kind described in Sub-Paragraph 8.1(A) above, or
    (2)   is paying or has in the last two years paid any such benefit

to (in either case) any Relevant Employee or any widow, widower, child or dependant of any Relevant Employee.

(C) *All Details Disclosed* All material details relating to the Pension Scheme are contained in or annexed to the Disclosure Letter including (but without limitation) the following:

    (1) true and complete copies of the following documents referable to the Pension Scheme, *viz*:

        (a) all deeds, rules and other governing documents of current effect;

        (b) all announcements, booklets and the like of current effect which have been issued to any of the employees of the Company;

        (c) the latest completed actuarial valuation report and any document (including a draft) containing the results or preliminary results of any subsequent actuarial valuation;

        (d) the latest completed audited accounts and any subsequent accounts or draft accounts;

        (e) an accurate list of all Pensionable Employees and Life Assurance Employees at the date of this Agreement with such data as is necessary to establish their respective entitlements under the Pension Scheme;

        (f) the schedule of contributions;

    (2) details of all amendments (if any) to the Pension Scheme which have been announced or are proposed but which have not yet been formally made;

    (3) details of all discretionary increases (if any) to pensions in payment or in deferment under the Pension Scheme which have been granted in the ten years prior to the date of this Agreement or which are under consideration;

    (4) details of all discretionary practices (if any) which may have led any person to expect additional benefits in a given set of circumstances (by way of example, but without limitation, on retirement at the behest of the Company or in the event of redundancy); and

    (5) details of the rate at which and basis upon which the Company currently contributes to the Pension Scheme, any change to that rate and/or basis which is proposed or which is under consideration and all contributions paid to the Pension Scheme by the Company in the three years prior to the date of this Agreement.

(D) *Membership* Every person who has at any time had the right to join, or apply to join, the Pension Scheme has been properly advised of that right. No Relevant Employee has been excluded from membership of the Pension Scheme or from any of the benefits thereunder in contravention of Art 119 of the Treaty of Rome, the Pensions Act 1995 or other applicable laws or requirements or the provisions of the Pension Scheme or otherwise.

(E) *No Pay Restructuring* There has not in the last four years been any restructuring of the earnings of all or any of the employees of the Company (by way of example, but without limitation, consolidation of bonuses into basic pay).[170]

(F) *Transfer Payments* No transfer value has been paid (directly or indirectly) to the Pension Scheme from another arrangement for any employee of the Company under which any benefits referable to that employee contravened Art 119 of the Treaty of Rome, s 62 of the Pensions Act 1995 or other applicable law or requirement.

(G) *Death Benefits Insured* All benefits (other than any refund of members' contributions with interest where appropriate) payable under the Pension Scheme on the death of any person while in employment to which the Pension Scheme relates are insured fully under a policy with an insurance company of good repute and there are no grounds on which that company might avoid liability under that policy.

(H) *Augmentation*   No power under the Pension Scheme has been exercised in relation to any employee of the Company:
  (1) to provide terms of membership of the Pension Scheme (whether as to ben-
       efits or contributions) which are different from those generally applicable to
       members of the Pension Scheme;
  (2) to provide any benefits which would not but for the exercise of that power
       have been payable under the Pension Scheme; or
  (3) to augment any benefits under the Pension Scheme.

(I) *Contributions*   Contributions to the Pension Scheme are not paid in arrear and all
contributions and other amounts which have fallen due for payment by the Company have been paid. The Company has (to the extent that it will be required to
do) discharged its liability (if any) to pay or reimburse (whether wholly or in part)
to anyone who has paid any costs, charges or expenses which have been incurred
by or in connection with the Pension Scheme.

(J) *Company's Obligations*   The Company:
  (1) has been admitted to participation in the Pension Scheme on the same terms
       as apply generally to other employers participating in the Pension Scheme;
  (2) has observed and performed those provisions of the Pension Scheme which
       apply to it;
  (3) is not indebted to the Pension Scheme by virtue of s 75 of the Pensions
       Act 1995; [and][171]
  (4) may (without the consent of any person or further payment) terminate its li-
       ability to contribute to the Pension Scheme at any time subject only to giving
       such notice (if any) as is expressly provided for in the documentation con-
       taining the current provisions governing the Pension Scheme[172] [.] [and
  (5) has at all material times held or been named in a contracting-out certificate
       referable to the Pension Scheme.]

(K) *Compliance*   The Pension Scheme:
  (1) is an exempt approved scheme; and
  (2) complies with and has at all times been administered in accordance with all
       applicable laws, regulations and requirements (including those of the Board
       of Inland Revenue and of trust law).

(L) *Disputes*   None of the Pension Scheme, the Company or any member of the Vendor's Group is engaged or involved in any proceedings which relate to or are in
connection with the Pension Scheme or the benefits thereunder and no such proceedings are pending or threatened and so far as the Vendor is aware there are no
facts likely to give rise to any such proceedings. In this Sub-Paragraph 'proceedings' included any litigation or arbitration and also includes any investigation or
determination by the Pensions Ombudsman or the Occupational Pensions Advisory Service and any complaint under any internal dispute resolution procedure established in connection with the Pension Scheme.

9 Damages for Breach of Pension Warranties[173]

9.1 In determining the damages flowing from any breach of Warranties contained in
Paragraph 8, the Company shall be deemed to be under a liability:

(A) to provide and to continue to provide any benefits of a kind referred to in that Paragraph which are now provided or have been announced or are proposed; and

(B) to maintain and to continue to maintain (without benefits being reduced) the Pension Scheme and any other arrangements of a kind described in that Paragraph
which are now in existence or are proposed and any discretionary practices of a
kind referred to in that Paragraph which have hitherto been carried on.

SCHEDULE 6

PENSIONS

[C   Company has own money purchase scheme][174]

1   Interpretation

1.1   Definitions

In this Schedule, where the context admits:

'Company' means the Company and the Subsidiaries or such one or more of them as the context requires;

'Pension Scheme' means [the retirement benefits scheme known as [   ] which was established by a deed dated [   ] (or the trustees from time to time of that scheme as the context requires);] [Scheme A [,] [and] [Scheme B] [and Scheme C] (or such one or [other] [more] of them as the context requires);]

'Relevant Employee' means any past or present employee of the Company or of any predecessor to all or part of its business[.][;]

['Scheme A' means the retirement benefits scheme known as [   ] which was established by a trust deed dated [   ] (or the trustees from time to time of that scheme as the context requires);] [and]

'Scheme B' means the retirement benefits scheme known as [   ] which was established by a trust deed dated [   ] (or the trustees from time to time of that scheme as the context requires) [.] [; and

'Scheme C' means the retirement benefits scheme known as [   ] which was established by a trust deed dated [   ] (or the trustees from time to time of that scheme as the context requires).]

1.2   Employees

References in this Schedule to employees includes directors.

2   Warranties and Representations[68; 175]

2.1   The Vendor hereby warrants and represents[68] to and for the benefit of the Purchaser in the following terms:

(A)   *No Other Arrangements*   Save for the Pension Scheme the Company is not a party to nor participates in nor contributes to any scheme, agreement or arrangement (whether legally enforceable or not) for the provision of any pension, retirement, death, incapacity, sickness, disability, accident or other like benefits (including the payment after cessation of employment with the Company of medical expenses) for any Relevant Employee or for the widow, widower, child or dependant of any Relevant Employee.

(B)   *No Assurances etc*   Neither the Company *nor any member of the Vendor's Group:*

    (1)   has given any undertaking or assurance (whether legally enforceable or not) as to the continuance, introduction, improvement or increase of any benefit of a kind described in Sub-Paragraph 2.1(A) above, or

    (2)   is paying or has in the last two years paid any such benefit,

to (in either case) any Relevant Employee or to any widow, widower, child or dependant of any Relevant Employee.

(C) *All Details Disclosed*   All material details relating to the Pension Scheme
     are contained in or annexed to the Disclosure Letter including, but without limita-
     tion, the following:

    (1)   true and complete copies of the following documents referable to the Pen-
        sion Scheme, *viz*:

        (a)   all deeds, rules and other governing documents;

        (b)   all announcements, booklets and the like of current effect;

        (c)   the latest completed actuarial valuation report;[176]

        (d)   the latest completed audited accounts;

        (e)   all administration and other agreements to which the Pension Scheme
            is a party;

        (f)   all insurance policies (if any) and annuity contracts (if any) and all pro-
            posals (if any) to effect any such policies or contracts which are with
            any insurer for consideration;

        (g)   an accurate list of all employees of the Company for whom contribu-
            tions are being paid, or are payable, by the Company, showing the
            amount of contributions in respect of each employee;

        (h)   an accurate list with the names and addresses of all the trustees;

        (i)   the memorandum and articles of association of any trustee which is a
            company and an accurate list with the names and addresses of the di-
            rectors and secretary of that company; and

        (j)   internal dispute resolution procedure, payment schedule and statement
            of investment principles for the purposes of the Pensions Act 1995;

    (2)   details of the arrangements made or being considered (or confirmation that
        none have been made or are being considered) to comply with ss 16 to 21 of
        the Pensions Act 1995;

    (3)   details of the investments and assets of the Pension Scheme;

    (4)   details of all amendments (if any) to the Pension Scheme which have been
        announced or are proposed but which have not yet been formally made;

    (5)   details of all discretionary increases (if any) to pensions in payment or in de-
        ferment under the Pension Scheme which have been granted in the ten years
        prior to the date of this Agreement or which are under consideration;

    (6)   details of all discretionary practices (if any) which may have led any person
        to expect additional benefits in a given set of circumstances (by way of ex-
        ample, but without limitation, on retirement at the behest of the Company or
        in the event of redundancy).

(D) *Membership*   Every person who has at any time had the right to join, or apply to
     join, the Pension Scheme has been properly advised of that right. No Relevant Em-
     ployee has been excluded from membership of the Pension Scheme or from any
     of the benefits thereunder in contravention of Art 119 of the Treaty of Rome, the
     Pensions Act 1995 or other applicable laws or requirements or the provisions of
     the Pension Scheme or otherwise.

(E) *Benefits*   All benefits which are not money purchase benefits and which are pay-
     able under the Pension Scheme on the death of any person while in employment
     to which the Pension Scheme relates are insured fully under a policy with an in-
     surance company of good repute and there are no grounds on which that company
     might avoid liability under that policy. All other benefits payable, or prospective-
     ly or contingently payable, under the Pension Scheme are money purchase bene-
     fits. In this Sub-Paragraph 'money purchase benefits' has the same meaning as in
     s 181(1) of the Pension Schemes Act 1993.

(F) *Transfer Payments*   No transfer value has been paid (directly or indirectly) to the
     Pension Scheme from another arrangement for any member of the Pension

Scheme under which any benefits referable to that member contravened Art 119 of the Treaty of Rome, s 62 of the Pensions Act 1995 or other applicable law or requirement.

(G) *Contributions and Expenses* Contributions to the Pension Scheme are not paid in arrear and all contributions and other amounts which have fallen due for payment have been paid punctually. No fee, charge or expense relating to or in connection with the Pension Scheme has been incurred but not paid. If any such fee, charge or expense has been paid by any person other than the Pension Scheme the Pension Scheme has reimbursed that person if and to the extent that the Pension Scheme is or may become liable so to do.

(H) *Company's Obligations* The Company:
   (1) has observed and performed those provisions of the Pension Scheme which apply to it; [and]
   (2) may (without the consent of any person or further payment) terminate its liability to contribute to the Pension Scheme at any time subject only to giving such notice (if any) as is expressly provided for in the documentation containing the current provisions governing the Pension Scheme[177] [.] [; and
   (3) has at all material times held or been named in a contracting-out certificate (within the meaning of s 7(1) of the Pension Schemes Act 1993) referable to the Pension Scheme.]

(I) *No Other Employer* The Company is the only employer for the time being participating in the Pension Scheme. No employer which has previously participated in the Pension Scheme has any claim under the Pension Scheme and in respect of any such employer the period of participation has been terminated and benefits have been provided in accordance with the provisions of the Pension Scheme.

(J) *Administration* All documentation and records in respect of the Pension Scheme are up to date and so far as the Vendor is aware complete and accurate in all material respects.

(K) *Investments* Save for any deposit with a bank or building society the only assets which the Pension Scheme has held are insurance policies and annuity contracts with insurance companies of good repute.

(L) *Compliance* The Pension Scheme:
   (1) is an exempt approved scheme (within the meaning of s 592(1) of the Income and Corporation Taxes Act 1988);
   (2) has properly and punctually accounted to the Inland Revenue for all and any tax for which the Pension Scheme is liable or accountable; and
   (3) has at all times complied with and been administered in accordance with all applicable laws, regulations and requirements (including those of the Board of Inland Revenue and of trust law).

(M) *Disputes* None of the Pension Scheme, the Company *or any member of the Vendor's Group* is engaged or involved in any proceedings which relate to or are in connection with the Pension Scheme or the benefits thereunder and no such proceedings are pending or threatened and so far as the Vendor is aware there are no facts likely to give rise to any such proceedings. In this Sub-Paragraph 'proceedings' includes any litigation or arbitration and also includes any investigation or determination by the Pensions Ombudsman or the Occupational Pensions Advisory Service and any complaint under any internal dispute resolution procedure established in connection with the Pension Scheme.

(N) *Indemnities* In relation to the Pension Scheme or funds which are or have been held for the purposes thereof neither the Company nor the Pension Scheme has given an indemnity or guarantee to any person (other than in the case of the Company any general indemnity in favour of the trustees or administrator under the documentation governing the Pension Scheme).

3   Damages for Breach of Pension Warranties[178]

3.1   In determining the damages flowing from any breach of Warranties contained in Paragraph 2, the Company shall be deemed to be under a liability:

(A)   to provide and to continue to provide any benefit of a kind referred to in that Paragraph which is now provided or has been announced or is proposed; and

(B)   to maintain and to continue to maintain (without benefits being reduced) the Pension Scheme and any other arrangements of a kind described in that Paragraph which are now in existence or are proposed and any discretionary practices of a kind referred to in that Paragraph which have hitherto been carried on.

SCHEDULE 6

PENSIONS

[D   Company participates in group money purchase scheme][179]

1   Interpretation

1.1   Definitions

In this Schedule, where the context admits:

'Company' means the Company and the Subsidiaries or such one or more of them as the context requires;

'Interim Period' means the period from and including the day next following the Completion Date to and including [   ] (or such earlier date as the Purchaser may by not less than one month's notice in writing to the Vendor specify or such later date as the Vendor and the Purchaser may agree in writing) except that if for any reason the Company is unable to participate in the Pension Scheme in accordance with Sub-Paragraph 2.1 until the date which would (apart from this exception) be the last day of the Interim Period the Interim Period shall end on the last day the Company participates in the Pension Scheme;

['Life Assurance Employee' at any time means a person who at that time is both an employee of the Company and covered by the Pension Scheme for certain death-in-service benefits but is not a Pensionable Employee;]

'Pension Scheme' means [the retirement benefits scheme known as [   ] which was established by a deed dated [   ] (or the trustees from time to time of that scheme as the context requires);] [Scheme A [,] [and] [Scheme B] [and Scheme C] (or such one or [other] [more] of them as the context requires);]

'Pensionable Employee' at any time means a person who at that time is both an employee of the Company and is, or but for being absent from work would be, in pensionable service under the Pension Scheme;

'Relevant Employee' means any present or past employee of the Company or of any predecessor to all or any part of its business;

['Scheme A' means the retirement benefits scheme known as [   ] which was established by a trust deed dated [   ] (or the trustees from time to time of that scheme as the context requires);]

['Scheme B' means the retirement benefits scheme known as [   ] which was established by a trust deed dated [   ] (or the trustees from time to time of that scheme as the context requires);]

['Scheme C' means the retirement benefits scheme known as [   ] (or the trustees from time to time of that scheme as the context requires);]

'Scheme Member' means a person who is at any time on or after Completion both an employee of the Company and a Pensionable Employee.

'Statutory Transfer Provision' means Chapter IV, Part IV of the Pension Schemes Act 1993.

1.2   Employees

References in this Schedule to employees includes directors.

1.3   Purchaser's Group Reorganisation

If during the Interim Period any of the Pensionable Employees is transferred from the employment of the Company to another company within, or otherwise connected with, the Purchaser's Group (the 'New Employer'), the Vendor shall, at the request of the Purchaser, use all reasonable endeavours to procure that the New Employer is duly admitted to participation in the Pension Scheme with effect from the date of such transfer or if more than one such transfer occurs with effect from the date of the first such transfer. If for any reason the New Employer is not so admitted then in respect of the employees transferred to it the day next following the date of such transfer shall in relation to those employees be the last day of the Interim Period and this Schedule shall take effect accordingly. Subject to the New Employer being so admitted, the New Employer and the Company shall be treated as one for the purposes of Paragraphs 1 to 3 (inclusive).[180]

[1.4   Separate Application

Paragraphs 2 and 3 and for the purposes of those Paragraphs, Paragraph 1, apply separately to each Pension Scheme.]

2   The Pension Scheme

2.1   Vendor's Undertakings

The Vendor undertakes to the Purchaser for its own benefit and as trustee and agent for the Company:

(A)   to procure that subject to the consent of the Board of Inland Revenue being obtained (which consent the Vendor shall use all reasonable endeavours to procure), the Company is permitted to participate in the Pension Scheme throughout the period which would (apart from the exception to the definition of 'Interim Period') be the Interim Period;

(B)   to procure that no power or discretion under the Pension Scheme is exercised in a way which would or might affect the Company and/or all or any of its employees save with the consent of the Purchaser;

(C)   to indemnify and to keep indemnified and to hold harmless on a continuing basis the Company against all and any liability to make any payment to or in connection with the Pension Scheme other than to pay contributions pursuant to Sub-Paragraph 2.2(A); and

(D)   to procure that the Pension Scheme continues in full force and effect and does not cease to have active members (within the meaning of the Pensions Act 1995) until after the Company has ceased to participate in it.[181]

2.2   Purchaser's Undertaking

The Purchaser shall procure that the Company:

(A)   pays or procures to be paid to the Pension Scheme the employer contributions which accrue under the terms of the Pension Scheme during the Interim Period in respect of the Pensionable Employees [and the Life Assurance Employees] from time to time, such contributions shall be deemed to be payable at [the same rate as is in force at the date of this Agreement] [an annual rate of:

    (1)   in relation to a Pensionable Employee, [   ] per cent of [   ] from time to time;

    (2)   in relation to a Life Assurance Employee, [   ] per cent of [   ] from time to time;]

plus the contributions (if any) payable during the Interim Period by the Pensionable Employees; and

(B) complies in all other respects with the provisions of the Pension Scheme during the Interim Period.[182]

[2.3 Contracting-out

The Vendor and the Purchaser undertake to co-operate with each other with a view to procuring that the employment of the Pensionable Employees is contracted-out of the state earnings related pension scheme by reference to the Pension Scheme at all applicable times during the Interim Period.][183]

3 Benefits and Options[184]

3.1 The Vendor undertakes to the Purchaser for its own benefit and as trustee and agent for the Company and the Scheme Members to procure that:

(A) benefits will be provided under the Pension Scheme for each Scheme Member who on ceasing to be in pensionable service under the Pension Scheme does not qualify for short service benefits (within the meaning of s 71 of the Pension Schemes Act 1993) as if he had qualified for such benefits unless the Scheme Member elects to take a refund of his contributions;[185]

(B) the Pension Scheme notifies each Scheme Member in writing as soon as practicable after he ceases to be in pensionable service under the Pension Scheme and in any event within 30 days thereafter of the options available to him under the Pension Scheme and the funds accumulated for his benefit under the Pension Scheme and all other information concerning the Pension Scheme and those options which the Scheme Member may reasonably require in order to make an informed decision as to which (if any) option to exercise;[186]

(C) any Scheme Member who on ceasing to be in pensionable service under the Pension Scheme does not acquire a right to a transfer value under Statutory Transfer Provision is given the option under the Pension Scheme of a transfer value as if he had acquired such a right;[187]

(D) the transfer value paid in respect of any Scheme Member shall not be less than it would have been had Statutory Transfer Provision required the amount of the transfer value to be the value of the funds accumulated for the benefit of the Scheme Member adjusted (upwards or downwards) for the investment return obtained on those funds up to the date the transfer value is paid;[188]

(E) subject to Sub-Paragraph 3.1(D) the amount of any transfer value for a Scheme Member is the cash equivalent (within the meaning of Statutory Transfer Provision) without any reduction pursuant to reg 8(4), Occupational Pension Schemes (Transfer Values) Regulations 1996);

(F) if a Scheme Member requests in writing that a transfer value be paid in respect of him in a manner permitted under Statutory Transfer Provision the Pension Scheme gives effect to that request as soon as practicable and in any event within 60 days of that request being made; and

(G) the Purchaser is forthwith on request advised in writing of the respective amounts of the transfer values for the Scheme Members and is supplied with such information and evidence as the Purchaser may request to enable the Purchaser to verify those amounts.

4 Warranties and Representations[68; 189]

4.1 The Vendor hereby warrants and represents[68] to and for the benefit of the Purchaser in the following terms:

(A) *No Other Arrangements*   Save for the Pension Scheme the Company is not a party to nor participates in nor contributes to any scheme, agreement or arrangement (whether legally enforceable or not) for the provision of any pension, retirement, death, incapacity, sickness, disability, accident or other like benefits (including the payment after cessation of employment with the Company of medical expenses) for any Relevant Employee or for the widow, widower, child or dependant of any Relevant Employee.

(B) *No Assurances etc*   Neither the Company nor any member of the Vendor's Group:

(1)   has given any undertaking or assurance (whether legally enforceable or not) as to the continuance, introduction, improvement or increase of any benefit of a kind described in Sub-Paragraph 4.1(A) above, or

(2)   is paying or has in the last two years paid any such benefit,

to (in either case) any Relevant Employee or to any widow, widower, child or dependant of any Relevant Employee.

(C) *All Details Disclosed*   All material details relating to the Pension Scheme are contained in or annexed to the Disclosure Letter including, but without limitation, the following:

(1)   true and complete copies of the following documents referable to the Pension Scheme, viz:

(a)   all deeds, rules and other governing documents;

(b)   all announcements, booklets and the like of current effect;

(c)   the latest completed actuarial valuation report;

(d)   the latest completed audited accounts;[176]

(e)   payment schedule (within the meaning of s 87 of the Pensions Act 1995);

(f)   an accurate list of all employees of the Company for whom contributions are being paid, or are payable, by the Company showing the amount of contributions in respect of each employee;

(2)   details of the investment in which the funds referable to the Pensionable Employees are held;

(3)   details of all amendments (if any) to the Pension Scheme which have been announced or are proposed but which have not yet been formally made;

(4)   details of all discretionary increases (if any) to pensions in payment or in deferment under the Pension Scheme which have been granted in the ten years prior to the date of this Agreement or which are under consideration; and

(5)   details of all discretionary practices (if any) which may have led any person to expect additional benefits in a given set of circumstances (by way of example, but without limitation, on retirement at the behest of the Company or in the event of redundancy).

(D) *Membership*   All Relevant Employees who have at any time had the right to join, or apply to join, the Pension Scheme have been properly advised of that right. No Relevant Employee has been excluded from membership of the Pension Scheme or from any of the benefits thereunder in contravention of Art 119 of the Treaty of Rome, the Pensions Act 1995 or other applicable laws or requirements, or the provisions of the Pension Scheme or otherwise.

(E) *Benefits*   All benefits (other than money purchase benefits) which are payable under the Pension Scheme on the death of any person while in employment to which the Pension Scheme relates are insured fully under a policy with an insurance company of good repute and there are no grounds on which that company might avoid liability under that policy. All other benefits payable, or prospectively or contingently payable, under the Pension Scheme are money purchase benefits. In this Sub-Paragraph 'money purchase benefits' has the same meaning as in s 181(1) of the Pension Schemes Act 1993.

(F) *Transfer Payments* No transfer value has been paid (directly or indirectly) to the Pension Scheme from another arrangement for any Relevant Employee under which the benefits referable to that Relevant Employee contravened Art 119 of the Treaty of Rome, s 62, Pensions Act 1995 or other applicable law or requirement.

(G) *Contributions* Contributions to the Pension Scheme are not paid in arrear and all contributions and other amounts which have fallen due for payment have been paid punctually. The Company has (to the extent that it will be required to do) discharged its liability (if any) to pay or reimburse (whether wholly or in part) anyone who has paid any costs, charges or expenses which have been incurred by or in connection with the Pension Scheme.

(H) *Company's Obligations* The Company:
   (1) has been admitted to participation in the Pension Scheme on the same terms as apply generally to other employers participating in the Scheme;
   (2) has observed and performed those provisions of the Pension Scheme which apply to it; [and]
   (3) may (without the consent of any person or further payment) terminate its liability to contribute to the Pension Scheme at any time subject only to giving such notice (if any) as is expressly provided for in the documentation containing the current provisions governing the Pension Scheme[190] [.][; and
   (4) has at all material times held or been named in a contracting-out certificate (within the meaning of s 7(1) of the Pension Schemes Act 1993) referable to the Pension Scheme.]

(I) *Compliance* The Pension Scheme:
   (1) is an exempt approved scheme (within the meaning of s 592(1) of the Income and Corporation Taxes Act 1988); and
   (2) has at all times complied with and been administered in accordance with all applicable laws, regulations and requirements (including those of the Board of Inland Revenue and of trust law).

(J) *Disputes* None of the Pension Scheme, the Company or any member of the Vendor's Group is engaged or involved in any proceedings which relate to or are in connection with the Pension Scheme and no such proceedings are pending or threatened and so far as the Vendor is aware there are no facts likely to give rise to any such proceedings. In this Sub-Paragraph 'proceedings' includes any litigation or arbitration and also any investigation or determination by the Pensions Ombudsman or the Occupational Pensions Advisory Service and any complaint under any internal dispute resolution procedure established in connection with the Pension Scheme.

5 Damages for Breach of Pension Warranties[191]

5.1 In determining the damages flowing from any breach of Warranties contained in Paragraph 4, the Company shall be deemed to be under a liability:

(A) to provide and to continue to provide any benefits of a kind referred to in that Paragraph which are now provided or have been announced or are proposed; and

(B) to maintain and to continue to maintain (without benefits being reduced) the Pension Scheme and any other arrangements of a kind described in that Paragraph which are now in existence or are proposed and any discretionary practices of a kind referred to in that Paragraph which have hitherto been carried on.

SCHEDULE 7

PARTICULARS OF PROPERTIES

Freehold Properties

Description	Relevant owner	Title number or date and description of root of title	Details of documents containing or referring to matters subject to which the property is sold (other than tenancies)	Current use	Consideration £

Leasehold Properties

Demised premises	Title number (if applicable)	Date and parties to lease	Term	Current principal yearly rent	Current use	Consideration £

SCHEDULE 8

VENDOR PROTECTION[192]

1 Guarantees

The Purchaser shall use its best endeavours to secure the release of the Vendor from the guarantees and other contingent liabilities listed in the Disclosure Letter for the purpose of this Paragraph (offering its own covenant in substitution if requested by the Vendor) and shall in the meantime indemnify the Vendor and keep the Vendor indemnified against any liability (including costs damages and expenses) thereunder or which may be incurred in relation thereto.

2 Loan Accounts

At Completion the Purchaser shall procure that the Company and the Subsidiaries shall repay to the Vendor *[and its subsidiaries]* the amounts owing to *[them]* as specified in the Disclosure Letter.

3 Limitation of Liability[193]

The following Paragraphs of this Schedule shall operate to limit the liability of the Vendor under or in connection with the Tax Deed, the Warranties and the Disclosure Letter and accordingly, in this Schedule, 'Relevant Claim' means any claim under or in connection with the Warranties or the Disclosure Letter [including for the avoidance of doubt, any claim for misrepresentation or negligent misstatement].[194]

4 Financial Limits

4.1 Aggregate limit

The aggregate liability of the Vendor in respect of Relevant Claims[195] and claims under the Tax Deed shall be limited to £[   ].

4.2 Thresholds

The Vendor shall not be liable in respect of a Relevant Claim unless:

[(A) the liability of the Vendor in respect of that Relevant Claim (and all other Relevant Claims arising out of or related to the same or similar subject matter) exceeds £[   ][196]; and]

(B) the aggregate liability of the Vendor in respect of all Relevant Claims (excluding any for which liability is excluded by Sub-Paragraph 4.2(A)) exceeds £[   ] in which case the Vendor shall be liable for the whole amount and not merely the excess over £[   ].

5 Time Limits

5.1 Notice to Vendor

The Vendor shall have no liability in respect of any Relevant Claim unless the Purchaser shall have given notice in writing to the Vendor of such claim specifying (in reasonable detail) the matter which gives rise to the claim, the nature of the claim and the amount claimed in respect thereof not later than:

(A)   in the case of a Relevant Claim under or in connection with or any of the Warranties contained in Schedule 4 (Taxation)) the applicable time limits specified in Sub-Clause 3.2 of the Tax Deed; or[197]

(B)   in any other case, the date [   ] years after the date of this Agreement.[197]

6   Recovery from Third Parties

6.1   Accounting to Vendor

If the Vendor pays to or for the benefit of the Purchaser an amount in respect of any Relevant Claim and any of the Purchaser, the Company or any of the Subsidiaries subsequently receives from any other person any payment in respect of the matter giving rise to the Relevant Claim, the Purchaser shall thereupon pay to the Vendor an amount equal to the payment received, after having taken into account any cost, liability (including tax liability) or expense in respect thereof and except to any extent that the liability of the Vendor in respect of the Relevant Claim was reduced to take account of such payment.[198]

7   No Duplication of Recovery

7.1   No Double Recovery

The Purchaser shall not be entitled to recover damages or otherwise obtain reimbursement or restitution more than once in respect of the same loss.

7.2   Claims under Warranties or Tax Deed

In the event that the Purchaser is entitled to claim under the Tax Deed or under the Warranties contained in Schedule 4 (Taxation) in respect of the same subject matter, the Purchaser may claim under either or both but payments under the Tax Deed shall *pro tanto* satisfy and discharge any claim which is capable of being brought under the Warranties contained in Schedule 4 in respect of the same subject matter and *vice versa*.

[8   Relevance of Limitations in Circumstances of Fraud etc

The provisions of Paragraphs 4 and 5 shall not apply in respect of any Relevant Claim or any claim under the Tax Deed if it is (or the delay in the discovery of which is) the consequence of fraud, wilful misconduct or wilful concealment by the Vendor *or any member of the Vendor's Group* or officer or employee or former officer or employee of the Vendor *or any member of the Vendor's Group*].[199]

SIGNED by [	*]*	*)* [200]
duly authorised for and on		*)*
behalf of [	*] PLC*	*)*

SIGNED by [	]	)
duly authorised for and on		)
behalf of [	] PLC	)

Notes

Parties and Recitals

1   Attempt has been made in this precedent to accommodate both the situation where the vendors are individuals (when there may be more than one vendor shareholder) and where the vendor is a company (public or private, listed or otherwise). Clauses particularly affected by the nature of the vendor are italicised and will need deletion or modification as appropriate; where relevant references to the 'vendor' should be changed to 'vendors' in the plural. References to the 'vendor's group' may not be relevant to individual vendors, or the definition may require modification to include the vendors' other business interests, where that is appropriate. The suggested amendments may not suit every circumstance and the draftsman will tailor them to his own circumstances. In cases of ambiguity, comment is made in the Notes. It is assumed that either or both of versions A and C of the pensions provisions (Schedule 6, at p 434 and p 451) will apply to the sale by individual vendors, but that Versions B and D, which involves transfer from a group scheme, will not.

2   Add a guarantor, if appropriate.

Clause 1: Interpretation

3   This definition is used in the warranties and in the preparation of completion accounts in Schedule 5. Consider whether it is appropriate to include in addition (notably for the purpose of the warranties) the individual accounts of the Company and any of its material subsidiaries. Separate warranties on individual accounts may have the effect of reducing the materiality threshold (in relation, for example, to a liability which is not included in the accounts). It may, however, mean (for example) that where there is an overvalued asset reflected in the accounts of one subsidiary which is the basis of a warranty claim, credit is not given for an undervalued asset in another subsidiary unless there is a specific item in the vendor protection provisions (Schedule 8) which has that effect.

4   Retain the definition of 'Completion' even if completion is to be simultaneous with the signature of the agreement.

5   The disclosure letter qualifies the warranties given in Schedules 3, 4 and 6 (cl 8.1). The agreement provides for certain items to be included in (or annexed to) the disclosure letter (*see* the list on p 627). Also, Schedule 8, para 1, refers to guarantees and other contingent liabilities of the vendors to be listed in the disclosure letter for the purpose of indemnity. The scheme of the agreement is to oblige the vendors to make all disclosures by way of the disclosure letter. The accuracy of the disclosure letter is warranted: Schedule 3, para 2.12(C). A precedent disclosure letter will be found on p 623. *See further* Note 44.

6   This period is likely to run from the Balance Sheet Date to the most recent management accounts data—management accounts should be as recent as possible.

7   *See* precedent on p 637. *See also* p 237.

8   This term could include companies which are not strictly 'subsidiaries' within the meaning of the Companies Act 1985, s 736. Particular care should be taken by the vendor in relation to the scope of the warranties and disclosures against them, if that is the case. 'Bodies corporate' will encompass overseas subsidiaries.

9   See precedent on p 483.

10   Ensure that the definition ties in to those provisions of the Agreement which are intended to be warranted and against which disclosures are intended to operate - not indemnities which would not be subject to disclosure. For pensions, it will depend on which schedule(s) are relevant. *See further* Note 44.

11   Vendors will bear this in mind when considering the warranties and in some cases (eg Schedule 3, para 2.1(B)) they may resist it. The provision requires diligent enquiry by the vendor. It is suggested that, even if due and careful enquiry is to be made, it will not be assumed that the vendor will know everything which is in its possession or capable of discovery on an exhaustive investigation. See *William Sindall PLC v Cambridgeshire County Council* [1994] 1 WLR 1016 and the cases referred to therein. If time is short or if secrecy must be maintained during the negotiations it is prudent for the vendor to specify that its enquiries are confined to named individuals. In such a case, the purchaser should be satisfied that the named individuals have the necessary breadth and depth of knowledge and perhaps seek assurance that such is the case.

12   This clause is required where there is more than one vendor shareholder eg where the target is held by a number of individuals. It can equally be used where some person other than the vendor shareholder (such as a guarantor or parent company, or directors) also joins in certain provisions of the agreement, such as for the purpose of giving the warranties. See the commentary on joint and several liability in Chapter 9 at p 178; see also cl 11.5.

Clause 2: Sale of Shares

13   *See* Chapter 10 at p 187 for a discussion of covenants for title. Note that the implied covenants do not cover anything which the purchaser actually or constructively knows, but this provision is varied in cl 8.2.

Clause 3: Consideration

14   Clause 3.2 provides for a vendor placing (*see* p 237) using the 'SDRT saving' approach (*see* p 244). It seems best to specify the consideration as shares, rather than as a sum of money to be satisfied by the issue of shares, as it may be argued on the authority of *Spargo's Case* (1873) 8 LR Ch App 407 that the latter amounts to an issue for cash requiring the authority of a special resolution under the Companies Act 1985, s 95, but see *Stanton (Inspector of Taxes) v Drayton Commercial Investment Co Ltd* [1982] STC 585 where the consideration was stated as a price to be satisfied by the issue of shares at an agreed value and it was held that the consideration was shares, and their value, for tax purposes, was the value agreed between the parties (*see also* the Companies Act 1985, s 738(2)). The sub-clause contemplates that the vendors have stipulated a fixed cash sum to be realised by a placing as opposed to a fixed number of shares or a number of shares to be ascertained by eg reference to the quoted price. For a precedent vendor placing agreement, *see* p 637. The purchaser may wish to include a provision restricting the disposal of any of the consideration shares which are not to be placed. In such a case, it should note the limitations on such arrangements in consequence of the Companies Act 1985, s 150.

15   See, for instance, Table A, reg 104, relating to the apportionment of dividends. The purchaser's articles should be checked.

Clause 4: Conditions

16 For a discussion of the location of the beneficial ownership in the interim period see *Sainsbury v O'Connor* [1991] STC 318 and the cases there cited. Vendors may insist that the purchaser undertakes to convene the necessary meeting and to apply for, and use its best endeavours to obtain, a listing for the consideration shares.

17 Amend as appropriate and delete if no shareholder consent is required. An increase of capital or authorisation of allotment under the Companies Act 1985, s 80 may be required. Shareholder approval by the purchaser to the acquisition may be required (including, possibly, in respect of any other member of the vendor's or purchaser's group which is listed) and approvals may be required even though the consideration is cash: *see* p 7 and Chapters 10 and 11 of the Stock Exchange Yellow Book.

18 If there is a placing the brokers will insist that their obligations are conditional upon the listing of the consideration shares so that the inclusion of this condition in the acquisition agreement itself becomes vital. In any event, the vendors are likely to insist upon it if they are retaining consideration shares. *See* p 245 as to the implications of including a condition in this form.

19 Whether or not the vendors will agree to this is a matter of negotiation. They may insist that the purchaser remains bound to pay cash if the placing agreement is rescinded or fails to become unconditional.

20 *See generally*, Chapter 4. The conditions may need to be modified to fit the circumstances.

21 Where EC merger control applies, in principle it is not necessary to consider the national merger regimes of individual member states (although there are exceptions applicable to certain sectors eg media, defence). Thus the conditions are not always alternatives. If there are overseas subsidiaries or activities, local competition rules may apply. Condition (E) is expressed in subjective terms, although sometimes objectivity is introduced.

22 As to directors agreeing to recommend the acquisition to shareholders, despite changing circumstances and whether they will be in breach of their fiduciary duties, see *Fulham Football Club Ltd v Cabra Estates* [1994] 1 BCLC 363, although see also *John Crowther Group v Carpets International* [1990] BCLC 460; even if bound effectively, the directors' duties would nonetheless require them to put an alternative offer to shareholders. Otherwise, make sure the purchaser knows or circumscribes what it is obliged to do to procure satisfaction of the conditions, particularly those relating to competition or regulatory matters where the condition might be capable of satisfaction if an undertaking is given by the purchaser to a regulatory authority, yet that undertaking is in unacceptable terms.

Clause 5: Completion

23 Even where completion is simultaneous with signing this clause should be retained as a checklist.

24 Item (2) may be necessary if the vendors have granted pre-emption rights to third parties. Pre-emption rights under the target's articles ought not be relevant in the case of a single corporate vendor registered as the holder of all the target's shares.

25 Delays in stamping the transfers where adjudication is required will often mean that the purchaser will not be registered for some time after completion and in such

a case it is a useful precaution to take a power of attorney. Inclusion of the power of attorney in the agreement would require the agreement to be executed as a deed and, in any event, the power should be granted by the registered holder(s) who are not necessarily the vendor(s). For a precedent power of attorney *see* p 635. *See also* the commentary in Chapter 10 at p 190.

26   *See* precedent letter of resignation on p 633. Note that the acknowledgement that the director has no claim for compensation does not necessarily bar a claim for redundancy pay or for unfair dismissal under Employment Rights Act 1996, s 203; hence the concluding words of the sub-clause. In a case where there is any real possibility of a director claiming compensation the conciliation officer or compromise agreement procedure should be used (*see* p 73).

27   Vendors agreeing to this should note the provisions of the Companies Act 1985, s 394, which provides for the form of such notices of resignation and their filing at the Companies Registration Office.

28   A purchaser may wish the books (other than the register of members which should be checked on completion) to be handed over at the target's offices rather than at the completion meeting. The purchaser should be satisfied that the register of members actually reflect the vendor's (or registered) shareholding it has contracted to acquire and insist that books are written up if not. If there are problems, it may be necessary to delay signing to sort out the position so as to ensure that the purchaser gets what it is paying for.

29   This is probably of reduced significance now it is possible for the subsidiaries to have a single shareholder (Companies Act 1985, s 24) although many subsidiaries will still have two shareholders. The purchaser will certainly wish to change nominees if they are directors who are retiring.

30   This may not be possible if the properties are mortgaged; the purchaser should, however, insist on the appropriate documents and releases if mortgages and charges are to be released at completion (including, in particular, those which support cross guarantees of the vendor group's banking arrangements). Any additional documentation for delivery should be added.

31   The vendor's certificate is relatively uncommon and the purchaser will typically have investigated title: *see* the commentary in Chapter 9 at p 153.

32   Unless it is the vendors themselves who are to enter into the service agreements it will be appropriate to obtain commitments from the executive(s) concerned or for the service agreement to be entered into at the time of signing (on a conditional basis, if completion is deferred).

33   Notwithstanding delay in registration pending stamping of transfers it is good practice for the board of the target to approve the transfers at completion so as to perfect the purchaser's to the extent then possible.

34   The guarantees and obligations to be discharged will arise out of disclosure and due diligence. For example, there may be cross guarantees or charges over target assets that relate to the vendor group's financing arrangements which should be discharged at completion. However, the obligation in this clause is expressed in general terms so that the vendor, for the avoidance of doubt, remains obliged to discharge the obligation even if not disclosed.

35   Eg if there are indemnities for specific matters (such as for environmental obligations or disclosed litigation) the terms of which are not otherwise included in the

agreement. Sometimes interim handover arrangements (eg for computer systems) are set out in a separate document, when this too should be mentioned.

36   If this sub-clause is not included and time is not made of the essence, the party not in default will have to make it so by giving reasonable notice if it wishes to rescind by reason of failure to complete. The sub-clause is obviously unnecessary if completion is simultaneous with exchange. Note cl 8.8 with regard to the right of rescission. Contrast with th Agreement for Sale (Assets), cl 6.4 which takes a slightly different approach.

Clause 6: Purchaser's Right of Access

37   Any accountants' investigation should have been concluded before exchange of contracts, but it is always useful for a purchaser to have access to the target's books. Vendors may object to this while the agreement remains conditional.

Clause 7: Restriction of Vendor's Group

38   *See generally,* Chapter 4 at p 31. If the vendor is an intermediate holding company, it would be advisable to obtain a direct covenant from the ultimate holding company, which is in a position to procure that the covenant can be enforced.

39   Restrictive covenants imposed on the vendor will need consideration under Art 85 of the Treaty of Rome, the Restrictive Trade Practices Act 1976 and the common law restraint of trade doctrine. As a general principle the covenant should be limited to the activities of the business sold, be reasonable in its geographic scope for the protection of that business and should usually be limited to a maximum of five years (two, if only goodwill is transferred), although it should be noted that this period is not always justified under the common law rules, for which reason a shorter period is often adopted. Broader or longer covenants may be subject to scrutiny from the EC and/or UK competition authorities although, of course, special circumstances will sometimes make such covenants justifiable. Purchaser covenants eg which protect the vendor's retained business will rarely be justifiable. Note that in this precedent the periods run from the date of the agreement; to make them longer the completion date is sometimes specified, but beware of the effect on time limitations when a long period between signing and completion is contemplated. Sometimes the vendor will seek an exception to deal with the situation where it later acquires a company or business which itself carries on competing business—this is usually agreed to provided the exception is confined to the acquisition of an entity which has only incidental competing business (which is not then actively developed).

40   This restriction may be difficult to justify; for this reason sub-cl (C) and sub-cl (D) are separate and in different terms and intended to be capable of severance.

41   It is possible that such an open-ended provision for effectively rewriting the covenant could render the whole covenant void for uncertainty; however some purchasers feel that such an expression of contractual intention will facilitate severance if necessary.

42   See Chapter 4 at p 32. Note that the Restrictive Trade Practices Act 1976 may require registration of the agreement even though the restriction on the vendor is reasonable in terms of scope and duration, etc.

Clause 8: Warranties and Deposit

43   If there is more than one vendor all references to the vendor in cl 8 (in particular—but also other clauses) should be amended to the plural.

44   This is unlikely to work in all cases: *see* Chapter 9 at p 167. The case of *Eurocopy v Teesdale* [1991] BCLC 1067, suggests that a purchaser may not be able to rely on such a clause where it has actual knowledge of certain facts not disclosed in the disclosure letter. As a result, to the extent a purchaser has knowledge of a matter which may be in breach of the warranties, the agreement should either make it clear that notwithstanding that particular item of knowledge, the purchaser is still entitled to claim or alternatively, should contain a specific indemnity in respect of the item in question (a further alternative sometimes used in cases where the item is quantifiable is for a provision to be made for it in any completion accounts).

45   *See* Note 13 and Chapter 10 at p 187.

46   *See* Chapter 9 at p 168 for a discussion as to the measure of damages on contractual warranty claims and the 'pound for pound' clause.

47   Obviously not relevant if signing and completion are simultaneous.

48   This is sometimes drafted as a restatement of the warranties at completion. If that approach is taken then, unlike this clause, there will be an absolute right to rescind, even where the breach of warranty was outside the vendor's control. The vendor might then negotiate an exception for breaches outside its control. The restatement approach obviously offers greater protection for the purchaser and puts the vendor on risk for all matters arising between contract and completion. The agreed approach will depend in part why there is a delay between signing and completion. If for reasons associated with the purchaser, the vendor will take a tougher line against carrying responsibility or consequence in the event of new matters arising between signing and completion. This area, and the related area of rescission in the event of breach, can be the subject of lengthy negotiation—there is rarely a 'right' answer.

49   This clause often supplements cl 8.5 (frequently in shorter form). While arguably offering no additional protection to the purchaser, it has merit to focus the vendor on some matters relating to conduct of the target business between exchange and completion which are uppermost in the purchaser's mind. A vendor will often seek to use the 'list' approach in cl 8.6 as a substitute for cl 8.5. While not objectionable in principle it is probably to be avoided in practice. The protection offered by cl 8.5 relates to all the warranties and is in considerable detail. To offer the same protection the list would need to be much more extensive (indeed, approaching the length and content of the warranties themselves).

50   Or include a definition of 'material contract' if there are certain types of contracts that the purchaser is particularly concerned about.

51   The circumstances in which rescission is permitted, and whether for any, or only, material breach, and what then is regarded as material (eg referable to profits, assets or some other criteria) is for negotiation.

52   It is difficult to draft these provisions satisfactorily. If the period referred to in sub-cl 8.11 is not consistent with the limitation period (as reduced, if applicable: see eg Schedule 8, para 5) and if the purchaser notifies a claim and withholds a larger amount than that eventually due, any excess will be available by way of set-off against another claim notified after the end of the period stipulated in sub-cl 8.11.

If any of the vendors is a company, it is open to question whether these sub-clauses evidence a charge registrable under the Companies Act 1985, s 395 *et seq.* It is suggested that they do not, but nothing is lost by registration and the point should be considered on each occasion. The Agreement for Sale (Assets), at p 519, takes a different approach with the funds retained by the purchaser rather than deposited with a bank.

53 Consider whether all interest should, in fact, accrue to the vendor. Any payments to the purchaser are in respect of damages which should be assessed on a loss basis and should, perhaps, take into account the time value of money.

54 Another alternative is a two-stage retention; (1) in respect of completion accounts adjustments and (2) in respect of general warranty claims. If there is any element of deferred consideration, an express right of set-off is sometimes included (although it is generally thought unnecessary).

Clause 9: Confidentiality

55 Note the clause affects both vendor and purchaser, which may not always be appropriate (although see cl 9.3). Disclosure may be necessary to auditors, insurers, bankers, directors and senior employees who are involved in the acquisition process.

Clause 10: Announcements

56 The purchaser will need to be free to deal with announcements to customers, suppliers, employees etc. The vendor may wish to have some influence over these, in which case the clause will require modification.

Clause 11: Provisions relating to the Agreement

57 The vendor will generally prefer that the warranties are not assignable, and will argue that it is willing to give the warranties only to a purchaser whose identity it knows. If the purchaser intends that an assignee should be able to recover directly from the vendor for its own loss, this will need to be addressed specifically with the vendor agreeing to the point so that there is no doubt as to what was intended. See for example *Linden Gardens Trust Ltd v Lenesta Sludge Disposals Ltd* [1994] 1 AC 85 (the *St Martins Property* decision).

58 A vendor will seek a provision of this type for the purpose of excluding liability in respect of pre-contractual misrepresentation, confining the purchaser's remedies instead to those statements included as warranties in the agreement. As the provision seeks to exclude liability for misrepresentation it will be subject to the requirement of reasonableness in the Misrepresentation Act 1967, s 3 and it is for this reason the clause does not seek to exclude liability where there is fraud. The limitation on the purchaser's remedies for such representations should be read in conjunction with the vendor protection provisions contained in Schedule 8 (p 461), where the limitations are expressed to apply in respect of all claims, including misrepresentation claims and, it is thought, should also be regarded (at least to the extent of misrepresentation) as subject to s 3 of the 1967 Act. As a result, the schedule also excludes those limitations in respect of fraud and, in that case, similar matters (para 8 at p 462).

The clause included in the precedent will leave open the possibility of claims for misrepresentation in respect of those pre-contractual representations which are then repeated as warranties in the agreement; the vendor may seek to exclude the purchaser's remedies for such representations by limiting the purchaser's remedies to *breach of contract* in respect of the warranties contained in the agreement eg 'no fact or matter which renders any of the Warranties incorrect or is inconsistent with any of them shall give rise to any claim against the Vendor other than a claim for breach of contract in respect of the Warranties concerned and (save in respect of fraud) the Purchaser shall not in respect of any such fact or matter have any claim for misrepresentation'. It will be noted that the exception in respect of fraud is also applicable. By limiting the purchaser's remedies to the contractual remedy, the different measure of damages for misrepresentation (which is based on the tortious measure) would be precluded.

See further the discussion in Chapter 9 at p 163 and in particular, *Thomas Witter Ltd v TPB Industries Ltd* [1996] 2 All ER 573.

59   This provision may not be enforceable in all circumstances. Oral agreements may be effective for a variety of reasons. It is no longer necessary for a deed to be amended by a document which is also a deed—an agreement under hand is sufficient, provided there is consideration (Supreme Court Act 1981, s 49).

60   *See* Note 12. This Agreement has been prepared on the basis of a single vendor giving the warranties. However it may be appropriate that a holding company of the vendor be joined in or, if there is more than one shareholder, all will give warranties. In either case, such a clause will be relevant.

61   Amend as appropriate. Overseas service may not be appropriate. It may be appropriate to specify personal service during business hours.

Clause 12: Law and Jurisdiction

62   There are various possible jurisdiction clauses: (1) exclusive (given here); (2) non-exclusive; and (3) exclusive for one party but not for the other. An exclusive submission to the English (or other) courts is particularly suitable for an English law contract, while a non-exclusive submission may permit a subsequent tactical decision to be taken on the forum most likely to be advantageous to the intending plaintiff's case. The intention of the third alternative might be to require the vendor to have recourse solely to the English courts, while allowing the purchaser to sue in the English courts but also elsewhere if that should appear more advantageous after a dispute has arisen. The effectiveness of these clauses depends in part on whether proceedings are intended to be brought outside the UK and whether such other jurisdictions are states which have ratified the Brussels Convention and/or the Lugano Convention which have the effect, for parties in ratifying states, to prevent 'forum shopping'.

63   Only if one or more of the parties are outside the United Kingdom for the service of documents.

Schedule 3: Warranties and Representations

64   For general comment on warranties, *see* p 165. The warranties contained in the schedule are extensive and it is most unlikely that they would all be appropriate in any particular transaction. Consider what additional warranties are appropriate to the transaction. When negotiating warranties, bear in mind the distinction between what are essentially information gathering warranties, primarily intended to produce information, and those that are in substance designed to place the risk of the

warranty being incorrect on the vendor. Accepting qualification to the latter plainly requires careful thought as the qualification may result in risk transferring to the purchaser (eg under the principle of *caveat emptor*). If there is more than one vendor, amend all references to the 'vendor' to the 'vendors'.

65   *See* the discussion in Chapter 10 at p 207 concerning computer systems (on an assets acquisition). If assets are owned and contractual arrangements are with the target group on a standalone basis, computer arrangements should be relatively straightforward, although documentation should be checked for change of control clauses. If there is dependence on vendor group systems, then interim operating arrangements may need to be agreed.

66   The definition is intended to include most forms of intellectual property right recognised in English law. It should be reviewed and adapted having regard to the nature of the target's business.

67   The definition of connected persons is wide-ranging and, in relation to an individual, includes relatives, partners, trustees of settlements of which the individual is a settlor and companies controlled by the individual; it also includes companies under common control. Other definitions are sometimes used (eg Companies Act 1985, s 346), but are narrower.

68   A vendor may wish to delete the reference to 'representations' (*see* Note 58).

69   These warranties in a number of respects go to the heart of what is to be sold and amendment will be made with care. Note the overlap with the title of what is to be conveyed (cl 2.1 at p 381); and *see generally* the discussion in Chapter 10 at p 187. When negotiating vendor limitations, a purchaser will often resist any limits on the warranties contained in Paragraphs 2.1(A), (B) and (C) and 2.2 (so-called 'fundamental warranties') as these go to the root of what is being acquired and the vendor's ability to sell it.

70   Other warranties also cover compliance with laws issues (eg Property, para 2.8(I)(d), (e); Environmental, para 2.4(I)(2)(a)). Disclosure will generally operate to qualify all relevant warranties to the extent of the disclosure concerned. If warranties are qualified by amendment, however, it will offer protection only if all relevant warranties are so qualified. As a result, it is becoming increasingly common to take a 'locked box' or 'ringfencing' approach to warranties and provide that, eg environmental warranties only cover environmental matters so that environmental matters are not, for example, covered by this warranty. If such an approach is desired it will be necessary to incorporate appropriate wording. The purchaser will vigorously resist such an approach unless it can be wholly confident that gaps in its protection are not thereby created. If it is accepted, it may stipulate that disclosure must be specific to, and only qualify, specified warranties. *See*, however, Note 44.

71   Debt collection actions in the ordinary course of business of less than a specified amount (individually and in the aggregate) are commonly excepted to reduce the disclosure burden. Whether that is appropriate and what the disclosure threshold would be plainly depends on the business. A purchaser will often omit the wording in square brackets, preferring to make up its own mind about the effect.

72   *See* comment about 'ringfencing' at Note 70.

73   *See* Chapter 16 for the effect of insolvency/liquidation on share sales.

74   *See* Note 3 for the definition of the Audited Accounts to be warranted. Consider whether consolidated accounts, individual accounts, or both, should be warranted. The Agreement for Sale (Assets) at p 565 contains a fuller records warranty.

75   The vendors will object to warranting that the accounts are 'true and accurate in all material respects' preferring to restrict their warranty to the wording of the auditors' report on the accounts (which, of course, may vary depending upon the target). The judgment of the House of Lords in *Caparo Industries v Dickman* [1990] 1 All ER 568 means that, save where there is an express assumption of responsibility by the auditors to the purchaser, the audited accounts alone cannot be relied upon to provide redress to the purchaser against the auditors in the event that they are wrong. *See further* Chapter 9 at p 137.

76   The vendor will prefer 'proper' provision or, alternatively, provision for all material liabilities.

77   Changes in stock valuation or in the bases and policies of accounting can, of course, affect the recorded profits of the target. Such policies should be stated by way of note to the accounts (see Statement of Standard Accounting Practice No 2: 'Disclosure of Accounting Policies').

78   The wording of this warranty will frequently be the subject of negotiation as the vendor will, depending on its procedures for preparation of management accounts, be concerned not to warrant them as 'accurate'. Vendors will also be alert to ensure, by appropriate words in the disclosure letter, that they do not indirectly warrant the 'accuracy' of management accounts under (eg warranty 2.12(C)). This is a point which may also apply to other annexures to the disclosure letter.

79   The wording reflects an attempt to identify by disclosure possible differences between accounting policies adopted in the management and audited accounts.

80   Note the relationship with cl 8.5. Consider whether a longer period is appropriate (eg the previous 12 months) and whether other matters (eg margins) should be covered. See the equivalent provision in he Agreement for Sale (Assets) at p 567.

81   The vendors may object to giving warranties as to the 'prospects' of the company and may wish this to be qualified 'to the best of their knowledge and belief.'

82   This is likely to be highly contentious particularly as it depends on the purchaser's management going forward. A definition of working capital (eg stock, prepayments and debtors, less creditors and accruals) may be required. Alternatively the vendor could be asked to warrant historical working capital levels and working capital at completion thus showing that current working capital levels are in line with historical averages. If the acquisition is a Super Class 1 transaction for the purchaser or involves issuing listing particulars the purchaser may seek some form of comfort on working capital from the vendor to underpin the statement it is required to make in its circular or listing particulars (which must include the target), and on which its sponsor is required to report (*see generally*, Chapter 11 at p 229).

83   See Chapter 3 at p 21 relating to consents and approvals.

84   Vendors who themselves seek insurance against liability under warranties will find insurers wary of this warranty.

85   If completion accounts are prepared, the parties sometimes agree to forgo such a warranty. The warranty serves a function, however, even where there are completion accounts. Note that the vendor is given a 'cushion' to the extent of current

year profits, if any (but not losses). It may be appropriate to specify a figure for the comparison.

86   See the Agreement for Sale (Assets), sub-paras 2.7(B), (C) and (D) at p 569 for extended asset warranties. These may be adapted and included if felt appropriate.

87   Insurers of warranty liabilities will normally exclude such a warranty from cover. Some (alternative) protection from bad debts may be available through completion accounts.

88   'Listed Intellectual Property' is generally confined to registered intellectual property, eg patents and registered trade marks, although where it is possible to identify other forms of unregistered intellectual property (eg copyright in drawings, software programs and updates, publishers' listings of titles, portfolios of designs etc) details should also be set out in the Disclosure Letter or in a schedule.

89   This is an important intellectual property warranty to obtain for the purchaser. It is designed to identify licences (express or implied) under which the target company is using intellectual property rights; if any are revealed check if they terminate on change of ownership. It is quite common for a company to commission copyright works from a third party but fail to put in place the necessary assignment of such rights to the company in which case the rights may belong to the third party. Also, the target company may be part of a larger group of companies and may have the benefit of implied licences relating to, for example, the use of software. Such matters should be disclosed under this warranty by the vendor and where appropriate the purchaser will request formal licences be put in place.

90   A warranty that all the intellectual property rights used by the target *are valid and enforceable* will not be given lightly and is often qualified by reference to the vendor's knowledge. For example, the granting of patents and registered trade marks by the Patent Office/Trade Marks Registry does not mean that such rights are valid: the validity of these rights can be challenged on a number of grounds. The warranty is also designed to identify matters such as non-use of a registered trade mark, delay in taking action and/or acquiescence in relation to an infringing act which may have consequences for later use or enforcement of rights.

91   Often qualified by the vendor's awareness.

92   Often amended as monitoring internal controls on confidentiality can be difficult.

93   Warranties (13) to (15) are additional options that depend on the nature of business being acquired.

94   Most forms of advertising, marketing and sales promotion in the UK fall within the provisions of codes of practice which have been adopted voluntarily by the advertising industry. These relate, for example, to the truthfulness and tastefulness of advertisements. Failure to comply may result in adverse publicity and a tendency to be shunned by potential advertising media.

95   The extent to which these warranties will be agreed will depend in part on the extent to which the purchaser will be relying on its inspections, searches and other investigations (such as structural surveys) and the quality and quantity of information supplied by the vendor.

96   Where warranties turn on 'materiality' consider the qualification in the light of any '*de minimis*' level for claims agreed in the vendor protection provisions (Schedule 8); consider specifying a monetary value for materiality. This point is, of course, of application to any of the warranties.

97   To cover the position where, even though not legally binding, a proposal has been put to a customer/potential customer which may prove to be 'morally' binding.

98   It is envisaged that the schedule of employees will show not only remuneration but also length of service, age, position held etc. In the case of a target with a large number of employees, the purchaser may waive the requirement except in respect of employees earning more than a specified amount.

99   Vendors will often seek to resist any warranty of information contained or referred to in the Disclosure Letter. Its main reasons are that (i) the Disclosure Letter is intended to protect the vendor, not provide an additional basis of claim for the purchaser (a 'shield' not a 'sword' is the usual expression) (ii) to the extent disclosures are inaccurate, they will not be 'fair' and the purchaser in such circumstances will not be precluded from claiming (iii) such a 'blanket' warranty will cut across others which have been carefully drawn. One compromise is for certain documents to be identified and warranted as accurate. The purchaser should insist on much of the warranty as the Disclosure Letter is a document on which it relies.

100   Vendors who dishonestly conceal material facts may be liable under the Financial Services Act 1986, s 47 (*see* p 133).

Schedule 4: Taxation

101   In the case of individual vendors selling a single United Kingdom tax-resident company, delete warranties 2.1(F) and 2.2(B) and (C).

102   If the company is not an investment company or there is no investment company in the target group, delete warranty 2.3(C).

103   If the company is not a close company, delete warranties 2.4(2)–(8), and amend warranty 2.4(1) accordingly.

104   If the company has no interest in a controlled foreign company, delete the remainder of warranty 2.5(C).

105   Consider whether the company's activities come within the scope of the legislation affecting sub-contractors in the construction industry for the purposes of warranty 2.10(E) and delete as appropriate.

106   If the vendor is a listed company, delete warranty 2.13 in its entirety.

Schedule 5: Adjustment of Consideration

107   The schedule sets out a framework for preparation of completion accounts—it may not be appropriate for all circumstances but can be used as a base for calculation of most forms of adjustment. It is highly desirable that the parties' accountants are involved in setting out the criteria for preparation of the completion accounts—especially where they have been involved in due diligence, when they will be familiar with particular aspects of the target's books which may require special attention. Take particular care, where completion accounts are prepared, with their relationship to the tax deed. If the consideration is adjusted by reference to completion accounts it would be usual for the tax deed to operate by reference to completion accounts rather than previous audited accounts, failing which there may be problems of mismatching, double counting or giving credit to the vendor more than once for eg overprovisions for tax in the accounts. *See further* the Tax Deed, Note 23 at p 498.

108 If goodwill or other intangible assets appear as assets in the audited accounts, ex-
     clusion of these amounts in the completion accounts will mean that the vendor will
     require that the different basis be taken into account in setting the reference figure
     for net tangible assets in para 5.

109 If the target companies do not form a group of companies for which consolidated
     accounts are prepared, it will be necessary to discuss how the accounts should be
     prepared and aggregated/consolidated.

110 Consider whether there is a need for a profit and loss account: it may not be nec-
     essary in all transactions; however from the purchaser's point of view it may give
     an indication of the profitability of the company since the balance sheet date, as-
     sisting the purchaser to identify warranty claims at an early stage.

111 It is helpful for the parties and their accountants to agree on a *pro forma* comple-
     tion balance sheet so at least the layout and line items are agreed in advance.

112 If other financial standards or guidance notes are appropriate, add (after discussion
     with the accountants).

113 Discuss with the purchaser's accountants. They may prefer, where no specific re-
     quirement is given, for the policies to 'default' back to GAAP rather than the ven-
     dor's accounting policies. The purchaser will, of course, need to be satisfied about
     the vendor's policies. Also problems sometimes arise with the hindsight which is
     applied in preparing audited accounts. If circumstances arise after completion
     which make it clear, with hindsight, that an asset was worth less or that a bad debt
     provision should be made, the usual rule is to reflect the new information. Whether
     or not this is appropriate for completion accounts is difficult—the purchaser will
     want to provide at completion based on all available information, but the vendor
     may disagree because the matter will be out of its control. The vendor may seek a
     specific requirement that nothing done after completion by the purchaser will im-
     pair the value of an asset or increase a provision as at the completion date but ac-
     cepting that what is done by others may nonetheless affect the position.

114 These provisions must be discussed with the purchaser's accountants and ampli-
     fied where necessary. The key question is whether the 'net tangible assets' will be
     clearly shown. See *Shorrock v Meggitt PLC* [1991] BCC 471 and the paper enti-
     tled 'The Involvement of Accountants in Commercial Agreements' issued in No-
     vember 1991 by the Institute of Chartered Accountants.

115 Fixing asset values in this way means that the purchaser will need to have satisfied
     itself about the value of the assets it is acquiring.

116 It is likely that there will be detailed provisions for valuing stock which will need
     to address the specific circumstances of the target business. Some stock may have
     a short shelf life and others may require different treatment (eg packaging). Fin-
     ished stock and raw materials may be valued differently. Specific provisions in re-
     lation to obsolete stock may be required following any financial due diligence.
     Similarly, work-in-progress will often be the subject of specific valuation rules
     and in either case, a maximum value for stock or work in progress is sometimes
     seen (*see* Chapter 10 at p 193).

117 Volume discounts may be triggered and payable after completion, where a propor-
     tion of the business with the customer has been pre-completion, for which the ven-
     dor has taken the benefit of the trading profit.

118 Ensure there is no overlap with sub-para (A), where other wants of repair are re-
     ferable to the policies used in the audited accounts. Sometimes it is thought appro-
     priate to provide that where the damage is insured, credit is to be given in respect
     of the insurance only if the insurer has accepted liability.

119 These are termination payments to senior staff, if any. *See* Chapter 5 for financial
     assistance considerations in respect of such payments; however, their inclusion in
     the accounts does not mean that the target group need bear the payment.

120 This can be an area of contention. The vendor will be keen, in the disclosure letter,
     to disclose all that it can in the nature of liabilities, both actual and contingent, to
     preclude claims under the warranties but will be alarmed to find that full provision
     for all such amounts is to be included in the completion accounts. Conversely, the
     purchaser will not, having identified matters for which it requires the vendor to be
     responsible, want to have any dispute when it comes to preparing the accounts as
     to the amount of the provision. The solutions (if the vendor retains responsibility)
     are a combination of agreed provision for liabilities which are certain in amount
     and dealing with liabilities which are uncertain by indemnity from the vendor,
     without provision being made in the completion accounts.

121 For example, the costs of preparing the accounts; pension provisions are some-
     times suggested, but care should be taken as there will be overlap with Schedule
     6. A funding deficit (if any) will be dealt with under those provisions. Another dif-
     ficult area is where there are overseas subsidiaries, eg how these should be reflect-
     ed in the accounts, and any local accounting rules which will need to be taken into
     account. The accountants will be consulted on such matters.

122 The procedure for preparation of completion accounts can take a number of forms.
     This precedent contemplates that the purchaser, with its accountants, will prepare
     the first draft for agreement by the vendor (and its accountants) failing which the
     matter will be referred to arbitration if it cannot be agreed. Sometimes the first
     draft will be prepared by the vendor's accountants. Sometimes the parties will do
     the work themselves and involve the accountants only at an intermediate stage, if
     there is preliminary dispute, and sometimes the accountants will be instructed
     jointly by the parties. The joint instruction of a firm of accountants can cause dif-
     ficulties when there is genuine difference between the parties. Whichever is the
     best approach is a matter of judgement, and often negotiation—each party will
     want control. It is important that both parties have access to the relevant people
     and information. The vendor will sometimes require that the same individuals em-
     ployed in the target business and previously responsible for preparation of ac-
     counts also have involvement in preparation of completion accounts. It is
     increasingly becoming the practice of the accountants (particularly where jointly
     instructed) to require an appointment letter to be signed, containing limits on its
     liability and an indemnity (*see* Chapter 9 at p 141).

123 For authority on the words 'act as expert and not as arbitrator' see *Nikko Hotels
     (UK) Ltd v MEPC PLC* [1991] 28 EG (disapproving *Burgess v Purchase & Sons
     (Farms) Ltd* [1983] WLR 361). In *Nikko Hotels* it was held that unless it can be
     shown that expert has not performed its task, his decision will be final binding and
     conclusive, and thus not open for review ie if he answers to the question but in the
     wrong way, his decisions will still be binding. That decision should be viewed in
     the light of the House of Lords' decision in *Mercury Communications Ltd v Di-
     rector General Of Telecommunications* [1996] 1 WLR 48 where it was held, in a
     different context, that where a matter was referred for determination (by the Di-

rector General) his decision was open to review by the court should he misinterpret the matter referred.

124 Alternatively, the parties may agree an estimated completion NAV figure, based eg on management accounts, against which to adjust.

125 The drafting attempts to ensure that the purchaser is not precluded from claiming damages is a result of a breach of warranty because the matter concerned is taken into account in the completion accounts. However, the amount taken into account is deducted from the claim.

Schedule 6: Pensions

A   Company has own final salary scheme

126 The exclusion of debts of the target may be inappropriate if there are to be completion accounts.

127 The valuation of the assets of the pension scheme requires careful consideration in conjunction with the actuary. With an insured scheme, it would be normal to refer to the face (as distinct from the surrender) value of the policy.

128 If pensionable pay is increased only annually under the pension scheme the purchaser should ensure that the assumed increases in pensionable pay apply from the last annual review date and not from completion. Alternatively, the purchaser may require the past service liabilities to be based on actual earnings at completion. Check that there have been no unusual increases in earnings which count for pension, (eg consolidation of bonuses)—see para 4(E) of the schedule.

129 *See* p 113.

130 The vendor may wish to aggregate if the surplus in one scheme can be used to offset a deficit in another.

131 The vendor may wish to argue for an adjustment in respect of any surplus, see p 90.

132 *See* Note 123.

133 The vendor should note that if it ends up paying more than the purchase price to the purchaser the excess will be a taxable receipt by the purchaser. The effect of any gross up clause should not be overlooked in the circumstances.

134 The vendor may wish to argue that an adjustment should be made for tax relief (*see* p 89).

135 If exchange and completion are not to be simultaneous, the purchaser should ensure that it is adequately protected during the intervening period. The schedule relies on cl 8.5. The purchaser should ensure that all matters against which it requires protection are referred to in the warranties. Conversely, the vendor should bear in mind the limited control which it has over the pension scheme. *See also* the Agreement for Sale (Shares), Note 48 at p 468.

136 *See* p 87.

137 *See* p 85.

138 *See* p 113.

139 Recent pay restructuring (eg consolidation of bonus into basic pay) may have a material effect on the funding of the pension scheme which should be taken into account when valuing the liabilities.

140 *See* p 114.

141 To guard against, eg the company having given a covenant to the trustees to pay contributions over a number of years (eg for a benefit augmentation).

142 *See* p 81.

143 Material only if the purchaser is relying on the actuarial valuation report. Also, *see* p 89.

144 *See* p 112.

B   Company participates in group final salary scheme

145 If the pension scheme is contracted-out on a protected rights basis, the vendor should provide for a deduction in respect of any age-related rebates which will as a consequence of the transfer be payable to the purchaser's scheme.

146 As the transaction takes place at completion, commercially this is the most logical time as at which to calculate the Basic Amount. It can then be appropriately adjusted on a basis which is broadly financially neutral to both parties for subsequent contributions for Transferring Employees and investment return. Consideration should, however, be given to whether doing the calculation in this way is consistent with the Pension Scheme rules. The share sale is not in this context material to the trustees of the Pension Scheme, the rules of which will normally provide for the transfer payment to be calculated at the end of the Interim Period.

147 *See* Note 128 *above*.

148 *See* p 113.

149 The schedule is drafted on the assumption that defined benefits will always exceed any protected rights underpin.

150 The appropriate method of investment adjustment will depend upon how the pension scheme is invested, the investments held in respect of active members (as distinct from pensioners) and the number of employees involved. There is no particular justification for either side trying to make a profit out of the transitional arrangements and so the adjustment should be one which can reasonably be obtained by the pension scheme.

151 If pensionable pay is increased annually under the pension scheme the vendor may wish to provide for the Membership Transfer Date to fall before the next annual review date so as to immunise the scheme from pay increases granted after completion.

152 Suitable where purchaser's scheme may be a retirement benefits scheme or a personal pension scheme.

153 It may be possible to dispense with the need for consents, although other Payment Conditions would then be required (*see* p 104). If consents are to be obtained, the vendor may wish to approve the form in which they are given.

154 *See* p 104.

155 The vendor may seek to aggregate the transfer values if a deficit in one scheme can be made good by transferring surplus from another.

156 This gives the purchaser the flexibility to transfer the employment of employees to another company in the purchaser's group without disrupting the transitional arrangement.

157 *See* p 102.

158 To provide protection for the company both during the Interim Period (eg the trustees of the Pension Scheme requiring contributions at a different rate than contemplated in the schedule) and after the end of the Interim Period (eg sex equality or under general indemnity under the Pension Scheme, *see* p 100).

159 The vendor may require the purchaser to contribute to the administration expenses either by making a direct payment to the vendor or by an additional deduction being made in (B) of the definition of 'Transfer Value'. The vendor may also wish to include protective provisions preventing the target from increasing the liabilities under the pension scheme during the transitional period (*see* p 99). In addition the vendor may want the purchaser to undertake to procure that the company exercises its discretions under the Pensions Act 1995 as it may reasonably direct (*see* p 98).

160 *See* p 97.

161 *See* p 100.

162 The vendor should consider whether any undertaking from the purchaser with regard to the level of future service benefits is required. Also the vendor should consider in conjunction with the pension scheme trustees whether any additional provisions are required to ensure that the transfer value is applied for the benefit of the transferring employees, *see* p 103. As to the extent to which it may be lawful for the company to vary benefits *see* p 107.

163 Delete reference to MP Employees if paragraph 4.4 deleted.

164 Stamp duty should not be payable, *see* p 106.

165 The vendor may wish to include an excess clause, *see* p 96.

166 *See* Note 133 *above*.

167 The purchaser should ensure that the shortfall provisions do not constitute a penalty (see *Export Credits Guarantee Dept v Universal Oil Products Company* [1983] 2 All ER 205 and *Alder v Moore* [1961] 1 All ER 1). The vendor may require allowance to be made in calculating the shortfall for tax relief and any of the Transferring Employees' benefits not transferred to the Purchaser's Scheme (*see* p 95).

168 *See* Note 123 *above*.

169 *See* Note 135 *above*.

170 *See* Note 139 *above*.

171 *See* p 100.

172 *See* Note 141 *above*.

173 *See* p 112.

C   Company has own money purchase scheme

174 The schedule is drafted on the assumption that the scheme is insured. If it is self-administered, more extensive warranties may be required, as in the schedule for final salary schemes.

175 *See* Note 135 *above.*

176 There may not be an actuarial valuation report (see IR 12 (1991), paras 13.3 and 16.6).

177 *See* Note 141 *above.*

178 *See* p 112.

D   Company participates in group money purchase scheme

179 *See* Note 174 *above.*

180 *See* Note 156 *above.*

181 As to (C), *see* Note 158 *above.* As to (D) *see* the reference to the Deficiency Regulations on p 111.

182 The vendor may require a contribution towards the pension scheme expenses.

183 *See* Note p 97.

184 The vendor may wish to impose on the purchaser some obligation with regard to the provision of future service benefits.

185 *See* p 111.

186 Expands on the statutory requirements.

187 As to when the statutory transfer option is not available, *see* p 103.

188 It is not particularly satisfactory to rely on the statutory requirements. They impose a duty on the trustees to pay the transfer value within six months of the application. Penal interest is payable if payment is delayed, without reasonable excuse, beyond that period but otherwise no interest need be paid (Chapter IV, Part IV, Pension Schemes Act 1993 and The Occupational Pension Schemes (Transfer Values) Regulations 1996 (SI No 1847), reg 10(2)).

189 *See* Note 135 *above.*

190 *See* Note 141 *above.*

191 *See* p 112.

Schedule 7: Vendor protection

192 *See generally,* Chapter 9 at p 174. As these clauses are exclusion clauses, they will be construed *contra proferentum.* The vendor should ensure they are clear.

193 The schedule includes the basic limitations. Other limitations on liability are often put forward by the vendor. For example: a provision that proceedings have to be commenced within a certain time after a claim; deduction for insurance recoveries; deduction for compensation from other sources and the other provisions described at p 174. It would seem, however, that recoveries by the target should be taken into account in assessing damages without the need for express provision to that effect. The vendor will often seek conduct of claims against the target in

respect of which it may be liable under warranties or indemnities. Where completion accounts are prepared, the vendor will often require a provision which specifies that there should be no claim in respect of amounts included in those accounts. Again, it would seem that such matters would be taken into account in any event (which may not be so of matters already included in the audited accounts). An example of wording would to meet this point be eg 'the Vendor shall not be liable in respect of a Relevant Claim to the extent that allowance, provision or reserve in respect of the matter giving rise to the Relevant Claim is made in the Completion Accounts or such matter is otherwise taken into account or reflected in the preparation of the Completion Accounts'. Take extreme care that the credit is not given more than once eg refer either to the completion accounts or to the audited accounts but not, as a general rule, to both.

194 Note that while liability is limited in respect of the the 'Tax Deed', the 'Warranties' and the 'Disclosure Letter' a 'Relevant Claim' does not include a claim under the Tax Deed. This is because the Tax Deed itself contains certain provisions which operate to limit or have the effect of limiting the vendor's liability for claims under that deed (*see eg* clauses 2.3, 3.2, 3.7, of the Tax Deed, at pp 488–90). It is sometimes agreed that limitations similar to those provisions should apply more generally to claims under the agreement and in such a case the inclusion of claims under the Tax Deed in the definition of 'Relevant Claim' may result in a limitation being applied twice. Where additional limitations are to apply more generally in relation to the agreement, check very carefully how they relate to the Tax Deed. If there is any doubt, the purchaser may decide, for the sake of certainty, to specify that credit or limitation should never the applied more than once. Note also that the limitations do not apply more generally in respect of claims under the 'Agreement'.

195 Sometimes suggested the limit applies to all claims under the agreement. The purchaser will resist this because it would include claims for failure to deliver title to shares, for breach of restrictive covenant, and other 'fundamental' matters. The figure is often set at the amount of consideration, but there is no reason why it should not be higher. Consider excluding certain warranties from the provision (eg paras 2.1 and 2.2 on p 398).

196 This is a 'small claims' threshold, to eliminate immaterial 'nuisance' claims. If accepted by the purchaser it should set the threshold having regard to the nature of the target's business. The provision will often be resisted if warranties have been qualified so as to relate only to 'material' matters, since the threshold for claims will by this means already have been raised. This exclusion, and the more general threshold (sub-para (B)), is not expressed in the precedent to apply to claims under the Tax Deed, although there is no reason in principle why the parties should not agree that the thresholds apply to all claims and indeed, sometimes do.

197 *See* the Tax Deed, cl 3.2 at p 489. Consider whether the limit should be different depending on the different warranties eg environmental matters may merit a longer period.

198 A more vendor-friendly provision would, for example, give credit to the vendor where the purchaser is entitled to a benefit from a third party, even if it does not claim it.

199 *See* Note 58. The purchaser will, of course, wish to include such a provision in any event.

200 Ensure that checks on who will sign is made at an early stage and that the necessary signing authorities or powers of attorney (where required) are in place. Where overseas companies or a number of vendors are involved, this can occasionally take time to organise.

Appendix II

Tax Deed

Contents

THIS DEED[1] dated the [   ] day of [   ] 19[   ] and made

BETWEEN:

(1) [   ] PLC[2] a company registered in England under number
     [   ] whose registered office is at [   ] (the 'Vendor');

(2) [   ] PLC a company registered in England under number [   ]
     whose registered office is at [   ] (the 'Purchaser'); and

(3) [   ] LIMITED a company registered in England under number
     [   ] whose registered office is at [   ] (the 'Company').

WHEREAS

This Deed has been entered into pursuant to an agreement dated [   ] made
between the Vendor and the Purchaser ('the Agreement') under which the Purchaser has
agreed to purchase the Sale Shares from the Vendor, with the intention that an amount
equal to certain Tax Liabilities of the Company and certain Tax Liabilities of the Purchaser relating to the Sale Shares or the Company shall be paid by the Vendor to the
Purchaser.

NOW IT IS HEREBY AGREED as follows:

1 Interpretation

1.1 Definitions

In this Deed, unless the contrary intention appears:

words and expressions defined in the Agreement have the same meaning in this
Deed and any provisions in the Agreement concerning matters of construction or
interpretation shall also apply in this Deed;

'Accounting Period' has the same meaning as in s 12 of the Taxes Act;

'Actual Tax Liability' means
(A) a liability of the Company to make an actual payment of Tax or of an amount
     in respect of Tax either immediately or contingently[3] whether satisfied[4] or
     unsatisfied at Completion whether or not such Tax is also or alternatively
     chargeable against or attributable to any other person; and
(B) a liability of the Purchaser or a member of the Purchaser's Group[5] to make
     an actual payment of Tax or of an amount in respect of Tax in connection
     with the Sale Shares (other than stamp duty and stamp duty reserve tax on
     the transfer or sale thereof), the Company or any amount paid or due to the
     Purchaser under this Deed;
'ACT' means advance corporation tax;
'Auditors' means the Company's auditors from time to time;
'Business Day' means a day (other than a Saturday) when banks are open for the
transaction of normal banking business in London;
'Claim' means any assessment, notice, demand or other document issued or action
taken by or on behalf of any Tax Authority or any form of self-assessment from
which it appears that the Company, the Purchaser or any member of the Purchaser's Group is subject to, or is sought to be made subject to, or might become subject to, any Tax Liability;
'Company' includes [each of] the Subsidiar[y/ies];

'Deemed Tax Liability' means, in any of the circumstances set out in column (1) below, an amount determined as set out in column (2) below:

(1)	(2)
Either:	
1 The Unavailability of all or any part of any Relief to the Company.]	[1 The amount of Tax payable by the Company which would not have been payable had such Relief been available on the basis of rates of Tax current at the date when such Relief was found to be Unavailable[6] or, in the case of a right to repayment of Tax, the amount of the repayment which is found to be Unavailable.]
or:	
[1 The Unavailability of all or any part of any Relief which has been taken into account in preparing the Audited Accounts as an asset or to reduce or eliminate taxable profits or a provision for Tax or deferred Tax.]	[1 Either (a) the amount of Tax payable by the Company which would not have been payable if such Relief had been available; or (b) the amount by which such provision was so reduced; or (c) in the case of a right to a repayment of Tax, the amount of the repayment which is found to be Unavailable; or (d) in the case of any other Relief taken into account as an asset, that proportion of the amount so taken into account as corresponds to the proportion of the Relief which is Unavailable.]
2 The use of a Relief which has been taken into account in preparing the Audited Accounts (either by way of reduction of taxable profits or by way of set-off against a Liability to pay Tax) to reduce an Actual Tax Liability in respect of which the Purchaser would, but for that reduction or set off, have been able to make a claim against the Vendor under this Deed.	2 The amount by which such Actual Tax Liability is reduced by such use of the Relief.
3. The use of a Purchaser's Relief to reduce an Actual Tax Liability in respect of which the Purchaser would, but for that use, have been able to make a claim against the Vendor under this Deed.	3 The amount by which such Actual Tax Liability is reduced by the use of the Purchaser's Relief.

'Distribution' includes anything which is, or is deemed to be, a dividend or distribution for Tax purposes and shall also include any other Event which gives rise to an obligation to account for ACT or amounts corresponding to or similar to ACT;

'Event' includes (without limitation):
(A) any act, omission, transaction or Distribution whether or not the Company is a party thereto;[7]
(B) the death of any person;[8]
(C) the failure by any person to avoid an apportionment or Distribution of income (whether or not it is or was possible by taking action after Completion to avoid such apportionment or Distribution);[9]
(D) the Company ceasing to be a member of any group or associated with any person;[10]
(E) Completion; and
(F) any event which is treated as having occurred for the purposes of any legislation;

and references to the result of an Event occurring on or before Completion shall include the combined result of two or more Events one or more of which shall have taken place on or before Completion;[11]

'Purchaser's Group' means the Purchaser and those companies (other than the Company) which may be treated for relevant Tax purposes as being, or as having at any time been, either a member of the same group of companies as the Purchaser or otherwise associated with the Purchaser;

'Purchaser's Relief' means
(A) any Relief arising to the Purchaser or any member of the Purchaser's Group;
(B) any Relief arising as a consequence of, or by reference to, an Event occurring (or deemed to have occurred) or income earned after the Balance Sheet Date;[12] and
(C) any Relief the availability of which was taken into account in the Audited Accounts;[12]

'Relief' means any relief, allowance or credit in respect of Tax or any right to repayment of Tax (including any payment receivable in consideration for the surrender of ACT or group relief) or any deduction, exemption or set-off relevant in computing income, profits or gains for the purposes of Tax pursuant to any legislation or otherwise;[13]

'Tax' and 'Taxation' includes (without limitation) corporation tax, ACT, the charge under s 419 of the Taxes Act, income tax, capital gains tax, the charge under s 601(2) of the Taxes Act, value added tax, the charge to tax under Sched 9A of the Value Added Tax Act 1994, excise duties, customs and other import duties, inheritance tax, stamp duty,[14] stamp duty reserve tax, capital duties, national insurance contributions, local authority council taxes, petroleum revenue tax, foreign taxation and duties, amounts payable in consideration for the surrender of group relief or ACT or refunds pursuant to s 102 of the Finance Act 1989 and any payment whatsoever which the Company may be or become bound to make to any person as a result of the operation of any enactment relating to any such taxes or duties and all penalties charges and interest relating to the foregoing or resulting from failure to comply with the provisions of any enactment relating to Tax;

'Tax Authority' means any person entitled to enforce or collect Tax;

'Tax Liability' means an Actual Tax Liability or a Deemed Tax Liability;

'Taxes Act' means the Income and Corporation Taxes Act 1988;

'Unavailability' means in relation to a Relief, the setting-off, reduction, modification, clawback, counteraction, nullification, disallowance or cancellation of or withdrawal of or failure to obtain that Relief; and

references to any 'income earned' means any profits, gains or income earned, accrued or received or deemed for Tax purposes to be earned, accrued or received (including, for the avoidance of doubt, any increases in the values of any assets of the Company since their acquisition).

1.2   Inheritance Tax Charge Time of Liability for Purposes of this Deed

In determining for the purposes of this Deed whether a charge on or power to sell, mortgage or charge any of the shares or assets of the Company is in existence at any time, the fact that any Tax is not yet payable or may be payable by instalments shall be disregarded. Such Tax shall be treated as becoming due, and the charge or power to sell, mortgage or charge as arising, on the date of the transfer of value or other Event on or in respect of which it becomes payable or arises.[15]

2   Covenant by the Vendor

2.1   Covenant

Subject to the provisions of this Deed, the Vendor covenants to pay to the Purchaser[16] an amount equal to:

(A)   any Actual Tax Liability arising in connection with:
    (1)   any Event occurring on or before Completion; or
    (2)   any income earned on or before, or in respect of any accounting period ending on or before, the date of Completion;
(B)   any Deemed Tax Liability arising as a consequence of, or by reference to, an Event occurring (or deemed to have occurred) on or before Completion;
(C)   any Tax Liability arising as a result of the application of s 767A of the Taxes Act provided that such Actual Tax Liability is in respect of an undischarged liability of the Vendor or of a company controlled (as defined by s 767B(4) of the Taxes Act) by the Vendor in the three years ending on or before Completion;[17]
[(D)   *any Tax Liability arising as a consequence of or by reference to any of the following occurring or being deemed to occur at any time after Completion:*[18]
    (1)   the disposal by any Relevant Company of any asset or of any interest in or right over any asset; or
    (2)   the making by any Relevant Company (or by any person in pursuance of a scheme or arrangement with any Relevant Company) of any payment or deemed payment which constitutes a chargeable payment for the purposes of s 214 of the Taxes Act; or
    (3)   any Relevant Company ceasing to be resident in the United Kingdom for Tax purposes
    and, for the purposes of this Sub-Clause, the term 'Relevant Company' shall mean the Vendor and any company (other than the Company) that may be treated for Tax purposes as being, or as having at any time been, either a member of the same group of companies as the Vendor or otherwise associated with the Vendor;][19]
[(E)   *any Tax Liability in respect of inheritance tax which:*
    (1)   is at Completion in the form of a charge on, or gives rise to a power to sell, mortgage or charge, any assets of the Company or the Sale Shares; or
    (2)   after Completion takes the form of a charge on or gives rise to a power to sell, mortgage or charge, any assets of the Company or the Sale Shares as a

> *result of the death of any person after Completion which would, if the death had occurred immediately before Completion and the inheritance tax payable as a result had not been paid, have existed at Completion; or*
>
> *[(3)   arises as a result of a transfer of value occurring or being deemed to occur on or before Completion (whether or not in conjunction with the death of any person whenever occurring) which increased or decreased the value of the estate of the Company;]* [20]

(F)   any reasonable costs and expenses properly incurred and payable by the Purchaser or the Company in connection with any Tax Liability giving rise to a claim made under this Deed.

2.2   Adjustment to Consideration

Any payments made pursuant to Clause 2.1 shall, so far as possible, be treated as an adjustment to the consideration paid by the Purchaser for the Sale Shares.[21]

2.3   Limits of Vendor's Liability under this Deed[22]

The Vendor's liability under this Deed arising from any Tax Liability shall be limited in accordance with the provisions of Schedule 8 to the Agreement and to the extent that:

(A)   provision or reserve in respect of that Tax Liability has been made in the Audited Accounts[23] or to the extent that payment or discharge of such claim has been taken into account in the Audited Accounts;[24]

(B)   provision or reserve in respect of that Tax Liability has been made in the Audited Accounts which is insufficient only by reason of any increase in rates of Tax or change in law or published practice after the date hereof having retrospective effect;

(C)   it is a Tax Liability for which the Company is or may become liable as a result of transactions entered into by the Company in the ordinary course of trading[25] after the Balance Sheet Date and for the purposes of this Sub-Clause the following shall not be regarded as arising in the ordinary course of trading:

    (1)   any liability under Part VIII of the Taxes Management Act 1970 (charges on non-residents) or s 126 or Sched 23 of the Finance Act 1995 (UK representatives);

    (2)   any liability under Part XVII of the Taxes Act 1988 (anti-avoidance);

    (3)   any liability in respect of any Distribution; and

    (4)   any liability arising from the disposal or acquisition of or deemed disposal or acquisition of any asset other than trading stock;

(D)   it is a Tax Liability which would not have arisen but for a voluntary act or transaction, which could reasonably have been avoided, carried out by the Purchaser (or persons deriving title from it) or the Company after the date of Completion otherwise than in the ordinary course of business and which the Purchaser was aware could give rise to a claim, but so that this exclusion shall not extend to any voluntary act carried out with the approval, concurrence or assistance of the Vendor[26] other than any liability in connection with the following:

    [(1)   ;

    (2)   .]

2.4   Disclosure not relevant[27]

The Vendor's obligation to make payments under Clause 2.1 shall not be affected by the Purchaser's (or its officers, employees, agents or advisers) knowledge or the disclosure, in the Disclosure Letter or otherwise, of the Tax Liability giving rise to the payment, or of the circumstances giving rise to that Tax Liability.

3 Notice and Mitigation

3.1 Notice of Claim

If the Purchaser shall become aware of any Claim which is likely to give rise to a liability on the Vendor under Clause 2.1, it shall if possible not later than 14 days prior to the expiry of any time for appeal give notice or procure that notice is given to the Vendor setting out reasonable particulars of the Claim but no failure by the Purchaser to comply with this Sub-Clause shall affect the Vendor's obligations under Clause 2.1.[28]

3.2 Time Limit for Claims under this Deed[22]

No claim shall be brought by the Purchaser under this Deed unless notice in writing of such claim specifying (in reasonable detail) the matter which gives rise to the claim has been given to the Vendor not later than:

[(A) nine years and one month after the end of the accounting period of the company concerned in which Completion occurs in respect of corporation tax on chargeable gains;][29]
[(B) twelve years after the date of this Deed in relation to claims arising from the re-computation for tax purposes of the value of a transaction pursuant to s 770 of the Taxes Act;][30] and
(C) six years and one month after the end of the accounting period of the company concerned in which Completion occurs, in all other cases.

3.3 Information and Assistance

The Purchaser shall, and shall procure that the Company shall, take such action and give such information and assistance in connection with the affairs of the Company as the Vendor may reasonably and promptly by written notice request to avoid, resist, appeal, or compromise a Claim or pay an amount in respect of the Tax Liability provided that:

(A) the Purchaser and the Company shall not be obliged to appeal against any assessment, notice, demand or decision if, having given the Vendor notice in accordance with Clause 3.1, the Purchaser has not, by the later of 14 days from receipt by the Vendor of such notice, and 7 days prior to the expiry of any time for appeal, received instructions in writing from the Vendor to do so;
(B) the Purchaser and the Company shall not be obliged to comply with any request of the Vendor which involves contesting any assessment for Tax before any tribunal, court or other appellate body (a) unless they have been advised in writing by leading Tax counsel instructed by agreement between the Purchaser and the Vendor at the expense of the Vendor that an appeal against the assessment will, on the balance of probabilities, be successful, or (b) if the Purchaser can demonstrate to the reasonable satisfaction of the Vendor that in the opinion of the Purchaser such action would involve the disclosure of information confidential to the Company's business or result in a material adverse effect on the financial results of the Company's business;[31] and
(C) the Purchaser and the Company shall not be obliged to take any action which in the opinion of the Purchaser is likely to increase the liability to Tax of any company in the Purchaser's Group.

3.4 No Settlement of a Claim Without Consent

Following receipt of any instructions as referred to in Clause 3.3(A) the Purchaser shall procure that the Claim is not settled or otherwise compromised without the Vendor's prior written consent, such consent not to be unreasonably withheld or delayed.

3.5   Action Required by Vendor

The action which the Vendor may request under Sub-Clause 3.3 above shall include (without limitation but subject to the provisions of Sub-Clauses 3.3(A) to (C)) the Company applying to postpone (so far as legally possible)[32] the payment of any Tax but shall not include allowing the Vendor to take on or take over the conduct of any proceedings of whatsoever nature arising in connection with the Claim in question.

3.6   Recovery from Other Persons[22]

Where the Company is entitled to recover from some other person (not being the Company or any Subsidiary but including any Tax Authority[33]) any sum in respect of any Claim the amount of the Claim shall nevertheless be payable in full by the Vendor on the due date ascertained in accordance with Clause 4 and the Purchaser shall:

(A)   procure that the Vendor is promptly notified of such entitlement;

(B)   take such action as the Vendor may reasonably and promptly by written notice request to enforce such recovery; and

(C)   account to the Vendor for an amount equal to any amount so recovered by the Company (including any interest or repayment supplement included in such recovery less any Tax chargeable on the Company in respect of that interest) not exceeding the amount paid by the Vendor under Clause 2 in respect of that Claim save to the extent that to do so would leave the Company and the Purchaser together in a worse position than they would have been in had the Tax Liability in question not arisen.

3.7   Over-provisions[22]

If, at the request and cost of the Vendor, the Auditors shall certify that any provision for Tax (not being a provision for deferred taxation)[34] contained in the Audited Accounts is an over-provision, the value of such over-provision shall be set against the liability of the Vendor under Sub-Clause 2.1, except in so far as such over-provision is attributable to the effect of a change in rates of Tax after the date hereof, but no deduction shall be made from any payment which the Vendor shall be obliged to make hereunder unless such certificate is in existence on the due date for that payment. In the event that such a certificate is given after the Vendor has made a payment hereunder, the Purchaser shall refund to the Vendor (without interest) any payment made by the Vendor to the extent that such over-provision could have been set against such payment if the certificate had been in existence on the due date of payment. The Purchaser shall procure that the Company shall co-operate in obtaining any such certificate if the Vendor shall so request.

3.8   Indemnity for Costs etc

Notwithstanding anything in the Agreement or this Deed neither the Purchaser nor the Company shall be obliged to take any steps to reduce the amount of any Claim or to recover any amount from any other person unless the Vendor shall first indemnify and secure the Company and the Purchaser to their satisfaction against all losses (including any additional Tax Liability), costs, interest, damages and expenses which they may so incur.

4 Date for Payment

4.1 Date for Payment

Where any amount is required to be paid to the Purchaser by the Vendor in respect of an Actual Tax Liability, the Vendor shall pay such amount in cleared funds three Business Days before the date on which the Tax in question is due for payment to the relevant Tax Authority or, if later, ten Business Days following the date on which the Purchaser notifies the Vendor of its liability to make such payment.[35]

4.2 Notification of Amount

Where any amount is required to be paid by the Vendor other than in respect of an Actual Tax Liability, the Purchaser will notify the Vendor in writing of the amount which the Vendor is required to pay and the Vendor shall pay such amount in cleared funds on or before the date ten Business Days after the date on which it receives or is deemed to receive such notice in accordance with Sub-Clause 11.1(G) save that where the payment is in respect of a Deemed Tax Liability relating to the Unavailability of a right to repayment of Tax, payment shall be made on the date on which that repayment would otherwise have become due. Any dispute as to the amount contained in such notice shall be determined by the Auditors acting as experts and not arbitrators (at the cost of the Vendor.)

4.3 When Tax becomes Due

References to a date on which Tax becomes due for payment include a reference to the date on which it would have become due were it not for the availability of any Purchaser's Relief.[36]

4.4 Business Days

Any payment which becomes due on a day which is not a Business Day shall be paid on the previous Business Day, and any payment which is made after noon on any day shall, for the purposes of calculating interest, be deemed to have been paid on the next following Business Day.

4.5 Due Date and Interest

The Vendor shall make all payments under this Deed in immediately available funds before noon on the due date for payment without deduction or withholding on any account (save as expressly provided in this Deed) and if any amount is not paid when due the Vendor shall pay to the Purchaser interest on such amount accruing from day to day (as well after judgment as before) at the rate of [   ] per cent per annum above the base rate of [   ][37] Bank PLC from time to time from the due date until the date of actual payment (or the next Business Day if such day of actual payment is not a Business Day), compounded quarterly.

5 Deductions and Withholdings

5.1 No Deductions etc

Any amount payable pursuant to this Deed shall be paid free and clear of all deductions, withholdings, counter-claims or set-off whatsoever, save only as may be required by law.[38]

5.2   Deductions and Witholdings Required by Law

If any deductions or withholdings are required by law to be made from any sums, the Vendor shall be obliged to pay the Purchaser such amount as will, after the deduction or withholding has been made, leave the Purchaser with the same amount as it would have been entitled to receive in the absence of such requirement to make a deduction, withholding or set-off provided that if the Purchaser subsequently receives a credit for such deduction or withholding then such credit shall be applied in accordance with the provisions of Clause 7.

5.3   Accounting for Deductions and Withholdings

If the Vendor is required by law to make a deduction or withholding as is referred to in Sub-Clause 5.2, the Vendor shall:

(A)   make such deduction or withholding;

(B)   account for the full amount deducted or withheld to the relevant authority in accordance with applicable law; and

(C)   provide to the Purchaser the original, or a certified copy, of a receipt or other documentation evidencing the above.

6   Gross-Up

6.1   If any amount paid or due to the Purchaser under this Deed is a taxable receipt of the Purchaser then the amount so paid or due (the 'Net Amount') shall be increased to an amount which after subtraction of the amount of any Tax on such increased amount which arises, or would, but for the availability of any Relief arise, shall equal the Net Amount provided that if any payment is initially made on the basis that the amount due is not taxable in the hands of the Purchaser and it is subsequently determined that it is, or *vice versa*, such adjustments shall be made between the Purchaser and the Vendor as may be required.

7   Credits and Reductions

7.1   If any Claim represents Tax for which credit is or may become due to the Company at a later date or in respect of which it is subsequently found that there arises a corresponding credit or right to repayment of Tax, the amount of the Claim shall nevertheless be payable in full by the Vendor on the due date ascertained in accordance with Clause 4[39] but if subsequently any reduction is made in the Claim or it is found that the Vendor's liability in respect of the Claim falls short of the amount claimed or such credit or repayment is received by the Company, the Purchaser shall promptly repay to the Vendor an amount equal to such reduction, shortfall, credit or repayment (after deduction of any reasonable costs incurred in obtaining it and any Actual Tax Liability in respect of it) up to the amount previously paid by the Vendor in respect of that Claim and without interest[40], save to the extent that interest or repayment supplement is included (or allowed) in such credit, repayment, reduction or shortfall. For this purpose, no credit shall be taken to have been received by the Company unless it shall have relieved the Company of a present obligation to pay Tax.

8   *Group Arrangements*

8.1   *Group Relief, ACT and Tax Refunds[41]*

(A)   *In respect of the accounting period ended on [199   ] the [Vendor] and its subsidiaries ('surrendering companies') shall surrender group relief, ACT or* tax refunds to such of [the Company and the Subsidiaries] as can utilise the same ('claimant companies') and the [Purchaser] shall procure that [   ] per cent of the amount so surrendered (in the case of group relief) and 100 per cent of the amount surrendered (in the case of ACT or tax refunds) shall be paid by each relevant claimant company to the relevant surrendering company on or before [199   ].

(B)   The amount of group relief, ACT or tax refunds surrendered shall be determined by the surrendering companies but shall not, in the case of group relief and ACT, exceed the maximum amount which can be utilised by the claimant companies by way of relief from liability to corporation tax after utilising all other reliefs (including other group relief available to them).

(C)   If any part of the amounts so surrendered shall not be allowed to the claimant company by way of a relief from corporation tax the surrendering company shall refund to the claimant company forthwith the amount paid by the claimant company in respect of that part of the amount so surrendered.

8.2   Surrender in Settlement of Tax Liability

The Vendor may, so far as is lawfully possible, satisfy its obligation to make any payment to the Purchaser in respect of a liability arising under this Deed by surrendering or procuring the surrender of group relief or ACT for nil consideration to reduce or eliminate the Tax Liability giving rise to that liability.

8.3   Co-operation

The parties shall co-operate to secure the agreement of the Inland Revenue of the tax computations relating to the accounting period referred to above and shall take all necessary action to procure the surrenders aforesaid.

8.4   Agency

To the extent that each of the Vendor and the Company assumes obligations pursuant to this Clause 8 or Clause 9, it does so both in its own capacity and as agent for the Vendor's subsidiaries and the Subsidiaries respectively.

8.5   Disputes

In the event of any dispute with the Inland Revenue concerning a surrender of group relief or ACT the provisions of Clauses 3.3 to 3.5 and 3.8 hereof shall apply mutatis mutandis to the conduct of that dispute as if references therein to the Purchaser and the Company were references to the claimant company and as if references to the Vendor therein were references to the surrendering company.

9   Value Added Tax Group Registration[42]

9.1   Application for Registration

On or before the date of Completion, the Vendor shall procure that an application is made to HM Customs & Excise pursuant to s 43(5) of the Value Added Tax Act 1994 for the exclusion from the Vendor's group registration of [such of the Company and the Subsidiaries as are currently within that group registration] and for such exclusion to take effect at the earliest date permitted.

9.2   Continuing Representative Pending VAT Registration

Until such application has taken effect, the parties shall furnish or procure to be so furnished such information as may be required to enable [insert name of the continuing representative member of the group] to make the returns required in respect of the group.

9.3   Supplies by Vendor's VAT Group After Completion

In the context of supplies of goods or services made by the members of the Vendor's VAT group to third parties for the period commencing immediately after Completion and ending on the date the Company is excluded from the Vendor's group registration such payments shall be made by the Company to the Vendor or by the Vendor to the Company as shall ensure that the resulting position for VAT purposes for the Company and the remaining members of the Vendor's VAT group including the Vendor is the same as would have been the case had the Company ceased to be a member of the Vendor's VAT group from the date of this Deed, provided that to the extent such supplies of goods and services are required to be ignored for VAT purposes as made to or by the Company while it is a member of the Vendor's VAT group by or to another member of that VAT group those supplies shall also be ignored for the purposes of this Sub-Clause 9.3.

9.4   Interpretation With Regard to VAT

For all the purposes of this Deed, in respect of VAT for which the Company is jointly and severally liable with other members of the Vendor's VAT group registration (other than VAT the liability for which arises as a result of the Company's activities after Completion), then references to Completion shall be treated as references to the date upon which the Company is excluded from the Vendor's group registration.

[9.5   VAT Deferment Schemes[42]

The parties shall assist each other in establishing and seeking approval of HM Customs & Excise to [number] new VAT deferment schemes ('the New Schemes') pursuant to the provisions of the Customs Duties (Deferred Payment) Regulations 1976 ('the Regulations') to be operated by the Company. The parties shall procure that the existing VAT deferment schemes operated by the Company prior to Completion ('the Old Schemes') be cancelled with effect from Completion along with the existing bank guarantee given by [   ] Bank PLC to HM Customs & Excise in connection with the Old Schemes and the release of indemnities given to [   ] Bank PLC in support of such guarantee. For the avoidance of doubt, neither the Purchaser nor the Vendor shall be obliged to give any person any indemnity, security, or any other comfort whatsoever in support of any bank guarantee or indemnity required to be given in respect of the establishment and approval of the New Schemes. It is hereby agreed that each party shall bear its own costs in connection with the establishment of the New Schemes, the cancellation of the Old Schemes and the consequential cancellation and substitution of guarantees and indemnities. It is further agreed that such payments shall be made as may be appropriate to ensure that the resulting position between all the companies and bodies concerned with all such importations as are covered by the Old Schemes and the New Schemes is the same as it would have been if the New Schemes shall have been approved pursuant to the Regulations immediately after the date of Completion.]

10 Conduct of Tax Affairs

10.1 Assistance to Vendor

The Vendor (which may act through a duly authorised agent for the purposes of this Sub-Clause) shall at its own cost prepare the Company's statutory accounts and tax returns for accounting periods ended on or prior to Completion. The Purchaser shall procure that such returns and accounts are authorised, signed and submitted by the Company to the appropriate authority without amendment or with such amendments as the Vendor shall agree (such agreement not to be unreasonably withheld) and that the Vendor is given all such assistance as may be required to agree the said returns with the appropriate authorities. The Vendor shall prepare all documentation and deal with all matters (including correspondence) relating to the said returns and the Purchaser shall procure that such access to the books, accounts and records of the Company is afforded as may be required to enable the Vendor to prepare the said returns and accounts and conduct related matters in accordance with the Vendor's rights under this Sub-Clause.

10.2 Vendor's Actions

The Vendor shall take no action after Completion the effect of which is likely to increase the amount of Tax payable by the Company in respect of accounting periods after the Balance Sheet Date or likely to prejudice the business or tax affairs of the Company without the prior written consent of the Purchaser. Unless such action is taken with the prior written approval of the Purchaser any resulting increase in a Tax Liability of the Company shall be treated as if it were a Tax Liability arising prior to Completion.

11 Incorporation of Provisions from the Agreement

11.1 The provisions set out in the Agreement (in the following Sub-Clauses of the Agreement) with regard to:

(A) *Joint and Several Liabilities (Sub-Clause 1.3);*
(B) [Assignment (Sub-Clause 11.1)];[43]
(C) Rights etc Cumulative and Other Matters (Sub-Clause 11.4);
(D) *Release of One Vendor (Sub-Clause 11.5);*
(E) Invalidity (Sub-Clause 11.7);
(F) Counterparts (Sub-Clause 11.9); and
(G) Notices (Sub-Clause 11.11)

shall have effect for the purposes of this Deed as if incorporated herein (save that references to 'the Agreement' shall be references to this Deed).

12 Law and Jurisdiction

12.1 English Law

This Deed shall be governed by, and construed in accordance with, English law.

12.2 Jurisdiction [and Process Agent]

The provisions of Sub-Clause 12.2 [and 12.3] of the Agreement shall have effect with regard to the jurisdiction for [and service of process in respect of] disputes for the purposes of this Deed.

IN WITNESS WHEREOF this Deed was executed by the parties on the day and year first above written.

Notes

1   For a general discussion *see* Chapter 14. This document is drafted as a deed rather than a schedule to the Agreement for Sale (Shares) for administrative convenience (particularly where the commercial lawyers are not advising on tax matters) although it will have a limitation period of 12 years for a deed as opposed to six years for a contract. If there are overseas companies in the group, other provisions will be needed.

2   See the Agreement for Sale (Shares), Note 1 at p 463. This precedent may also be used as a basis both where the vendor is a corporate entity, and where there are several individual vendors. Clauses which require consideration, or the inclusion of which will depend on or be affected by the status of the vendors as individuals (or where there is a corporate vendor which is itself owned by individuals) are shown in italics.

Clause 1: Interpretation

3   Capital gains that have accrued but have not been realised and perhaps for which no deferred tax provision has been made may also be included in the scope of the indemnity. Vendors may wish to make an amendment to the deed on this point.

4   A 'satisfied claim' is included to prevent the vendor from avoiding liability by paying off the claim before completion but after the balance sheet date and thereby reducing the net assets of the target.

5   'Actual Tax Liability' includes claims made against the purchaser in order to cover any potential liability levied on the purchaser under TCGA 1992, s 190 or the VAT Act 1994, s 43. This is sometimes inappropriate, eg non-UK resident purchaser.

6   The reference to rates of taxation current at the date of the loss of the relief is arbitrary but to specify or even ascertain when the economic loss is suffered by the target is, in practice, impossible.

7   For example, the target or a subsidiary ceasing to be a member of a group (see also note 10) or another former group company (ie a member of the vendor's group) deciding not to surrender group relief but to disclaim capital allowances instead. It also covers secondary liabilities.

8   This covers liabilities under the Inheritance Tax Act 1984.

9   This covers close company apportionment (for accounting periods beginning before 1 April 1989) and also controlled foreign companies (where the target's interest could be as low as 10 per cent).

10 See Taxes Act 1988, s 410 (group relief), s 240 (ACT carry forward) and TCGA 1992, s 179.

11 The 'combined events' clause. An acceptable limitation is that pre-completion events are outside the ordinary course and post completion events are within it. For example, if the purchaser disposes of an asset after completion in the ordinary course of business and a gain has been rolled over/held over into the asset without the purchaser being aware of the matter, this clause is intended to catch the increased liability arising.

12 This allows the purchaser to make a claim where a loss or relief (most commonly trading losses) available to the target is lost. If the purchaser is not paying for the

losses, then the vendor may seek to limit the purchaser's rights to recover. If the purchaser is buying on the basis of profit projections which take into account the availability of tax losses as a tax shelter, then he may require the vendor to indemnify the purchaser for the loss of any losses (and perhaps warrant the existence of the losses). If the purchaser is buying at a price calculated by reference to net asset value, the vendor may wish to exclude any loss save to the extent that it has been taken into account in computing (and so reducing or eliminating) any provision for taxation or deferred taxation. The clause also covers the situation where the purchaser uses one of its own reliefs post-completion to relieve what would otherwise be a tax liability of the target for which the purchaser could claim against the vendor under the tax deed.

13   Includes foreign tax credit for which unilateral/double tax relief available.

14   The definition of tax includes stamp duty; however, the schedule is not an indemnity for stamp duty but an adjustment to the price, so the Stamp Act 1891, s 117 should not apply.

15   An inheritance tax point. Inheritance tax may be relevant in three circumstances: (a) where there has been a gift to the company; (b) where there has been a gift by the company; and (c) where there has been a gift of the company.

Clause 2: Covenant by the Vendor

16   Some vendors insist, particularly if there are other parties to the agreement, that the purchaser applies the monies to satisfy the relevant taxation claim (usually a liability of the target) so as to ensure the relevant taxation claim is extinguished. This is acceptable provided the target has no enforceable right to the monies paid as this can result in the company having a *Zim* right (*see* p 335).

17   Section 767A of the Taxes Act 1988 was introduced to stop companies from selling subsidiaries with tax liabilities, after stripping out all their assets with the result that the Inland Revenue had to recover tax from an insolvent company.

18   Any problems which it is agreed will be for the vendor's account should be referred to here, particularly if they could be said to have arisen in the ordinary course of business since the balance sheet date (see clause 2.3(C)).

19   This additional sub-clause is required because it covers limited specified events which occur after completion whereas the rest of the Deed covers only the period up to completion. The provisions cover specific secondary liabilities which may be visited on the target post-completion as a result of subsequent acts by the vendor. The clause may not always be relevant. For example, Taxes Act 1988, s 214 will be applicable only if the target has been the subject of a previous demerger.

20   *See* Note 15 *above*. Delete if dealing with a listed vendor.

21   This merely states what TCGA 1992, s 49 already states. There was a question in the past as to whether s 49 applies where the sale is a 'share for share' exchange on which there is no disposal for capital gains purposes (TCGA 1992, s 127) on the basis that s 49 applies only where there is a disposal. The Revenue accept under ESC D52 that TCGA 1992, 49(1)(*c*) will by concession apply on a share for share exchange so that any payment by the vendor to the purchaser will be added to the vendor's capital gains base cost in his new shares.

22   Avoid double counting between these provisions and any vendor limitation provisions in the agreement. *See* the Agreement for Sale (Shares), Notes 193 and 194 at p 480.

23   'Audited Accounts' and 'Balance Sheet Date' may be supplemented or replaced by 'Completion Accounts' and 'Completion Accounts Date' where the fifth schedule to the Agreement for Sale (Shares) applies and if there is a pound for pound adjustment, where there is no limitation to the application of such a clause. *See further* the Agreement for Sale (Shares), Note 107 at p 474.

24   If there is a liability which is unsatisfied, there should be a provision; if it has been satisfied, such satisfaction (ie payment or discharge) will have been taken into account as net assets (ie cash) will be reduced.

25   Business is wider than trading and may be more appropriate if a holding company is being purchased (although of course it is more favourable to the vendor).

26   There is often long debate over this last phrase. A common qualification is that the purchaser was aware, or ought reasonably to have been aware. Those acting for the purchaser will resist deletion of the phrase as it then makes the exclusion absolute—ie any act of the purchaser whether he knew of the consequences or not.

27   Disclosure should not apply to clause 2.1 of the Tax Deed. If there is any matter which the vendor wishes to exclude, then it should be dealt with by express exclusion in clause 2.3 referring specifically to the tax liability, ie to the type of tax involved and the amount in question, rather than the circumstances giving rise to the claim. For example, the vendor discloses that it has made an interest free loan to a director and has not reported it on form P11D as a benefit in kind (Taxes Act 1988, s 160). The director is also a shareholder and the target is close. There is therefore a liability on the target to account for tax pursuant to the Taxes Act 1988, s 419 (loans to participators).

Clause 3: Notice and Mitigation

28   The words from 'but no failure...' to the end are often deleted by the vendor. A suggested compromise would be to add 'save to the extent the vendor is prejudiced thereby'.

29   Only in particular cases (eg multinational or acquisitive groups)—this is not standard practice. The need for a nine year time limit arises from the Inland Revenue's interpretation of how the roll-over relief time limits work. Gains can be rolled over into expenditure incurred three years after the disposal giving rise to the gain (TCGA 1992, s 152(3)) and a claim to shelter that gain can be made up to six years after the expenditure has been incurred (see Capital Gains Manual 60600).

30   Only in particular cases (eg multinational or acquisitive groups)—this is not standard practice. The exception for claims under the Taxes Act 1988, s 770 is necessary as a result of the decision of the Court of Appeal in *Glaxo Group Limited and Others v IRC* [1996] STC 191.

31   This is a compromise to resolve the conflict between the purchaser's management time and the vendor's desire to fight a claim to the death.

32   Certain taxes, eg ACT and VAT, cannot be postponed, and with other taxes, the amount not in dispute must be paid.

33   For example, one may wish to bring proceedings against a tax authority in another jurisdiction. Contrast this provision with the equivalent provision applicable to

warranty claims (including tax warranty claims) in the Agreement for Sale (Shares), Schedule 8 para 6.1 at p 462 which gives credit to the vendor only where the purchaser receives the relevant benefit. A purchaser may decide to make the two provisions consistent.

34 This does not cover an over-provision for deferred taxation as it is not an over-provision in the amount of taxation that is due, only an over-estimate of the amount which may become due in the opinion of the directors as applied in accordance with SSAP 15.

Clause 4: Date for Payment

35 This is again arbitrary; although it is possible to set out a clause which would specify the date when the economic loss is suffered, in practice the date may not be ascertainable. Further, if the purchaser has previously acquired the share capital of another company and the acquisition agreement contained such a provision, then he may find that he cannot fulfil his obligation to mitigate his loss by deferring the date tax becomes due by using reliefs available to him, in respect of both agreements.

36 This includes (a) relief from the purchaser's group or (b) relief the economic burden of which has been borne by the purchaser (ie which arises after completion) but if a corporate vendor satisfies a tax liability by using group relief or surrendering ACT for no payment by the target this will extinguish a tax liability.

37 This rate should be sufficiently high to encourage the vendor to pay because the interest cost to the vendor is greater than his cost of funds.

Clause 5: Deductions and Withholdings

38 As in the case of interest.

Clause 7: Credits and Reductions

39 If the tax liability is in respect of ACT not paid, then the vendor must make payment notwithstanding that the Company will eventually receive credit for the ACT against its corporation tax liability. When credit is received, the vendor is repaid.

40 Neither the vendor nor the purchaser have had the use of such monies—the relevant taxation authority has. Therefore the vendor, who is supposed to be providing a full indemnity, should not be entitled to interest.

Clause 8: Group Arrangements

41 If the target has no subsidiaries and is not being sold by a UK resident company delete this clause.

Clause 9: Value Added Tax Group Registration

42 Delete this clause if the target is not in the vendor's VAT group registration, or the vendor does not have a VAT group registration. *See also* the Agreement for Sale (Assets), Note 81 at p 615 concerning the release of guarantees for VAT deferment schemes, where these are relevant.

43 If the purchaser has the right to assign the benefit of the warranties and/or its rights under the tax deed, the vendor should ensure that on any such assignment it is not

obliged to pay more than it would have been obliged to pay had the benefit of the warranties/deed not been assigned. This could arise, for example, because of the application of *Zim* (*see* Note 16 *above*) or the assignment of the benefit of such rights to a company in a jurisdiction which taxes indemnity payments. The assignment clause should be amended accordingly.

Appendix III

Agreement for Sale (Assets)

Contents

THIS AGREEMENT dated the [   ] day of [   ] 19[   ] and made

BETWEEN:

(1) [   ] LIMITED a company registered in England under number
     [   ] whose registered office is at [   ] (the 'Vendor');

(2) [   ] LIMITED a company registered in England under number
     [   ] whose registered office is at [   ] (the 'Purchaser');
     and

[(3) [   ] LIMITED a company registered in England under number
     [   ] whose registered office is at [   ] (the '[Vendor's]
     Guarantor')]¹.

WHEREAS:

The Vendor wishes to sell (or procure the sale) and the Purchaser wishes to acquire the goodwill and other associated assets of the business of [   ] carried on by [the Vendor] [under the name [   ]] and to assume certain obligations relating to such business in each case on and subject to the terms of this Agreement.²

NOW IT IS HEREBY AGREED as follows:

1 Interpretation

1.1 Definitions

In this Agreement, where the context admits:

'Affiliate' means, in respect of any body corporate, a body corporate which is its subsidiary or holding company, or a body corporate which is a subsidiary of that holding company, and each such body corporate;

'Assumed Liabilities'³ means those liabilities of the Vendor in relation to the Business at the Transfer Date [specified in the list annexed to the Disclosure Letter [(but excluding, for this purpose the Creditors)] and] to the extent that the same are provided for or otherwise taken into account in the Completion Accounts;

'Audited Accounts'⁴ means the audited balance sheet of the Vendor made up as at the Balance Sheet Date and the audited profit and loss account of the Vendor in respect of the financial year ending on the Balance Sheet Date including, in each case, the notes thereto and the directors' report and auditor's report; true copies of all of which are annexed to the Disclosure Letter;

'Balance Sheet Date' means [   ] 19[   ];

'Book Debts'⁵ means all debts and other amounts owing and due to the Vendor in respect of [goods and services supplied] in the Business as at the Transfer Date [as shown in the Completion Accounts] [other than:

'Business'⁶ means the entire business of [   ] [hitherto carried on by the Vendor from the Premises];

'Business Assets' means the assets of the Business to be sold and purchased as specified in Sub-Clause 2.1 (Sale and Purchase);

'Business Day' means a day (other than Saturday or Sunday) on which banks are open for ordinary banking business in London;

(A) Prepayments;

(B) debts owed to the Vendor on any closed account of a customer [or] with which the Vendor is at the Transfer Date no longer prepared to transact business;

(C) any debts in respect of which the Vendor has prior to the date of this Agreement instructed solicitors to commence proceedings for recovery of such debts; and

(D) any debts which at the Transfer Date have been outstanding for more than [90] days from the due date for payment];

'Completion'[7] means completion of the sale and purchase of the Business in accordance with Clause 6 (Completion);

'Completion Accounts' has the meaning given in Schedule 4;

'Contracts'[8] means the Specified Contracts and the Lease Contracts;

['Creditors'[9] means the [aggregate amounts owing by the Vendor to the] trade creditors of the Vendor in the ordinary course of the Business as at the Transfer Date [to the extent of which provision or reserve (but not note only) is made in the Completion Accounts;]

'Current Assets'[10] means the Prepayments and the assets of the kinds described in Schedule 1 and used by the Vendor in the Business as at the Transfer Date [and, to the extent applicable, ascertained in accordance with Schedule 4];

'Disclosure Letter'[11] means the letter dated the date hereof written and delivered by or on behalf of the Vendor to the Purchaser in agreed terms;

'Employees'[12] means all the employees of the Vendor employed in the Business at the Transfer Date (and at the date hereof consists of those persons specified in the list attached to the Disclosure Letter);

'Encumbrance' includes any interest or equity of any person (including any right to acquire, option or right of pre-emption) or any mortgage, charge, pledge, lien, assignment, hypothecation, security interest (including any created by law), title retention or other security agreement or arrangement or a rental, hire purchase, credit sale or other agreement for payment on deferred terms;

['Excluded Assets'[13] means

[(A) cash in hand or at the bank and all cheques and other securities representing the same [other than those (if any) representing any of the Book Debts hereby agreed to be sold];

(B) the Book Debts;

(C) any right to use or continue to use after [Completion] any trade or service name or mark of the Vendor or any member of the Vendor's Group [other than the Listed Intellectual Property Rights]; and

(D) [specify any other exclusions eg insurance prepayments where purchaser to implement own insurance at Completion]];

['Excluded Liabilities'[14] means [   ];]

'Fixed Assets'[15] means the Movable Fixed Assets and the Immovable Fixed Assets;

'Freehold Premises' means the freehold premises particulars of which are set out in Part IA of Schedule 3 (and includes any part thereof and/or any building, structure and/or works thereon);

'Goodwill' means all the goodwill, interest and connection of the Vendor in and concerning the Business together with the right to represent the Purchaser as carrying on the Business as a going concern in succession to the Vendor;

'Immovable Fixed Assets'[15] means all fixtures and fittings and other fixed plant, machinery, equipment and hardware (as defined in Paragraph 1 of Schedule 6) physically attached to the Premises [now and] at the Transfer Date (excluding landlord's fixtures and fittings at the Leasehold Premises) [and at the date hereof [includes/consists] of the items set out in Part I of Schedule 2];

'Intellectual Property'[16] means patents, trade marks, service marks, rights (registered or unregistered) in any designs; applications for any of the foregoing; trade or business names; copyright [(including rights in computer software) and topography rights; know-how; secret formulae and processes; lists of suppliers and customers and other confidential and proprietary knowledge and information; rights protecting goodwill and reputation; database rights and rights under licences and consents in relation to such things and all rights or forms of protection of a similar nature to any of the foregoing or having equivalent effect anywhere in the world];

'Intellectual Property Agreements' means agreements or arrangements relating in any way whether wholly or partly to Intellectual Property;

'Intellectual Property Rights' means all Intellectual Property owned or used by the Vendor in relation to the Business in any part of the world (other than the Listed Intellectual Property Rights);

'Interest Rate' means interest at a rate equal to [   ] per cent above the base lending rate from time to time of [   ] Bank Plc;

'Leased Assets' has the meaning given under 'Lease Contracts';

'Lease Contracts'[17] means those contracts and other contractual arrangements (including, without limitation, finance leases, but excluding leases of real property) entered into by or on behalf of the Vendor in the ordinary course of the Business and remaining unperformed as at the Transfer Date pursuant to which tangible assets used by the Vendor in or in connection with the Business at that date (together the 'Leased Assets') have been supplied to or are held by the Vendor on hire or other rental, lease, licence, hire purchase or on other terms such that title thereto does not pass or has not passed to the Vendor (but excluding any such contract or contrctual arrangements in respect of (i) the Fixed Assets and (ii) any tangible assets which would have been owned by the Vendor but for any retention of title or like clause) [and at the date hereof [includes/consists of] those contracts specified in the first column of Part III of Schedule 2];

'Leasehold Premises' means the leasehold [or other] premises particulars of which are set out in Part IIA of Schedule 3 (and includes any part thereof and/or any building, structure and/or works thereon);

'Listed Intellectual Property'[18] means the intellectual property referred to in the list annexed to the Disclosure Letter;

'Listed Intellectual Property Agreements' means the Intellectual Property Agreements set out in the list annexed to the Disclosure Letter;

'Management Accounts'[19] means the management accounts of the Vendor for the period from the Balance Sheet Date to [   ] 19[   ], true copies of which are annexed to the Disclosure Letter;

'Movable Fixed Assets'[15] means all the plant and machinery, tools and equipment, vehicles, office furniture, Hardware (as defined in Paragraph 1 of Schedule 6) and other tangible assets used by the Vendor in or in connection with the Business now and/or at the Transfer Date (other than the Immovable Fixed Assets and the Leased Assets) [and at the date hereof [includes/consists of] the items set out in Part II of Schedule 2;

['New Lease'[20] means the lease of the New Leasehold Premises to be granted to the Purchaser in accordance with Part III of Schedule 5;]

['New Leasehold Premises'[20] means the premises particulars of which are set out in Part III of Schedule 3 (and includes any part thereof and/or any building, structure and/or works thereon);]

'Premises'[21] means the Freehold Premises, the Leasehold Premises and the New Leasehold Premises and each of them (as the case may be);

'Prepayments' means the prepayments made and other amounts paid by the Vendor in respect of the Business and attributable in whole or in part to the period after the Transfer Date [as shown in the Completion Accounts];

'Provisional Consideration' has the meaning given in Clause 3.1 (Amount);

'Records'[22] means all the books, files, records and other documents of the Vendor relating wholly or mainly to the Business or any of the Business Assets and in whatever medium so held including, without limitation the following:

(A) all books of account, ledgers, payroll records, income records, information relating to clients, customers and suppliers and other books, documents and computer records which relate to or are relevant to the Business;

(B) all promotional material, sales publications, catalogues, price lists, advertising materials, surveys, reports and other technical materials and sales matter relating to the Business [excluding any right to publish any such material bearing any trade or service name or mark of the Vendor or any member of the Vendor's Group (other than the Listed Intellectual Property Rights)]; [and]

(C) (subject to Clause 14 (Value Added Tax)) all VAT records relating to the Business;
(but excluding any records the Vendor is required by law to retain including, without limit, all national insurance and PAYE records)

the 'Regulations' means The Transfer of Undertakings (Protection of Employment) Regulations 1981 and any subsequent re-enactment or modification thereof;

'Specified Contracts'[8] means those contracts and contractual arrangements of the Vendor in relation to the Business [details of which are set out in the Disclosure Letter] [and including the Systems Contracts and Listed Intellectual Property Agreements];

'Systems Contracts'[23] means the licensing, maintenance and support contracts and contractual arrangements of the Vendor in relation to the Computer Systems (as defined in Paragraph 1 of Schedule 6) details of which are set out in the Disclosure Letter;

'Taxation' or 'Tax' includes (without limitation) corporation tax, advance corporation tax, income tax, capital gains tax, the charge under s 601(2) of the Taxes Act 1988, value added tax, the charge to tax under s 419 of the Taxes Act 1988, customs and other import duties, inheritance tax, stamp duty, stamp duty reserve tax, capital duties, national insurance contributions, local authority council taxes, petroleum revenue tax, foreign taxation and duties, and any payment whatsoever which the Vendor may be or become bound to make to any person as a result of the operation of any enactment relating to any such taxes or duties, and all penalties, charges and interest relating to any of the foregoing or resulting from a failure to comply with the provisions of any enactment relating to taxation;

['Third Party Rights'[24] means all rights of the Vendor against third parties arising out of or in connection with the Business Assets or the conduct of the Business prior to the Transfer Date (including, but not limited to,

(A)   all rights under or in respect of manufacturer's or supplier's warranties, guarantees and other contractual obligations and assurances (express or implied);
(B)   all rights against any person in respect of any defect in the title, construction or condition of the Premises or in respect of any work or treatment carried out on the Premises;
(C)   all rights against sub-contractors [and others],
but excluding any claim by or right of the Vendor in respect of
(1)   taxation; or
(2)   insurance (other than that relating to any Business Asset hereby agreed to be sold);][31]

the 'Transfer' means the transfer of the Business pursuant to this Agreement;

'Transfer Date'[25] means the close of business on [the date of Completion];

'VAT' means Value Added Tax;

'Vendor's Group' means the Vendor and each of its Affiliates; and

'Warranties'[26] means the warranties and representations set out in Part IV of Schedule 5 (Property Warranties), Paragraph 2 of Schedule 6 (Warranties and Representations) and Paragraph [3/4/5/8] of Schedule 7 (Pensions).

1.2   Construction of Certain References

In this Agreement, where the context admits:

(A)   words and phrases the definitions of which are contained or referred to in Part XXVI of the Companies Act 1985 shall be construed as having the meanings thereby attributed to them;
(B)   references to statutory provisions shall be construed as references to those provisions as amended or re-enacted or as their application is modified by other provisions from time to time and shall include references to any provisions of which they are re-enactments (whether with or without modification);
(C)   where any statement is qualified by the expression 'so far as the Vendor is aware' or 'to the best of the Vendor's knowledge and belief' or any similar expression, that statement shall be deemed to include an additional statement that it has been made after due and careful enquiry;[27]
(D)   references to Clauses and Schedules are references to clauses and schedules of and to this Agreement, references to Sub-Clauses or Paragraphs are, unless otherwise stated, references to Sub-Clauses of the Clause or Paragraphs of the Schedule in

which the reference appears, and references to this Agreement include the Schedules; and

(E) references to any document being in 'agreed terms' or in 'agreed form' are to that document in the form signed or initialled by or on behalf of the parties for identification.

1.3 Joint and Several Liabilities[28]

[All warranties, representations, indemnities, covenants, agreements and obligations given or entered into by more than one person in this Agreement are given or entered into jointly and severally.]

1.4 Headings

The headings and sub-headings are inserted for convenience only and shall not affect the construction of this Agreement.

1.5 Schedules

Each of the Schedules shall have effect as if set out herein.

2 Sale of Business Assets

2.1 Sale and Purchase

Subject as hereinafter expressly provided the Vendor shall sell with full title guarantee[29] [(or to the extent it is not the owner thereof shall procure the sale, with full title guarantee by the same)][30] and free from all encumbrances to the Purchaser and the Purchaser (with a view to carrying on the Business as a going concern in succession to the Vendor) shall purchase with effect from the Transfer Date:

(A) the Current Assets;
(B) the Freehold Premises;
(C) the Leasehold Premises;
(D) the Movable Fixed Assets;
(E) the Immovable Fixed Assets;
(F) the Intellectual Property Rights;
(G) the Goodwill;
(H) the Listed Intellectual Property;
(I) the Records;
(J) the benefit (subject to the burden in so far as it relates to the period following the Transfer Date) of the Contracts;
(K) the Third Party Rights;
(L) [Others];[31] and
(M) subject to Clause 2.2 (Exclusions), all other property, assets and rights of the Vendor used in or [principally] for the purposes of the Business or in connection with such Business Assets or any of them.

2.2 Exclusions

(A) The sale and purchase pursuant to this Agreement shall not include the Excluded Assets.
(B) The Vendor acknowledges and agrees that the Purchaser shall not assume or have any liability or obligation in respect of the Business which is not specifically assumed by it under this Agreement [and, without limitation, the Purchaser shall

have no responsibility in respect of the Excluded Liabilities]. Accordingly, the Vendor hereby agrees to indemnify the Purchaser and hold it harmless against any obligation or liability of the Vendor in respect of the Business [(including the Excluded Liabilities)] not specifically assumed by the Purchaser under this Agreement.

2.3   Risk and Insurance

[(A)] Risk in respect of the Business Assets agreed to be sold and purchased hereunder shall pass to the Purchaser on the Transfer Date [and accordingly the Vendor shall carry on the Business between the date hereof and the Transfer Date for its own benefit and at its own risk].[25]

[(B)] The Vendor shall maintain in force all the insurance policies referred to in the Disclosure Letter and shall procure that the interest of the Purchaser under or pursuant to this Agreement in respect of the Fixed Assets and the Premises shall be noted on all insurance policies effected by or for the benefit of the Vendor in respect thereof. If any of the Fixed Assets or the Premises shall be lost, destroyed or damaged prior to the Transfer Date the Purchaser may at its option either

(1)   require the consideration payable hereunder to be abated or adjusted as a result or

(2)   require that the insurance monies (if any) recoverable in respect thereof shall be paid to it and the Vendor shall direct the insurance company accordingly and in such event any such insurance monies received by the Vendor shall be held by it on trust for the Purchaser absolutely.[32]

[(C)] The Vendor shall use all reasonable endeavours to procure that the Purchaser's interest is noted as aforesaid on all insurance policies in respect of the Premises in respect of which insurance is effected by a person other the Vendor.

2.4   No Sale of Part Only

Subject as provided in Sub-Clause 7.1 (Pending Third Party Consents) the Purchaser shall not be obliged to complete the purchase of any of the Business Assets unless the purchase of all such assets is effected simultaneously.

3   Consideration

3.1   Amount

The consideration for the sale and purchase of the Business Assets shall [(subject to Sub-Clause 3.2 (Adjustment))] be the sum of £[   ] (the 'Provisional Consideration') which shall (subject as aforesaid) be apportioned between the Business Assets as follows:[33]

(A)   for the Current Assets the sum of £[   ] [(subject to adjustment as provided in Schedule 4)];

(B)   for the Freehold Premises the sum of £[   ];[33]

(C)   for the Leasehold Premises the sum of £[   ];[33]

(D)   for the Movable Fixed Assets the sum of £[   ];

(E)   for the Immovable Fixed Assets the sum of £[   ];[33]

(F)   for the Goodwill the sum of £[   ];

(G)   for the Listed Intellectual Property the sum of £[   ];[33]

(H)   for the Records the sum of £[   ];

(I)   for the benefit (subject to the burden) of the Contracts the sum of £[   ];

(J)   for the Intellectual Property Rights the sum of £[   ];

(K) for the Third Party Rights the sum of £[   ];

(L) [specify any other][31]

and the Purchaser shall in addition discharge the Assumed Liabilities in accordance with Clause 7.3 (Assumed Liabilities). The apportionment of consideration is given for the sake of convenience only and the Vendor agrees that the Purchaser's remedies shall not in any way be limited or affected by the amount apportioned to any particular Business Asset or category of Business Assets.

3.2 Adjustment[34]

(A) The Provisional Consideration shall be subject to adjustment in accordance with Schedule 4 (Adjustment of Consideration).

(B) The apportionment of the Provisional Consideration (as so adjusted) between the Business Assets shall be as set out in the Completion Accounts prepared pursuant to Schedule 4.

3.3 Method and Timing for Payment of Consideration[35]

The consideration for the Business Assets shall be payable as follows:

(A) An amount equal to the Provisional Consideration [(less the Retention referred to in Clause 11.8 (Retention))] shall be paid by the Purchaser to the Vendor in cash at Completion.

(B) The amount and method of payment in respect of any adjustment to the Provisional Consideration shall be determined in accordance with Paragraph 5 of Schedule 4.

4 The Premises

The provisions of Schedule 5 (Terms Applicable to the Premises) shall have effect in relation to the Premises.

5 Conditions

Completion is conditional upon:

[(A) the passing at a duly convened and held general meeting of the [Purchaser/Vendor/   ]] of a resolution in the agreed form to approve the [acquisition/sale] of the Business Assets and other arrangements on the terms of this Agreement;][36]

[(B) consents in writing in terms satisfactory to the Purchaser being received from the Reversioner (as defined in Paragraph 1 of Part II of Schedule 5) of [each of] the Leasehold Premises to the assignment of such Leasehold Premises to the Purchaser pursuant to this Agreement;][37]

(C) [specify any other conditions eg UK/EC competition conditions[38] or consents of third parties to assignment of significant contracts];

and in the event that the above conditions shall not have been satisfied [or waived by the Purchaser] on or before [   ] 19[   ] this Agreement shall lapse and no party shall make any claim against any other in respect hereof, save for any antecedent breach.[39]

6 Completion

6.1 Date and Place of Completion

Completion shall take place at the offices of [   ] [immediately following the execution hereof] [or] [at [   ] on [   ] 19[   ] [or] [within 48 hours of this Agreement becoming unconditional].

6.2 Vendor's Obligations[40]

On Completion the Vendor shall deliver or cause to be delivered to the Purchaser:

(A) the Current Assets and all relative documents of title;

(B) duly executed transfer(s)/conveyance(s) of the Freehold Premises [and the Immovable Fixed Assets situated thereon] in agreed terms together with all title deeds and documents relating thereto in accordance with the schedules of title deeds in agreed terms;

(C) duly executed assignment(s)/transfer(s) of the Leasehold Premises [and the Immovable Fixed Assets situated thereon] in agreed terms together with all title deeds and documents relating thereto in accordance with the schedules of title deeds in agreed terms (including, without limit, all necessary consents to the assignment/transfer thereof in favour of the Purchaser);

(D) the Movable Fixed Assets, the Leased Assets and all documents of title and registration documents relating thereto;

(E) [an assignment of Goodwill in agreed terms;][41]

(F) an assignment of each of the Listed Intellectual Property in agreed terms;[41]

(G) assignments of each of the Contracts, the Intellectual Property Rights, the Third Party Rights and the Lease Contracts each in such form as the Purchaser shall reasonably require;;[41]

(H) the Records;

(I) a letter containing full details of any changes to the list(s) of Employees, Fixed Assets, [Premises], Leased Assets, Listed Intellectual Property, the Contracts and the Lease Contracts set out in this Agreement and/or the Disclosure Letter between the date hereof and the Transfer Date/Completion;

(J) [an engrossment of the New Lease duly executed by the Vendor [and relevant consents];][20]

(K) [a deed in a form approved by the Purchaser, duly executed by the relevant chargees, unconditionally releasing [the Business Assets] from the security of all relevant charge(s) (including those charges details of which are set out in the Disclosure Letter) and consenting to their sale pursuant to this Agreement;][42]

(L) [a letter of non-crystallisation in a form approved by the Purchaser duly executed by or on behalf of the relevant chargee(s) in relation to all relevant charge(s) (including those charges details of which are set out in the Disclosure Letter);][42]

(M) [other - specify].[43]

6.3 Purchaser's Obligations

At Completion the Purchaser shall:

(A) pay the Consideration for the Business Assets as provided by Sub-Clause 3.3 (Method and Timing for Payment of Consideration), any payment in cash to be [by banker's draft drawn on a [City of London] branch of a clearing bank and made in favour of the Vendor or as it may direct]; and

(B) [deliver to the Vendor a counterpart of the New Lease duly executed by the Purchaser.][20]

6.4 Failure to Complete[44]

If in any respect the provisions of Sub-Clause 6.2 (Vendor's Obligations) are not complied with on the date for Completion set by Sub-Clause 6.1 (Date and Place of Completion) the Purchaser may:

(A) defer Completion to a date not more than 28 days after the date set by Sub-Clause 6.1 (and so that the provisions of this Sub-Clause 6.4 apart from this item 6.4(A) shall apply to Completion as so deferred); or

(B) proceed to Completion so far as practicable (without prejudice to its rights hereunder); or

(C) rescind this Agreement.

7 Consents, Contracts and Assumed Liabilities

7.1 Pending Third Party Consents[45]

Without prejudice to any other provisions of this Agreement, the Vendor shall obtain all such consents as may be necessary for the transfer of the Business Assets to the Purchaser with effect from the Transfer Date and the Vendor declares itself with effect from the Transfer Date trustee for the Purchaser in respect of all such Business Assets until the same shall, with any necessary consents from third parties, have been finally assigned to the Purchaser. The Vendor undertakes that until completion of such assignments it will with effect from the Transfer Date act under the direction of the Purchaser and as its agent in all matters relating to such Business Assets. The Vendor shall be fully and effectively indemnified by the Purchaser in so acting.

[7.2 Treatment of Contracts[46]

In respect of the Contracts:

(A) the Vendor shall with effect from the Transfer Date assign or hold to the order of the Purchaser or procure the assignment to the order of the Purchaser of all the Contracts which are capable of assignment without the consent of other parties;

(B) in the case of those of the Contracts not so capable of assignment the Vendor shall, as soon as practicable following Completion, use all reasonable endeavours to obtain, at the Vendor's cost and expense, all necessary consents for the assignment of the same or to arrange the novation thereof on terms acceptable to the Purchaser; and

(C) in respect of the benefit of the Contracts, unless and until such consents are obtained or novation is effected (and in respect of the burden of performance of the Contracts after Transfer Date, unless and until such novation is effected) the Vendor shall, at the option of the Purchaser, following Completion either:

(1) unless contractually prevented from so doing, sub-contract the same to the Purchaser on the same terms (*mutatis mutandis*) and for the same remuneration as apply to the Contracts in question; or

(2) act in connection therewith in all respects as the Purchaser may from time to time reasonably direct;

and so that (without prejudice to the generality of the foregoing) the Purchaser shall perform the obligations and liabilities arising under the Contracts in question so far as any such obligation or liability arises after the Transfer Date (provided that (i) no such obligation or liability is attributable to a breach of duty or contract of the Vendor prior to the Transfer Date and (ii) such obligations have been notified by the Vendor to the Purchaser prior to the date hereof) and the full benefit of all contractual rights, benefits and claims thereunder whether arising before or after the Transfer Date shall vest in and be held on trust by the Vendor for the Purchaser absolutely.][47]

7.3   Assumed Liabilities

The Purchaser shall assume responsibility as from Completion for the payment or performance of the Assumed Liabilities and shall indemnify and hold harmless the Vendor in respect of the same.[48]

8   Mutual Covenants[49]

8.1   Vendor's Covenants

Save as otherwise herein expressly provided the Vendor covenants with the Purchaser that:

(A)   the Vendor will pay, satisfy, discharge and fulfil all costs, claims, expenses, liabilities, obligations and undertakings whatsoever relating to the Business arising in respect of or by reference to any period up to the Transfer Date and will indemnify and hold harmless the Purchaser in respect of the same; and

(B)   in the event of any breach or delay by the Vendor in performing whatever is required of it under Sub-Clause (A), the Purchaser shall be entitled (but in no way obliged) [if it reasonably considers it to be in its commercial interests so to do] to do, on behalf of the Vendor, whatever is reasonably required to satisfy or discharge any such liability and obligation and the Vendor will indemnify and hold harmless the Purchaser from and against all cost, claims, liabilities and expenses which the Purchaser may thereby reasonably suffer or incur.[50]

8.2   Purchaser's Covenant

Save as otherwise herein expressly provided the Purchaser covenants with the Vendor that it will pay, satisfy, discharge, and fulfil all costs, claims, expenses, liabilities, obligations and undertakings whatsoever relating to the Business in respect of any period commencing on the Transfer Date and will indemnify and hold harmless the Vendor in respect of the same.

[8.3   Product Liability Etc

After the Transfer Date the Purchaser shall as agent for the Vendor meet and discharge all claims for fulfilment of warranties given by the Vendor which arise after that date in respect of products sold or supplied or services provided by the Vendor in the course of the Business before the Transfer Date and the Vendor shall on demand indemnify the Purchaser (at cost) for all costs charges and expenses incurred by the Purchaser in respect thereof except to the extent that the costs, charges and expenses in question are recovered by the Purchaser from manufacturers or suppliers or other third parties.][51]

8.4   Taxation

The Vendor acknowledges that the Purchaser shall not be liable in any respect of any liability of the Vendor for taxation arising from its conduct of the Business or ownership or disposal of the assets to be purchased pursuant to this Agreement and the Vendor shall fully and effectually indemnify and hold harmless the Purchaser in respect of the same.

8.5 Apportionment[52]

[If no completion accounts are to be drawn up, a clause providing for apportionments (prepayments and accruals on a time or other agreed basis) will need to be included. It would be usual to prepare a statement after, say, 28 days and for disputes to be referred to a third party. Apart from the usual gas, electricity, wages and other amounts (which, if in relation to property, should be consistent with the property provisions of the Agreement), consideration should be given to excess mileage charges on leased vehicles, volume/overriding discounts on trading contracts, holiday pay etc.]

9 Pre and Post Completion Obligations

9.1 Pre Completion Obligations[53]

(A) The Purchaser or its representatives shall be entitled following exchange of this Agreement to have access during normal business hours to the Premises and the Employees and the Records and to take copies of and extracts from the Records at its own expense.

(B) Prior to Completion the Vendor shall take such action as the Purchaser may request to ensure that immediately prior to and at Completion all the Immovable Fixed Assets will be in a state of actual severance from the respective Premises.

9.2 Post Completion Obligations

(A) All monies or other items belonging to the Purchaser which are received by the Vendor on or after Completion in connection with the Business or any of the Business Assets shall immediately be paid or passed by the Vendor to the Purchaser.

(B) The Purchaser shall be entitled following Completion (after giving reasonable notice) to have access during normal business hours to any of the books of account, financial or other records which relate partly to the Business and which are retained by the Vendor following Completion and at the Purchaser's expense to take copies of and extracts from the same.

(C) The Vendor shall forthwith at its own expense change its name to any name not including the words '[   ]' or any colourable imitation thereof and shall supply a copy of such Certificate of Incorporation upon Change of Name to the Purchaser when effected.[54]

9.3 Trade Debtors and Creditors[55]

[(A) The Purchaser shall not acquire the Book Debts and accordingly the Vendor shall remain entitled to the Book Debts.

(B) For the period of [six] months after Completion the Purchaser shall as agent for the Vendor collect and receive the Book Debts.

(C) In performing its obligations under Sub-Clause (B), the Purchaser shall not be obliged to take any action to recover the Book Debts beyond the usual debt collection procedures previously adopted by the Vendor (as disclosed in writing by the Vendor to the Purchaser) but excluding litigation, [and the Vendor shall indemnify the Purchaser against all costs, charges, expenses and liability whatsoever which the Purchaser may incur in connection therewith]. The Purchaser shall not without the consent of the Vendor compromise or waive any of the Book Debts.[56]

(D) Monies received by the Purchaser referable to the Book Debts may be mixed with and dealt with in the same manner as money belonging to the Purchaser.

(E)   Where sums are received which are referable or appropriated to a particular obligation or Book Debt the Purchaser shall apply such sums against such obligation or Book Debt. Any money received by the Purchaser which is not appropriated to a particular obligation or Book Debt may be appropriated as the Purchaser thinks fit.[57]

(F)   The Purchaser shall not assume any liability in respect of the Creditors and accordingly the Vendor shall discharge such Creditors in accordance with Clause 8.1 (Vendor's Covenants).

(G)   Notwithstanding Sub-Clause (F) for a period of [six] months after Completion, the Purchaser shall, on behalf of and as agent for the Vendor, if and to the extent it receives any amounts referable to the Book Debts, apply such amounts in reduction or discharge of the Vendor's liabilities to Creditors on such basis and in respect of whichever of the Creditors as the Purchaser thinks fit.

(H)   Upon the expiry of the period of six months referred to in Sub-Clause (G):

(1)   the Purchaser shall provide to the Vendor appropriate evidence as to the Book Debts which have been collected and the Creditors which have been discharged, together with a cheque for the balance (if any) of the Book Debts which have been collected after allowing for payment of any outstanding Creditors; and

(2)   the Vendor shall thereafter be solely responsible for the collection of any of the Book Debts and in so doing where the debtor is a continuing customer or debtor of the Business the Vendor shall give the Purchaser not less than 21 days' notice of its intention to commence proceedings.[58]]

10 Restriction of Vendor['s Group][59]

10.1 Restricted Business[60]

In this Clause, 'Restricted Business' means [   ] within [country or area] and which directly or indirectly competes with the Business [carried on at the date of this Agreement].

10.2 Covenants

The Vendor undertakes with the Purchaser and its successors in title that it will not and that it will procure that none of its Affiliates will:

(A)   for the period of [   ][60] after the date of this Agreement, either on its own account or in conjunction with or on behalf of any person, firm or company, carry on or be engaged, concerned or interested (directly or indirectly and whether as principal, shareholder, director, employee, agent, consultant, partner or otherwise) in carrying on any Restricted Business (other than as a holder of less than 5 per cent of any class of shares or debentures listed on the London Stock Exchange or any other recognised stock exchange);

(B)   for the period of [   ][60] after the date of this Agreement, either on its own account or in conjunction with or on behalf of any person, firm or company, solicit or endeavour to entice away from the Business any person who at the date of this Agreement is (or who within a period of one year prior to the date of this Agreement has been) a director, officer, manager, employee or servant of the Business whether or not such person would commit a breach of contract by reason of leaving service or office;

(C)   for the period of [   ][60] after the date of this Agreement, either on its own account or in conjunction with or on behalf of any person, firm or company, in connection with any Restricted Business, deal with, solicit the custom of or endeavour to entice away from the Business any person who at the date of this Agreement is (or who within a period of one year prior to the date of this Agreement has been) a customer of the Business whether or not such person would commit a breach of contract by reason of transferring business;

(D) for the period of [   ][60] after the date of this Agreement, either on its own account or in conjunction with or on behalf of any person, firm or company, in connection with any Restricted Business endeavour to entice away from the Business any person who at the date of this Agreement is (or who within a period of one year prior to the date of this Agreement has been) a supplier of the Business whether or not such person would commit a breach of contract by reason of transferring business;[61] and

(E) at any time after the date of this Agreement, directly or indirectly use or attempt to use in the course of any business on its own account or in conjunction with or on behalf of any person, firm or company, any trade or service mark, trade name, design or logo (whether registered or not and including the Listed Intellectual Property) used in the Business or any other name, logo, trade or service mark or design which is or might be confusingly similar thereto [exceptions for group logos etc].

10.3 Vendor to Procure Compliance

The Vendor undertakes to take all such steps as shall from time to time be necessary to ensure compliance with the terms of Sub-Clause 10.2 by employees and agents of the Vendor or any of its Affiliates.

10.4 Separate Covenants

Each of the undertakings in Sub-Clauses 10.2 and 10.3 shall be construed as a separate and independent undertaking and if one or more of the undertakings is held to be void or unenforceable, the validity of the remaining undertakings shall not be affected.

10.5 Reasonableness

The Vendor agrees that the restrictions and undertakings contained in Sub-Clauses 10.2 and 10.3 are reasonable and necessary for the protection of the Purchaser's legitimate interests in the goodwill of the Business, but if any such restriction or undertaking shall be found to be void or voidable but would be valid and enforceable if some part or parts of the restriction or undertaking were deleted, such restriction or undertaking shall apply with such modification as may be necessary to make it valid and enforceable.[62]

10.6 Void or Unenforceable Restrictions

Without prejudice to Sub-Clause 10.5, if any restriction or undertaking is found by any court or other competent authority to be void or unenforceable the parties shall negotiate in good faith to replace such void or unenforceable restriction or undertaking with a valid provision which, as far as possible, has the same legal and commercial effect as that which it replaces.

10.7 Registration[63]

Any provision of this Agreement, or of any agreement or arrangement of which it forms part, by virtue of which such agreement or arrangement is subject to registration under the Restrictive Trade Practices Act 1976 shall only take effect the day after particulars of such agreement or arrangement have been duly furnished to the Director General of Fair Trading pursuant to s 24 of that Act.

10.8 Confidential Information Concerning the Business

The Vendor shall not and shall procure that no other member of the Vendor's Group nor any officer or employee of the Vendor nor any member of the Vendor's Group shall make use of or divulge to any third party (other than to the Vendor's professional advisers for the purpose of this Agreement in which case the Vendor shall use all reasonable endeavours to procure that such advisers keep such information confidential on terms equivalent to this Clause) any confidential information relating to the Business save only:

(A) insofar as the same has become public knowledge otherwise than, directly or indirectly, through the Vendor's breach of this Sub-Clause 10.8 or the failure of the officers, employees or professional advisers referred to above to keep the same confidential; or

(B) to the extent required by law or by any supervisory or regulatory body.

11 Warranties and Retention

11.1 General

The Vendor hereby warrants and represents to the Purchaser in the terms of the Warranties and acknowledges and accepts that the Purchaser is entering into this Agreement in reliance upon each of the Warranties.

11.2 Purchaser's Knowledge

The Warranties are given subject to matters fairly disclosed in this Agreement or in the Disclosure Letter, but no other information relating to the Business of which the Purchaser has knowledge (actual or constructive) shall prejudice any claim made by the Purchaser under the Warranties or operate to reduce any amount recoverable.[64] The provisions of s 6(2) of the Law of Property (Miscellaneous Provisions) Act 1994 are hereby excluded.[65]

11.3 Warranties Independent

Each of the Warranties shall be separate and independent and, save as expressly provided, shall not be limited by reference to any other Warranty or anything in this Agreement.

11.4 Damages[66]

Without restricting the rights of the Purchaser or the ability of the Purchaser to claim damages on any basis in the event that any of the Warranties is broken or proves to be untrue or misleading, the Vendor hereby covenants to pay, on demand, to the Purchaser:

(A) the amount necessary to put the Purchaser and the Business into the position which would have existed if the Warranties had not been broken and had been true and not misleading; and

(B) all costs and expenses incurred by the Purchaser, directly or indirectly, as a result of such breach.

11.5 Pending Completion[67]

The Vendor shall procure that (save only as may be necessary to give effect to this Agreement) it shall not do, allow or procure any act or omission before Completion which would constitute a breach of any of the Warranties if they were given at any and at all times from the date hereof down to Completion or which would make any of the

Warranties inaccurate or misleading if they were so given. In particular, the Vendor shall procure that items (1) to (7) of Paragraph 2.6(A) of Schedule 6 shall be complied with at all times from the date hereof down to Completion.[68]

11.6 Further Disclosure by Vendor[67]

The Vendor shall forthwith disclose in writing to the Purchaser any matter or thing which may arise or become known to the Vendor after the date hereof and before Completion which is inconsistent with any of the Warranties or which might make any of them inaccurate or misleading if they were given at any and at all times from the date hereof down to Completion or which is material to be known to a purchaser for value of the Business.

11.7 Rescission[67]

In the event of any matter or thing that is mentioned in Sub-Clause 11.5 becoming known to the Purchaser before Completion or in the event of it becoming apparent on or before Completion that the Vendor is in [material][69] breach of any of the Warranties or any other term of this Agreement the Purchaser may at its option either:

(A) rescind this Agreement by notice in writing to the Vendor; or

(B) proceed to Completion but without prejudice to its rights to claim for breach of this Agreement or such Warranties.

11.8 Retention[70]

The Purchaser shall be entitled to retain out of the monies payable to the Vendor under or pursuant to the provisions of Sub-Clause 3.3 (Method and Timing for Payment of Consideration) above the sum of £[   ] (the 'Retention') as a retention against claims which it may make against the Vendor under or by reason of any breach of the Warranties or any of the other provisions of this Agreement and any amounts so applied by the Purchaser shall *pro tanto* satisfy the liability concerned.

11.9 Interest[70]

Interest shall accrue or be deemed to accrue to the Retention as if it had been placed with [   ] Bank Plc in such an interest bearing deposit account as the Purchaser shall specify for the period from Completion and pending its release in accordance with the provisions of Sub-Clause 11.10. All such interest (or deemed interest) (net of any tax required by law to be deducted therefrom) shall be paid to and form part of the Retention and accordingly shall belong and be paid to the Vendor subject to the provisions of this Agreement. The Purchaser's *bona fide* certificate as to the amount of interest which would have accrued to the Retention if it had been placed in the said deposit account and/or as to the amount of tax (if any) required (or which would have been required) to be deducted therefrom shall be final and binding on the parties hereto (save in respect of manifest error).

11.10 Release[70]

In the event that the Purchaser shall not have notified the Vendor in writing of any claim hereunder before [   ] 19[   ] (the 'Release Date') the Retention (including accrued interest (or such that is deemed to be accrued hereunder)) shall (net of any tax required (or deemed to be required) by law to be deducted therefrom) be released to the Vendor whose receipt shall be an absolute discharge. In the event that on or before the Release Date the Purchaser shall have notified any such claim to the Vendor it shall use its best endeavours to quantify the amount claimed and any balance shall be so released on that date. Upon final determination of the total amount (if any) falling to be applied by the Purchaser under this Clause any remaining balance of the Retention (after deducting the amount of any fully determined claim) shall be released and paid to the Vendor provided that no amount shall be released before the Release Date.

11.11 Waiver of Claims

The Vendor undertakes to the Purchaser that it will not make or pursue any claims which it has or may have against any of the Employees in respect of or arising out of the Warranties or any information supplied by them to or on behalf of the Vendor or its professional advisers or agents on or prior to the date hereof.

12 Employees of the Business[71]

12.1 Contracts of Employment

The Purchaser acknowledges and agrees that the respective contracts of employment of the Employees shall have effect from and after the Transfer Date as if originally made between each of the Employees and the Purchaser and that (*inter alia*) the provisions of regs 5 and 7 of the Regulations shall apply.

12.2 Informing Employees

As soon as practicable after [exchange of this Agreement/the Transfer Date/this Agreement becoming unconditional] the Vendor shall prepare and sign a letter to each Employee in a form agreed with the Purchaser outlining the consequences of the Transfer and a copy of such letter shall be delivered to each Employee by the Vendor.

12.3 Vendor Indemnity[72]

The Vendor covenants with the Purchaser that the Vendor will indemnify the Purchaser and hold the Purchaser harmless against all and any costs, claims, expenses, liabilities, demands, losses and actions (including legal costs on an indemnity basis) arising from any claims arising from facts or events occurring:

(A)   prior to the Transfer Date and/or which arise or are alleged to arise against the Purchaser by virtue of the operation of the Regulations in connection with this Agreement; or

(B)   at any time whether before or after the Transfer Date and which are brought by any person other than an Employee and which arise or are alleged to arise against the Purchaser by virtue of the operation of the Regulations in connection with this Agreement.

In this Clause 12 'person' means any individual or organisation (including, without limitation, trade unions and elected representatives).

12.4 Conduct of Claims

In the event that any of the Employees or other person brings a claim against the Vendor or the Purchaser arising out of or in connection with the Transfer, the Vendor and the Purchaser shall [at their own respective expense] give to the other as soon as practicable after any request therefor all co-operation, assistance and information which may be reasonably relevant to the claim.

12.5 Confidentiality and Other Restrictions

The Vendor hereby agrees to assign to or otherwise hold for the Purchaser with effect from the Transfer Date the benefit of any confidentiality or other undertakings or restrictions given to the Vendor by any present or former employees of the Vendor in the Business where such undertakings or restrictions or the benefit thereof are not novated to or otherwise vested in the Purchaser by virtue of the Regulations and accordingly the Vendor hereby agrees pending formal assignment or novation of the same and at the request of the Purchaser to take such steps, actions and proceedings as the Purchaser shall reasonably require to enforce such undertakings and restrictions (or any of them) for the benefit and at the cost of the Purchaser.

13 Pensions

The provisions of Schedule 7 (Pensions) shall have effect.

14 Guarantees

14.1 Release of Existing Guarantees

The Purchaser shall use [its best/all reasonable endeavours] to procure that as soon as reasonably practicable after Completion [the Vendor] the [Vendor's] Guarantor and each member of the Vendor's Group shall be released from all such guarantees and indemnities given by them or any of them (other than under this Agreement) in respect of:

(A) the obligations and liabilities of the Business as at the Transfer Date hereby expressly agreed to be assumed by the Purchaser (if any); and/or
(B) the benefit and burden of [the Contracts] from and after the Transfer Date hereby agreed to be assumed by the Purchaser

and of which (in each case) full particulars (including, the extent or limit of such liability) are contained in the Disclosure Letter and pending such release the Purchaser shall with effect from the Transfer Date indemnify [the Vendor] the [Vendor's] Guarantor and each such member of the Vendor's Group and keep each of them fully and effectively indemnified from and against all liabilities in connection therewith (up to but to no greater extent than that disclosed).

14.2 Obligations of the [Vendor's] Guarantor

(A) In consideration of the Purchaser entering into this Agreement at the request of the [Vendor's] Guarantor (as it hereby acknowledges), the [Vendor's] Guarantor hereby covenants with the Purchaser as primary obligations of it:
   (1) to procure that the Vendor shall duly perform all its obligations under this Agreement;
   (2) if and whenever the Vendor shall be in default in the payment when due of any amount payable under this Agreement the [Vendor's] Guarantor shall within [two] days after being given notice to that effect by the Purchaser pay all amounts then payable by the Vendor as though the [Vendor's] Guarantor instead of the Vendor was expressed to be the principal debtor; and
   (3) to indemnify the Purchaser against all [reasonable] costs and expenses (including legal fees) which the Purchaser may pay or incur in collecting any amount payable by the Vendor or the [Vendor's] Guarantor and referred to in Sub-Clause (A)(2).
(B) Any amount not paid by the Vendor and not recoverable from the [Vendor's] Guarantor on the basis of a guarantee (whether because of any legal limitation,

disability or incapacity on the part of the Purchaser or the Vendor or any other matter or thing whether known to the Purchaser or not) shall nevertheless be recoverable from the [Vendor's] Guarantor on the basis of an indemnity.[73]

(C) The [Vendor's] Guarantor acknowledges that its liability under this Clause shall not be discharged or affected in any way by time being given to the Vendor or by any other indulgence or concession being granted to the Vendor or by any other act, omission, dealing, matter or thing whatsoever (including without limitation any change in the Memorandum or Articles of Association of the Vendor or the [Vendor's] Guarantor, any amendment to this Agreement or the liquidation, dissolution, reconstruction or amalgamation of the Vendor or the [Vendor's] Guarantor or the illegality or enforceability of this Agreement) which but for this provision might operate to release the [Vendor's] Guarantor from its obligations under this Clause.[74]

(D) The guarantee contained in this Sub-Clause 14.2 is a continuing guarantee and shall remain in full force and effect until all obligations of the Vendor hereby guaranteed have been discharged in full. It is in addition to and shall not prejudice nor be prejudiced by any other guarantee, indemnity or other security or right against any third party which the Purchaser may have for the due performance of the obligations concerned.

15 Value Added Tax[75]

15.1 Transfer as Going Concern

All amounts expressed in this Agreement as payable by the Purchaser are expressed [exclusive] of any VAT which may be chargeable thereon.[76]

[First alternative form of Sub-Clause 14.1:[77]

The Purchaser and the Vendor intend that art 5 of the Value Added Tax (Special Provisions) Order 1995 shall apply to the transfer of the Business Assets hereunder and accordingly:

(A) the Vendor and the Purchaser shall on the date of Completion give notice of such a transfer to HM Customs & Excise; and

(B) on Completion the Vendor shall deliver to the Purchaser all records referred to in s 49(1) of the Value Added Tax Act 1994, relating to the Business (the Vendor shall be entitled to retain photocopies of such records and shall also be entitled at its own expense to, and the Purchaser shall permit, the Vendor or its agents access to the originals of such records upon giving reasonable notice to the Purchaser) and the Vendor agrees that it has not and will not seek a direction that the Vendor be entitled to keep such records].

[or]

[Second alternative form of Sub-Clause 14.1:[78]

The Purchaser and the Vendor intend that art 5 of the Value Added Tax (Special Provisions) Order 1995 shall apply to the transfer of the Business Assets hereunder and accordingly:

(A) the Vendor and the Purchaser shall on the date of Completion give notice of such a transfer to HM Customs & Excise; and

(B) [the Vendor shall make a request to HM Customs & Excise under s 49(1)(*b*) of the Value Added Tax Act 1994 and shall if HM Customs & Excise so direct retain all records referred to in the said s 49(1) relating to the Business and shall upon the Purchaser's written request and at the Purchaser's expense deliver copies of the said records to the Purchaser and shall also allow the Purchaser or its agents upon giving reasonable notice to the Vendor access to the originals of such records.]

15.2 Payment of VAT

(A) The Vendor and the Purchaser shall use all reasonable endeavours to secure that pursuant to the said art 5, the sale of the Business Assets pursuant to this Agreement is treated as neither a supply of goods nor a supply of services for the purposes of VAT [and the Vendor and the Purchaser shall agree the form of a letter to be sent to their respective VAT offices seeking confirmation that art 5 applies to the transfer of Business Assets].

(B) The Vendor [has/has not] made [, or will prior to Completion make,] an election pursuant to Sched 10 para 2 of the Value Added Tax Act 1994 in respect of [any of the Premises/these Premises identified [by an asterisk in Schedule 3/in the Disclosure Letter] (the 'VAT Premises')]. Notwithstanding the provisions of this Clause or the said art 5, the Vendor shall be entitled to charge VAT and the Purchaser shall, subject to Sub-Clause 14.2(D) pay to the Vendor an amount equal to such VAT in respect of the VAT Premises, unless the Purchaser has prior to Completion produced to the Vendor certified copies of both an election made by it pursuant to the said Sched 10 para 2 in respect of the VAT Premises and notification thereof.

(C) In the event that an amount is paid by the Purchaser to the Vendor in respect of VAT which is not properly chargeable then the Vendor shall be obliged to repay to the Purchaser an amount equal to such [alleged] VAT.[79]

(D) In the event that VAT is chargeable on the transfer of the Business Assets hereunder or any of them pursuant to the Agreement then subject to receipt by the Purchaser of the tax invoices relating thereto, the Purchaser shall pay to the Vendor an amount equal to the amount of VAT payable in respect of such transfer.

15.3 Pre and Post Completion Supplies[80]

All VAT payable in respect of goods and services supplied or deemed to be supplied by the Vendor in connection with the business prior to Completion and all interest payable thereon and penalties attributable thereto shall be paid to HM Customs & Excise by the Vendor and the Vendor shall be entitled to receive and to retain for its own benefit all reimbursement or credit from HM Customs & Excise for VAT borne by the Vendor on goods and services supplied to the Vendor prior to Completion and any payments received in respect of VAT overpaid to HM Customs & Excise prior thereto.

15.4 Capital Goods Schems[81]

In relation to assets to which Part XV of the Value Added Tax Regulations 1995 (Capital Goods Scheme) ('Part XV') apply, the Vendor agrees that any recovery of input tax on the Premises [and the Computer Hardware] after the date of this Agreement shall be retained by the Purchaser and the Purchaser undertakes that it will not make any claim against the Vendor in respect of any adjustment of input tax relating to such items pursuant to Part XV. The Vendor agrees to provide to the Purchaser on request such information in respect of its recovery of input tax and adjustments thereto as shall be required by the Purchaser to comply fully with its obligations under Part XV.

16 Confidentiality

16.1 Confidentiality[82]

Subject to Sub-Clauses 16.2 (Permitted Disclosures) and to Clause 17 (Announcements) and without prejudice to Sub-Clause 10.8 (Confidential Information Concerning the Business), each party:

(A)   shall treat as strictly confidential information obtained or received by it as a result of entering into or performing its obligations under this Agreement and relating to the negotiations relating to, or the provisions or subject matter of, this Agreement or the other party ('confidential information'); and

(B)   shall not, except with the prior written consent of the other party (which shall not be unreasonably withheld or delayed), publish or otherwise disclose to any person any confidential information.

16.2 Permitted Disclosures

Sub-Clause 16.1 (Confidentiality) shall not apply if and to the extent that [the party proposing to make such disclosure can demonstrate that]:

(A)   such disclosure is required by law or by any securities exchange or regulatory or governmental body having jurisdiction over it (including the London Stock Exchange Limited, the Panel on Take-overs and Mergers or the Serious Fraud Office) and whether or not the requirement has the force of law;

(B)   the confidential information was lawfully in its possession prior to its disclosure by the other party (as evidenced by written records) and had not been obtained from that other party; or

(C)   the confidential information has come into the public domain other than through its fault or the fault of any person to whom the confidential information has been disclosed in accordance with Sub-Clause 16.1(B) [, provided that any such disclosure shall not be made without prior [notice to]/[consultation with] the other party].

16.3 Continuance of Restrictions

The restrictions contained in this Clause on the part of the Vendor shall survive Completion.

17 Announcements

17.1 Restriction[83]

Subject to Sub-Clause 17.2 (Permitted Announcements), neither the Vendor nor the Purchaser shall make any announcement whether to the public, to the customers or suppliers of the Business, or to all or any of the Employees concerning the subject matter of this Agreement without the prior written approval of the other [(which shall not be unreasonably withheld or delayed).]

17.2 Permitted Announcements

Sub-Clause 17.1 (Restriction) shall not apply if and to the extent that such announcement is required by law or by any securities exchange or regulatory or governmental body having jurisdiction over it (including but not limited to the London Stock Exchange Limited, The Panel on Take-overs and Mergers or the Serious Fraud Office) and whether or not the requirement has the force of law and provided that any such announcement shall be made only after consultation with the other party.

17.3 Continuance of Restrictions

The restrictions contained in this Clause on the part of the Vendor shall survive Completion.

18 Provisions Relating to this Agreement

18.1 Assignment[84]

This Agreement shall be binding upon and enure for the benefit of the successors of the parties but shall not be assignable, save that the Purchaser may at any time assign all or any part of its rights and benefits under this Agreement, including the Warranties and any cause of action arising under or in respect of any of them, to any transferee of all or any part of the Business Assets or to any Affiliate of the Purchaser who may enforce them as if he had also been named in this Agreement as the Purchaser.

18.2 Whole Agreement[85]

(A) This Agreement, together with any documents referred to in it, constitutes the whole agreement between the parties relating to its subject matter and supersedes and extinguishes any prior drafts, agreements, undertakings, representations, warranties, assurances and arrangements of any nature, whether in writing or oral, relating to such subject matter.

[(B) The Purchaser acknowledges that it has not been induced to enter into this Agreement by any representation, warranty, promise or assurance by the Vendor or any other person save for those contained in this Agreement and in the Disclosure Letter. The Purchaser agrees that (except in respect of fraud) it shall have no right or remedy in respect of any representation, warranty, promise or assurance save for those contained in this Agreement. The Purchaser acknowledges that its legal advisers have explained to it the effect of this Sub-Clause 17.2(B).[85]]

(C) No variation of this Agreement shall be effective unless made in writing and signed by each of the parties.[86]

18.3 Agreement Survives Completion

The Warranties and all other provisions of this Agreement, in so far as the same shall not have been performed at Completion, shall remain in full force and effect notwithstanding Completion.

18.4 Rights etc Cumulative and Other Matters

(A) The rights, powers, privileges and remedies provided in this Agreement are cumulative and are not exclusive of any rights, powers, privileges or remedies provided by law or otherwise.

(B) No failure to exercise nor any delay in exercising any right, power, privilege or remedy under this Agreement shall in any way impair or affect the exercise thereof or operate as a waiver thereof in whole or in part.

(C) No single or partial exercise of any right, power, privilege or remedy under this Agreement shall prevent any further or other exercise thereof or the exercise of any other right, power, privilege or remedy.

[18.5 Release of One Vendor[87]

The Purchaser may release or compromise the liability [of any of the Vendors] hereunder without affecting the liability of the other Vendor.]

18.6 Further Assurance

At any time after the date hereof the Vendor and the [Vendor's] Guarantor shall, at the request and cost of the Purchaser, execute or procure the execution of such documents and do or procure the doing of such acts and things as the Purchaser may reasonably require for the purpose of vesting the respective Business Assets hereby agreed to be sold in the Purchaser or its nominees and/or otherwise giving to the Purchaser the full benefit of all the provisions of this Agreement.

18.7 Invalidity

If any provision of this Agreement shall be held to be illegal, void, invalid or unenforceable under the laws of any jurisdiction, the legality, validity and enforceability of the remainder of this Agreement in that jurisdiction shall not be affected, and the legality, validity and enforceability of the whole of this Agreement in any other jurisdiction shall not be affected.

18.8 Payment to the Vendor

[Any payment falling to be made to the Vendor under any provision of this Agreement may be made to the Vendor's solicitors, [   ], whose receipt shall be an absolute discharge.]

18.9 Counterparts

This Agreement may be executed in any number of counterparts, which shall together constitute one Agreement. Any party may enter into this Agreement by signing any such counterpart.

18.10 Costs

Each party shall bear its own costs arising out of or in connection with the preparation, negotiation and implementation of this Agreement save that if this Agreement is lawfully rescinded by the Purchaser the Vendor shall pay to the Purchaser its accountancy legal and [   ] costs in relation to the investigation of the Business prior to the date hereof and the preparation and negotiation of this Agreement and the documents referred to herein [up to an aggregate limit of £[   ] (inclusive of VAT)].

18.11 Notices[88]

(A) Any notice or other communication required to be given under this Agreement or in connection with the matters contemplated by it shall, except where otherwise specifically provided, be in writing in the English language and shall be addressed as provided in Sub-Clause (B) and may be:
  (1) personally delivered, in which case it shall be deemed to have been given upon delivery at the relevant address; or
  (2) if within the United Kingdom, sent by first class pre-paid post, in which case it shall be deemed to have been given two Business Days after the date of posting; or

(3) [if from or to any place outside the United Kingdom, sent by pre-paid priority airmail, in which case it shall be deemed to have been given seven Business Days after the date of posting; or]

(4) sent by fax, in which case it shall be deemed to have been given when despatched, subject to confirmation of uninterrupted transmission by a transmission report[, or sent by telex, in which case it shall be deemed to have been given when despatched, provided the recipient's answer back code is duly received by the sender at the start and end of the message,] provided that any notice despatched by fax [or telex] after 5 pm (at the place where such fax [or telex] is to be received) on any day shall be deemed to have been received at [8am] on the next Business Day.

(B) The addresses and other details of the parties referred to in Sub-Clause (A) are, subject to Sub-Clause (C):

Name:

[For the attention of:]

Address:

Fax number:

[Telex number:]

(C) Any party to this Agreement may notify the other parties of any change to its address or other details specified in Sub-Clause (B), provided that such notification shall be effective only on the date specified in such notice or five Business Days after the notice is given, whichever is later[.][, and provided also that any new address shall be in the United Kingdom.]

19 Law and Jurisdiction

19.1 English Law

This Agreement shall be governed by, and construed in accordance with, English law.

19.2 Jurisdiction[89]

In relation to any legal action or proceedings to enforce this Agreement or arising out of or in connection with this Agreement ('proceedings') each of the parties irrevocably submits to the jurisdiction of the English courts and waives any objection to proceedings in such courts on the grounds of venue or on the grounds that the proceedings have been brought in an inconvenient forum.

[19.3 Process Agent[90]

The Vendor appoints [   ] of [   ] as its process agent to receive on its behalf service of process in any proceedings in England. Service upon the process agent shall be good service upon the Vendor whether or not it is forwarded to and received by the Vendor. If for any reason the process agent ceases to be able to act as process agent, or no longer has an address in England, the Vendor irrevocably agrees to appoint a substitute process agent with an address in England acceptable to the Purchaser and to deliver to the Purchaser a copy of the substitute process agent's acceptance of that appointment within 30 days. In the event that the Vendor fails to appoint a substitute process agent, it shall be effective service for the Purchaser to serve the process upon the last known address in England of the last known process agent for the Vendor notified to the Purchaser, notwithstanding that such process agent is no longer found at such address or has ceased to act.]

AS WITNESS the hands of the duly authorised representatives of the parties the day and year first above written.

SCHEDULE 1

THE CURRENT ASSETS[10]

[(A) All stocks of raw materials, components and consumables including, without lim-
it, fuel, office supplies, packaging and labelling, spares and spare parts; [and]
(B) All stocks of partly finished goods and all work-in-progress; [and]
(C) All stocks of unsold finished goods; [and]
[(D) All cash in hand, in transit and at the bank and all cheques and securities repre-
senting the same [and not representing any of the Book Debts hereby agreed to be
sold]; [and]]
(E) Prepayments; [and]
(F) [Specify any other].]

SCHEDULE 2

THE IMMOVABLE FIXED ASSETS, THE MOVABLE FIXED ASSETS,
THE LEASE CONTRACTS

PART I

(The Immovable Fixed Assets)

Description   Premises as which situated   Consideration

PART II

(The Movable Fixed Assets)

PART III

(The Lease Contracts)

Description of Lease Contract   Description of Leased Asset(s)
                                                     held thereunder

SCHEDULE 3

THE FREEHOLD PREMISES, THE LEASEHOLD PREMISES, THE NEW LEASEHOLD PREMISES

Part IA: Freehold Premises

Description	Relevant owner	Title number or date and description of root of title	Details of documents containing or referring to matters subject to which the premises are sold (other than tenancies)	Current use	Consideration £

Part IB: Tenancies to which Freehold Premises are subject

Demised premises	Date and parties to lease	Current tenant	Term	Current principal yearly rent	Next or outstanding rent review

Part IIA: Leasehold Premises

Demised premises	Title number (if applicable)	Date and parties to lease	Relevant assignor	Term	Current principal yearly rent	Current Use	Consideration £

Part IIB: Tenancies to which Leasehold Premises are subject

Demised premises	Date and parties to sub-lease	Current sub-tenant	Term	Current principal yearly rent	Next or outstanding rent review

Part III: New Leasehold Premises

Number	Short description	Relevant grantor	Nature of grantor's interest	Current use	Details of grantor's interest, if leasehold		
					Date of lease	Parties	Term
1			[ ]hold				
2							
3							
4							
5							

SCHEDULE 4

ADJUSTMENT OF CONSIDERATION[91]

1 Interpretation

In this Schedule, where the context admits:

1.1   'the Audited Accounts' and 'the Balance Sheet Date' and any other defined term used in this Schedule shall have the same meanings as in the Agreement and the Schedules;

1.2   'Completion Accounts' means the accounts prepared in accordance with Paragraph 2 (Completion Accounts) and agreed or determined in accordance with Paragraph 4 (Procedure);

1.3   'Net Tangible Assets' means the sum of the values of
(1)   the Fixed Assets;
(2)   the Current Assets;
(3)   the Premises;

less

(4)   the Assumed Liabilities;
[if relevant: add Book Debts; deduct Creditors; adjust for any specific item]
(all as shown in or derived from the Completion Accounts).

1.4   'the Provisional Consideration' means the consideration for the sale and purchase of the Business Assets stated in Clause 3.1 (Amount);

1.5   'Purchaser's Accountants' means [   ];

1.6   'SSAP' means Statements of Standard Accounting Practice in force at the date hereof; and

1.7   'Vendor's Accountants' means [   ].

2 Completion Accounts

2.1 Preparation

The Purchaser shall, as soon as practicable, and in any event within [42] days after Completion, procure that accounts for the Business shall be prepared in accordance with the Schedule and the parties shall use their best endeavours to secure compliance with this Schedule by their respective accountants. The Vendor shall promptly supply all such information and provide access to all such records and personnel as the Purchaser shall reasonably require for such purpose.

2.2 Description

The Completion Accounts shall consist of a balance sheet of the Business drawn up as at the Transfer Date [which shall be substantially in the form of the *pro forma* accounts in the agreed terms].[92]

2.3 General Requirements

Subject to the specific requirements of Sub-Paragraph 2.4 which shall take priority over the general requirements set out below, the Completion Accounts shall:

(A)   make full provision for all [actual, future and contingent liabilities of the Business including][93] the Assumed Liabilities;

(B)   be prepared under the historic cost convention in accordance with the requirements of all relevant statutes and generally accepted accounting principles, SSAPs and Financial Reporting Standards [(as if the Business was a company registered under the Companies Act 1985)];[94]

(C)   [apply and adopt the same basis and policies of accounting as applied or adopted for the purposes of the Audited Accounts][95]

2.4   Specific Requirements[96]

In preparing the Completion Accounts:

(A)   [the Fixed Assets and the Premises shall be included at the value at which they were included in the Audited Accounts (or, if acquired after the Balance Sheet Date, at their cost) less, in each case, depreciation on a *pro rata* basis at the rates used in the Audited Accounts and less, in each case, provisions for damage or impairment or other want of repair [on the same basis used in preparing the Audited Accounts];]

(B)   those of the Current Assets representing stock shall be determined in accordance with Paragraph 3 (Stock Valuation) and valued [on the same basis as used in the Audited Accounts (details of which are described in the Disclosure Letter)] and full provision shall be made for unusable, unsaleable, slow moving or deteriorated stocks;[97]

(C)   no value shall be attributed to any Business Asset except to the extent the purchaser shall have the full benefit of it after Completion;

(D)   [no value shall be attributed to the Goodwill, the Intellectual Property Rights, the Listed Intellectual Property Rights, the Third Party Rights, the Specified Contracts, the Lease Contracts (or the Leased Assets) or the Records;]

(E)   no provision or reserve for taxation shall be made in the Completion Accounts;[98]

(F)   [full provision shall be made for any Book Debts outstanding and uncollected at the Transfer Date for a period of more than 60 days past their due date and proper provision or reserve shall be made for all other bad or doubtful debts comprised in the Book Debts];[99]

(G)   full provision shall be made for any repairs or other servicing required in relation to the Fixed Assets;[100]

(H)   full provision shall be made in respect of the cost of making good dilapidations and/or wants of repair on or to the Premises;

(I)   [consider provision on a *pro rata* basis for holiday pay or bonuses due in respect of Employees; for overriders, excess mileage charges, hire purchase payments, other items which may not accrue evenly etc.][101]

(J)   [specify any other specific requirements—these should be checked (where applicable) with the Purchaser's accountants].

3   Stock Valuation

For the purposes of the preparation of the Completion Accounts, the value of the Current Assets (comprising stock) shall be ascertained in accordance with the following provisions of this Paragraph:

(A)   The Vendor and the Purchaser shall cause a stocktaking to be made on the Completion Date of all the Current Assets.

(B)   Unless otherwise agreed by the parties such stocktaking shall consist of a physical check of the amount, quality and condition of all such Current Assets (comprising stock) situated on the Premises at the Transfer Date and an inspection of the books and records and contractual documentation for all Current Assets not so situated together with confirmation from the person or persons having physical possession of such stock of the extent of any interest in or encumbrance claimed over such stock (if any).

(C)   When such stocktaking has been completed the Current Assets shall be valued by the Purchaser in accordance with Paragraph 2 and included in the Completion Accounts.

4   Procedure[102]

4.1   Submission of Draft

(A)   As soon as the Completion Accounts shall have been prepared the Purchaser shall send a copy to the Vendor together with such working papers used in connection with the preparation of the same as it considers necessary or appropriate to understand and agree the Completion Accounts and shall in addition, and at the same time, send to the Vendor its calculation of the Net Tangible Assets.

(B)   Unless the Vendor shall within 21 days of receipt of the Completion Accounts (and associated papers and calculation as provided in Sub-Paragraph (A)) serve a notice in writing on the Purchaser that it objects to the Completion Accounts (identifying the reason for any objection and the amount(s) or items(s) in the Completion Accounts and/or calculation which is/are in dispute) (such notification being, for the purposes of this Paragraph 4, an 'Objection Notice') the Vendor shall be deemed to have agreed to the Completion Accounts and the Purchaser's calculation of the Net Tangible Assets for all purposes of this Agreement.

4.2   Agreement of Draft

If, within the period referred to in Sub-Paragraph 4.1 (B), the Vendor shall give the Purchaser an Objection Notice then the Purchaser and the Vendor shall use their best endeavours to reach agreement upon adjustments to the draft and the value of Net Tangible Assets.

4.3   Independent Accountant[103]

In the event that the Vendor and the Purchaser are unable to reach agreement within 28 days following service of the Objection Notice, either the Vendor or the Purchaser shall be entitled to refer the matter or matters in dispute to an independent firm of chartered accountants agreed upon between them or (failing agreement) to be selected (at the instance of either party) by the President for the time being of the Institute of Chartered Accountants for England and Wales. Such independent firm of chartered accountants shall act as experts not as arbitrators and shall determine the matter or matters in dispute and certify the Net Tangible Assets accordingly and whose decision shall, save in the event of fraud or manifest error be binding. The costs of the independent firm of accountants shall be borne by the Vendor and the Purchaser [equally or in such proportions as the said accountants shall direct].

4.4   Report

If the Vendor accepts, or is deemed to accept, that the said draft complies with Paragraph 2 the Purchaser['s Accountants] shall sign a report to the effect that the Completion Accounts comply with Paragraph 2 and any Completion Accounts so reported on, or (if Sub-Paragraph 4.3 shall apply) the final draft of the Completion Accounts as determined by the independent firm of accountants, shall be the Completion Accounts for the purposes of this Agreement and shall be final and binding on the parties.

4.5 Information and Explanations

The Purchaser and the Purchaser's Accountants shall provide such information and explanations relating to the draft Completion Accounts and their preparation as the Vendor's Accountants, or any independent firm of chartered accountants appointed pursuant to Paragraph 4.3, shall reasonably require.

5 Adjustment of Consideration

5.1 Increase or Reduction

When the Completion Accounts have become binding, the Provisional Consideration shall forthwith:

(A) be increased by the amount (if any) by which the Net Tangible Assets of the Business as at the Transfer Date as shown by the Completion Accounts are greater than [£   ][104]; or (as the case may be)

(B) be reduced by the amount (if any) by which the Net Tangible Assets of the Business as at the Transfer Date as shown by the Completion Accounts are less than [£   ][104].

5.2 Payment

Any increase or reduction in the Provisional Consideration shall be paid by the Purchaser or the Vendor (as appropriate) within 14 days after the Completion Accounts have become binding as aforesaid and any amount not paid when due shall carry interest (accrued daily and compounded monthly) at the Interest Rate.

6 Interaction with Other Provisions[105]

[Subject to the due performance of Paragraph 5, if the Purchaser shall have any claim against the Vendor under this Agreement in respect of any liability, deficiency or value of any asset which is taken into account in the Completion Accounts the amount of such liability, deficiency or value of any asset so taken into account shall be deducted from the amount of the Purchaser's claim but, save as aforesaid, preparation and acceptance of the Completion Accounts by the Purchaser shall be without prejudice to any claim which the Purchaser may have against the Vendor under or in respect of any breach of this Agreement.]

SCHEDULE 5

TERMS APPLICABLE TO THE PREMISES[106]

PART I

Terms Applicable to the Freehold Premises

1 Interpretation

1.1   In this Part I of this Schedule, where the context admits :
'Relevant Owner' means the party so named in Part IA of Schedule 3 and in whom the legal estate of each of the Freehold Premises is vested at the date hereof and 'Relevant Owners' shall be construed accordingly;
'Tenancy' means the lease or tenancy particulars of which are set out in Part IB of Schedule 3 and shall include any document supplemental thereto and 'Relevant Tenancy' and 'Tenancies' shall be construed accordingly.

1.2   References in this Part of this Schedule to Paragraphs and Sub-Paragraphs shall unless the context requires otherwise be to those in this Part of this Schedule.

1.3   References to any Act of Parliament include references to any statutory modification or re-enactment thereof for the time being in force and any order, instrument, regulation or bye-law made or issued thereunder.

2 Title and Matters Affecting the Freehold Premises

2.1   Each of the Freehold Premises are sold subject to and (where applicable) with the benefit of such of the following matters as relate to them:

(A)   all matters contained or referred to in the relevant Tenancy (so far as it is subsisting on the date of Completion);

(B)   all matters in the nature of easements, rights, exceptions, reservations, restrictions, covenants and conditions;

(C)   in relation to the Freehold Premises title to which is registered at HM Land Registry:
(1)   entry numbers [   ] in the Property Register and entry numbers [   ] in the Charges Register of title number [   ] as at the [   ] 19[   ] (being the date of office copy entries supplied to the Purchaser's solicitors [other than entry numbers [   ]];
[repeat for each registered title]

(D)   in relation to the Freehold Premises title to which is not registered at HM Land Registry all matters contained or referred to in the documents listed in the fourth column of Part IA of Schedule 3

in each case so far as the same are now subsisting, binding on the Freehold Premises and capable of taking effect.

2.2   Title to each of the Freehold Premises having been deduced to the Purchaser prior to the date hereof the Purchaser shall accept the same and shall not raise any enquiry, requisition or objection in relation thereto.

2.3   The Purchaser shall not be entitled to make any enquiry, requisition or objection with regard to any document which the Vendor's solicitors have disclosed to the Purchaser's solicitors in writing on or before the date hereof as not being in the Vendor's possession nor shall the Purchaser require the Vendor or the relevant Owner to obtain an examined or certified copy of any such document.

2.4   The Purchaser shall be deemed to have full notice of the current use of each of the Freehold Premises as shown in Schedule 3 and shall not be entitled to request any information or to raise any objection or requisition with regard thereto.

3   The Transfer

3.1   The Vendor shall sell or procure that the relevant Owner shall sell the Freehold Premises with full title guarantee[107] and the Purchaser shall purchase the Freehold Premises.

3.2   The assurance of each of the Freehold Premises shall be in duplicate and executed by the Purchaser as well as by the Vendor or the relevant Owner and the Purchaser shall, at the Vendor's expense, arrange for the duplicate assurance of each of the Freehold Premises to be stamped and denoted against the original and after stamping and denoting shall return the same to the Vendor's solicitors as soon as reasonably practicable.

3.3   The Purchaser shall in the assurance of each of the Freehold Premises covenant with the relevant Owner as follows:

(A)   (by way of indemnity only) that the Purchaser and its successors in title will thenceforth perform and observe:

    (1)   the obligations of the owner of the Freehold Premises or otherwise binding on the relevant Owner, in the case of Freehold Premises title to which is registered at HM Land Registry, arising under the documents and matters referred to in the Property and Charges Registers of the registered title to the Freehold Premises or, in the case of Freehold Premises title to which is not registered at HM Land Registry, all matters contained or referred to in the documents listed in column (4) of Part IA of Schedule 3 as appropriate in each case so far as the same are still subsisting and capable of being enforced; and

    (2)   the obligations of the grantor or lessor under the Tenancies and the conditions contained in the Tenancies and binding the grantor or lessor;

(B)   fully and effectually to indemnify the relevant Owner in respect of all such obligations and conditions referred to in Sub-Paragraph 3.3(A) and against all actions, claims, costs, demands, expenses, liabilities and losses arising in consequence of any breach thereof by the Purchaser.

3.4   The assurance of each of the Freehold Premises shall contain a declaration to the effect that the covenant implied on the part of the relevant Owner by the Law of Property (Miscellaneous Provisions) Act 1994, s 3 shall be limited so that the relevant Owner's liability shall not extend to:

(A)   any matters or categories of matters to which the disposition is expressly made subject; and

(B)   any charges, encumbrances, and other third party rights created granted or imposed after the date of this Agreement (other than by the relevant Owner).

4   Incorporation of National Conditions

4.1   The National Conditions of Sale (20th Edition) shall be deemed to be incorporated herein and apply separately in relation to each of the Freehold Premises so far as the same are not varied by or inconsistent with the conditions herein contained and are applicable to a sale by private treaty save that National Conditions 1, 2, 3, 4, 5, 6, 7, 8, 10, 11, 13(3), 15(2), 15(3), 15(4), 18(4), 19, 20, 21 and 22 shall not apply.

5   Completion

5.1   Completion of the sale and purchase of each of the Freehold Premises shall take place on Completion when vacant possession will be given (save in respect of any part of the Freehold Premises subject to a Tenancy and save for property belonging to suppliers of gas, water, electricity, telephone or other like services).

[6   Rent Review and Renewal of Tenancies[108]

6.1   This Paragraph shall apply in relation to any of the Tenancies:

(A)   in respect of which the lessor was entitled to a review of the yearly or other fixed rent with effect from a date (a 'Review Date') prior to or being the date of Completion; or

(B)   which is subject to proposed renewal (whether or not pursuant to the Landlord and Tenant Act 1954) or to payment of (or any application for an order as to) an interim rent pursuant to the Landlord and Tenant Act 1954 and the contractual term has expired prior to the date of Completion

but (in any such case) where the amount of rent payable from any date (a 'Relevant Date') relevant to this Paragraph (including under any renewal of any Tenancy) has not been determined as at the date of Completion.

6.2   The Purchaser shall use its reasonable endeavours to conclude the said rent reviews and renewals and to obtain the interim rent orders (if any) to which this Paragraph applies as soon as reasonably practicable after Completion. The Purchaser shall not without the consent of the Vendor (such consent not to be unreasonably withheld or delayed) be entitled to conclude any such matters on any basis other than:

(A)   (in the case of a review) in accordance with the rent review provisions of the relevant Tenancy; and

(B)   (in the case of a renewal or interim rent) in accordance with the provisions of the Landlord and Tenant Act 1954.

6.3   As soon as reasonably practicable after the determination or agreement of any such matter as aforesaid the Purchaser shall give written notice thereof to the Vendor and pending such determination or agreement the Purchaser shall on the request and at the cost of the Vendor keep the Vendor informed as to progress therein and the state of negotiations or proceedings.

6.4   Paragraph 7 shall apply to all rent and interest received or receivable by the Vendor or the relevant Owner or the Purchaser in respect of any such matters as aforesaid.]

[7   Income from Freehold Premises[109]

7.1   Rents received by the Vendor or the relevant Owner from tenants or occupiers of each of the Freehold Premises in advance and which relate to any period following the Transfer Date shall be apportioned as at the Transfer Date on an equal daily basis over the relevant year based on the amounts then payable under the relevant Tenancy.

7.2   Rents under any Tenancies which have fallen due for payment to the relevant Owner on or before Completion but which shall not have actually been received by the Vendor or the relevant Owner shall be apportioned as between the Vendor and the Purchaser as and when the same are actually received by the Purchaser (or the Vendor or the relevant Owner as the case may be) after Completion.

7.3   The Purchaser shall within 14 days of receipt pay to the Vendor any arrears of rent or other sums received from any tenant in respect of any period prior to the Transfer Date such arrears being duly apportioned under Sub-Paragraph 7.1 where appropriate.

7.4 The Vendor will within 14 days of receipt pay to the Purchaser any arrears of rent or other sums received from any tenant by the Vendor or the relevant Owner in respect of any period after the Transfer Date and which shall have been paid to the Vendor or the relevant Owner such arrears being duly apportioned under Sub-Paragraph 7.1 where appropriate.

7.5 The Purchaser shall on the request and at the cost of the Vendor at any time after the Transfer Date assign such rights as may be necessary to enable the relevant Owner to recover any arrears of rent or other sums payable under the Tenancy for any period prior to Completion and the Purchaser shall at the Vendor's cost execute a deed or deeds of assignment thereof in such terms as the Purchaser shall approve.]

[8 Management of the Freehold Premises

8.1 The Vendor shall procure the continuance of the management of each of the Freehold Premises in accordance with the principles of good estate management until Completion but no lease, underlease, tenancy or occupational licence of all or any part of any Freehold Premises shall be granted, surrendered or agreed to be granted or surrendered by the Vendor or the relevant Owner, nor shall the terms thereof be varied or agreed to be varied, nor shall any licence or consent be granted until Completion except:

(A) with the prior written consent of the Purchaser (which the Purchaser agrees shall not be unreasonably withheld or delayed in the case of any matter to which the consent of the relevant Owner is required as lessor or grantor of any of the Tenancies where such consent is not to be unreasonably withheld or delayed); or

(B) in pursuance of:

    (1) any legally enforceable agreement subsisting at the date hereof; or

    (2) any application made on or before the date hereof for the lessor's or grantor's consent to any act, matter or thing under the terms of any of the Tenancies and to which the consent of the relevant Owner is not to be unreasonably withheld under the relevant Tenancy

the existence of which agreement or application has (in either case) been disclosed in writing to the Purchaser's solicitors on or before the date hereof including the renewal of any tenancy on terms settled on or before the date hereof.

8.2 Until Completion the Vendor shall upon the request of the Purchaser provide the Purchaser with such information as the Purchaser reasonably requires as to matters relating to the then current management of each of the Freehold Premises.

8.3 The Vendor shall on Completion or (if later) forthwith on receipt of the same account to the Purchaser for any refund of insurance premium relating to any of the Freehold Premises and actually received by the Vendor or the relevant Owner in respect of the period after Completion and expiring on the date of renewal of the relevant insurance policy to the extent that such premium shall have been paid by persons having an interest under any Tenancy.]

9 Surety Covenants

9.1 On Completion the Vendor will if required by the Purchaser by separate deed (to be prepared by the Purchaser's solicitors in a form previously approved by the Vendor's solicitors) assign or procure that the relevant Owner assigns to the Purchaser so far as the same remain in force and effect the benefit of the covenants relating to the Tenancies entered into with the Vendor or the relevant Owner by any sureties to or guarantors or assignees of any of the Tenancies.

10 No Merger

10.1   The terms of this Part I of this Schedule (or any part thereof) shall not merge on Completion and shall continue in full force and effect to the extent that anything remains to be performed and observed hereunder.

11 Miscellaneous

11.1   In the event of any conflict between the provisions of this Part of this Schedule and the other provisions of this Agreement the provisions of this Part of this Schedule shall prevail.

PART II

Terms Applicable to the Leasehold Premises[108]

1 Interpretation

1.1   In this Part II of this Schedule, where the context admits:
'an Assignment' and 'to Assign' include a transfer or to transfer;
'Lease' means the lease or underlease of each of the Leasehold Premises vested in the relevant Assignor at the date hereof and shall include any document supplemental thereto and 'Leases' and 'Relevant Lease' and 'Relevant Leases' shall be construed accordingly;
'Premises Completion Date' means in relation to each of the Leasehold Premises the later of (a) the Transfer Date or (b) 10 working days after notice is given to the Purchaser's solicitors of the grant of the Reversioner's Licence;
'Relevant Assignor' means the party so named in Part IIA of Schedule 3 and in whom a Lease is vested and 'relevant Assignors' shall be construed accordingly;
'Reversioner' means in respect of the Leasehold Premises (and each of them respectively) the immediate landlord and/or any superior landlord of the relevant Assignor whose licence is required to the assignment of the relevant Lease or if Paragraph 7 applies, to the grant of an Underlease to the Purchaser;
'Reversioner's Licence' means any necessary licence or licences or consents required from the relevant Reversioner [either] to the assignment of the relevant Lease to the Purchaser [or if Paragraph 7 applies to the grant of an Underlease to the Purchaser];
'Tenancy' means the lease or tenancy particulars of which are set out in Part IIB of Schedule 3 and shall include any document supplemental thereto and 'Relevant Tenancy' and 'Tenancies' shall be construed accordingly.

1.2   References in this Part of this Schedule to Paragraphs and Sub-Paragraphs shall unless the context requires otherwise be to those in this Part of this Schedule.

1.3   References to any Act of Parliament include references to any statutory modification or re-enactment thereof for the time being in force and any order, instrument, regulation or bye-law made or issued thereunder.

2 Title and Matters Affecting the Leasehold Premises

2.1   Each of the Leasehold Premises are sold subject to and (where applicable) with the benefit of such of the following matters as relate to them:

(A)   all matters contained or referred to in the relevant Tenancy (so far as it is subsisting on the date of Completion);

(B)   the rents reserved by and the lessee's covenants and conditions and the exceptions and reservations and other matters contained in or arising in respect of the relevant Lease or the relevant Leases or subject to which the relevant Lease or the relevant Leases is or are granted;

(C)   all matters in the nature of easements, rights, exceptions, reservations, restrictions, covenants and conditions;

(D)   in relation to the Leasehold Premises title to which is registered at HM Land Registry:

(1)   entry numbers [   ] in the Property Register and entry numbers [   ] in the Charges Register of title number [   ] as at the [   ] 19[   ] (being the date of office copy entries supplied to the Purchaser's solicitors [other than [entry numbers [   ]];

[repeat for each registered title]

in each case so far as the same are now subsisting, binding on the Leasehold Premises and capable of taking effect.

2.2   Title to each of the Leasehold Premises having been deduced to the Purchaser prior to the date hereof the Purchaser shall accept the same and shall not raise any enquiry, requisition or objection in relation thereto.

2.3   The Purchaser shall not be entitled to make any enquiry, requisition or objection with regard to any document which the Vendor's solicitors have disclosed to the Purchaser's solicitors in writing on or before the date hereof as not being in the Vendor's possession nor shall the Purchaser require the Vendor to obtain an examined or certified copy of any such document.

2.4   The Purchaser shall be deemed to have full notice of the current use of each of the Leasehold Premises as shown in Schedule 3 and shall not be entitled to request any information or to raise any objection or requisition with regard thereto.

2.5   The Purchaser shall raise no enquiry, requisition or objection founded on the fact (if such be the case) that the Leases or any of them are or is found to be an underlease.

3   The Assignment

3.1   The Vendor shall sell or shall procure that the relevant Assignor shall sell the Leasehold Premises with full title guarantee and the Purchaser shall purchase the Leasehold Premises.

3.2   The assurance of each of the Leasehold Premises shall be in duplicate and executed by the Purchaser as well as by the Vendor or the relevant Assignor and the Purchaser shall at the Vendor's expense arrange for the duplicate assurance of each of the Leasehold Premises to be stamped and denoted against the original and after stamping and denoting shall return the same to the Vendor's solicitors as soon as reasonably practicable.

3.3   The Purchaser shall in the assurance of each of the Leasehold Premises covenant with the relevant Assignor as follows:

(A)   (by way of indemnity only) that the Purchaser and its successors in title will thenceforth perform and observe:

(1)   all the obligations of the lessee under the relevant Lease or relevant Leases;

(2)   (where appropriate) the obligations of the owner of the relevant Leasehold Premises or otherwise binding on the relevant Assignor arising under the documents and matters referred to in the Property and Charges Registers of

the title or titles under which the Leasehold Premises are registered at HM Land Registry so far as the same are still subsisting and capable of being enforced; and

(3)   the obligations of the grantor or lessor under the Tenancies and the conditions contained in the Tenancies and binding the grantor or lessor;

(B)   fully and effectually to indemnify the relevant Assignor in respect of all such obligations and conditions referred to in Sub-Paragraph 3.3(A) and against all actions, claims, costs, demands, expenses, liabilities and losses arising in consequence of any breach thereof by the Purchaser.

3.4   The assurance of each of the Leasehold Premises shall contain declarations to the effect that:

(A)   the covenants implied on the part of the relevant Assignor by the Law of Property (Miscellaneous Provisions) Act 1994, s 4 shall be limited so that no such covenant shall extend to any breach of covenant or other provision in the relevant Lease or relevant Leases relating to the state or condition of the relevant Leasehold Premises and (where appropriate) the assurance shall contain a request by the parties thereto to the Chief Land Registrar to note such limitation in the registers of the relevant title(s);

(B)   the covenant implied on the part of the relevant Assignor by the Law of Property (Miscellaneous Provisions) Act 1994, s 3 shall be limited so that the relevant Assignor's liability shall not extend to:

(1)   any matters or categories of matters to which the disposition is expressly made subject; and

(2)   any charges, encumbrances and other third party rights created granted or imposed after the date of this Agreement (other than by the relevant Assignor).

4   Incorporation of National Conditions

4.1   The National Conditions of Sale (20th Edition) shall be deemed to be incorporated herein and apply separately in relation to each of the Leasehold Premises so far as the same are not varied by or inconsistent with the conditions herein contained and are applicable to a sale by private treaty save that National Conditions 1, 2, 3, 4, 5, 6, 7, 8, 10, 11(5), 11(6), 13(3), 15(2), 15(3), 15(4), 18(4), 19, 20, 21 and 22 shall not apply.

5   Completion

5.1   Either vacant possession (save for property belonging to suppliers of gas, water, electricity, telephone or other like services and landlord's fixtures and fittings) or a right of occupation under Paragraph 10 of this Part of this Schedule of each of the Leasehold Premises will be given on Completion subject in either case to any part of the Leasehold Premises subject to a Tenancy.

5.2   Completion of the assignment of each of the Leasehold Premises to the Purchaser shall take place on the relevant Premises Completion Date.

6   Reversioner's Licence

6.1   As soon as practicable after the date hereof the Vendor shall (where the Reversioner's Licence is required) make or procure to be made at the cost of the Vendor application to the relevant Reversioner for the Reversioner's Licence.

6.2   As soon as practicable after the date hereof the Purchaser shall supply to the Vendor such information and references regarding the financial position and suitability of the Purchaser as the Reversioner shall reasonably require and the Purchaser shall in such connection provide such further assistance as the Reversioner may reasonably require.

6.3   The Vendor and the Purchaser shall use their respective best endeavours to obtain the relevant Reversioner's Licence which obligations shall unless the parties otherwise agree include an application to the Court for a declaration that the Reversioner is unreasonably withholding or delaying consent (if such consent is not forthcoming within a reasonable period) provided that the Purchaser shall not be required to pay any premium as consideration for the Reversioner's Licence.

6.4   For the avoidance of doubt all costs of obtaining the Reversioner's Licence including (without prejudice to the generality of the foregoing) the Reversioner's solicitors', surveyors', and/or agents' fees costs and disbursements and administrative charges charged by the Reversioner and all costs incurred in connection with any such Court application shall be borne by the Vendor.

6.5   The Vendor or relevant Assignor in its application for the Reversioner's Licence shall be entitled on behalf of the Purchaser to offer to the Reversioner the direct covenant of the Purchaser to pay the rent reserved by and to perform and observe the covenants, obligations and conditions on the part of the lessee contained in the relevant Lease for the residue of the term granted by the relevant Lease (save and to the extent that the Purchaser is released by virtue of the Landlord and Tenant (Covenants) Act 1995).

6.6   The Purchaser shall when required by the Vendor enter into the covenant by deed with the relevant Reversioner referred to in Sub-Paragraph 6.5 in such form as may reasonably be required by that Reversioner.

6.7   If by a date [six months] from the date hereof the Reversioner's Licence has not been obtained then at the request of the Purchaser the Vendor or the relevant Assignor shall make an application to the appropriate Court for a declaration that the relevant Reversioner is unreasonably withholding or delaying consent and the Purchaser shall provide such assistance as may reasonably be required of it in respect of such application to the Court.

6.8   Any application to the Court under Sub-Paragraph 6.7 shall be made at the sole cost and expense of the Vendor.

[7   Grant of Underlease if Reversioner Refuses Consent to an Assignment[110]

7.1   If any Reversioner's Licence is refused and (where an application has been made to the Court pursuant to Sub-Paragraph 6.7) the Court declares that the Reversioner has not unreasonably withheld its consent or licence to the assignment of the relevant Lease to the Purchaser then the Purchaser may by notice in writing to the Vendor (an 'Underletting Notice') require the relevant Assignor to grant an underlease (the 'Underlease') of the relevant Leasehold Premises whereupon save as otherwise stated the provisions of this Part of this Schedule shall apply (*mutatis mutandis*) to the grant and acceptance of the Underlease as if references to assignments were references to underlettings and reference to 'the date hereof' in Sub-Paragraph 6.7 was deleted and substituted by 'the date of the Underletting Notice'.[111]

7.2   The Underlease shall be for a term equal to the unexpired residue of the term of the relevant Lease (less three days) as at the Premises Completion Date and shall contain the same provisions as those contained in the relevant Lease (*mutatis mutandis*) with such amendments as the Purchaser shall reasonably require and shall be at a rent equal to the rent reserved by the relevant Lease or (if higher and if so required by the terms of the relevant Lease) the open market rent.

7.3   If the Vendor and the Purchaser are unable to agree the terms of the Underlease within one month of the date of the Underletting Notice then the terms of the Underlease shall be determined by a sole solicitor with not less than ten years' relevant experience in the letting of property similar to the relevant Leasehold Premises acting as an expert and not as an arbitrator such solicitor to be agreed upon by the Vendor and the Purchaser and in default of agreement within ten days to be appointed by or on behalf of the President for the time being of the Law Society or his duly appointed deputy.

7.4   All costs and expenses in connection with the grant and acceptance of the Underlease including (without limitation) the costs and expenses incurred or suffered by the Reversioner including (without prejudice to the generality of the foregoing) the Reversioner's solicitors', surveyors' and/or agents' fees, costs and disbursements and administrative charges charged by the Reversioner shall be borne by the Vendor.

8   Purchaser may Require an Assignment in Breach of the Terms of Lease if Reversioner's Consent Refused[112]

8.1   The Purchaser may at any time after the date of this Agreement by written notice to the Vendor (an 'Assignment Notice') require the Vendor to assign or to procure that the relevant Assignor assigns the relevant Leasehold Premises to the Purchaser without the Reversioner's Licence being obtained.

8.2   Within ten working days of the date of the Assignment Notice the Vendor shall assign or procure the assignment by the relevant Assignor and the Purchaser shall take an assignment of the relevant Leasehold Premises.

8.3   The Purchaser shall in such assignment indemnify and keep the relevant Assignor indemnified against all outgoings, actions, claims, costs, demands, expenses and losses arising in respect of the relevant Leasehold Premises after the Transfer Date including (without limitation but subject to the provisions of Sub-Paragraph 10.2(D)) below all rents, rates, insurance premiums, service charge payments and other sums due from or payable by the lessee under the relevant Lease and all other outgoings and expenses relating to the relevant Leasehold Premises throughout the remainder of the term granted by the relevant Lease.

[9   Purchaser to Vacate Premises and Premises to Revert to Vendor if Reversioner's Consent Not Obtained

9.1   If either:

(A)   the licence or consent of the relevant Reversioner to the assignment [or the underletting] of any of the Leasehold Premises has not been granted within [six months] of the date hereof (subject to such longer period or periods as the Vendor and the Purchaser shall agree in writing); or

(B)   (if earlier) the court has either ordered the Purchaser to cease occupation of the relevant Leasehold Premises or declared that the refusal of consent by the relevant Reversioner to the assignment [or the underletting] of the relevant Leasehold Premises to the Purchaser is not unreasonable

then the Purchaser may by written notice to the Vendor (an 'Exclusion Notice') forthwith exclude such Leasehold Premises from the sale and purchase pursuant to this Agreement whereupon:

(1)   the Purchaser shall vacate the Leasehold Premises referred to in the Exclusion Notice as soon as reasonably practicable;

(2)   the Purchaser shall be released from its obligation to take an assignment of the Lease [or accept the grant of an Underlease] of the Leasehold Premises referred to in the Exclusion Notice and the Vendor shall cease to hold such Leasehold Premises on trust for the Purchaser and shall have no further obligation to seek or obtain the relevant Reversioner's Licence but in either case without prejudice to any antecedent breach of the terms and provisions hereof;

(3)   the Purchaser shall notwithstanding the exclusion of the Leasehold Premises referred to in the Exclusion Notice from the sale and purchase pursuant to this Agreement [retain the remainder of the [Business Assets now located at such Leasehold Premises and] [continue to employ any Employees employed thereat as at the date of the Exclusion Notice] [but shall as soon as reasonably practicable procure that all such Business Assets are removed from such Leasehold Premises];]

(4)   the Vendor shall within five days after the date on which the Purchaser vacates the Leasehold Premises referred to in the Exclusion Notice repay to the Purchaser a sum equal to the consideration attributable to such Leasehold Premises as set out in Part IIA of Schedule 3 together with interest on such sum calculated at the Interest Rate for the period commencing on the date of payment by the Purchaser and ending on the date of repayment pursuant to this Sub-Paragraph 9.1.]

10 Occupation of Leasehold Premises from the Transfer Date

10.1   The Purchaser shall be entitled on or after [Completion/the Transfer Date] to go into occupation of the Leasehold Premises (which expression shall be deemed to include each of them as appropriate) as licensee of the relevant Assignor.

10.2   The Purchaser (whether or not it goes into occupation) shall in any event be subject to the following provisions:

(A)   the Purchaser shall pay or otherwise indemnify the relevant Assignor against all outgoings and expenses relating to the Leasehold Premises with effect from or by reference to any period commencing on or after the Transfer Date (save for those yearly rents in respect of which a licence fee is payable pursuant to Sub-Paragraph 10.2(D));

(B)   the Purchaser shall be entitled to the income (if any) from the Leasehold Premises arising with effect from or by reference to any period commencing on or after the Transfer Date;

(C)   the Purchaser shall indemnify the relevant Assignor against all damages, proceedings, costs, expenses, actions, losses, claims, demands and liabilities (including third party risks) arising from the possession or occupation of the relevant Leasehold Premises by the Purchaser and in particular (but without limitation) will observe and perform all the covenants, conditions and obligations (other than the liability to pay rents under the Leases to which Sub-Paragraph 10.2(E) shall apply) owed to the Reversioner Provided that this Sub-Paragraph shall not apply to:

(1)   occupation of the relevant Leasehold Premises by the Purchaser in breach of the terms of the relevant Lease;

(2)   the erection or installation of any temporary fascia or other signs whether or not pursuant to any other obligations under this Agreement; and/or

(3)   the carrying on by the Purchaser of the relevant part of the Business currently carried on from the relevant Leasehold Premises

all of which breaches as between the parties hereto the Vendor and the relevant Assignor shall accept;

(D)   during such period as the Purchaser shall be entitled to occupy the relevant Lease-hold Premises the Purchaser shall pay to the Vendor a licence fee on demand at the same annual rate as the yearly rents from time to time payable under the relevant Lease but so that nothing herein contained shall be construed as creating a legal demise or any rights in any of the relevant Leasehold Premises greater than a licence; and

(E)   the Vendor shall pay to the Reversioner the rents due under the relevant Lease and all other monies due thereunder immediately the same shall become due.

10.3   If in pursuance of the requirement of the Reversioner or an order of the court made on the application of the Reversioner the Purchaser is required to cease occupation of any of the Leasehold Premises then the Purchaser shall as soon as reasonably practicable vacate the relevant Leasehold Premises so as to comply therewith.

10.4   The Vendor shall or shall procure that the relevant Assignor shall during the period commencing on the date of this Agreement and expiring on [the earlier of] the date of assignment to the Purchaser of the relevant Leasehold Premises [or the date of the grant to the Purchaser of an Underlease of the relevant Leasehold Premises pursuant to Paragraph 7] use all reasonable endeavours to enforce the covenants on the part of the lessor contained in the relevant Lease.

11 Forfeiture Proceedings

11.1   If any Reversioner shall take proceedings (other than those referred to in Sub-Paragraph 10.3) to forfeit any Lease then the Vendor shall take or procure to be taken such action (including applying for relief against forfeiture) as the Vendor may reasonably think fit or (if so requested by the Purchaser) as the Purchaser may reasonably require in order to preserve the relevant Lease (and the Purchaser shall give all such assistance as may reasonably be required of it) and the costs of any such action shall be borne by the Vendor if the breach complained of shall have commenced prior to Completion or shall be a breach of the type referred to in Sub-Paragraph 10.2(C) but otherwise by the Purchaser.

11.2   The Vendor will give or procure to be given written notice to the Purchaser within seven days of receipt of any such proceedings.

11.3   In the event that any Lease shall be forfeited and no relief against forfeiture is granted then the Purchaser shall vacate the relevant Leasehold Premises as soon as reasonably practicable whereupon the relevant Leasehold Premises shall be excluded from the sale and purchase pursuant to this Agreement without prejudice to any antecedent breach of the provisions hereof but so that subject thereto the parties' obligations in respect of the relevant Leasehold Premises shall cease and neither party shall be under any liability to make any further payments to the other nor reimburse any payments made.

[12 Rent Review under Leases

12.1   Where at the date of this Agreement or at any time prior to the Premises Completion Date applicable to any Leasehold Premises there shall remain outstanding under any Lease a rent review then:

(A)   the Vendor or the relevant Assignor will prior to the relevant Premises Completion Date:

(1) use its best endeavours to agree or procure to have agreed or procure to have determined under the rent review provisions of the relevant Lease a reviewed rent which is as low a rent as is reasonably achievable;

(2) keep the Purchaser fully informed of all material matters relating to such review;

(3) procure that all reasonable representations made by the Purchaser in respect of such review are promptly passed on to the relevant Reversioner; and

(4) not agree and shall procure that there shall not be agreed by negotiation any rent review without the prior consent of the Purchaser (such consent not to be unreasonably withheld or delayed where such revised rent has been assessed strictly in accordance with the provisions of the relevant Lease);

(B) the Vendor or the relevant Assignor shall be entitled with the consent of the Purchaser (which consent shall not be unreasonably withheld or delayed where such referral is strictly in accordance with the terms of the relevant Lease) to refer or procure to be referred any such rent review to a third party for determination;

(C) forthwith on the settlement or determination of the relevant rent review the Vendor shall notify the Purchaser of the amount of the reviewed rent and provide a certified copy of any relevant rent review memorandum or determination;

(D) if any such settlement or determination shall take place prior to the relevant Premises Completion Date the Purchaser shall account to the Vendor by way of a licence fee under Sub-Paragraph 10.2(D) for an amount equal to the difference between the rent previously payable and the revised rent (if any) agreed or determined pursuant to the relevant rent review in respect of the period commencing on the later of either the relevant review date and the Transfer Date and ending on the date on which such difference shall be payable pursuant to the relevant Lease;

(E) if any such settlement or determination shall take place after the relevant Premises Completion Date the Vendor shall forthwith after demand by the Purchaser accompanied by evidence of the amount of the reviewed rent and a copy of any relevant rent review memorandum or determination pay to the Purchaser such amount as shall be equal to the difference between the rent previously payable and the revised rent (if any) determined pursuant to the relevant rent review together with interest thereon (if applicable) in respect of the period commencing on the relevant review date and ending on the Transfer Date.]

[13 Rent Review and Renewal of Tenancies[108]

13.1 This Paragraph shall apply in relation to any of the Tenancies:

(A) in respect of which the lessor was entitled to a review of the yearly or other fixed rent with effect from a date (a 'Review Date') prior to or being the relevant Premises Completion Date; or

(B) which is subject to proposed renewal (whether or not pursuant to the Landlord and Tenant Act 1954) or to payment of (or any application for an order as to) an interim rent pursuant to the Landlord and Tenant Act 1954 and the contractual term has expired prior to the relevant Premises Completion Date

but (in any such case) where the amount of rent payable from any date (a 'Relevant Date') relevant to this Paragraph (including under any renewal of any Tenancy) has not been determined as at the relevant Premises Completion Date.

13.2 The Purchaser shall use its reasonable endeavours to conclude the rent reviews and renewals and to obtain the interim rent orders (if any) to which this Paragraph applies as soon as reasonably practicable after the relevant Premises Completion Date. The Purchaser shall not without the consent of the Vendor (such consent not to be unreasonably withheld or delayed) be entitled to conclude any such matters on any basis other than:

(A)   (in the case of a review) in accordance with the rent review provisions of the relevant Tenancy; and

(B)   (in the case of a renewal or interim rent) in accordance with the provisions of the Landlord and Tenant Act 1954.

13.3   As soon as reasonably practicable after the determination or agreement of any such matter as aforesaid the Purchaser shall give written notice thereof to the Vendor and pending such determination or agreement the Purchaser shall on the request and at the cost of the Vendor keep the Vendor informed as to progress therein and the state of negotiations or proceedings.

13.4   Paragraph 14 shall apply to all rent and interest received or receivable by the Vendor or the relevant Assignor or the Purchaser in respect of any such matters as aforesaid.]

[14 Income from Leasehold Premises[109]

14.1   Rents received by the Vendor or the relevant Assignor from tenants or occupiers of each of the Leasehold Premises in advance and which relate to any period following the Transfer Date shall be apportioned as at the Transfer Date on an equal daily basis over the relevant year based on the amounts then payable under the relevant Tenancy.

14.2   Rents under any Tenancies which have fallen due for payment to the Vendor or the relevant Assignor on or before Completion but which shall not have actually been received by the Vendor or the relevant Assignor shall be apportioned as between the Vendor and the Purchaser as and when the same are actually received by the Purchaser (or the Vendor or the relevant Assignor as the case may be) after Completion.

14.3   The Purchaser shall within 14 days of receipt pay to the Vendor any arrears of rent or other sums received from any tenant in respect of any period prior to the Transfer Date arrears being duly apportioned under Sub-Paragraph 14.1 where appropriate.

14.4   The Vendor will within 14 days of receipt pay to the Purchaser any arrears of rent or other sums received from any tenant by the Vendor or the relevant Assignor in respect of any period after the Transfer Date and which shall have been paid to the Vendor or the relevant Assignor such arrears being duly apportioned under Sub-Paragraph 14.1 where appropriate.

14.5   The Purchaser shall on the request and at the cost of the Vendor at any time after the Transfer Date assign such rights as may be necessary to enable the Vendor or the relevant Assignor to recover any arrears of rent or other sums payable under the Tenancy for any period prior to Completion and the Purchaser shall at the Vendor's cost execute a deed or deeds of assignment thereof in such terms as the Purchaser shall approve.]

[15 Management of the Leasehold Premises

15.1   The Vendor shall procure the continuance of the management of each of the Leasehold Premises in accordance with the principles of good estate management until Completion but no lease, underlease, tenancy or occupational licence of all or any part of any Leasehold Premises shall be granted, surrendered or agreed to be granted or surrendered by the relevant Assignor nor shall the terms thereof be varied or agreed to be varied, nor shall any licence or consent be granted thereunder until Completion except:

(A)   with the prior written consent of the Purchaser (which the Purchaser agrees shall not be unreasonably withheld or delayed in the case of any matter to which the consent of the relevant Assignor is required as lessor or grantor of any of the Tenancies where such consent is not to be unreasonably withheld or delayed); or

(B) in pursuance of:

(1) any legally enforceable agreement subsisting at the date hereof; or

(2) any application made on or before the date hereof for the lessor's or grantor's consent to any act, matter or thing under the terms of any of the Tenancies and to which the consent of the relevant Assignor is not to be unreasonably withheld under the relevant Tenancy

the existence of which agreement or application has (in either case) been disclosed in writing to the Purchaser's solicitors on or before the date hereof including the renewal of any tenancy on terms settled on or before the date hereof.

15.2   Until Completion the Vendor or the relevant Assignor (as the case may be) shall upon the request of the Purchaser provide the Purchaser with such information as the Purchaser reasonably requires as to matters relating to the then current management of each of the Leasehold Premises.]

16 Surety Covenants

16.1   On Completion the Vendor will if required by the Purchaser by separate deed (to be prepared by the Purchaser's solicitors in a form previously approved by the Vendor's solicitors) assign or procure that the relevant Assignor assigns to the Purchaser so far as the same remain in force and effect the benefit of the covenants relating to the Tenancies entered into with the Vendor or the relevant Assignor by any sureties to or guarantors or assignees of any of the Tenancies.

17 No Merger

17.1   The terms of this Part of this Schedule (or any part thereof) shall not merge on completion of any assignment or grant and shall continue in full force and effect to the extent that anything remains to be performed and observed hereunder.

18 Miscellaneous

18.1   In the event of any conflict between the provisions of this Part of this Schedule and the other provisions of this Agreement the provisions of this Part of this Schedule shall prevail.

PART III

Terms Applicable to the New Leasehold Premises[113]

1   Interpretation

1.1   In this Part III of this Schedule, where the context admits:

'Lease' means in respect of each of the New Leasehold Premises the lease or underlease, if any, under which the relevant Grantor holds such premises details of which are set out in Part III of Schedule 3 and shall include any document supplemental thereto and 'Leases' and 'Relevant Lease' and 'Relevant Leases' shall be construed accordingly;

'Lease Completion Date' means:

(1) in relation to each of the New Leasehold Premises to which Sub-Paragraph 3.2 does not apply, Completion; and

(2)   in relation to each of the New Leasehold Premises to which Sub-Paragraph 3.2 applies, the later of (a) Completion or (b) ten working days after notice is given to the Purchaser's solicitors of the grant of the Reversioner's Licence and/or the Order as the case may be;

'New Lease' means the lease or underlease of each of the New Leasehold Premises to be granted to the Purchaser in the form of the draft in agreed terms annexed hereto and 'New Leases' and 'Relevant New Lease' and 'Relevant New Leases' shall be construed accordingly;

'Order' means an order of a court of competent jurisdiction authorising the inclusion in the New Lease of a provision excluding the operation of the Landlord and Tenant Act 1954 (as amended) ss 24–28 (inclusive) in relation to the tenancy to be granted by the New Lease;

'Relevant Grantor' means the party so named in Part III of Schedule 3 and in whom a Lease is vested at the date hereof and 'Relevant Grantors' shall be construed accordingly;

'Reversioner' means in respect of those of the New Leasehold Premises to which Sub-Paragraph 3.2(A) applies (and each of them respectively) the immediate landlord and/or any superior landlord of the relevant Grantor whose licence is required to the grant of the relevant New Lease;

'Reversioner's Licence' means any necessary licence required from the relevant Reversioner to the grant of the relevant New Lease to the Purchaser.

1.2   References in this Part of this Schedule to Paragraphs and Sub-Paragraphs shall unless the context requires otherwise be to those in this Part of this Schedule.

1.3   References to any Act of Parliament include references to any statutory modification or re-enactment thereof for the time being in force and any order, instrument, regulation or bye-law made or issued thereunder.

2   Title and Matters Affecting the New Leasehold Premises

2.1   Each of the New Leasehold Premises are let subject to such of the following matters as relate to them:

(A)   the rents to be reserved by and the lessee's covenants and conditions and the exceptions and reservations and other matters to be contained in or arising in respect of the relevant New Lease or subject to which the relevant New Lease is to be granted;

(B)   all matters in the nature of easements, rights, exceptions, reservations, restrictions, covenants and conditions;

(C)   in relation to the New Leasehold Premises title to which is registered at HM Land Registry:

(1)   entry numbers [   ] in the Property Register and entry numbers
[   ] in the Charges Register of title number [   ] as at the
[   ] 19[   ] (being the date of office copy entries supplied to the
Purchaser's solicitors [other than [entry numbers [   ]];

[repeat for each registered title]

in each case so far as the same are now subsisting, binding on the New Leasehold Premises and capable of taking effect.

2.2   The [originals or copies of the Leases [and copies of such Property and Charges registers] having been supplied to or made available for inspection by the Purchaser or the Purchaser's Solicitors,] [title to each of the New Leasehold Premises having been deduced to the Purchaser prior to the date hereof the Purchaser shall accept the same and] the Purchaser shall be deemed to purchase with full knowledge thereof and shall not raise any enquiry requisition or objection in relation thereto.

2.3   The Purchaser shall not be entitled to make any enquiry, requisition or objection with regard to any document not now in the Vendor's possession nor shall the Purchaser require the Vendor to obtain an examined or certified copy of any such document.

2.4   The Purchaser shall be deemed to have full notice of the current use of each of the New Leasehold Premises as shown in Schedule 3 and shall not be entitled to request any information or to raise any objection or requisition with regard thereto.

2.5   The Purchaser shall raise no enquiry, requisition or objection founded on the fact (if such be the case) that the Leases or any of them is found to be an underlease.

3   Grant and Acceptance

3.1   The Vendor shall grant or shall procure the relevant Grantor[s] to grant the New Lease[s] and the Purchaser shall accept and execute the counterpart of the New Lease[s] on the Lease Completion Date.

3.2   The obligations of the Vendor, the relevant Grantor[s] and the Purchaser to complete the grant and acceptance of the New Lease[s] are conditional:

(A)   in the case of the New Leasehold Premises numbered [   ] in Part III of Schedule 3 on the obtaining of the Reversioner's Licence; and/or

(B)   in the case of the New Leasehold Premises numbered [   ] in Part III of Schedule 3 on the obtaining of the Order.

4   Incorporation of National Conditions

4.1   The National Conditions of Sale (20th Edition) shall be deemed to be incorporated herein and apply separately in relation to each of the New Leasehold Premises so far as the same are not varied by or inconsistent with the conditions herein contained and are applicable to a sale by private treaty save that National Conditions 1, 2, 3, 4, 5, 6, 7, 8, 10, 11(5), 11(6), 13(3), 15(2), 15(3), 15(4), 18(4), 19, 20, 21 and 22 shall not apply.

5   Completion

5.1   Either vacant possession (save for property belonging to suppliers of gas, water, electricity, telephone or other like services and landlord's fixtures and fittings) or a right of occupation under Paragraph 8 of each of the New Leasehold Premises will be given on the Transfer Date.

5.2   Completion of the grant of each of the New Leases to the Purchaser shall take place on the relevant Lease Completion Date.

6   No Merger

6.1   The terms of this Part III of this Schedule (or any part thereof) shall not merge on completion of the grant of any New Lease and shall continue in full force and effect to the extent that anything remains to be performed and observed hereunder.

7   Reversioner's Licence and Order

7.1   As soon as practicable after the date hereof the Vendor shall (where the Reversioner's Licence is required) make or procure to be made at the cost of the Vendor application to the relevant Reversioner for the Reversioner's Licence.

7.2   As soon as practicable after the date hereof the Purchaser shall supply to the Vendor such information and references regarding the financial position and suitability of the Purchaser as the Reversioner shall reasonably require and the Purchaser shall in such connection provide such further assistance as the Reversioner may reasonably require.

7.3   The Vendor and the Purchaser shall use their respective best endeavours to obtain the relevant Reversioner's Licence which obligations shall unless the parties otherwise agree include an application to the Court for a declaration that the Reversioner is unreasonably withholding or delaying consent (if such consent is not forthcoming within a reasonable period) Provided that the Purchaser shall not be required to pay any premium as consideration for the Reversioner's Licence or provide or procure the provision of any collateral security for the performance of the lessee's covenants in the relevant New Lease or the relevant Lease or otherwise incur any expenditure or liability to secure the grant of the Reversioner's Licence.

7.4   For the avoidance of doubt all costs of obtaining the Reversioner's Licence including (without prejudice to the generality of the foregoing) the Reversioner's solicitors', surveyors', and/or agents' fees costs and disbursements and administrative charges charged by the Reversioner and all costs incurred in connection with any such Court application shall be borne by the Vendor.

7.5   The Vendor or the relevant Grantor in its application for the Reversioner's Licence shall be entitled on behalf of the Purchaser to offer to the Reversioner the direct covenant of the Purchaser to perform and observe the covenants, obligations and conditions on the part of the lessee contained in the relevant Lease (other than the covenant to pay rent) and further to pay the rents reserved by and perform and observe the covenants and conditions on the part of the lessee contained in the relevant New Lease in each case for the residue of the term granted by the relevant New Lease (save and to the extent that the Purchaser is released by virtue of the Landlord and Tenant (Covenants) Act 1995).

7.6   The Purchaser shall when required by the Vendor enter into the covenant by deed with the relevant Reversioner referred to in Sub-Paragraph 7.5 in such form as may reasonably be required by that Reversioner.

7.7   If by a date [six months] from the date hereof the Reversioner's Licence has not been obtained then at the request of the Purchaser the Vendor or the relevant Grantor shall make an application to the appropriate Court for a declaration that the relevant Reversioner is unreasonably withholding or delaying consent and the Purchaser shall provide such assistance as may reasonably be required of it in respect of such application to the Court.

7.8   Any application to the Court under Sub-Paragraph 7.7 shall be made at the sole cost and expense of the Vendor.

[7.9   As soon as practicable after the date hereof the Vendor or the relevant Grantor and the Purchaser shall jointly apply to the [Mayor's and City of London Court] for the Order such application to be in the form to be prepared by the Vendor's solicitors and agreed by the Purchaser's solicitors (each acting reasonably) and the Vendor or the relevant Grantor and the Purchaser hereby irrevocably agree that the said Court shall have jurisdiction in relation to such application notwithstanding the location and the rateable value of the relevant New Leasehold Premises and neither the Vendor, the relevant Grantor nor the Purchaser shall make any application to the said Court to withdraw such application without the consent of the other(s).]

7.10   If the relevant Reversioner's Licence and/or the Order in respect of any of the relevant New Leasehold Premises have not been obtained within [six months] of the date hereof or (if earlier) if the Court has declared that the refusal of consent by the Reversioner to the underletting of the relevant New Leasehold Premises to the Purchaser is reasonable then the Purchaser may at any time thereafter by written notice to the Vendor (a 'Termination Notice') require the following provisions to have effect:

(A) the Purchaser shall vacate the relevant New Leasehold Premises as soon as reasonably practicable after the date of the Termination Notice;

(B) the Vendor shall be released from its obligations to grant or procure the grant of the relevant New Lease to the Purchaser and the Purchaser shall be released from its obligation to take the relevant New Lease;

(C) the Purchaser shall retain the remainder of the Business Assets now located at the relevant New Leasehold Premises and continue to employ any Employees employed thereat as at the date of the Termination Notice but shall as soon as reasonably practicable after the date of the Termination Notice procure that all such Business Assets are removed from such New Leasehold Premises.

8 Occupation of New Leasehold Premises from Completion

8.1   The Purchaser shall be entitled on or after [Completion/ the Transfer Date] to go into occupation of each of the New Leasehold Premises as licensee of the relevant Grantor.

8.2   Whether or not the Purchaser goes into occupation on or after [Completion/ the Transfer Date] the Purchaser shall:

(A) pay to the Vendor by way of mesne profits payments equal to the rents reserved by and other sums due under each of the New Leases;

(B) observe and perform all the covenants (other than the payment of rent) on the part of the lessee and the conditions contained in each of the New Leases as if the same had been granted on (and for a term commencing on) the Transfer Date provided that until the actual completion of the New Leases the Purchaser shall not be entitled to exclusive possession of the New Leasehold Premises and it is hereby expressly declared that nothing herein contained or arising in consequence hereof or the payment of such mesne profits shall create or be deemed to create any demise or be deemed to give any interest greater than that of a licensee; and

(C) indemnify the relevant Grantor against all damages, proceedings, costs, expenses, actions, losses, claims, demands and liabilities (including third party risks) arising from the possession or occupation of the New Leasehold Premises by the Purchaser Provided that this Sub-Paragraph shall not apply to:

    (1) occupation of the relevant New Leasehold Premises by the Purchaser in breach of the terms of the relevant Lease;

    (2) the erection or installation of any temporary fascia or other signs whether or not pursuant to any other obligations under this Agreement; and/or

    (3) the carrying on by the Purchaser of the relevant part of the Business currently carried on from the relevant New Leasehold Premises

all of which breaches as between the parties hereto the Vendor and the relevant Grantor shall accept.

8.3   If in pursuance of the requirement of the Reversioner or an order of the Court made on the application of the Reversioner the Purchaser is required to cease occupation of any of the New Leasehold Premises then the Purchaser shall vacate the relevant New Leasehold Premises as soon as reasonably practicable so as to comply therewith.

9 Forfeiture Proceedings

9.1   If at any time before the completion of any New Lease the relevant Lease shall be forfeited and no relief against forfeiture is granted then the Purchaser shall as soon as reasonably practicable vacate the relevant New Leasehold Premises whereupon the relevant New Leasehold Premises shall be excluded from the sale and purchase pursuant to this Agreement but without prejudice to any antecedent breach of the provisions hereof.

10 Miscellaneous

10.1   In the event of any conflict between the provisions of this Part of this Schedule and the other provisions of this Agreement the provisions of this Part of this Schedule shall prevail.

PART IV

Property Warranties and Representations

1   Interpretation

1.1   In this Part IV of this Schedule, the 'Proprietor' means the relevant Owner (in the case of each of the Freehold Premises); the relevant Assignor (in the case of each of the Leasehold Premises); the relevant Grantor (in the case of each of the New Leasehold Premises); and the terms 'relevant Owner', 'relevant Assignor' and 'relevant Grantor' shall have the meanings respectively given to them in Parts I, II and III of this Schedule.

2   Warranties and Representations[117]

The Vendor hereby warrants and represents[117] to and for the benefit of the Purchaser in the following terms.

2.1   Title to the Premises

(A)   The particulars of the Premises shown in Schedule 3 are true and correct.
(B)   The Proprietor is solely legally and beneficially entitled to and has good and marketable title to and exclusive occupation of the relevant Premises.
(C)   Each of the Premises is held free from any mortgage or charge (whether legal or equitable, fixed or floating), encumbrance, sub-lease, tenancy, licence or right of occupation, rent charge, exception, reservation, easement, quasi-easement or privilege (or agreement for any of the same).
(D)   The lease, sub-lease, tenancy or agreement for any of the same under which any of the Premises are held by the Proprietor is valid and subsisting against all persons, including any person in whom any superior estate or interest is vested.
(E)   There are appurtenant to each of the Premises all rights and easements necessary for its current use and enjoyment (without restriction as to time or otherwise) and the access for each of the Premises is over roads adopted by the local authority and maintained at public expense.

2.2   Matters Affecting the Premises

(A)   None of the Premises or any part thereof is affected by any of the following matters or is to the knowledge of the Vendor or the Proprietor likely to become so affected:
    (1)   any outstanding dispute, notice or complaint or any exception, reservation, right, covenant, restriction or condition which is of an unusual nature or which affects or might in the future affect the use of any of the Premises for

the purpose or purposes for which it is now used (the 'Current Use') or which affects or might in the future affect the value of the Premises; or

(2)   any notice, order, demand, requirement or proposal of which the the the Vendor or the Proprietor is aware made or issued by or on behalf of any government or statutory authority, department or body for acquisition, clearance, demolition or closing, the carrying out of any work upon any building, the modification of any planning permission, the discontinuance of any use or the imposition of any building or improvement line, the alteration of any road or footpath or which otherwise affects any of the Premises or their current use or value; or

(3)   any compensation received as a result of any refusal of any application for planning consent or the imposition of any restrictions in relation to any planning consent; or

(4)   any commutation or agreement for the commutation of rent or payment of rent in advance of the due date of payment thereof; or

(5)   any outstanding claim or liability (contingent or otherwise) whether under the Planning Acts (as that expression is defined in the Town and Country Planning Act 1990) or otherwise; or

(6)   any outgoings except uniform business rates and water rates; or

(7)   the requirement of consent from any third party to the charging of the Premises or any of them.

(B)   Each of the Premises is in a good state of repair and condition and fit for the current use and no deleterious material (including, without limit, high alumina cement, woodwool, calcium chloride, sea-dredged aggregates or asbestos material) was used in the construction, alteration or repair thereof or of any of them and there are no development works, redevelopment works or fitting out works outstanding in respect of any of the Premises.

(C)   All restrictions, conditions and covenants (including any imposed by or pursuant to any lease, sub-lease, tenancy or agreement for any of the same and whether the Proprietor is the landlord or the tenant thereunder and any arising in relation to any superior title) affecting any of the Premises have been observed and performed and no notice of any breach of any of the same has been received or is to the knowledge of the Vendor or the Proprietor likely to be received.

(D)   The current use of the Premises and all machinery and equipment therein and the conduct of any business therein complies in all respects with all relevant statutes and regulations including without prejudice to the generality of the foregoing the Factories Act 1961, the Offices Shops and Railway Premises Act 1963, the Fire Precautions Act 1971, the Health and Safety at Work etc, Act 1974 and with all rules regulations and delegated legislation thereunder and all necessary licences and consents required thereunder have been obtained.

(E)   There are no restrictive covenants or provisions, legislation or orders, charges, restrictions, agreements, conditions or other matters which preclude or limit the current use of any of the Premises and the current user is the permitted user under the provisions of the Planning Acts (as that expression is defined in the Town and Country Planning Act 1990) (including without limit Town and Country Planning Act 1971, s 52; Town and Country Planning Act 1990, s 106 or Highways Act 1980, s 278) and regulations made thereunder and is in accordance with the requirements of the Local Authorities and all restrictions, conditions and covenants imposed by or pursuant to the Planning Acts have been observed and performed and no agreements have been entered into with any public authority or statutory authority in respect of the Premises whether pursuant to the Planning Acts or otherwise.

(F)   All necessary planning permissions, listed building consents, bye-law consents, building regulation consents and other permissions and approvals (whether or not required by Statute) for the construction, extension and alteration of the Premises have been obtained and complied with, and none of those permissions, consents and approvals has been given on a personal or temporary basis nor does it require the removal at any time of the works so authorised.

(G)   Any necessary action to protect the interests of the Proprietor has been taken under the Landlord and Tenant Act 1954 and in relation to rent review provisions in relation to any lease, sub-lease, tenancy or agreement for any of the same and whether the Proprietor is the landlord or the tenant thereunder and all appropriate time limits have been complied with and no rent reviews are outstanding at the date hereof or exercisable prior to the Transfer Date.

(H)   In relation to any lease, sub-lease, tenancy or agreement for any of the same under which the Proprietor is the landlord:

(1)   the rents collected by the Proprietor have not exceeded the sums lawfully recoverable;

(2)   no forfeiture proceedings have been taken or are contemplated;

(3)   no notice has been served by the Proprietor which is still outstanding;

(4)   no works have been carried out which could give rise to a claim against the Proprietor for compensation or which would have to be disregarded on any rent review;

(5)   all consents and conditions contained therein have been observed and performed to date; and

(6)   brief details of such leases, sub-leases, tenancies or agreements for any of the same are set out in Parts IB and IIB of Schedule 3 and such details are true and correct.

(I)   None of the Premises is used for any purpose other than the [current use specified in respect of each of the Premises in Parts IA, IIA, and III of Schedule 3].

(J)   Where the interest of the Proprietor in any of the Premises is leasehold, there is no right for the landlord to determine the lease except in the event of non-payment of rent or other breach of covenant by the tenant.

(K)   All replies by or on behalf of the Vendor or the Proprietor to enquiries relating to any of the Premises made by or on behalf of the Purchaser were when given and are now true and correct.

SCHEDULE 6

WARRANTIES AND REPRESENTATIONS[114]

1 Interpretation

In this Schedule, where the context admits:

'Operator of the Business' or 'Operator' means any person carrying on the Business at the date hereof and includes the Vendor and any member of the Vendor's Group and, after the Transfer Date, means the Purchaser;[115]

'Computer Systems' means the Hardware, Software and Data;

'Data' means any data or information used by or for the benefit of the Business at any time and stored electronically at any time;

'Hardware' means any computer equipment used by or for the benefit of the Business at any time including, without limitation, PCs, mainframes, screens, terminals, keyboards, disks, printers, cabling, associated and peripheral electronic equipment but excluding all Software;

'Software' means any set of instructions for execution by microprocessor used by or for the benefit of the Business irrespective of application, language or medium;

any question whether a person is connected with another shall be determined in accordance with Income and Corporation Taxes Act 1988, s 839 (subject to the deletion of the words from 'Except' to 'arrangements' in subs (4) thereof) which shall apply in relation to this schedule as it applies in relation to that Act;[116]

[reference to any Act, statutory instrument, regulation, bye-law or other requirement of English law and to any English legal term for any action, remedy, method of judicial proceeding, legal document, legal status, court, official or any legal concept or thing shall in respect of any jurisdiction other than England be deemed to include that which most nearly approximates in that jurisdiction to the English legal term;] and

where, in this Schedule, a term is defined in and for the purposes of a particular Paragraph or Sub-Paragraph, the relevant definition shall apply, where the context admits, for all other purposes of this Schedule.

2 Warranties and Representations[117]

The Vendor hereby warrants and represents[117] to and for the benefit of the Purchaser in the following terms:

2.1 The Vendor and the Vendor's Group

(A) *Capacity*   The Vendor has full power and authority to enter into and perform this Agreement and has full power and authority to carry on the Business as it is now being carried on and to sell the Business and the Business Assets (and each of them) to the Purchaser on the terms of this Agreement and may execute and deliver this Agreement and perform its obligations under this Agreement without in any such case requiring or obtaining the consent of its shareholders any other person, authority or body and this Agreement constitutes valid and binding obligations on the Vendor in accordance with its terms.

(B) *Competing interests*   Neither the Vendor nor any other member of the Vendor's Group nor any person connected with such member has any interest, direct or indirect in any company or business (other than the Business) which is or is likely to be or become competitive with the Business, [save as the registered holder or beneficial owner of not more than 5 per cent of any class of securities of any company which is listed in the Official List of The London Stock Exchange Limited or dealt in on the Alternative Investment Market].

(C) *Branches and Associations*   No part of the Business has ever been conducted through a branch, agency or permanent establishment (as that expression is defined in the relevant double taxation relief orders current at the date of this Agreement) outside the United Kingdom. The Vendor is not, and has not agreed to become, in relation to the Business, a member of any partnership, joint venture, consortium or other unincorporated association, body or undertaking in which it is to participate with any other in any business or investment.

2.2   Licences, Litigation and the Law

(A) *Compliance with Laws*[118]   The Business has been conducted in all material respects in accordance with all applicable laws and regulations of the United Kingdom and any other relevant foreign country or authority and there is no order, decree or judgment of any court or any governmental or other competent authority or agency of the United Kingdom or any other relevant foreign country outstanding against the Business or the Vendor which may have a material adverse effect upon the Business or the Business Assets.

(B) *Licences etc*

   (1)   All licences, consents, permits, approvals and authorisations (public and private) necessary and/or desirable for utilising any of the Business Assets in the Business or carrying on effectively any aspect of the Business or any business now being carried on at any of the Premises [(other than landlords' or superior landlords' licences, consents, permits, approvals or authorisations in connection with the Premises details of which are specified in the Disclosure Letter)] have been obtained by the Vendor, are in full force and effect and are not limited in duration or subject to onerous conditions.

   (2)   All reports, returns and information required by law or as a condition of any licence, consent, permission, approval or other authorisation to be made or given to any person or authority in connection with the Business have been made or given to the appropriate person or authority.

   (3)   The utilisation of any of the Business Assets or the carrying on of any aspect of the Business or any business now being carried on at any of the Premises is not in breach of any of the terms and conditions of any of such licences, consents, permits, approvals and authorisations and so far as the Vendor is aware there is no circumstance which indicates that any such licence, consent, permit, approval or authorisation is likely to be suspended, cancelled or revoked or why any of them should expire within a period of [one] year from the date of this Agreement.

   (4)   [Full particulars of all licences, consents, permits, approvals and authorisations which are referred to in Sub-Paragraph (1) are referred to in the Disclosure Letter and] the Vendor is not aware of any reason why such licences, consents, permits, approvals or authorisations [(other than landlords' or superior landlords' licences, consents, permits or approvals in connection with the Premises)] should not be capable of being transferred to or, as the case may be, obtained by, or on behalf of, the Purchaser without the necessity of any special arrangement or expense.

   (5)   At and after Completion there will be no restriction on the right of the Purchaser to carry on the Business which is not now applicable to the Vendor.

(C) *Breach of statutory provisions*   Neither the Vendor, nor any of its officers, agents or employees (during the course of their duties in relation to the Business) have committed, or omitted to do, any act or thing the commission or omission of which is, or could be, in contravention of any Act, Order, Regulation, or the like in the United Kingdom or elsewhere which is punishable by fine or other penalty and no notice in respect thereof has been received.

(D) *Litigation*

    (1)   Neither the Business nor the Vendor nor any of its officers or agents nor any of the employees of the Business is engaged in or the subject of any litigation, arbitration, administrative or criminal proceedings, whether as plaintiff, defendant or otherwise, [which adversely affects or is likely to have an adverse effect on the Business and/or the Business Assets and/or the ability of the Vendor or any purchaser to carry on the Business in the same manner and to the same extent as previously carried on].

    (2)   No such litigation or arbitration, administrative or criminal proceedings are pending, threatened or expected by or against the Business or the Vendor or any such officers, agents or employees, and so far as the Vendor is aware, there are no facts or circumstances likely to give rise to any such litigation or arbitration or administrative or criminal proceedings.

    (3)   Neither the Business nor the Vendor nor any other member of the Vendor's Group (or any officer or employee of any of them) nor so far as the Vendor is aware any predecessor of the Vendor has or have been a party to any undertaking or assurance given to any court or governmental agency or the subject of any injunction relating to the Business and/or the Business Assets which is still in force.

(E) *Fair Trading*

    (1)   No agreement practice or arrangement carried on by the Vendor or any Affiliate in connection with or in relation to the Business or to which the Vendor is a party (including, but not limited to, any Contract):

        (a)   is or ought to have been registered in accordance with the provisions of the Restrictive Trade Practices Acts 1976 and 1977 or contravenes the provisions of the Resale Prices Act 1976 or is or has been the subject of any enquiry, complaint, investigation or proceeding under any of those Acts; or

        (b)   is or has been the subject of an enquiry, complaint, investigation, reference or report under the Fair Trading Act 1973 (or any previous legislation relating to monopolies or mergers) or the Competition Act 1980 or constitutes an anti-competitive practice within the meaning of the 1980 Act; or

        (c)   infringes Art 85 of the Treaty of Rome establishing the European Economic Community or constitutes an abuse of a dominant position contrary to Art 86 of that Treaty or infringes any regulation or other enactment made under Art 87 and/or Art 235 of that Treaty or is or has been the subject of any enquiry, complaint, investigation or proceeding in respect thereof; or

        (d)   has been notified to the Directorate General for Competition of the European Commission and/or to the EFTA Surveillance Authority; or

        (e)   is by virtue of its terms or by virtue of any practice for the time being carried on in connection with it a 'Consumer Trade Practice' within the meaning of s 13 of the Fair Trading Act 1973 and susceptible to or under reference to the Consumer Protection Advisory Committee or the subject matter of a report to or an order of the Secretary of State, in the latter case under the provisions of Part II of that Act; or

        (f)   infringes any other competition, restrictive trade practice, anti-trust, fair trading or consumer protection law or legislation applicable in any jurisdiction in which the Business is carried on or in which the activities of the Business may have an effect.

(2)   In relation to the Business, the Vendor has not given and is not in default or contravention of any assurance or undertaking (written or oral) to the Restrictive Practices Court, the Director General of Fair Trading, the Secretary of State for Trade and Industry, the European Commission, the EFTA Surveillance Authority or the Courts of Justice of the European Communities or to any other court, person or body and is not subject to or in default or contravention of any Article, Act, decision, regulation, order or other instrument or undertaking relating to any matter referred to in this Sub-Paragraph 2.2(E).

(3)   (a)   None of the activities of the Vendor as currently conducted could give rise to the imposition of any anti-dumping duty or other sanction under any trade regulation legislation in respect of any products manufactured by the Business or in which the Business trades.

(b)   No anti-dumping duty or other sanction under any trade regulation legislation is or has been in force in any area in which the Business is carried on or intended to be carried on in respect of products manufactured by the Business or in which the Business trades.

(c)   No undertaking has been given by the Vendor to any governmental authority under any anti-dumping or other trade regulation legislation.

(4)   (a)   In relation to the Business, the Vendor is not and has not been in receipt of any aid which could be construed as falling within Art 92(1) of the Treaty of Rome other than:

(i)   aid in operation at the date of UK Accession to the Community which is treated as existing aid pursuant to Art 93(1); or

(ii)   aid or any alteration to existing aid falling within Art 92(3) which has been duly notified to the European Commission pursuant to Art 93(3) and approved by the European Commission.

(b)   The Vendor is not aware of any pending or threatened investigation, complaint, action or decision in relation to the receipt or alleged receipt by it of any aid or alleged aid.

(F)   *Product Liability*

(1)   There is no claim in respect of Product Liability (as hereinafter defined) outstanding or threatened against or expected by the Vendor in relation to the Business and so far as the Vendor is aware there are no circumstances which are likely to give rise to any such claim. For this purpose 'Product Liability' means a liability arising out of death, personal injury or damage to property caused by a defective product or defective services sold supplied or provided by the Vendor in relation to the Business on or prior to the date hereof.

(2)   The Vendor has not prior to the date hereof and will not have prior to [the Transfer Date/Completion] manufactured, sold or supplied products or services during the course of the Business which:

(a)   is, was, or will become, in any material respect faulty or defective; or

(b)   do not comply in any material respect with any warranty or representation expressly or impliedly made by or on behalf of the Vendor in respect of it or with all applicable regulations, standards and requirements in respect thereof; and/or

(c)   was sold as supplied on terms that the Vendor accepts an obligation to service or repair or replace such products after delivery.

(3)   The Vendor has not received a prohibition notice, a notice to warn or a suspension notice under the Consumer Protection Act 1987 in relation to any products of the Business.

(G)   *Inducements*   So far as the Vendor is aware no officer, agent or employee of the Vendor in relation to the Business has paid any bribe (monetary or otherwise) or used any of the Business Assets unlawfully to obtain an advantage for any person.

2.3   Environmental[118]

(A)   *Definitions*   For the purpose of this Sub-Paragraph 2.3, the following terms shall have the following meanings:

'Environment' means all or any of the media of air, water and land (wherever occurring) and in relation to the media of air and water includes without limitation the air and water within buildings and the air and water within other natural or man-made structures above or below ground;

'Environmental Law' means all or any applicable EU, national or local law or regulation arising through statute, subordinate legislation, or common law or any relevant code of practice, guidance, note, standard or other advisory material issued by any competent authority relating to Environmental Matters and in relation to Sub-Paragraph (B)(5) below includes Part IIA of the Environmental Protection Act 1990 whether or not in force;

'Environmental Liability or Liabilities' means all costs, expenses, liabilities, claims, damages, penalties or fines arising from:

(1)   any legal requirement, direction, notice, order or obligation served or imposed by any competent authority or court of competent jurisdiction under Environmental Law; or

(2)   the carrying out of any investigatory, monitoring, precautionary, remedial or engineering works (whether on the Premises or elsewhere) which are necessary to avoid the issue, service or imposition of any notice, requirement or obligation by any competent authority or court of competent jurisdiction under Environmental Law; or

(3)   the carrying out of any investigatory, monitoring, precautionary, remedial or engineering works (whether on the Premises or elsewhere) which are necessary in order to ensure the continued operation of the Business or the protection of the goodwill of the Business and otherwise taking into account the interests of the Business; or

(4)   the repair, replacement or rebuilding of any part of the Premises or any disruption of the Business caused or necessitated by the carrying out of any investigatory, monitory, precautionary, remedial or engineering works (whether on the Premises or elsewhere) in connection with the Environmental Matters;

including in each case all reasonable legal, consulting, monitoring, laboratory and other professional fees and other reasonable costs and expenses associated therewith;

'Environmental Matters' means the pollution of the Environment, the protection of the Environment and human health, health and safety of employees in the work place, the protection of natural amenity, production, the disposal, release, use, storage, spillage, deposit, escape, discharge, leak, emission, recovery, transport of, or radiation from any Hazardous Material or Waste;

'Environmental Permits' means the permits, licences, consents or authorisations required under Environmental Law in relation to the carrying on of the Business or the occupation or use of the Premises;

'Hazardous Material' means any pollutant, or any hazardous, toxic, radioactive, noxious, corrosive or caustic substance whether in solid, liquid or gaseous form; 'Waste' includes any unwanted or surplus substance irrespective of whether it is capable of being recycled or recovered.

(B) *Environmental Matters*

    (1) The Business and the Business Assets have complied at all times with Environmental Law.

    (2) All Environmental Permits have been lawfully obtained and are in full force and effect and at all times all conditions and limitations in all Environmental Permits have been complied with by the Operator of the Business.

    (3) The Vendor is not aware of any circumstances which would make it impossible or difficult for the Business to comply with the conditions or limitations in any Environmental Permits in the future and the Vendor has received no communication revoking, suspending, modifying or varying any of the Environmental Permits and is not aware of any circumstances which might give rise to any such communication being received.

    (4) The Vendor is not in relation to the Business or the Business Assets engaged in any litigation, arbitration, administrative or criminal proceedings or negotiations with any person or body relating to any Environmental Liability and no litigation, arbitration, administrative or criminal proceedings or negotiations with any person or body relating to any actual or potential Environmental Liability are pending, threatened or envisaged by or against the Vendor.

    (5) The Vendor has not in relation to the Business or the Business Assets received at any time any communication failure to comply with which would constitute a breach of Environmental Law or compliance with which could be secured by further proceedings under Environmental Law or which relates in any way to any actual or potential Environmental Liability on the part of the Vendor and the Vendor is not aware of any circumstances, including without limitation the existence of any contractual obligation on the part of the Company, which might give rise to any such communication being received.

2.4 The Vendor's Solvency

(A) *Winding Up* No order has been made, petition presented or resolution passed for the winding up of the Vendor and no meeting has been convened for the purpose of winding up the Vendor. The Vendor has not been a party to any transaction which could be avoided in a winding up.

(B) *Administration and Receivership* No steps have been taken for the appointment of an administrator or receiver (including an administrative receiver) in respect of the Vendor and/or of all or any part of the Business Assets.

(C) *Compositions* The Vendor has not made or proposed any arrangement or composition with its creditors or any class of its creditors.

(D) *Insolvency* The Vendor is not insolvent, is not unable to pay its debts within the meaning of the insolvency legislation applicable to the Vendor and has not stopped paying its debts as they fall due.

(E) *Unsatisfied Judgments* No distress, execution or other process has been levied against the Vendor or action taken to repossess any of the Business Assets [which has not been satisfied in full]. No unsatisfied judgment is outstanding against the Vendor.

(F) *Floating Charges* No floating charge created by the Vendor has crystallised and, so far as the Vendor is aware, there are no circumstances likely to cause such a floating charge to crystallise.

(G) *Analogous Events*   No event analogous to any of the foregoing has occurred in or outside England.

2.5   Accounts, Records and Taxation[119]

(A) *Accounts*[120]
  (1) *Accounts*   The Audited Accounts:
      (a) were prepared in accordance with the requirements of all relevant statutes and accounting practices generally accepted in the United Kingdom at the time they were audited and commonly adopted by companies carrying on business similar to the Business;
      (b) show a true and fair view[119] of the assets and liabilities of the Vendor and the Business as at, and the profits of the Vendor and the Business for the accounting reference period ended on, the Balance Sheet Date; and
      (c) are not affected by any unusual or non-recurring items; and
      (d) apply bases and policies of accounting which have been consistently applied in the audited financial statements of the Vendor and the Business for the three accounting reference periods ending on the Balance Sheet Date.
  (2) *Provisions for liabilities*   Full[119] provision has been made in the Audited Accounts for all actual liabilities of the Vendor relation to the Business the Business outstanding at the Balance Sheet Date and proper provision (or note) in accordance with accounting practices generally accepted in the United Kingdom at the time they were audited has been made in the Audited Accounts for all other liabilities of the Vendor and in relation to the Business then outstanding whether contingent, quantified, disputed or not, including the cost of any work or material for which payment has been received or credit taken, any future loss which may arise in connection with uncompleted contracts and any claims against the Vendor and the Business in respect of completed contracts.
  (3) *Valuation of stock and work in progress*[119]
      (a) For the purposes of the Audited Accounts all stock in trade was valued at the lower of cost and net realisable value and all work in progress was valued on a basis excluding profit, including proper provision for losses which are or could reasonably be anticipated.
      (b) None of the stock in trade of the Business is obsolete, redundant (being out of fashion or demand), slow moving or likely to realise less than its book value.
      (c) The respective amounts of raw materials, work in progress, finished goods, packaging and promotional material held or on order by the Business are appropriate and normal for its present level of business.
  (4) *Management accounts*[119]   The Management Accounts have been carefully prepared in accordance with accounting policies consistent with those used in preparing the Audited Accounts[119] and on a basis consistent with the management accounts prepared in the preceding [year]. The cumulative profits assets and liabilities of the Business stated in the Management Accounts [have not been materially misstated and are not materially inaccurate] and the Vendor does not consider the Management Accounts misleading.
(B) *Books and Records*
  (1) All the books and other material comprised in the Records which are to be delivered or otherwise made available to the Purchaser in accordance with the terms of this Agreement:

(a)   have been fully, properly and accurately maintained on a consistent basis and are and will at the Transfer Date be up to date and contain true complete and accurate records of all aspects of the Business and/or the Business Assets to which they relate and of all matters required by law to be entered therein;

(b)   do not contain or reflect any material inaccuracies or discrepancies;

(c)   are within the possession and control of the Vendor; and

(d)   give a true and fair view of the financial, contractual and trading position of the Business and of its fixed and current assets and liabilities (actual and contingent) and debtors and creditors (as appropriate) and all other matters which ought or would normally be expected to appear therein

and no notice or allegation that any of the same is incorrect or should be rectified has been received;

(2)   Without prejudice to the generality of the foregoing, the Records will fully reflect and provide full and sufficient details of:

(a)   all entitlements of customers of the Business to any special terms, discounts, rebates, allowances and the like in respect of or by reference to the terms on which goods or services have been supplied by the Vendor to such customers prior to the Transfer Date;

(b)   the names and addresses of all customers and suppliers of the Business, all dealings between the Vendor and such customers and/or suppliers during the last [six] years together with full details of all known or likely defaulters;

(c)   all items of Current Assets and Fixed Assets held at the Transfer Date together with proof of ownership thereof; and

(d)   the location of all tangible Business Assets which are not physically located on the Premises at the Transfer Date and the terms and conditions upon which they are being held.

(C)   *Taxation*[121]

(1)   The Vendor has maintained all records for taxation (including, without limit, VAT and PAYE) and other purposes required to be kept by it in relation to the Business and the Business Assets, all proper payments and returns have been made to the Inland Revenue and Commissioners of Customs and Excise and none of the same are subject to or are likely to be the subject of any dispute.

(2)   The Vendor has duly paid or has procured to be paid all stamp duty on the Contracts and all other relevant documents to which it is a party or in which it is interested and which are liable to stamp duty.

(3)   No assets to be transferred to the Purchaser pursuant to this Agreement other than those Premises listed in the Disclosure Letter are capital items for the purposes of Part XV of the Value Added Tax Regulations 1995 ('Part XV'); the period of adjustment (as defined in Part XV) has not expired in respect of those Premises; and all adjustments required to be made pursuant to Part XV on or before the date hereof have been made and declared to HM Customs & Excise in the appropriate manner.

(4)   There are not in existence any circumstances whereby any such power as is mentioned in s 212 of the Inheritance Tax Act 1984 could be exercised in relation to any of the Business Assets.

(5)   No Inland Revenue Charge (as defined in s 237 of the Inheritance Tax Act 1984) is outstanding over any of the Business Assets.

(6) The Disclosure Letter contains details and copies of all elections, together with the relevant notification, made by the Vendor pursuant to para 2 of Sched 10 to the Value Added Tax Act 1994.

(7) The Vendor is not and has not since 1 August 1989 been in relation to any land, building or civil engineering work a developer within the meaning of para 5(5) of Sched 10 to the Value Added Tax Act 1994.

(8) (a)[121] The Vendor has complied with all statutory provisions and regulations relating to value added tax and has duly paid or provided for all amounts of value added tax for which the Vendor is liable in relation to the Business.

   (b) All supplies made by the Vendor in relation to the Business are taxable supplies and the Vendor is not and the Purchaser will not be denied credit for any input tax by reason of the operation of s 26 of the Value Added Tax Act 1994 and regulations made thereunder.

   (c) All input tax for which the Vendor in relation to the Business has claimed credit has been paid by the Vendor in respect of supplies made to it relating to goods or services used or to be used for the purpose of the Business.

   (d) The Vendor is not and has not been, for value added tax purposes, a member of any group of companies and no act or transaction has been effected in consequence whereof the Vendor is or may be held liable for any value added tax chargeable against some other company.

   (e) No supplies have been made to the Vendor to which the provisions of s 8 of the Value Added Tax Act 1994 might apply.

   (f) The Vendor has not committed any offence contrary to ss 60 or 72 Value Added Tax Act 1994 nor has it received any penalty liability notice pursuant to s 64(3), surcharge liability notice pursuant to s 59, or written warning issued pursuant to s 76(2) of that Act.

   (g) The Vendor has not been and is not liable to be registered for VAT otherwise than pursuant to the provisions of para 1 of Sched 1 to the Value Added Tax Act 1994.

   (h) The Vendor has not been required to give security under para 4 Sched 11 to the Value Added Tax Act 1994.

2.6   The Conduct of Business and the Effect of Sale

(A) *Business since the Balance Sheet Date*[122]   Since the Balance Sheet Date:

   (1) the Business has been carried on in the ordinary and usual course so as to maintain it as a going concern and without any interruption or alteration in the nature, scope or manner of the Business;

   (2) there has been no material deterioration in the financial or trading position or prospects or turnover of the Business;[123]

   (3) there has been no significant event or occurrence (including, but not limited to the loss of any significant customer or supplier) which has had or may following Completion have a material adverse affect on the Business (or any of the Business Assets) or its or their respective value, profitability or prospects;[123]

   (4) the Vendor has paid creditors of the Business in accordance with their respective credit terms or (if not) within the time periods usually applicable to such creditors and save as disclosed there are no debts outstanding by the Vendor in relation to the Business which have been due for more than four weeks;

(5) the Vendor has not done or omitted to do anything which might prejudicially affect the Goodwill; and

(6) there has been no unusual change in the Business' stock in trade [or work in progress].

[(B) No substantial customer or supplier [representing more than 5 per cent of sales or supplies of any product or service] of the Business has [since the Balance Sheet Date] preceding the date of this Agreement:

(a) ceased or indicated an intention to cease trading or reduce its level of trading with or supplying or level of supplies to the Business;

(b) changed or is likely to change the terms on which it is prepared to trade with or supply the Business;]

(C) *Consequence of Acquisition of the Business by the Purchaser*

(1) The acquisition of the Business and/or the Business Assets (or any of them) by the Purchaser or compliance with the terms of this Agreement:

(a) will not cause the Business (or the operator thereof) to lose the benefit of any right or privilege it presently enjoys or relieve any person of any obligation to the Business or such operator (whether contractual or otherwise) or enable any person to determine any such obligation or any contractual right or benefit enjoyed by the Business or such operator or to exercise any right whether under an agreement with such operator or otherwise in respect of the Business;

(b) will not give rise to or cause to become exercisable any right of preemption relating to the Business or any of the Business Assets; and

(c) will not result in a breach of, or constitute a default under

(i) the terms, conditions or provisions of any agreement, understanding, arrangement or instrument (including, but not limited to, any of the Contracts) or

(ii) any order, judgment or decree of any court or governmental agency to which the Vendor or any current or previous operator of the Business are party or by which, in either case, the Vendor or the Business or any of the Business Assets is bound or subject;

and to the best of the knowledge and belief of the Vendor the goodwill of the Business and its relationship with clients, customers, suppliers and employees will not be adversely affected thereby.

(2) Without prejudice to the generality of the foregoing the execution and/or performance of this Agreement will not relieve any other party to any of the Contracts from any of its respective obligations thereunder or enable it to determine any of them.

(3) The Vendor is not aware of any circumstances (whether or not connected with the Purchaser and/or the sale of the Business Assets hereunder) indicating that, nor has it been informed or is otherwise aware that any person who now has business dealings with the Business would or might cease to do so from and after Completion.

(D) *Grants* [The Vendor (or other operator of the Business) has not applied for or received any financial assistance from any supranational, national or local authority or government agency.]

[Full particulars of all grants received from any supranational, national or local authority or government agency (and all applications for any such) [and in respect of which there remains any obligation to repay all or part thereof] are given in the Disclosure Letter and there are no circumstances (including the sale of the Business) which might lead to the whole or part of any such grant or other financial assistance becoming repayable or forfeited].

[2.7 The Business and its Assets

(A) *Net Asset Value*[124]   The value of the [Business Assets] at [the date of this Agreement] [Completion] determined in accordance with the same accounting policies as those applied in the Audited Accounts (and on the basis that each of the Fixed Assets is valued at a figure no greater than the value attributed to it in the Audited Accounts or, in the case of any Fixed Asset acquired by the Vendor after the Balance Sheet Date, at a figure no greater than cost) [is not] [will not be] less than the value of the Business Assets at the Balance Sheet Date as shown in the Audited Accounts].

(B) *Business Assets*[125]

    (1)   The Vendor is the owner both legally and beneficially and has good and marketable title to (or is otherwise able to procure the sale hereunder to the Purchaser by the legal and beneficial owner who has good and marketable title to) all the Business Assets free from any encumbrance or any third party claim and all such assets are within the control or possession of the Vendor.

    (2)   No encumbrance is outstanding nor is there any agreement or commitment to give or create or allow any encumbrance over or in respect of the whole or any part of the Business Assets and no claim has been made by any person that he is entitled to any such encumbrance.

    (3)   No asset is shared by the Business (or by the Vendor in relation to the Business) with any other person (including, but not limited to, both the Vendor and/or any member of the Vendor's Group in relation to any other business carried on by them or any of them) and the Business does not require or depend for its continuation or for the continuation of the method or manner or scope of operation of its business in the same way or manner or on the same basis as heretofore upon any assets, premises, facilities or services owned or supplied by the Vendor or any of its respective subsidiaries (other than assets already included within the Business Assets) or any person connected with the Vendor or any third party (whether or not so connected).

    (4)   [Save for the Excluded Assets] the Business Assets comprise all of the assets, rights and privileges (other than cash, stock in trade or stocks of materials and work in progress which have been sold or used in the ordinary course of the Business) which are currently or have since [the Balance Sheet Date] been used or required by the Vendor to carry on the Business.

    (5)   To the best of the knowledge, information and belief of the Vendor there is no dispute or circumstances likely to give rise to a dispute directly or indirectly relating to all or any of the Business Assets which would materially affect the trading or financial position or prospects of the Business.

(C) *Book Debts*   [Save to the extent of the provision or reserve therefor contained or reflected in the Completion Accounts] the Book Debts are good and collectable in the ordinary course of business and will realise their full face value within three months after the Transfer Date. The rights of the Vendor and/or the Business in respect of the Book Debts are valid and enforceable and are not subject to any defence, right of set-off or counter claim, withholding or other deduction and no act has been done or omission permitted whereby any of them has ceased or might cease to be valid and enforceable in whole or in part. No amount included in the Audited Accounts as owing to the Vendor at the Balance Sheet Date has been released for an amount less than the value at which it was included in the Audited Accounts or is now regarded by the Vendor as irrecoverable in whole or in part. The Vendor has not factored or discounted any of its debts or other receivables or agreed to do so.

(D) *Condition and use of Fixed Assets*   Each of the Fixed Assets:

    (1)   is in good repair and condition (bearing in mind its age and level of use) is in satisfactory working order and has been regularly and properly serviced and maintained and none is dangerous, inefficient, obsolete or in need of renewal or replacement;

    (2)   is not unsafe, dangerous or in such a physical condition as to contravene the Health and Safety at Work etc Act 1974 and any other statutes or regulations or orders having the force of law or the terms of any contract (express or implied) to which the Vendor (or other operator of the Business) is a party with any of its employees or customers or any third party or otherwise contravenes or infringes any law applicable to the Vendor (or such other operator) or obligation to which it is subject or would otherwise be in breach of a duty of care which it owes;

    (3)   is capable of being properly used over its estimated useful life for the requirements of the Business for the same purposes and to no lesser extent than heretofore; and

    (4)   is not surplus to the current or proposed requirements of the Business.

(E) *Levels, value and quality of Current Assets*

    (1)   All Current Assets (including, without limit, stock and work-in-progress) represented in the Audited Accounts were valued as at the Balance Sheet Date at the lower of cost or net realisable value.

    (2)   Each of the Current Assets [(other than cash in sterling and cheques representing the same)] is capable of being sold in the ordinary course of the Business at, or is otherwise (on the basis of the lower of cost and net realisable value) worth in aggregate not less than, the value [attributed to them by Sub-Clause 3.1 of the Agreement] [thereof as shown or to be shown in the Completion Accounts].

    (3)   All stocks of finished products comprised in the Current Assets are in good condition, meet all relevant statutory regulatory and industry accepted standards and contractual specifications and are capable of being sold in the ordinary course of the Business in accordance with their current price list without discount, rebate or allowance to a purchaser.

    (4)   The levels of stocks of materials and partly and fully finished products respectively which are comprised in the Current Assets are sufficient for the normal requirements of the Business and are adequate (but not excessive) in relation to the current and anticipated trading requirements of the Business as a whole.

(F) *Intellectual Property Rights*

    (1)   The Vendor is the sole legal and beneficial owner [free from encumbrances] of the Intellectual Property Rights and the Listed Intellectual Property and (where such property is capable of registration) the registered proprietor thereof and (save for copyrights and unregistered design rights not included in the Listed Intellectual Property) owns no other Intellectual Property in relation to the Business.[126]

    (2)   Save as may appear from the Listed Intellectual Property Agreements no person has been authorised to make any use whatsoever of any Intellectual Property owned by the Vendor and used in the Business.

    (3)   Save as may appear from the Listed Intellectual Property Agreements all the Intellectual Property used by the Vendor in the Business is owned by the Vendor and the Vendor does not use in the Business any Intellectual Property in respect of which any third party has any right, title or interest.[127]

    (4)   All the Intellectual Property rights owned by the Vendor and/or used in the Business are valid and enforceable [and [so far as the Vendor is aware] noth-

ing has been done, omitted or permitted whereby any of them has ceased or might cease to be valid and enforceable].[128]

(5)   None of the processes or products of the Vendor and/or used in the Business infringes any Intellectual Property or any right of any other person relating to Intellectual Property or involves the unlicensed use of confidential information disclosed to the Vendor in relation to the Business by any person in circumstances which might entitle that person to make a claim against the Vendor in relation to the Business.[129]

(6)   None of the Listed Intellectual Property or Intellectual Property Rights is being used, claimed, applied for, opposed or attacked by any person.

(7)   The Vendor is not aware of any infringement of the Listed Intellectual Property or Intellectual Property Rights or of any rights relating to them by any person.

(8)   There are no outstanding claims against the Vendor or the Business for infringement of any Intellectual Property or of any rights relating to it used (or which has been used) in the Business and [during the last three years] no such claims have been settled by the giving of any undertakings which remain in force. The Vendor has not received any actual or threatened claim that any of the Intellectual Property Rights or Listed Intellectual Property Rights is invalid [nor is the Vendor aware of any reason why any patents should be amended].

(9)   Confidential information and know-how used in the Business is kept strictly confidential [and the Vendor operates and fully complies with procedures which maintain such confidentiality. The Vendor is not aware of any such confidentiality having been breached.] The Vendor has not disclosed (except in the ordinary course of its business) any of its know-how, trade secrets or list of customers to any other person.[130]

(10) All application and renewal fees, costs, charges, taxes [and other steps] required for the maintenance [or protection] of the Listed Intellectual Property have been duly paid on time [or taken] and none of such rights are subject to any existing challenge or attack by a third party or competent authority [and there are no outstanding patent office or trade marks registry deadlines which expire within three months of Completion.]

(11) The Listed Intellectual Property Agreements are all the Intellectual Property agreements to which the Vendor is a party and each of them is valid and binding and the Vendor is not in breach of any of the provisions of such agreements.

(12) The Vendor has, if required to do so under the Data Protection Act 1984 duly registered as a data user in respect of the Business and has complied with the data protection principles as set out in that Act.

(13) [All current advertising, marketing and sales promotions by the Business comply with all applicable codes of practice and self-regulatory schemes. The Vendor has not been disciplined under any scheme or code in respect of any such advertising, marketing or sales promotion and no complaint has been made against it in respect thereof and there are no outstanding complaints or disciplinary proceedings against the Vendor in respect thereof.][131]

(14) [All persons retained or employed by the Vendor who, in the course of their work in the Business will or might reasonably be expected to bring into existence Intellectual Property or things protected by Intellectual Property are, so far as is reasonably practicable, individually bound by agreements with the Vendor whereby all Intellectual Property which such persons may bring into existence during their work in the Business vests in the Vendor and all

such agreements contain terms which, so far as is reasonably practicable, prevent such persons disclosing any confidential information about the Vendor and the Business.]

(15) [None of the Intellectual Property owned or used in the Business is subject to compulsory licensing or the granting of any licences of right nor, so far as the Vendor is aware, will it become so by operation of law.]

(16) The Business does not use on its letterhead, brochures, sales literature or vehicles nor does it otherwise carry on its business under any name other than under the name(s) set out in the Disclosure Letter.

(G) *Computer Systems*

(1) The Hardware has been satisfactorily maintained and supported and has the benefit of an appropriate maintenance and support agreement terminable by the contractor by not less than 24 months' notice.

(2) The Hardware and Software have adequate capability and capacity for the projected requirements of the Business for not less than four years following Completion for the processing and other functions required to be performed for the purposes of the Business.

(3) Disaster recovery plans are in effect and are adequate to ensure that the Hardware, Software and Data can be replaced or substituted without material disruption to the Business.

(4) In the event that any person providing maintenance or support services for the Hardware, Software and Data ceases or is unable to do so, the Business has all necessary rights and information to procure the carrying out of such services by employees or by a third party without undue expense or delay.

(5) The Business has sufficient technically competent and trained employees to ensure proper handling, operation, monitoring and use of its computer systems.

(6) The Business has adequate procedures to ensure internal and external security of the Hardware, Software and Data, including (without limitation) procedures for preventing unauthorised access, preventing the introduction of a virus, taking and storing on-site and off-site back-up copies of Software and Data.

(7) Where any of the records of the Business are stored electronically, the Vendor is the owner of all hardware and software licences necessary to enable it to keep, copy, maintain and use such records in the course of the Business and does not share any hardware or software relating to the records with any person.

(8) The Vendor has all the rights necessary (including rights over the source code) to obtain, without undue expense or delay, modified versions of the Software which are required at any time to improve in any regard the operation and/or efficiency of the Software.

(9) The Vendor owns, and is in possession and control of, original copies of all the manuals, guides, instruction books and technical documents (including any corrections and updates) required to operate effectively the Hardware and the Software.

(10 The Hardware and Software have never unduly interrupted or hindered the running or operation of the Business, and have no defects in operation which so affect the Business.

(H) *Title Retention*   The Vendor has not acquired or agreed to acquire any of the Business Assets on terms that property therein or title thereto does not pass until full payment is made or (if it has) the property therein or title thereto has now fully passed to the Vendor and no supplier or other third party has any rights or claims against or in respect of such Business Assets accordingly.

(I) *Insurances*[132]

    (1) [Full particulars of all the insurance policies (including, without limitation, the limit and basis of cover under each policy and the amount of the applicable excess) in which the Vendor has an interest in relation to the Business (the 'Insurances') are given in the Disclosure Letter.] The Insurances afford the Business adequate cover against fire and such other risks as persons carrying on a similar business as the Business commonly cover by insurance and in particular:

        (a) the Business Assets are insured in their full replacement value;

        (b) the Computer Systems are insured for all foreseeable risks to their full replacement value, together with incidental expenses, including, without limitation, costs and expenses of data recovery and reconstruction; and

        (c) the Business and the Business Assets have now, and have at all material times been fully covered against accident, damage, injury, third party loss (including Product Liability), loss of profits and other risks normally insured against by persons carrying on a similar business as the Business.

    (2) All the Insurances are in full force and effect and will be maintained in full force without alteration pending Completion, there are no circumstances which might lead to any liability under any of the Insurances being avoided by the insurers or the premiums being increased. In relation to the Insurances there are no special or unusual terms, restrictions or rates of premium and all premiums have been paid on time. There is no claim outstanding under any Insurance nor is the Vendor aware of any circumstances likely to give rise to a claim nor (if the Vendor was to renew the Insurances) is the Vendor aware of any circumstances as to why the insurers would refuse to renew them.

(J) *Trade Associations*   Full particulars of all trade or business associations of which the Vendor is a member of in relation to the Business are set out in the Disclosure Letter, and the Vendor is now and has been at all material times in compliance in all material respects with the regulations or guidelines laid down by any such trade or business association and all reports, comments and recommendations made by any such association [during the six years prior to the date of this Agreement] are annexed to the Disclosure Letter.

(K) *Terms of Business*   True and complete copies of the standard terms upon which the Vendor carries on the Business or provides goods or services to any person in relation to the Business are annexed to the Disclosure Letter and the Vendor does not provide and has not provided any goods or services to any person on terms which differ from its standard terms in relation to the Business as annexed.

2.8 Contracts and Contractual Arrangements

(A) *The Contracts*[133]

    (1) [Full and complete copies/All material terms] of the Contracts entered into prior to the date hereof have been disclosed to the Purchaser in writing in or by the Disclosure Letter.

    (2) Each of the Contracts is valid and binding on the parties thereto and is capable of being assigned by the Vendor to the Purchaser without the consent of the other party/parties thereto (save to the extent otherwise expressly stated in the Disclosure Letter) and no notice of termination of any such Contract has been received or served by the Vendor.

(3)   The Vendor is not aware of the invalidity of, or of any grounds for determination, rescission, avoidance or repudiation, of any of the Contracts.

(4)   Save for the Contracts, there are not now in force in relation to the Business or the Business Assets (or any of them) nor will there be in force at the Transfer Date any agreements, undertakings, understandings, arrangements or other engagements, whether written or oral to which the Vendor or any member of the Vendor's Group is a party or has the benefit of or is otherwise subject, the benefit of which would be required to be assigned to or otherwise vested in it to enable a purchaser of the Business and the Business Assets to carry on the Business and/or to enjoy all the rights and privileges attaching thereto and/or to any of the Business Assets in the same manner and scope and to the same extent and on the same basis as the Vendor has so carried it on or enjoyed prior to the date hereof.

(5)   There are not now nor will there be at the Transfer Date any agreements, undertakings, understandings, arrangements or other engagements, whether written or oral, in relation to the Business to which the Vendor or any member of the Vendor's Group is a party or has the benefit of or is otherwise subject, the burden of which has passed or will pass or will be alleged to pass to the Purchaser (other than the Contracts).

(6)   [None of the Contracts][The Vendor is not now and will not at the Transfer Date in relation to the Business be a party to or subject to any agreement, transaction, obligation, commitment, understanding, arrangement or liability (including, without limit, any of the Contracts) which]:

(a)   is of [six] months or greater duration or is incapable of complete performance in accordance with its terms within [six] months after the date on which it was entered into or undertaken or is otherwise of a length that is greater than is customary in businesses of a similar nature to the Business; or

(b)   is known by the Vendor to be likely to result in a loss to the Vendor or to the Business on completion of performance; or

(c)   cannot readily be fulfilled or performed by the Vendor on time and without undue or unusual expenditure of money or effort; or

(d)   involves or is likely to involve obligations, restrictions, expenditure or receipts of any unusual onerous or exceptional nature; or

(e)   is a contract for services (other than contracts for the supply of electricity or other normal office services); or

(f)   requires the Vendor to pay any commission, finder's fee, royalty or the like; or

(g)   involves liabilities which may fluctuate in accordance with an index or rate of currency exchange; or

(h)   is (save for the Lease Contracts) a contract for the supply of assets to the Vendor on hire, lease, hire purchase, conditional sale, credit or deferred payment terms; or

(i)   is dependent on the guarantee or covenant of or security provided by any other person; or

(j)   is in any way otherwise than in the ordinary course of business.

(7)   There are no agreements or arrangements relating to the Business or any part thereof to which the Vendor or any member of the Vendor's Group is a party (including, but not limited to the Contracts) which in any way restricts the freedom of the Vendor to carry on the Business in whole or in part or to use or exploit any of the Business Assets in any part of the world as it thinks fit.

(B) *Substantial or significant contracts*   No contract, agreement, transaction, obligation, commitment, understanding, arrangement or liability entered into by the Vendor in connection with the Business and now outstanding or unperformed (and, without limiting the generality of the foregoing, none of the Contracts) involves any of the following:

    (1)   obligations on the part of the Vendor which will cause or are likely to cause the Vendor to incur expenditure or an obligation to pay money in excess of £[   ];

    (2)   obligations on the part of the Vendor to purchase any specified minimum quantity or any specified minimum percentage of its total requirement for [   ] or other stock in trade from any one supplier;

    (3)   the supply by the Vendor of [   ] or other products or services whether by way of lease or outright sale or otherwise to any one customer such that the value of such supplies exceeds or is likely to exceed (if the Vendor were to carry on the Business after the Transfer Date) [five per cent] of the total turnover of the Vendor in relation to the Business in the financial year ending [   ] 19[   ] or in any subsequent year.

(C) *Defaults*

    (1)   Neither the Vendor nor the Business nor any other party to any agreement with the Vendor or the Business is in default thereunder, and the Vendor is not aware of any invalidity or grounds for termination, avoidance, rescission or repudiation of any agreement to which it or the Business is a party which in any such case would be material[134] in the context of the financial or trading position of the Business or in the context of the Business Assets] nor (so far as the Vendor is aware) are there any circumstances likely to give rise any such event.

    (2)   Full details of any customers (or any persons to whom the Vendor in the course of Business has supplied goods or services in the twelve months ending on the date hereof) who have defaulted (or who are believed by the Vendor to be likely to default) [in any material respect] in the payment when due of any monies to the Vendor or the Business are specified in the Disclosure Letter.

(D) *Powers of Attorney*   There are not in force at the date hereof nor will there be in force at the Transfer Date any power of attorney or other authority (express, implied or ostensible) given by or on behalf of the Vendor in connection with the Business or the conduct thereof or any of the Business Assets which is still outstanding or effective to any person to enter into any contract, commitment or obligation on behalf of or which might affect the Business or the conduct thereof or any of the Business Assets (save to competent and responsible Employees to enter into routine contracts in the ordinary course of business in the normal course of their duties).

(E) *Non-arm's length contracts*   The Vendor has not in relation to the Business been a party to, nor has the profits or financial position of the Business during the last three years been affected by any agreement or arrangement which is not entirely of an arm's length nature.

(F) *Tenders, etc*   No offer, tender, or the like is outstanding which is capable of being converted into an obligation of the Vendor in respect of the Business by an acceptance or other act of some other person [and the Vendor is not in negotiations with, nor has it put proposals forward or entered into discussions with any customer or supplier for the renewal of any existing business or acquisition of any new business.][135]

(G) *Documents*   All title deeds and agreements relating to the Business and/or the Business Assets to which the Vendor is party (including, without limit, the Contracts) and other documents relating to the Business and/or the Business Assets owned by or which ought to be in the possession or control of the Vendor are in the possession or control of the Vendor, are properly stamped, are free from any encumbrance and will be delivered or made available to the Purchaser on Completion.

2.9   Employees

(A) *Particulars of Employees*

    (1)   The Employees are all employed by the Vendor in the Business at the date of this Agreement and notice of termination will not be given by the Vendor on or before the Transfer Date. There are no other individuals employed at the date of this Agreement in the Business wheresoever. There will be no other individuals employed at the Transfer Date in the Business wheresoever.

    (2)   All contracts of service of any of the Employees are terminable on not more than three months' notice without compensation, (other than compensation payable in accordance with the Employment Rights Act 1996).

    (3)   The particulars shown in the Disclosure Letter show true and complete details of ages and lengths of continuous service of all of the Employees and by reference to each of the Employees' remuneration payable and other benefits provided or which the Vendor is bound to provide (whether now or in the future) to each category of the Employees at the Transfer Date or any person connected with any such person and (without limiting the generality of the foregoing) include particulars of all profit sharing, incentive, bonus, commission arrangements and any other benefit to which any such category of the Employees is entitled or which is regularly provided or made available to them (including details of their notice period and their entitlement to holiday) in any case whether legally binding on the Vendor or not.

    (4)   There are no subsisting contracts for the provision by any person of any consultancy services to the Business.

    (5)   None of the Employees has given notice terminating his contract of employment.

    (6)   None of the Employees is under notice of dismissal or has any outstanding dispute with the Vendor or any other member of the Vendor's Group in connection with or arising from his employment nor is there any liability outstanding to such persons except for remuneration or other benefits accruing due and no such remuneration or other benefit which has fallen due for payment has not been paid.

    (7)   During the period of six months ending with the execution of this Agreement neither the Vendor nor any member of the Vendor's Group nor any other person carrying on the Business has directly or indirectly terminated the employment of any person employed in or by the Business where the reason or principal reason for such termination was the transfer of the Business.

    (8)   None of the Employees belongs or has belonged at any material time to an independent trade union recognised by the Vendor or any member of the Vendor's Group in relation to the Business.

    (9)   There are no employee representatives representing all or any of the Employees.

    (10) The Vendor has complied with all of its statutory obligations to inform and consult appropriate representatives as required by law.[136]

(11) There is no plan, scheme, commitment, custom or practice relating to redundancy affecting any of the Employees more generous than the statutory redundancy requirements.

(12) All plans for the provision of benefits to the Employees comply in all respects with all relevant statutes, regulations or other laws and all necessary consents in relation to such plans have been obtained and all governmental filings in relation to such plans have been made.

(13) There are no loans owed by any of the Employees to any of the Vendor or any member of the Vendor's Group.

(14) Since [the last review date/the Balance Sheet Date,] no change has been made in (i) the rate of remuneration, or the emoluments or pension benefits or other contractual benefits, of any officer of the Vendor or any of the Employees or (ii) the terms of engagement of any such officer or any of the Employees.

(15) There are no training schemes, arrangements or proposals whether past or present in respect of which a levy may henceforth become payable by the Vendor, or a member of the Vendor's Group under the Industrial Training Act 1982 (as amended by the Employment Act 1989) and pending the Transfer Date no such schemes, arrangements or proposals will be established or undertaken.

(16) There is no outstanding undischarged liability to pay any governmental or regulatory authority in any jurisdiction any contribution, taxation or other duty arising in connection with the employment or engagement of any of the Employees.

(17) None of the Employees will become entitled by virtue of their contract of service to any enhancement in or improvement to their remuneration, benefits or terms and conditions of service only by reason of the execution of this Agreement or the completion of the sale and purchase under or pursuant to this Agreement.

(18) Neither the Vendor nor any member of the Vendor's Group have in the last twelve months, entered into any informal or formal agreement to amend or change the terms and conditions of employment of any of the Employees (whether such amendment or change is to take effect prior to or after the Transfer Date).

(B) *Service Contracts* There is not outstanding any contract of service between the Vendor and any of its directors, officers or employees relating to the Business which is not terminable by the Vendor without compensation (other than any compensation payable by statute) on not more than three months' notice given at any time.

(C) *Pensions* Except for the Pension Scheme[s] defined in Schedule 7 the Vendor is not under any present or future liability to pay to any of the Employees or to any other person who has been in any manner connected with the Business any pension, superannuation allowance, death benefit, retirement gratuity or like benefit or to contribute to any life assurance scheme, medical insurance scheme, or permanent health scheme and the Vendor has not made any such payments or contributions on a voluntary basis nor is it proposing to do so.

(D) *Disputes with Employees* There is no:

(1) outstanding claim by any person who is now or has been an employee of the Vendor or any member of the Vendor's Group in relation to the Business or any dispute outstanding with any of the said persons or with any unions or any other body representing all or any of them in relation to their employ-

ment in the Business or of any circumstances likely to give rise to any such dispute;

(2)   industrial action involving any employee, whether official or unofficial, currently occurring or threatened; or

(3)   industrial relations matter which has been referred to ACAS or any similar governmental agency in the applicable jurisdiction for advice, conciliation or arbitration.

2.10   Miscellaneous[137]

[(A)   *Overdraft*   The bank overdraft and all other amounts owed to bankers and other lenders by the Vendor to be assumed by the Purchaser as forming part of the Creditors at [Completion/the Transfer Date] will not exceed a total amount of £[   ] (inclusive of accrued interest).]

[(B)   *Sureties*

(1)   Neither the Vendor nor any member of the Vendor's Group nor any third party has given any, nor do any of the Contracts contain any, guarantee of or security for, any overdraft loan, loan facility or off-balance sheet financing granted to the operator of the Business or owner of the Business Assets or of any other obligations of such person or persons, nor has any person other than the Vendor given any guarantee of or security for any overdraft loan, loan facility or off-balance sheet financing granted to the Vendor or such operator or owner as aforesaid.]

(2)   There is not now outstanding in respect of the Business or any of the Business Assets any guarantee or warranty or agreement for indemnity or for suretyship given by or for the accommodation of the Business or in respect of the Business Assets.

(C)   *Off-Balance Sheet Financing*   Save for the Lease Contracts particulars of which are given in this Agreement or the Disclosure Letter, the Vendor has not in relation to the Business engaged in any borrowing or financing which is not reflected in the Audited Accounts.

(D)   *All Material Matters Disclosed*   All information contained or referred to in this Agreement (including the Schedules and the documents in the agreed terms) and in the Disclosure Letter or any annexure thereto or which has otherwise been disclosed by or on behalf of the Vendor to the Purchaser [or its advisers/others] on or prior to the date hereof is true and accurate in all [material] respects and the Vendor is not aware of any other fact or matter which renders any such information misleading because of any omission or ambiguity or for any other reason.[138] The Vendor has disclosed to the Purchaser all information and facts relating to the Business (including financial information) which are or may be material for disclosure to a purchaser of the Business and/or the Business Assets on the terms of this Agreement and all information and facts so disclosed are true and accurate in all [material] respects.[139]

SCHEDULE 7

PENSIONS

[A   Vendor has own final salary scheme]

1   Interpretation

1.1   Definitions

In this Schedule, where the context admits:

'Actuarial Assumptions' means the actuarial assumptions and method set out in a letter in agreed terms dated [   ] from the Vendor's Actuary to the Purchaser's Actuary;

'Actuary' means a Fellow of the Institute of Actuaries or of the Faculty of Actuaries or of any successor body of such Institute or Faculty;

'Pension Scheme' means [the retirement benefits scheme known as [   ] which was established by a deed dated [   ] (or the trustees from time to time of that scheme as the context requires);] [Scheme A] [;] [Scheme B] [and Scheme C] (or such one or [other] [more] of them as the context requires);]

'Purchaser's Actuary' means [   ] (or such other Actuary as the Purchaser may appoint for the purposes of this Schedule);

['Scheme A' means the retirement benefits scheme known as [   ] which was established by a trust deed dated [   ] (or the trustees from time to time of that scheme as the context requires);]

['Scheme B' means the retirement benefits scheme known as [   ] which was established by a trust deed dated [   ] (or the trustees from time to time of that scheme as the context requires);]

['Scheme C' means the retirement benefits scheme known as [   ] which was established by a trust deed dated [   ] (or the trustees from time to time of that scheme as the context requires);]

'Shortfall' means the amount (if any), determined in accordance with the Actuarial Assumptions, by which the capital value at the Transfer Date of the benefits which are then payable, or prospectively or contingently payable, under the Pension Scheme exceeds the value at the Transfer Date of the then assets of the Pension Scheme. For the purposes of this definition:

(A)   when calculating the value of the assets of the Pension Scheme no account shall be taken of:

   (1)   any debts of the Vendor to the Pension Scheme[140], or

   (2)   any contributions payable to the Pension Scheme after the Transfer Date,

   but subject thereto the assets shall be valued in accordance with the Actuarial Assumptions;[141]

(B)   when calculating the liabilities of the Pension Scheme no account shall be taken of any benefits in respect of service after the Transfer Date but allowance shall be made in accordance with the Actuarial Assumptions for:

   (1)   projected increases in earnings up to the assumed date of cessation of pensionable service;[142] and

   (2)   increases to pensions in payment or in deferment;

(C)   when calculating the liabilities of the Pension Scheme allowance shall also be made in accordance with the Actuarial Assumptions for any refund of contributions and any benefits in pension form payable in the event of death while in service but, save where death occurs before the Transfer Date, no account shall be taken of any other lump sum death-in-service benefits;

(D) any improvement to the benefits under the Pension Scheme which has been announced before the Transfer Date shall be deemed to have been duly effected under the Pension Scheme and to have come into force before the Transfer Date; and

(E) the Pension Scheme shall be deemed to be under an overriding obligation to provide benefits [(including guaranteed minimum pensions within the meaning of the Pension Schemes Act 1993)] which are attributable to any period of employment after 16 May 1990 on a basis which does not discriminate between men and women and without reducing the benefits of either sex;[143]

'Vendor's Actuary' means [   ] (or such other Actuary as may be appointed by the Vendor for the purposes of this Schedule).

1.2 Employees

References in this Schedule to employees includes directors.

[1.3 Schedule Applies Separately to Each Pension Scheme

Paragraphs 2 to 4 and, for the purposes of those Paragraphs, Paragraph 1 apply separately to each Pension Scheme.][144]

2 The Pension Scheme

2.1 Purchaser to become Principal Employer

The Vendor undertakes to the Purchaser to procure that subject to the consent of the Inland Revenue (which consent the Vendor shall use all reasonable endeavours to procure) the Purchaser becomes the principal employer under the Pension Scheme with effect from the Transfer Date.[145]

[2.2 Retirement of Trustee(s)

The Vendor undertakes to the Purchaser to procure that [   ] [and [   ]] retire(s) as (a) trustee(s) of the Pension Scheme with effect from the Transfer Date.]

2.3 Damages for Breach

In assessing damages flowing from any breach of the provision of this Paragraph 2 it shall be deemed to be within the power of the Vendor to procure everything which in this Paragraph the Vendor has undertaken to procure.

3 Calculation of Shortfall[146]

3.1 Data

The Vendor and the Purchaser shall each use all reasonable endeavours to procure that all such information as the Vendor's Actuary or the Purchaser's Actuary or any independent Actuary appointed under Sub-Paragraph 3.3 may reasonably request for the purposes of this Schedule is supplied promptly to such Actuary and that all such information is complete and accurate in all respects.

3.2 Agreement of Shortfall

The Purchaser's Actuary shall determine the amount (if any) of the Shortfall and shall submit his findings in writing to the Vendor's Actuary for agreement. If the Vendor's Actuary and the Purchaser's Actuary agree the amount (if any) of the Shortfall, the Vendor shall procure that the Vendor's Actuary and the Purchaser shall procure that the Purchaser's Actuary jointly certify that amount as the Shortfall.

3.3 Dispute

If the Vendor's Actuary and the Purchaser's Actuary fail to agree the amount (if any) of the Shortfall within two months from the date the Purchaser's Actuary first submits his findings to the Vendor's Actuary in accordance with Sub-Paragraph 3.2, the matter may, at the option of either the Vendor or the Purchaser, be referred to an independent Actuary to be agreed between the Vendor and the Purchaser or, in default of agreement within 14 days from the first nomination of an Actuary by one party to the other, to be appointed by the President for the time being of The Institute of Actuaries (or any successor body) on the application of either the Vendor or the Purchaser. The certificate of the independent Actuary as to the amount (if any) of the Shortfall shall, save in the event of fraud or manifest error, be final and binding on the parties and, in so certifying, the independent Actuary shall be deemed to be acting as an expert and not as an arbitrator.[147] His costs shall be borne by the Vendor and the Purchaser [equally or in such other proportions as he shall direct].

4 Payment of Shortfall

4.1 The Vendor shall within a period of 14 days commencing on and including the date the amount (if any) of the Shortfall is certified as aforesaid pay, by way of further adjustment so far as possible to the Provisional Consideration,[148] to the Purchaser (or to a third party, as the Purchaser may direct) a sum in cash equal to the amount shown in the certificate as being the Shortfall[149] together with interest thereon (accruing daily and compounded monthly) from and including the Transfer Date to but excluding the date final payment is made in accordance with this Paragraph (as well after judgment as before). Such interest shall be at the Agreed Rate up to and including the last day in the aforesaid 14-day period and thereafter at the Agreed Rate plus [   ] per cent per annum. In this Paragraph 'Agreed Rate' means the base rate from time to time of [   ] Bank Plc plus [   ] per cent per annum.

5 Warranties and Representations[117; 150]

5.1 The Vendor hereby warrants and represents[117] to and for the benefit of the Purchaser in the following terms:

(A) *No Other Arrangements* Save for the Pension Scheme no member of the Vendor's Group is a party to or participates in or contributes to any scheme, agreement or arrangement (whether legally enforceable or not) for the provision of any pension, retirement, death, incapacity, sickness, disability, accident or other like benefits (including the payment after cessation of employment with the Vendor of medical expenses) for any Employee or for the widow, widower, child or dependant of any Employee.

(B) *No Assurances etc* No member of the Vendor's Group:

    (1) has given any undertaking or assurance (whether legally enforceable or not) as to the continuance, introduction, improvement or increase of any benefit of a kind described in Sub-Paragraph 5.1(A) above, or

(2)   is paying or has in the last two years paid any such benefit,

to (in either case) any Employee or to any widow, widower, child or dependant of any Employee.

(C)   *All Details Disclosed*   All material details relating to the Pension Scheme are contained in or annexed to the Disclosure Letter including, but without limitation, the following:

(1)   true and complete copies of the following documents referable to the Pension Scheme, *viz*:

(a)   all deeds, rules and other governing documents;

(b)   all announcements, booklets and the like of current effect;

(c)   the latest completed actuarial valuation report and any document (including any draft) containing the results or preliminary results of any subsequent actuarial valuation;

(d)   the latest completed audited accounts and any subsequent accounts or draft accounts;

(e)   all investment management, custodian, administration and other agreements to which the Pension Scheme is a party;

(f)   all insurance policies (if any) and annuity contracts (if any) and all proposals (if any) to effect any such policies or contracts which are with any insurer for consideration;

(g)   an accurate list of all active members, deferred members and pensioners with such data as is necessary to establish their respective entitlements under the Pension Scheme;

(h)   an accurate list with the names and addresses of the trustees;

(i)   the memorandum and articles of association of any trustee which is a company and a list with the names and addresses of the directors and secretary of that company;

(j)   internal dispute resolution procedure, schedule of contributions and statement of investment principles for the purposes of the Pensions Act 1995;[151]

(2)   details of the arrangements made or being considered (or confirmation that none have been made or are being considered) to comply with ss 16 to 21 of the Pensions Act 1995;[152]

(3)   details of the investments and other assets of the Pension Scheme;

(4)   details of all amendments (if any) to the Pension Scheme which have been announced or are proposed but which have not yet been formally made;

(5)   details of all discretionary increases (if any) to pensions in payment or in deferment under the Pension Scheme which have been granted in the ten years prior to the date of this Agreement or which are under consideration;

(6)   details of all discretionary practices (if any) which may have led any person to expect additional benefits in a given set of circumstances (by way of example, but without limitation, on retirement at the behest of the Vendor or in the event of redundancy); and

(7)   details of the rate at which and basis upon which the Vendor currently contributes to the Pension Scheme, any change to that rate and/or basis which is proposed or which is under consideration and all contributions paid to the Pension Scheme by the Vendor in the three years prior to the date of this Agreement.

(D)   *Membership*   Every person who has at any time had the right to join, or apply to join, the Pension Scheme has been properly advised of that right. No person has been excluded from membership of the Pension Scheme or from any of the benefits thereunder in contravention of Art 119 of the Treaty of Rome, the Pensions

Act 1995 or other applicable laws or requirements or the provisions of the Pension Scheme or otherwise.[153]

(E)   *No pay restructuring*   There has not in the last four years been any restructuring of the earnings of all or any of the members or prospective members of the Pension Scheme (by way of example, but without limitation, consolidation of bonuses into basic pay).[154]

(F)   *Transfer payments*   No transfer value has been paid (directly or indirectly) to the Pension Scheme from another arrangement for any member of the Pension Scheme under which any benefits referable to that member contravened Art 119 of the Treaty of Rome, s 62 of the Pensions Act 1995 or other applicable law or requirement.[155]

(G)   *Death Benefits Insured*   All benefits (other than any refund of members' contributions with interest where appropriate) payable under the Pension Scheme on the death of any person while in employment to which the Pension Scheme relates are insured fully under a policy with an insurance company of good repute and there are no grounds on which that company might avoid liability under that policy.

(H)   *Contributions and Expenses*   Contributions to the Pension Scheme are not paid in arrear and all contributions and other amounts which have fallen due for payment have been paid. No fee, charge or expense relating to or in connection with the Pension Scheme has been incurred but not paid. If any such fee, charge or expense has been paid by any person other than the Pension Scheme the Pension Scheme has reimbursed that person if and to the extent that the Pension Scheme is or may become liable so to do.

(I)   *Augmentation*   No power under the Pension Scheme has been exercised in relation to any Employee or, since the date as at which the last actuarial valuation of the Pension Scheme to be completed prior to the date of this Agreement was undertaken, in respect of any other person:
   (1)   to provide terms of membership of the Pension Scheme (whether as to benefits or contributions) which are different from those generally applicable to the members of the Pension Scheme; or
   (2)   to provide any benefits which would not but for the exercise of that power have been payable under the Pension Scheme; or
   (3)   to augment any benefits under the Pension Scheme.

(J)   *Vendor's Obligations*   The Vendor:
   (1)   has observed and performed those provisions of the Pension Scheme which apply to it; [and]
   (2)   may (without the consent of any person or further payment) terminate its liability to contribute to the Pension Scheme at any time subject only to giving such notice (if any) as is expressly provided for in the documentation containing the current provisions governing the Pension Scheme[156] [.][; and
   (3)   has at all material times held or been named in a contracting-out certificate (within the meaning of s 7(1), Pension Schemes Act 1993) referable to the Pension Scheme.]

(K)   *No Other Employer*   The Vendor is the only employer for the time being participating in the Pension Scheme. No employer which has previously participated in the Pension Scheme has any claim under the Pension Scheme and in respect of any such employer the period of participation has been terminated and benefits have been provided in accordance with the provisions of the Pension Scheme.

(L)   *Administration*   All documentation and records in respect of the Pension Scheme are up to date and so far as the Vendor is aware complete and accurate in all material respects.

(M)   *Investments*   None of the assets of the Pension Scheme:

(1)   is invested in any description of employer-related investments (within the meaning of s 40, Pensions Act 1995); or

(2)   save for deposits with banks, building societies and other financial institutions and save for any instrument creating or acknowledging an indebtedness listed on any recognised stock exchange of repute, is loaned to any person; or

(3)   is subject to any encumbrance or agreement or commitment to give or create any encumbrance.

(N) *Compliance*   The Pension Scheme:

(1)   is an exempt approved scheme (within the meaning of s 592(1) of the Income and Corporation Taxes Act 1988);

(2)   has properly and punctually accounted to the Board of Inland Revenue for all and any tax for which the Pension Scheme is liable or accountable;

(3)   is not liable to taxation on any income from or capital gains on any of the funds which are or have been held for the purposes of the Pension Scheme[157]; and

(4)   has at all times complied with and been administered in accordance with all applicable laws, regulations and requirements (including those of the Board of Inland Revenue and of trust law);

(O) *Actuarial*[158]   The report dated [   ] of [   ] on the actuarial valuation of the Pension Scheme as at [   ] (the 'Valuation Date') (a true copy of the report being annexed to the Disclosure Letter) shows a true and fair view of the respective actuarial values of the assets and liabilities of the Pension Scheme at the Valuation Date on the basis of the actuarial assumptions and method detailed in that report. Since the Valuation Date nothing has occurred, been done or been omitted to be done which may affect materially the level of funding of the benefits under the Pension Scheme.

(P) *Disputes*   None of the Pension Scheme, the Vendor or any member of the Vendor's Group is engaged or involved in any proceedings which relate to or are in connection with the Pension Scheme or the benefits thereunder and no such proceedings are pending or threatened and so far as the Vendor is aware there are no facts likely to give rise to any such proceedings. In this Sub-Paragraph 'proceedings' includes any litigation or arbitration and also includes any investigation or determination by the Pensions Ombudsman or the Occupational Pensions Advisory Service and any complaint under any internal dispute resolution procedure established in connection with the Pension Scheme.

(Q) *Indemnities*   In relation to the Pension Scheme or funds which are or have been held for the purposes thereof neither the Vendor nor the trustees or administrator of the Pension Scheme has given an indemnity or guarantee to any person (other than in the case of the Vendor any general indemnity in favour of the trustees or administrator under the documentation governing the Pension Scheme).

6   Damages for Breach of Pension Warranties[159]

6.1   In determining the damages flowing from any breach of Warranties contained in Paragraph 5, the Purchaser shall be deemed to become at Completion under a liability:

(A) to provide and to continue to provide any benefit of a kind referred to in that Paragraph which is now provided or has been announced or is proposed; and

(B) to maintain and to continue to maintain (without benefits being reduced) the Pension Scheme and any other arrangements of a kind described in that Paragraph which are now in existence or are proposed and any discretionary practices of a kind referred to in that Paragraph which have hitherto been carried on.

SCHEDULE 7

PENSIONS

[B   Vendor participates in group final salary scheme]

1 Interpretation

1.1 Definitions

In this Schedule, where the context admits:

'Actuarial Assumptions' means the actuarial assumptions and method set out in the Actuary's Letter;

'Actuary' means a Fellow of The Institute of Actuaries or of The Faculty of Actuaries or of any successor body to such Institute or Faculty;

'Actuary's Letter' means a letter in agreed terms dated [   ] from the Vendor's Actuary to the Purchaser's Actuary;

'Adjusted Transfer Value' means [the Transfer Value multiplied by the Investment Adjustment from and including the Membership Transfer Date to and including the Payment Date;][160]

'Basic Amount' means an amount, determined in accordance with the Actuarial Assumptions, equal to the capital value at the Transfer Date of the benefits which are payable under the Pension Scheme to or in respect of the Transferring Employees, such benefits being calculated as if the Purchaser were to continue participating in the Pension Scheme indefinitely.[161]

For the purposes of this definition:

(A)   benefits include any benefits which are contingently or prospectively payable;

(B)   when calculating the value of the benefits payable under the Pension Scheme no account shall be taken of any benefits in respect of service after the Transfer Date but allowance shall be made in accordance with the Actuarial Assumptions for:

(1)   projected increases in earnings up to the assumed date of cessation of pensionable service;[162] and

(2)   increases to pensions in payment or in deferment;

(C)   when calculating the value of the benefits payable under the Pension Scheme allowance shall also be made in accordance with the Actuarial Assumptions for any refund of contributions and any benefits in pension form payable in the event of death while in service but no account shall be taken of any other lump sum death-in-service benefits;

(D)   any improvement to the benefits under the Pension Scheme which has been announced before the Transfer Date shall be deemed to have been duly effected under the Pension Scheme and to have come into force before the Transfer Date; and

(E)   the Pension Scheme shall be deemed to be under an overriding obligation in respect of members who are, or but for being absent from work would have been, in pensionable service at the Transfer Date to provide benefits (including guaranteed minimum benefits in respect of service) after 16 May 1990 on a basis which does not discriminate between men and women and without reducing the benefits of either sex;][163]

'Contracting-out Benefits' means guaranteed minimum pensions, section 9(2B) rights and protected rights (or such of them as are applicable);[164]

'Interest' means, in respect of any period and any principal sum, an amount of interest (accruing daily and compounded monthly) at a rate equal to the base rate from time to time of [   ] Bank Plc plus [   ] per cent per annum;

'Interim Period' means the period from the Transfer Date to but excluding the Membership Transfer Date;

['Investment Adjustment' means, in relation to any period, one plus, when expressed as a fraction, the rate of investment return (whether positive or negative) during that period on a notional portfolio comprising [   ] per cent in the FT-SE Actuaries All-Share Total Return Index and [   ] per cent in the FT-Actuaries British Government Fixed Interest Over 15 Year Index (as published in the *Financial Times*) with allowance for income to be reinvested at monthly intervals. For the purposes of this definition the notional return shall be measured by taking the respective figures on the indices published for the close of business on the last business day preceding the commencement of the relevant period and for the close of business on the last business day preceding the day upon which that period ends;][165]

['Life Assurance Employee' means an Employee who is covered by the Pension Scheme for certain death-in-service benefits but is not a Pensionable Employee;]

'Membership Transfer Date' means the first day of the first calendar month to commence after the date which is [   ] months after the Transfer Date (or such earlier date as the Purchaser may by not less than one month's notice in writing to the Vendor specify or such later date as the Vendor and the Purchaser may agree in writing) except that if for any reason the Purchaser is unable to participate in the Pension Scheme in accordance with Sub-Paragraph 3.1 until the date which would (apart from this exception) be the Membership Transfer Date then the 'Membership Transfer Date' means the day next following the date upon which the Purchaser ceases so to participate in the Pension Scheme or if the Purchaser is unable to participate at all it means the day next following the Completion Date;[166]

'Payment Conditions'[167] means:

(A) if the Purchaser's Scheme is a retirement benefits scheme, the Purchaser notifying the Vendor in writing that[:
    (i)] the Purchaser's Scheme is an exempt approved scheme or that the Board of Inland Revenue has confirmed that the Purchaser's Scheme may accept a transfer payment from the Pension Scheme; [and
    (ii) where the employment of the Transferring Employees is to be contracted-out by reference to the Purchaser's Scheme, the Purchaser's Scheme may accept transfer values in respect of Contracting-out Benefits in accordance with the contracting-out requirements of the Pension Schemes Act 1993 and any applicable regulations made thereunder];

(B) if the Purchaser's Scheme is a personal pension scheme, the Purchaser's Scheme is approved under Chapter IV, Part XIV of the Income and Corporation Taxes Act 1988 and if the Transferring Employees have Contracted-out Benefits under the Pension Scheme it is an appropriate scheme;

'Payment Date' means the earlier of:

(A) the date upon which the Adjusted Transfer Value is paid in accordance with Sub-Paragraph 5.2; and

(B) the date which is 14 days after the later of:
    (1) the date upon which the amount of the Transfer Value is certified in accordance with Sub-Paragraph 5.1 or 7, as the case may be; and
    (2) the date upon which the Payment Conditions are first satisfied;

'Pension Scheme' means [the retirement benefits scheme known as [   ] which was established by a deed dated [   ] (or the trustees from time to time of that scheme, as the context requires);] [Scheme A [;] [Scheme B] [and Scheme C] (or such one or [other] [more] of them as the context requires;]

'Pensionable Employee' means an Employee who is, or (but for being absent from work or but for not fulfilling any relevant eligibility conditions) would be, in pensionable service under the Pension Scheme;

'Purchaser's Actuary' means [   ] (or such other Actuary as the Purchaser may appoint for the purposes of this Schedule);

'Purchaser's Scheme' means the scheme or schemes nominated by or at the instance of the Purchaser pursuant to Sub-Paragraph 4.1 (or the trustees or managers thereof as the context requires);

['Scheme A' means the retirement benefits scheme known as [   ] which was established by a trust deed dated [   ] (or the trustees from time to time of that scheme as the context requires);]

['Scheme B' means the retirement benefits scheme known as [   ] which was established by a trust deed dated [   ] (or the trustees from time to time of that scheme as the context requires);]

['Scheme C' means the retirement benefits scheme known as [   ] which was established by a trust deed dated [   ] (or the trustees from time to time of that scheme as the context requires);]

'Transferring Employee' means a person who:

(A) immediately prior to the Membership Transfer Date is a Pensionable Employee;

(B) accepts the offer of membership of the Purchaser's Scheme to be made pursuant to Sub-Paragraph 4.2; and

(C) consents in writing on or before the date which is [   ] days after the Membership Transfer Date (or before such other date as the Vendor and the Purchaser shall agree) to a transfer payment being made in respect of him to the Purchaser's Scheme from the Pension Scheme;[168]

'Transfer Value' means an amount equal to the sum of:

(A) the Basic Amount multiplied by the Investment Adjustment for the period from and including the day next following the Transfer Date to and including the Membership Transfer Date; plus

(B) the aggregate contributions paid in respect of the Interim Period to the Pension Scheme by or in respect of the Transferring Employees [(other than, in relation to any Transferring Employee, any such contributions paid while he was a Life Assurance Employee)] less [   ] in respect of the cost of insuring the death-in-service benefits in respect of the Transferring Employees together with Interest on the balance from the date of payment of each such contribution to the Membership Transfer Date;

reduced, but only if [the Purchaser's Scheme is a retirement benefits scheme and] the employment of the Transferring Employees is not to be contracted-out by reference to the Purchaser's Scheme, by an amount equal to the sum (determined by applying the Actuarial Assumptions *mutatis mutandis*) of:

(1) the amount on the day next before the Membership Transfer Date of the protected rights of the Transferring Employees under the Pension Scheme; minus

(2) the discounted value on the day before the Membership Transfer Date of any age-related payment payable in respect of the Transferring Employees on or

after the Membership Transfer Date in respect of any period before that date; plus

(3) the capital value on the date next before the Membership Transfer Date of the guaranteed minimum pensions and section 9(2B) rights payable under the Pension Scheme to or in respect of the Transferring Employees;[169]

'Vendor's Actuary' means [   ] (or such other Actuary as the Vendor may appoint for the purposes of this Schedule).

1.2   Statutory Terms

In this Schedule, where the context admits, 'exempt approved scheme', 'personal pension scheme' and 'retirement benefits scheme' have the same meanings as in the Income and Corporation Taxes Act 1988; 'appropriate scheme', 'contracted-out', 'contracted-out scheme', 'contracting-out certificate', 'guaranteed minimum', 'guaranteed minimum pension' and 'protected rights' shall have the same meanings as in the Pension Schemes Act 1993; 'age-related payment' and 'section 9(2B) rights' have the same meanings as in The Occupational Pension Schemes (Contracting-out) Regulations 1996 and 'schedule of contributions' has the same meaning as in the Pensions Act 1995.

1.3   Employees

References in this Schedule to employees includes directors.

1.4   Indices

Where in this Schedule or in the Actuary's Letter there is a reference to any index on a particular date and the index for that date is not published or otherwise ascertainable the index for that date shall be determined by the Vendor's Actuary and agreed by the Purchaser's Actuary, or in default of such agreement within one month of the Vendor or the Purchaser giving notice to the other that a dispute has arisen, determined by an independent Actuary pursuant to Paragraph 7.

1.5   Separate Application

Paragraphs 2 to 7 (inclusive) and for the purposes of those Paragraphs Paragraph 1 apply separately to each Pension Scheme. Where more than one scheme is nominated as the Purchaser's Scheme pursuant to Sub-Paragraph 4.1, those Paragraphs shall, where the context so requires, also apply separately to each of those schemes and the Transferring Employees referable to that scheme. No more than one such scheme may for the purposes of this Schedule be referable to any particular Transferring Employee. If apart from this provision more than one such scheme would be referable to a Transferring Employee, the Purchaser shall notify the Vendor as to which such scheme is to be treated as referable to him.[170]

1.6   Purchaser's Group Reorganisation

If during the Interim Period any of the Pensionable Employees are transferred from the employment of the Purchaser to another company within, or otherwise connected with, the Purchaser's Group (the 'New Employer'), the Vendor shall, at the request of the Purchaser, use all reasonable endeavours to procure that the New Employer is duly admitted to participation in the Pension Scheme with effect from the date of such transfer or if more than one such transfer occurs with effect from the date of the first such transfer. If for any reason the New Employer is not duly admitted to participation in the Pension Scheme then in respect of the employees transferred to it the day next following the date of such transfer shall be the Membership Transfer Date in relation to those employees and this Schedule shall take effect accordingly. Subject to the New Employer being so admitted, the New Employer and the Purchaser shall be treated as one for the purposes of Paragraphs 1 to 7 (inclusive).[171]

2 Data

2.1 Data to be Supplied

The Vendor and the Purchaser shall each use all reasonable endeavours to procure that all such information as the Vendor's Actuary or the Purchaser's Actuary or any independent Actuary appointed under Paragraph 7 may reasonably request for the purposes of this Schedule is supplied promptly to such Actuary.

2.2 Non-availability of Data

If any information requested by an Actuary is not (whatever the reason) made available by the date which is 42 days after the date the request is made, he may make reasonable assumptions as to the information requested and any assumptions so made by an independent Actuary appointed under Paragraph 7 shall (in the absence of manifest error) be treated as facts for any and all of the purposes of this Schedule.

2.3 Data Accuracy Warranty

The Vendor hereby warrants to the Purchaser for itself and as trustee and agent for the Purchaser's Group and the Purchaser's Scheme that all such information which it or any member of the Vendor's Group or the Pension Scheme provides or procures to be provided for any purpose relevant to this Schedule shall be true, complete and accurate in all material respects as at the date the information is required for the purpose of this Schedule and shall contain no omission material to the calculation of the Transfer Value or material to any other calculation or determination for the purposes of this Schedule.

3 The Pension Scheme

3.1 Deed of Adherence

At or forthwith following the Transfer Date the Purchaser shall execute and deliver and the Vendor shall use its best endeavours to procure that the other parties to the deed hereinafter referred to execute and deliver a deed [in agreed terms] providing for the Purchaser to participate in the Pension Scheme throughout the period which would (apart from the exception to the definition of 'Membership Transfer Date') be the Interim Period. [The deed shall be in such terms as the Vendor, the Purchaser and the Pension Scheme agree (such agreement not to be unreasonably withheld or delayed by either the Vendor or the Purchaser and the Vendor shall procure that such agreement is not unreasonably withheld or delayed by the Pension Scheme)].

3.2 Vendor's Undertakings

The Vendor undertakes to the Purchaser:

(A) to use all reasonable endeavours to procure that subject to:
   (1) a deed of adherence being executed and delivered by the parties thereto in accordance with Sub-Paragraph 3.1; and
   (2) the consent of the Board of Inland Revenue to the participation of the Purchaser in the Pension Scheme throughout the period which would (apart from the exception to the definition of 'Membership Transfer Date') be the

Interim Period (such approval the Vendor shall use all reasonable endeavours to obtain);

the Purchaser is permitted to participate in the Pension Scheme throughout that period;

(B)   to procure that until after payment has been made in full in accordance with Paragraph 5 no power or discretion under the Pension Scheme is exercised in a way which would or might affect the Purchaser and/or all or any of its employees save with the consent of the Purchaser;

(C)   to use all reasonable endeavours to procure that none of the Employees is discriminated against in the exercise of any discretionary power (including, without limitation, the grant of discretionary pension increases) under the Pension Scheme;

(D)   to procure that if the Purchaser's Scheme is a retirement benefits scheme no payment is made by the Pension Scheme which would or might result in the Purchaser's Scheme not obtaining approval under or, as the case may be, ceasing to be approved under the Income and Corporation Taxes Act 1988, s 591 or in the pensionable service completed by a Transferring Employee under the Pension Scheme not being treated as continuous with the pensionable service completed by him under the Purchaser's Scheme for the purpose of determining the maximum benefits which may be paid under the Purchaser's Scheme without prejudicing the obtaining of approval of or, as the case may be, the approval of the Purchaser's Scheme as aforesaid;[172]

(E)   to indemnify and to keep indemnified and to hold harmless on a continuing basis the Purchaser against all and any liability to make any payment to or in connection with the Pension Scheme (including, but without limitation, the amount (if any) the Actuary to the Pension Scheme certifies pursuant to Sub-Paragraph 3.5) other than to pay contributions pursuant to Sub-Paragraph 3.3(A);[173] and

(F)   to procure that the Pension Scheme is maintained in full force and effect and does not cease to have active members until after the Purchaser has ceased to participate in the Pension Scheme.

3.3   Purchaser's Undertaking

The Purchaser shall:

(A)   pay or procure to be paid to the Pension Scheme the employer contributions which accrue to the Pension Scheme during the Interim Period in respect of the Pensionable Employees [and the Life Assurance Employees] from time to time, such contributions to be deemed to be payable at [the same rate as is in force at the date of this Agreement] [the same rate as is generally payable from time to time by other employers participating in the Pension Scheme] [an annual rate of:

(1)   in relation to a Pensionable Employee, [   ] per cent of [   ] from time to time;

(2)   in relation to a Life Assurance Employee, [   ] per cent of [   ] from time to time];

plus the contributions (if any) payable during the Interim Period by the Pensionable Employees; and

(B)   complies in all other respects with the provisions of the Pension Scheme during the Interim Period.[174]

[3.4   Contracting-out in Interim Period

The Vendor and the Purchaser undertake to co-operate with each other with a view to procuring that the employment of the Pensionable Employees is contracted-out by reference to the Pension Scheme at all applicable times during the Interim Period.][175]

3.5   Statutory Debt

The Vendor shall procure that as soon as reasonably practicable after the Membership Transfer Date (and in any event within three months from that date) the Actuary to the Pension Scheme shall in accordance with all applicable statutory requirements and professional guidance, either certify in writing:

(A)   the amount which is due from the Purchaser to the Pension Scheme pursuant to s 75 of the Pensions Act 1995; or

(B)   that no such amount is due.

The obligation on the Vendor contained in this Sub-Paragraph 3.5 above shall include, if necessary to comply with the prevailing statutory requirements and professional guidance then applicable, procuring that the Pension Scheme carries out a minimum funding valuation for the purposes of s 57(1)(a), Pensions Act 1995.[176]

4   The Purchaser's Scheme

4.1   Purchaser to Provide Scheme

For the purposes of this Schedule the Purchaser shall nominate or procure the nomination of one or more [of the following:

(A)] retirement benefits schemes which are, or which are designed to be capable of being, exempt approved schemes[.][;

(B)   personal pension schemes which are approved under Chapter IV, Part XIV of the Income and Corporation Taxes Act 1988.]

4.2   Purchaser to Offer Membership[177]

The Purchaser shall procure that those of the Employees on the Membership Transfer Date who were Pensionable Employees immediately prior to that date are offered membership of the Purchaser's Scheme.

4.3   Final Salary Past Service Credit

The Purchaser shall procure that on payment being made in full in accordance with Sub-Paragraphs 5.2 and 5.3 the Transferring Employees [(other than the MP Employees as defined in Sub-Paragraph 4.4)][178] are credited with benefits under the Purchaser's Scheme in respect of service prior to the Membership Transfer Date which are, in the opinion of the Purchaser's Actuary, substantially no less favourable overall than the benefits which would have been payable under the Pension Scheme in respect of such service had the Purchaser continued to participate in the Pension Scheme on indefinite basis but disregarding any changes to the benefits under the Pension Scheme on or after the Transfer Date and having due regard to whether a transfer is made from the Pension Scheme to the Purchaser's Scheme in respect of the Contracting-out Benefits under the Pension Scheme of the Transferring Employees. The benefits so credited shall be payable in accordance with and subject to the terms and conditions of the Purchaser's Scheme including (but without limitation) the powers of amendment and discontinuance.

[4.4   Money Purchase Alternative

The Purchaser may (at its option) provide benefits under this Paragraph for such (or all) of the Transferring Employees as the Purchaser determines (the 'MP Employees') in lieu of the benefits which would otherwise be provided pursuant to Sub-Paragraph 4.3. For each of the MP Employees the Purchaser shall on payment being made in full in accordance with Sub-Paragraphs 5.2 and 5.3 procure that an amount equal to that part of the Adjusted Transfer Value as is referable to the MP Employee is credited to an account under the Purchaser's Scheme designated to the MP Employee and that amount adjusted for investment return (positive or negative) less relevant expenses shall (subject to the requirements for approval of the Purchaser's Scheme by the Board of the Inland Revenue) be applied to provide money purchase benefits for or in respect of the MP Employee and his service before the Membership Transfer Date.]

5 Payment of Transfer Value

5.1 Calculation

Immediately following the Membership Transfer Date the Vendor shall procure that the Vendor's Actuary calculates the amount of the Transfer Value and submits his findings in writing to the Purchaser's Actuary. If the Purchaser's Actuary agrees the amount of the Transfer Value, the Vendor shall procure that the Vendor's Actuary and the Purchaser shall procure that the Purchaser's Actuary jointly certify that amount as the Transfer Value. If, however, the Vendor's Actuary and the Purchaser's Actuary fail to agree within two months from the date upon which the Vendor's Actuary first submits his findings to the Purchaser's Actuary as aforesaid, the matter may, at the option of either the Vendor or the Purchaser, be referred to an independent Actuary pursuant to Paragraph 7.

5.2 Payment

The Vendor shall use all reasonable endeavours to procure that the Pension Scheme transfers to the Purchaser's Scheme on the Payment Date the Adjusted Transfer Value in cash (or if the Vendor and the Purchaser so agree transfers assets equal in value to the Adjusted Transfer Value).[179]

5.3 Shortfall[180]

If the sum (if any) duly transferred from the Pension Scheme to the Purchaser's Scheme in respect of the Transferring Employees on the Payment Date is less than the Adjusted Transfer Value (the amount of the difference being referred to in this Paragraph as the 'Shortfall'), the Vendor shall forthwith pay, by way of adjustment so far as possible to the Provisional Consideration,[181] to the Purchaser (or to a third party as the Purchaser may direct) an amount in cash equal to the Shortfall together with interest thereon (accruing daily and compounded monthly) from and including the Payment Date to but excluding the date upon which final payment is made in accordance with this Paragraph (as well after judgment as before). Such interest to be at the base rate from time to time of [   ] Bank Plc plus [   ] per cent per annum.[182]

5.4 Payment on Account

If the Purchaser so requests, the Vendor shall use its best endeavours to procure that as soon as practicable after receiving such request (but not before the Membership Transfer Date) a payment on account of the amount payable pursuant to Sub-Paragraph 5.2 is made to the Purchaser's Scheme. Such payment shall be equal to [   ] per cent of the amount which the Vendor's Actuary, in consultation with the Purchaser's Actuary, reasonably estimates to be the amount of the Adjusted Transfer Value. In the event of a payment on account being made in accordance with this Paragraph, the Pension Scheme shall be deemed to have transferred on the Payment Date to the Purchaser's Scheme (in addition to the amount (if any) actually transferred on the Payment Date) an amount equal to the payment made in accordance with this Paragraph [multiplied by the Invest-ment Adjustment for the period from and including the day next following that upon which that payment is made to and including the Payment Date.]

5.5 Apportioning Adjusted Transfer Value

The Vendor shall if the Purchaser so requests arrange for the Purchaser's Scheme to be notified in writing in respect of each Transferring Employee:

(1)   the amount of the Adjusted Transfer Value referable to him;
(2)   the amount of the part (if any) of the Adjusted Transfer Value which is the cash equivalent of his accrued rights to guaranteed minimum pensions;
(3)   the amount of the part (if any) of the Adjusted Transfer Value which is the cash equivalent of his section 9(2B) rights; and
(4)   the amount of the part (if any) of the Adjusted Transfer Value which is the cash equivalent of his protected rights;

where such cash equivalents shall be calculated and verified in a manner consistent with s 97, Pension Schemes Act 1993.

6   Additional Voluntary Contribution

6.1   For the purpose of the foregoing provisions of this Schedule there shall be disre-garded:

(A)   any benefits under the Pension Scheme which are attributable to additional volun-tary contributions made to it by the members of the Pension Scheme and in respect of which the members are not entitled to benefits based on their final pensionable earnings (however defined);
(B)   any such contributions; and
(C)   any transfer in respect of any such benefits or contributions.

The Vendor shall nevertheless use all reasonable endeavours to procure that the Pension Scheme transfers to the Purchaser's Scheme on the Payment Date for the benefit of the Transferring Employees all such funds and assets of the Pension Scheme which repre-sent any such contributions made by the Transferring Employees and the investment return on them.

7   Disputes

7.1   Any dispute between the Vendor's Actuary and the Purchaser's Actuary concern-ing the amount of the Transfer Value or any other matter to be agreed between them in accordance with this Schedule may, at the option of either the Vendor or the Purchaser, be referred to an independent Actuary to be appointed by agreement between the Ven-dor and the Purchaser or, in default of agreement within 14 days from the first nomina-tion of an Actuary by one party to the other, by the President for the time being of The Institute of Actuaries (or of any successor body) on the application of either the Vendor or the Purchaser. The independent Actuary shall act as an expert and not as an arbitra-tor.[183] His decision shall, save in the event of fraud or manifest error, be final and bind-ing on the parties and his costs shall be borne by the Vendor and the Purchaser [equally or in such other proportions as he directs].

8   Warranties and Representations[117; 184]

8.1   The Vendor hereby warrants and represents[117] to and for the benefit of the Pur-chaser in the following terms:

(A) *No Other Arrangements*   Save for the Pension Scheme no member of the Vendor's Group is a party to or participates in or contributes to any scheme, agreement or arrangement (whether legally enforceable or not) for the provision of any pension, retirement, death, incapacity, sickness, disability, accident or other like benefits (including the payment after cessation of employment with the Vendor of medical expenses) for any Employee or for the widow, widower, child or dependant of any Employee.

(B) *No Assurances etc*   No member of the Vendor's Group:

    (1) has given any undertaking or assurance (whether legally enforceable or not) as to the continuance, introduction, improvement or increase of any benefit of a kind described in Sub-Paragraph 8.1(A) above, or

    (2) is paying or has in the last two years paid any such benefit

    to (in either case) any Employee or any widow, widower, child or dependant of any Employee.

(C) *All Details Disclosed*   All material details relating to the Pension Scheme are contained in or annexed to the Disclosure Letter including (but without limitation) the following:

    (1) true and complete copies of the following documents referable to the Pension Scheme, *viz*:

        (a) all deeds, rules and other governing documents of current effect;

        (b) all announcements, booklets and the like of current effect which have been issued to any of the Employees;

        (c) the latest completed actuarial valuation report and any document (including a draft) containing the results or preliminary results of any subsequent actuarial valuation;

        (d) the latest completed audited accounts and any subsequent accounts or draft accounts;

        (e) an accurate list of all Pensionable Employees and Life Assurance Employees at the date of this Agreement with such data as is necessary to establish their respective entitlements under the Pension Scheme;

        (f) the schedule of contributions;

    (2) details of all amendments (if any) to the Pension Scheme which have been announced or are proposed but which have not yet been formally made;

    (3) details of all discretionary increases (if any) to pensions in payment or in deferment under the Pension Scheme which have been granted in the ten years prior to the date of this Agreement or which are under consideration;

    (4) details of all discretionary practices (if any) which may have led any person to expect additional benefits in a given set of circumstances (by way of example, but without limitation, on retirement at the behest of the Vendor or in the event of redundancy); and

    (5) details of the rate at which and basis upon which the Vendor currently contributes to the Pension Scheme, any change to that rate and/or basis which is proposed or which is under consideration and all contributions paid to the Pension Scheme by the Vendor in the three years prior to the date of this Agreement.

(D) *Membership*   Every person who has at any time had the right to join, or apply to join, the Pension Scheme has been properly advised of that right. No Employee has been excluded from membership of the Pension Scheme or from any of the benefits thereunder in contravention of Art 119 of the Treaty of Rome, the Pensions Act 1995 or other applicable laws or requirements or the provisions of the Pension Scheme or otherwise.

(E) *No pay restructuring* There has not in the last four years been any restructuring of the earnings of all or any of the Employees (by way of example, but without limitation, consolidation of bonuses into basic pay).[185]

(F) *Transfer payments* No transfer value has been paid (directly or indirectly) to the Pension Scheme from another arrangement for any employee under which any benefits referable to that Employee contravened Art 119 of the Treaty of Rome, s 62 of the Pensions Act 1995 or other applicable law or requirement.

(G) *Death Benefits Insured* All benefits (other than any refund of members' contributions with interest where appropriate) payable under the Pension Scheme on the death of any person while in employment to which the Pension Scheme relates are insured fully under a policy with an insurance company of good repute and there are no grounds on which that company might avoid liability under that policy.

(H) *Augmentation* No power under the Pension Scheme has been exercised in relation to any Employee:

(1) to provide terms of membership of the Pension Scheme (whether as to benefits or contributions) which are different from those generally applicable to members of the Pension Scheme;

(2) to provide any benefits which would not but for the exercise of that power have been payable under the Pension Scheme; or

(3) to augment any benefits under the Pension Scheme.

(I) *Contributions* Contributions to the Pension Scheme are not paid in arrear and all contributions and other amounts which have fallen due for payment by the Vendor have been paid. The Vendor has (to the extent that it will be required to do) discharged its liability (if any) to pay or reimburse (whether wholly or in part) to anyone who has paid any costs, charges or expenses which have been incurred by or in connection with the Pension Scheme.

(J) *Vendor's obligations* The Vendor:

(1) has been admitted to participation in the Pension Scheme on the same terms as apply generally to other employers participating in the Pension Scheme;

(2) has observed and performed those provisions of the Pension Scheme which apply to it;

(3) is not indebted to the Pension Scheme by virtue of s 75 of the Pensions Act 1995; [and][186]

(4) may (without the consent of any person or further payment) terminate its liability to contribute to the Pension Scheme at any time subject only to giving such notice (if any) as is expressly provided for in the documentation containing the current provisions governing the Pension Scheme[187] [.] [and

(5) has at all material times held or been named in a contracting-out certificate referable to the Pension Scheme.]

(K) *Compliance* The Pension Scheme:

(1) is an exempt approved scheme; and

(2) complies with and has at all times been administered in accordance with all applicable laws, regulations and requirements (including those of the Board of Inland Revenue and of trust law).

(L) *Disputes* None of the Pension Scheme, the Vendor or any member of the Vendor's Group is engaged or involved in any proceedings which relate to or are in connection with the Pension Scheme or the benefits thereunder and no such proceedings are pending or threatened and so far as the Vendor is aware there are no facts likely to give rise to any such proceedings. In this Sub-Paragraph 'proceedings' includes any litigation or arbitration and also includes any investigation or determination by the Pensions Ombudsman or the Occupational Pensions Advisory Service and any complaint under any internal dispute resolution procedure established in connection with the Pension Scheme.

9 Damages for Breach of Pension Warranties[188]

9.1 In determining the damages flowing from any breach of Warranties contained in Paragraph 8, the Purchaser shall be deemed to become at Completion under a liability:

(A) to provide and to continue to provide any benefits of a kind referred to in that Paragraph which are now provided or have been announced or are proposed; and

(B) to maintain and to continue to maintain (without benefits being reduced) the Pension Scheme and any other arrangements of a kind described in that Paragraph which are now in existence or are proposed and any discretionary practices of a kind referred to in that Paragraph which have hitherto been carried on.

SCHEDULE 7

PENSIONS

[C   Vendor has own money purchase scheme][189]

1   Interpretation

1.1   Definitions

In this Schedule, where the context admits:

'Pension Scheme' means [the retirement benefits scheme known as [   ] which was established by a deed dated [   ] (or the trustees from time to time of that scheme as the context requires);] [Scheme A [;] Scheme B] and [Scheme C] (or such one or [other] [more] of them as the context requires);]

['Scheme A' means the retirement benefits scheme known as [   ] which was established by a trust deed dated [   ] (or the trustees from time to time of that scheme as the context requires);] [and]

'Scheme B' means the retirement benefits scheme known as [   ] which was established by a trust deed dated [   ] (or the trustees from time to time of that scheme as the context requires) [.] [; and

'Scheme C' means the retirement benefits scheme known as [   ] which was established by a trust deed dated [   ] (or the trustees from time to time of that scheme as the context requires).]

1.2   Employees

References in this Schedule to employees includes directors.

2   The Pension Scheme[190]

2.1   Purchaser to Become Principal Employer

The Vendor undertakes to the Purchaser to procure that subject to the consent of the Inland Revenue (which consent the Vendor shall use all reasonable endeavours to procure), the Purchaser becomes the principal employer of the Pension Scheme with effect from the Transfer Date.

[2.2   Retirement of Trustees

The Vendor undertakes to the Purchaser to procure that [   ] [and [   ]] retire(s) as (a) trustee(s) of the Pension Scheme with effect from the Transfer Date.]

2.3   Damages for Breach

In assessing damages flowing from any breach of the provisions of this Paragraph 2 it shall be deemed to be within the power of the Vendor to procure everything which in this Paragraph the Vendor has undertaken to procure.

3   Warranties and Representations[117; 191]

3.1   The Vendor hereby warrants and represents[117] to and for the benefit of the Purchaser in the following terms:

(A)   *No Other Arrangements*   Save for the Pension Scheme no member of the Vendor's Group is a party to or participates in or contributes to any scheme, agreement or arrangement (whether legally enforceable or not) for the provision of any pension, retirement, death, incapacity, sickness, disability, accident or other like benefits (including the payment after cessation of employment with the Vendor of medical expenses) for any Employee or for the widow, widower, child or dependant of any Employee.

(B)   *No Assurances etc*   No member of the Vendor's Group:
   (1)   has given any undertaking or assurance (whether legally enforceable or not) as to the continuance, introduction, improvement or increase of any benefit of a kind described in Sub-Paragraph 3.1(A) above, or
   (2)   is paying or has in the last two years paid any such benefit,
   to (in either case) any Employee or to any widow, widower, child or dependant of any Employee.

(C)   *All Details Disclosed*   All material details relating to the Pension Scheme are contained in or annexed to the Disclosure Letter including, but without limitation, the following:
   (1)   true and complete copies of the following documents referable to the Pension Scheme, *viz*:
      (a)   all deeds, rules and other governing documents;
      (b)   all announcements, booklets and the like of current effect;
      (c)   the latest completed actuarial valuation report;[192]
      (d)   the latest completed audited accounts;
      (e)   all administration and other agreements to which the Pension Scheme is a party;
      (f)   all insurance policies (if any) and annuity contracts (if any) and all proposals (if any) to effect any such policies or contracts which are with any insurer for consideration;
      (g)   an accurate list of all Employees for whom contributions are being paid, or are payable, by the Vendor, showing the amount of contributions in respect of each Employee;
      (h)   an accurate list with the names and addresses of all the trustees;
      (i)   the memorandum and articles of association of any trustee which is a company and an accurate list with the names and addresses of the directors and secretary of that company; and
      (j)   internal dispute resolution procedure, payment schedule and statement of investment principles for the purposes of the Pensions Act 1995;
   (2)   details of the arrangements made or being considered (or confirmation that none have been made or are being considered) to comply with ss 16–21, Pensions Act 1995;
   (3)   details of the investments and assets of the Pension Scheme;
   (4)   details of all amendments (if any) to the Pension Scheme which have been announced or are proposed but which have not yet been formally made;
   (5)   details of all discretionary increases (if any) to pensions in payment or in deferment under the Pension Scheme which have been granted in the ten years prior to the date of this Agreement or which are under consideration;
   (6)   details of all discretionary practices (if any) which may have led any person to expect additional benefits in a given set of circumstances (by way of ex-

ample, but without limitation, on retirement at the behest of the Vendor or in the event of redundancy).

(D) *Membership*   Every person who has at any time had the right to join, or apply to join, the Pension Scheme has been properly advised of that right. No Employee has been excluded from membership of the Pension Scheme or from any of the benefits thereunder in contravention of Art 119 of the Treaty of Rome, the Pensions Act 1995 or other applicable laws or requirements, or the provisions of the Pension Scheme or otherwise.

(E) *Benefits*   All benefits which are not money purchase benefits and which are payable under the Pension Scheme on the death of any person while in employment to which the Pension Scheme relates are insured fully under a policy with an insurance company of good repute and there are no grounds on which that company might avoid liability under that policy. All other benefits payable under the Pension Scheme are money purchase benefits. In this Sub-Paragraph 'money purchase benefits' has the same meaning as in s 181(1) Pension Schemes Act 1993.

(F) *Transfer payments*   No transfer value has been paid (directly or indirectly) to the Pension Scheme from another arrangement for any member of the Pension Scheme under which any benefits referable to that member contravened Art 119 of the Treaty of Rome, s 62 of the Pensions Act 1995 or other applicable law or requirement.

(G) *Contributions and Expenses*   Contributions to the Pension Scheme are not paid in arrear and all contributions and other amounts which have fallen due for payment have been paid punctually. No fee, charge or expense relating to or in connection with the Pension Scheme has been incurred but not paid. If any such fee, charge or expense has been paid by any person other than the Pension Scheme the Pension Scheme has reimbursed that person if and to the extent that the Pension Scheme is or may become liable so to do.

(H) *Vendor's Obligations*   The Vendor:

    (1)   has observed and performed those provisions of the Pension Scheme which apply to it; [and]

    (2)   may (without the consent of any person or further payment) terminate its liability to contribute to the Pension Scheme at any time subject only to giving such notice (if any) as is expressly provided for in the documentation containing the current provisions governing the Pension Scheme[193] [.] [; and

    (3)   has at all material times held or been named in a contracting-out certificate (within the meaning of s 7(1) of the Pension Schemes Act 1993) referable to the Pension Scheme.]

(I) *No Other Employer*   The Vendor is the only employer for the time being participating in the Pension Scheme. No employer which has previously participated in the Pension Scheme has any claim under the Pension Scheme and in respect of any such employer the period of participation has been terminated and benefits have been provided in accordance with the provisions of the Pension Scheme.

(J) *Administration*   All documentation and records in respect of the Pension Scheme are up to date and so far as the Vendor is aware complete and accurate in all material respects.

(K) *Investments*   Save for any deposit with a bank or building society the only assets which the Pension Scheme has held are insurance policies and annuity contracts with insurance companies of good repute.

(L) *Compliance*   The Pension Scheme:

    (1)   is an exempt approved scheme (within the meaning of s 592(1) of the Income and Corporation Taxes Act 1988);

(2)   has properly and punctually accounted to the Inland Revenue for all and any tax for which the Pension Scheme is liable or accountable; and

(3)   has at all times complied with and been administered in accordance with all applicable laws, regulations and requirements (including those of the Board of Inland Revenue and of trust law).

(M) *Disputes*   None of the Pension Scheme, the Vendor or any member of the Vendor's Group is engaged or involved in any proceedings which relate to or are in connection with the Pension Scheme or the benefits thereunder and no such proceedings are pending or threatened and so far as the Vendor is aware there are no facts likely to give rise to any such proceedings. In this Sub-Paragraph 'proceedings' includes any litigation or arbitration and also includes any investigation or determination by the Pensions Ombudsman or the Occupational Pensions Advisory Service and any complaint under any internal dispute resolution procedure established in connection with the Pension Scheme.

(N) *Indemnities*   In relation to the Pension Scheme or funds which are or have been held for the purposes thereof neither the Vendor nor the Pension Scheme has given an indemnity or guarantee to any person (other than in the case of the Vendor any general indemnity in favour of the trustees or administrator under the documentation governing the Pension Scheme).

4   Damages for Breach of Pension Warranties[194]

4.1   In determining the damages flowing from any breach of Warranties contained in Paragraph 3, the Purchaser shall be deemed to become at Completion under a liability:

(A)   to provide and to continue to provide any benefit of a kind referred to in that Paragraph which is now provided or has been announced or is proposed; and

(B)   to maintain and to continue to maintain (without benefits being reduced) the Pension Scheme and any other arrangements of a kind described in that Paragraph which are now in existence or are proposed and any discretionary practices of a kind referred to in that Paragraph which have hitherto been carried on.

SCHEDULE 7

PENSIONS

[D   Vendor participates in group money purchase scheme][195]

1 Interpretation

1.1   Definitions

In this Schedule, where the context admits:

'Interim Period' means the period from the Transfer Date to and including [   ] (or such earlier date as the Purchaser may by not less than one month's notice in writing to the Vendor specify or such later date as the Vendor and the Purchaser may agree in writing) except that if for any reason the Purchaser is unable to participate in the Pension Scheme in accordance with Sub-Paragraph 2.1 until the date which would (apart from this exception) be the last day of the Interim Period the Interim Period shall end on the last day the Purchaser participates in the Pension Scheme;

['Life Assurance Employee' means an Employee who is covered by the Pension Scheme for certain death-in-service benefits but is not a Pensionable Employee;]

'Pension Scheme' means [the retirement benefits scheme known as [   ] which was established by a deed dated [   ] (or the trustees from time to time of that scheme as the context requires);] [Scheme A [;] [Scheme B] [and Scheme C] (or such one or [other] [more] of them as the context requires);]

'Pensionable Employee' means an Employee who is, or (but for being absent from work or but for not fulfilling any relevant eligibility conditions) would be, in pensionable service under the Pension Scheme;

['Scheme A' means the retirement benefits scheme known as [   ] which was established by a trust deed dated [   ] (or the trustees from time to time of that scheme as the context requires);]

['Scheme B' means the retirement benefits scheme known as [   ] which was established by a trust deed dated [   ] (or the trustees from time to time of that scheme as the context requires);]

['Scheme C' means the retirement benefits scheme known as [   ] (or the trustees from time to time of that scheme as the context requires);]

'Statutory Transfer Provision' means Chapter IV, Part IV of the Pension Schemes Act 1993.

1.2   Employees

References in this Schedule to employees includes directors.

1.3   Purchaser's Group Reorganisation

If during the Interim Period any of the Pensionable Employees is transferred from the employment of the Purchaser to another company within, or otherwise connected with, the Purchaser's Group (the 'New Employer'), the Vendor shall, at the request of the Purchaser, use all reasonable endeavours to procure that the New Employer is duly admitted to participation in the Pension Scheme with effect from the date of such transfer or if more than one such transfer occurs with effect from the date of the first such transfer. If for any reason the New Employer is not so admitted then in respect of the employees transferred to it the day next following the date of such transfer shall in relation to those employees be the last day of the Interim Period and this Schedule shall take effect accordingly. Subject to the New Employer being so admitted the New Employer and the Purchaser shall be treated as one for the purposes of Paragraphs 1 to 3 (inclusive).[196]

[1.4   Separate Application

Paragraphs 2 and 3 and for the purposes of those Paragraphs Paragraph 1 apply separately to each Pension Scheme.]

2   The Pension Scheme

2.1   Vendor's Undertakings

The Vendor undertakes to the Purchaser:

(A)   to procure that subject to the consent of the Board of Inland Revenue being obtained (which consent the Vendor shall use all reasonable endeavours to procure), the Purchaser is admitted to participate in the Pension Scheme throughout the period which would (apart from the exception to the definition of 'Interim Period') be the Interim Period;

(B)   to procure that no power or discretion under the Pension Scheme is exercised in a way which would or might affect the Purchaser and/or all or any of the Employees save with the consent of the Purchaser;

(C)   to indemnify and to keep indemnified and to hold harmless on a continuing basis the Purchaser against all and any liability to make any payment to or in connection with the Pension Scheme other than to pay contributions pursuant to Sub-Paragraph 2.2(A); and

(D)   to procure that the Pension Scheme continues in full force and effect and does not cease to have active members (within the meaning of the Pensions Act 1995) until after the Purchaser has ceased to participate in it.[197]

2.2   Purchaser's Undertaking

The Purchaser shall:

(A)   pay or procure to be paid to the Pension Scheme the employer contributions which accrue under the terms of the Pension Scheme during the Interim Period in respect of the Pensionable Employees [and the Life Assurance Employees] from time to time, such contributions shall be deemed to be payable at [the same rate as is in force at the date of this Agreement] [an annual rate of:
   (1)   in relation to a Pensionable Employee, [   ] per cent of [   ] from time to time;
   (2)   in relation to a Life Assurance Employee, [   ] per cent of [   ] from time to time;]
   plus the contributions (if any) payable during the Interim Period by the Pensionable Employees; and

(B)   complies in all other respects with the provisions of the Pension Scheme during the Interim Period.[198]

[2.3   Contracting-out

The Vendor and the Purchaser undertake to co-operate with each other with a view to procuring that the employment of the Pensionable Employees is contracted-out of the state earnings related pension scheme by reference to the Pension Scheme at all applicable times during the Interim Period.][199]

3 Benefits and Options[200]

3.1 The Vendor undertakes to the Purchaser for its own benefit and as trustee and agent for the Pensionable Employees to procure that:

(A) benefits will be provided under the Pension Scheme for each Pensionable Employee who on ceasing to be in pensionable service under the Pension Scheme does not qualify for short service benefits (within the meaning of s 71 of the Pension Schemes Act 1993) as if he had qualified for such benefits unless the Pensionable Employee elects to take a refund of his contributions;[201]

(B) the Pension Scheme notifies each Pensionable Employee in writing as soon as practicable after he ceases to be in pensionable service under the Pension Scheme and in any event within 30 days thereafter of the options available to him under the Pension Scheme and the funds accumulated for his benefit under the Pension Scheme and all other information concerning the Pension Scheme and those options which the Pensionable Employee may reasonably require in order to make an informed decision as to which (if any) option to exercise;[202]

(C) any Pensionable Employee who on ceasing to be in pensionable service under the Pension Scheme does not acquire a right to a transfer value under Statutory Transfer Provision is given the option under the Pension Scheme of a transfer value as if he had acquired such a right;[203]

(D) the transfer value paid in respect of any Pensionable Employee shall not be less than it would have been had Statutory Transfer Provision required the amount of the transfer value to be the value of the funds accumulated for the benefit of the Pensionable Employee adjusted (upwards or downwards) for the investment return obtained on those funds up to the date the transfer value is paid;[204]

(E) subject to Sub-Paragraph 3.1(D) the amount of any transfer value for a Pensionable Employee is the cash equivalent (within the meaning of Statutory Transfer Provision) without any reduction pursuant to reg 8(4) of the Occupational Pension Schemes (Transfer Values) Regulations 1996;

(F) if a Pensionable Employee requests in writing that a transfer value be paid in respect of him in a manner permitted under Statutory Transfer Provision the Pension Scheme gives effect to that request as soon as practicable and in any event within 60 days of that request being made; and

(G) the Purchaser is forthwith on request advised in writing of the respective amounts of the transfer values for the Pensionable Employees and is supplied with such information and evidence as the Purchaser may request to enable the Purchaser to verify those amounts.

4 Warranties and Representations[117; 205]

4.1 The Vendor hereby warrants and represents[117] to and for the benefit of the Purchaser in the following terms:

(A) *No Other Arrangements* Save for the Pension Scheme the Vendor is not a party to nor participates in nor contributes to any scheme, agreement or arrangement (whether legally enforceable or not) for the provision of any pension, retirement, death, incapacity, sickness, disability, accident or other like benefits (including the payment after cessation of employment with the Vendor of medical expenses) for any Employee or for the widow, widower, child or dependant of any Employee.

(B) *No Assurance etc* No member of the Vendor's Group:

(1) has given any undertaking or assurance (whether legally enforceable or not) as to the continuance, introduction, improvement or increase of any benefit of a kind described in 4.1(A) above, or

(2) is paying or has in the last two years paid any such benefit,

to (in either case) any Employee or to any widow, widower, child or dependant of any Employee.

(C) *All Details Disclosed*   All material details relating to the Pension Scheme are contained in or annexed to the Disclosure Letter including, but without limitation, the following:

(1) true and complete copies of the following documents referable to the Pension Scheme, *viz*:

(a) all deeds, rules and other governing documents;

(b) all announcements, booklets and the like of current effect;

(c) the latest completed actuarial valuation report;[192]

(d) the latest completed audited accounts;

(e) payment schedule (within the meaning of s 87 of the Pensions Act 1995);

(f) an accurate list of all Employees for whom contributions are being paid, or are payable, by the Vendor showing the amount of contributions in respect of each employee;

(2) details of the investment in which the funds referable to the Pensionable Employees are held;

(3) details of all amendments (if any) to the Pension Scheme which have been announced or are proposed but which have not yet been formally made;

(4) details of all discretionary increases (if any) to pensions in payment or in deferment under the Pension Scheme which have been granted in the ten years prior to the date of this Agreement or which are under consideration; and

(5) details of all discretionary practices (if any) which may have led any person to expect additional benefits in a given set of circumstances (by way of example, but without limitation, on retirement at the behest of the Vendor or in the event of redundancy).

. (D) *Membership*   All Employees who have at any time had the right to join, or apply to join, the Pension Scheme have been properly advised of that right. No Employee has been excluded from membership of the Pension Scheme or from any of the benefits thereunder in contravention of Art 119 of the Treaty of Rome, the Pensions Act 1995 or other applicable laws or requirements, or the provisions of the Pension Scheme or otherwise.

(E) *Benefits*   All benefits (other than money purchase benefits) which are payable under the Pension Scheme on the death of any person while in employment to which the Pension Scheme relates are insured fully under a policy with an insurance company of good repute and there are no grounds on which that company might avoid liability under that policy. All other benefits payable, or prospectively or contingently payable, under the Pension Scheme are money purchase benefits. In this Sub-Paragraph 'money purchase benefits' has the same meaning as in s 181(1), of the Pension Schemes Act 1993.

(F) *Transfer Payments*   No transfer value has been paid (directly or indirectly) to the Pension Scheme from another arrangement for any Employee under which the benefits referable to that Employee contravened Art 119 of the Treaty of Rome, s 62 of the Pensions Act 1995 or other applicable law or requirement.

(G) *Contributions*   Contributions to the Pension Scheme are not paid in arrear and all contributions and other amounts which have fallen due for payment have been paid punctually. The Vendor has (to the extent that it will be required to do) discharged its liability (if any) to pay or reimburse (whether wholly or in part) anyone who has paid any costs, charges or expenses which have been incurred by or in connection with the Pension Scheme.

(H) *Vendor's Obligations*   The Vendor:

   (1)   has been admitted to participation in the Pension Scheme on the same terms as apply generally to other employers participating in the Scheme;

   (2)   has observed and performed those provisions of the Pension Scheme which apply to it; [and]

   (3)   may (without the consent of any person or further payment) terminate its liability to contribute to the Pension Scheme at any time subject only to giving such notice (if any) as is expressly provided for in the documentation containing the current provisions governing the Pension Scheme[206] [.][; and

   (4)   has at all material times held or been named in a contracting-out certificate (within the meaning of s 7(1) of the Pension Schemes Act 1993) referable to the Pension Scheme.]

(I) *Compliance*   The Pension Scheme:

   (1)   is an exempt approved scheme (within the meaning of s 592(1) of the Income and Corporation Taxes Act 1988); and

   (2)   has at all times complied with and been administered in accordance with all applicable laws, regulations and requirements (including those of the Board of Inland Revenue and of trust law).

(J) *Disputes*   None of the Pension Scheme, the Vendor or any member of the Vendor's Group is engaged or involved in any proceedings which relate to or are in connection with the Pension Scheme and no such proceedings are pending or threatened and so far as the Vendor is aware there are no facts likely to give rise to any such proceedings. In this Sub-Paragraph 'proceedings' includes any litigation or arbitration and also includes any investigation or determination by the Pensions Ombudsman or the Occupational Pensions Advisory Service and any internal dispute resolution procedure established in connection with the Pension Scheme.

5   Damages for Breach of Pension Warranties[207]

5.1   In determining the damages flowing from any breach of Warranties contained in Paragraph 4, the Purchaser shall be deemed to become at Completion under a liability:

(A)   to provide and to continue to provide any benefits of a kind referred to in that Paragraph which are now provided or have been announced or are proposed; and

(B)   to maintain and to continue to maintain (without benefits being reduced) the Pension Scheme and any other arrangements of a kind described in that Paragraph which are now in existence or are proposed and any discretionary practices of a kind referred to in that Paragraph which have hitherto been carried on.

SCHEDULE 8

VENDOR PROTECTION[208]

1   Limitation of Relevant Claims

1.1   The provisions of this Schedule shall operate to limit the liability of the Vendor under or in connection with the Warranties and the Disclosure Letter and accordingly, in this Schedule, 'Relevant Claim' means any claim under or in connection with any of the Warranties or the Disclosure Letter [including, for the avoidance of doubt, any claim for misrepresentation or negligent misstatement].[209]

2   Financial limits

2.1   Aggregate limit

The aggregate liability of the Vendor in respect of Relevant Claims[209] shall be limited to £[   ].

2.2   Thresholds

The Vendor shall not be liable in respect of a Relevant Claim unless:

[(A) the liability of the Vendor in respect of that Relevant Claim (and all other Relevant Claims arising out of or related to the same or similar subject matter) exceeds £[   ][209]; and]

(B) the aggregate liability of the Vendor in respect of all Relevant Claims (excluding any for which liability is excluded by Sub-Paragraph 2.2(A)) exceeds £[   ] in which case the Vendor shall be liable for the whole amount and not merely the excess over £[   ].

3   Time limits

3.1   Notice to Vendor

The Vendor shall have no liability in respect of any Relevant Claim unless the Purchaser shall have given notice in writing to the Vendor of such claim specifying (in reasonable detail) the matter which gives rise to the claim, the nature of the claim and the amount claimed in respect thereof not later than the date [   ] years after the date of this Agreement.[210]

4   Recovery from Third Parties

4.1   Accounting to Vendor[209]

If the Vendor pays to or for the benefit of the Purchaser an amount in respect of any Relevant Claim and the Purchaser subsequently receives from any other person any payment in respect of the matter giving rise to the Relevant Claim, the Purchaser shall thereupon pay to the Vendor an amount equal to the payment received, after having taken into account any cost, liability (including tax liability) or expense in respect thereof and except to any extent that the liability of the Vendor in respect of the Relevant Claim was reduced to take account of such payment.

[5 Relevance of Limitations in Circumstances of Fraud etc

5.1   The provisions of Paragraphs 2 and 3 shall not apply in respect of a Relevant Claim if it is (or the delay in the discovery of which is) the consequence of fraud, wilful misconduct or wilful concealment by the Vendor or any member of the Vendor's Group or officer or employee or former officer or employee of the Vendor or any member of the Vendor's Group].[209]

SIGNED by [ ]	)[211]
duly authorised for and on	)
behalf of [ ] Limited	)

SIGNED by [ ]	)
duly authorised for and on	)
behalf of [ ] Limited	)

SIGNED by [ ]	)
duly authorised for and on	)
behalf of [ ] Limited	)

Notes

Parties and Recitals

1   If a guarantor of the purchaser is required include and modify cl 14.2. A guarantor of the vendor is particularly relevant because after sale, the vendor may be only a cash 'shell'.

2   Add other recitals as necessary to explain transaction; including, for example, any pre-sale hive-down.

Clause 1: Interpretation

3   The treatment of liabilities assumed by the purchaser is a difficult area and this agreement offers only one suggested approach. It is drafted on the basis that the purchaser is willing to assume responsibility for specified categories of liability only (not including trade creditors, see cl 9.3(F)), up to a limited amount. The agreed liabilities to be assumed are quantified in completion accounts. If the actual liability for any particular item is greater than the amount taken into account, the purchaser should ensure he can recover from the vendor under cl 8.1. If, as is common, the consideration is adjusted on the basis of completion accounts the liabilities assumed by the purchaser will then be taken into account in the purchase price. Whether or not assumed liabilities are taken into account in this way is for negotiation and will presumably affect the consideration. Of course, if no completion accounts are to be prepared the purchaser will wish to see its exposure to assumed liabilities contained in some other way, perhaps to an overall maximum amount. The method for the purchaser to take on assumed liabilities will generally be by the purchaser agreeing to indemnify the vendor (see cl 7.3). In any event define the liabilities to be assumed carefully, eg exclude tax liabilities, including tax arising out of the sale itself. If trade creditors were to be assumed by the purchaser (*see* Chapter 10 at p 195) then it would be appropriate to treat those 'Creditors' as 'Assumed Liabilities' and cl 9.3 would be amended.

4   This definition will require modification if the business assets of several companies are acquired or if only part of the vendor company's businesses are to be sold. In the latter case consider whether it is desirable that divisional or *pro forma* accounts showing the performance of the actual business assets to be acquired be made available and, ideally, warranted.

5   The definition of book debts will be affected by the approach adopted in relation to the payment of creditors and collection of debtors. The proposed definition would be relevant for the agency approach (described at (b) on p 195) and the reference to completion accounts should be deleted. If, however, the debts were to be acquired such debts would be included in completion accounts (and the reference to those accounts be retained). In either case prepayments (such as insurance and rent) are treated as current assets and if the purchaser is to receive the benefit of these amounts the vendor will wish that they be taken into account in an apportionment clause or the completion accounts. The definition excludes bad debts. *See further* Note 9 and Chapter 10 at p 195.

6   This too will require careful definition particularly where the vendor carries on more than the business being sold or from several premises. The vendor will wish to exclude, specifically, the businesses and activities not sold. Note that key provisions of the agreement relate back to this definition, eg the warranties (Sched 6) and restrictive covenant (cl 10).

7   Retain the definition of 'Completion' even if completion is to be simultaneous with the signature of the agreement.

8   This definition encompasses identifiable contracts only, not all contractual arrangements. It may be appropriate to distinguish between different types of contracts, eg if certain contracts require specific novation or consent. It might be appropriate for the definition to be wider eg 'all contracts, contractual arrangements, engagements or orders (excluding contracts of employment) entered into in the ordinary course of the business and remaining unperformed in whole or in part at the Transfer Date including (but not limited to) the Specified Contracts and the Lease Contracts'. *See* Chapter 10 at p 209.

9   These are intended to cover trade creditors, not general liabilities. These creditors are discharged out of book debts (see cl 9.3(F)), and the closing words of the definition would be deleted. If the purchaser were to acquire book debts and assume responsibility for discharging creditors as an assumed liability, it would, it is suggested, wish to quantify its exposure to the extent of the creditors included in completion accounts (if they are to be prepared). In such case, the closing words of the definition would be included. Exactly which creditors, if any, are to be assumed by the purchaser needs consideration in every case and further clarification in the definition may be desirable. There will usually be a distinction to be drawn between current or trade creditors, which a purchaser will often choose to discharge as part of the trading of the business acquired (although not necessarily assume) and contingent or long term creditors in the nature of funding, which will generally be excluded.

10 See the list at Sched 1, which should be amended to fit the circumstances of the transaction.

11 The disclosure letter qualifies the warranties given in Scheds 5, 6 and 7 (cl 11.2). The agreement provides for certain items to be included in (or annexed to) the disclosure letter (*see* the list on p 627). The scheme of the agreement is, like the precedent Agreement for Sale (Shares), to warrant the disclosure letter and to oblige the vendors to make all disclosures by way of the disclosure letter. A precedent disclosure letter will be found on p 623. *See further* Note 64.

12 If the warranty in the form set out in Sched 6, para 2.9 is adopted, reference should be made to an agreed or disclosed list of employees. Where there is a gap between signing and the transfer date be clear that changes are disclosed and the purchaser is protected from the effect of any changes, since it will assume responsibility for all employees at the transfer date (and possibly some who have been dismissed before) as a matter of law, *see* Chapter 6 at p 73.

13 Whether any assets are to be excluded depends on the scope of what is to be acquired, and whether the vendor owns any other assets. There is invariably overlap and uncertainty in definitions and the list of exclusions will develop in the course of negotiations. Cash and cash equivalents are usually excluded (when they should be deleted from Sched 1). Ensure that what is excluded is consistent with what is intended to be sold, eg item (C) will be an exclusion from the intellectual property assets to be acquired. *See* Notes 6 and 9 for the treatment of book debts and Chapter 10 on p 192.

14 Generally speaking, it is not necessary to specify liabilities that are being excluded as the purchaser will take over only liabilities specifically assumed. Certain liabilities will however attach to the purchaser by virtue of the assets acquired. For example, employment liabilities and liabilities arising out of the occupation of

property, including certain environmental matters. If any such liability is to be retained by the vendor, the purchaser will need protection by way of indemnity—*see* cl 12.3, which gives an indemnity in respect of pre-acquisition employment liabilities (there is no similar specific protection for property or environmental liabilities). It may, as an alternative to an indemnity if that cannot be agreed, be possible to agree an appropriate provision in the completion accounts or seek warranties (but *see* Note 64). Such liabilities will otherwise be inherited without limit. While other, general, liabilities are not automatically assumed, it is often desirable to specify certain exclusions, for the avoidance of doubt, such as taxation. *See* cl 2.2.

15   A distinction is made between movable and immovable fixed assets as stamp duty is payable on the latter but not the former, where title passes by delivery (*see* Chapter 12 at p 288).

16   This definition is intended to include most forms of intellectual property right recognised in English law. It should be reviewed and adapted having regard to the nature of the business being acquired. Note its use in connection with the intellectual property warranties (Sched 6, para 2.7(F)).

17   This definition includes finance leases which for accounting purposes are treated as assets owned by the vendor and hence treated in the vendor's accounts as fixed assets. Such assets should be noted, particularly when drawing up rules for preparation of any completion accounts.

18   The list will be a useful checklist for registered intellectual property rights. Where specific unregistered rights (such as copyright) are known these could also be added. Whether or not listed, the scheme of the agreement is to transfer to the purchaser all intellectual property (save for any excluded assets).

19   Management accounts should be as recent as possible (preferably within two months prior to signing). It is sometimes desirable to insist on their preparation before signature of the agreement.

20   Only if relevant. *See* Chapter 10 at p 199.

21   If the business assets include any interest in freehold or leasehold land this Agreement is likely to be a contract for the disposition of an interest in land within the meaning of the Law of Property (Miscellaneous Provisions) Act 1989 and caution should be exercised to ensure all terms are included. *See* Chapter 10 at p 199.

22   *See* Chapter 10 at p 216 and, in respect of VAT records, Chapter 12 at p 295.

23   Detailed consideration of computer systems will be necessary, particularly if the vendor is part of a group and also in respect of the terms of transfer of equipment, and of maintenance agreements and software licences. It will be necessary to consider, for example, whether new software licences are required and whether any interim operating arrangements with the vendor or members of its group will be required until the business is integrated into the purchaser's operations. *See* Chapter 10 at p 207.

24   This definition should be carefully reviewed in each case so as to encompass rights which the purchaser may require to support or which relate to the assets and business it has acquired. *See* Chapter 10 at p 213.

25   A transfer date may differ from the time of completion which will generally take place during banking hours or otherwise at a time convenient for a handover of the business. Current assets (eg where there is a stocktake) will be ascertained at the

transfer date. If there is to be a period between completion and the transfer date, the conduct of the business during such time and for whose risk/benefit the business carried on should accrue will need to be addressed. In any event consideration should be given which of 'Completion' or the 'Transfer Date' is appropriate in all clauses where they appear, to meet the circumstances of the transaction.

26   Make sure this includes all warranties, but not indemnities.

27   See the Agreement for Sale (Shares), Note 11 at p 464.

28   This is relevant if more than one person is joined in as warrantor or in respect of other obligations, eg any shareholders or directors or the vendor's guarantor. *See* Chapter 9 at p 178 regarding joint and several liability. *See also* cl 18.5. This precedent contemplates only one vendor, and that the guarantor will not give warranties jointly and as such the clause will not usually be relevant in which case it should be deleted.

Clause 2: Sale of Business Assets

29   *See* Chapter 10 at p 187 for a discussion of covenants for title. Note that the implied covenants do not cover anything which the purchaser actually or constructively knows, but this provision is varied in cl 11.2.

30   May be required if certain assets are owned by vendor's subsidiaries. Alternatively join all owners as vendor (various consequential amendments will be required).

31   Book Debts would be included, if the purchaser has agreed to acquire them (*see* Note 6).

32   The purchaser should insure from the point at which it is on risk. If there is any delay between signing and completion then, unless it has an absolute right to rescind in the event of destruction of or damage to the business assets, the contract should provide for insurance to be maintained to the transfer date the benefit of which will accrue to of the purchaser, and appropriate arrangements for adjustment to the price in the event of losses (including insured losses). Note that the clause deals principally with insurance of fixed assets and premises and not stock (on the assumption that a completion accounts adjustment will sort out any problems) or liability insurance (on the footing that such liabilities are not to be assumed by the purchaser). The insurance position during the period needs to match the risk allocation and the purchaser's right to withdraw in the event of problems. *See* Chapter 10 at p 215.

Clause 3: Consideration

33   The apportionment is for tax and stamp duty purposes. A more detailed apportionment will sometimes be necessary if there is more than one item within each category. This can be included in the relevant schedule or list. *See* Chapter 12 at p 279.

34   The consideration is commonly adjusted by reference to the Current Assets (eg stock and work in progress). The precedent contemplates a more comprehensive set of completion accounts by reference to which price is adjusted rather than, for example, relying on warranties if assets prove not to exist or to be in a poor condition. Although in this draft warranties on asset values are also proposed (*see* para 2.7 at p 569) they may be strongly resisted by the vendor. Whatever approach is adopted is clearly a matter for negotiation.

35 The precedent assumes consideration will be discharged in cash. *See* Chapter 11 at p 251 if the purchaser's shares are to form part of the consideration.

Clause 5: Conditions

36 *See* Chapter 11 and see also the Agreement for Sale (Shares), Note 17 at p 465.

37 Consider whether the entire agreement or the acquisition of any of the Premises is to be made conditional on landlord's licences (*see* Chapter 10 at p 200 and see also Sched 5). Such a condition is unlikely save for the most exceptional case. If a new lease is to be granted, reversioner's consent under Part III of Schedule may be required. This may merit a condition.

38 *See* the Agreement for Sale (Shares), cl 4.1(E) at p 383 for examples of UK and EU competition conditions.

39 Consider whether any of the parties should be under any obligation to use its best/ reasonable endeavours to procure fulfilment of any relevant condition or whether any conditions should be capable of waiver. *See* the Agreement for Sale (Shares), cl 4.2 and cl 4.3 at p 383 and the related notes.

Clause 6: Completion

40 Even where completion is simultaneous with signing, retain as a checklist.

41 Precedent assignments can be found as follows: patents, p 659; trademarks, p 661; copyright, p 665; assignments of goodwill, contracts and other assignments are straightforward and have not been included.

42 Obviously, unless releases are obtained business assets will be transferred subject to such charges. Consider whether releases from other encumbrances are necessary.

43 Other completion matters might include, for example, evidence of any relevant name changes; specific classes of asset may require some other form of document to convey title and if so, should be included. If there are indemnities for specific matters (eg environmental) not otherwise included in the agreement, these should be listed. Sometimes interim handover arrangements (eg for computer systems) are set out in a separate document, when these too should be mentioned.

44 See the Agreement for Sale (Shares), cl 5.4 at p 385.

Clause 7: Consents, Contracts and Assumed Liabilities

45 This clause is intended as a general catch-all for those situations where consents are required. Certain of the business assets are dealt with more specifically (eg contracts (cl 7.2); leasehold premises (Sched 5)).

46 Individual contracts which are critical to the business may deserve further specific treatment, for example arranging consents or novation as part of the completion process. *See* Chapter 10 at p 211.

47 The vendor may require indemnity for so acting.

48 The terms of this clause may require modification depending on the nature of the Assumed Liabilities; if the limit of the purchaser's liability for such amounts is not included elsewhere, this would be a useful place to put it.

Clause 8: Mutual Covenants

49   These mutual covenants will often overlap with other risk-sharing clauses eg cl 12 (employees of the business); check the clauses are consistent, mutually exclusive or that those which take priority over others is clear.

50   The purchaser will often require the right to discharge obligations he does not agree to assume to protect the Goodwill he has acquired. For example, trade creditors (*see further* cl 9.3). *See also* Chapter 10 at p 216.

51   Whether a clause of this nature is included obviously depends on the nature of the Business being acquired. It is included because the vendor will not be able to rectify defects if he no longer has the Business. The purchaser may wish to limit his exposure. The price for fulfilling warranty claims on products supplied by the vendor is, of course, for negotiation.

52   An apportionment clause is an alternative to completion accounts—particularly in a smaller acquisition. *See also* Chapter 10 at p 198.

Clause 9: Pre and Post Completion Obligations

53   The purchaser will require comfort, if there is delay between signing and completion, that there has been no material change to the business. Note that under cl 11.5, the vendor agrees to ensure that the warranties are not broken within this period, so far as within its control. It is not uncommon however, to set out in addition specific restrictions on the activities of the vendor. For example, restricting appointment of additional employees, entering into capital commitments, material contracts, creation of charges, etc. *See* the Agreement for Sale (Shares), cl 8.6 at p 388 and in particular, Note 49 at p 468 with regard to its relationship with the purchaser's right to rescind.

54   Consider whether this should be a completion obligation under cl 6.

55   There are a number of options available in relation to trade debtors (eg book debts) and creditors as described in Chapter 10 at p 197. The contract provides for the second approach, the 'agency' route. Note, however, that if debtors appear significantly to exceed creditors, consideration will need to be given to funding the shortfall; buying them (if that approach is chosen) may not be a good idea.

56   Decide whether the purchaser is to be paid a commission or fee for collection of book debts for the vendor.

57   One point is whether the purchaser may appropriate monies received from customers to whom it has made supplies after completion ahead of a pre-completion book debt. The vendor will usually require a first in, first out approach, unless there is a clear dispute or alternative appropriation by the customer.

58   Consider whether proceedings should be prohibited or alternatively whether the purchaser should be entitled to purchase the debt and itself pursue or negotiate with the customer.

Clause 10: Restriction of Vendor's Group

59   *See generally*, Chapter 4 at p 31. If the vendor is an intermediate holding company, it would be advisable to obtain a direct covenant from the ultimate holding company, which is in a position to procure that the covenant can be enforced.

60   *See* the Agreement for Sale (Shares), Note 39 at p 467.

61   *See* the Agreement for Sale (Shares), Note 40 at p 467.

62   *See* the Agreement for Sale (Shares), Note 41 at p 467.

63   *See* Chapter 4 at p 32. Note that the Restrictive Trade Practices Act 1976 may re-
     quire registration of the agreement even though the restriction on the vendor is rea-
     sonable in terms of scope and duration, etc.

Clause 11: Warranties and Retention

64   *See* Agreement for Sales (Shares), Note 44 at p 468.

65   *See* Note 29 and Chapter 10 at p 185.

66   The 'pound for pound' clause is of less relevance in many business asset acquisi-
     tions; a precise value is being placed on each individual asset being acquired and
     the purchaser will expect to be fully compensated if any asset turns out to be worth
     less than warranted; although note that the purchaser will not wish to be limited to
     the apportioned value of assets and will wish to be compensated for damage to
     goodwill, see cl 3.1. The vendor may argue that such a clause is not necessary or
     alternatively that it is not in any event warranting asset values. *See* Chapter 9 at
     p 167 for its relevance on a share acquisition; if liabilities are to be discharged by
     the purchaser, the clause might nonetheless be appropriate.

67   Obviously not relevant if signing and completion are simultaneous.

68   *See* the Agreement for Sale (Shares), Note 48 at p 468.

69   *See* the Agreement for Sale (Shares), Note 51 at p 468.

70   The Agreement for Sale (Shares) takes a slightly different approach, requiring de-
     posit with a bank. *See also* Notes 52 to 54 to that Agreement, at p 468–9.

Clause 12: Employees of the Business

71   *See* Chapter 6 as to the effect of the transfer of a business on employment contracts
     which will transfer, with accrued rights, by operation of law. Consider whether all
     those individuals identified by the purchaser as being necessary for the continu-
     ance of the business after completion will automatically transfer or whether spe-
     cific arrangements will be necessary, for example, where they are employed by
     other members of the vendor's group.

72   The indemnity is necessary to ensure that the purchaser can transfer the cost of
     pre-completion liabilities back to the vendor.

Clause 14: Guarantees

73   Retain the indemnity provision to deal with the situation where the underlying ob-
     ligation of the vendor becomes void or otherwise unenforceable when the guaran-
     tee provisions in sub-cl (A) would fall away.

74   To avoid discharge of the guarantee by certain events which might otherwise
     automatically do so. However, where any material change is to be made to the
     underlying agreement between the parties it would be advisable to seek the guar-
     antor's consent in any event.

Clause 15: Value Added Tax

75   For the VAT treatment of the transaction, *see generally* Chapter 12 at p 293. Clause 15 sets out two alternative clauses dealing with VAT, each on the basis that the purchaser does not take on the vendor's VAT number but does receive the VAT records. Take care that other provisions of the agreement dealing with Records do not conflict with VAT provisions.

76   The purchaser may prefer that all sums should be expressed to be inclusive of VAT but this is often unacceptable to a vendor as a VAT charge will reduce the consideration in circumstances where, in any event, VAT will in most cases be recoverable by the purchaser.

77   The first alternative form of sub-cl 15.1 is applicable where the purchaser acquires all the VAT records in accordance with the Value Added Tax Act 1994, s 49 (Chapter 12 at p 295).

78   The second alternative form of sub-cl 15.1 is applicable where the vendor retains the VAT records.

79   This refers to a case where VAT has been charged on the sale where it was not appropriate eg where a vendor has incorrectly taken the view that VAT is chargeable. Sometimes vendors object to this provision without realising that it is necessary to ensure that they can recover VAT incorrectly charged by Customs & Excise, as the effect is to overcome any argument by Customs & Excise that the vendor has been unjustly enriched. If Customs & Excise can successfully argue the point, then they have a statutory defence to any repayment of VAT (Value Added Tax Act 1994, s 80).

80   This deals with the apportionment of liabilities for VAT in respect of pre and post completion supplies and entitlement to VAT refunds. In practice the vendor should recover all VAT which it has paid but not yet recovered in relation to supplies made to the business before completion and the vendor should account for VAT on supplies made by the business before completion but on which the VAT has not yet been accounted for to Customs & Excise. In fact, the matter is often fudged and left to the vendor and purchaser to agree their respective liabilities with the relevant VAT office.

81   Delete if not relevant. The capital goods scheme adjusts the recovery of VAT over a period of time where a business has purchased land or buildings costing more than £250,000 or computer hardware costing more than £50,000. It applies to purchases made after 1 April 1990. The amount of VAT recovered on the initial purchase is adjusted over a five or ten year period. If the person who bought the asset sells it on as part of the transfer of a business as a going concern then the historic VAT recovery rates are inherited by the purchaser and the amount which the purchaser can recover by way of VAT on the asset, at worst, might have to pay back to Customs & Excise, will be affected by what has happened in the past. A further clause might be included if the vendor has in place a VAT deferment scheme for the target business. A VAT deferment scheme will usually be in operation with a business which import goods or material from outside the EC. The scheme defers the point at which duty becomes payable. HM Customs & Excise usually require the company with such a scheme to give guarantees. It is important when acting for the vendor to ensure that those guarantees are cancelled following completion, together with the vendor's VAT deferment account number. The purchaser must make its own VAT deferment account arrangements. Where VAT deferment ar-

rangements exist, a clause will need to be included in the agreement to deal with the point. *See* eg the Tax Deed, at p 494.

Clause 16: Confidentiality

82   *See* the Agreement for Sale (Shares), Note 55 at p 469.

Clause 17: Announcements

83   *See* the Agreement for Sale (Shares), Note 56 at p 469.

Clause 18: Provisions relating to this Agreement

84   *See* the Agreement for Sale (Shares), Note 57 at p 469.

85   *See* the commentary on the equivalent provision in the Agreement for Sale (Shares), at Note 58 at p 470. Note also, however, that exclusion clauses in an agreement for the sale of business assets will, depending on the character of assets involved, be subject not only to the provisions of the Misrepresentation Act 1967, s 3 but, in addition, the Unfair Contract Terms Act 1977, s 2(2) as regards exclusion of eg negligent misstatement.

86   *See* the Agreement for Sale (Shares), Note 59 at p 470.

87   As noted above, the agreement has been prepared on the basis of a single vendor who gives the warranties. However it may be appropriate that the vendor's guarantor or directors or shareholders give warranties in which case cl 11 in particular will need amending to provide for additional warrantors and joint and several liability.

88   Amend as appropriate. Overseas service may not be appropriate. It may be appropriate to specify personal service during business hours.

Clause 19: Law and Jurisdiction

89   This clause is prepared on the basis of both parties agreeing to a simple, exclusive jurisdiction. *See* the Agreement for Sale (Shares), Note 62 at p 470 for other choices.

90   Only if one or more of the parties is outside the United Kingdom for service of documents.

Schedule 4: Adjustment of Consideration

91   The schedule sets out a framework for preparation of completion accounts; it may not be appropriate where, for example, a limited exercise to value stock or other current assets is required. It is highly desirable that the parties' accountants are involved in setting out the criteria for preparation of the completion accounts—especially where they have been involved in due diligence, when they will be familiar with particular aspects of the target's books which may require special attention. Note that while based on Companies Acts accounts for the vendor in relation to the business, completion accounts need not comprise a full set of accounts because, eg, certain liabilities (such as tax) will not be reflected as they will not form that part of the target's business which is being taken on by the purchaser.

92   It is helpful for the parties and their accountants to agree on a *pro forma* completion balance sheet so at least the layout and line items are agreed in advance. While this is also true of a share acquisition it is perhaps more important in the asset context because, as noted above, the accounts may reflect only part of the whole business (eg book debts, inventory, fixed assets).

93   Generally, only if such liabilities are to be assumed. *See also* Notes 3 and 9.

94   If other financial standards or guidance notes are appropriate, add (after discussion with the accountants). Where the business comprises only part of the business carried on by the vendor, care is needed to ensure items are sufficiently clearly identified.

95   *See* the Agreement for Sale (Shares), Note 113 at p 475.

96   Discuss with purchaser's accountants and amplify where necessary. *See also* the Agreement for Sale (Shares), Note 114 at p 475.

97   It is likely that there will be detailed provisions for valuing stock which will need to address the specific circumstances of the target business. Some stock may have a short shelf life and others may require different treatment (eg packaging). Finished stock and raw materials will be valued differently. *See* Chapter 10 at p 193. Specific provisions in relation to obsolete stock may be required following any financial due diligence. Similarly, work-in-progress will often be the subject of specific valuation rules and in either case, there is sometimes seen a maximum value for stock or work in progress.

98   The purchaser will not normally assume any liability for taxation. It may, however, agree to discharge the vendor's most recent VAT liability when that should be reflected either as an Assumed Liability or otherwise be specifically addressed—the completion accounts would be a useful way of dealing with it.

99   Only if Book Debts are acquired, *see* Note 6.

100   The purchaser will wish to provide for any item which will become its responsibility after completion by virtue of the acquisition of the assets, but is attributable to the vendor's period of ownership—unless specifically included in the definition on p 504, they will not be 'Assumed Liabilities' as they are a function of ownership or use.

101   In order to accrue such items. The Vendor will wish to have credit for prepayments to the extent they are not taken into account under normal principles and the purchaser will wish to provide for liabilities it will inherit which are referable in part to the vendor's period of ownership.

102   *See* the Agreement for Sale (Shares), Note 122 at p 476.

103   *See* the Agreement for Sale (Shares), Note 123 at p 476 in relation to the appointment of an 'expert'.

104   The parties may prefer to use an estimated completion NAV figure as a basis for adjustment, otherwise the base figure (or a means of ascertaining it) will need to be agreed.

105   *See* the Agreement for Sale (Shares), Note 125 at p 477.

Schedule 5: Terms Applicable to the Premises

106   The schedule is prepared from the purchaser's standpoint. A vendor is likely to seek to impose more onerous provisions on a purchaser eg as to the provision of guarantees or other security to a reversioner when seeking the reversioner's consent and the costs of obtaining that consent. *See* Sched 5, part II, para 6.2 at p 544 and para 6.4 at p 545.

107   *See* Chapter 10 at p 187 for discussion of full title guarantee in the context of property transfers.

108   The terms contain provisions to deal with the situation where the leaseholds themselves are subject to existing tenancies.

109   If completion accounts are used or an apportionment clause is adopted, ensure consistency of approach—the paragraph may be amended if covered by those provisions.

110   Paragraphs 7 to 9 contain different methods for dealing with the situation where the reversioner's licence is refused. It is unlikely that all the methods will be appropriate in any one transaction and should be considered as alternatives since some of the provisions conflict.

111   Such an underlease will be a 'new tenancy' for the purpose of the Landlord and Tenant (Covenants) Act 1995, with the result that the undertenant will cease to be liable under the undertenant's covenants on an authorised assignment of the underlease but subject to the terms of any authorised guarantee agreement which the undertenant may be required to enter into.

112   This paragraph is drafted in the alternative to para 7. If however para 8 is to apply and is to take effect after failure to obtain reversioner's licence to the grant of an underlease, para 8.1 will require redrafting.

113   Where the relevant grantor's title to the new leasehold premises is freehold, appropriate amendments must be made throughout this part of Sched 5, eg to delete references to the need to obtain the reversioner's licence.

Schedule 6: Warranties and Representations

114   The warranties are in standard form and are fairly comprehensive but are unlikely to cover every aspect of a particular target's business. More so than a corporate acquisition, warranties on an assets acquisition require detailed modification to suit the circumstances. Seeking excessive warranties at the outset may undermine the purchaser's negotiating position. Consider what additional warranties are appropriate to the transaction. The standard warranties include a number of matters which address liabilities or obligations which may not, in fact, be assumed when it may be safe to ignore the point and delete or modify the warranty. However, such matters, even if not assumed by the purchaser, may be of relevance to the overall performance of the business, its goodwill, and its profitability going forward. *See* also the commentary on warranties in the Agreement for Sale (Shares), Note 64 at p 470 and thereafter.

115   The warranties as drafted assume the vendor is the operator of the Business and will require revision if it is not.

116   *See* the Agreement for Sale (Shares), Note 67 at p 471.

117   *See* the Agreement for Sale (Shares), Note 68 at p 471.

118 *See* the Agreement for Sale (Shares), Note 70 at p 471.

119 *See further* the Notes 74 to 79 to the Agreement for Sale (Shares), at p 472 for further comment on the accounts warranties.

120 It may be appropriate to seek warranties about specific aspects of the Audited Accounts, eg those assets and liabilities which are to be assumed. Warranties on turnover and profitability are obvious candidates. If only part of the vendor's business is included in the sale, *pro forma* or divisional accounts should be warranted; these may not be audited and as far as possible, should be the subject of any accountant's investigation (*see* Chapter 9 at p 137).

121 For general comment on tax warranties on an acquisition of business assets, see Chapter 14 at p 336 and Chapter 12 at p 292. Tax warranties in such transactions are usually minimal as the purchaser does normally assume the pre-acquisition tax liabilities of the vendor in respect of the business. Instead, the liabilities are retained by the vendor. Where the purchaser does not take over the vendor's VAT number, delete warranties 2.5(C)(8)(a) to (h).

122 Note the relationship with clause 11.5. Consider whether the warranty should cover a longer period eg the previous 12 months' trading, and whether other specific matters, eg margins should be covered.

123 The vendors may object to giving warranties as to the 'prospects' of the company and may wish this to be qualified 'to the best of their knowledge and belief.'

124 A vendor will generally expect the purchaser to rely on its own assessment of asset values and (if given) on any accounts warranties—thus such a warranty will be resisted in many cases. *See also* the Agreement for Sale (Shares), Note 85 at p 472.

125 These warranties in a number of respects go to the heart of what is to be sold and amendment will be made with care. Note the overlap with the title of what is to be conveyed (cl 2.1 at p 509); and *see generally* the discussion in Chapter 10 at p 187.

126 *See* the Agreement for Sale (Shares), Note 88 at p 473.

127 Intellectual property licences, like any other agreement/contract will require assignment/novation. *See also* the Agreement for Sale (Shares), Note 89 at p 473.

128 *See* the Agreement for Sale (Shares), Note 90 at p 473.

129 Often qualified by the vendor's awareness.

130 Often amended as monitoring internal controls on confidentiality can be difficulty.

131 *See also* the Agreement for Sale (Shares), Notes 93 and 94 at p 473.

132 The purchaser will, of course, usually take out its own insurances. However, the existence and validity of insurances will be important as regards fixed assets, if it is to benefit from claims under them (eg between signing and completion) and the existence of uninsured liability claims against the vendor will tend to impair the purchaser's goodwill. *See also* the Agreement for Sale (Shares), Note 84 at p 472.

133 Make sure the warranty ties in with what is being taken on—eg is it all contracts or some only that are to be covered by the warranty?

134 *See* the Agreement for Sale (Shares), Note 96 at p 473.

135 To cover the position where, even though not legally binding, a proposal has been put to a customer/potential customer which may prove to be morally binding.

136 *See* Chapter 6 at p 76 relating to employee consultation requirements on a transfer of business.

137 *See* also warranties on any circular and/or sale memorandum: Agreement for Sale (Shares) at p 418.

138 *See* the Agreement for Sale (Shares), Note 99 at p 474.

139 Again, a vendor will often seek to resist.

Schedule 7: Pensions

A   Vendor has own final salary scheme

140 *See* the Agreement for Sale (Shares), Note 126 at p 477.

141 *See* the Agreement for Sale (Shares), Note 127 at p 477.

142 *See* the Agreement for Sale (Shares), Note 128 at p 477.

143 *See* p 113.

144 *See* the Agreement for Sale (Shares), Note 130 at p 477.

145 Consideration should be given as to whether the purchaser's accession as principal employer should be made a condition precedent to completion.

146 *See* the Agreement for Sale (Shares), Note 131 at p 477.

147 *See* the Agreement for Sale (Shares), Note 123 at p 476.

148 It may be more tax efficient for the adjustment to the consideration for specific assets. *See* Chapter 12 at p 287.

149 *See* the Agreement for Sale (Shares), Note 134 at p 477.

150 *See* the Agreement for Sale (Shares), Note 135 at p 477.

151 *See* p 87.

152 *See* p 85.

153 *See* p 113.

154 *See* the Agreement for Sale (Shares), Note 139 at p 478.

155 *See* p 114.

156 *See* the Agreement for Sale (Shares), Note 141 at p 478.

157 *See* p 81.

158 *See* the Agreement for Sale (Shares), Note 143 at p 478.

159 *See* p 112.

B   Vendor participates in group final salary scheme

160 *See* the Agreement for Sale (Shares), Note 145 at p 478.

161 *See* the Agreement for Sale (Shares), Note 146 at p 478.

162 *See* the Agreement for Sale (Shares), Note 128 at p 477.

163 *See* p 113.

164 *See* the Agreement for Sale (Shares), Note 149 at p 478.

165 *See* the Agreement for Sale (Shares), Note 150 at p 478.

166 *See* the Agreement for Sale (Shares), Note 151 at p 478.

167 *See* the Agreement for Sale (Shares), Note 152 at p 478.

168 *See* the Agreement for Sale (Shares), Note 153 at p 478.

169 *See* p 104.

170 *See* the Agreement for Sale (Shares), Note 155 at p 479.

171 *See* the Agreement for Sale (Shares), Note 156 at p 479.

172 *See* p 102.

173 *See* the Agreement for Sale (Shares), Note 158 at p 479.

174 *See* the Agreement for Sale (Shares), Note 159 at p 479.

175 *See* p 97.

176 *See* p 100.

177 *See* the Agreement for Sale (Shares), Note 162 at p 479.

178 Delete reference to MP Employees if paragraph 4.4 is deleted.

179 Stamp duty should not be payable, *see* p 106.

180 The vendor may wish to include an excess clause, *see* p 96.

181 *See* Note 148 *above*.

182 *See* the Agreement for Sale (Shares), Note 167 at p 479.

183 *See* the Agreement for Sale (Shares), Note 123 at p 476.

184 Where exchange and completion are not simultaneous, cl 11.5 is relied on. *See more generally* the Agreement for Sale (Shares), Note 135 at p 477.

185 *See* the Agreement for Sale (Shares), Note 139 at p 478.

186 *See* p 100.

187 *See* the Agreement for Sale (Shares), Note 141 at p 478.

188 *See* p 112.

C   Vendor has own money purchase scheme

189 *See* the Agreement for Sale (Shares), Note 174 at p 480.

190 *See* Note 145 *above*.

191 *See* Note 184 *above*.

192 *See* the Agreement for Sale (Shares), Note 176 at p 480.

193 *See* the Agreement for Sale (Shares), Note 141 at p 478.

194 *See* p 112.

D   Vendor participates in group money purchase scheme

195 *See* the Agreement for Sale (Shares), Note 174 at p 480.

196 *See* the Agreement for Sale (Shares), Note 156 at p 479.

197 As to (C), *see* p 100 and as to (D) *see* p 111.

198 The vendor may require a contribution towards pension scheme expenses.

199 *See* p 97.

200 *See* the Agreement for Sale (Shares), Note 184 at p 480.

201 *See* p 111.

202 Expands on the statutory requirements.

203 As to when the statutory transfer option is not available, *see* p 103.

204 *See* the Agreement for Sale (Shares), Note 188 at p 480.

205 *See* Note 184 *above*.

206 *See* the Agreement for Sale (Shares), Note 141 at p 478.

207 *See* p 112.

Schedule 8: Vendor Limitations

208 *See generally* Chapter 9 at p 176. There tends to be a broader range of limitations which will be put forward in a share transaction eg giving credit for overprovisions in accounts will not tend to be relevant to the asset transaction. Of course, an asset sale will not generally involve any form of tax deed and some of the tricky points which can arise on a share sale, which require a matching of limitations with the tax deed, will not be relevant to the asset sale.

209 *See further* the Agreement for Sale (Shares), Notes 193 at p 480 and Notes 196 and 199 at p 481.

210 Consider extending time limit for claim in respect of taxation and eg environmental warranties to 6 years.

211 *See* the Agreement for Sale (Shares), Note 200 at p 482.

Appendix IV

Disclosure Letter[1]

[On letterhead of the Vendor or Vendor's solicitors]

[STRICTLY CONFIDENTIAL]

[THE DIRECTORS
[PURCHASER PLC
REGISTERED OFFICE ADDRESS]

OR

[THE PURCHASER'S SOLICITORS
ADDRESS]

Dated [   ] 199[   ]

Dear Sirs

[Target Name] (the 'Company')

1   Disclosure Letter and Interpretation

1.1   We refer to the Agreement (the 'Agreement') to be entered into today between (1) [Vendor Plc/Limited] (the 'Vendor') and (2) [Purchaser PLC Limited] (the 'Purchaser') providing for the sale and purchase of the *entire issued share capital of the Company/ the Business of [   ] carried on by the Company, as more particularly described in the Agreement* (the 'Acquisition').

1.2   The Disclosure Letter referred to in the Agreement comprises:

(A)   this letter;

(B)   the Disclosure Schedule attached hereto (the 'Disclosure Schedule'); and

(C)   the Disclosed Documents Index attached hereto (the 'Disclosed Documents Index').

1.3   Unless otherwise defined herein, or unless the context otherwise requires, words and expressions defined in the Agreement shall bear the same meanings in this Disclosure Letter.

2   Disclosures

2.1   The Purchaser acknowledges and agrees that the Warranties[2] are given subject to all facts and matters fairly disclosed in or by virtue of the Disclosure Letter and that the Purchaser shall have no claim in respect of any of the Warranties in relation to any such fact or matter.

2.2   The Purchaser acknowledges and agrees that:

(A)   notwithstanding that reference may in some cases be made in the Disclosure Letter to particular Warranties or other provisions of the Agreement, all disclosures made in or by virtue of the Disclosure Letter are made on the basis that they shall have effect in relation to each of the Warranties and the Purchaser shall not be entitled to claim that any fact or matter has not been disclosed to it by reason of the relevant disclosure not being specifically related to any one or more of the Warranties;

[(B)   neither the Disclosure Letter nor any disclosure made in or by virtue of it shall constitute or imply any representation, warranty, assurance or undertaking by the Vendor not expressly set out in the Agreement and neither the Disclosure Letter nor any such disclosure shall have the effect of, or be construed as, adding to or extending the scope of any of the Warranties.][3]

2.3   The Disclosure Letter shall be deemed fairly to disclose, and the Purchaser acknowledges and agrees that there shall be treated as so disclosed, the following:

(A)   the contents of the Disclosure Schedule;[4]

(B)   the contents of all documents listed in the Disclosed Documents Index;[4]

(C)   the contents of the Agreement and the contents of all documents referred to in the Agreement as being in Agreed Terms (whether or not the same are, in fact, signed by or on behalf of the parties for identification);

(D)   all information and all documents available from:
  (1)   searches on [   ] 199[   ] of the public files maintained by the Registrar of Companies in England and Wales in respect of the Vendor, the Company and each of the [Subsidiaries]/the Vendor;
  (2)   searches on [   ] 199[   ] of the Central Registry of Winding-up Petitions in England and Wales in respect of each of the companies referred to in sub-clause (1);
  (3)   searches on [   ] 199[   ] of the following public registries in respect of the companies shown below:[5]

  RegistryCompany/Subsidiary

  [   ][   ]
  [   ][   ]

(E)   the contents of:
  (1)   the statutory registers and books; and
  (2)   the books of minutes of the meetings of directors, holders of shares and where applicable holders of other securities;
  kept by the Company and the Subsidiaries/the Vendor;

(F)   all information:
  (1)   contained in replies to enquiries (and additional and further enquiries) and requisitions on title relating to any real property or leasehold interest made by the Purchaser's Solicitors [and listed in Part [   ] of the Disclosed Documents Index];
  (2)   contained in the documents of title to the *Properties/Premises* (copies of which have been supplied to the Purchaser's Solicitors) [and the other doc-

uments, entries and searches] listed in Part [   ] of the Disclosed Documents Index;

(3) available from the Purchaser's searches or enquiries in respect of the *Properties/Premises* at HM Land Registry, the Land Charges Registry, or any local [(or other competent)] authority (including statutory undertakings [eg Coal Board, National Rivers Authority]) ;

(4) [which might be revealed by a physical inspection on [   ] 199[   ] of the *Properties/Premises* by a prudent purchaser and his professional advisers;]

(5) [contained in any draft or final valuation report obtained by the Purchaser relating to any of the *Properties/Premises*];

(6) [contained in any certificate of title obtained by the Purchaser in respect of any of the *Properties/Premises*;]

(G) [all information available from searches or enquiries on [   ] 199[   ] of HM Patent Office or the United Kingdom Trade Marks Registry];[6]

(H) [the contents of any draft or final report relating to the Company [or any of the *Subsidiaries/the Business* prepared for the Purchaser by *[accountants/actuaries/ employee benefit consultants/environmental auditors etc]*;]

(I) [the information made available to [   ] (as actuaries acting for the Purchaser) in connection with their actuarial review of [the Pension Scheme(s) as listed in Part [   ] of the Disclosed Documents Index];]

(J) all information contained in the [statutory] accounts of the Company[, the Subsidiaries /the Vendor for periods ended on or before the Balance Sheet Date [and in the Management Accounts];]

(K) [the contents of the Information Memorandum dated [   ] 199[   ] relating to the Company;]

(L) [the contents of the documents made available for inspection in the data room used in connection with the Acquisition as listed in the Data Room Index;][4]

(M) all information contained in correspondence on or before [the day prior to the date of this letter] between the Vendor, and any other adviser of the Vendor's Solicitors on the one hand and the Purchaser, the Purchaser's Solicitors and any other adviser of the Purchaser in connection with the Agreement or the Acquisition;[4]

(N) [refer to any previously supplied documents which are now listed in the Disclosed Documents Index].

2.4 [In the event of there being any inconsistency between any document or information (other than the Disclosure Schedule) referred to in Paragraph 2.3[(B)] above and any description or summary in respect of the same subject matter in the Disclosure Schedule, the terms of such document or information shall prevail, unless expressly otherwise specified in the Disclosure Schedule.]

3 Acknowledgement

Signature by you of the enclosed copy of this letter constitutes an acknowledgment of receipt of the Disclosure Letter and your acceptance of its terms. Please sign and return the enclosed copy of this letter.

[[IF ON THE VENDOR'S SOLICITORS' LETTERHEAD:]

4   Disclaimer

This letter is written on behalf of the Vendor and is given on the basis that no liability shall arise on the part of this firm or any of its partners or employees in respect of it.]

Yours faithfully

[Name]
duly authorised for and on behalf of [Vendor]

[ON COPY:

We acknowledge receipt of the letter of which this is a copy and of all documents comprising the Disclosure Letter as referred to therein. We accept and agree the terms of the Disclosure Letter.

Date:
duly authorised for and on behalf of [Purchaser Name]]

DISCLOSURE SCHEDULE

This is the Disclosure Schedule to the Disclosure Letter dated [   ] 199[   ] from [Vendor/Vendor's Solicitors] to [Purchaser/Purchaser's solicitors] relating to the sale and purchase of the entire issued share capital of *[Target]/Business description.*

References in this Disclosure Schedule to [numbered documents] are references to the document(s) indexed with such reference in the Disclosed Documents Index referred to in the Disclosure Letter.

Headings and paragraph or clause numbers below corresponding to those in Schedules [   ] to the Agreement are included for convenience only and do not in any respect limit the application of any disclosure.

The following disclosures are made:

[insert specific disclosures]

DISCLOSED DOCUMENTS INDEX

This is the Disclosed Documents Index for the purposes of the Disclosure Letter dated
[   ] 199[   ] from [Vendor/Vendor's Solicitors] to [Purchaser/Purchaser's Solicitors] relating to the sale and purchase of the entire issued share capital of
[Target]/Business description.

[list documents]

The precedent Agreement for Sale (Shares) at p 375 contemplates that certain documents be annexed to or contained in the Disclosure Letter as follows (references are to the relevant clause in the precedent agreement, unless the item in question is a defined term)

Audited Accounts

Management Accounts

Title deeds to the Properties (cl 5.2(D)(3))

Guarantees to be discharged at Completion (cl 5.2(H))

Accrued remuneration (cl 8.6 (R))

Listed Intellectual Property (Sched 3, para 1)

Listed Intellectual Property Agreements (Sched 3, para 1)

Memorandum and Articles of Association (Sched 3, para 2.2(C))

Grants (Sched 3, para 2.7(E))

Company's Insurances (Sched 3, para 2.7(F))

Trading Name (Sched 3, para 2.7(G))

Trade Associations (Sched 3, para 2,7(H))

Terms of Business (Sched 3, para 2.7(I))

Defaulting customers (Sched 3, para 2.9(E)(2))

Sureties and guarantees (Sched 3, para 2.9(F))

Financial facilities (Sched 3, para 2.10(B))

Bank balances (Sched 3, para 2.10(D))

List of Employees (Sched 3, para 2.11(B)(3))

Sale Memorandum (Sched 3, para 2.12(B))

Transferred tax refunds (Sched 4, para 2.1(F))

Arrangements and concessions with tax authorities (Sched 4, para 2.1(G))

Group income elections (Sched 4, para 2.2(B))

Arrangements relating to the surrender of ACT (Sched 4, para 2.2(C))

Arrangements relating to group relief (Sched 4, para 2.3(A))

Past changes of ownership (Sched 4, para 2.3(C)(1))

Notifications under The Movements of Capital (Required Information) Regulations 1990 (Taxes Act 1988, s 765) (Sched 4, para 2.5(A))

Interests in foreign companies (Sched 4, para 2.5(C))

Base values (Sched 4, para 2.6(A))

Particulars under TCGA 1992, s 35 and Schedule 4 TCGA 1992 (Sched 4, para 2.6(A)(2))

Claims for rollover relief (Sched 4, para 2.6(B))

Pre-entry losses (Sched 4, para 2.6(C))

Elections (Sched 4, para 2.7(A))

Clearances (Sched 4, para 2.7(B))

Claims to defer unrealised exchange gains (Sched 4, para 2.8(C)(2))

Debts to which Chapter II of Part II Finance Act 1993 does not apply (Sched 4, para 2.8(C)(3))

Qualifying contracts with non-resident persons (Sched 4, para 2.8(D)(2))

Connected loan relationships (Sched 4, para 2.9(B) and 2.9(C) and 2.9(G))

Debtor relationships (Sched 4, para 2.9(D))

Dispensations and PAYE audits (Sched 4, para 2.10(B))

VAT elections (Sched 4, para 2.12(A)(8) and 2.12(A)(11))

Guarantees for release (Sched 8, para 1)

Loan accounts for repayment (Sched 8, para 2)

The precedent Agreement for Sale (Assets) at p 501 contemplates that certain documents be annexed to or contained in the Disclosure Letter as follows (references are to the relevant clause in the precedent agreement, unless the item in question is a defined term)

Assumed Liabilities

Audited Accounts

List of Employees

Listed Intellectual Property

Listed Intellectual Property Agreements

Management Accounts

Specified Contracts

Systems Contracts

Insurance policies (cl 2.3(B)) and (Sched 6, para 2.7(I))

Charges for release at completion (cl 6.3(K) and (L))

VAT Premises (cl 15.2(B))

Stock valuation (Sched 4, para 3)

Landlords' consents (Sched 6, para 2.2(B)(1))

Authorisation (Sched 6, para 2.2(B)(4))

VAT elections (Sched 6, para 2.5(C)(6))

Grants (Sched 6, para 2.6(C))

Trade associations (Sched 6, para 2.7(J))

Terms of business (Sched 6, para 2.7(K))

Consents to assignment of contract (Sched 6, para 2.8(A)(4))

Customers who have defaulted (Sched 6, para 2.8(C)(2))

Notes

1   This precedent is appropriate for use with the Agreement for Sale (Shares) and the Agreement for Sale (Assets) although prepared primarily with the former in mind. Appropriate amendment will be necessary, generally indicated by italicised alternatives.

2   Consider whether disclosure against other provisions eg, indemnities, Deed of Tax Indemnity (rare) is appropriate. Consequential changes will be necessary.

3   This would not be appropriate if the Warranties contemplate that the disclosure letter is warranted (eg the Agreement for Sale (Shares), Sched 3, para 2.12; the Agreement for Sale (Assets), Sched 6, para 2.10).

4   The purchaser will often insist these documents are bundled and not merely indexed, so it knows exactly what is disclosed.

5   List other registers, eg overseas registries for any foreign subsidiary.

6   These general disclosures could be very wide in ambit. Consider limiting them to specified companies, trade marks/patents etc.

Appendix V

Completion Board Minutes

[These minutes may be reproduced and adapted in relation to Subsidiaries.]

[TARGET] LIMITED

MINUTES of a Meeting of the Board of Directors of the Company held on [   ]
19[   ] at [   ] am/pm at [   ].

PRESENT

being a quorum.

IN ATTENDANCE

1   Transfers

There were produced to the meeting duly executed transfer forms, together with the relative share certificates, in respect of the following transfers:

Transferor	*Transferee*	*Class of Shares*	*No of Shares*

IT WAS RESOLVED that the transfers be and they are hereby approved and (subject to the transfer documents being duly stamped) that the names of the transferees be entered in the register of members of the Company in respect of the shares represented by the respective transfer forms and that the common seal of the Company be affixed to certificates issued in respect of the shareholdings of the transferees in accordance with the Articles of Association of the Company and that such certificates be issued to the transferees accordingly.

2   Appointment of Additional Directors

IT WAS RESOLVED that, upon conclusion of the meeting, the following persons who have consented to so act be appointed new directors of the Company with immediate effect:

[insert directors' names]

There were produced to the meeting forms 288 duly signed by the above consenting to act as directors of the Company.

3   Resignation of Directors

There was produced to the meeting letters of resignation from   as directors of the Company and IT WAS RESOLVED that such resignations be and are hereby accepted with effect from the conclusion of the meeting.

4   Appointment of New Secretary

There was produced to the meeting a letter of resignation from   as secretary of the Company and IT WAS RESOLVED that such resignation be and it is hereby accepted with effect from the conclusion of the meeting and that, with effect from the conclusion of the meeting   be appointed as secretary of the Company in his place.

There was produced to the meeting a form 288 duly signed by the above consenting to act as secretary of the Company.

5   Registered Office

IT WAS RESOLVED that the registered office of the Company be changed to   and that a form 287 be completed in respect thereof.

6   Bankers

IT WAS RESOLVED that the authority of the Company's bankers,   Bank Plc,   Branch, be revoked and such branch be notified accordingly forthwith and that the Company open a bank account with   Bank Plc,   Branch and that the resolutions contained in the Bank's standard form and mandate, a copy of which is attached to these minutes, be and are hereby passed and that [any director or the secretary] be and are hereby authorised to sign cheques and all other documents relating to such account in accordance with such resolutions.

7   Auditors

There was produced to the meeting written resignation of   with effect from [   ] 19[   ] together with their statement as auditors of the Company pursuant to Companies Act 1985, s 394(1). IT WAS RESOLVED that such resignation be accepted with effect from the conclusion of the meeting and that   of   be appointed auditors of the Company with effect from the conclusion of the meeting.

8   Filings

IT WAS RESOLVED that the secretary be instructed to submit all forms and documents to the registrar of companies as necessary.

9   Conclusion

There being no further business, the meeting concluded.

Chairman

Letters of Resignation

The Directors,
[TARGET] LIMITED[1]

[Registered office]

Dated [   ] 19[   ]

Dear Sirs

[TARGET] LIMITED ('THE COMPANY')

I hereby resign from the office of [director/secretary [of], and as an employee of,] the Company with effect from the conclusion of the board meeting at which this letter is presented, and I acknowledge and confirm that [, save in respect of any statutory rights,][2] I have no claim of whatsoever kind outstanding for compensation or otherwise against the Company, its servants, officers, agents or employees in respect of the termination of my appointment or otherwise whatsoever.

Yours faithfully

SIGNED and DELIVERED as a   )
DEED by the said [   ]   )
in the presence of:)

Notes

1   Modify for subsidiaries, as appropriate.
2   *See* the Agreement for Sale (Shares), clause 5.2(B), and the note thereon (p 383).

The Directors
[TARGET] LIMITED[1]

[Registered office]

Dated [   ] 19[   ]

Dear Sirs

[TARGET] LIMITED ('THE COMPANY')

We hereby resign as auditors of the Company and, in accordance with the Companies Act 1985, s 394, we confirm that there are no circumstances connected with our resignation which we consider should be brought to the notice of the members or creditors of the Company.

We further confirm that there are no sums owing to us by the Company at the date hereof on any account.

Yours faithfully

[Auditors]

Notes

1   Modify for subsidiaries as appropriate.

Appendix VII

Power of Attorney

To whom it may concern:

[Vendor or nominee of registered holder] [Plc/Limited] (the 'Member') of [address] being the registered holder of [   ] ordinary shares (the 'Shares') in [Target] Limited (the 'Company'), having by an agreement (the 'Agreement') dated [   ] 19[   ] between [Vendor] and [Purchaser] Plc (the 'Attorney') sold the Shares to the Attorney, together with all rights now and hereafter attaching thereto, hereby as the deed of the Member:

(a) irrevocably appoints the Attorney as the Member's attorney to exercise in the absolute discretion of the Attorney all rights attaching to the Shares or exercisable by the Member in his capacity as a member of the Company, and without prejudice to the generality of the foregoing the powers exercisable by the Attorney shall include the power to execute, deliver and do all deeds, instruments and acts in the Member's name and on his behalf in pursuance of the foregoing, and shall include the power to sub-delegate this power;

(b) undertakes and agrees not, save upon the written request of the Attorney, to exercise any rights attaching to the Shares or exercisable by the Member in his capacity as a member of the Company or to appoint any other person to exercise such rights;

(c) undertakes and agrees, save as may be provided to the contrary in the Agreement, that any moneys, securities or other benefits, or notices, documents or other communications which may be received after the date hereof by the Member (including any officer, employee, banker or other agent thereof) from the Company or any third party in respect of the Shares or in the Member's capacity as a member of the Company shall be received by the Member (including as aforesaid) and held in trust for the Attorney and, without prejudice to the generality of the obligations imposed by the foregoing, promptly to procure the forwarding to the Attorney for the attention of [the Secretary] all such benefits or communications and to account to the Attorney for all benefits arising therefrom;

(d) agrees and undertakes upon written request by the Attorney to ratify all deeds, instruments and acts exercised by the Attorney in pursuance of this power;

(e) agrees that in acting hereunder the Attorney may act by its secretary or any director or person acting pursuant to authority conferred by its board of directors or any director; and

(f) declares that such power, undertaking and agreement shall cease and determine upon the Member ceasing to be a member of the Company, but without prejudice to any power exercised prior to such date and shall not, save as may be required by law, terminate on [the commencement of any winding up of the Member or appointment of any administrator or receiver] OR [the Member's previous death, bankruptcy or mental disorder], and shall, save as aforesaid, in connection with the Shares be accordingly binding upon [any liquidator, administrator or receiver] OR [any personal representative, trustee in bankruptcy or trustee in respect of any mental disorder].

This deed shall be governed by and construed in accordance with English law.

Dated [   ] 19[   ]

THE COMMON SEAL of [   ]   )
LIMITED was affixed to this   )
deed in the presence of:)

   Director

   Secretary

OR

SIGNED and DELIVERED as a   )
DEED by the said [   ]   )
)
in the presence of:)

Appendix VIII

Vendor Placing Agreement[1]

Contents

THIS AGREEMENT dated the [   ] day of [   ] 19[   ] and made

BETWEEN:

(1)   [   ] LIMITED a company registered in England under number
      [   ] whose registered office is at [   ] (the 'Company');
      and
(2)   [   ] LIMITED a company registered in England under number
      [   ] whose registered office is at [   ] (the 'Bank').

WHEREAS:

(A)   By an Agreement dated [   ] between the Company and [the Ven-
      dors], [the Vendors] have agreed to sell, and the Company has agreed to purchase,
      on the terms and subject to the conditions set out therein all of the issued shares in
      the capital of [target] in consideration for the issue by the Company to the Bank
      and/or its nominee(s) and/or the Placees of such number of fully paid Ordinary
      Shares as shall pursuant to the Placing result in the receipt by the Vendors of an
      amount equal to the Placing Proceeds.
(B)   On the terms and subject to the conditions of this Agreement the Company has re-
      quested the Bank to implement the Placing.

NOW IT IS HEREBY AGREED as follows:

1   Interpretation

1.1   Definitions

In this Agreement, unless the context otherwise requires:

      'Acquisition Agreement' means the agreement dated [   ] between
      the [Vendors and the Company] in the agreed form;
      'Admission' means the London Stock Exchange admitting the Placing Shares to
      the Official List and such admission becoming effective in accordance with para-
      graph 7.1 of the Listing Rules;
      'Business Day' means a day on which dealings take place on the London Stock
      Exchange;
      'the Circular'[2] means the circular letter from the Company to its shareholders in
      the agreed form giving details, *inter alia*, of the acquisition to be made pursuant
      to the Acquisition Agreement and the Placing [and incorporating a notice conven-
      ing the EGM];
      'Completion' means Completion of the Acquisition Agreement;
      ['EGM' means the extraordinary general meeting of the Company to be convened
      for [   ], notice of which is set out in the Circular (and including any
      adjournment of such meeting)];
      'the Group' means the Company and its subsidiaries;
      'Indemnified Person' has the meaning given in Clause 11;
      'the Indemnities' means the indemnities contained in Clause 11;
      'the Listing Rules' means the listing rules made under s 142 of the Financial Ser-
      vices Act 1986 (as amended from time to time);
      'the London Stock Exchange' means The London Stock Exchange Limited;
      'Ordinary Shares' means ordinary shares of [   ] each in the capital of
      the Company;

'Placees' means persons to whom the Placing Shares are offered under the Placing;

'the Placing' means the proposed placing by the Bank of the Placing Shares on the terms of this Agreement;

'the Placing Price' means the price at which the Placing Shares will be placed by the Bank, namely [   ] pence per Ordinary Share;

'the Placing Proceeds' means £[   ];

'the Placing Shares'[3] means a total of [   ] Ordinary Shares;

'the Press Announcement' means the press announcement in the agreed form giving details of the Placing and the acquisition proposed to made pursuant to the Acquisition Agreement;

'the Registrars' means [   ];

['The Resolution(s)' means the resolution(s) set out in the notice convening the EGM incorporated in the Circular];

'the Vendors' means [   ]; and

'the Warranties' means the warranties, representations and undertakings set out in Schedule 1 and given pursuant to Clause 10.

1.2   Construction of Certain References

In this Agreement, where the context admits:

(A)   words and phrases the definitions of which are contained or referred to in Part XXVI Companies Act 1985 shall be construed as having the meanings thereby attributed to them;

(B)   references to statutory provisions shall be construed as references to those provisions as amended or re-enacted or as their application is modified by other provisions from time to time and shall include references to any provisions of which they are re-enactments (whether with or without modification);

(C)   where any of the Warranties is qualified by reference to the awareness, knowledge and/or belief of any person, that statement shall be deemed to include an additional statement that it has been made after due and careful enquiry;[4]

(D)   references to Clauses and Schedules are references to clauses and schedules of and to this Agreement, references to Sub-Clauses or Paragraphs are, unless otherwise stated, references to sub-clauses of the Clause or paragraphs of the Schedule in which the reference appears, and references to this Agreement include the Schedules; and

(E)   references to any document being in 'agreed terms' or in 'agreed form' are to that document in the form signed or initialled by or on behalf of the parties for identification.

1.3   Headings

The headings and sub-headings are inserted for convenience only and shall not affect the construction of this Agreement.

1.4   Schedules

The Schedules shall have effect as if set out herein.

2   Conditions

2.1   Conditions[5]

The obligations of the Bank under this Agreement are conditional upon:

[(A) the release of the Press Announcement to the London Stock Exchange at or before 8.00 am on [*date of the agreement*];]

[(B) approval by the London Stock Exchange of the Circular, prior to its despatch to the shareholders of the Company;]

[(C) the Circular being posted to the shareholders of the Company no later than [   ];]

[(D) the passing of the Resolutions, without amendment, at a duly convened EGM of the Company;]

(E) Admission occurring not later than 9.30 am on [*anticipated date of completion*];

[(F) none of the Warranties being or having become untrue, inaccurate or misleading in any respect at any time before Admission and no fact or circumstance having arisen and nothing having been done or omitted to be done which would render any of the Warranties untrue or inaccurate in any respect if it was repeated as at Admission;][6]

(G) the Bank not having exercised any of its rights to terminate this Agreement under Clause 14;[6]

(H) the Acquisition Agreement having become unconditional and having been completed in accordance with its terms (save for the condition set out in Clause 4.1(D) of the Acquisition Agreement and the Company's obligations under Clause 5.3 thereof).[7]

2.2   Conditions Not Fulfilled

If any of such conditions shall not have been fulfilled (or waived by the Bank) in all respects or if any of such conditions shall have ceased to be capable of being fulfilled by the time and date specified or by such later time and/or date as the Bank may agree (or, if no such time and/or date is specified, by 5pm on [*longstop*], or such later time and/or date as the Bank may agree) the obligations of the Bank under this Agreement shall cease and determine and neither party shall have any claim against the other for costs, damages, charges, compensation or otherwise save for antecedent breach and save that:

[(A) the Company shall pay to the Bank the amounts payable (or liable to be paid) by it under Clause 9;] and[8]

(B) the indemnity set out in Clause 11, and Clauses 15 and 16, shall remain in full force and effect.

2.3   Reasonable Endeavours

The Company undertakes to use its reasonable endeavours to procure that each of the conditions set out in Sub-Clause 2.1 is fulfilled by the due time and/or date referred to in each case (or by such later time and/or date as the Bank may agree).

3   Delivery of Documents

3.1   Documents to be Delivered at Signing

The Company shall immediately on execution of this Agreement, deliver, or procure that there are delivered, to the Bank:

(A) a certified copy of the minutes of the meeting of the Directors at which resolutions were passed approving the Acquisition Agreement and authorising the execution of this Agreement by the Company, and authorising the despatch of the Press Announcement [together with a copy of all documents referred to as being produced at such meeting];

(B) a certified copy of the Acquisition Agreement; and

(C) a copy of the Press Announcement.

[3.2 Documents to be Delivered on Approval of Circular[9]

Immediately following the approval of the Circular by the London Stock Exchange the Company shall deliver to the Bank:

(A) a copy of the Circular;

(B) a certified copy of the minutes of the meeting of the Directors containing resolutions approving the Circular and authorising its despatch and authorising the application to the London Stock Exchange for the admission of the Placing Shares to the Official List [together with a copy of all documents referred to as being produced at such meeting];

(C) a certified copy of the statements signed by each director of the Company accepting responsibility for the information contained in the Circular;[10]

(D) a certified copy of the verification notes relating to the information contained in the Circular signed by each director of the Company;[11]

[(E) a certified copy of the letters from the Company's auditors addressed to the Company and the Bank reporting on the working capital and indebtedness position of the Group and confirming the accuracy of certain financial information in the Circular;]][12]

[3.3 Documents to be Delivered Following EGM

On or before the close of business on the day upon which the EGM is held the Company shall deliver to the Bank a certified copy of the minutes of the EGM;]

[3.4 Documents Required to be Available under Listing Rules

The Company shall procure that further copies of the Circular are published and made available by or on behalf of the Company in accordance with paragraphs 5.28, 8.4 to 8.6 inclusive of the Listing Rules.][13]

3.5 Waiver or Extension of Time of Delivery

The Bank may, in its discretion, waive the requirement that the Company deliver to it any of the documents listed in [Sub-Clauses 3.1 to 3.4] or may extend the time for delivery of any of the documents. Any waiver or extension may be granted by the Bank on such terms as it thinks fit.

4 Application for Listing

4.1 Company to Make Application

The Company at its own expense will make an application for admission of the Placing Shares to the Official List and will so far as within its powers obtain by [   ] (or such later date as the Bank may agree) the agreement of the London Stock Exchange to Admission and for such purposes the Company will supply all such information, give all such undertakings, execute all such documents, pay all such fees and do or procure to be done all such things as may reasonably be required to comply with the requirements of the London Stock Exchange in relation to such application and with the Listing Rules.

4.2 Bank to Assist

The Bank undertakes to the Company that it will take all reasonable steps to assist with the application for admission of the Placing Shares to the Official List by [*completion date*].

5   Placing of the Placing Shares

5.1   Subject to Sub-Clause 2.1 the Bank agrees:

(A)   as agent for the Company to use its reasonable endeavours to procure subscribers for the Placing Shares; and

(B)   in the event of the Bank not being able to procure subscribers for any Placing Shares, by [   ]pm on [   ] itself as principal to subscribe for and receive the allotment of and pay for such Placing Shares;

such subscription and allotment in each case to be at a price per share equal to the Placing Price.

6   The Company's Obligations

6.1   Company's Obligations

The Company agrees with the Bank that it will:

(A)   at Completion allot and issue, credited as fully paid, the Placing Shares to the Bank and/or its nominee(s) and/or the Placees specified by the Bank and approve the due registration as holders of the Placing Shares of the Bank and/or its nominee(s) and/or the Placees as may have been notified by the Bank, such allotment of the Placing Shares being conditional upon Admission occurring by not later than [9.30] am on [*completion date*] (or such later time and/or date as the Bank may agree);

(B)   forthwith after allotment deliver to the Bank a certified copy of the minutes of the meeting of its directors allotting the Placing Shares; and

(C)   procure that the Registrars shall:
    (1)   effect registration of Placees notified by the Bank, and, to the extent that the Bank accepts and pays for any Placing Shares as principal, the Bank itself (or its nominee(s)), as members of the Company and the registered holders of the Placing Shares; and, subject thereto
    (2)   issue definitive certificates in respect of the Placing Shares, and shall make the same available to the persons entitled thereto by delivery to the Bank for itself or on their behalf by] [and/or that instructions are given to CRESTCo Limited to credit the appropriate stock accounts nominated by the Placees/ Bank not later than] [   ] (or such later date as the Bank may agree).

6.2   Terms of Allotment of Placing Shares

The Placing Shares allotted under Sub-Clause 6.1 shall be allotted and issued subject to the Memorandum and Articles of Association of the Company and credited as fully paid free from all claims, liens, charges, encumbrances and equities and on terms that they rank *pari passu* in all respects with the existing Ordinary Shares [and shall rank for dividend in respect of all dividends made, paid or declared after[   ]].

7   Payment

7.1   Payment by Bank

The Bank shall make payment or procure the payment of the Placing Proceeds by bank transfer for same day value to the credit of the Vendors' solicitors account (account number [   ]; sort code [   ] at [Bank] [Branch]) on [   ] (or such later date as the Company shall notify to the Bank as being the effective date of Completion).

7.2   Payment Constitutes Discharge

Payment of the Placing Proceeds in accordance with Sub-Clause 7.1 shall be a complete discharge by the Bank of its obligations to the Company under this Agreement.

8   Authority of Registrars

8.1   The Company confirms to the Bank that it will provide the Registrars with all authorisations and information as will enable the Registrars to perform their duties in accordance with the terms of this Agreement and will authorise the Registrars to act in accordance with the proper instructions of the Bank.

9   Fees, Commissions and Expenses

9.1   Fees and Commission[8]

[Whether or not this Agreement becomes unconditional] the Company shall pay to the Bank:

[(A)   a fee of [£   ] as remuneration for its services under this Agreement]; and/or

[(B)   a commission of an amount equal to [   ] per cent of the Placing Price multiplied by the total number of the Placing Shares.]

9.2   Expenses and Stamp Duty[14]

The Company shall pay all the costs, charges and expenses howsoever of or incidental to the [Acquisition Agreement and the transactions contemplated thereby; the Circular; and the Placing] including but not limited to stock exchange listing fees, printing and advertising costs, postage and registrars' fees, the Bank's legal fees and reasonable out of pocket expenses and the Company's legal and accounting expenses (in all cases together with value added tax thereon) and the Company shall in addition bear the cost of the stamp duty and/or stamp duty reserve tax (if any) which is payable in respect of the arrangements for the allotment and issue of all or any Placing Shares as contemplated by this Agreement.

9.3   VAT Payable by Company

In respect of any reimbursement of expenses by the Company to the Bank, the Company shall in addition pay to the Bank:

(A)   if any reimbursement in respect of expenses constitutes part of the consideration for any supply of services to the Company, such amount as equals any value added tax charged to the Bank in respect of the said expenses which is not recoverable by the Bank together with any amount representing any value added tax properly chargeable in respect of the consideration for that supply (including such irrecoverable value added tax); and

(B)   if any such expenses constitute disbursements incurred by the Bank as agent on behalf of the Company, an amount equal to any value added tax charged thereon to the Bank.

9.4   VAT Invoice

Any value added tax properly chargeable in respect of any amount payable to the Bank under this Clause 9 shall be paid on production of an appropriate VAT invoice.

9.5   Time for Payment

All fees, commission and other amounts (together with any value added tax thereon) will be payable for value on the date of payment not later than the date of payment by the Bank to the Vendors under Clause 7 or the second business day after the date on which the obligations of the Bank shall cease and determine under Sub-Clause 2.2 or be terminated under Sub-Clause 14.1.

10 Warranties, Representations and Undertakings

10.1   Warranties by the Company

The Company warrants, represents and undertakes to the Bank as an inducement to the Bank to enter into this Agreement[15], as at the date hereof [and at all times during the period up to and including Admission as if repeated by reference to the facts and circumstances existing at all such times,][16] in the terms set out in Schedule 1.

10.2   Company to Notify Bank

The Company undertakes to notify the Bank immediately if it comes its knowledge at any time up to Admission that any of the Warranties was not true or accurate or was misleading in any material respect when given or made [and/or has ceased to be true or accurate in any material respect or has become misleading in any material respect by reference to the facts or circumstances from time to time subsisting.]

10.3   Company Not to Cause Warranty to be Untrue

Except to the extent necessary to implement this Agreement the Company undertakes to the Bank not to do, or omit to do, anything which would cause any of the Warranties to become untrue, inaccurate or misleading at any time before Admission.

11 The Bank's Indemnity

11.1   No Claims Against Bank

No claim shall be made against the Bank or any of its [associated companies] or any of the [directors] [partners] employees or agents[17] of the Bank or any such [associated company] (each, an 'Indemnified Person') by the Company to recover any damage, loss, liability, cost, charge or expense which the Company may suffer or incur or claim to have suffered or incurred by reason of or arising out of the carrying out by the Bank or on its behalf of its obligations and services hereunder or otherwise in connection with or incidental to the Placing provided that such damage, loss, liability, cost, charge or expense does not arise from the negligence, fraud or wilful default of the Bank in carrying out, or the breach by any Indemnified Person of, any of its obligations under this Agreement or the breach by any Indemnified Person of any of its duties or obligations under the Financial Services Act 1986 or the regulatory system[18] (as defined in the rules of The Securities and Futures Authority Limited).

11.2 Indemnity[19]

The Company hereby undertakes with the Bank (for itself and as trustee for each other Indemnified Person) that it will indemnify each Indemnified Person and at all times keep each Indemnified Person indemnified against all losses, claims, costs, charges, expenses, liabilities, actions, demands, proceedings and judgments which any Indemnified Person may suffer or incur (except those which this Agreement specifically contemplates will be borne by any Indemnified Person) or which may be brought or threatened to be brought against or incurred by any of them and against all losses, costs, charges and expenses (including legal fees) and taxes which any Indemnified Person may suffer or incur as a result thereof (including without limitation, all such losses, costs, charges and expenses (including legal fees) and taxes as each Indemnified Person may pay or incur in responding to, disputing or considering any such actual or potential actions, claims, demands or proceedings) and which in any such case arises out of or in connection with:[20]

(A) any breach or alleged breach of any of the Warranties or fact or circumstances which causes any of the Warranties to become untrue inaccurate or misleading before Admission; or

(B) any breach by the Company of any of its obligations hereunder; or

(C) the performance by an Indemnified Person of its obligations hereunder or otherwise in connection with the Placing

and which does not in any such case arise from the negligence, fraud or wilful default of the Bank in carrying out, [or the breach by the Bank (or any other Indemnified Person) of, any of its obligations under this Agreement or the breach by any Indemnified Person of any of its or their duties or obligations under the Financial Services Act 1986 or the regulatory system (as defined in the rules of The Securities and Futures Authority Limited) or the Bank's subscription for Placing Shares under this Agreement.].[21]

11.3 Notification of Claim

If the Bank becomes aware of any claim relevant for the purposes of this Clause 11 in respect of which indemnity may be sought from the Company, the Bank shall promptly notify the Company thereof and shall consult with the Company and provide the Company with such information and documentation relating to such claim as the Company may reasonably require.

11.4 No Deductions or Withholdings

All sums payable to an Indemnified Person under this Clause 11 shall be paid free and clear of all deductions or withholdings unless the deduction or withholding is required by law, in which event the payer shall pay such additional amount as will be required to ensure that the net amount received by the Indemnified Person will equal the full amount which would have been received by it had such deduction or withholding not been made. If the United Kingdom Inland Revenue or any other taxing authority in any jurisdiction brings into any charge for taxation any sum payable under any indemnity contained in this Clause 11, the amount so payable shall be increased by such amount as will ensure that after deduction of the taxation so chargeable there shall remain a sum equal to the amount that would otherwise be payable under such indemnity. If an Indemnified Person subsequently receives a credit for any such deduction or withholding, the Bank shall or shall procure that such Indemnified Person shall forthwith repay to the Company an amount equal to the amount of the credit so received.

12 Announcements

12.1 Announcements etc after Admission

Save as required by law or the London Stock Exchange or as agreed with the Bank, no press conference, public announcement, public statement or public communication (other than the Press Announcement [and the Circular]) concerning any member of the Group which is material in the context of the Placing shall be made or despatched between the date of this Agreement and the expiry of the period of [20] Business Days following Admission without the prior approval of the Bank in writing (such approval not to be unreasonably withheld or delayed).

12.2 Entering into Obligations etc after Admission

The Company shall not and shall procure that no member of the Group shall, between the date of this Agreement and the expiry of the period of [20] Business Days following Admission, enter into, or incur any obligation to make any commitment or agreement or put itself in a position where it is obliged to announce that any commitment or agreement may be entered into or made, which in any such case, is material in the context of the Placing, without the prior approval of the Bank in writing (such approval not to be unreasonably withheld or delayed).

13 Acquisition Agreement

13.1   The Company undertakes to the Bank that:

(A)   it will not agree to any alteration, revision or amendment of any of the terms of the Acquisition Agreement (or any document entered into pursuant thereto) to any extent which is material in the context of the Placing or waive any such term or grant any time for performance or other indulgence under any such document or proceed to Completion without full satisfaction of the terms and conditions of the Acquisition Agreement or exercise or choose not to exercise any right to rescind the Acquisition Agreement without, in any such case, prior consultation with the Bank and, if the Bank reasonably so requires, its prior consent in writing;

(B)   it will duly and punctually perform its obligations at Completion in accordance with the Acquisition Agreement.

14 Termination

14.1 Termination

If at any time prior to [Admission]:

(A)   it comes to the knowledge of the Bank that any of the Warranties was untrue or inaccurate or misleading in any material respect when made and/or that any of the Warranties has ceased to be true or accurate in any material respect or has become misleading in any material respect by reference to the facts and circumstances from time to time subsisting[6]; or

(B)   the Company shall fail in any material respect to comply with any of its obligations hereunder;

the Bank may, in its absolute discretion, terminate this Agreement, by notice in writing to the Company received prior to [Admission].

14.2 Consultation

The Bank shall use its reasonable endeavours to consult with and grant time or indulgence to the Company prior to exercising its right to terminate hereunder.

14.3 Effect of Termination

In the event of termination hereunder, the provisions of Sub-Clause 2.2 shall apply, *mutatis mutandis*, as if the conditions set out in Sub-Clause 2.1 shall have become incapable of satisfaction on the date of such termination.

15 General

15.1 Assistance

The Company will give all such assistance and provide all such information as the Bank shall reasonably require for the purposes of this Agreement and will execute all such documents and do all such acts and things as the Bank may reasonably require in order to give effect to the terms of this Agreement.

15.2 Time of the Essence

Any time, date or period mentioned in this Agreement may be extended by mutual agreement between the parties hereto or otherwise as provided herein, but as regards any time, date or period originally fixed or so extended as aforesaid time shall be of the essence. [All references in this Agreement to a time of day are to London time.]

15.3 Rights etc Survive Completion

(A) Subject as otherwise provided in this Agreement, each of the Warranties and the Indemnities shall remain in full force and effect notwithstanding completion of this Agreement.
(B) The Warranties and the Indemnities shall be in addition to and shall not be construed to limit, affect or prejudice any other right or remedy available to the Bank.
(C) No neglect, delay or indulgence on the part of the Bank in enforcing the Warranties or the Indemnities or any other terms or conditions hereof shall be construed as a waiver thereof and no single or partial exercise of any rights or remedy under this Agreement will preclude or restrict the further exercise or enforcement of any such right or remedy.

15.4 Invalidity

If any provision of this Agreement shall be held to be illegal or unenforceable the enforceability of the remainder of this Agreement shall not be affected.

15.5 Release of or Compromise with One Indemnified Person

Any release, waiver or compromise which the Bank may agree to or effect as regards any one Indemnified Person in connection with the Indemnities shall not affect the rights of any other Indemnified Person.

15.6 Notices[22]

(A) Save as specifically otherwise provided in this Agreement any notice or other communication required to be given under this Agreement or in connection with the matters contemplated by it shall, except where otherwise specifically provid-

ed, be in writing by facsimile or by first class post and shall be addressed as follows:

Name:

[For the attention of:]

Address:

Fax Number:

Name:

[For the attention of:]

Address:

Fax Number:

(B)   Any notice given to the Company by the Bank under Clause 14.1 may also be giv-
en by any [Partner] [Director] of the Bank to any Director of the Company either
personally or by telephone (to be confirmed in writing) and shall have immediate
effect.

15.7 Agreement Binding on Successors

This Agreement shall be binding on each party's successors and personal representatives and estates (as the case may be).

15.8 Counterparts

This Agreement may be entered into in any number of counterparts which shall together
constitute one Agreement. Any party may enter this Agreement by signing any such
counterpart.

16 Law and Jurisdiction

16.1 English Law

This Agreement shall be governed by, and construed in accordance with, English law.

16.2 Jurisdiction

In relation to any legal action or proceedings to enforce this Agreement or arising out
of or in connection with this Agreement ('proceedings') each of the parties irrevocably
submits to the jurisdiction of the English courts and waives any objection to proceedings in such courts on the grounds of venue or on the grounds that the proceedings have
been brought in an inconvenient forum.

IN WITNESS whereof this Agreement has been entered into the day and year first
above written.

SCHEDULE 1

THE WARRANTIES

1 The Press Announcement [and the Circular]

1.1 The Press Announcement contains all such information required by the Listing Rules and the information contained in the Press Announcement is in accordance with the facts and all statements of fact contained in the Press Announcement are true and accurate and are not misleading. All statements, forecasts, estimates and expressions of opinion, intention and expectation contained in the Press Announcement are fairly and honestly given and have been made after due and proper consideration and are reasonably based.

1.2 All information supplied to the Bank for the purposes of the Placing is true and accurate in all material respects and in accordance with the facts and not incomplete or misleading and all statements, forecasts, estimates and expressions of opinion, intention and expectation so supplied have been made after due and proper consideration, are fair and honest and represent reasonable expectations based on facts known or which ought on reasonable enquiry to have been known to the Company.

1.3 There are no other facts relating to the Group or the directors of the Company known or which could on reasonable enquiry be known to the Company the omission of which makes any statement in the Press Announcement incorrect or misleading in any material respect or which in the context of the proposed issue of the Placing Shares are material for disclosure to a subscriber or potential subscriber thereof.

[1.4   [2]The Circular contains or when issued will contain all information which investors and their investment advisers would reasonably require and reasonably expect to find therein [for the purpose of making an informed assessment of the assets and liabilities, financial position, profits and losses and prospects of the Group and of the rights attaching to the Placing Shares having regard to the particular nature of the Group, the Placing Shares, the persons likely to consider their subscription or acquisition and to the fact that certain matters may reasonably to be expected to be within the knowledge of professional advisers of any kind which those persons may reasonably be expected to consult] and all statements of fact contained in the Circular for which the directors of the Company are responsible will when the same is despatched to the shareholders of the Company be true and accurate in all material respects and not misleading and there are no other facts known or which reasonably ought to be known to the Company which are material for disclosure therein or the omission of which would make any statement in the Circular misleading and all forecasts estimates and expressions of opinion expectation and intention contained therein are and will be made after due and proper consideration and will be fair and honest and reasonably based].

2 Financial Records

2.1 The audited [consolidated] financial statements of the [Group] ('the Accounts') for the financial period ended on [   ] ('the Accounts Date'):

(A) have been prepared in accordance with all relevant statutes, Statements of Standard Accounting Practice and Financial Reporting Standards and with generally accepted United Kingdom accounting principles, practices and standards consistently applied;

(B) give a true and fair view of the state of affairs of the Group as at the Accounts Date and of the profit or loss for the period ending on the Accounts Date; and

(C)   fairly set out the assets, liabilities, reserves, profits and source and application of funds of the Group and either make proper provision for or, where appropriate in accordance with generally accepted United Kingdom accounting principles and practices, include a note in respect of all material liabilities or commitments, whether actual, deferred, contingent or disputed, of the Group as at the relevant date.

3   Current Financial Period

3.1   [Save as disclosed in the Group's Interim Statement], since the Accounts Date:

(A)   the business of the Group has been carried on in the ordinary and usual course and there has been no material adverse change, nor any development likely to give rise to a material adverse change, in the financial or trading position or prospects of the Group and no material depletion in the net assets of the Group taken as a whole;

(B)   no member of the Group has acquired or disposed of or agreed to acquire or dispose of any business or any material asset or assumed or acquired any material liabilities (including contingent liabilities) other than in the ordinary course of business;

(C)   no member of the Group has entered into any contracts or commitments of a long term or unusual nature which in the context of the Placing are material for disclosure; and

(D)   save as publicly announced no dividend or other distribution has been, or is treated as having been, declared, paid or made by the Company.

4   Working Capital[12]

4.1   All of the Group's term loans and overdraft facilities are in full force and effect. No event has occurred or is likely to occur which (with the giving of notice or the lapse of time or both or the making of any relevant determination by any bank) may cause any such loan to be repayable prior to its stated date of maturity or cause the bank's commitment thereunder to be cancelled.   So far as the Company is aware all undrawn amounts under such facilities are capable of drawdown and all conditions precedent to such drawdown have been met or can be met by the Group.

[4.2   The information supplied by the Company to [auditors] for the purpose of preparing their reports and letters to the Company and to the Bank in relation to the Placing and the working capital projection referred to in the Circular is true and accurate in all material respects and not misleading in any material respect and the working capital report has been carefully compiled by the Company on the basis of the assumptions stated therein and presented on a basis consistent with the accounting principles adopted by the Company in relation to the preparation of the Accounts and the assumptions upon which the working capital report has been based are made after diligent enquiry and are fair and reasonable in the context of Group taken as a whole.]

5   Insolvency

5.1   No member of the Group has taken any action nor, to the best of the knowledge, information and belief of the Company, have any other steps been taken or legal proceedings started or threatened against any [material] member of the Group for its winding-up or dissolution or for it to enter into any arrangement or composition for the benefit of creditors, or for the appointment of a receiver, administrator, administrative receiver, trustee or similar officer of it or any of its properties, revenues or assets nor have any orders been made for any of the foregoing.

6   Other Events of Default

6.1   To the best of the knowledge, information and belief of the Company no event has occurred or is likely to occur which constitutes or results in or may constitute or result in a default or the acceleration of any obligation under any agreement, instrument or arrangement to which any member of the Group is a party or by which it or any of its properties, revenues or assets are bound which would in any such case have a material adverse effect on the businesses, assets, financial or trading position or prospects of the Group.

7   Litigation

7.1   No member of the Group nor any person for whom any such company is or may be vicariously liable has any claim outstanding against them or is engaged in any litigation or arbitration, prosecution or other proceedings or governmental or official investigation or inquiry which individually or collectively is of material importance to the Group and to the best of the knowledge, information and belief of the Company, no such litigation, arbitration, prosecution or other proceedings or governmental or official investigation or inquiry are threatened or pending nor are there any circumstances which are likely to give rise to any of the same.

8   Effect of Placing

8.1   The Placing and the Admission will comply with all agreements or arrangements to which members of the Group are a party or by which they or any of their property is bound and will not exceed or infringe any restrictions or the terms of any contract, obligation or commitment by or binding upon the Company's Board of Directors, or result in the imposition or variation of any material rights or obligations of any member of the Group.

8.2   Neither the Placing and its associated transactions nor the performance of this Agreement by the Company will infringe or exceed any borrowing limits, powers or restrictions of, or the terms of any contract, indenture, security obligation, commitment or arrangement binding on any member of the Group.

9   Licences

9.1   Members of the Group have obtained all material licences, permissions, authorisations, approvals and consents required for the carrying on of their respective businesses and such licences, permissions, authorisations, approvals and consents are in full force and effect and there are no circumstances of which the Company is aware whereby any of such licences, permissions, authorisations, approvals or consents will be revoked or not renewed, in whole or in part, in the ordinary course of events and members of the Group have so far as the Company is aware complied with all legal and other requirements which are applicable to their respective businesses.

10 Shares

10.1   There are in force no options or other agreements which call for the issue of, or afford to any person the right to call for the issue of, any shares in the capital of the Company.

10.2   The Placing Shares will, upon allotment and issue, be free from all claims, charges, liens, encumbrances and equities and will rank *pari passu* in all respects with the existing Ordinary Shares.

11 Capacity

11.1   The Company has capacity to enter into and perform this Agreement and the Acquisition Agreement [without any sanction or consent by members of the Company or any class of them,] and all other authorisations, approvals, consents and licences required for the entering into of this Agreement by the Company have been obtained and remain in full force and effect.

12 Compliance with Securities Laws

12.1   The Placing, and the issue of the Press Announcement [the Circular] in the manner contemplated by this Agreement will comply with the Acts, the Financial Services Act 1986, the Rules and Regulations of the London Stock Exchange, the Listing Rules, and all other applicable laws, rules and regulations of the United Kingdom and elsewhere.

```
SIGNED by [              ]              )
duly authorised for and on                    )
behalf of [              ] LIMITED     )


SIGNED by [              ]              )
duly authorised for and on                    )
behalf of [              ] LIMITED     )
```

SCHEDULE 2

Documents in the Agreed Form

Acquisition Agreement
Circular
Placing Letter
Press Announcement

Notes

1   This agreement is for use in connection with eg for the Agreement for Sale (Shares). If used in connection with an assets acquisition modification would be necessary to take into account, *inter alia*, the Companies Act 1985, s 103. The vendor placing agreement will generally be drafted by the bank's lawyers, reflecting the bank's preferred approach on various points. Thus the primary purpose of this document is as an aid to the purchaser's solicitor when presented with such a document for review. The bank's document will often be longer eg as to warranties.

2   If the acquisition for any reason requires shareholder consent (eg Super Class 1; to increase share capital or disapply pre-emption rights, *see* p 7), or if there is any open offer (which this agreement does not contemplate), then a circular to the company's shareholders will need to be issued in connection with the vendor placing. The circular may include listing particulars, if the issuer's share capital is to be increased by 10 per cent or more, although this agreement does not contemplate listing particulars nor, indeed, a prospectus in respect of unlisted shares (*see* p 250). Where listing particulars are required the agreement would need modification to reflect their approval by the Stock Exchange and the possibility that under the Financial Services Act 1986, s 147, supplementary listing particulars may be required.

3   The placing shares will be all of the consideration shares allotted as consideration pursuant to the acquisition agreement, unless the vendors elect to receive some of the shares. Where a substantial number of shares are to be received and retained by the vendors, the bank may require that the vendors accept restrictions on the timing of disposals so as to prevent immediate sales which could upset the market in the period following the placing.

4   See the Agreement for Sale (Shares), Note 11 at p 464.

5   It will be noted that items which are included as conditions are elsewhere repeated as obligations of the company. Although not strictly necessary, it is common to produce a list of the important obligations in this form; the company will prefer to minimise the conditions (although sometimes it is preferable for the item in question to be expressed as a condition when, if the transaction proceeds (eg the condition is not invoked) its obligations in respect of the item in question may then become 'spent').

6   The bank will usually seek, as a condition, continued accuracy of the warranties even though it commonly seeks in addition that the warranties be repeated at admission and that it should have a right to terminate for breach (*see* cl 10.1 at 644 and cl 14.1 at p 646). It is preferable that the bank either has the right to terminate or that the rolling accuracy of warranties is a condition. One difference between the two is the burden of proof. Repeating warranties at admission is, of course, different as it may give the bank a right to damages which survives the placing even where the breach was outside the company's control. To that extent at least such a provision will normally be the subject of negotiation. The parties will wish to balance the respective rights and remedies and the right to terminate if there is breach. This will be particularly significant if the period between contract and completion is lengthy. This agreement does not include the right on the part of the Bank to terminate in the event of *force majeure* which, in exceptional circumstances, may be required by the Bank and will be a matter for negotiation eg as to what constitutes *force majeure*, sometimes most satisfactorily defined by refer-

ence to a percentage fall in the FT-SE index or relevant sector index, over a (very short, eg the morning of the placing) period of time.

7   It will be a matter for negotiation whether the acquisition agreement is also conditional upon the vendor placing agreement becoming unconditional. If it is not and the purchaser has an obligation to pay cash if the placing is terminated, then this condition will be straightforward. If the placing and acquisition are dependent upon each other, however, care will need to be taken with this condition and the equivalent condition in the acquisition agreement to ensure that the conditions are not 'circular'.

8   Since it is common for fees to be payable even if conditions are not satisfied or if there is termination, the company will wish to limit conditionality and be satisfied that, so far as possible, fulfilment of conditions is within its control.

9   In fact, it will often be the case that the circular is approved and items 3.1 and 3.2 occur at the same time; if there are listing particulars, there may be a brief gap pending final approval and delivery to the Registrar of Companies (Financial Services Act 1986, s 149).

10   The Listing Rules require the directors to accept responsibility for the content of listing particulars and Super Class 1 circulars and it is usual for a formal responsibility statement to be given. It is a useful opportunity to advise directors of their obligations. Not relevant for other circulars (eg Companies Act 1985, s 80).

11   Only where a Super Class 1 circular or listing particulars are proposed. Verifications notes are designed to test the factual accuracy and reasonable basis of statements and opinions in the circular and take the form of questions to which a formal response is given, backed by documentation where relevant. Such notes have a particular role where listing particulars are prepared as (it is thought), they will represent evidential support in defence of a claim under Financial Services Act 1986, s 150. Warranties of verification notes are sometimes sought but often resisted, for much the same reason as a vendor will resist warranting a disclosure letter (*see* the Agreement for Sale (Shares), Note 99 at p 474).

12   A working capital statement is required for a Super Class 1 circular or listing particulars (see the Listing Rules, Ch 10 (app); para 6.E.16). Otherwise, delete.

13   Where listing particulars are published, paras 8.4 to 8.6 of the Listing Rules require the particulars to be available at the stock exchange's Companies Announcement Office, at the company's registered office and at any paying agent. Similar rules apply (under para 5.28) where there is an issue without listing particulars, when the circular should contain the information required by para 5.28 and will suffice.

14   The structure of this agreement is to use the SDRT saving approach, described at p 244. In other cases, it is usual for the purchaser to bear the stamp duty/SDRT costs in respect of the placing shares, although where the placing has been arranged at the request of the vendors, this is a matter which may be open to negotiation. In such case the purchaser should be reminded of this additional stamp duty cost of a vendor placing.

15   Note the words 'as an inducement to enter into this agreement'. While, it is suggested, the words are no more than evidential, they are included to take account of the judgment of the Court of Appeal in *Barclays Bank plc v British & Commonwealth Holdings plc* [1996] 1 BCLC 1 (at p 45) and otherwise to show reliance for the purpose of any misrepresentation claim (it does not seem to be practice to in-

corporate a *Thomas Witter v TBP Industries* style limitation clause in such agreements (*see* p 161). The warranties set out in this precedent are conventional, although the bank and the purchaser should consider whether they are appropriate, and the extent to which any additional warranties should be included (for example in respect of an interim financial statement published since the accounts date, environmental matters or any specific aspect of the company's business).

16 *See* Note 6 concerning updating of warranties. Warranties are sometimes expressed to be for the bank and as trustee for the placees. This is plainly to be avoided by the company. The bank may argue that the placee is otherwise left without remedy: the position would, however, need to be analysed in light of the particular circumstances and marketing structure.

17 Check who is to be indemnified, the definition can sometimes be drawn surprisingly wide.

18 The rules of the SFA (Conduct of Business Rule 5.24–1) do not permit its member firms (as most banks will be) to restrict or exclude liability for their breach of the 'regulatory system'.

19 The purchaser's adviser should consider the financial assistance implications of giving such an indemnity although it seems, following *Barclays v B&C* that it may be regarded as an inducement to enter into the agreement rather than 'assistance' (*see* Note 15). It may be appropriate to negotiate limitations on its liability under the indemnity (and indeed the warranties), including the time limit for bringing claims and a claims handling procedure.

20 The matters which are the subject of indemnity are sometimes stated in much fuller form eg arising from the content of the press announcement or any circular, or from breach of securities and other laws. In most cases, sub-clause (A) will cover the point, as the warranties are broadly drawn (although a bank's desire for the indemnity to be more specifically stated is understandable and often agreed).

21 These exclusions will be for negotiation—the SFA rules do not prohibit indemnities. The exclusion dealing with the bank's subscription for placing shares is thought necessary to ensure that, in such event, there is no unlawful financial assistance.

22 A fuller notice clause can be found in the Agreement for Sale (Shares) cl 11.11 at p 393.

Appendix IX

Placing Letter[1]

[BANK] LIMITED

(Registered in England No 658567)

To: [The Placees]

Dear Sirs

Purchaser plc ('Purchaser')
Conditional Placing of   **new Ordinary Shares**
('the Placing Shares') at [**]p per share ('the Offer Price')**

Further to our telephone conversation earlier today concerning the proposed acquisition of Target Limited, we confirm your conditional commitment to subscribe Placing Shares at a price of [   ]p per share.

The Placing Shares will be free of stamp duty, stamp duty reserve tax and commission.

The Placing Shares will rank *pari passu* in all respects with the existing issued Ordinary Shares of Purchaser and will carry the right to receive in full all dividends and other distributions declared, made or paid hereafter, save that they will not rank for the [interim/final] dividend in respect of the financial year ending [   ] 19[   ].

The Bank has entered into a placing agreement (the 'Placing Agreement') whereby it has agreed, to subscribe or procure subscribers for the Placing Shares.

The Placing Agreement and your commitment are conditional[2] upon, *inter alia*, the following conditions being fulfilled on or prior to [   ] (or such later time or date as the Bank may agree):

(i)   Admission of the Consideration Shares to the Official List of the London Stock Exchange and such Admission becoming effective in accordance with the Rules of the London Stock Exchange;

(ii)   completion of the Acquisition Agreement between Purchaser and the Vendors, save in respect of certain matters relating to the Placing Agreement and payment; and

(iii)   the Placing Agreement having become unconditional in all respects and not having been terminated in accordance with its terms.

In consideration of your commitment to subscribe Placing Shares, we confirm that the following commissions[3] will be paid:

[minimum commission, and any additional 'success' element]

Payment for the Placing Shares will be required in full not later than [   ] (or such later date as may be notified to you). Share certificates are expected to be despatched on [   ]/instructions to CREST Co Limited to credit stock accounts as notified to us by you on or before [   ] are expected to be given on [   ].]. Dealings in the Placing Shares are expected to commence on [   ] for normal account settlement.

You will be sent a cheque for the amount of the commissions due to you within five business days of the Placing Agreement becoming unconditional in all respects or, in the event that any of the above conditions are not satisfied by [   ] within five business days of such date.

By agreeing to subscribe the Placing Shares, on the terms and subject to the conditions of this letter, you confirm and represent that you are not a US person or a resident of Canada[4] and that you are not applying for the Placing Shares on behalf of or with a view to resale of such shares to a US person or a resident of Canada and that you undertake to advise any purchaser of the Placing Shares from you of the restrictions on resales of such shares to such persons.

Yours faithfully

for and on behalf of
[BANK] LIMITED

Notes

1   The Bank or broker will have a preferred form of Placing Letter and this specimen is included by way of example.

2   Clearly, the conditions and the date by which they are to be satisfied should be consistent with the Placing Agreement.

3   Commissions are generally paid out of (and not in addition to) commissions payable by the Company under the Placing Agreement.

4   It is common for the Placing Letter to contain wording of this nature. It is intended as a protection against breaking the securities laws of the USA and Canada. Where shares might be distributed into the USA or Canada, consideration should be given to seeking local advice on such matters.

Appendix X

Patent Assignment

THIS ASSIGNMENT is dated the [   ] day of [   ] and made

BETWEEN:

(1) [   ] LIMITED a company registered in England under number
     [   ] whose registered office is at [   ] (the 'Assignor');

(2) [   ] LIMITED a company registered in England under number
     [   ] whose registered office is at [   ] (the 'Assignee');
     and

[(3) [   ] LIMITED a company registered in England under number
     [   ] whose registered office is at [   ] (the 'Guaran-
     tor')][1]

WHEREAS:

(A) The Assignor is the owner of the various patents and patent applications particu-
     lars of which are set out in the Schedule hereto ('the Patents').
(B) The Assignor has agreed to assign the Patents to the Assignee.

NOW IT IS HEREBY AGREED as follows:

1   Assignment

1.1   In consideration of the sum of [   ] pounds (£[   ]) now paid
by the Assignee (receipt of which sum the Assignor hereby acknowledges) the Assignor
HEREBY ASSIGNS with full title guarantee to the Assignee absolutely free from all
liens, charges, security interests and/or encumbrances whatsoever:

(A) the Patents including the right to be registered as proprietor thereof, and including
     any patent application forming part of the Patents to the intent that upon the appli-
     cation proceeding to grant the resultant registration shall vest in the Assignee; and
(B) the right to take action and claim damages in respect of all past infringements
     thereof including the rights conferred by publication of any relevant patent appli-
     cation.

2   Further Assurance

2.1   The Assignor hereby covenants that at the cost and request of the Assignee at any time and from time to time it will execute such deeds or documents and do such acts or things as may be necessary or desirable to give effect to this Assignment.[2]

3   Guarantee

3.1   The Guarantor agrees that the provisions of Clause [15.2] of the Agreement shall have effect as if set out in full herein and as if references therein to the Agreement were references to this Assignment.

4   Law and Jurisdiction

4.1   This Assignment shall be governed by and construed in all respects in accordance with English law and the parties hereto submit to the [exclusive][3] jurisdiction of the English Courts.

SCHEDULE

(The Patents)

[   ]

IN WITNESS WHEREOF the Assignment has been executed the day and year first above written.

Signed by   )
duly authorised for   )
and on behalf of   )
[   ] LIMITED   )
in the presence of   )

Signed by   )
duly authorised for   )
and on behalf of   )
[   ] LIMITED   )
in the presence of   )

Signed by   )
duly authorised for   )
and on behalf of   )
[   ] LIMITED   )
in the presence of   )

Notes

1   The purchaser may feel it can dispense with a guarantee in this assignment and rely on the agreement itself.
2   Consider security power of attorney under Powers of Attorney Act 1974, s 4.
3   *See* Note 62 to the Agreement for Sale (Shares), at p 470.

Appendix XI

Trade Mark Assignment

THIS ASSIGNMENT is dated the [   ] day of [   ] and made

BETWEEN:

(1) [   ] LIMITED a company registered in England under number
     [   ] whose registered office is at [   ] (the 'Assignor');

(2) [   ] LIMITED a company registered in England under number
     [   ] whose registered office is at [   ] (the 'Assignee');
     and

[(3) [   ] LIMITED a company registered in England under number
     [   ] whose registered office is at [   ] (the 'Guaran-
     tor')]¹.

WHEREAS:

(A) The Assignor is the proprietor of the trade marks and service marks registered or
     unregistered or the subject of applications for registration in [the United Kingdom]
     listed in the Schedule hereto ('the Trade Marks').

(B) The Assignor has agreed to assign all its rights title and interest in and to the Trade
     Marks to the Assignee for the consideration hereinafter mentioned.

NOW IT IS HEREBY AGREED as follows:

1 Assignment

1.1   In consideration of the sum of [   ] pounds (£[   ]) now paid by the
Assignee to the Assignor (receipt of which sum the Assignor hereby acknowledges) the
Assignor HEREBY ASSIGNS with full title guarantee to the Assignee absolutely free
from all liens, charges, security interests and/or encumbrances whatsoever the Trade
Marks and all and any rights in and to the Trade Marks including the benefit of any applications for registration with the intention that when the applications are granted the
registrations will vest in the Assignee together with any common law rights and all the
goodwill associated with, symbolised by or attaching to the Trade Marks.

2   Right to Bring Proceedings

2.1   The Assignment hereby effected shall include the right for the Assignee to bring proceedings against any third party in respect of the Trade Marks (including proceedings against any third party for infringement of the Trade Marks or for passing-off or for otherwise infringing the rights of the Assignor in the Trade Marks). The Assignor hereby agrees and undertakes to render to the Assignee (at its request) all such assistance with any proceedings which may be brought by or against the Assignee against or by any third party in relation to the Trade Marks and the Assignee shall indemnify the Assignor in respect of all costs and expenses (including reasonable legal costs) actually incurred by it in providing the Assignee with such assistance.

3   Further Assurance

3.1   The Assignor hereby covenants that at the cost and request of the Assignee at any time and from time to time it will execute such deeds or documents and do such acts or things as may be necessary or desirable to give effect to this Assignment.[2]

4   Guarantee

4.1   The Guarantor agrees that the provisions of Clause 15.2 of the Agreement shall have effect as if set out in full herein and as if references therein to the Agreement were references to this Assignment.

5   Law and Jurisdiction

5.1   This Assignment shall be governed by and construed in accordance with the laws of England and the parties hereto submit to the [exclusive][3] jurisdiction of the English Courts.

SCHEDULE

Registrations/Applications for registration

Mark	*Class*	*No*	*Specification of goods/services*

Unregistered Marks

Mark	*Date first used*	*Goods/services in respect of which the mark has been used*

IN WITNESS WHEREOF the Assignment has been executed the day and year first above written.

Signed by   )
duly authorised for   )
and on behalf of   )
[   ] LIMITED   )
in the presence of   )

Signed by   )
duly authorised for   )
and on behalf of   )
[   ] LIMITED   )
in the presence of   )

Signed by   )
duly authorised for   )
and on behalf of   )
[   ] LIMITED   )
in the presence of   )

Notes

1   The purchaser may feel it can dispense with a guarantee in this assignment and
     rely on the agreement itself.
2   Consider a security power of attorney under Powers of Attorney Act 1974, s 4.
3   *See* Note 62 to the Agreement for Sale (Shares), at p 470.

Appendix XII

Copyright Assignment

THIS ASSIGNMENT is dated the [   ] day of [   ] and made

BETWEEN:

(1) [   ] LIMITED a company registered in England under number
     [   ] whose registered office is at [   ] (the 'Assignor');
(2) [   ] LIMITED a company registered in England under number
     [   ] whose registered office is at [   ] (the 'Assignee');
     and
[(3) [   ] LIMITED a company registered in England under number
     [   ] whose registered office is at [   ] (the 'Guaran-
     tor')]¹.

WHEREAS:

(A) The Assignor is the legal and beneficial owner of the Copyright in the Works (as
     defined herein) used in the Business (as defined herein).
(B) The Assignor has agreed to assign all Copyright in the Works and all other rights,
     title and interest in the Works to the Assignee.

NOW IT IS HEREBY AGREED as follows:

1 Interpretation

1.1 In this Assignment, where the context admits:

'The Business' means [   ];
'Copyright' means copyright, design right and all other rights in the nature of
copyright and design right in the Works and shall include the exclusive right to do
and to authorise others to do all acts restricted by the Copyright, Designs and Patents Act 1988 both in the United Kingdom and in all other countries of the world
in which Copyright may subsist in the Works; and
'The Works' means [   ] including without prejudice to the
generality of the foregoing, the works more particularly described for the purposes
of identification in the Schedule hereto.

2   Assignment

2.1   In consideration of the sum of [   ] pounds (£[   ]) now paid by the Assignee to the Assignor (receipt of which the Assignor hereby acknowledges) the Assignor hereby assigns with full title guarantee to the Assignee absolutely free from all liens, charges, security interests and/or encumbrances whatsoever all the Copyright in the Works worldwide including the right to take action and claim damages and other remedies in respect of any infringement of the Copyright in the Works or for possession of infringing copies whatsoever or wheresoever occurring.

3   Assignor's Covenants

3.1   The Assignor hereby covenants and warrants that:

(a)   the Works are original works and are not copies or substantial copies of any other work;

(b)   the Works were designed, created and produced by employees of the Assignor whose terms of employment did not excluded s 11(2) of the Copyright, Designs and Patents Act 1988 or were commissioned by the Assignor from third parties who have assigned to the Assignor all Copyright in such part of works as were designed, created or produced by them;

(c)   the Assignor has all rights in and title to the Copyright in the Works and is free to enter into an assignment of such rights to the Assignee; and

(d)   prior ro the date hereof no assignment of the Copyright in the Works or licence or any other right in respect of the Copyright in the Works has been made or granted to any third party.

4   Further Assurance

4.1   The Assignor hereby covenants that at the cost and request of the Assignee at any time and from time to time it will execute such deeds or documents and do such acts or things which may be necessary or desirable for the purposes of securing or absolutely vesting the Copyright in the Works in the Assignee or to give effect to this Assignment.[2]

5   Guarantee

5.1   The Guarantor agrees that the provisions of Clause 15.2 of the Agreement shall have effect as if set out in full herein and as if references therein to the Agreement were references to this Assignment.

6   Law and Jurisdiction

6.1   This Assignment shall be governed by and construed in accordance with the laws of England and the parties hereto submit to the [exclusive][3] jurisdiction of the English Courts.

SCHEDULE

(The Works)

IN WITNESS WHEREOF the Assignment has been executed the day and year first above written.

Signed by   )
duly authorised for   )
and on behalf of   )
[   ] LIMITED   )
in the presence of   )

Signed by   )
duly authorised for   )
and on behalf of   )
[   ] LIMITED   )
in the presence of   )

Signed by   )
duly authorised for   )
and on behalf of   )
[   ] LIMITED   )
in the presence of   )

Notes

1   The purchaser may feel it can dispense with a guarantee in this assignment and rely on the agreement itself.
2   Consider a security power of attorney under Powers of Attorney Act 1974, s 4.
3   *See* Note 62 to the Agreement for Sale (Shares), at p 470.

Appendix XIII

Offer Circular

If you are in any doubt about this offer you should consult a person authorised under the Financial Services Act 1986, who specialises in advising on the sale of shares and debentures.[1]

RECOMMENDED OFFER

by

PURCHASER PLC[2]

to acquire the whole[3] of the share capital of

TARGET LIMITED

The terms of the offer contained

in this document are recommended by all

the directors of

Target Limited[4]

Acceptances should be received by 3.00 pm on Tuesday 18 December 1996. The procedure for acceptance is set out on page [   ].

Notes

1   Schedule 4 to The Financial Services Act 1986 (Investment Advertisements) (Exemptions) (No 2) Order 1995 (SI No 1536), para 8.
2   Schedule 4, para 6. Schedule 4, para 7. Note that the offer must be recommended by all the directors.

3   The offer must be for all of the shares of the relevant class in the target, other than those held by or on behalf of the offeror. Schedule 4, para 2.

4   The offer must be recommended by all the directors other than any director who is the purchaser or a director of the Purchaser. Schedule 4, para 2(a) and para 7; there is no provision for cases in which some directors are unable to participate.

TARGET LIMITED

(Registered in England No 7654321)

Directors:	Registered Office:
A Feather	The Glade
R Bow	Oakdene
J Quiver	Nottingham NX4 8MB

27 November 1996

To the shareholders

Dear Sir or Madam

Recommended cash offer for your shares

Your board and the board of Purchaser PLC ('Purchaser') reached agreement on the terms of an offer to be made by Purchaser for the whole of the share capital of Target Limited ('Target'). Details of this offer are set out in the accompanying letter from Purchaser. As you will see, you are being offered 200p in cash for each ordinary share of £1 of Target. Your directors and their financial advisers, Merchant Bank Limited, consider that the offer is fair and reasonable, having regard to the net asset value of Target and its profit record.

The financial effects of accepting the offer are set out in paragraph 5 of the letter from Purchaser and your attention is also drawn to paragraph 6 headed 'Taxation on Capital Gains'.

Your directors have received assurances from Purchaser that the rights of all employees of Target will be fully safeguarded.

Your directors unanimously recommend shareholders to accept the offer. Your directors, and certain other shareholders, who together hold 2,629,800 shares (representing 43.83 per cent of the issued share capital of Target) have irrevocably undertaken to accept the offer in respect of their entire holdings.

Copies of the accounts of Target for the year ended 30 September 1996[1] and of Purchaser for the year ended 31 December 1995 and the letter from Merchant Bank Limited dated 27 November 1996 addressed to the board of Target containing their advice on the financial implications of the offer are enclosed with this letter.[2] A statement by your board is set out in paragraph 2 of Appendix IV of the accompanying letter from Purchaser.[3]

Yours faithfully

A Feather
Chairman

Notes

1   Schedule 4, para 12(a).
2   Schedule 4, para 12(b).
3   Schedule 4, para 12(c).

PURCHASER PLC

(Registered in England No 123456789)

Directors:	Registered office:
R Hood (Chairman)	Grove House
L John	Sherwood Gardens
A A Dale	Nottingham NX2 3LZ
M Marion	
F Tuck MA	
W Scarlett	

27 November 1996

To the shareholders of Target Limited

Dear Sir or Madam

Recommended Offer by Purchaser Plc

1   Introduction

As stated in the accompanying letter from your chairman, agreement has been reached between your directors and Purchaser Plc ('Purchaser') for Purchaser to make an offer ('the offer') to acquire, at a price of 200p in cash per share,[1] all the issued ordinary shares of Target Limited ('Target').

This document sets out the terms of the offer.

Notes

1   The consideration must be cash, shares or debentures—Schedule 4, para 2(f).

2   The Offer

Purchaser, as principal, hereby offers to acquire, on and subject to the terms and conditions set out herein, all the 6,000,000 ordinary shares of £1 each of Target ('Target shares') now in issue on the basis of 200p in cash for each Target share.

The Target shares will be acquired free from all liens, charges, equities and encumbrances and together with all rights and advantages now or hereafter attaching thereto, including rights to all dividends and other distributions declared, made or paid hereafter. Signature of the enclosed form of acceptance will constitute a warranty by the accepting shareholder to that effect in respect of the Target shares for which the offer is accepted.

Your directors have agreed to accept the offer in respect of their shareholdings[1] and, as stated in your chairman's letter, unanimously recommend all shareholders to accept the offer. Save pursuant to its agreement with Target directors and certain other shareholders who have together irrevocably undertaken to accept the offer in respect of 2,629,800 Target shares, Purchaser does not own or have any interest in, any Target shares.[2]

Notes

1   Schedule 4, para 12(d).
2   Schedule 4, para 11(a). See further note 1 to para 3 below.

3   Conditions of the Offer[1]

The offer is subject to the following conditions and the further conditions and terms set out in Appendix I:

(a)   valid acceptances being received by 3.00 pm on 18 December 1996 (or such later date(s) as Purchaser may from time to time decide and notify shareholders, subject to paragraph 2(c) of Appendix I) in respect of 90 per cent of the shares comprised in the offer or such lesser percentage as Purchaser may decide, provided that the offer will not become unconditional unless Purchaser shall have acquired or agreed to acquire pursuant to or during the offer:
  (i)   shares carrying more than 50 per cent of the voting rights then exercisable in general meetings of Target; and
  (ii)   shares carrying more than 50 per cent of the voting rights attributable to the equity share capital of Target;[2]
(b)   approval by the shareholders of Purchaser (for which purpose an extraordinary general meeting has been convened for 13 December 1996); and
(c)   notification being received that the Board of Inland Revenue are satisfied that the exchange to be effected under the share election referred to in paragraph 4 will be effected for *bona fide* commercial reasons and will not form part of any such scheme or arrangements as are mentioned in the Taxation of Chargeable Gains Act 1992, s 137(1).[3]

The offer will be open for acceptance by every shareholder for at least 21 days from the date of this document.[4] In the event that the conditions set out above have not been fulfilled by the later of the dates referred to in paragraph 1 of Appendix I, the offer will lapse.

The offer is not conditional upon shareholders of Target approving or consenting to any payment or other benefit being made or given to any director or former director of Target in connection with, or as compensation or consideration for, his ceasing to be a director, or loss of any office held in conjunction with any directorship or, in the case of a former director, loss of any office which he held in conjunction with his former directorship and which he continued to hold after ceasing to be a director.[5]

The directors of Target have the right to decline to register any transfer of Target shares but have resolved to sanction any transfer of Target shares to Purchaser made pursuant to the offer. Save as aforesaid there are no restrictions on the transfer of Target shares other than those imposed by law.[6]

Notes

1   It will be for consideration in any particular case whether it is appropriate for conditions concerning changes in the target's business since its last published accounts or the purchaser not becoming aware that information supplied to it is incorrect or misleading or that regulatory authorities (eg regarding competition issues (*see* p 31)) do not take action which prevents or affects such offers. Most takeovers of public companies conducted under the terms of the City Code on Takeovers and Mergers contain such terms. Copies of public takeover documents, by way of example, are available from [   ]. Such conditions are typically expressed in terms that they can be waived by the purchaser since it will not always be clear whether they are satisfied the conditions are no substitute for warranties and will not give the purchaser a remedy if broken but will enable the purchaser to withdraw in the event

of material adverse change. There is no reason why a separate warranty agreement should not be sought from principal shareholders in the target, together with irrevocable undertakings on their part to accept the offer. The Agreement for Sale (Shares) can be adapted for such purpose. If an irrevocable undertaking to accept is taken, careful consideration should be given to the provisions of the Companies Act 1985, ss 428–430F. A particular point to note is subs 428(5); unless the undertaking to accept the offer complies with that section shares accepted pursuant to it will not count towards the nine-tenths threshold for acceptances in order to operate the compulsory acquisition provisions.

2　　This follows the wording of para 2(c) of Schedule 4. The Purchaser will usually include a 90 per cent acceptance condition in similar form so as to enable operation of the Companies Act 1985, s 428 *et seq*.

3　　*See* p 264.

4　　The period of 21 days begins on the day after the day on which the document is issued. Schedule 4, para 2(d).

5　　Schedule 4, para 2(e). This is required by para 9 of Schedule 4 to be stated 'clearly' and is accordingly contained in the letter itself rather than relegated to an appendix.

6　　Schedule 4, para 11(h).

4　Share Election

Holders of Target shares who validly accept the offer by 3pm on 18 December 1996 may irrevocably elect ('the share election') to receive, subject to the limitation set out below, ordinary shares of £1 each in Purchaser ('Purchaser shares') instead of all or part of the cash consideration which they would otherwise receive under the offer. For the purpose of the share election, the value of each Purchaser share will be taken to be 130p, which is based on the middle market quotation of 130p at the close of business on 26 November 1996 (the latest practicable date for the purposes of finalising the terms of the offer).

The maximum number of Purchaser shares which may be issued under the share election will be limited to a total of 900,000 Purchaser shares, representing in value approximately 10.2 per cent of the total consideration. If share elections cannot be satisfied in full, such elections will be scaled down *pro rata* and the unsatisfied balance of the consideration will be paid in cash.

No fractions of a Purchaser share will be issued to Target shareholders accepting the offer. Such fractions will be aggregated and sold and the net proceeds will be distributed to the Target shareholders entitled thereto, but so that no individual amount of less than £2.50 will be distributed.

The Purchaser shares to be issued pursuant to the share election will rank *pari passu* in all respects with the existing Purchaser shares and will rank in full for all dividends declared, made or paid after the date of their allotment. The first dividend to which Target shareholders accepting the offer and making the share election will be entitled will be the final dividend in respect of Purchaser's financial year ending 31 December 1996 which would normally be paid in May 1997. There are no restrictions on the transfer of fully paid Purchaser shares save those imposed by law.[1]

Notes

1　　Schedule 4, para 11(g)(iii).

5　Financial Effects of Acceptance[1]

The effects of acceptance as shown below do not take account of the incidence of taxation. Your attention is drawn to paragraph 6.

(a) Capital Value

Target shares have not been quoted on any stock exchange and no meaningful comparison of capital values may therefore be made. On the basis of the statement of the net tangible assets of Target set out in Appendix II, derived from the most recent audited accounts, the net assets attributable to each Target share at 30 September 1996 were 34.2p.

(b) Income

The income available to shareholders of Target who accept the offer is dependent on individual circumstances and the manner in which the cash proceeds are reinvested.

A holder of 100 existing Target shares who accepts the offer and makes the share election would, if the election were satisfied in full, receive 153 Purchaser shares. On the assumptions:

(i)   that the cash consideration is reinvested to yield 10 per cent gross (which could be achieved by reinvesting the cash consideration in government securities); and

(ii)   of gross annual dividends for Purchaser at the rate announced in respect of its latest financial year ended 31 December 1995;

an accepting shareholder who received consideration (a) wholly in cash and (b) wholly in Purchaser shares, will benefit from an increase in income as follows:

	All cash consideration	*All share consideration*
	£	£
Income from 100 Target shares	2.00	2.00
Income from £200 cash reinvested	20.00	—
Income from 153 Purchaser shares	–	9.95
Increase in income	£18.00	£7.95

Notes

1   Schedule 4, para 11(g)(iv).

6   Taxation on Capital Gains

To the extent that they receive and retain their consideration in Purchaser shares, Target shareholders will not, under present legislation, be deemed to have made a disposal for the purposes of United Kingdom capital gains tax. To the extent that shareholders receive their consideration in cash, they will be treated for capital gains tax purposes as making a disposal, or part disposal, as the case may be and may, therefore, depending on their circumstances, incur a liability to tax.

If you are in any doubt as to your tax position, you should consult your professional adviser.

7 Business of Target

Target was incorporated in 1894 to acquire a business which had been manufacturing archery targets since shortly before the battle of Agincourt in 1415. It now carries on business from a freehold factory, having a floor area of approximately 12,000 square feet, at Nuthall near Nottingham and its European operations are conducted from Poitiers, France. Target is also engaged in fast food retailing through its 'Bullseye' franchise. 'Bullseye' has outlets throughout the United Kingdom and United States of America.

Purchaser expects, following acquisition, to realise certain of Target's non-core operations, notably 'Bullseye'.

Further information relating to Target is set out in Appendix II.

8 Management and Employees

Purchaser has given assurances that it will have regard to the interests of employees of Target and that the rights of such employees, including existing pension entitlements, will be fully safeguarded.

9 Business of Purchaser

The Purchaser group is an international group with widespread interests in leisure industries. Companies in the Purchaser group are engaged in toxophily, windsurfing and other trivial pursuits. The turnover of the Purchaser group in the year ended 31 December 1995 amounted to some £32.5 million and profits before tax amounted to some £2.6 million. The Purchaser group has approximately 2,000 employees worldwide. Further information on Purchaser is set out in Appendix III.

During the current economic climate conditions in the leisure industry continue to be difficult. Despite this, the Purchaser group has experienced a significant increase in sales in 1996 and the directors of Purchaser believe that prospects are excellent. They intend to continue their policy of expansion of the group's core business.[1]

Notes

1   Schedule 4, para 11(g)(i).

10 Procedure for Acceptance

To accept the offer you should complete and sign part A of the enclosed form of acceptance and transfer in accordance with the instructions thereon.

To exercise the share election you should complete and sign part A and part B of the enclosed form of acceptance and transfer in accordance with the instructions thereon.

You should return the completed form together with your share certificates and any other documents of title for the number of shares for which you wish to accept the offer in the enclosed pre-paid, pre-addressed envelope to Purchaser Plc, Grove House, Sherwood Gardens, Nottingham NX2 3LZ (ref Target Offer) so as to arrive as soon as possible and in any event not later than 3.00 pm on 18 December 1996. The share election ceases to be available thereafter.

Even if any document of title is not readily available, the form should nevertheless be completed and returned so as to arrive by the time and date stated and the document of title forwarded to Purchaser as soon as possible thereafter. Purchaser reserves the right to treat as valid any acceptance which is not entirely in order or not accompanied by the relevant documents of title, but in any case the consideration due will not be despatched until the acceptance is completely in order and the remaining documents or satisfactory indemnities have been received.

11 Settlement

No acknowledgement of receipt of documents will be issued but in the event of the offer becoming unconditional in all respects and provided the form of acceptance and transfer and your share certificates and other documents of title (if any) are in order, a cheque and, where applicable, definitive share certificates in respect of Purchaser shares will be posted in accordance with the authority contained in the form within seven days of the offer becoming unconditional in all respects or of the receipt of a valid acceptance (including all necessary documents of title or satisfactory indemnities therefor) whichever is the later.[1]

Application will be made to the London Stock Exchange for the Purchaser shares to be issued pursuant to the offer to be admitted to the Official List. It is expected that dealings in such shares will commence on the first dealing day following that on which the offer becomes or is declared unconditional in all respects. Pending despatch of definitive certificates, transfers will be certified against the register.

If the offer lapses the completed form and share certificates and other documents of title (if any) will be returned to accepting shareholders by first class post not later than seven days thereafter.

All documents and payments sent by or to shareholders or their agents are sent at shareholders' risk.

Settlement of the consideration to which any shareholder is entitled under the terms of the offer will be implemented in full in accordance with the terms of the offer without regard to any lien, right of set-off, counter-claim or other analogous right to which Purchaser may otherwise be or claim to be entitled as against such shareholder.

Notes

1   Schedule 4, para 11(f).

12 Additional Information

The Appendices to this letter contain:

I   Further conditions and terms of the offer.
II   Further information relating to Target.
III   Further information relating to Purchaser.
IV   General information.

13 Documents Available for Inspection

Paragraph 7 of Appendix IV lists certain documents relating to Target and Purchaser which will be available for inspection free of charge at the place and at the time specified therein.[1]

Notes

1   Schedule 4, para 10.

Yours faithfully

R Hood, *Chairman*

APPENDIX I

FURTHER CONDITIONS AND TERMS OF THE OFFER

1 Lapse[1]

If conditions (b) and (c) set out in paragraph 3 on page [684] of this document are not fulfilled prior to whichever is the later of 26 January 1997 and the expiration of 21 days after the offer becomes unconditional as to acceptances by fulfilment of condition (a)[2], then the offer will lapse.

Notes

1   There is no requirement to specify that the offer will, lapse after a certain period, but it will normally be desirable. For compulsory acquisition under the Companies Ac 1985, ss 428–430F, the purchaser must have satisfied the requirement that it has by virtue of acceptance of the offer acquired or contracted to acquire nine-tenths of the shares to which the offer relates before the end of the period of four months beginning with the date of the offer (s 429(3)).

2   Where regulatory conditions are included (see Note 1 to para 3 of the offer letter, p 672) thought should be given to whether such a provision is appropriate, if there is a risk of some conditions remaining outstanding for a considerable period.

2 Acceptance Period

(a)   If the offer becomes unconditional as to acceptances, it will remain open until further notice and Purchaser will give not less than fourteen days' notice in writing to shareholders before it is closed.[1]

(b)   The offer will not be revised or increased.

(c)   The offer will not be capable of becoming unconditional as to acceptances after 3.00 pm on 26 January 1997 nor will it be kept open after that time unless it has previously become unconditional as to acceptances.[2]

Notes

1   Schedule 4, para 11(d).

2   Schedule 4, para 11(c).

3 Announcements

On the business day next following the day on which the offer is due to expire, or the day on which the offer becomes unconditional as to acceptances, Purchaser will notify shareholders by letter of the total number of shares (as nearly as practicable) for which acceptances of the offer have been received.

In any announcement of an extension of the offer the next expiry date will be stated. In computing the number of shares represented by acceptances, there may be included for the above purposes acceptances not in all respects in order or subject to verification.

4 Rights of Withdrawal

An acceptance shall be irrevocable.

5   General

(a)   If circumstances arise in which an offeror is able compulsorily to acquire shares of any dissenting minority under Part XIIIA of the Companies Act 1985, Purchaser intends so to acquire those shares.[1]

(b)   The form of acceptance and transfer (including the instructions and notes thereon) shall be deemed to be an integral part of this document.

Notes

1   Schedule 4, para 11(e).

APPENDIX II

FURTHER INFORMATION RELATING TO TARGET[1]

1   Secretary and Registered Office

A Quiver
The Glade, Oakdene, Nottingham NX4 8MB

2   Share Capital

The present called up share capital of Target is as follows:

	Authorised	Allotted and fully paid
Ordinary shares of 10p each	6,000,000	6,000,000

3   Results Summary[1]

The following is a summary of certain results of Target based on the published audited accounts for the five years ended 30 September 1996:

	Year ended 30 September				
	1992 *£000s*	*1993* *£000s*	*1994* *£000s*	*1995* *£000s*	*1996* *£000s*
Turnover	2,370	2,710	3,051	3,751	4,310
Profit before taxation	555	605	772	938	990
Profit after taxation	333	363	421	450	462

Total amount of dividends paid	90	100	110	120	120
	===	===	===	===	===
Earnings per share	5.6p	6.1p	7.0p	7.5p	7.7p
Rate per cent of dividends paid	1.5%	1.7%	1.8%	2.0%	2.0%

4 Net Assets

The following is a summary of the net assets of Target at 30 September 1996 based on the published audited balance sheet at that date:

	£000s	£000s
Fixed assets		
Tangible assets		1,705
Current assets		
Stocks	475	
Debtors	845	
Cash at bank and in hand	342	
	1,662	
Current liabilities—Amounts falling due within one year	(815)	
Net current assets		847
Total assets less current liabilities		2,552
Creditors—amounts falling due after more than one year	150	
Provisions for liabilities and charges	352	
		502
Net assets attributable to shareholders		2,050

5   Abridged Accounts

The financial information set out above does not constitute statutory accounts of Target within the meaning of the Companies Act 1985. Statutory accounts of Target for the five years ended 30 September 1992 have been delivered to the Registrar of Companies. The auditors of Target have made unqualified reports under the Companies Act 1985, s 235 in respect of all such accounts.[2]

Notes

1   Schedule 4, para 11(g)(ii).
2   Companies Act 1985, s 240(3).

APPENDIX III

FURTHER INFORMATION RELATING TO PURCHASER[1]

1   Secretary and Registered Office

M Marion
Grove House, Sherwood Gardens, Nottingham NX2 3LZ

2   Share Capital

The present called up share capital of Purchaser is as follows:

	Authorised	Allotted and fully paid
Ordinary shares of £1 each	12,500,000	10,000,000

Purchaser has not issued any share capital since 31 December 1995, the date of the latest audited accounts of Purchaser and Purchaser has no securities in the nature of loan notes or debenture stock in issue at the date of the offer.

3   Results Summary[1]

The following is a summary of certain results of Purchaser based on its published audited consolidated accounts for the five years ended on 31 December 1995.

	Year ended on 31 December				
	1991 *£000s*	*1992* *£000s*	*1993* *£000s*	*1994* *£000s*	*1995* *£000s*
Turnover	18,243	20,656	25,755	29,336	32,453
Profit before taxation	2,857	2,861	2,432	2,305	2,593

Profit after taxation	2,097	1,902	1,621	1,202	1,379
Total amount of dividends paid	300	300	337	450	650
	===	===	===	===	===
Earnings per share	28.0p	25.4p	21.6p	12.0p	13.8p
Rate per cent of dividends paid (net)	4.0%	4.0%	4.5%	4.5%	6.5%

4 Summary of Consolidated Audited Balance Sheet of Purchaser as at 31 December 1995[2]

	£000s	£000s
Fixed assets[3]		
Tangible assets	18,309	
Investments	1,441	
		19,750
Current assets[3]		
Stocks	2,290	
Debtors	4,826	
Investments	613	
Cash at bank and in hand	302	
	8,031	
Creditors—amounts falling due within one year		
Finance debt	1,185	
Other creditors	4,113	
	5,298	
Net current assets		2,733
Total assets less current liabilties		22,483
Creditors—amounts falling due after more than one year		

Finance debt	4,283
Other creditors	<u>1,777</u>
	6,060
Provisions for liabilties and charges	<u>657</u>
	<u>15,766</u>

Represented by:

Capital and reserves

Called-up share capital	10,000
Share premium account	906
Reserves	<u>4,860</u>
	<u>15,766</u>

5 Half-year results to 30 June 1996

The following information has been extracted from the announcement on 16 September 1996 regarding the unaudited consolidated results of the Purchaser group for the six months ended 30 June 1996:

	Six months ended 30 June		Year ended 31 December
	1996 £000s	1995 £000s	1995 £000s
Turnover	22,175	15,260	32,453
Profit before taxation	1,967	1,240	2,593
Profit after taxation	1,102	678	1,379
	===	===	===
Earnings per share	11.0p	6.8p	13.8p
Dividends per share			
Interim	2.5p	2.0p	2.0p
Final			4.5p

In his accompanying remarks the chairman of Purchaser, Mr R Hood, commented on the improved profitability following the acquisition in 1995 of F Tuck & Sons Limited and M Marion & Sons Limited, both of which were now starting to make useful contributions to the group's results. As a consequence of these better prospects for the group, a higher interim dividend had been paid and it is hoped to match this increase again when the final dividend is declared.

6 Abridged Accounts

The financial information set out above does not constitute statutory accounts of Purchaser within the meaning of the Companies Act 1985. Statutory accounts of Purchaser for the five years ended 31 December 1995 have been delivered to the Registrar of Companies. The auditors of Purchaser have made unqualified reports under the Companies Act 1985, s 235 in respect of all such accounts.[4]

Notes

1   Schedule 4, para 11(g)(ii).
2   Schedule 4, para 11(n).
3   Inclusion of asset values in the accounts are not regarded as within the scope of para 11(o) of Schedule 4, which requires inclusion of asset valuations in certain circumstances.
4   Companies Act 1985, s 240(3).

APPENDIX IV

GENERAL INFORMATION

1 Responsibility

(a)   The directors of Purchaser and Target are responsible for the information contained in this document and those accompanying it insofar as it relates to their respective companies and to themselves and to the best of their respective knowledge and belief (having taken all reasonable care to ensure that such is the case) the information is in accordance with the facts and does not omit any material fact, and each of them accepts responsibility accordingly.[1]

(b)   The directors of Purchaser hereby state that the information in relation to Purchaser and to Purchaser shares contained in this document by virtue of sub-paragraph 12(e) of Schedule 4 to The Financial Services Act 1986 (Investment Advertisements) (Exemptions) (No 2) Order 1995, is correct.[2]

Notes

1   Schedule 4, para 12(g).
2   Schedule 4, para 12(e).

2 Statement of Directors of Target[1]

The directors of Target, acting as a board, hereby state that:

(a)   There has not been any material change in the financial position or prospects of Target since 30 September 1996, the date to which the latest available accounts of Target are made up.

(b)   The interests which the directors of Target have in the securities of Target which are required to be entered in the register kept by Target under the Companies Act 1985, s 325 are as follows:

Director	*Ordinary shares held beneficially*		
	Held personally	*Family interests*	*Percentage*
A Feather	1,080,000	195,000	21.25
R Bow	588,000	76,500	11.07
J Quiver	24,000	–	0.4

(c)   None of the directors of Target has any interests in the securities of Purchaser which would be required to be entered in the register kept by Purchaser under the Companies Act 1985, s 325, if any such director were a director of Purchaser.

(d)   Save for the undertaking referred to in paragraph 3 below none of the directors of Target has any material interest in any contract entered into by Purchaser or in any contract entered into by any member of the group of which Purchaser is a member.

Notes

1   Schedule, para 12(c). It is convenient, although slightly odd, to include this in the offer circular. The Schedule only requires the circular to be 'accompanied' by such a statement. It could be included in the letter from the chairman of the target set out at the front of the circular but would look even odder there.

3   Acceptance by Directors of Target[1]

The directors of Target have undertaken to accept the offer in respect of their beneficial shareholders and to procure acceptance in respect of their family shareholdings as set out in paragraph 2(b) above. These shareholdings represent in total 32.72 per cent of the Target shares.

Notes

1   Schedule, para 12(d).

4   Disclosure of Interests[1]

(a)   The following dealings in Target shares by the directors of Target and their families have taken place since 28 November 1995:

Director	*Date of Transaction*	*Nature of Transaction*	*Number of Shares*	*Price per Share*
A Feather	20 Dec 1995	Sale	3,000	£1.50
	14 Feb 1996	Purchase	1,200	£1.60
R Bow	3 March 1996	Purchase	3,000	£1.50

Save as aforesaid, none of the directors of Target nor any person who has been a director of Target since 28 November 1995 has dealt in the share capitals of Target or Purchaser since 28 November 1995.

(b) Neither Purchaser nor any person acting on behalf of Purchaser holds any securities of Target.

(c) None of the directors of Purchaser has dealt in the share capital of Purchaser or Target since 28 November 1995.

Notes

1   Schedule, para 11(m).

5   General

(a) It is not proposed in connection with the offer that any payment or other benefit shall be made or given to any director or former director of Target in connection with or as compensation or consideration for his ceasing to be a director or loss of any office held in conjunction with a directorship or, in the case of a former director, loss of any office which he held in conjunction with his former directorship and which he continued to hold after ceasing to be director.[1]

(b) Following the acquisition of Target, Mr A Feather is to be appointed a director of Purchaser. Save as aforesaid there is no arrangement made between Purchaser or any person with whom Purchaser has an agreement of the type described in the Companies Act 1985, s 204 and any of the directors or shareholders of Target or any persons who have been such directors or shareholders in the period since 28 November 1995 having any connection with or dependence on the offer.[2]

(c) There is no agreement or arrangement whereby any of the shares in Target acquired by Purchaser pursuant to the offer will or may be transferred to any other person. However, Purchaser reserves the right to transfer any of such shares to a nominee on its behalf or any company from time to time being a member of the Purchaser group of companies.[3]

(d) All expenses of and incidental to the preparation and circulation of this document and any stamp duty payable on transfers of Target shares pursuant to the offer will be paid by Purchaser.

(e) There has not been, within the knowledge of Purchaser, any material change in the financial position or prospects of Target since 30 September 1996, the date of the latest available accounts of Target.[4]

(f) Merchant Bank Limited has given (and has not withdrawn) its consent to the issue of this document with the reference to its name in the form and context in which it appears.

Notes

1   Schedule 4, para 11(i).
2   Schedule 4, para 11(j).
3   Schedule 4, para 11(l).
4   Schedule 4, para 11(k).

6   Material Contracts[1]

The following contracts entered into by the Purchaser in the period of two years immediately preceding the date of the offer (not being contracts entered into in the ordinary course of business) are, or may be, material:

(i)   agreement dated 1 April 1995 for the acquisition by Purchaser of F Tuck & Sons Limited from Mr F Tuck and members of his family for £1,185,000; and

(ii)   agreement dated 17 July 1995 for the acquisition by Purchaser of M Marion & Sons Limited from Miss M Marion for £3,200,000.

There are no such agreements by Target which are considered to be material.

Notes

1   Schedule 4, para 11(g)(v).

7   Documents Available for Inspection[1]

Copies of the following documents will be available for inspection free of charge at the offices of Coke & Littleton, 1 Moor Alley, London EC3Z 2FL between 10.00 am and 4.00 pm on weekdays (Saturdays and public holidays excepted) so long as the offer remains open for acceptance:

(i)   the memorandum and articles of association of each of Target and Purchaser;

(ii)   the audited accounts of Target for the two years ended 30 September 1995 and 1996;

(iii)   the audited consolidated accounts of Purchaser for the two years ended 31 December 1994 and 1995 and Purchaser's announcement dated 15 September 1996 in respect of its half-year results to 30 June 1996;

(iv)   the letter dated 27 November 1996 from Merchant Bank Limited to the Board of Target;

(v)   the written consent of Merchant Bank Limited referred to in paragraph 5 (f) above;

(vi)   the contracts referred to in paragraph 6 above; and

(vii)   the existing contracts of service between Target and its directors and between Purchaser and its directors, each of which has been entered into for a period of more than a year.

Notes

1   Schedule 4, paras 2(g) and 10.

Appendix XIV

Outline Checklist

1 Consents and Approvals

1.1 Does the acquisition require any consent from creditors or vendors of target (p 21)?

1.2 (*Shares*) Is the target party to any contracts which may terminate or accelerate rights on change of control (eg joint venture, banking) which require consent from the other party?

1.3 (*Assets*) Do any material contracts of the target business require consent of another party in order to be assigned to the purchaser, including intellectual property and computer licences?

1.4 If consideration is shares, is it necessary to increase purchaser's capital and is any consent needed to issue shares (eg under purchaser's articles, loan stock trust deeds, etc) (p 25)?

1.5 Is consent of purchaser's, or vendor's shareholders required (p 25)?

1.6 If vendor or purchaser (or the holding company of either) is listed, what are the London Stock Exchange requirements (p 219)? Does the transaction involve a sale to or by a director or former director such that there may be a requirement for shareholder approval as a transaction with a related party or Companies Act 1985, s 320?

1.7 (*Shares*) Does the target have any special qualification requiring third party consent to a change in control (p 23)?

1.8 (*Assets*) Does the target business require any licence (public or private)? Can the vendor's licences be transferred to the purchaser? Will the purchaser require new licences? What are the timeframe and criteria to obtain such licence (p 30)?

1.9 (*Assets*) Do the property interests to be transferred include leases and will landlord's consent be required to assignment? Can the acquisition proceed with consent to be obtained subsequently (p 199)?

1.10 If target is technically public (or has had its shares listed or issued on prospectus within the last ten years), can dispensation from the City Code on Takeovers and Mergers be obtained (p 2)?

1.11 Is clearance required under the Taxation of Chargeable Gains Act 1992, s 138 (p 264), or under the Income and Corporation Taxes Act 1988, ss 707 (p 277) s 765 (p 278) or 776 (p 277)?

1.12 Are there any agreements or contract terms which are restrictive of competition which may have European competition or UK restrictive trade practices implications (p 31)?

687

1.13 Does the acquisition fall within the criteria of the Fair Trading Act 1973, s 64 (p 37) or for EC Merger Control (p 39)?

1.14 Are there any overseas subsidiaries where local consents may be required? Is advice on overseas laws required?

1.15 Is any shareholders' meeting of the target necessary, to approve any matter or to modify any pre-emption provision in its articles?

2   Information concerning target and any subsidiaries

2.1 Full company search against vendor, target and target's subsidiaries (p 135). Winding up search against target and corporate vendors; bankruptcy only search of Land Charges Register against individual vendors (p 136).

2.2 If relevant, searches at the Patent Office or the Trade Mark Registry (p 136)?

2.3 Particulars of share capital, names of registered holders and beneficial owners and details of any option scheme or arrangement relating to shares.

2.4 Memorandum and Articles.

2.5 List of directors.

2.6 Report and accounts for three previous years and latest management accounts.

2.7 Accountants' Report.

2.8 Details or matters outside the ordinary course of business since the balance sheet date (eg dividends, customer losses, etc).

2.9 Details of target's tax affairs.

2.10 Details of government and other grants: are they repayable eg on change of control; are there conditions attached?

2.11 Details of all borrowing and charges.

2.12 Details of properties.

2.13 Environmental review eg of the target's activities, its disposal of waste and of its environmental licences. Where desired, a Phase I or Phase II investigation (p 151).

2.14 Property and other asset valuations, where relevant.

2.15 Details of insurances and claims record.

2.16 Details of guarantees given by or on behalf of the target.

2.17 Details of any intellectual property owned by the target which it uses under licence, or which it itself licences. Obtain copy licences. Check whether any rights are shared with members of the vendor's group.

2.18 Details of litigation and potential litigation and of any investigations into the target's business. Has it given any undertakings or is it subject to any injunctions or restriction?

2.19 Details of licences and approvals which affect the target business (whether from companies or individuals or public or quasi-public authorities (p 23).

2.20 Details of non-arm's length contracts and of contracts or arrangements with, and liabilities owing to or from, the vendors.

2.21 Copies of material contracts. Do they contain onerous provisions? Are they terminable on change of control (*shares*) or do they require consent to assignment (*assets*)? Will the sale mean that any rights under them will be triggered or accelerate? Should include joint venture, distributorship, franchise, computer, intellectual property contracts etc as well as major trading agreements.

2.22 Details of material customer and supply arrangements.

2.23 Details of employees, including employment terms, copy service agreements and union agreements. Check employee restrictive covenants. Are there important employees who will not transfer/be employed by the target for whom special arrangements need to be made?

2.24 Details of share or other incentive arrangements; particularly those which will not continue following completion, eg cannot be transferred.

2.25 Pensions questionnaire (p 118).

2.26 Details of ownership and use of computer systems—hardware, software and peripherals—and of licensing of software; access to source codes; security of systems (eg offsite storage) and disaster recovery arrangements; maintenance arrangements.

2.27 Other information regarded as important by purchaser.

3 Taxation

3.1 Are there any special reliefs available to the vendors (eg roll-over relief, retirement relief, etc) or are they liable to be subject to any special charge (p 255)?

3.2 (*Shares*) Is the target a close company (p 231)?

3.3 (*Shares*) Is the target a member of a group (p 299)?

3.4 (*Shares*) Does the target have allowable losses (p 313)?

3.5 Are there any inheritance tax implications (p 324)?

3.6 How much stamp duty/stamp duty reserve tax will be payable; (*Assets*) Can stamp duty be saved, eg by offshore execution (p 290)?

3.7 What are the arrangements for the VAT Registration (p 325)?

3.8 (*Assets*) What will be the VAT treatment of the transaction? Is the consideration inclusive or exclusive of VAT (p 293)?

3.9 (*Assets*) How is the consideration to be apportioned between the assets to be acquired?

3.10 (*Shares*) Particulars of all corporation tax computations (whether agreed or not) for the last six accounting periods together with all correspondence and details of all accounting periods which remain open and amounts due.

3.11 (*Shares*) Particulars of any matter in dispute with a tax authority including amounts due.

3.12 (*Shares*) Particulars of any amount deductible in computing the gain on the disposal of a capital asset of the target where the book cost of the asset in the latest accounts is less, including the extent of the deficit and specific details of all roll-over claims whether made or anticipated and for which no provision for tax has been made.

3.13 (*Shares*) Particulars of tax written down values of capital assets on which capital allowances have been claimed for the most recent completed accounting period and details of all capital expenditure subsequently incurred on which the vendor intends to claim capital allowances.

3.14 Details of last PAYE and customs visit.

4 Preparation of the Agreement

4.1 Will any pre-sale structuring be required? Will it involve a transaction at an undervalue or financial assistance (p 11)? What are the tax implications? What consents will be required?

4.2 If the target's shares are widely held, should the acquisition be by way of offer under the Financial Services Act 1986 (Investment Advertisements) (Exemptions) (No 2) Order 1995 (SI No 1536) (p 28)?

4.3 What is the consideration and how is it calculated? How will it be paid and funded?

4.4 If the consideration for the acquisition is shares in the purchaser, what are the rights attached to the consideration shares in particular with regard to entitlement to dividend? What are the provisions in the purchaser's articles with regard eg to apportionment of dividends?

4.5   If the purchaser's shares are listed, will listing particulars need to be prepared (p 220)? Will ABI guidelines require clawback to be available to existing shareholders (p 9)? If the purchaser's shares will not be listed, is any prospectus required (p 250)?

4.6   Should there be an 'earn out' or other deferred payment arrangement? What are the performance criteria and how will they be measured? How will earn out consideration be funded?

4.7   Should there be a deposit or retention, or other arrangement to be used as security for warranty and other claims? (*Assets*) Should there be a retention pending consent to assignment or certain contracts, eg computer licences (p 209)?

4.8   Will all the target's directors retire? Are there to be any new service agreements for directors? Are existing agreements adequate?

4.9   Will the target's auditors change at completion?

4.10 Is the target's title to its property to be investigated or is a certificate to be obtained (p 154)?

4.11 (*Assets*) Are there any leasehold premises? Is landlord's consent to assignment required and when will such consent be obtained? What arrangements for obtaining consent and for occupation in the meantime will be proposed?

4.12 Should completion be conditional upon the obtaining of any necessary consent or approval? What undertakings should be taken to ensure the conditions are satisfied? Should either party be able to waive any condition?

4.13 What special warranties are required?

4.14 What documents and/or statements or assurances has the purchaser relied upon in its evaluation of the target? Have they been discussed with the purchaser and are they clearly covered by the warranties? Has the scope and effect of the warranties been discussed with the purchaser?

4.15 If acting for the vendor, have the warranties been discussed with the vendor, and has proper care been taken in preparing the disclosure letter?

4.16 (*Assets*) Will the sale be a transfer of the business as a going concern and will all employee contracts automatically transfer to the purchaser (p 73)? Are there any employees for whom special arrangements for transfer will be required or (*Shares or assets*) are new service agreements to be entered into? (*Shares or assets*) Will there be redundancies? Who will bear the cost? (*Assets*) What consultation to the transfer is required?

4.17 Is the vendor or any member of its group involved in any competing business or likely to become so? Should the purchaser require the vendor to accept restrictive covenants? For what activities and for how long (p 31)?

4.18 Are there any specific matters with regard to taxation (eg continuation of group relief arrangements) which ought to be incorporated in the sale agreement?

4.19 Are there loans by the vendors to the target to be repaid on completion? Are any guarantees given by the vendors on behalf of the target to be released?

4.20 Is the target entering into any transaction as part of the sale arrangements? Is the target to repay any indebtedness at completion? Are there financial assistance implications under the Companies Act 1985, s 151 (p 43)?

4.21 If the purchaser's shares form part of the consideration, should there be restrictions on their disposal?

4.22 (*Shares*) Are all the target's shares being acquired?

4.23 Are completion accounts required? Have the purchaser's accountants been involved in settling the criteria for preparation of those accounts? How will completion accounts interact with other provisions of the agreement, eg treatment of debtors/creditors (*assets*)?

4.24 Are any limitations on the vendor's liability under warranties appropriate?

4.25 Do the vendors have any special characteristics which require consideration? Minors will not have the capacity to enter into a binding agreement; a bankrupt will become bound (usually) by his trustee in bankruptcy; trustees may be subject to limitations in their trust deed and will often be reluctant to accept joint and several liability under warranties; a vendor who is subject to mental disorder may be difficult to bind if there is no enduring power of attorney; receivers must be authorised by their appointing instrument and liquidators must be duly appointed. Check any special considerations where the vendor is incorporated and/or resident overseas. In any of these circumstances, it may be prudent to retain a proportion of the consideration until any issued are determined.

4.26 Are there multiple vendors? Should liability be joint and several and, if acting for the vendor, should each vendor's liability be individually limited?

4.27 Does the purchaser have any special characteristics (eg are they members of management, and if so how is the acquisition to be funded)?

4.28 What continuing arrangements need to be put in place with the vendor or members of the vendor's group, eg formalising supply arrangements? Are there any interim arrangements needed (eg for administration or computer facilities) until the purchaser can put in place its own arrangements?

4.29 Does the purchaser intend to sell all or part of the target after completion or to reorganise intragroup? Check that the full benefit of warranties and indemnities can be transferred, and the tax impact.

4.30 (*Assets*) Prepare inventories of assets to be sold: moveable and immoveable fixed assets; contracts, intellectual property and agreements; inventory or classification of stock and work-in-progress.

4.31 (*Assets*) How will debtors and creditors be dealt with?

4.32 Should there be any specific indemnities eg for environmental matters or for matters which have been revealed by due diligence or disclosure?

5 Accounting

5.1 Does any accountants' report recommend special warranties be taken? Are there disclosed contingencies which should be excluded from the transaction?

5.2 What will be the accounting treatment of the acquisition?

5.3 If shares are to be issued as consideration, will merger relief be available under the Companies Act 1985, s 131 (p 125)?

6 Procedure

6.1 Preparation of timetable, list of parties, list of documents. Make sure the timetable is not too ambitious: even the smallest transaction is complicated and will take time to negotiate.

6.2 Heads of agreement, with or without exclusivity and/or confidentiality provisions (p 183).

6.3 Conduct due diligence; agree form of due diligence report with purchaser and ensure that there is liaison with any accountants who are preparing an acquisition report.

6.4 Instruct overseas lawyers on local law issues, if there are any overseas subsidiaries or businesses. Prepare foreign law opinion letters, if required.

6.5 Title investigation (p 153).

6.6 Investigation of funding of pension scheme (Chapter 7).

6.7 Preparation and agreement of contracts.

6.8 Preparation and agreement of disclosure letter.

6.9   Preparation and agreement of all ancillary documents: service agreements, placing agreement (*shares*); trade mark, patent, copyright, leasehold assignments and freehold transfers (*assets*), releases from charges (*shares or assets*) and letters of non-crystallisation (*assets*).

6.10 Submission of proof circular and any temporary documents of title to consideration shares for London Stock Exchange approval (if applicable).

6.11 Exchange of contracts (with announcement by press release if desired or required by the London Stock Exchange) (p 223).

6.12 Despatch of circular (if shareholder consent required).

6.13 Preparation and agreement of ancillary documents for completion. Prepare completion agenda. Check availability and authority (eg board resolution, power of attorney, trust deed) for those who are to sign documentation.

6.14 EGM, at which necessary shareholder approvals are given.

6.15 Application for listing of consideration shares (if applicable).

6.16 Completion.

6.17 All necessary secretarial matters including filings at Companies Registration Office.

6.18 Stamp transfers and transfers/assignments/contract (Stamps Form 22 for assets transaction) within 30 days.

6.19 File agreements with the Registrar of Restrictive Trade Practices if they contain registrable restrictions, before the restrictions take effect and in any event with three months.

6.20 (*Assets*) After stamping, record patent, trademark, design right assignments with the relevant registries and register (or apply for first registration of) any freehold transfers or registrable leasehold assignments.

Index

Circulars—*contd*
  copies, 224
  Exchange approval, 224–5
  fraud prevention, 28
  indebtedness statement, 224
  investment advertisement, 28
  offer, 669–86
  related party,224. *See also* Related party
    circular
  requirement, 224
  resubmission, 224
  submission of documents, 224–5
  Super Class 1. *See* Super Class 1 circular
  Yellow Book requirements, 224
City Code on Take-overs and Mergers, 2–3, 26
Clawback—
  ABI guidelines, 9
  meaning, 9
Close company—
  act of company, 323
  apportionment test, 322
  associates, 321
  control test, 321–2
  corporation tax, 323
  definition, 321
  director, 322
  distributions, 324
  generally, 321
  inheritance tax, 324–5, 328
  investment holding, 322–3
  loans to participators, 323–4
  material interest in, 323
  nominees, 321
  non-resident, 322
  open company, 321
  participators, 321–2
  pay and file, 324
  shortfall apportionment, 323
  subsidiaries, 322
  VAT, 325–6
  warranties, 324
Coal sector mergers, 39
Cold calls—
  solicitors, 4
Collective agreements, 67
Commons registration, 156
Companies Announcement Office (CAO),
  220, 223
Companies Court, 136, 357
Companies Registration Office, 155–6
Companies Registry, 135–6, 357
Company name preservation, 371
Competition law, 31–42
  1989 orders, 33–4
  accountants' acquisition report, 145
  clearances, 25
  deregulation, 34
  EC. *See* EC competition law

Competition law—*contd*
  generally, 31
  mergers. *See* Mergers
  non-notifiable agreements, 34
  practical points, 34–5
  restraint of trade, 31–2
  restrictive covenants—
    restraint of trade, 31–2
    restrictive trade practices. *See* Restrictive
      trade practices
  restrictive trade practices. *See* Restrictive
    trade practices
  turnover threshold, 34
  United Kingdom law, 31–5
Completion—
  accounts, 202
  board minutes, 631–2
Compulsory winding up, 364–5
Computer—
  communications routes, 208
  copyright on software, 208
  data protection, 22
  hardware, 207–8
  licensing, 210
  maintenance, 207–8
  shared facilities, 208–9
  software, 208
  support and maintenance, 207–8
  transfer, 207–9
'Concentrations', 39
Conflict of laws, 340–1
Connected persons, 25
Consents—
  See also Approvals
  asset acquisition, 30
  Companies Act 1985 section 103, 26–7
  generally, 21
  Taxes Acts, under, 29–30
Consideration—
  capital gains tax instalment payment, 263–4
  insolvency, retention on, 353
  stamp duty, 280, 291
  Super Class 1 circular, 221–2, 225
Constructive dismissal, 67
  pensions, 110–11
Constructive trust—
  financial assistance, breach of rules, 60
Consumer credit licences, 30
Contracted out pensions, 81–2, 97–8
Contracts, 209–13
  Agreement for Sale, 213
  assignment, 209–13
  benefit, 211–12, 288
  burden, 212–13
  computer licensing, 210
  consent to assignment, 210–12
  defence of counterparty, 212
  employment, 211